AF846612

Logic, Argumentation & Reasoning

Interdisciplinary Perspectives from the Humanities and Social Sciences

Volume 3

Series Editor

Shahid Rahman

For further volumes:
http://www.springer.com/series/11547

Logic, Argumentation & Reasoning

The Series is developed in partnership with the Maison Européenne des Sciences de l'Homme et de la Société (MESHS) at Nord - Pas de Calais and the UMR-STL: 8163 (CNRS). Aims & Scope: The scientific objectives of the series, where humanities and social sciences are conceived as building interdisciplinary interfaces, are:

This series publishes volumes that link practices in the Humanities and Social Sciences, with theories in Logic, Argumentation and Reasoning, such as: Decision theory and action theory, Argumentation Theories in: cognitive sciences, economy, sociology, law, logic, philosophy of sciences. The series is open towards research from the Analytic and the Continental traditions, and has four main focus areas: Pragmatic models and studies that develop a dynamic approach to reasoning in which argumentation is structured as an interaction or as a game, in which two or more participants play moves defined by the type of argumentation in question, communication, language and techniques of argumentation: studies between the practical and theoretical dimensions of argumentation, as well as the relationships between argumentation and other modes of communication, reception, persuasion and power: studies in which reasoning practice is considered from the point of view of its capacity to produce conviction of persuasion, and focusing on understanding what makes an argument performative, Diachronic transformations of reasoning practices studies that emphasize the invention and renewal of reasoning forms, with respect to its performance and its effectiveness.

General Editor
Shahid Rahman (Lille, UMR 8163)

Managing Editor
Laurent Keiff (Lille, UMR 8163)

Area Editors

Argumentation and Pragmatics
Marcelo Dascal (Tel Aviv)
Erik Krabbe (Groningen)
Frans H. van Eemeren (Amsterdam)
John Woods (British Columbia/King's College)

Argumentation and Rhetoric
Fabienne Blaise (Lille, MESHS-Nord Pas de Calais)
Gabriel Galvez-Behar (Lille, MESHS-Nord Pas de Calais)
André Laks (Sorbonne, Paris IV)
Ruth Webb (Lille, UMR 8163)

Decision Theory, Mathematics, Economy
Jacques Dubucs (IHPST-Paris 1)
Fredéric Jouneau (Lille)
Richard Sobel (Lille)

Cognitives Sciences. Computer Sciences
Yann Coello (Lille)
Eric Gregoire (CRIL-Lens)
Henry Prakken (Utrecht)
François Recanati (ENS, Paris)

Epistemology and Philosophy of Science
André Fuhrmann (Frankfurt)
Gerhard Heinzmann (Nancy)
Göran Sundholm (Leyden)

Logic
Michel Crubellier (Lille, UMR 8163)
Dov Gabbay (King's College)
Sven Ove Hansson (Stockholm)
Tero Tulenheimo (Lille, UMR 8163)

Political Science and Sociology
Jean-Gabriel Contamin (Lille)
Franck Fischer (Rutgers)
Josh Ober (Stanford)
Marc Pichard (Lille, MESHS-Nord Pas de Calais)

Manuel Rebuschi • Martine Batt
Gerhard Heinzmann • Franck Lihoreau
Michel Musiol • Alain Trognon
Editors

Interdisciplinary Works in Logic, Epistemology, Psychology and Linguistics

Dialogue, Rationality, and Formalism

Springer

Editors
Manuel Rebuschi
LHSP – Archives H. Poincaré (UMR 7117)
MSH Lorraine (USR 3261) CNRS
Université de Lorraine
Nancy, France

Gerhard Heinzmann
MSH Lorraine (USR 3261) CNRS
Université de Lorraine
Nancy, France

Michel Musiol
MSH Lorraine (USR 3261) CNRS
ATILF (UMR 7118)
Université de Lorraine
Nancy, France

Martine Batt
Laboratoire de Psychologie de l'Interaction et des Relations Intersubjectives (InterPsy – EA 4432)
Université de Lorraine
Nancy, France

Franck Lihoreau
Faculdade de Ciências Sociais e Humanas
Instituto de Filosofia da Linguagem
Universidade Nova de Lisboa
Lisboa, Portugal

Alain Trognon
Laboratoire de Psychologie de l'Interaction et des Relations Intersubjectives (InterPsy – EA 4432)
Université de Lorraine
Nancy, France

ISSN 2214-9120 ISSN 2214-9139 (electronic)
ISBN 978-3-319-03043-2 ISBN 978-3-319-03044-9 (eBook)
DOI 10.1007/978-3-319-03044-9
Springer Cham Heidelberg New York Dordrecht London

Library of Congress Control Number: 2014932162

© Springer International Publishing Switzerland 2014
This work is subject to copyright. All rights are reserved by the Publisher, whether the whole or part of the material is concerned, specifically the rights of translation, reprinting, reuse of illustrations, recitation, broadcasting, reproduction on microfilms or in any other physical way, and transmission or information storage and retrieval, electronic adaptation, computer software, or by similar or dissimilar methodology now known or hereafter developed. Exempted from this legal reservation are brief excerpts in connection with reviews or scholarly analysis or material supplied specifically for the purpose of being entered and executed on a computer system, for exclusive use by the purchaser of the work. Duplication of this publication or parts thereof is permitted only under the provisions of the Copyright Law of the Publisher's location, in its current version, and permission for use must always be obtained from Springer. Permissions for use may be obtained through RightsLink at the Copyright Clearance Center. Violations are liable to prosecution under the respective Copyright Law.
The use of general descriptive names, registered names, trademarks, service marks, etc. in this publication does not imply, even in the absence of a specific statement, that such names are exempt from the relevant protective laws and regulations and therefore free for general use.
While the advice and information in this book are believed to be true and accurate at the date of publication, neither the authors nor the editors nor the publisher can accept any legal responsibility for any errors or omissions that may be made. The publisher makes no warranty, express or implied, with respect to the material contained herein.

Printed on acid-free paper

Springer is part of Springer Science+Business Media (www.springer.com)

Contents

Contributors

Maxime Amblard LORIA, UMR 7503, Université de Lorraine, CNRS, Inria, Vandœuvre-lès-Nancy, France

Guillaume Aucher University of Rennes 1, INRIA, Rennes, France

Martine Batt Laboratoire de Psychologie de l'Interaction et des Relations Intersubjectives (InterPsy – EA 4432), Université de Lorraine, Nancy, France

Jean Caelen Laboratoire d'Informatique de Grenoble (UMR 5217), Domaine universitaire, Grenoble, France

Marcelo Dascal Philosophy Department, Tel-Aviv University, Ramat Aviv, Tel-Aviv, Israel

Gerhard Heinzmann MSH Lorraine (USR 3261) CNRS, Université de Lorraine, Nancy, France

Franck Lihoreau Faculdade de Ciências Sociais e Humanas, Instituto de Filosofia da Linguagem, Universidade Nova de Lisboa, Lisboa, Portugal

Michel Musiol MSH Lorraine (USR 3261) CNRS, ATILF (UMR 7118), Université de Lorraine, Nancy, France

Eric Pacuit Tilburg Institute for Logic and Philosophy of Science, Tilburg University, Warandelaan, AB Tilburg, The Netherlands

Sylvain Pogodalla LORIA, UMR 7503, Université de Lorraine, CNRS, Inria, Vandœuvre-lès-Nancy, France

Manuel Rebuschi LHSP – Archives H. Poincaré (UMR 7117), MSH Lorraine (USR 3261) CNRS, Université de Lorraine, Nancy, France

Oliver Schlaudt Philosophisches Seminar, Universität Heidelberg, Heidelberg, Germany

Christian Thiel Institut für Philosophie, Universität Erlangen-Nürnberg, Erlangen, Germany

Frédérick Tremblay LHSP – Archives H. Poincaré (UMR 7117), Université de Lorraine, Nancy, France

Alain Trognon Laboratoire de Psychologie de l'Interaction et des Relations Intersubjectives (InterPsy – EA 4432), Université de Lorraine, Nancy, France

Frédéric Verhaegen MSH Lorraine (USR 3261) CNRS, Laboratoire APEMAC, EPSaM (EA 4360), Université de Lorraine, Nancy, France

Denis Vernant Département de philosophie – ARSH, Université Pierre-Mendes-France, Grenoble, France

Anne Xuereb Laboratoire d'Informatique de Grenoble (UMR 5217), Domaine universitaire, Grenoble, France

Tomoyuki Yamada Division of Philosophy and Cultural Sciences, Graduate School of Letters, Hokkaido University, Sapporo, Hokkaido, Japan

Chapter 1
General Introduction

Manuel Rebuschi, Martine Batt, Gerhard Heinzmann, Franck Lihoreau, Michel Musiol, and Alain Trognon

As witnessed by its title, the papers collected in this book aim to provide a renewed perspective on the relationships between dialogue, rationality, and formalism. More precisely, the goal of this volume is to shed light on the use of formalisms in psychological and philosophical explanations of the rationality of interactive agents. This book grew out of an interdisciplinary scientific project called DiaRaFor ("Dialogue, Rationality, Formalisms") and hosted by the MSH Lorraine (Lorraine Institute for Social Sciences and Humanities) from 2007 to 2011. The project was led by two Lorraine research teams, the *LHSP–Archives Henri Poincaré* (UMR 7117), and the *Laboratoire de Psychologie de l'Interaction et des Relations*

M. Rebuschi (✉)
LHSP – Archives H. Poincaré (UMR 7117), MSH Lorraine (USR 3261) CNRS, Université de Lorraine, 91, avenue de la Libération, BP 454, 54001 Nancy, France
e-mail: manuel.rebuschi@univ-lorraine.fr

M. Batt • A. Trognon
Laboratoire de Psychologie de l'Interaction et des Relations Intersubjectives (InterPsy – EA 4432), Université de Lorraine, Campus Lettres et Sciences Humaines, 3, Place Godefroy de Bouillon, 54015 Nancy, France
e-mail: martine.batt@univ-lorraine.fr; alain.trognon@univ-lorraine.fr

G. Heinzmann
MSH Lorraine (USR 3261) CNRS, Université de Lorraine, 91, avenue de la Libération, BP 454, 54001 Nancy, France
e-mail: gerhard.heinzmann@univ-lorraine.fr

F. Lihoreau
Faculdade de Ciências Sociais e Humanas, Instituto de Filosofia da Linguagem, Universidade Nova de Lisboa, Avenida de Berna, 26 – 4° piso, 1069-061 Lisboa, Portugal
e-mail: franck.lihoreau@fcsh.unl.pt

M. Musiol
MSH Lorraine (USR 3261) CNRS, ATILF (UMR 7118), Université de Lorraine, 44, avenue de la Libération, 54063 Nancy, France
e-mail: michel.musiol@univ-lorraine.fr

M. Rebuschi et al. (eds.), *Interdisciplinary Works in Logic, Epistemology, Psychology and Linguistics*, Logic, Argumentation & Reasoning 3,
DOI 10.1007/978-3-319-03044-9_1, © Springer International Publishing Switzerland 2014

Intersubjectives (InterPsy, EA 4432), in conjunction with several external researchers. Specific collaboration was implemented with a team of psychiatrists working at the *Centre Hospitalier Universitaire* (University Hospital) of Rouen.

The goal of the project was to compare recent accounts in the formalization of natural language (dynamic logics and formal semantics) with informal conceptions of interaction (dialogue, natural logic, and attribution of rationality) that had been developed in both psychology and epistemology. Like the project, the book is divided into four parts: historical and systematic studies; the formalization of context in epistemology; the formalization of reasoning in interactive contexts in psychology; the formalization of pathological conversations.

The book's chapters are partly direct products of the research conducted within the project, and partly written by international scholars working on issues adjacent to those of the DiaRaFor project. In the remainder of this introduction, we will briefly present the objectives of each part and the nature of the papers contained therein.

1.1 Part I: "Historical Context"

In the last century scientific philosophy has seen the birth of two epistemological currents, namely the better-known logical empiricism and, as a reaction against that, several continental European methodologies associated with the Erlangen School of Germany. Both have developed a logical analysis of scientific discourse and proposed to reconstruct theoretical terms on the basis of non-theoretical data. Both seek to distance themselves from German idealism and the German metaphysical tradition, and are famous for their seemingly draconian rejection of Heidegger (Lorenzen, Beth, Piaget). Recent studies on logical empiricism suggest, however, a more nuanced verdict concerning the influence of German metaphysics, and the same observation must be made with respect to the Erlangen School.

The topic of the first part of this book is motivated by the realization that the currents "around" the Erlangen School explicitly proposed a logical analysis of science—a logic of science—as well as an operational reconstruction of psychological concepts, while at the same time distinguishing themselves from their predecessors, who had been the target of Quine's celebrated 'Two Dogmas'.

The three papers in this part of the book provide insights into the difficulties of characterizing the very beginning of a conceptual reassessment of the project of rational reconstruction from a pragmatic point of view, including both the epistemological and psychological sides of the issue.

In "Phenomenology, "*Grundwissenschaft*" and "*Ideologiekritik*": Hermann Zeltner's Critique of the Erlangen School", **Christian Thiel** sheds light not only on a little-known German philosopher but, more importantly, on the intellectual circle that existed at the beginning of Kamlah and Lorenzen's collaboration in Erlangen. Following Carl Friedrich Gethmann's assertion that "constructive philosophy is phenomenology after the linguistic turn", one might conjecture that, as Kamlah was influenced by Heidegger, so Zeltner was influenced by the supervisor of his *habilitation*, Moritz Geiger, who succeeded Husserl in Göttingen in 1932, such that both confirm Gethmann's thesis. Nevertheless, Thiel's carefully organized historic-systematic examination and testimony (Zeltner sat on the jury for his own *habilitation*) arrives at a different claim: (1) just as it is difficult to say "to what extent phenomenology was at the core of Geiger's philosophy", so it is difficult to say to what extent Zeltner "was a phenomenologist, regarding either the subjects of investigation or the methods employed"; (2) Zeltner's term "*Grundwissenschaft*" is directed as much against Plato's ontology as against Kant's epistemology. As far as geometry is concerned, it means that we must internalize (*mitvollziehen*) the meaning of geometrical norms as "prescriptions of actions in the physical world, in order to grasp the real meaning of mathematical propositions". This argument comes very near to Lorenzen's position, although his discussion of it was not in respect to a system of geometrical propositions. Nevertheless, although there were some common systematic (though non-phenomenological) features in common between the Erlangen School and its local philosophical counterparts, there was no significant discussion or exchange between the two. Thiel's paper is a precious argument against historical links hastily accepted. It is a masterpiece of "*Ideologiekritik*".

The second paper, "Geometry as a Measurement-Theoretical A Priori: Lorenzen's Defense of Relativity Against the Ontology of Its Proponents", by **Oliver Schlaudt**, describes and motivates Lorenzen's normative approach to geometrical space as an object constituted by spatial measuring operations and highlights the consequences of this approach for the interpretation of the theory of relativity. What is often conceived of as "fact" is, in the tradition of Poincaré's conventionalism, the outcome of a process of interpretation that also depends on a priori elements. In Lorenzen, "*a priori*" simply denotes the consequences of linguistic and technical methods established by convention within the reconstruction of scientific theories. In this carefully argued article, the author shows convincingly how Lorenzen transcends the customary realism/anti-realism quarrel: his pragmatic approach reflects both Helmholtz and Mach on the one hand and the neo-Kantian thinkers Kries and Cassirer on the other. His arguments thus leverage two opposing currents, a critical one and a constructive one, which respectively inherit empiricist and rationalist positions. He replaces the circles used by these modes of thought with the so-called theory of forms, i.e. the objects of a purely "basic geometry", with an operationally defined plane surface as the most fundamental form, ranging from topology to geometry strictly speaking. The originality of Lorenzen's approach is finally clarified by a confrontation with the earlier positions of Helmholtz, Russell, and especially Couturat.

The correspondence between Beth and Piaget, edited and annotated by **Gerhard Heinzmann**, **Alain Trognon**, and **Frédérick Tremblay**, was kindly made available to us by the Beth Foundation in Amsterdam. It constitutes a very exceptional document that fits perfectly into a book about the DiaRaFor project. It is, in fact, a dialogue, more precisely an epistolary dialogue, but at the same time it has all the properties of a critical discussion conducted within the framework of an interdisciplinary scientific project. It focuses on the relationship between "natural mind" and "formal thinking", a long-standing issue in epistemology and one of the main points discussed by the members of Lorenzen's Erlangen School. The dialogue concludes with "Psychology and Epistemology of Mathematics" and a basic declaration of the separateness of research on the "laws of thought" and research on logic. The missing link that would have allowed a closer intellectual agreement between Piaget and Beth was to come much later, with the "pragmatic turn" of logic. The semantic tableaus presented by Beth during the Geneva seminar on Genetic Epistemology and then within his discussion with Lorenzen[1] hold the key to his pragmatic insights.

1.2 Part II: "Epistemology, Context, Formalism"

The second part of the book is devoted to formal epistemology. Since Hintikka's seminal 1962 work *Knowledge and Belief,* the considerable development of epistemic and doxastic logics—mainly in such areas as computer science, economy, and game theory—has led them quite far from their original core area, namely a priori conceptual reasoning (a.k.a. philosophy). Epistemology, on the other hand, has remained relatively isolated from such technical developments. Since the early 2000s, however, a strong renewed interest in philosophical issues has been expressed by a number of prominent epistemic logicians (see Benthem 2006; Hendricks 2006). All the while, dynamic epistemic logic (DEL) has incorporated (modeled) concrete features of agent actions into the abstract framework of epistemic and doxastic logic. The overall picture of formal epistemology is now that of a lively discipline attempting eagerly to account for a more realistic, cognitively plausible conception of knowledge.

The papers in Part II show the distance that has been covered by contemporary epistemology since the original formulation of doxastic and epistemic logics half a century ago. Dynamics is concerned not only with epistemic and general actions but also with changes in context, especially conversational context. In addition to formulating his own specific conception, Lewis's contextualist perspective on knowledge corroborated a view reminiscent of what cognitive scientists had already begun stressing at the time: that knowledge was no longer to be apprehended from God's perspective but rather in relation to contexts of ascription, thereby bringing epistemology back down to a more worldly arena.

Whence the direct connection between Part II and this book's overall purpose. At the frontier between epistemology and pragmatics, different agents' roles in dialogue must be taken into account in order to provide finer-grained descriptions of real-life attitude ascriptions. A number of classical puzzles can be revisited in light

[1] This correspondence will be published in a forthcoming volume.

of this new insight. The four papers collected here all reflect this new dynamic and more "concrete" trend in epistemology.

The first chapter, "Principles of Knowledge, Belief and Conditional Belief", by **Guillaume Aucher**, offers a sharp review of different axiomatic systems for knowledge and belief which have been proposed in the epistemic logic literature. The author thereby isolates and addresses a number of nagging problems that have helped shape the modern history of the logic of knowledge. The paper also investigates the conditions for the formal interdefinability of the two notions of belief and knowledge, and establishes that certain important and intricate principles for reasoning about knowledge can be derived from a set of intuitively simple interaction axioms relating knowledge and conditional belief.

In "Procedural Information and the Dynamics of Belief", **Eric Pacuit** offers an overview of recent advances in DEL and introduces the key ideas and definitions of the operations that dynamically alter agents' beliefs during social interaction. The paper focuses on *procedural information,* that is, information about the protocol specifying which of a number of options are feasible and permissible for the agents at any given moment. It also discusses the role played by this kind of information in situations of interaction and learning.

In "Reasoning About Knowledge in Context", **Franck Lihoreau** and **Manuel Rebuschi** propose a new semantics, based on the notion of *contextual models,* that makes it possible to express and compare—within a unique formal framework—different views on the roles of various notions of context in knowledge ascriptions. Skeptical and moderate invariantism, contextualism, and subject-sensitive invariantism are thus examined. A dynamic formalism is also proposed that offers new insights into a classical skeptical puzzle.

Finally, **Tomoyuki Yamada**'s chapter, "The Epistemic Closure Principle and the Assessment Sensitivity of Knowledge Attributions", addresses the debate between relativism and contextualism over the vexed issue of the semantics of knowledge ascriptions. The interest in relativism on this issue has recently been renewed by authors who defend the idea, championed by Macfarlane, of the assessment sensitivity of epistemic attributions, i.e., that their truth is somehow relative to the context of a "judge" or assessor rather than to the attributor's context. Yamada's paper challenges this notion with an argument grounded in new, alternative formulations of the principle of epistemic closure.

1.3 Part III: Reasoning in Interactive Context

Pure logic has been built up against the psycho-sociology of thought; Frege theorized its advent at the beginning of the twentieth century. In the present volume, the Beth-Piaget correspondence (pp. 45–93) bears witness to the solidity of that construction in the 1950s.

At the beginning of the twenty-first century however, the so-called "Wall of Frege", to use Van Benthem's evocative metaphor (Benthem 2008), was poised to fall. A loyal cooperation without second thoughts could now replace the "armed peace" that had prevailed between logic as a "discipline of foundations" on the one hand and the human and social sciences as the study of empirical thought on the other. This collaboration was set to perfect a reconciliation that had begun around 1980. We recently re-examined this reconciliation (Trognon and Batt 2011) by following two special editions of the journal *Synthese*. A "mild" psychologism reconciling pure logic with the human and social sciences through the concept of "rational agency", with social psychology as an interface, may take the place of what has remained the rule until recently, namely antipsychologism, as driven by Hintikka for instance. Van Benthem asserts that "logic is of course not experimental, or even theoretical, psychology and it approaches human reasoning with purposes of its own. And a logical theory is not useless if people do not quite behave according to it. But the boundary is delicate. And I think the following should be obvious: if logical theory were *totally disjoint* from actual reasoning, it would be no use at all, for whatever purpose!" (Benthem 2008, p. 69). He goes on to say that " 'human behaviour' as brought to light by psychology is not just a set of protocol sentences in simple-minded experiments, but a hierarchy of description levels, ranging from plain observable facts to sophisticated higher-order description. Viewed that way, the fit with logical theory becomes much more plausible, in both directions" (Benthem 2008, p. 80).

The third part of our volume is meant as a step in the direction in which van Benthem and other logicians want to take their colleagues: the meeting point between logic and the human and social sciences.

Martine Batt and **Alain Trognon** portray the microgenesis of the solution to an arithmetic division problem by showing two children dialoguing in order to solve it. In their chapter "From Dialogue to Calculation", they employ the method of "interlocutory logic", which involves leveraging logical knowledge "controlled" by the progression of the dialogue. This allows them to precisely locate the turning point in the children's work and illustrate the representation of the division they accomplish in their dialogue, thus bringing to light an interlocutory model of representation achieved through experimental developmental psychology.

In "Dialogue of Rationalities: A Case Study" **Marcelo Dascal** demonstrates that human rationality is not reducible to "mathematical" rationality (or "hard" rationality). Rather, it coexists peacefully with soft rationality. These two rationalities complete each other due to the very features that distinguishes them in a dialogue of rationalities. Dascal discovers this theorization in the "Preliminary Discourse on the Conformity of Faith and Reason", which opens the *Essais de Theodicée* of Leibniz, whom he calls "perhaps *the* rationalist par excellence".

Finally, **Denis Vernant**'s proposal of a "logic of veridicality" will probably be very useful in research on inter-discourse and cooperative multi-agent dialogues. This logic now allows us to examine "the combining of different agents' veridictional actions in relation to the same proposal". Its principles are presented in the chapter entitled "Pragmatics of Veridicity".

1.4 Part IV: "Conversation, Pathology, Formalization"

The fourth part of the book focuses on research at the intersection between linguistics and psychology. For cognitive psychologists, studying subjects' effective reasoning through thought patterns in conversation (non-directed dialogue) is a natural way to pinpoint possible disorders. This is particularly the case in psychopathology, where surface deviances can reflect more or less profound dysfunction. Indeed, conversations are complex human activities involving a wide array of competences. Disorders can occur at any level, from phonetic recognition or syntactic competence to social interaction and logical capability.

Some linguists, on their end, have tried to account for the pragmatic features of dialogue using formal semantic tools. Among the main developments of the past few decades, after Lewis and Montague's attempts in the 1970s at formalizing (fragments of) natural language, there have been key achievements yielded by Hans Kamp's DRT (Discourse Representation Theory) (see Kamp and Reyle 1993). This formal framework, shaped to fit the dynamic aspects of discourse, was eventually subjected to several extensions in order to account for phenomena such as underspecification or presupposition as well as rhetorical links in monologue and dialogue. This is dealt with especially closely by Nicholas Asher and Alex Lascarides's (2003) SDRT (Segmented DRT), which opens up new prospects in both pragmatics and psycholinguistics.

Two of the papers in this part focus on linguistic issues, while the other two are concerned with the use of language analysis in psychopathology.

In the first chapter, "Modeling the Dynamic Effects of Discourse: Principles and Frameworks", **Maxime Amblard** and **Sylvain Pogodalla** offer an overview of various accounts of dynamic phenomena in linguistics, more particularly in formal natural language semantics. The authors introduce several phenomena, such as presupposition, anaphora and modal subordination, that challenge traditional truth-theoretical semantics. They then present several formalisms capable of handling these phenomena: DRT and SDRT as well as dynamic predicate logic and continuation semantics.

Jean Caelen and **Anne Xuereb**'s chapter, entitled "Dialogue Analysis: Pragmatic and Rhetorical Aspects", explores the pragmatic and rhetorical aspects of dialogue and dialogue interpretation. After a conceptual survey of the issue, they offer their analysis of a real-life conversation between a doctor and a patient. According to the authors, such analyses support their conception of dialogues as strategic games, i.e., as constituting a special kind of action-oriented practice grounded in a more general praxeology.

In "Investigating Discourse Specificities in Schizophrenic Disorders", **Michel Musiol** and **Frédéric Verhaegen** present a pragmatic and psychological framework used to account for schizophrenic discourse. They offer a rational background for this, from psychological and psychiatric viewpoints to more formal studies such as that presented in the following paper. In their approach, the authors distinguish between several types of discontinuities occurring in conversations between a psychologist and a schizophrenic patient.

In the final chapter, "Using SDRT to Analyze Pathological Conversations", **Manuel Rebuschi**, **Maxime Amblard**, and **Michel Musiol** present ongoing research into the formalization of conversations between schizophrenic individuals and ordinary speakers. This work is based on the collection and transcription of empirical data and on informal pragmatic analyses performed by psychologists. Because significant irregularities are identified, the authors propose using SDRT to analyze and discuss the specific features of the extraordinary rationality exhibited by schizophrenic speakers, from the interpreter's point of view.

Acknowledgements The editorial work for this project was supported by the MSH-Lorraine (USR 3261), the LHSP–Archives Henri Poincaré (UMR 7117), and the *Laboratoire de Psychologie de l'Interaction et des Relations Intersubjectives* (InterPsy, EA 4432). We would like to thank several colleagues who lent their help in reviewing the papers published here: Nicholas Asher, Valérie Aucouturier, Alain Blanchet, Marcel Bromberg, Eric Grillo, Roger Pouivet, Jean Paul Roux, Henk Visser, and Tomoyuki Yamada. Finally, we would like to give special thanks to Doug Herman for revising the English, and to Sandrine Avril for her invaluable role in the technical editing process.

References

N. Asher, A. Lascarides, *Logics of Conversation* (Cambridge University Press, Cambridge/New York, 2003)

V.F. Hendricks, *Mainstream and Formal Epistemology* (Cambridge University Press, Cambridge, 2006)

H. Kamp, U. Reyle, *From Discourse to Logic: Introduction to Model Theoretic Semantics of Natural Language, Formal Logic and Discourse Representation Theory* (Kluwer Academic, Dordrecht/Boston, 1993)

A. Trognon, M. Batt, Some aspects of the current situation in research on dialogue logic, in *Logical Properties of Dialogue*, ed. by A. Trognon, M. Batt, J. Caelen, D. Vernant (Presses Universitaires deNancy, Nancy, 2011), pp. 7–25

J. van Benthem, Epistemic logic and epistemology: the state of their affairs. Philos. Stud. **128**, 49–76 (2006)

J. van Benthem, Logic and reasoning: do the facts matter? Studia Logica **88**, 67–84 (2008). Special Issue: Psychologism in Logic? Edited by Hannes Leitgeb

Part I
Historical Context

Chapter 2
Phenomenology, "Grundwissenschaft" and "Ideologiekritik": Hermann Zeltner's Critique of the Erlangen school

Christian Thiel

This paper is visibly connected neither to relations between the Erlangen school and logical empiricism, nor to any problems of logic. I will instead be concerned with whether Wilhelm Kamlah and Paul Lorenzen were possibly influenced by the discussion of phenomenological issues by certain philosophers active in Erlangen shortly before or during the development of the so-called Erlangen school in the Mid-1960s. My claim is that there was *no* real discussion or exchange of ideas between the protagonists of constructive philosophy and those in the Erlangen Institute closer to phenomenology, neo-Kantianism, or "new ontology", although some of them were concerned with similar problems and, like Hermann Zeltner, attempted to establish a dialogue from time to time.

The topic of this local and more traditional context of the Erlangen school has, to my knowledge, not yet been taken up anywhere, and it may well turn out that this omission does not amount to a great loss. My own interest derives of course from the fact that I was once involved on both sides, which also means that I must leave an objective evaluation to others and to the future.

Let me begin with a remark on the title of my paper. Whereas I may assume some common understanding of the word "phenomenology", the two German words in quotes may need some explanation, and moreover Hermann Zeltner is likely to be unknown to the majority of my readers. I have taken the word "Grundwissenschaft" from Zeltner's paper "Philosophie als Grundwissenschaft" published posthumously in memory of Wilhelm Kamlah in 1978. I have chosen the term "Ideologiekritik" as a catch-word suggested by Zeltner's monograph *Ideologie und Wahrheit: Zur Kritik der politischen Vernunft,* published in 1966. I will come back to these terms a little

C. Thiel (✉)
Institut für Philosophie, Universität Erlangen-Nürnberg, Bismarckstr. 1,
91054 Erlangen, Germany
e-mail: Thiel-Erlangen@t-online.de

M. Rebuschi et al. (eds.), *Interdisciplinary Works in Logic, Epistemology, Psychology and Linguistics*, Logic, Argumentation & Reasoning 3,
DOI 10.1007/978-3-319-03044-9_2, © Springer International Publishing Switzerland 2014

later. Let us begin with the context in which Hermann Zeltner appears connected to the Erlangen school, a context I regard as necessary to appreciate his life as well as the thought of his later years.

Of course, philosophy at Erlangen did not start with the vague set of persons later called (by others) the "Erlangen school". When I began studying at Erlangen in 1956, there was Wilhelm Kamlah, who had taken over the only philosophy chair in 1954. There was also Rudolf Zocher, who had already accomplished his *Habilitation* (the qualification as university lecturer) in 1925 but had made almost no progress in his academic career because he had refused to comply with the demands of the Nazis. There was also Hermann Zeltner, already over 50 but only recently *habilitated*—for reasons I will present in a moment. The bulk of the teaching load was taken by Hans R.G. Günther, a pupil of Eduard Spranger, aged almost 60, who had lost his chair at the German University in Prague and held a poorly salaried position at Erlangen although he had never been a member of the Nazi party. He finally left for Freiburg in 1958 when he was asked to choose where to retire. I attended lecture courses and seminars with all of them, and later also with Wolfgang Albrecht after he had completed his *Habilitation* in 1958. This was the staff and the situation before Paul Lorenzen arrived in 1962 to fill the newly created second philosophy chair. I supplemented my philosophical schedule with lecture courses by Hans Joachim Schoeps, Hans Liermann and Ruprecht Matthaei.

Considering the small philosophy staff, phenomenology was fairly well represented. Zocher, who had published an impressive analysis and critique of Husserl's phenomenological approach in 1932 offered two graduate seminars on Husserl's *Logical Investigations.* Albrecht gave a seminar on Husserl's *Formal and Transcendental Logic,* followed by another on the *Cartesian Meditations,* and Zeltner taught an introduction to phenomenology focussing on Husserl and Heidegger. Remembering Gethmann's now famous slogan that "constructive philosophy is phenomenology after the linguistic turn" (Gethmann 1991), it is tempting to suspect that this context exerted a strong phenomenological influence on Kamlah even though he had just taken a different turn himself, offering a lecture course on "Begriff, Aussage, Wahrheit, Wissenschaft" and a graduate seminar entitled "Das Wahrheitsproblem". This suspicion would seem all the more plausible since Kamlah and Zeltner shared a common past. So I must ask the reader's patience in taking a look at their lives: rather a glimpse in the case of Kamlah who is no doubt better known, and a slightly more explicit overview in the case of Zeltner.

Wilhelm Kamlah was born the son of a Lutheran parson on September 3, 1905 in Hohendorf an der Bode. After graduating from the *Domgymnasium* in Halberstadt, he studied theology, and later also musicology, history and philosophy at Marburg, Tübingen, Heidelberg and Göttingen. Among his teachers, Kamlah specifically recalled Rudolf Bultmann and the young provocative Martin Heidegger in Marburg, as well as Hans Lipps in Göttingen. He calls Heidegger his philosophy teacher even after the renunciation of his partisanship in 1954, and mentions Hans Lipps along with Arnold Gehlen as forerunners for his own philosophical anthropology in 1982 (Kamlah 1982). For a short time, one of his fellow students was Zeltner, perhaps in musicology where Kamlah worked on his edition of Heinrich Schütz's *Geistliche*

Chormusik between 1928 and 1935, which was later incorporated into Schütz's collected works. Zeltner paid tribute to this achievement in his 1973 paper entitled "Anfang und Ausgang der Schütz-Bewegung" (Zeltner 1973).

In 1932, Kamlah married Kläre Nohl (1908–1988), one of four daughters of the pedagogue Herman Nohl. After the Nazis came to power, the Nohl family was considered "jüdisch versippt" (i.e., related by marriage or ancestry to jews). Kamlah lost his post as assistant in the historical seminar in 1936, and 1 year later also that of director of the academic orchestra. A difficult period for the family followed, their only income being that from Kläre Kamlah's violin lessons (one of her pupils was Margarethe Zeltner, Hermann Zeltner's wife). Although Kamlah was drafted in 1939, sent to the front and severely wounded, he managed to win the support of sociologist Eduard Baumgarten at the University of Königsberg and to obtain his *Habilitation* in the winter semester of 1941–1942. In 1945 he was able to transfer to Göttingen as *Privatdozent,* was promoted to university reader in 1950, and in 1951 became associate professor at the Technical University of Hannover. He began to engage in logic and in a philosophical critique of language, perhaps based on a lingering stimulus from Hans Lipps (killed in action in 1941), but in my opinion more likely due to discussions with Paul Lorenzen, whom he had met and come to know just in those years. Kamlah accepted a call to become chair of philosophy at Erlangen in 1954, and later developments are well documented. For an excellent biographical and intellectual survey I refer the reader to Martin Langanke's paper "Fundamentalphilosophie und philosophische Anthropologie im Werk Wilhelm Kamlahs" (Langanke 2003).

Hermann Zeltner was born on July 5, 1903 in Nürnberg to the physician Dr. Edwin Zeltner and his wife Maria, née Altmann. He graduated from the Melanchthon-Gymnasium with his *Abitur* in 1922 and studied theology, philosophy and musicology in Erlangen, Munich, Tübingen, Göttingen and Münster. He first prepared for a theological profession, entering the *Predigerseminar* in Nürnberg, but decided to add three semesters in philosophy from 1928 to 1929 in Göttingen. There, he obtained his doctorate *summa cum laude* with a dissertation entitled "Schellings philosophische Idee und das Identitätssystem" (Zeltner 1929), supervised by the phenomenologist Moritz Geiger, who accepted Zeltner as a candidate for *Habilitation* early in 1933.

Geiger, who was Jewish, and moreover had involved himself in a fight over the Göttingen International Office with Hans Lipps, who was an ardent national socialist, was removed from his professorship at the end of 1933. Georg Misch was willing to step in for Geiger as far as Zeltner's *Habilitation* was concerned, but he was likewise dismissed in 1934. Zeltner nevertheless applied for the *venia legendi* in 1935, presenting his work "Studien zur Logik der existentiellen Reflexion" to Herman Nohl, who would have awarded him the desired qualification. But Nohl was also considered politically unreliable (in fact he was discharged in 1937), and so Hans Lipps (who was at that time filling Misch's chair) was asked to assess Zeltner's *Habilitationsschrift.* Lipps told Zeltner that he was by no means willing to accept the thesis, and that he considered a revision of it useless. Zeltner was forced to withdraw his thesis and his application. It is not without irony that, in the same year, Karl Jaspers recommended Zeltner's appointment to the philosophy chair at the University of Frankfurt despite his still lacking the *venia legendi,* and that this chair was finally filled by none other than Hans Lipps.

After this failure at a university career, Zeltner became a librarian and was in the Prussian library service at Halle-Wittenberg from 1935 to 1945, including military service from 1939 to 1945, when he was discharged by the Soviet military administration. A difficult time followed. Zeltner had married in 1931 and had four children. He had to eke out a living as a piano teacher, chorus leader, synodal secretary and teacher at an ecclesiastical girls school in Frankonia. Finally, he was accepted into the Bavarian library service in 1948, and promoted to vice-director of the university library of Erlangen in 1949. He was entrusted with teaching philosophy courses at the University in 1951, wrote a second habilitation thesis and finally got his *venia legendi* in 1955 at the age of 52. Zeltner quit the library service and was appointed to an unsalaried professorship in 1961. He spent the winter semester of 1966–1967 as visiting professor at the University of Bern in Switzerland, substituting for Wilhelm Kamlah at Erlangen twice, before and after this foreign appointment. Zeltner retired in 1968 and died in Erlangen in 1975.

Zeltner is not widely known today, and wasn't either during his life-time. The only philosophical dictionary with a short entry on him is Kröner's *Philosophisches Wörterbuch,* since its 19th edition published in 1974 (Schischkoff 1974). This neglect may be due to his position outside of any philosophical movement, and to the fact that he did not produce a pioneering or epoch-making *opus magnum,* probably as a consequence of his broad field of activities. I remember his colloquium for advanced students on information theory, half of the participants in which were staff members from philosophy or related disciplines. I regret having missed another colloquium that he conducted jointly with Finnish physiologist and philosopher Yrjö Reenpää, nuclear physicist Wolfgang Finkelnburg and bio-cybernetics-pioneer Wolf-Dieter Keidel. Even the formal sciences cast a spell on him, as shown by an unpublished manuscript of 75 pages, quoted in Zeltner's CV and entitled "Logik und Mathematik" that I have tried to re-discover, so far without success. Most significant perhaps, Zeltner was for many years a highly competent reviewer and critic of concerts and other music performances for local newspapers and journals, his contributions to which number in the hundreds.

A survey of his work in philosophy proper is somewhat easier, since among numerous contributions there are two clear foci. The first is Zeltner's research on Schelling and his presentation of it to the educated public. Manfred Schröter, the pope of Schelling scholarship, as it were, praised Zeltner's book on Schelling (Zeltner 1954) as "the best introduction to Schelling in existence".[1] Zeltner used it (I assume on Kamlah's advice) as his *Habilitationsschrift* in Erlangen. He was involved in the critical Academy edition of Schelling's works, the first volume of which he co-edited. Volume II is dedicated to the memory of Hermann Zeltner.

[1]Closing statement of the short description as a blurb for Zeltner's book, printed on its dust-cover: "die beste Einführung in Schelling, die wir besitzen."

The second focus is social philosophy, with emphasis on the theory and critique of ideology. It is not only expounded in the monograph *Ideologie und Wahrheit* (Zeltner 1966), but also developed in several papers, and last but not least in Zeltner's contribution to the *Festschrift* for Paul Lorenzen, published only posthumously in 1978. Like Zeltner's contribution to the volume *Vernünftiges Denken* (Zeltner 1978b), originally intended as a *Festschrift* for Wilhelm Kamlah, but transformed into a memorial volume by the vicissitudes of life.

Before taking up, or rather digging up, Zeltner's relations to Kamlah and Lorenzen, let me return for a moment to his Göttingen period and to the role of his academic teacher and *Doktorvater* Moritz Geiger (1880–1937). Zeltner held him in highest esteem. He owned all or nearly all of his writings, and in his office one could see a portrait of Geiger, marked on the back side as Zeltner's property. And he published an unusually long commemorative paper on Geiger in the *Zeitschrift für philosophische Forschung* in 1960 (Zeltner 1960). Geiger had studied in Munich with Alexander Pfänder and Theodor Lipps (who supervised his dissertation). He was co-editor of Husserl's *Jahrbuch für Philosophie und phänomenologische Forschung* and succeeded Husserl as chair in Göttingen in 1932. One would expect his relevance to the philosophy of mathematics as well as to constructive philosophy because of two of his writings. First, the monograph *Systematische Axiomatik der Euklidischen Geometrie* (Geiger 1924), summarized in a lecture before the *Göttinger Mathematische Gesellschaft* 1 year later (Geiger 1926). Geiger is claiming here that Hilbert's axioms of geometry are perfect for the derivation of geometry as a discipline, but lack the perspicuity and simple internal structure of our intuition of space, which one would expect them to represent as nicely as Peano's axioms represent the calculatory basis of arithmetic.[2] The second pertinent text is a very detailed review of Oskar Becker's *Mathematische Existenz* (Becker 1927) in the *Göttingische gelehrte Anzeigen* of 1928 (Geiger 1928), prompting a similarly detailed defensive reply from Becker (Becker 1929). But Geiger did not pursue these studies any further, moving instead towards phenomenological aesthetics and beyond. Herbert Spiegelberg, in his well-known survey on *The Phenomenological Movement* (Spiegelberg 1961), could give the paragraph on Geiger the heading "From Phenomenological Esthetics toward Metaphysics". He found it difficult "to tell how far phenomenology was and remained the core of Geiger's philosophy" (*op. cit.* I 206). I would not have gone into so much detail myself if I had not felt obliged to ask the same question about Zeltner: to what extent was he a phenomenologist, either regarding the subject of his investigations, or regarding the methods employed?

At the beginning of his paper "Philosophie als Grundwissenschaft" (Zeltner 1978b), Zeltner explains that he is far from claiming any foundational role for philosophy in the realm of science *as such,* but will investigate whether philosophy can supply foundations or justifications for *specific* disciplines. Hugo Dingler

---

[2]Bernays, in his short notice of the book in the *Jahrbuch über die Fortschritte der Mathematik,* saw in it "... the first undertaking to motivate a significant axiom system from internal reasons" ("... das erste Unternehmen [...], ein bedeutendes Axiomensystem aus inneren Gründen zu motivieren.")

believed that this could be done for geometry, and Kant, in his *Prolegomena,* was convinced that pure mathematics and pure natural science would get a philosophical foundation by exhibiting the conditions of their possibility. The question of whether a similar procedure might be effective in the humanities, say for law or for social philosophy, alerts us to the problem that an attempted foundation might turn out to be no more than an ideological underpinning, and therefore something that would bear the name of *foundation* unjustly. Closer analysis shows that a "Grundwissenschaft", which may be translated approximately as "basic science" or "foundational knowledge", cannot take the form of an *ontology* as in Plato's doctrine of ideas, nor the form of an *epistemology* like Kant's in the case of, say, ethics or anthropology. Zeltner's proposal is a third way, based on an elucidation (but also a critique) of Lorenzen's foundation of geometry. He aims to show that in following the prescriptions of geometrical norms, we must internalize ("mitvollziehen") their meaning as prescriptions of *actions* in the physical world, in order to grasp the real meaning of mathematical propositions. Zeltner thinks that Lorenzen's approach is valuable but still insufficient, since it may well lead to practical geometry as we find it already with the ancient Egyptians, but not yet to a well-founded structure or system of mathematical propositions. As Zeltner does not elaborate this argument any further, I will not delve into this question either. Zeltner's point is that we need a kind of reciprocity between a discipline and the co-ordinated part of "Grundwissenschaft". In reflecting e.g., on geometry, we pick the *philosophically* relevant aspects of the geometer's actions, remembering with Kant that space is not a concept but pure intuition. I do not know whether Zeltner and Lorenzen ever made any attempt to discuss these particular foundational questions.

It is a great pity that Zeltner's unexpected death at the end of 1975 prevented a discussion of his paper published posthumously in the *Festschrift* for Lorenzen in 1978–1979 (Zeltner 1979). Zeltner cites, analyzes and cautiously criticizes passages from Lorenzen's "Rules of Reasonable Argumentation" (Lorenzen 1974) (in the 1974 version of *Konstruktive Wissenschaftstheorie*) and from Lorenzen and Schwemmer's *Konstruktive Logik, Ethik und Wissenschaftstheorie,* published in 1973. Although we have not yet reached Lorenzen's late political philosophy here, I would find it fascinating to see the early struggles for a consistent and fertile concept of "*normative genesis*" confronted with Zeltner's historically underpinned proposals for exposing, dismantling and finally overcoming *ideologies.* It is true that the terminologies of these would-be dialogue partners are light-years apart from each other, and Zeltner's argumentation is complex and often terse. But in my view the two philosophers have nowhere else been closer to a bulk of common questions (and therefore to each other). Already, the title is significative and promising: "Klopfzeichen. Normative Genese und Ideologiekritik—Ferneres zum Kallikles-Gespräch (Platon, Gorgias 481 C ff.)" (Zeltner 1979).

"Klopfzeichen" are rapping sounds or signs exchanged by prisoners in neighbouring cells, aiming at establishing communication, or to send each other messages later on. Zeltner obviously wanted to indicate that he felt, in the Erlangen institute, like a prisoner deprived of contact with his fellow sufferers. At the same time he intended to send a signal that he wished to change this situation. It was no doubt an invitation to an exchange of ideas, and the pairing of the terms "Normative Genese" and "Ideologiekritik" shows clearly where Zeltner located the common ground. The second title refers back to Zeltner's paper "Ideologie und Idee: Zum Kallikles-Gespräch" in *Zeitschrift für philosophische Forschung* 1974 (reprinted, like Zeltner 1979, in Zeltner 1978a). Kallikles is one of Socrates' dialogue partners in Plato's dialogue *Gorgias,* and in Zeltner's view the first literary person to express a suspicion of ideology *(Ideologieverdacht)* at work in his discussion of the needs of individuals and of the polis, and of the appropriate kind of order for an ideal social community. The older text was originally written for a *Festschrift* for Helmut Berve (one of the great historians of ancient Greece), and uses a historical background to reflect theoretically on the normative questions hidden in traditional ways of thinking. By contrast, the "Klopfzeichen" explicitly compare the argumentation in the *Gorgias* with Lorenzen's proposals for finding justified norms for people living together in a community, by constructing a normative genesis in contradistinction to the factual genesis we find in actual history. Implicitly, contemporary debates on "freedom from repression" in such a common endeavour are taken into account, and Zeltner's doubt about the possibility of an "herrschaftsfreier Diskurs" goes nicely with reflections in the Erlangen school on the equity of rights in a rational dialogue, the necessity of expert advice, and the consideration of the interests of non-participants. A lively discussion between these "locked-in" philosophers would indeed have been a great event, perhaps with a valuable outcome. That Lorenzen, in turn, read Zeltner's writings carefully, is documented by his annotations in the nine offprints he received from Zeltner, most of them with short but friendly dedications (among which "dem treuen Erlanger" on the first page of a 1966 paper probably refers to Lorenzen's decision to stay at Erlangen and decline three nearly simultaneous calls to other universities).

Little is known about the personal relations of Zeltner to Kamlah and Lorenzen. About the relations between Zeltner and Kamlah I do not know anything. Andreas Kamlah (one of Wilhelm Kamlah's two sons) stated in a letter to me dated 6 November, 2008, that his parents had not had any personal relationships with Hermann Zeltner, and that he did not recall ever having seen him in the Kamlah family's house. Admittedly, I know almost as little about Zeltner and Lorenzen. The friendly dedications mentioned above point to good relations but nothing is known about a closer relationship, say, in the form of mutual private invitations or discussions, as between Kamlah and Lorenzen in their "untroubled" time.

Correspondence is lacking, small wonder between persons living in the same town and seeing each other often in their shared place of study. I do not interpret Zeltner's outspoken protest against my definition of "foundational debate" and "foundational crisis" in my Habilitationsschrift—he had been asked to be the second referee of it—as an attack on Lorenzen or on myself, even though it led to a request for two further assessments by Kamlah and the sociologist Werner Mangold.

A last word on Gethmann's description of methodical constructivism as "phenomenology after the linguistic turn". I have, earlier in this paper, supported the judgment that Geiger was no full-blooded phenomenologist, while Misch, as forceful defender of Wilhelm Dilthey's philosophy of life against Husserl and Heidegger, should be counted rather as what he is: a proponent of *Lebensphilosophie.*

Gethmann, as an expert both on phenomenology and on Lebensphilosophie, cannot have mixed them up, not even by misinterpreting the title of Misch's book *Phänomenologie und Lebensphilosophie* (Misch 1931). Only Wilhelm Kamlah, who has some superb phenomenological analyses of *Lebenswelt* and the general *condition humaine* in his book *Der Mensch in der Profanität* of 1949, probably wrote under the impression of Heidegger's *Sein und Zeit.* Yet even here, we do not find a *dependence* on Heidegger if we focus our attention on the concept of "Lebenswelt" and its role in the oft-quoted formulation of scientific thought as a "refining stylization of that which has always constituted the practical life of men and women."[3] Returning to the situation at Erlangen, the information so far available seems to corroborate my claim (in answer to the question posed at the beginning of this paper) of the absence of any significant discussion or exchange between the constructivists and the more traditional thinkers in this potential market-place of philosophical ideas.

References

O. Becker, *Mathematische Existenz. Untersuchungen zur Logik und Ontologie mathematischer Phänomene*. Max Niemeyer, Halle a.d.S. (1927) (Monograph edition of the paper in *Jahrbuch für Philosophie und phänomenologische Forschung* 8, 441–809); Tübingen, 1973

O. Becker, Über den sogenannten 'Anthropologismus' in der Philosophie der Mathematik. (Eine Erwiderung in Sachen der 'Mathematischen Existenz'). Philosophischer Anzeiger **6**(3), 369–387 (1929)

M. Geiger, *Systematische Axiomatik der Euklidischen Geometrie* (Benno Filser, Augsburg, 1924)

M. Geiger, Systematische Axiomatik der Euklidischen Geometrie. Zusammenfassender Bericht über den Inhalt des gleichnamigen Buches des Vortragenden. Jahresbericht der Deutschen Mathematiker-Vereinigung, **34**(Teil II), 103–104 (1926)

M. Geiger, [Review of] "Oskar Becker, *Mathematische Existenz*" [q.v.]. Göttingische gelehrte Anzeigen **190**(9), 401–419 (1928)

C.F. Gethmann, Phänomenologie, Lebensphilosophie und Konstruktive Wissenschaftstheorie. Eine historische Skizze zur Vorgeschichte der Erlanger Schule, in *Lebenswelt und Wissenschaft. Studien zum Verhältnis von Phänomenologie und Wissenschaftstheorie*. Volume 1 of Neuzeit und Gegenwart. Philosophische Studien (Bouvier, Bonn, 1991), pp. 28–77

W. Kamlah, *Der Mensch in der Profanität. Versuch einer Kritik der profanen durch vernehmende Vernunft* (W. Kohlhammer, Stuttgart, 1949)

W. Kamlah, *Philosophische Anthropologie. Sprachkritische Grundlegung und Ethik* (Bibliographisches Institut, Mannheim/Wien/Zürich, 1982)

M. Langanke, Fundamentalphilosophie und philosophische Anthropologie im Werk Wilhelm Kamlahs. Deutsche Zeitschrift für Philosophie **51**, 639–657 (2003)

P. Lorenzen, Regeln vernünftigen Argumentierens, in *Konstruktive Wissenschaftstheorie*. Number 93 in SuhrkampTaschenbuch Wissenschaft (Suhrkamp, Frankfurt-am-Main, 1974), pp. 47–97

[3]Paul Lorenzen, (1974, 5): "... eine Hochstilisierung dessen, was man im praktischen Leben immer schon tut".

P. Lorenzen, Methodical thinking, in *Constructive Philosophy* (The University of Massachusetts Press, Amherst, 1987), pp. 3–29. Trans. by K.R. Pavlovic from "Methodisches Denken", *Ratio* 7 (1965), 1–23, repr. in: id., *Methodisches Denken*, Suhrkamp: Frankfurt am Main 1968, 1974, 24–59

P. Lorenzen, O. Schwemmer, *Konstruktive Logik, Ethik und Wissenschaftstheorie*. Volume 700 of Hochschultaschenbücher (Bibliographisches Institut, Mannheim/Wien/ Zürich, 1973)

G. Misch, Lebensphilosophie und Phänomenologie. Eine Auseinandersetzung der Diltheyschen Richtung mit Heidegger und Husserl. Philosophischer Anzeiger, Vols. 3 (1928–1929) and 4 (1930) (Monographic edition: B.G. Teubner, Leipzig/Berlin, 1931), Stuttgart 1975 with a "Nachwort" to the 3rd edition

G. Schischkoff (ed.), *Philosophisches Wörterbuch*. Volume 13 of Kröners Taschenausgabe, 19th edn. (Alfred Kröner, Stuttgart, 1974)

H. Spiegelberg, *The Phenomenological Movement. A Historical Introduction, I* (Martinus Nijhoff, The Hague, 1961)

H. Zeltner, *Schellings philosophische Idee und das Identitätssystem* (Carl Winters Universitätsbuchhandlung, Heidelberg, 1931) *Beiträge zur Philosophie,* 20; Phil. Diss. Göttingen 1929

H. Zeltner, *Schelling*. Volume XXXIII of Frommanns Klassiker der Philosophie (Friedrich Frommann Verlag, Stuttgart, 1954)

H. Zeltner, Moritz Geiger zum Gedächtnis. Zeitschrift für philosophische Forschung **14**, 452–466 (1960)

H. Zeltner, *Ideologie und Wahrheit. Zur Kritik der politischen Vernunft* (Friedrich Frommann Verlag, Stuttgart-Bad Cannstatt, 1966)

H. Zeltner, Anfang und Ausgang der Schütz-Bewegung. Wilhelm Kamlah zu Ehren. Gottesdienst und Kirchenmusik **4**, 117–123 (1973)

H. Zeltner, Ideologie und Idee. Zum Kallikles-Gespräch (Platon, Gorgias 481 C ff.). Zeitschrift für philosophische Forschung **28**, 3–16 (1974)

H. Zeltner, *Existentielle Kommunikation. Ausgewählte Aufsätze zur Philosophie und Soziologie. Gedenkschrift zum 75. Geburtstag von Hermann Zeltner*. Volume 24 of Erlanger Forschungen, Reihe A: Geisteswissenschaften (Universitätsbund Erlangen-Nürnberg, Erlangen, 1978a)

H. Zeltner, Philosophie als Grundwissenschaft, in *Vernünftiges Denken. Studien zur praktischen Philosophie und Wissenschaftstheorie*, ed. by J. Mittelstraß, M. Riedel (Walter de Gruyter, Berlin/New York, 1978b), pp. 148–157

H. Zeltner, Klopfzeichen. Normative Genese und Ideologiekritik – Ferneres zum Kallikles-Gespräch (PLATON, Gorgias 481 C ff.), in *Konstruktionen versus Positionen. Beiträge zur Diskussion um die Konstruktive Wissenschaftstheorie*, ed. by K. Lorenz. Allgemeine Wissenschaftstheorie, Vol. II (Walter de Gruyter, Berlin/New York, 1979), pp. 245–255

R. Zocher, *Husserls Phänomenologie und Schuppes Logik. Ein Beitrag zur Kritik des intuitionistischen Ontologismus in der Immanenzidee* (Ernst Reinhardt, München, 1932)

Chapter 3
Geometry as a Measurement-Theoretical A Priori: Lorenzen's Defense of Relativity Against the Ontology of Its Proponents

Oliver Schlaudt

3.1 Introduction

In the 1970s Paul Lorenzen presented several papers in which he rejected major parts of the interpretation usually given to the geometric basic concepts both of special relativity (length contraction, time dilatation) and general relativity (curved space) (Lorenzen 1976, 1977, 1979). These papers give expression to an original point of view which challenges a lot of things usually taken for granted in the interpretation of relativity. The argument briefly reads like this:

Already Poincaré in his analysis of applied geometry showed that geometric statements do not simply represent "facts" but on the contrary essentially depend on conventions. In particular the development of non-Euclidean geometries and relativity theories strongly sensitised us to the role of conventions. These conventions cannot be subtracted from the statements in order to achieve pure reality, for one simply cannot speak about reality without using a "language". Poincaré's analysis thus shows that there is no way to defend the point of view that geometry somehow describes space, the latter being understood as an object of empirical research. This is the basic anti-realist attitude Lorenzen essentially shared. However there is more in Lorenzen's approach: Lorenzen, interested in operationalizing the basic concepts of physics, thought of geometry as a normative theory of measurement. According to this point of view, geometry does not deal with nature, but with how to do spatial measurements; it is normative, not descriptive. If there is any sense in speaking about space as an entity or as an object, this entity must be thought of as constituted by the measuring operations.

O. Schlaudt (✉)
Philosophisches Seminar, Universität Heidelberg, Schulgasse 6, 69117 Heidelberg, Germany
e-mail: olivier.schlaudt@univ-lorraine.fr; oliver.schlaudt@urz.uni-heidelberg.de

M. Rebuschi et al. (eds.), *Interdisciplinary Works in Logic, Epistemology, Psychology and Linguistics*, Logic, Argumentation & Reasoning 3,
DOI 10.1007/978-3-319-03044-9_3, © Springer International Publishing Switzerland 2014

The challenging point in this approach is that for reasons of uniqueness and reproducibility geometry, now understood as a theory of measurement, is confined to Euclidean geometry. At face value it seems that Lorenzen's thus conflicts with general relativity, based on non-Euclidean geometry. But, as Lorenzen stressed, this is only true if one presupposes that relativistic phenomena have to be accounted for in geometric terms. The language of curved space-time however is only an interpretation of the data, replacing the dynamical interpretation dominating Newtonian mechanics. In so far as the geometric interpretation is ruled out by Lorenzen's approach, there is still the alternative of pursuing the dynamical interpretation.

I will not engage in a discussion of Lorenzen's alternative account of relativistic effects—this is a topic for experts on relativity. Instead, I will focus on two topics which constitute the originality of Lorenzen's approach: First, Lorenzen's idea of space as an object constituted by the spatial measuring operations. This approach offers an interesting way to give an account of the role of measuring instruments, neglected in most philosophical investigations of geometry. Moreover, it challenges the distinction between pure and applied geometry. Secondly, Lorenzen's approach stresses the point that what is conceived as a "fact" in empirical science is in reality the outcome of a process of interpretation. This process, as one may put it, is governed by tacit interpretation principles, which themselves are interrelated with other methodological basic concepts such as *understanding*, *explanation*, *causality* etc. Both points transcend the customary realism-antirealism quarrel in an original way. As a restriction however it should be stated that Lorenzen's approach is bound up with the way the problem of non-Euclidean geometry was put in the tradition of Riemann, von Helmholtz, and also Carnap in his famous study *Der Raum* of 1922, who focussed on space in the traditional meaning, whereas General Relativity involves four-dimension space-time where space and time depend on each other. Poincaré already in 1912 broached the issue of space-time, (cf. Walter 2009 and Poincaré 1912), but anyhow, as can be seen in Carnap's *Der Raum*, the traditional approach persisted. Put in Lorenzen's terms, to attack the problem of space-time would involve a theory of indirect measurement, for it is dealing with different frames of reference which can be linked with each other only by the way of indirect measurement.

In this paper, I will first give a sketch of some basic characteristics of Lorenzen's philosophy in order to show that interpretation is indeed an important issue in his philosophy of science, though it is usually not set out in terms of interpretation (Sect. 3.2). Next I will present Lorenzen's idea of a "measurement-theoretical a priori" (*messtheoretisches Apriori* (Lorenzen 1980), English (Lorenzen 1987)) which gives sense to his constitutional theory of space. I will cite two historical examples in order to motivate the idea of a priori elements in science (Sect. 3.3). Finally, I will show how Lorenzen applied this to geometry (Sect. 3.4).

3.2 Truth, Facts, and Interpretation in Lorenzen

One might wonder whether it is just to reframe Lorenzen's thought in terms of interpretative principles, a notion which admittedly is not prominent in Lorenzen's methodological basic writings. In relation to the Lorentz transformation however he indeed explicitly spoke of an "*Interpretationsproblem*":

> Lorentz-contraction and Einstein-dilatation raise the problem of interpretation: Do physical objects contract or is the measurement of length modified by motion? Do processes decelerate or is the measurement of time modified by motion? This interpretational problem of the Lorentz-Einstein algorithm (*Formelapparat*) already was debated by Lorentz and Einstein. Lorentz interpreted the alterations as real effects, whereas Einstein interpreted them as effects caused by the measuring procedure. (Lorenzen 1976, p. 386)

Elsewhere Lorenzen emphasised that between both interpretations there is no empirical difference and thus no empirical way to bring about a decision (Lorenzen 1979, p. 1); however a decision can be made and has to be made for methodological reasons:

> One might get the impression that the question whether length contraction is to be understood in geometrical or mechanical terms is a mere quarrel about words. This is wrong, for it makes a difference whether empirical physics (= mechanics) must be preceded by non-empirical Protophysics (= geometry and kinematics) in order to comprehend measurement *adequately*. (Lorenzen 1979, p. 3)

The issue of interpretation thus can indeed be found in Lorenzen's more specialised writings on relativity. I furthermore hold that the problem of interpretation is in fact an important issue of his epistemological thought as sketched in *Logical Propaedeutic. Pre-School of Reasonable Discourse* (Kamlah and Lorenzen 1967). In this book, a sort of founding document of the Erlangen School written in collaboration with Wilhelm Kamlah, Lorenzen rejected the opinion that sentences or propositions somehow represent existing facts the world is thought to be made up of. The reason for this rejection essentially repeats the Kantian argument that cognition cannot be immediately compared to its object:

> Truth, it is said, consists in the agreement of cognition with its object. [...] Now I can compare the object with my cognition, however, only by cognizing it. Hence my cognition is supposed to confirm itself, which is far short of being sufficient for truth. For since the object is outside me, the cognition in me, all I can ever pass judgement on is whether my cognition of the object agrees with my cognition of the object. (Kant 1992, pp. 557–558)

Lorenzen's argument has the very same structure apart from the fact that he replaced cognitions by sentences, i.e., mentalistic by linguistic entities. Kant's argument then reads like this: We cannot refer to facts in order to justify statements about the world, because we could do so only by referring to these facts linguistically, i.e., in the form of the statement we want to justify. Lorenzen finally put the argument in the following way: The word "fact" does not denote an existing entity we can point at; the word "fact" is rather an element of the meta-discourse indicating that we speak about true statements in a way invariant to sameness of content (Kamlah and Lorenzen 1967, Chap. IV, Sects. 2 and 3). This definition refers to true statements and thus rests on Lorenzen's consensus theory of truth also set out in *Logical Propaedeutic* ((Kamlah and Lorenzen 1967, Chap. IV, Sect. 1); here, by the way, Lorenzen is quite close to Habermas (1973)). Truth hence is not introduced with reference to reality, i.e., as adequate representation of reality, but the other way round reality (as the whole of all facts) is introduced with reference to truth. The lesson to be drawn from this is that reality, or facts, is not simply given to us. It is what is finally expressed by sentences or propositions. Lorenzen's considerations turn out to be closely related to Sellar's critique of empiricism, i.e., his critique of the "myth of the given", and I think that the process of mediation involved in giving us facts that are not immediately given might quite reasonably be described as interpretation. According to this view, facts are the linguistic outcome of interpretation. The whole point of Lorenzen's critique of relativity then is that the conditions of the possibility of producing data constrains the interpretation of these data.

3.3 The Measurement-Theoretical A Priori

3.3.1 The Case of Relativity Theory

In relativity theory the distinction between empirical data and interpretative principles is even more evident since relativity—as Einstein put it in 1905—started with methodological considerations about the operationalibility of the basic quantities time and length. If one looks at relativity in a prosaic way, the following story may be told: At the beginning of relativity theory the number of basic terms which count as unproblematic is reduced with respect to classical physics. Simultaneity, e.g., remains valid only for events which occur at neighboring points in space. Simultaneity at distant places is ruled out as a basic term. It has rather to be constructed by means of the new basic terms. Based on the new set of basic terms and a small number of procedural principles a new calculus is established. From a behaviouristic point of view this calculus is so far nothing more than new way to design calculations. It is then supplemented by a physical interpretation which goes beyond the empirical content of the basic terms and principles. One finds that the scientific community refers to "length contraction", "time dilatation", and "curved space". Here we observe a fundamental shift with respect to classical physics which surpasses the abandon of certain basic terms formerly held to be irreducible: While classical theories treated the behaviour of bodies in space and the course of events in time, relativity theory is said to be a theory of space and time itself. These utterances are surprising in light of the careful or even scrupulous methodological foundation of relativity: What should it mean to say that space is curved and time dilates? How can it be justified to transcribe properties observed in bodies in space and time to space and time themselves?

The story I have told here was admittedly designed to make these utterances appear highly metaphysical. Nevertheless the doubts it serves to raise have a rational and justifiable core. (It should be added for sake of impartiality that these kinds of doubt raising strategies always work symmetrically: Once one accepts that it is a difficult step to transcribe properties to space and time themselves, one will also be aware of the analogous difficulties in ascribing properties to bodies in time and space, for these properties too are not observed, but *inferred* on the basis of data interpreted as their utterances. We are comparing two interpretational schemes with each other, not an interpretation with reality.) The doubts risen here call forth the twofold endeavour on the one hand to ask systematically for the meaning of the utterances in question and on the other hand to develop strategies to defend them. These two parts clearly reflect respectively empiricist and rationalist positions. A careful reading of Lorenzen's papers shows arguments indebted to both positions. On the one hand one finds critical remarks known from von Helmholtz, Mach, Carnap and Reichenbach, and on the other hand there are efforts to make a priori statements about space and time which pick up traditional kantian arguments known, e.g., from von Kries and Cassirer. By "a priori" Lorenzen *nota bene* did not mean the possibility of deriving in an a priori way statements which physicists worked hard to find by experience.[1] The meaning of "a priori" adopted here is rather related to the neo-kantian position: In so far as the object of investigation is defined, shaped, or constituted by the means of its investigation, the study of these means will allow us to make statements about the form of possible empirical results, as also becomes clear in the following quotation form *Logical Propaedeutic*:

> Does the justification of these truths require empirically true sentences or does they follow from nothing but reasonable conventions of linguistic means (which then in turn will be used by us e.g., in empirically true sentences)? This is what is behind the dispute between empiricists and apriorists. (Kamlah and Lorenzen 1967, p. 202)

In this framework the term "a priori" obviously does not refer to non-empirical sources of knowledge situated in some faculty of the subject. It is of course this sense which makes this term appear dubious and suspect. In Lorenzen on the contrary "a priori" simply indicates consequences of linguistic means established by convention within the reconstruction of scientific theories. Therefore "a priori" in particular is used as a binary predicate: "p is a priori in relation to q". I think that this relative notion of a priori grasps best the meaning we find in Lorenzen. In particular it shows the difference to Dingler, the forerunner of the Erlangen School

[1] Cf. Reichenbach's critique of Kraus: "On the basis of an apriorist philosophy, he wants to assert something about the behaviour of physical things; he wants to *deduce* physics from philosophy", in Reichenbach (1978, Vol. II, 8).

as its members themselves put it.[2] For Dingler indeed the whole system of physics had to be reconstructed by means of a priori principles. Contingency was plainly ruled out. All cases of experience inconsistent with the theory were systematically treated as the outcome of disturbance and error. Lorenzen on the contrary is concerned with *basing* scientific experience instead of *de*basing it. He asks for the necessary conditions, for instance, of quantitative measuring results. The whole point of his approach is that establishing the methods of scientific investigation constrains the range of interpretations which may be given to the empirical results obtained. It should also be mentioned that the restriction to linguistic means in the above quotation is dropped in Lorenzen's philosophy of physics, the so-called *Protophysics* which is essentially concerned with technical means of measurement.

3.3.2 Kant's Transcendental Philosophy

Lorenzen's term "measurement-theoretical a priori" clearly alludes to Kant. In his transcendental philosophy as presented in the *Critique of pure reason* (Kant 1787), Kant aims at the conditions of the possibility of knowledge, especially or even exclusively of scientific knowledge, as neo-kantian philosophers pointed out (Böhme 1986). In his solution of the antinomies of pure reason Kant presents a model of what these conditions might be and how a priori knowledge of scientific objects might be derived from them. In the antinomies, Kant discusses the hypotheses of atoms or of a beginning of the world in regard to time as well as a limit in space. In short one can say that he rejects both the hypothesis of finiteness as well as the contrary hypothesis of actual infiniteness of the world because both deal with the world as a *given totality*. For Kant the total world is never actually given, but only *given as a task* (*nicht gegeben, sondern aufgegeben*—B 526-7 and B 508-9). This *task* itself is to be resolved in a *regress* leading from a given entity to its causal, temporal or spatial conditions and from there to the pre-conditions and so on. This regress seems to be intended for modeling the process of scientific enquiry, and the knowledge of the methods of enquiry already allows Kant to gain a priori knowledge of the object of enquiry: The methods of science—e.g., measuring spatial and temporal distances—demand an in*de*finite size of the world, not more and not

[2] In his *Vorwort* to Dingler's *Aufbau der exakten Fundamentalwissenschaften*, Lorenzen presented Dinglers philosophy as a continuation of the Kantian transcendental philosophy *after its collapse in the face of empiricist attacks in nineteenth century* (Lorenzen 1964, p. 10). As an interpretation of Dingler's philosophy this may be regarded as too benevolent. As a characterization of his own point of view it may however be accepted. In particular it is evident from this that Lorenzen's concept of a priori is closely related to Reichenbach's "relative a priori" in being constitutive but not apodictic.

less. Hence the process of scientific investigation is indefinite.[3] If we reach e.g., in measuring space a point where we cannot proceed our very method of measurement rules out the hypothesis of an end of space itself and forces us to suppose an obstacle *in* space. The same holds for splitting matter: if we reach in splitting matter a particle which we are not able to split, there is nothing in our experience of this particle what would permit us to regard this particle as an atom, i.e., as indivisible. The particle has just to be regarded as not yet split and as demanding further efforts.— Here we are already concerned with a priori knowledge of the object of scientific investigation. We can conceptualise the possibility of this a priori knowledge in the following terms: We say that the scientific object is *constituted* by the means of its scientific investigation. Hence the scientific object cannot possess any properties which are ruled out by the very means of its investigation. The rules of scientific research *nota bene* do not allow us to deduce further a priori knowledge in the sense that they permit us to know a priori which concrete experiences we can expect in a certain case; but they allow the deduction of a priori knowledge in the sense that they rule out a priori a certain interpretation of our experiences and force us to adopt a different interpretation.

3.3.3 Examples

It will be helpful to sketch two examples from history of science which show that the abstract scheme taken from kantian philosophy applies to the natural sciences. These two examples are largely inspired by Cassirer's study *Substance and Function* (Cassirer 1923), whose conclusions I nonetheless do not necessarily share.

3.3.3.1 Conservation of Energy

It is well known that Leibniz was an advocate of the principle of conservation of mechanical energy or *vis viva*. Less known is the purpose this principle served in the framework of Leibnizian dynamics. Far from being an empirical law of nature or a hypothesis meant to be verified empirically, the principle of energy conservation belonged to the class of principles which we can characterise as an *measurement-theoretical a priori*: It was not the result of measurement, but served as a foundation of measurement procedures.

The principle of energy conservation firstly emerged in connection with the measurement of the so-called "force" of a moving body. It was clear that the force is a unique function of the velocity and the quantity of matter of the moving

[3]As is known, Kant considered the regress of splitting matter to be infinite. I agree with Wilhelm Wundt that this assumption rests on a mistake and that in effect every regress is indefinite—cf. Wundt (1910, pp. 82–83).

body, but its definite form was unknown.[4] Furthermore all participants of this controversy agreed on the fact that the force of a moving body can be measured only indirectly, namely by its effects. This is the point where conservation of energy comes into play: Leibniz insisted that the measurement of a cause by its total effect is valid if and only if the effect is "equipollent" to its cause, i.e., if the relevant quantity characterising the cause is exactly conserved in the total effect—nothing is lost and nothing is gained. This has straightforward consequences for the form of the function determining the force of a moving body: Once the effect and its measure are well-defined, the measure of force must be designed in such a way that the conservation of force is expressed in the numerical constancy of its measure (cf. McLaughlin 1996). The concrete form of the effect to be defined in order to measure the force of a moving body was the real object of the vis-viva-controversy. Leibniz chose the height to which a moving body ascends in the gravitational field of the earth. In connection with Galilei's law of falling bodies he directly obtained the well known measure of *vis viva*, mass times velocity squared. The Cartesians as well as Samuel Clarke chose the height divided by time, what lead to mass times velocity as the measure of the moving force. In Leibniz' reasoning we clearly and easily recognise that the conservation of energy is not an empirical result of quantitative research. On the contrary, it is a *condition of the possibility* of quantitative research and hence of scientific knowledge in its mathematical form.

Once the principle of energy conservation is adopted, we are thus able to measure energy and hence to treat it mathematically. But, as we have seen, apriorical principles frame our experience of the world in a twofold sense: They not only permit scientific access to the world (for example in shaping the phenomena in such a way as to enable them to enter into mathematical reasoning), but also oblige us to a certain interpretation of our experience and rule out other possible interpretations. This second sense also is valid in the case of energy conservation, for indeed by virtue of this principle any case of its violation is ruled out as basic fact and thus as a valid counter-example. In such cases the *phenomenal* loss of energy has to be reinterpreted as an *apparent* loss of energy. An example of such a case is the completely inelastic impact of two bodies of same mass and equal but opposite velocities. In such a collision the complete *vis viva* is destroyed since both bodies are at rest afterwards. Given this case—of course well known to him—Leibniz concluded that the *vis viva* is not destroyed, but transferred to the invisible constituent parts of the two bodies (Leibniz 1962, vol. 6, 230). At first sight this seems to be a simple ad-hoc-hypothesis designed in order to save a theory. The important point here is that Leibniz was *right* in his conclusion. By that I do not mean that the development of science confirmed his view some 200 years later. I mean that his conclusion was *in the framework of his theory* perfectly justified and even necessary: Once energy conservation is adopted in order to render the phenomena quantifiable, the detection of a loss of energy cannot indicate a

[4] As a straightforward presentation of this issue cf. Leibniz' letter to de l'Hospital, in Leibniz (2004, pp. 616–625).

violation of the principle of energy conservation. Even more: the principle of energy conservation is actually the foundation of the quantitative expression of the apparent loss of energy itself. But now the apparent loss of energy has to be understood as indicating that the physical system under investigation has changed: the conserved energy serves as a criterion of the identity of the system under investigation.[5] We see that interpretative principles impose an *evaluation of facts* which is expressed in the distinction between obvious and apparent phenomena. Indeed the rhetoric of appearance and reality (understood as the distinction between facts which result from an entanglement of phenomena and simple facts which are held to express a pure phenomenon) is essential to scientific discourse.

3.3.3.2 The Principle of Inertia

As a second example I refer to the principle of inertia. I am not going to elaborate on this example because the very same lesson can be drawn from it as from first one. Ernst Cassirer stressed the transcendental character of this principle in his study *Substance and Function*:

> Inertia is for Galileo [. . .] a postulate that we cannot do without in the scientific exposition of phenomena, but which is not itself a concrete sensible process of external reality. (Cassirer 1923, p. 169)

The principle plainly cannot be empirical in the simplest sense since nobody ever observed a movement not subjected to any force. But there is a deeper point: Without an equivalent principle it is not even clear what it means (in quantitative terms) to be subjected to an external force. Again a force can be determined only in terms of its effects, and thus these effects themselves have to be defined. The first step here consists in defining the absence of forces, as is well known from Newton's *Mathematical Principles of Natural Philosophy*: In order to grasp what happens if a force is acting we first have to know what happens if *no* force is acting, i.e., if nothing happens (cf. Damerow et al. 2004, pp. 71–72). At first a *baseline* has to be defined from which explanation departs.[6] Its fixation clearly has a *normative* meaning. It tells the scientist what has to be explained and how it has to be explained (e.g., in terms of acting forces). Such a fixation is necessary since it must always be possible to phrase facts to be explained in the form of an alternative: "why does x happen rather than y?". In classical mechanics this is done by means of the principle of inertia which states that a body not subjected to a force "endeavors to preserve in its present state, whether it be of rest, or of moving uniformly forward in a

[5]This is the—very plausible—interpretation of Freudenthal (1999).

[6]Of course inertia does not figure in Newton's *Mathematical Principles of Natural Philosophy* as an explanatory baseline, but is (in definition III) attributed to matter as a *faculty*, the *potentia resistendi*. Nevertheless, this does not change the functional role of inertia in the science of mechanics.

straight line". Having fixed this, one can ask why planets surround the sun rather than proceeding on a straight line.

From the necessity of such a baseline *nota bene* does not follow its uniqueness. The baseline of dynamical theories indeed changed within history: in aristotelian physics it was movement coming to rest, in newtonian mechanics movement of constant velocity and direction, in general relativity finally the free fall. Note that these principles of inertia cannot claim empirical truth since it is not possible to study forces independently of their dynamical effects. Nevertheless, we believe in a principle of inertia and reinterpret all its obvious violations as apparent violations, caused by invisible yet real forces whose mathematical expression rests totally on the principle in question. Thus it is justified to consider this principle as a measurement-theoretical a priori of the program of dynamics. Since it is not simply empirical one could say that it fixes a baseline *arbitrarily*, that it arbitrarily cuts a swath through reality. The establishment of a explanatory program as e.g., the dynamical program connected to inertia may then be studied from a sociological point of view.[7] From a philosophical point of view however it is possible to show that the principle in question is linked to a certain concept of *explanation*, i.e., explanation in terms of acting forces.

From this especially follows that inertia itself cannot be explained, at least not in terms of acting forces. It seems to some extent that such an explanation of inertia is aimed at in the context of "Mach's Principle". This principle states, according to Jammer (1993, p. 109), that the inertia of a body is determined by the masses of the universe and their distribution. From the literature it is not always evident what the discussion accompanying this principle exactly is about. But when e.g., Sciama claims in his paper *On the Origin of Inertia* of 1953 that

> inertia is not an intrinsic property of matter, but arises as a result of the interaction of matter with the rest of the matter in the universe (Sciama 1953, p. 35)

this strongly seems to be a *hysteron proteron*, since interaction is defined relatively to inertia and thus cannot explain inertia. Given a certain uniformly moving body it is of course possible to explain the constancy of its motion by showing that the net force acting on it is zero. But this does not explain inertia, on the contrary it presupposes inertia, since it is an explanation of the behavior of an inertial mass under certain circumstances. Inertia allows us to set up a quantitative calculus of forces in order to explain deviations from inertial motion. To apply this calculus to inertia itself is a misuse—unless the explanatory baseline is tacitly redefined. But this of course does not provide an explanation of previously unexplained facts. By redefining the explanatory baseline we simply redefine what a fact is. Applying the calculus of forces based on inertia to inertia itself is a kind of theoretical excess as it also appeared in the development of symbolic logic, when meta-theoretic principles of the calculus like the principles of excluded middle and of non-contradiction itself

[7] As Michael Wolff did with the older impetus theory, cf. Wolff (1978, 1987).

were translated in symbolic formulae. Lorenzen explicitly criticised this misuse of the symbolism in logic (Kamlah and Lorenzen 1967, pp. 206–207). Though this point is common sense among modern logicians, it seems that nobody ever considered this symbolic excess as a pitfall of algorithmic theories in general, comprising physics.

From these two examples it is clear, I think, that the concept of relative a priori, and in particular Lorenzen's concept of a measurement-theoretical a priori, can well be applied to the analysis of natural sciences and promises to be a fruitful instrument of philosophical analysis. Indeed theories contain principles which define a baseline in order (1) to define the phenomena to be explained and (2) to render them quantifiable. In addition, we saw that a conflict can occur between the use of a theory and its methodological presuppositions. This is of special interest for us, for Lorenzen's remarks on relativity are closely related to this point.

3.4 Geometry: Science of Space?

3.4.1 Geometry and Spatial Measurement

On the basis of the observations made in the preceding sections it is rather easy to present the consequences for the measurement of spatial quantities and for the theory of relativity as Lorenzen developed them. As I already stated at the beginning of this paper, Lorenzen's arguments consist of two opposed currents, a critical one and a constructive one, respectively inheriting empiricist and rationalist positions.

3.4.1.1 Lorenzen's Critique

At the end of the nineteenth century it was discovered that the *metrical* space can be characterised by the invariance of a certain differential form (the infinitesimal line segment *ds*) under infinitesimal rotations. Sophus Lie elaborated this idea in technical terms (Weyl 1990, p. 746). This approach to the geometrical space allows to systematically study and classify (Euclidean as well as non-Euclidean) geometries. It thereby entirely rests on the methods of analytic geometry as its proper medium. In this sense Riemann in his *Ueber die Hypothesen, welche der Geometrie zu Grunde liegen* considered space as a three-dimensional manifold, i.e., as a set of points having certain properties, in order to explicitly presuppose in a next step a *function* mapping these points on triples of real numbers $\{x_i | i = 1, 2, 3\}$, the *coordinates* of the points (Riemann 1990, p. 307). All his subsequent investigations of manifolds are based on this coordinate representation. In particular he defines a certain differential form of the coordinates, the infinitesimal line segment *ds*. This permits him to characterise all manifolds in which this expression is invariant under certain transformations as *metric spaces*. In these spaces, which are found to be manifolds of constant curvature, *ds* serves to define the *distance* between two points x and y:

$$s = \int_{\vec{x}}^{\vec{y}} ds = \int_0^1 \sqrt{\sum_i \left(\frac{dx_i(\lambda)}{d\lambda}\right)^2} d\lambda$$

In this way finally metric geometry is established, i.e. a geometry containing quantitative expressions about distances between points. We have to ask however—and Lorenzen indeed asked (Lorenzen 1984, pp. 81, 115–123, 209, 218, 232)—what the meaning of the coordinates figuring in this expression is (in the integration limits as well as in the integrand), if this expression itself serves to introduce the concept of distance. Aren't they already to be considered as numerical representations of distances? Riemann pretended to establish the meaning of metric expressions by means of analytic geometry, but in reality the analytic method presupposes measurement. Riemann started with a numerical representation without taking into account that such a representation can only be the result of measurement, not its precondition.

This is Lorenzen's critique, developed in *Elementargeometrie* from 1984, which indeed repeats Helmholtz' remarks on Riemann from 1870 (Helmholtz 1896, p. 15). This critique *nota bene* does exclude numerical manifolds as means to present and to study the various geometrical systems like Riemann did in his famous talk. It banishes them only from the foundations of geometry. The insight that numerical manifolds are not at all necessary for this purpose marked, as Hans Freudenthal emphasized (Freudenthal 1960, p. 7), a difficult step in the development of geometry. Lorenzen's critique in turn raises the question of how to establish spatial measurement. It thus evokes the complementary, constructive part of Lorenzen's approach.

3.4.1.2 Lorenzen's Foundation of Measurement

Indeed both, Helmholtz and Lorenzen, tried to solve the problem of the foundations of measurement. Helmholtz' proposal is well known. He replaced Riemann's *hypotheses* by the *empirical fact* of the existence of freely movable rigid bodies (Helmholtz 1883, 1896). This attempt to establish physical geometry however raises the question of how to define and to verify a body's rigidity without measuring. In fact Helmholtz defined rigidity in geometrical quantitative terms, namely as constancy of its length. Hence he again commits the circle he himself objected to Riemann as was shortly thereafter noticed by authors like Hölder (1900, pp. 5, 30), Dingler (1925, pp. 310–330), and Veronese (1891) (cf. Heath (1926, vol. III, pp. 226–227)).

Lorenzen, aware of these problems, chooses a different way to establish spatial measurement. The solution presented in the Erlangen School consists in so-called *theory of forms* (*Formentheorie*). It was part of the more general program of the so-called *Protophysik* to ground the natural sciences by giving non-circular operational definitions of the base quantities length, time, and mass (Janich 1985). I will only give a short account of the theory of forms for it is rather its consequences than its details which are of interest in the present context. The theory of forms is about the forms of spatial figures of one, two, or three dimensions without taking in account the actual magnitude of these objects. The forms are thus the object of the purely qualitative "basic geometry" (*Elementargeometrie*), ranging between topology—studying the properties of figures that are preserved under continuous *de*formations—and geometry in the strict sense—studying metric properties, i.e., both form and magnitude.[8] Beginning with an operationally defined plane surface as the most fundamental form and then successively joining more complicated forms like straight lines, right angles and so on it is finally possible to give account of the sameness of length of spatially separated line segments. This allows—if it works—a non-circular test of rigidity of physical bodies.[9]

The important point here is that the magnitude-invariant theory of forms implies the axiom of parallels and thus *Euclidean geometry*. As was already known to John Wallis, the existence of a relation of similarity between geometrical forms of different seize implies the axiom of parallels and hence Euclidean geometry (Rozenfeld 1988, p. 97). On the contrary, non-Euclidean geometry does not provide such a similarity since in non-Euclidean geometry the properties of figures (like the angular sum of a triangle) depend directly on their absolute magnitude. Advocates of the protophysical program went so far as to speak of the "enforcability of Euclidean geometry" (*Erzwingbarkeit der Euklidischen Geometrie*, Janich (1992)). For the interpretation of relativity it is however not even the most important question if it is really possible to realise or to put into practice Euclidean geometry. The important point is merely that there is no alternative in order to achieve unique data in reproducible measurement. To sum up the argument: Quantitative methods, which are to achieve unique data, require a foundation framed in non-quantitative terms. In geometry this foundation consists in a theory of forms which itself, according to Lorenzen, implies Euclidicity.

---

[8]As Michael Wolff recently has shown (Wolff 2001), Kant's notion of geometry corresponds perfectly to the idea of a theory of forms. The straight line for example is defined by Kant in purely qualitative terms as a self-similar line, i.e. as a line whose parts are similar both to each other and to the whole line. The quantitative archimedean property of being the shortest line connecting two points is inferred from this definition in a *synthetical* way, presenting thus a *synthetic a priori judgment*. Also Bertrand Russell (1896, p. 38) stressed that the straight line, "if it is to serve as the basis of metrical properties, has to be defined without reference to this properties" and thus in a purely qualitative way.

[9]Lorenzen's *Elementrageometrie* in fact fails to give a non-circular criterion of rigidity. Nevertheless this failure was not due to the strategy developed there. For a more promising realisation of this program cf. Janich (1976).

3.4.2 *Applied and Pure Geometry: Helmholtz, Russell, Couturat*

Lorenzen was not the first one to criticise Riemann and Helmholtz. Similar criticisms are found e.g., in the young Betrand Russell's nowadays rather disesteemed *Essay on the Foundations of Geometry* from 1897 as well as in the writings of a lot of other critical or neo-kantian authors from the epoch between the discovery of non-Euclidean geometries and their application in physics. There is no hint in Lorenzen that he was aware of, or interested in, this tradition, nor were to my knowledge these historical relations ever studied. I shall elaborate on this topic in order to make clear where Lorenzen nevertheless differs from these earlier approaches and hence wherein the originality of his own view consists.

Russell's approach, mainly inspired by the development of metageometry in the late nineteenth century, is characterised by a double step back, on the one hand from applied to pure geometry and on the other hand from the axioms of Euclidean geometry to those which are common to all geometries with constant curvature. The first step resulted from his critique of Helmholtz, who held that free mobility of rigid bodies is a condition of measurement. Russell noticed the failure to give a noncircular criterion of free mobility and rigidity (Russell 1897). Russell added that strictly speaking there are no rigid bodies, since all physical bodies deform when pushed. He concluded from this that free mobility does not refer to physical bodies, but to geometrical shapes. He thus withdrew from physical reality to pure geometry. This distinction later was taken up by Einstein in his famous talk *Geometrie und Erfahrung* of 1921, by way of which it exerted considerable influence e.g., on members of the Vienna Circle like Philipp Frank (1957, pp. 85–87); in a review of Nagel's *The Structure of Science* Grünbaum raised the question whether Poincaré's conventionalism applies to pure or to applied geometry, which shows that there was indeed an ambiguity in the status of geometry which is not always noticed (Grünbaum 1962, p. 303). In Russell's 1897 *Essay* "metrization" consequently did not stand for the operationalization of length, but meant introducing the concept of distance in projective geometry. Russell took up Riemann's insight that free mobility of geometrical figures is guaranteed in all spaces of constant curvature, i.e., besides Euclidean geometry, in Lobachevskian and in Riemannian geometry. He thus made a second retreat to projective geometry,[10] containing the axioms common to all three of these geometries, i.e., the axiom of free movability (as explained above), the axiom of dimension (space must have a finite whole number of dimensions), and the axiom of distance (two points must determine a unique spatial quantity, i.e., distance). Russell hold these axioms to be a priori true, since they are necessary and sufficient conditions of measure

[10]For more details on the notion of projective geometry and its use by Russell cf. Torretti (1978, pp. 303–307).

(in the sense of pure geometry, as explained above) and characterise space as a form of externality which necessarily is passive, indifferent, and homogeneous. Euclidean Space is characterised by three additional axioms (the axiom of parallels; the number of dimensions is three; two straight lines cannot enclose a space, cf. Russell 1897, Sect. 177) which Russell considered to be true as a matter of experience.

At this point Louis Couturat who wrote a extensive review of Russell's *Essay on the Foundations of Geometry* and who was the driving force behind its French translation attacked Russell's reasoning. He did so by turning Russell's argument against itself: When claiming that the truth of the axioms of Euclidean Geometry is a matter of experience, Russell silently made a step ahead to applied geometry. But in applied geometry, Couturat rightly insisted, every experiment on the true geometry is circular, for it rests on assuming the validity of the geometry to be proven for the measurement device (Couturat 1898, pp. 370–372; cf. also Couturat 1896, pp. 648–650). Couturat knew this critique from Poincaré to whom he indeed referred, but also other authors like Ernst Mach (1926, p. 419) emphasized that curvature of space cannot be detected in direct measurement since all deformations affect both the distances measured and the measuring device. Note that these arguments from Poincaré and Mach already suffice to reject realism in regard to physical geometry, for they show that experimental facts always depend on two factors: space (or at least a given mass distribution in space) and the measuring device. Poincaré reached solid ground by *conventionally* attributing certain properties to the latter. This allows referring the experimental data to spatial facts which, then, however rest on conventions. Though Lorenzen to my knowledge never referred to Poincaré, he would, I think, agree with the critical part of the argument. As regards the second part, we will see that he developed an alternative view.

From Poincarés and Mach's arguments against verification in geometry Couturat drew the conclusion that the truth of the axioms specifying Euclidean space must equally be a priori provable. It is interesting to see that this position need not necessarily to be a Kantian one. Indeed Couturat refused the idea of synthetic judgements based in intuition already in his discussion of Renouvier (Couturat 1893a, pp. 84–85).[11] He rather sought for a proof of the axioms in more general rational principles.[12] Since, as Russell had shown, these axioms are not preconditions of measurement, they must be a consequence of the preconditions of experience as such, i.e., consequences of properties which belong to space as a form of externality, being passive, indifferent, and homogeneous. Couturat held that an interdependence of form and magnitude would be in contradiction with this idea of space. Couturat's point was that in non-Euclidean geometries the properties of figures depend on

[11] Walter (2009, pp. 194–195), is thus wrong in counting Couturat among the neo-Kantians.

[12] As regards the role of rational principles in Couturat, cf. Bowne (1966).

their absolute magnitude or on the absolute magnitude of the universe, what he thought to be in contradiction with the relativity of magnitude. Thus there must be the possibility of similar figures of different size, which is equivalent to Euclidean geometry. Couturat put emphasis on the relativity of magnitude, which he considered to be the rational foundation of Euclidean geometry as an a priori truth (Couturat 1893a, pp. 76–79, 1893b, pp. 304–307). I do not think that this argument is right, for most natural laws state relations holding between absolute quantities (though expressed in a relative way), except those laws explicitly stated in terms of ratios, as Kepler's law or the law of the lever. In Lorenzen however, the argument takes a different turn: Lorenzen did not think of the dependence of form and magnitude as contradictory as such, but as circular in regard to the aim of establishing measurement. In so far as geometry serves as the practical fundament of measurement, it must not refer to quantity, that is, must not distinguish between similar figures of different absolute magnitude.

I shall elaborate on this point in order to make clear the differences between Couturat and Lorenzen. As we have seen, the distinction between pure and applied geometry is essential for Russsell, and even more for Couturat who held that all axioms of Euclidean geometry can be proven a priori. Accordingly, pure space must be Euclidean, and, as I should stress, the actual geometry of physical space is determined by that as Euclidean too. In Lorenzen, we find quite similar arguments, e.g., as regards his critique of Riemann and Helmholtz. The "direction of determination" between space and measurement, however, are opposed in Lorenzen. Lorenzen, with Dingler, didn't step back into pure geometry in view of the manifest problems of giving a noncircular criterion of rigidity. On the contrary, he attacked the problem of spelling out such a criterion. This is what protogeometry and protophysics is all about. It turned out that such a noncircular foundation of geometry is committed to Euclidean geometry. Euclidean geometry thus is a priori proven to be valid for pure geometry, because pure geometry studies space as it is constituted by measurement. In Lorenzen, the direction of determination hence does not point from pure to applied geometry, as in Couturat, but from applied to pure, i.e., from measurement to the object constituted by measurement. Despite some similarities in argumentation, Lorenzen worked out a totally different approach to geometry, attributing a constitutional role to the concrete instruments of research.

This discussion shows the originality of Lorenzen's approach to geometry, ascribing a constitutional role to the measuring instruments. In Russell and Couturat physical geometry was (partly or completely) determined by pure geometry. Later, especially adherents of Logical Empiricism felt the need to add an explicit "physical interpretation" of geometric basic terms in order to get to physical geometry. This probably was mainly due to Poincaré. Among these authors, Philipp Frank in particular absorbed some ideas from Dingler. He thus stressed the point that in these physical interpretations, technological procedures are involved (Frank 1957, p. 79). Though well-intentioned, this completely misses the point in Dingler and Lorenzen, for Frank, too, conceived technological practice as a later supplement to pure geometry. The inversion of this relation between theory and practice, I think, is the main interest of the philosophy of science of the Erlangen school.

3.4.3 Three Possible Critiques

In the preceding sections it was shown that a non-circular way to establish spatial measurement rests on a magnitude-invariant theory of forms which itself implies Euclidean geometry. I want to elaborate on the last step which led from the foundations of *spatial measurement* to the Euclidean *structure of space itself*. This step of course is anything but trivial. I will show the sense in which the step from the euclidicity of the measuring device to Euclidean space has to be understood and the extent to which this step is sound. I will do that by discussing three critiques.

3.4.3.1 Poincaré, Carnap, and Wind: Experience and Theory

First it may be (and has been) doubted whether spatial measurement really needs Euclidean measuring devices. Carnap discussed in his doctoral thesis the possibility of different "measure conventions" (Carnap 1922); Edgar Wind in his habilitation thesis *Experiment and Metaphysics* (*Das Experiment und die Metaphysik*, first published in 1934) took up the idea of measuring by means of non-rigid bodies (Wind 1934, pp. 90–91). Following Carnap and Poincaré, Wind sketched a procedure for performing measurements on the surface of the earth using a measuring device which he called a "wild body". This wild body is supposed to change its length depending on the latitude: Starting with a certain length at the north-pole, it is to shrink or contract approaching the equator. Wind of course recognised that such a thought-experiment would become physically meaningful if and only if one succeeded in finding or producing this wild body. He explicitly says:

> If such a body, whose behaviour in relation to an iron rod has been determined in a mathematically unique way, really exists, is a completely meaningful question to be answered by means of experiment. (Wind 1934, pp. 90–91)

From this it is perfectly clear that, in order to use such a wild body in measurements which are to produce unique and reproducible data, its "wild" behaviour must be anything but wild. On the contrary, it must be perfectly known and verifiable. Since this behaviour cannot be fixed in purely qualitative terms, its description already presupposes measurement. I do not deny that the usage of such a "wild body" may be convenient in some situations. But it does not discharge the scientist from fixing an antecedent measure which can be described in a non-quantitative way. Carnap, by the way, in his 1922 study committed the very same error as Wind, even though in a less evident way. What Carnap did indeed show in his study is that every spatio-temporal theory, once acquired, can be arbitrarily reparametrized with respect to the temporal and the spatial variables without loosing its empirical content or becoming self-contradictory—a more or less trivial point. The initial measure convention, as Carnap called it, is however anything but arbitrary. It is determined by the requirement of uniqueness and reproducibility.

3.4.3.2 Böhme's Critique: What Is the Subject Constituted?

Unlike Wind, Gernot Böhme accepted that the measuring devices have to be Euclidean in order to provide data in a unique and reproducible way. Nevertheless in a critique published in 1976 he attacked the step leading from the euclidicity of the measuring device to Euclidean space. Put in Kantian vocabulary he denied that Protophysics can be regarded as a theory of the constitution of the object of scientific enquiry: Though Protophysics aims at the conditions of the possibility of experience of objects, it does not show that these conditions really have to be regarded as conditions of the possibility of the objects themselves (Böhme 1976, p. 225). For example, Böhme argues, there might be (and actually are) objects in space of any non-Euclidean surface (like the earth) without forcing us to adopt a certain geometrical system in order to describe them. Böhme concludes that the requirement of Euclidean measuring devices merely is a constraint for the formulation of theories: Every theory of space, if it claims to be empirically meaningful and thus rests on measurement, just has to be Euclidean at the scale of the laboratory to which the measuring devices belong.[13] But this reasoning itself is not sound. Of course nobody denies the existence of material objects of spherical or any irregular surface. But these surfaces, as we perceive them with our senses, are not the scientific objects in question. What we are interested in is *how these objects enter into mathematical reasoning*. Spatial objects can be treated mathematically only insofar as they are transformed into spatial quantities, i.e., numerically expressible distances, surfaces and volumes. Rightly understood, these *quantities*, not the material objects instantiating them, are the proper objects constituted by the measurement procedures. In the case of geometry we thus could consider as the object constituted the *metrical space* understood as the embodiment of all spatial quantities. This metrical space may be visualised in the form of a three-dimensional lattice of infinite extension (Lorenzen 1984). In order to be reproducible this lattice however must be definable in purely qualitative terms and is consequently, as we have seen, Euclidean. Within this Euclidean lattice then of course can be mathematically represented objects of each surface, also non-Euclidean ones.

3.4.3.3 Reichenbach's Reply to Dingler

If one finally accepts that geometrical space somehow is constituted by the means of spatial measurement and that the measuring devices have to be Euclidean, one can nevertheless raise doubts that by means of the euclidicity of the measuring device the structure of space is determined as Euclidean too. This is what Reichenbach did

[13] A similar point of view is advanced by Michael Wolff (2001, pp. 227–232) and by Horst-Heino v. Borzeszkowski and Renate Wahsner (1995).

in a reply to Dingler. He insisted that from a logical point of view it is still possible to refute Euclidean geometry even though its validity has been presupposed:

> It can very well be demonstrated that space is *not* Euclidean even if it is at first assumed to be Euclidean; if by assuming $A = B$ one can, with the help of other statements, derive $A \neq B$, this is a contradiction, and therefore '$A \neq B$' must be true. (Reichenbach 1978, I, pp. 21–22)

What Reichenbach had in mind is an argument of the form "if p implies non-p, then non-p" which indeed is sound. Nevertheless Reichenbach's reply missed Dingler's point. Dingler was not concerned with logic but with *experience*. His (and Lorenzen's) point was that experiences made with Euclidean measuring rods cannot be considered as hints of a non-Euclidean structure of space. Non-Euclidean measuring results have instead to be related to objects *in* space. One sees that again the whole point is about the *interpretation* of experience.

3.4.4 Geometry and Dynamics

Having criticized Riemann's analytic approach to geometry Lorenzen developed the idea of a measurement-theoretical a priori in order to investigate what nevertheless might be said a priori about space. The result can be summarized as follows: Any discourse about space *itself* cannot be regarded as a matter of experience but, if it is not to be rejected all together, has to be understood as dealing with the preconditions of measurement and hence of numerically representing spatial quantities instantiated *in* space. This "space" may be visualised in the form of a threedimensional lattice of infinite extension. The quotation-marks are appropriate in view of the fact that this "space" is not subject of empirical investigations but the embodiment of the preconditions of the investigation of things in space.

As an important consequence it should be noted that in this picture the results of spatial measurement can no longer be interpreted as a hint of a non-Euclidean structure of space. On the contrary, they must always be related to physical deformations of entities in space. If e.g., in a cosmic triangulation it happens that the angular sum is found to differ from 180°, there are prima facie two possible explanations: First, the measurement may have been incorrect. This is the trivial case which I will leave aside. But secondly, it is always possible that the triangle realised, e.g., by lightrays is subjected to external forces deforming it. This ambiguity was Poincaré's main point. In this spirit the neo-kantian philosopher Johannes von Kries stated (1916, p. 23): If we emit a ray of light and this ray surprisingly returns to its origin, this does not show that straight lines always return to their origin (as would be the case in certain curved spaces) but that the ray of light deviates from the straight line. And of course it does so only under the influence of an external force. We recognise here the distinction between ideal and physical geometry. The point here is that whatever the behaviour of physical bodies might be, we have to maintain a certain form of ideal geometry. With Lorenzen we can say that this ideal geometry does not serve as a description of space, but as a transcendental theory of measurement. As Johannes von Kries clearly saw and as we have seen in our study of the principles of energy conservation and of inertia, such an ideal theory does not rule out any particular physical experience; it just commits us to a *dynamical* interpretation of the effects, which are at the same time defined as mathematically treatable entities only due to the aprioric principles in question.

These considerations contain in nuce the solution in fact suggested by Lorenzen, i.e., to revise mechanics instead of geometry. Lorenzen agreed on the point that relativistic mechanics demands for a revision of momentum conservation, for, say, in the simplest case of inelastic impacts

$$m_1u_1 + m_2u_2 = (m_1 + m_2)v$$

only approximately holds. But, as Lorenzen explicated

> Length contraction (described by the Lorentz transformation) is a subject of mechanics, not of geometry. (Lorenzen 1979, p. 3)

> Lorentz-contraction and time-dilatation, resulting from the Lorentz-metric, however can be regarded, like Lorentz himself did, as contractions of physical objects and decelerations of motions respectively. It is not necessary to speak about a revision of space and time. (Lorenzen 1977, p. 7)[14]

In this paper Lorenzen then again stressed the essential point that geometry is not an empirical hypotheses to be verified or disproved by measurements (Lorenzen 1977, p. 7), but a theory which is constitutive for measurement (Lorenzen 1977, p. 9). In a different paper, referring to Steven Weinberg, he more strongly makes clear that it "is simply a misuse of geometrical language to speak of a revision of geometry" (Lorenzen 1980, p. 299, 1987, p. 291). I already emphasized the critique of misusing geometrical and logical calculi. Instead, relativistic mechanics demands

[14] Lorenzen's point of view obviously is closely related to the revival of the Lorentzian approach to relativity in the recent work of Harvey Brown (1995). For a comparison of Lorenzen and Brown, both of them referring to Lorentz, it should be noted the they used the notion of kinematics in a quite different way: For Brown kinematics includes the comparison of different frames of reference while for Lorenzen it is restricted to movements in a single frame. Brown shows that Lorentz's approach still holds when the existence of the ether is denied—which is indeed a precondition of its reevaluation. More interesting for the present purpose is the reason of its reinvestigation. Brown links the discussion of the interpretation of the effects deduced from Lorentz-transformations directly to the concept of explanation. He suggests that an explanation must always be given in terms of a mechanism (Brown 1995, pp. 8, 24), a coupling (Brown 1995, p. 24), or an interaction (Brown 1995, p. 140), and thus that space-time is ruled out as an explanans—at least in special relativity for particles have no "space-time feelers" (Brown 1995, p. 24). In the case of general relativity Brown revises his opinion because here particles and the space-time-structure indeed *interact* (Brown 1995, p. 150).

a substitution of the basic elements of the fundamental equation $m\frac{dv}{dt} = K$ by its four-dimensional counterparts in order to pursue the Newtonian program:

> The Newtonian program of "explaining" or "predicting" actual movements by looking for an appropriate system of "forces" $K_1, K_2 \ldots$ to be inserted in form of a linear superposition $K = \sum_i K_i$ into the fundamental equation, is transformed into the Newton-Einstein program of finding an appropriate system of relativistic four-dimensional forces which is to be inserted into the revised fundamental equation. (Lorenzen 1977, p. 6)

Lorenzen thus held that, in special relativity, the Minkowski-metric must not be understood as a revision of geometry and that general relativity also does not present a revision of geometry, but a new theory of gravitation (Lorenzen 1979, p. 7).

References

G. Böhme, Ist die Protophysik eine Reinterpretation des Kantischen Apriori? in *Protophysik. Für und wider eine konstruktive Wissenschaftsphilosophie der Physik*, ed. by G. Böhme (Suhrkamp, Frankfurt a. M., 1976)

G. Böhme, Kant's epistemology as a theory of alienated knowledge, in *Kant's Philosophy of Physical Science*, ed. by R.E. Butts (Reidel, Dordrecht, 1986), pp. 335–350

H.-H.v. Borzeszkowski, R. Wahsner, *Messung als Begründung oder Vermittlung? Ein Briefwechsel mit Paul Lorenzen über Protophysik und ein paar andere Dinge* (Academia, Sankt Augustin, 1995)

G.D. Bowne, *The Philosophy of Logic 1880–1908* (Mouton, The Hague, 1966)

H. Brown, *Physical Relativity. Space-time Structure from a Dynamical Perspective* (Clarendon Press, Oxford, 1995)

R. Carnap, *Der Raum*, vol. 56 (Kant-Studien Ergänzungshefte, 1922)

E. Cassirer, *Substance and Function & Einsteins Theory of Relativity* (Open Court, Chicago, 1923)

L. Couturat, Compte rendu critique de l'*Année philosophique,* publié par F. Pillon. Revue de Métaphysique et de Morale **I**, 63–85 (1893a)

L. Couturat, Note sur la géométrie non euclidienne et la relativité de l'espace. Revue de Métaphysique et de Morale **I**, 302–309 (1893b)

L. Couturat, Études sur l'espace et le temps de MM. Lechalas, Poincaré, Delbœuf, Bergson, L. Weber, Evellin. Revue de Métaphysique et de Morale **IV**, 646–669 (1896)

L. Couturat, Compte rendu critique de B. Russell, *Essais sur les fondements de la géométrie*. Revue de Métaphysique et de Morale **IV**, 354–380 (1898)

P. Damerow, G. Freudenthal, P. McLaughlin, J. Renn, *Exploring the Limits of Preclassical Mechanics*, 2nd edn. (Springer, Berlin, 2004)

H. Dingler, Über den Zirkel in der empirischen Begründung der Geometrie. Kant-Studien **XXX**, 310–330 (1925)

A. Einstein, *Geometrie und Erfahrung. Erweiterte Fassung des Festvortrages gehalten an der Preussischen Akademie der Wissenschaften zu Berlin am 27. Januar 1921* (Springer, Berlin, 1921)

P. Frank, *Philosophy of Science: The Link between Science and Philosophy* (Prentice-Hall, Englewood Cliffs, 1957)

H. Freudenthal, Die Grundlagen der Geometrie um die Wende des 19. Jahrhunderts. Mathematisch-Physikalische Semesterberichte **7**, 2–26 (1960)

G. Freudenthal, Leibniz als Transzendentalphilosoph malgré lui. Der Status der Erhaltungssätze. *Studia Leibnitiana*, Sonderheft **29**, 9–29 (1999) *Labora diligenter*.

A. Grünbaum, Discussion: the structure of science. Philos. Sci. **29**(3), 294–305 (1962)

J. Habermas, Wahrheitstheorien, in *Wirklichkeit und Reflexion. Walter Schulz zum 60. Geburtstag*, ed. by H. Fahrenbach (Neske, Pfullingen, 1973), pp. 211–265
T.L. Heath, *The Thirteen Books of Euclid's Elements*, 3 vol., 2nd edn. (Cambridge University Press, Cambridge, 1926)
O. Hölder, *Anschauung und Denken in der Geometrie* (Teubner, Leipzig, 1900)
M. Jammer, *The Concept of Space: The History of Theories of Space in Physics* (Dover, New York, 1993)
P. Janich, Zur Protophysik des Raumes, in *Protophysik*, ed. by G. Böhme (Suhrkamp, Frankfurt a.M., 1976)
P. Janich, *Protophysics of Time: Constructive Foundation and History of Time Measurement* (Reidel, Dordrecht, 1985). Originally published in german language in 1969
P. Janich, Die technische Erzwingbarkeit der Euklidizität, in *Entwicklungen der methodischen Philosophie*, ed. by P. Janich (Suhrkamp, Franfurt a. M., 1992), pp. 68–84
W. Kamlah, P. Lorenzen, *Logische Propädeutik. Vorschule des vernünftigen Redens*, 3rd edn. (Bibliographisches Institut, Mannheim, 1967) (Metzler, Stuttgart, 1996)
I. Kant, *Kritik der reinen Vernunft* (2nd edition 1787). (Reimer, Berlin, 1787). Vol. III of *Kant's gesammelte Schriften. Herausgegeben von der Königl* (Preuß. Akademie der Wissenschaften. Erste Abteilung: Werke, 1904)
I. Kant, Lectures on logic, in *The Cambridge Edition of the Works of Immanuel Kant*, vol. 9 (Cambridge University Press, Cambridge, 1992)
G.W. Leibniz, *Mathematische Schriften* (Olms, Hildesheim, 1962). Reprint of the 1849 edition
G.W. Leibniz, Sämtliche Schriften und Briefe, in *Mathematischer, naturwissenschaftlicher und technischer Briefwechsel 1694– uni 1696*, vol. III.6B (Akademie Verlag, Berlin, 2004)
P. Lorenzen, Vorwort, in *Dingler's Aufbau der exakten Fundamentalwissenschaften* (Eidos, München, 1964)
P. Lorenzen, Eine Revision der Einsteinschen Revision. Philosophia Naturalis **16**, 383–391 (1976)
P. Lorenzen, Relativistische Mechanik mit klassischer Geometrie und Kinematik. Mathematische Zeitschrift **155**, 1–9 (1977)
P. Lorenzen, Die allgemeine Relativitätstheorie als eine Revision der Newtonschen Gravitationstheorie. Philosophia Naturalis **17**, 1–9 (1979)
P. Lorenzen, Geometrie als messtheoretisches Apriori der Physik. Physik und Didaktik **4**, 291–299 (1980)
P. Lorenzen, *Elementargeometrie* (Bibliographisches Institut, Mannheim, 1984)
P. Lorenzen, *Constructive Philosophy* (The University of Massachusetts Press, Amherst, 1987). Transl. by Karl Richard Pavlovic
E. Mach, Raum und Geometrie vom Standpunkt der Naturforschung, in *Erkenntnis und Irrtum* (Barth, Leipzig, 1926)
P. McLaughlin, Vis viva, in *Enzyklopädie Philosophie und Wissenschaftstheorie*, ed. by J. Mittelstraß, vol. 4 (Metzler, Stuttgart, 1996)
H. Poincaré, L'espace et le temps. Scientia **12**, 159–170 (1912)
H. Reichenbach, *Selected Writings 1909–1953*, 3 vols (Reidel, Dordrecht, 1978)
B. Riemann, Ueber die Hypothesen, welche der Geometrie zu Grunde liegen, in *Gesammelte mathematische Werke*, pp. 304–319 (Teubner und Springer, Berlin/Leipzig, 1854) 1990
B.A. Rozenfeld, *A History of Non-Euclidean Geometry: Evolution of the Concept of a Geometric Space* (Springer, New York, 1988)
B. Russell, Review of Hannequin's *L'hypothèse des atomes* (1896), in *Collected Papers*, vol. 2, Philosophical Papers 1896–1899 (Unwin Hayman, London, 1896) 1990
B. Russell, *An Essay on the Foundations of Geometry* (The University Press, Cambridge, 1897)
D.W. Sciama, On the origin of inertia. Mon. Not. R. Astron. Soc. **113**, 34–42 (1953)
R. Torretti, *Philosophy of Geometry form Riemann to Poincaré*, volume 7 of Episteme (Reidel, Dordrecht, 1978)
G. Veronese, *Fondamenti di geometria a più dimensioni e a più specie di unità rettilinee esposti in forma elementare. Lezioni per la Scuola di magistero in Matematica* (Tipografia del Seminario, Padova, 1891)

H. von Helmholtz, Ueber die Thatsachen, die der Geometrie zu Grunde liegen, in *Wissenschaftliche Abhandlungen*, vol. 2 (Barth, Leipzig, 1883)

H. von Helmholtz, Ueber den Ursprung und die Bedeutung der geometrischen Axiome, in *Vorträge und Reden*, vol. 2 (Vieweg, Braunschweig, 1896)

J. von Kries, *Logik. Grundzüge einer kritischen und formalen Urteilslehre* (JCB Mohr (Paul Siebeck), Tübingen, 1916)

S. Walter, Hypothesis and convention in Poincaré's defence of Galilei spacetime, in *The Significance of the Hypothetical in the Natural Sciences*, ed. by M. Heidelberger, G. Schiemann (de Gruyter, Berlin, 2009)

H. Weyl, Vorwort des Herausgebers [introduction to B. Riemann's *Ueber die Hypothesen, welche der Geometrie zu Grunde liegen* (1854)], in *Gesammelte mathematische Werke* (Teubner und Springer, Berlin/Leipzig, 1990)

E. Wind, *Das Experiment und die Metaphysik* (Suhrkamp, Frankfurt a. M., 2001)

M. Wolff, *Geschichte der Impetustheorie* (Suhrkamp, Frankfurt a. M., 1978)

M. Wolff, Impetus mechanics as a physical argument for copernicanism. copernicus, benedetti, galileo. Sci. Context **1**(2), 215–256 (1987)

M. Wolff, Geometrie und Erfahrung. Kant und das Problem der objektiven Geltung der Euklidischen Geometrie, in *Kant und die Berliner Aufklärung. Akten des IX. Internationalen Kant-Kongresses*, vol. 1 (de Gruyter, Berlin, 2001)

W. Wundt, Kants kosmologische Antinomien und das Problem des Unendlichen, in *Kleine Schriften* (Verlag Wilhelm Engelmann, Leipzig, 1910), pp. 77–132

Chapter 4
Correspondence Between Evert Willem Beth and Jean Piaget (1951–1955)

Gerhard Heinzmann, Alain Trognon, and Frédérick Tremblay

4.1 Introduction

4.1.1 The Historical Context: Beth on All Fronts

Piaget and Beth probably met for the first time at the second "entretiens" of Zurich in 1948, organized by the Swiss philosopher Ferdinand Gonseth, who, together with Gaston Bachelard, founded the international journal *Dialectica*.[1] As a contribution to the first volume of *Dialectica*, Beth, the Netherlands' first full professor of Logic

[1]We are indebted to Henk Visser of the Beth Foundation, for his generous help in procuring copies of this correspondence, and for his kind permission to publish it in this volume. The originals are located in the Beth Archive of the Noord-Hollands Archief (Public Records Office) in Haarlem: The Netherlands, File 386. We are grateful to Sandrine Avril for many valuable technical comments and suggestions.

G. Heinzmann (✉)
MSH Lorraine (USR 3261) CNRS, Université de Lorraine, 91, avenue de la Libération, BP 454, 54001 Nancy, France
e-mail: gerhard.heinzmann@univ-lorraine.fr

A. Trognon
Laboratoire de Psychologie de l'Interaction et des Relations Intersubjectives (InterPsy – EA 4432), Université de Lorraine, Campus Lettres et Sciences Humaines, 3, Place Godefroy de Bouillon, 54015 Nancy, France
e-mail: alain.trognon@univ-lorraine.fr

F. Tremblay
LHSP – Archives H. Poincaré (UMR 7117), Université de Lorraine, 91, avenue de la Libération, BP 454, 54001 Nancy, France
e-mail: frederick.tremblay@univ-lorraine.fr

M. Rebuschi et al. (eds.), *Interdisciplinary Works in Logic, Epistemology, Psychology and Linguistics*, Logic, Argumentation & Reasoning 3,
DOI 10.1007/978-3-319-03044-9_4, © Springer International Publishing Switzerland 2014

and Foundations of Mathematics (1948), published an outline on logic entitled "Hundred Years of Symbolic Logic. A Retrospect on the Occasion of the Boole-De Morgan Centenary" (Beth 1947).

The subject of the 1948 Zurich conference was "The power of intellect on reality". Beth's talk was entitled: "Les relations de la dialectique à la logique" (Beth 1948). There exist published reactions from Gonseth and Piaget on Beth's talk: Gonseth responded in a separate article on Beth's theses (Beth and Gonseth 1948), while the Piaget's observations were printed in a chapter called "Discussion" (Piaget 1948). Gonseth's critique concerns three main points:

1. Beth's refusal to accept the word "dialectic", even in a renewed interpretation.
2. Beth's adoption of Tarski's resolution of the truth problem. According to Gonseth, Tarski presupposes a simple class realism as an implicit "conservative" hypothesis.
3. Beth seems not to be aware of his tacit hypotheses.

Piaget's contribution to the discussion is an improvement on Gonseth's last point: Beth does not pay enough attention to the implicit hypotheses of the axiomatic method. In fact, Piaget's and Gonseth's common ground is a 6-year discussion and a joint publication (1946) about "Groupements, Groupes et latices" (Piaget and Gonseth 1946).[2]

In 1949, Piaget published a book entitled "Traité de logique. Essai de la logistique opératoire" (Piaget 1949) which Beth reviewed in the Italian journal of symbolic logic *Methodos* (1951). He very harshly denounces "the notorious failures" of Beth's book. The correspondence printed here begins with the Piaget encountering Beth's review (April 1951). Piaget sends Beth a public reply, also to be published in *Methodos*.

In the same year (1951), Beth too was subjected to harsh criticism. Else Barth, a scholar of Beth, writes in 1999:

> On 11 June 1951 Beth notifies Church of his dissatisfaction with a review Church has sent to him in advance for his information. It is a review of Beth's own *Fondements logiques des mathématiques* published in Paris and Louvain the year before (Beth 1950a). The review intended for publication in the *Journal of Symbolic Logic* [where Beth is a member of the editorial board], is negative, pointing out a number of technical inaccuracies and mistakes; it is however not yet printed, and Beth asks Church to ask the reviewer to revise it. [...] Church answers with a letter of 22 June, saying that he personally accepts the review and will publish it. Beth's reply on this on June 30 runs to three tightly typed pages. The second half is [of particular interest for us]:'It seems to me that your outlook on the situation as a whole is entirely mistaken and that, no less than the reviewer, [you] fail to realize the fact that the book was written for French readers. [Church wrote in his letter already that certain authors of books on logic mentioned by Beth, among which is the psychologist Piaget, may deceive the outsider, but not the serious student of modern logic]... For this reason, the publication of the review is unjust. Now your argument is that the books I mentioned are not recognized by logicians and therefore less harmful. But this is certainly not the opinion

[2]See also Gonseth's review of Piaget's "Classes, relations et nombres" (Piaget 1944–1945) and discussion in *Dialectica* (Piaget 1950; Gonseth 1950a,b).

> of prospective readers. In their opinion, the authors I mentioned are recognized specialists in logic, and this opinion will be cooperated by the reviews in the journal'. (Barth 1990, 1998–1999, pp. 5–6)

At the end of the letter, Beth submits his resignation from the editorial board of the *Journal*.[3] This incident is surely not without influence on the outcome of this correspondence and on Beth's careful but positive decision to continue collaborating with Piaget. But there is another reason for Beth to be careful.

At the end of World War II, a number of new societies for logic and philosophy of science came into existence. Most important to our context is the International Union for Philosophy of Science (IUPS), founded in 1950 by Gonseth. In the early 1950s, Gonseth tried getting the Association for Symbolic Logic, founded in 1936 and now strongly influenced by Tarski,

> ... to join forces in order to take advantage of the logic group's recognized strength and prestige. Tarski's Dutch colleague, Evert Beth belonged both to the logic association and to Gonseth's group and was a natural go-between.[4] The problem was that he, Tarski, and others in the association were put off by Gonseth's authoritarian way of conducting matters and by his lack of logical rigor. For this reason, Tarski and Beth discouraged the proposed alliance [...] In 1953, a putsch by Beth and his friends took place: the Dutch logician Arend Heyting was made president [...] and Everth Beth assumed the role of secretary. (Burdman and Feferman 2010, p. 162)

Whatever mistakes, prejudices and truth are concealed in this story, such events did not facilitate the dialogue between Beth and Gonseth's colleague Piaget. Nevertheless, the fact that Beth continued the dialogue, leading even to joint publications in 1955, 1957 and 1961,[5] bears witness to his intellectual integrity.

4.1.2 The Theoretical Context of the Correspondence

Before Frege, the psychological approach to logic was common and even predominant. After Frege and Husserl's attacks on psychologism, logicians banished psychology from their a priori considerations. This was the common "modern" attitude in the first half of the twentieth century. Although Beth started his work

[3]From Volume 17.1 (1952) on, Beth is absent from the editorial board of the journal.

[4]At the end of 1951, Beth worked with Tarski in Berkeley for 6 months (see letter 12 below).

[5]Beth and Piaget are co-editors of the proceedings of the Herzberg meeting (see Beth (1955) and Footnote 54, p. 82) and of the first volume of the series "Études d'épistémologie génétique" published by the recently (1955) founded "Centre international d'Épistémologie génétique" in Geneva. The volume is entitled "Épistémologie génétique et recherché psychologique", W. E. Beth, W. Mays and J. Piaget (1957) and contains the proceedings of a summer meeting in Piaget's Geneva Center [see below letters 13 and 14]. Beth's short contribution (pp. 131–134) is about "La logique formelle et la pensée naturelle" (Beth 1957).
The final result of the collaboration between Piaget and Beth is published as the 14th volume of the same series (Beth and Piaget 1961).

with a traditional psychological perspective on logic, he switched in the late 1930s, under the influence of Heinrich Scholz, to the "modern" way of doing logic.[6]

The "conservative" view, which did not distinguish psychology sharply enough as an empirical science versus logic as an a priori matter, could only have survived in a cultural circle unaware of the logical revolution of 1900. This was the case in France and in French speaking Switzerland, with the exception of Herbrand, Cavaillès, Rougier and some others. Quine's critique of the sharp distinction between a priori and a posteriori knowledge and his positive solution in his "Epistemology naturalized" came much later (Quine 1953, 1969) and was even more reductive than Piaget's attempt to keep logic and psychology together.

So, the problem we face is this: is there a moderate naturalistic way to put logic and psychology together while keeping the normative aspect of logic and the descriptive aspect of psychology? The question Piaget asks in his letter from April 16th, 1951 (letter 3 below) sounds very similar:

> It would be interesting to compare the range of psychological training and the order of logical construction. Does Aristotle's adage saying 'Thus what comes first in the production, comes last in the analysis' remains valid or is there rather a parallelism between production and analysis?

The alternative Piaget has in mind runs as follows: does only the logico-mathematical structure give us the possibility to *speak* of a structure of the operations of thought, or is it possible to establish a correspondence between the psychological and the logical structures? Neither Piaget nor Beth gives a clear answer or even succeeds in maintaining a precise and stable formulation of the problem.

An important part of Piaget's program has always been to uncover the psychological genesis of knowledge, especially scientific knowledge (physics, mathematics, logic) in the human mind. In other words, genetic epistemology "proposes to interpret the sciences as a result of the mental activity of man" (Beth and Piaget 1961, p. 325). Since "the thought of the logician is the most sophisticated form of human thought and it is psychologically impossible to account for human knowledge without including the activity of the logician as such" (Beth and Piaget 1961, p. 332), Piaget assigns a special role to logic. It is, he writes in 1947 (Piaget 1947, p. 297), "the axiomatic of the mind whereas the psychology of intelligence is the corresponding experimental science". In other publications, he identifies the relationship between the psychology of intelligence and logic with the relationship between physics and mathematics. Indeed, is logic itself just a non-reflected tool (an Aristotelian *organon*), or is there a closer relationship between psychology and logic in the sense of Aristotle's production and analysis? Piaget distinguishes two different points of view:

[6] See below, letter of April 13th (1951).

1. Logic as an a priori science and psychology as an experimental science are reciprocally autonomous. In this sense, Piaget is not interested in logic [letter 1; Beth and Piaget 1961, p. 325].
2. From the point of view of experimental psychology, the question arises whether the formation of the actual mechanism of thought can be connected with the laws of logic [letter 1; document 1′]. According to the above-mentioned alternative, two interpretations are possible:

(a) The "understanding of these laws [of logic] is the natural outcomes of mental development of which a number of intermediate phases can be identified". "In its subsequent reflection, the mind is able to see this conformity" (Beth and Piaget 1961, p. 328, cf. 325–326). "In reflecting later, the spirit shows itself able to see [...] even to some extent to justify the acceptance of the precepts of logic as 'laws of thought' (in the sense of normative laws)" (Beth and Piaget 1961, p. 326).

According to the first part of (a), the psychologist establishes a psychological genesis of logical operations (e.g., $\wedge$, $\vee$, $\rightarrow$, $\neg$) in comparison with the logician's "conventional" definition of these operations. "The structure for the psychologist is [...] the end product of a specific structuring development" cf. Beth and Piaget (1961, pp. 325–326). Excluding an exclusive use of an introspective method (Beth and Piaget 1961, p. 326), Piaget empirically finds (using logical assumptions) that there exists, between the 'logic' of the general coordination of actions and formal logic, an isomorphism, just as McCulloch and Pitts found an isomorphism between the structures of neural connections and logical structures (Beth and Piaget 1961, p. 329). With respect to a given meta-logic (its 'force' is not defined by Piaget), he shows in this way the psychological development of a system of formal logic. The validity of the result will depend on the care taken by the psychologist-experimenter whereas the logician has no objection to the method employed.

In contrast, the psychological study of adult thought cannot provide the justification needed in the second part of (a). If the comparing act is thought to give a foundation for the conventional definition, we encounter the issues dealt with in the arguments against psychologism. Since the psychological study will find itself in the position of using logic to establish a psychological result, such an interpretation is viciously circular. In fact, the reason for doubting the result of psychological study is an equally strong reason for doubting logical conventions.

> The norm can not depend on the facts. (Beth and Piaget 1961, p. 331).

> The psychologist cannot avoid appealing to logic and the ideal of formalization it entails; it is not sufficient to describe the psychology of the appearance of certain logical laws as facts. It remains to interpret the necessity that accompanies them, once established. (Beth and Piaget 1961, p. 332)

In 1961, both Piaget and Beth seem aware of the circular reasoning involved in (a). Pre-propositional operations supposed to be the basis of some simple intuitive logical structures are studied in an experiment which is itself governed by a complex logical structure (see document 1′, Footnote 18, p. 58).

(b) The connections concern the study of the psychological genesis of specific logical operations (e.g., $\wedge$, $\vee$, $\rightarrow$, $\neg$) in comparison with the genesis of the logical calculus of *thought.* In this interpretation, the psychological formation of primitive logical elements given by the conventional definitions of logicians is not conceived of as a foundation for logical conventions, but rather compared to its *psychological* extension to a logical calculus of thought, this being not simply a matter of *formalization.* In this interpretation, logic is *used* but not *founded* by Piaget's genetic epistemology. What we are comparing is not formal logic and the logic of thought, but different stages of the logic of thought using formal logic as a tool. Indeed, the conventional definitions of logical operations can be considered justified by their pertinent use in the analysis of the logic of thought.

One of the traps in the epistolary discussion between Piaget and Beth is to take an insufficiently careful approach to the different statuses of both interpretations or to confuse them explicitly. Neither Piaget nor Beth succeeds in defining the philosophical scope of their interaction as psychologist and logician.

Nevertheless, under the influence of Beth, Piaget's letter 5 takes a clear position in favor of view (*b*), although his development is by no means linear and stable. Indeed, by constantly identifying adult thought structure with a certain stage of a formal logical structure [document 1′ (p. 55); letter 5], he is, according to Beth, always confusing logic as a structure of thought with logic as a language structure [letter 6]. It is only by the use of logic that we can identify a logical structure in thought. Thus, it seems impossible to *describe* a structure of thought by logical means, because one cannot even grasp such a structure without logic. So, in letter 7, Piaget concedes that the logical structure is "not psychologically real or actual but that it corresponds only to a set of possibilia".

The epistolary dialogue shows another development of Piaget's thinking. Whereas he initially conceives of a hierarchy from elementary equilibriums to more extended ones (pp. 55, 57) showing, at the same time, an inverse parallelism between the *empirical* genesis of real structures and the *logical* development of formal structures, he later proceeds the other way around: he compares now earlier states of the empirical genesis of thought with respect to its absence in a fully developed logical structure. He is no longer considering the genesis of the logical structures, but using logic as a tool to compare different states of mental development.

The "political" circumstances mentioned above probably provoked an interruption of their correspondence between August, 51 and May, 53. Afterwards, the exchange addresses more private, formal and organizational matters.

Piaget invited Beth, in his letter from May 28th 1955, to attend the first Geneva conference at his International Center for Genetic Epistemology. The subject he chose was the study of "the relations between the logical structures and the activities of the subject", i.e., the problem their "correspondence started with" (see letter 13 below). Beth accepted the challenge but was unable to exploit the possibilities of his new methods of "semantic tableaux". The final remarks of his 4-page contribution were a laconically presented interpretation of the *naturalness* of his method:

> on peut se demander, enfin, si vraiment nos tableaux sémantiques correspondent à quelque réalité psychique. Or, ils constituent, me semble-t-il, une schématisation approximative de notre façon naturelle de raisonner. Pour montrer qu'il est ainsi, il n'est peut-être pas indispensable de recourir à des investigations proprement psychologiques. On peut faire appel à des faits historiques intéressants. (Beth 1957, p. 134)

Indeed, to find a logically appropriate expression of our natural reasoning is a purely logical aim, provided one knows what the natural reasoning is about. This is exactly Piaget's question Beth that eludes.

The two men end the systematic quarrel that shapes their correspondence by finding, in the joint 1961 volume, a meager compromise. Their activities as logician and psychologist refers to one another, not because they are interdependent, but because they are complementary (Beth and Piaget 1961, p. 332).

4.1.3 Editorial Policy

Our morphological or critical annotations are distinguished by Arabic numerals, the notes of the authors by lowercase letters. In our transcription, we indicate neither the pagination of the manuscript nor the breaks between words.

1. Piaget to Beth[7]

UNIVERSITÉ DE GENÈVE

Editorial symbols:

text	underlined words and passages, reproduced by the editors in italics
~~text~~	words and passages struck out by the authors
?... ?	undecipherable word
⟦text⟧	items added by the editors of the transcription
⌈...⌉	items removed by the editors

[7]Manuscript; 3 pages.

SCHOLA GENEVENSIS MDLIX

FACULTÉ DES SCIENCES

Genève, le 11 avril 1951

Mon cher Monsieur Beth,

J'ai lu votre beau livre sur la logique et les mathématiques[8] avec une grande admiration pour votre clarté et votre honnêteté intellectuelle (notamment à l'égard de l'intuitionnisme[9]). Cela m'a permis de supporter avec sérénité votre Compte-Rendu de *Methodos.*[10] Je ne dirai pas qu'il m'ait fait plaisir. Mais je puis vous assurer que je me suis mis suffisamment dans votre point de vue pour vous comprendre entièrement.

Il y a seulement une chose que je ne comprends pas : pourquoi croyez-vous que je m'intéresse à la logistique ? Pourquoi un homme de 50 ans, qui a fait ? 20 ? volumes de psychologies, qui a reçu des titres honorifiques de Harvard, de la Sorbonne, etc. ⟦,⟧ en serait-il assez fou pour s'occuper de ce qu'il connaît mal, s'il n'en avait pas besoin ? Et quels peuvent être ses besoins, sinon relatifs à la psychologie ?

C'est ce que j'essaye d'expliquer dans la réponse ci-jointe, que M. Bocheński m'a autorisé à faire.[11] Mais je ne veux pas la publier sans votre consentement et vos remarques, car, je le répète, les questions de personnes me paraissent bien secondaires à côté du seul problème qui me préoccupe depuis des années : celui des connexions possibles entre l'étude psychologique de la formation des opérations logiques, d'une part, et ~~la formalisation~~ le calcul logistique d'autre part.

J'espère vivement vous rencontrer aux ⟦pro⟧chains entretiens de Zürich.[12] Sinon il faut absolument que je vous voie un jour tranquillement, car je suis persuadé

---

[8]Beth (1950a).

[9]Piaget is by no means an intuitionist in Brouwer's sense. Nevertheless, insofar as logic for Brouwer describes regularities in already non-linguistic mathematical activities, for Piaget it describes certain steps in the equilibria of mental operations.

[10]Beth (1950b). In this extremely harsh review of Piaget's *Traité de logique. Essai de la logistique opératoire* (Piaget 1949), Beth denounces "the notorious failures of this book, especially since these failures are usually hidden by a false pretense of sophistication that can impress a lay reader in logic" (Piaget 1949, p. 258).

[11]Piaget encloses in his letter a typescript (see next text 1′) of his answer to Beth's review of Piaget's *Traité de logique*. An abbreviated version of this answer was published in *Methodos* 3 (see text 7′).

[12]Piaget and Beth were both participants in the second "Entretiens de Zurich" (1948) on "The Power of Intellect on Reality" (see *Dialectica* 2 (1948, 89–143), organized by the Swiss philosopher Ferdinand Gonseth. The third "Entretiens de Zurich" took place in April 1951. Beth did not participate in (see letter 2).

qu'après cette prise de contact vous me donnerez les indications les plus utiles une fois compris le problème que je me pose.

Veuillez croire, cher Monsieur Beth, à mes sentiments très dévoués.

J. Piaget

P.S. Mes respectueux hommages à Madame Beth, s.v.p., si elle se souvient de moi.

1′. Piaget's Answer to Beth's Review of his Book, *Traité de Logique*[13]

[s. d.]

À propos d'un « TRAITÉ DE LOGIQUE »

Réponse à M. E. W. Beth par Jean Piaget

L'étude critique que M. Beth a bien voulu consacrer à notre Traité de Logique répond certainement à un devoir qui s'est imposé à lui en tant que l'un des meilleurs défenseurs de la logistique axiomatique moderne. Comme elle [sic !], elle a droit à tout notre respect et nous ne saurions naturellement que prendre acte des remarques pertinentes et des observations qu'elle contient. Ce n'est donc pas sur le terrain sur lequel se place M. Beth que nous chercherons à lui répondre. Nous partirons au contraire de la supposition que, dans le domaine qui est le sien, il a vraisemblablement raison sur tous les points qu'il aborde, bien que certains d'entre eux puissent sans doute donner lieu à discussion.

Ce sur quoi nous nous sentons obligés de répondre, car le problème dépasse les considérations de compétences et de personnes, c'est sur la question centrale dont l'étude nous a conduit à recourir à la logistique et même à publier nos réflexions sur ce sujet, malgré les risques évidents d'une telle entreprise (l'article de Beth suffirait à le montrer) : existe-t-il des relations entre les structures logistiques[14] et le fonctionnement réel de l'esprit,—nous entendons par là les mécanismes de l'intelligence tels que la psychologie expérimentale cherche à les décrire,—et, si oui, par quelle méthode peut-on parvenir à déterminer ce genre de liaisons ?

Ce qui nous a frappé, en effet, dans la critique de M. Beth, est que, s'il a lu notre ouvrage avec une grande attention, il ne semble pas avoir examiné de même

[13]Manuscript in typescript (16 pages). Piaget published a short extract of this MS in *Methodos,* (Piaget 1951). See below the end of letter 7 and document 7′.

[14]The expression "structures logistiques" refers to primitive logical operations that will be compared to the more "concrete" operations of the logic of thought.

sa préface ni peut-être son introduction : il y aurait vu que notre but n'était en rien d'écrire une logique duement formalisée et axiomatisée, mais au contraire de pousser l'analyse des opérations comme telles—et une analyse demeurant explicitement intuitive—dans la direction, non pas du plus général au sens de plus abstrait, mais bien du plus élémentaire, au sens du plus concret et du plus proche des opérations mentales réelles (d'où le sous-titre se référant à une logistique opératoire avec cette signification particulière et peu usuelle[15]). Or, M. Beth conclut son article, avec une franchise digne de toute estime, que les erreurs contenues dans notre traité le rendent inutilisable en tant que Traité et lui enlèvent tout intérêt scientifique. Nous reviendrons sur les erreurs, dont certaines sont naturellement à reconnaître et à corriger honnêtement, mais dont d'autres (en particulier ce que M. Beth appelle les « déviations ») nous semblent dues à la différence des perspectives et des méthodes entre lui et nous. Pour ce qui est de la nécessité d'un Traité complet de logistique, chacun sait qu'on l'attend année après année des spécialistes eux-mêmes (en plus de l'excellent *Compendium* de Bocheński[16] et du bel ouvrage de Beth sur la logique et les mathématiques), mais qu'ils sont en réalité plus divisés qu'il ne pourrait sembler. Ce n'est donc pas sans raison qu'on a fini par s'adresser à un psychologue ne prétendant nullement être un logicien de métier. Ceci nous ramène à notre problème. Si notre ouvrage peut présenter quelque intérêt scientifique (et qu'on le nie nous rajeunit étrangement en nous rappelant nos débuts en psychologie proprement dite...) ce n'est évidemment pas du point de vue auquel il ne se place pas : celui de la pure logistique formalisée. C'est au point de vue des extensions possibles de la logistique dans la direction de l'analyse des opérations élémentaires. On connaît bien la relation entre la logistique et les mathématiques ou la physique : il s'agit en ce cas d'un rapport d'application ou de généralisation. Tout autre est le problème que nous avons cherché à poser : celui des relations entre les structures logistiques et, non pas les théories de la psychologie en tant que science, mais les structures mentales elles-mêmes telles qu'elles sont étudiées par la psychologie.

Notons d'emblée que ce problème peut n'intéresser en rien les logisticiens, puisqu'il s'agit d'une connexion simplement possible entre deux domaines hétérogènes : logique et psychologie. Pour un logisticien de tendance platonicienne ou pour un logisticien purement conventionnaliste, la question sera même dépourvue de sens. Il s'y ajoutera cette circonstance aggravante que tout psychologue abordant la logistique, en vue de rechercher les relations en question, le fera avec ses habitudes d'esprit particulières et provoquera de ce fait des résistances compréhensibles indépendamment des erreurs qu'il lui arrive de commettre... Seul un logicien préoccupé lui-même des attaches entre la logique et les aspects empiriques de la vie mentale comprendra l'intérêt du problème, mais encore faudrait-il qu'il soit psychologue autant que logicien pour parvenir à le résoudre. Bref, la question que

[15]The subtitle of his book, *Traité de logique. Essai de la logistique opératoire* also means that "logistique opératoire" refers to the logic of thought, which is in fact far from usual or self-evident.

[16]*Précis de logique mathématique* (Bocheński 1949). Reviewed by F. Kröner in *Dialectica,* 4 (1950), 78.

nous posons est celle dont la solution exige de toute nécessité une collaboration : or, psychologues et logiciens ne veulent en général pas collaborer.

Et pourtant la question se pose, et c'est pourquoi nous tenons à répondre à M. Beth, en toute objectivité et en toute sérénité, non pas comme un auteur qui répond à son critique, mais comme un chercheur s'adressant à un autre chercheur, persuadé qu'ils ont tous les deux raison et que les progrès de la recherche exigeraient leur collaboration.

La question se pose pour deux raisons complémentaires, l'une intéressant la psychologie et l'autre la position de la logique dans le système des sciences.

Du point de vue psychologique, il est frappant de constater que l'intelligence en son développement s'organise stade par stade en tendant, sur chaque palier, vers certaines formes d'équilibre : or, celles-ci sont caractérisées par les structures d'ensemble que constituent entre elles les opérations intellectuelles du sujet, au niveau d'évolution considéré. Il est donc nécessaire, si l'on veut expliquer de manière précise le développement des mécanismes mentaux, d'élaborer un langage adéquat permettant de décrire ces structures. Or, il se trouve que la logistique ou du moins l'algèbre opératoire utilisée par la logistique peut rendre ici les plus grands services à la recherche psychologique, ce qui parle évidemment en faveur d'une certaine correspondance entre les structures réelles de l'esprit (nous appelons « réel » par convention, ce qui ⟦est⟧ donné par l'expérimentation psychologique) et les structures formelles de la logistique.[17]

Remarquons seulement, en passant, que cette correspondance soulève de multiples problèmes et ne saurait donc être considérée comme simple. Par exemple, on admet couramment en logistique que la logique des classes ne saurait être fondée que sur celle des propositions, et non pas l'inverse, ce qui est sans doute exact au point de vue axiomatique. Il se trouve au contraire que, dans le développement mental, les opérations de classes et de relations s'organisent en systèmes restreints, mais bien définis, au même niveau que les nombres entiers et les nombres réels, mais bien avant que soient acquises les opérations de la logique bivalente. Il y aurait donc, en ce cas non pas parallélisme mais inversion de sens entre les structures réelles et les structures formalisées : le problème de la correspondance n'en reste pas moins intéressant pour autant. Il y a en tous cas là un problème général méritant d'être étudié pour lui-même, que les logiciens s'y intéressent ou non, et quelle que soit la place qu'il convienne de réserver à l'analyse de telles correspondances dans le système des sciences.

[17]Piaget's argumentation and terminology here are very confusing. The term "logistique opératoire" above means the logic of thought. By using the term "l'algèbre opératoire", Piaget suggests that what is most important for him is the use of primitive structural elements as tools to extend the first structural levels to the more concrete logic of thought (logistique opératoire). The two interpretations (2*a* and 2*b*) distinguished in the introduction are not separated sharply enough: whereas the second compares the psychological genesis of primitive structural operations to their extension to a logic of thought, the first compares formal structures and the logic of thought. Beyond this, Piaget seems to use the term "logic" with a double meaning: it designates not only the logic of the logician but also a structural tool.

Ceci nous conduit à la seconde raison d'étudier les liaisons entre les structures logistiques et les opérations réelles de l'esprit. On peut concevoir le système des sciences comme fondé sur une hiérarchie simple, tel que la logique constituerait la base de tout savoir ; de la logique procéderait alors les mathématiques, de celles-ci les sciences physiques, de celles-ci, les sciences biologiques, de telle sorte que psychologie et sociologie se trouveraient à l'autre extrémité de la série. En ce cas la question de la correspondance entre les structures logistiques et les structures mentales présenterait encore un vif intérêt au point de vue psychologique, mais sans réciprocité pour la logique. Seulement qu'arriverait-il si, pour une raison quelconque, on en venait au contraire à douter des droits de la logique à conserver son rang de commencement absolu ?

C'est ici que les choses risquent de se gâter pour la collaboration entre psychologues et logiciens et notamment pour la conciliation que je voudrais offrir à M. Beth. Il vaut donc mieux jouer franc jeu et éviter toute équivoque. Si l'on admet que la méthode axiomatique suffit à fournir un fondement à la connaissance déductive (nous disons bien un fondement et non pas une condition méthodologique indispensable, ce qui n'est pas la même chose, et n'est pas en discussion), alors il n'y a bien sûr pas à remonter au-delà, mais si l'on pense qu'une axiomatique est nécessairement la prise de conscience d'une structure sous-jacente, alors il est intéressant de chercher en quoi consiste cette structure. Que pourrait-elle en ce cas constituer d'autre qu'une structure mentale, si l'on ne veut pas se placer d'emblée à un point de vue métaphysique ?

Telles sont, en quelques mots, les deux raisons pour lesquelles il nous paraît indispensable, non pas seulement pour la psychologie, mais pour l'analyse épistémologique des rapports entre la logique et la psychologie, d'étudier aujourd'hui les correspondances possibles entre les structures formelles et les structures mentales. Deux problèmes se posent alors : à qui doit incomber un tel travail et selon quelles méthodes est-il à poursuivre ?

Pour l'exécution de la recherche, il n'y a que trois possibilités : ou qu'un logisticien apprenne assez de psychologie pour résoudre le problème, ou qu'un psychologue apprenne assez de logistique pour s'y essayer à son tour, ou qu'une collaboration s'établisse entre logisticiens et psychologues comme il en existe entre mathématiciens et physiciens.

La première possibilité ne s'est, à ma connaissance, pas présentée jusqu'ici. Il ne faut en effet pas confondre le problème que nous posons avec celui de la formalisation des théories psychologiques, lequel est tout différent. La troisième solution serait la plus féconde, il va de soi, et j'ai souvent cherché pour ma part une collaboration de ce genre. Je la suggère très sincèrement et très sérieusement à M. Beth, puisqu'il a montré dans son article les inconvénients de la seconde solution. Quant à celle-ci, j'ai dû m'en contenter, en écrivant un ouvrage logistique à l'intention de ceux qui s'intéressent au fonctionnement réel de la pensée et en insistant dans ma préface sur les lacunes de la formalisation dont je me suis servi. M. Beth y insiste à son tour et je ne le contredirai pas.

Mais il reste le problème des méthodes, et c'est ici que la critique de M. Beth , tout en étant donc parfaitement fondée au point de vue de l'axiomaticien, qui est le sien, ne me paraît pas toucher le nœud de la question.

Pour étudier les correspondances entre les structures formelles et les structures mentales, il ne suffit pas de confronter deux sortes de connaissances : (1) les connaissances expérimentales fournies par la psychologie sur les structures réelles s'organisant au cours du développement et (2) les connaissances formelles fournies par la logistique pure sur l'organisation des cadres de la déduction. Pour nous servir d'une comparaison un peu osée mais qui nous paraît exacte si l'on réduit les termes à leur juste proportion, la psychologie de l'intelligence est à l'égard de la logistique dans une relation analogue à celle de la physique expérimentale à l'égard des mathématiques. En effet, tout ce qui est physiquement constaté est exprimable en termes mathématiques mais la réciproque n'est pas vraie, car la logistique porte sur l'ensemble des structures possibles et seule une partie restreinte en est mentalement vécue. Dès lors, pour faire la théorie, en langage logistique, des structures mentales effectivement réalisables, il convient de constituer, à l'usage des sciences de l'esprit, l'équivalent de ce que les physiciens ont fait en fondant la physique mathématique : il est nécessaire de construire, à côté de la logistique pure, qui est axiomatique, une théorie logistique des opérations ou des structures mentales qui ne serait nullement une logistique « psychologiste »⟦,⟧ mais au contraire une psychologie logistique, c'est-à-dire une théorie écrite dans le langage de l'algèbre logistique mais portant sur les structures qui interviennent dans la vie mentale réelle. Or, ces structures étant dominées par des lois d'équilibre et tout équilibre se définissant par une compensation entre les transformations possibles d'un système, une telle théorie logistique des structures réelles demeurerait en premier lieu une science des possibles ; mais au lieu de partir des formes les plus générales, comme le fait une théorie déductive pure, elle étudierait au contraire, palier par palier, l'organisation de structures élémentaires ou restreintes, puis de plus en plus étendues.

En écrivant le « Traité de Logique » qu'on a bien voulu nous demander, nous avions en partie l'illusion qu'en faisant la théorie logistique des structures de l'intelligence telles que nous les avions étudiées dans le développement réel de la pensée, nous retrouverions certaines des structures formelles construites par les logisticiens purs : l'expérience nous a montré après coup, et l'article de M. Beth nous le prouve à nouveau, que nous nous engagions simplement sans le savoir sur la troisième des voies distinguées à l'instant, c'est-à-dire dans la direction d'une théorie logistique des opérations mentales par opposition à la logistique pure ou axiomatique. Un bel article de M. Kröner, dans *Dialectica*,[a] nous a reconnu le souci

[a]Kröner (1950).

de ne pas tomber dans le « psychologisme[18] ». M. Beth nous montre aujourd'hui que nous n'avons pas non plus fait de la logistique proprement dite. Comme nous avons tout de même traduit des faits—les mécanismes opératoires de la pensée sont le prototype des actes de l'intelligence—en langage logistique, il reste donc qu'il y a là une troisième direction possible de recherche.[b]

D'un tel point de vue, les critiques de M. Beth (de même que toutes celles qu'il aurait pu ajouter) prennent un grand intérêt, car, à part quelques erreurs de fait, faciles à corriger, elles montrent avant tout la différence considérable, dans les buts et dans les exigences, qui existe et doit exister entre la logistique pure et la théorie logistique des opérations mentales. Si nous reprenons la comparaison entre ces deux disciplines et les mathématiques opposées à la physique mathématique, la chose se comprend d'elle-même. On peut axiomatiser ou formaliser la physique mathématique (bien qu'elle n'ait pas commencé par là et ne puisse que difficilement aborder par cette méthode un problème entièrement nouveau), mais on ne demandera jamais à une théorie de physique mathématique de fournir la démonstration d'une vérité proprement mathématique : son but est de mathématiser la réalité physique et non pas de physicaliser les mathématiques. De même, le rôle d'une théorie logistique des opérations mentales élémentaires est de dégager les structures possibles que peuvent revêtir celles-ci, d'une façon suffisante pour permettre d'expliquer les structures réelles et de prévoir les lois de leur équilibration : or, ce but a été en partie atteint, car les idées contenues dans le Traité nous ont permis d'expliquer le passage de la logique de l'enfant (fondée uniquement sur les groupements de classes et de relations) à celle de l'adolescence (fondée sur le réseau des opérations interpropositionnelles bivalentes, conçu comme la généralisation de la structure du groupement[c]). Dès lors, quand M. Beth nous reproche des complications inutiles dans le développement des structures de relations et de propositions, et, surtout quand il nous reproche une conception naïve des mathématiques, il a raison de son point de vue, qui est celui de la généralité formalisée, mais nous avons raison du nôtre qui est celui de l'analyse des opérations élémentaires. Pour reprendre l'un de ses exemples, nous continuons de croire qu'il intervient une relation d'ordre dans la distinction des unités cardinales équivalentes 1+1+1... même si le logicien n'y a

---

[18]Piaget recognizes that this is an illusion if one interprets—as he has partially done—his intended comparison of psychology and logic as an attempt to find the formal logical structure through the analysis of the development of the logic of thought.

[b]Nous dégagerons cette troisième direction, de façon plus explicite, dans un ouvrage qui paraîtra prochainement aux Presses Universitaires de France et qui portera sur les transformations algébriques des 256 opérateurs ternaires de la logique des propositions bivalentes, sous le titre *Les transformations des opérations logiques.* [« *Essai sur les transformations des opérations logiques. Les 256 opérations ternaires de la logique bivalente des propositions* », Paris (1952) : PUF (Piaget 1952b), cf. letter 10].

[c]Dans un ouvrage avec B. Inhelder, à paraître d'ici quelques années. ⟦Cf. Piaget and Inhelder (1955)⟧.

point explicitement recours et utilise une définition par abstraction, car celle-ci ne se réfère point aux opérations préalables que l'esprit a exécutées en fait et que nous avons pour tâche de dégager.

Mais on ne demandera pas à une théorie logistique des opérations élémentaires réelles[19] de fonder l'axiomatisation, et c'est pourquoi les lacunes que M. Beth signale dans notre formalisation sont parfaitement exactes (et avouées). Par exemple, il est effectivement très important pour une théorie formalisée de distinguer la mention et l'usage d'une opération : cette distinction n'a qu'une signification secondaire si l'on se propose seulement d'étudier les structures opératoires comme telles. Par contre, on peut estimer que l'axiomatisation n'a pas la même valeur, à titre de fondement, en logique qu'en mathématique et qu'il y a un inévitable cercle vicieux à vouloir démontrer la logique par elle-même, puisque le logicien emploie exclusivement la métalogique et qu'il peut donc fonder une syntaxe puis, ensuite seulement, la compléter par une sémantique sans commettre aucun cercle. Mais les raisonnements du logicien qui construit la logique sont d'abord des actes mentaux, tandis que la logique qu'il construit est une théorie formelle : or ces actes mentaux contiennent déjà, si nous avons raison, toute une structure opératoire qui se retrouvera ensuite dans la théorie formelle, et c'est pourquoi il y a un cercle tout de même. De plus, et à s'en tenir au domaine formalisé, on sait qu'une syntaxe reçoit sa signification d'une métalangue, qui la reçoit elle-même d'une autre métalangue, etc. ; or, il existe des opérations communes à tous ces paliers successifs et ces opérations ne sont dès lors exprimables en aucun langage en tant que communes : qu'est-ce à dire sinon qu'il s'agit à nouveau d'opérations mentales, ce qui implique une fois de plus l'existence de structures sous-jacentes ? Il n'est donc pas si dénué de sens à chercher sous une axiomatique les structures sur lesquelles elle s'appuie, et si cette recherche ne sert en rien à la formalisation elle-même, elle nous semble riche d'enseignements au point de vue de l'étude des mécanismes opératoires de la pensée et même en ce qui concerne les fondements épistémologiques de la logique.

Il nous paraît donc inutile de reprendre une à une les critiques de M. Beth. Notons seulement que, à côté du reproche de n'avoir pas fait ce que nous avons voulu faire (tel qu'un exposé de la métalogique), il en est quelques-unes qui reposent sur de simples malentendus. Par exemple⟦,⟧ nous n'avons jamais « identifié » les axiomes de la logique des propositions et les règles d'opérations, mais seulement interprété les axiomes comme assumant en définitive eux aussi, un rôle de réglage : nous savons bien que cette interprétation est contraire à l'esprit de l'axiomatique, mais elle a été soutenue (G. Juvet) et nous la croyons vraie. Nous n'avons jamais dit que le fondement des mathématiques avait été cherché dans la seule logique des propositions (le texte même que cite M. Beth ne parle pas de fondements). Nous n'avons jamais pensé que le symbole $\neg P$ dans la logique de Griss, représente pour

[19] I.e., the logic of thought.

lui une négation : la classe complémentaire $\neg P$ est celle des éléments « autres » que P (d'où l'exclusion de toute classe nulle) ; mais il est légitime de penser que cette « altérité » englobe opératoirement malgré tout une négation. L'interprétation contestée par M. Beth des conséquences du théorème de Gödel est sans doute trop elliptique : nous pensons simplement qu'en étant obligé de recourir au transfini et à la récurrence transfinie⟦,⟧ on modifie entièrement l'économie logique de l'arithmétique, puisqu'on démontre la non-contradiction à partir du sommet et non plus de la base (voir les thèses de Cavaillès et de Lautmann ⟦sic !⟧. Quant aux pages sur Brouwer, elles se bornent (comme indiqué) au résumé des travaux trop peu cités de Wavre : mais je suis prêt à les rectifier dans le sens suggéré par M. Beth.

Par contre⟦,⟧ les critiques intéressantes de M. Beth sont celles qui manifestent l'opposition du point de vue axiomatique avec notre point de vue opératoire. Par exemple, il est bien exact que la métalogique aboutit à un système fermé, mais nous continuerons de croire qu'en considérant les opérations indépendamment de leur structure algébrique on se place à un point de vue atomistique⟦,⟧ alors que les questions de structure d'ensemble commandent tout le mécanisme de la pensée. De même, si désuètes que soient les discussions anciennes entre Poincaré et Couturat, ou la tradition algébrique de Peirce et Schröder, elles sont d'un grand intérêt au point de vue de ces structures opératoires, tandis que les théories récentes de la déduction ont déplacé la question. Déplacement légitime, cela va de soi, selon le but que l'on s'assigne, mais qui autorise des reprises si le but est autre. M. Beth nous répondra que le point de vue opératoire, tel que nous l'entendons, n'intéresse ni la logique formalisée ni les mathématiques depuis Frege. Nous n'avons pas cherché à démontrer le contraire. Nous disons seulement que, pour les besoins de la psychologie et de l'épistémologie génétique, la logique axiomatique ne suffit pas : il est donc nécessaire d'essayer de construire une théorie des opérations (~~logistiques~~) comme telles.[20]

Bref, du point de vue où il se place, M. Beth a incontestablement raison et je savais d'avance que je ne pourrais pas satisfaire les purs logiciens. Je dirai même plus : si mon but avait été de les satisfaire, je n'eusse naturellement pas écrit de Traité ! Mais si l'on croit à la possibilité d'une théorie logistique des opérations mentales, et en particulier des plus élémentaires, il faut avoir le courage d'essayer de la constituer avec les moyens dont on dispose. Certains logiciens ont compris la portée de cet essai et y ont vu une tentative encourageante pour la logistique elle-même.[d] Que d'autres dont les intérêts n'englobent pas la psychologie ne comprennent pas notre tentative, c'est dans l'ordre des choses. Je n'en félicite pas moins M. Beth de sa parfaite honnêteté intellectuelle.

[20]This confirms Piaget's very broad use of the term "logic" in the sense of "structural account".

[d]Voir Kröner, op. cit. ~~pp.~~

2. Beth to Piaget[21]

le 13 avril

Cher Monsieur Piaget, très honoré collègue,

Je vous remercie bien vivement de votre lettre et de votre gentillesse à me mettre au courant de votre réponse à mon compte-rendu. Ce geste témoigne à la fois d'une rare largeur d'esprit et d'une parfaite compréhension de mon point de vue et des circonstances dans lesquelles je me trouvais ; je ne pourrais que les admirer l'une et l'autre. Veuillez bien croire à mon appréciation de cette preuve de bonne volonté qui m'a profondément touché.

Ne voulant pas tarder à vous répondre, je vous prie de bien vouloir vous accommoder à un⌈e⌉ mode d'expression conditionnée par les imperfections de ma connaissance de votre langue et par des habitudes personnelles auxquelles il me serait difficile de renoncer.

Permettez-moi, à cette occasion, de faire—à ma façon—un peu de psychologie génétique en vous décrivant mon développement mental.

Ayant obtenu ma licence en mathématiques, je me suis intéressé au problème des fondements, et j'ai entamé plus particulièrement l'étude du problème de l'espace. Le choix de ce sujet m'a forcé d'élargir considérablement mon champ de travail et j'ai fini par obtenir, quelques années plus tard, la licence en psychologie. Puis, j'ai sout⟦enu⟧ une thèse sur le rôle de la raison et de l'intuition en mathématiques[22] et j'ai publié deux mémoires, couronné⌈e⌉s par la Société Mathématique sur la proposition de M. Mannoury, sur l'interprétation psycho-linguistique du symbolisme logique et sur le rôle de la perception du temps dans la pensée mathématique,[23] et un rapport sur l'état actuel de la psychologie de la pensée mathématique.[24]

À ce moment, je suis entré en relation⌈s⌉ avec M. Scholz qui m'a convaincu que, pour bien comprendre la logique et la recherche des fondements, il fallait abandonner le point de vue psychologique et adopter celui de la logique pure. Je peux vous assurer que d'abord la critique de M. Scholz m'a causé une déception profonde. Mais peu à peu je me suis rendu compte de son bien-fondé, et je n'ai jamais regretté les études renouvelées de logique et d'axiomatiques auxquelles il fallait me décider ; d'ailleurs, je ne crois pas non plus avoir perdu le temps consacré à l'étude de psychologie qui a assurément élargi ma formation intellectuelle.

---

[21] Manuscript in typescript ; 4 pages.

[22] Rede en Aanschouwing in de Wiskunde (Reason and Intuition in Mathematics) Dissertation, 1935 (Beth 1935).

[23] 'De significa van de pasigraphische systemen' (Beth 1936–1937) and 'Getalbegrip en tijdsaanschouwing' (Beth 1938–1939).

[24] 'Te psychologische argumenten en rischtlijnen voor de vernieuwing van het onderwijs in de wiskunde' (Beth 1939–1940).

Plus tard, ayant étendu mes relations internationales, j'ai été surpris que le point de vue de la logique pure, qui est à présent accepté à peu près partout, était absolument inconnu en France, où l'on continuait à faire de la logique comme je l'avais fait moi-même au début de ma carrière.[25] Aussi j'ai bien été content de pouvoir contribuer à la diffusion de la logique pure en France en publiant mes « Fondements logiques[26] ».

Vous comprendrez combien, dans ces circonstances, votre livre devait me choquer. Ce livre se présente comme un « Traité de logique » et un « Essai de logistique opératoire ». Il sera forcément acheté par des gens qui veulent comprendre, non pas la psychologie, mais la logique. Et la nature ne pourra pas les désabuser. Ayant terminé l'étude de votre livre, ils devront se croire au courant de la logique moderne et en état de juger, pour eux-mêmes, des questions logiques, d'autant plus que, pour une personne de culture française, la logique est une science qui, en quelque sorte, se rapporte à la pensée et que, par conséquent, les observations psychologiques ne constitueront pas, pour lui, quelque chose d'hétérogène par rapport à la logique qu'il voulait apprendre. Je ne nie pas qu'une telle personne, après la lecture de votre livre, aura acquis des connaissances en logique. Mais en même temps il aura pris, à l'égard de la logique, une attitude qui ne pourra que nuire à sa compréhension d'un livre de logique pure. Votre livre contribuera donc à faire subsister l'isolement de la France par rapport à l'état actuel des études logiques en d'autres pays.

Permettez-moi de me rapporter à la p. 2 de votre réponse, au milieu : « Pour ce qui ... pourrait sembler » ⟦see document 1′, p. 54⟧. Je ne crois pas que cette description puisse s'appliquer à la situation hors de la France. Il y a, surtout en anglais, toute une série de traités, au niveau élémentaire ou supérieur⌈e⌉, qui sont considérés de façon quasi-unanime comme acceptables. Il y a, par exemple, l'admirable « Introduction » de Tarski, pubié⟦e⟧ en polonais, allemand, anglais, russe, espagnol, hébreu, une traduction néerlandais⟦e⟧ étant en préparation.

Je crois donc que j'avais le droit, étant donné votre grand renom, la présentation de votre livre, l'état actuel des études logiques en France, et de la place où mon compte-rendu devait paraître, d'adopter exclusivement le point de vue de la logique pure, ce qui me forçait d'écrire comme je l'ai fait.

Il va sans dire que la situation aurait été différente si votre livre se serait [sic !] annoncé différemment, et même si vous seriez [sic !] restreint à développer les parties élémentaires de la logique. Dans ce cas j'aurais exprimé⌈s⌉, certes, certaines réserves, mais non pas des objections sérieuses. Vous avez vu, dans ce qui précède, que votre point de vue ne m'est pas entièrement étrange⟦r⟧, et vous comprendrez que la suggestion d'une collaboration—suggestion flatteuse, dont je suis fort reconnaissant—ne me pourrait être que sympathique. Il va de soi que

[25] Beth wants to insinuate that Piaget continues to defend what he himself has abandoned: a strong psychological position (formal logic reflects the logic of thought).

[26] In this work, the term "psychology" does not occur.

cette suggestion est trop importante pour être acceptée sans réflexion et discussion préalable, et je vous prie de bien vouloir permettre quelques observations à son égard.

Votre idée d'utiliser certaines structures logiques pour décrire certaines structures mentales révélées par la recherche psychologique me paraît parfaitement légitime au point de vue méthodique. Toutefois la situation actuelle de la logique me met dans la nécessité de regarder une telle application de la logique également sous un angle plus large, notamment par rapport au problème des relations entre logique et psychologie en général.[27]

On a fait de nombreux efforts pour établir une connexion entre la logique (y compris l'axiomatique) et la psychologie, et à mon avis les résultats en ont été extrêmement maigres ; il y a des cas où des résultats réels ont été acquis mais où, si l'on regarde les choses de près, ou la logique ou la psychologie n'a été appliquée qu'en apparence.

À mon avis, cela montre que, pour mettre en relation les deux sciences, il faut un trait d'union, et il me paraît que l'on pourrait utiliser la linguistique comme tel⟦le⟧. Dans ce cas, même la collaboration d'un psychologue orienté vers la logique et d'un logicien orienté vers la psychologie risquerait de s'exposer à des objections justifiées du côté des linguistes.

Pour prouver la nécessité de recourir à la linguistique, je peux faire appel à notre discussion même. Il me semble, en effet, que dans un sens nos divergences dérivent, en dernière analyse, de certaines divergences par rapport à notre façon de nous exprimer. Je ne veux pas dire que nos différends sont purement verbaux ; tout au contraire, le fait que nous travaillons, d'habitude, dans des domaines différents nous amène, naturellement, à adopter des modes différent⌈e⌉s à nous exprimer et, par conséquent, d'interpréter différemment un texte donné.

Je pense donc que, pour qu'une collaboration éventuelle puisse être féconde, il faudra (1) étudier les points de vue différents adoptés dans le passé par ceux qui ont cherché des connexions entre la psychologie et la logique, et (2) élaborer une terminologie commune permettant de confronter la logique et la psychologie sans risque de malentendu. Il est dommage que les circonstances ne me permettent pas de prendre part aux Entretiens de Zurich ; je suis d'accord avec vous qu'une prise de contact directe contribuerait à la compréhension mutuelle, et je serais bien content de pouvoir vous être utile. Espérons que l'occasion pour un⌈e⌉ échange de vues se présente bientôt !

Je me permets de vous remettre sous pli séparé, avec quelques autres tirages-à-part, celui de mon compte-rendu, arrivé très tardivement.

Ma femme me charge de vous assurer de son souvenir le meilleur.

Veuillez agréer, cher Monsieur et très honoré collègue, l'expression de mes sentiments les plus respectueux.

---

[27] Beth may referring both the situation of logic in France and to the difficult dialogue between the Gonseth group and the Tarski group about international institutions (see Introduction, Sect. 2). His argument therefore pertains to scientific policy.

3. Piaget to Beth[28]

UNIVERSITÉ DE GENÈVE
SCHOLA GENEVENSIS MDLIX

FACULTÉ DES SCIENCES

Genève, le 16 Avril 1951,

Cher Monsieur Beth,

Je reçois à l'instant votre aimable lettre et ne veux pas tarder à vous en remercier très vivement. Le seul fait que vous ne rejetiez pas l'idée d'une collaboration et en examiniez les conditions de possibilités est pour moi un grand encouragement.

Je tiendrai compte dans ma réponse de votre remarque au sujet des Traités existants comme Tarski, etc. Je parlerai naturellement de la seule langue française (et je reconnais pleinement avec vous la gaffe que j'ai commise en me soumettant à l'éditeur qui voulait imposer à mon ouvrage le titre de Traité et pas un autre !). Cela a été une surprise véritable et très excitante d'apprendre que vous êtes un ancien psychologue, qui a pour ainsi dire changé de religion.[29] C'est une raison de plus pour que nous cherchions à réaliser une collaboration qui suppose deux auteurs à points de vue opposés mais chacun compréhensif de celui de l'autre.

Je ne suis pas étonné de ce que vous me dites de la maigreur des résultats obtenus jusqu'ici dans les efforts pour établir une connexion entre la logique et la psychologie. Mais cela tient à mon avis au fait que le problème a été placé dans l'abstrait ou avec une trop grande généralité, ce qui le rend pour le moment insoluble.

Si je m'occupe néanmoins de la question et même avec une conviction telle que j'en viens à vous proposer une collaboration, c'est qu'il s'agit pour moi de problèmes limités—de portée générale mais de données bien délimitées.

Les problèmes sont ceux du développement même ou de la formation des opérations. En suivant le développement de la pensée, de 2–3 ans à l'adolescence (ou à l'état adulte)⟦,⟧ je me trouve en présence de stades successifs tels que l'on puisse

---

[28]Manuscript ; 6 pages.

[29]Beth changed his perspective under the influence of Scholz, who himself abandoned theology in favor of logic.

caractériser chacun par l'absence ou par l'apparition de telle ou telle opération. De plus, ces apparitions ne sont pas isolées, mais témoignent de l'intervention de structures (d'opérations solidaires et formant des systèmes).

Le problème est alors le suivant : (1) comment décrire les structures et les opérations qui en dépendent ? (2) comment décrire leurs filiations ?

Je pars donc de l'élémentaire et non pas du sommet, mais en rencontrant les questions les plus excitantes. Par exemple, en étudiant maintenant la pensée d'adolescent, je trouve à partir de 1–14 ans toute une organisation de la logique des propositions dont l'enfant est bien incapable (avant 11–12 ans il n'intervient que des systèmes concrets de classes et de relations et encore sous la forme très restreinte que j'ai appelée celle des groupements). Comment donc et surtout à partir de quoi s'effectue cette formation assez rapide de la logique des propositions ? etc. etc.[30]

Je suis entièrement d'accord avec vous que si nous songions sérieusement à une crise au point des rapports actuels ⟦entre⟧ logique et psychologie⟦,⟧ il nous faudrait d'abord (1) une étude historique et (2) une terminologie (ce second point m'intéresse⟦,⟧ je l'avoue⟦,⟧ plus que le premier, mais je me rallie au premier aussi dans la mesure de mes moyens). Mais je pense qu'il nous faudrait ensuite faire bien davantage : c'est une sorte de tableau en langage logistique des opérations réelles de la pensée sur les principaux paliers de sa constitution. Or ce troisième point soulève un problème très complexe : exprimer en un langage rigoureux une pensée qui ne l'est pas mais qui marche, par approximations successives, vers la rigueur !

J'ai naturellement sur ce troisième point un ensemble de résultats de fait et d'hypothèse, mais c'est de la psychologie et pas de la logique. Ce qui serait intéressant c'est de confronter l'ordre de formation psychologique et l'ordre de construction logique. L'adage d'Aristote πρῶτον μὲν ἐν τῇ γενέσει, ἔσχατον δὲ ἐν τῇ ἀναλύσει[31] est-il valable ici ou bien y a-t-il correspondance entre les deux ordres ?

Dites-moi ce que vous pensez de ce projet. Je pars la semaine prochaine faire quelques conférences à Oxford mais pourrais vous faire à mon retour un tableau plus détaillé des problèmes à discuter.

---

[30]Piaget indicates that propositional logic is acquired after rudimentary predicate logic. He then suggests, as part of the third point of his potential collaboration with Beth, "comparing the order of psychological formation with the order of logical construction." Still, he makes no explicit assumptions about the relationship between the actual acquisition of propositional logic and the "normative" construction of said logic.

[31]"Thus what comes first in the production, comes last in the analysis". It is not sure whether Piaget has fully grasped the sense of Aristotle's slightly different adage: τὸ ἔσχατον ἐν τῇ ἀναλύσει πρῶτον εἶnai ἐν τῇ γενέσει (Eth. Nic. III, 1112b24): "Thus what comes last in the analysis, comes first in the production". In fact, Aristotle's *production* and *analysis* are two operations concerning the same subject: one produces it, and the other gives its causes. This is the case both in theory and in practice. On the contrary, for Piaget the difference is identified with the difference: 'practical' (subjective; psychological) / 'theoretical' (objective; logical).

D'ici là veuillez croire, mon cher collègue, à mes sentiments très dévoués.

J. Piaget

P.S. I Merci beaucoup pour vos tirés à part. J'ai lu avec grand intérêt votre étude sur Kelsen et vos idées sur la non opposition du νόμος et de la φύσις. À propos du sens primitif de φύσις il existe une bonne étude de A. Burger chez Champion (1925) sur les mots de la racine φύ où il montre que φύσις est une sorte de poussée vitale (p. ex. φύσις δενδρῶν = la croissance des arbres) avant d'être la nature des choses (cité de mémoire).

P.S. II En relisant cette lettre⟦,⟧ j'ai un peu peur de vous inquiéter avec mon point 3. Il va de soi qu'on peut se borner au point 1 et 2. Si vous ne voulez pas aller plus loin, ou faire rentrer le point 3 comme cas particulier du 2 : « une terminologie permettrait de confronter la logique et la psychologie sans risque de malentendu ». On prendrait alors divers exemples parmi lesquels certains que j'aurais mis sous (3).

On pourrait toujours concevoir une partie (3) qui serait consacrée à l'énoncé d'une série de problèmes. À propos de chacun on indiquerait (a) le point de vue du logicien (b) le point de vue du psychologue et (c) la manière de les concilier ou la constatation de leur caractère actuellement inconciliable.

Cordialement vôtre⟦,⟧

J. P.

4. Beth to Piaget[32]

Amsterdam, le 7 mai 1951

Bern.[33] Zweerskade 23/I.

Cher Monsieur Piaget,

Je vous demande pardon d'être tard à répondre [sic !] votre lettre si importante du 16 avril. Vous comprendrez que ce n'est pas un⌈e⌉ manque d'intérêt mais des devoirs urgents qui sont les causes de ce retard.

Je suis entièrement d'accord avec vous que l'intérêt des points (1), (2) et (3) augmente dans cet ordre. Le point (1) pourrait être abandonné jusqu'à nouvel ordre,

[32] Manuscript in typescript ; 3 pages.

[33] Bernard.

et le point (2) pourrait être considéré de façon incidentelle ; toutefois, il importe de ne pas les négliger entièrement, leur élucidation pouvant servir à prévenir ou à corriger des malentendus.

C'est le point (3) qui est intéressant en soi, et j'espère que vous me permettrez de faire une observation à son égard, bien que je ne l'ai⟦e⟧ pas étudié récemment de manière systématique et que je n'ai⟦e⟧ qu'une connaissance fragmentaire de vos recherches psychologiques.

Au sujet de l'explication théorique du développement de la pensée on peut faire, en première approximation, deux hypothèses fondamentales et incompatibles, à savoir :

(i) ce développement est un processus spontané ;
(ii) il est imposé à l'individu par son milieu.[34]

J'ai l'impression que vous acceptez la première hypothèse et je vous concède au préalable que ce n'est que l'expérience psychologique qui pourra décider laquelle des deux hypothèses est exacte.

---

[34]Beth understands Piaget's position very well. Piaget cites the existence of four factors to account for mental development (Piaget and Inhelder (1966, pp. 121–126, French version): "organic growth and especially the maturation of the complex formed by the nervous system, and the endocrine systems", "the role of exercise and experience acquired in the action carried out on objects (in opposition to social experience)", "social interactions and transmissions". These three factors are considered "fundamental" but "insufficient". The only *truly causal* factor is "the process of equilibration" (cf. also Piaget in *Psychologie et pédagogie* (Piaget 1969, pp. 40–62, French version)). The primacy of the endogenous process in mental development is also underlined by the assertion of the primacy of the schemes of assimilation over those of accommodation. This was asserted as early as he wrote *Origins of intelligence in the child* (Piaget 1936, p. 415, French version), and such an assertion was always maintained by him. It is assimilation which remains "the mainspring of the cognitive act" (Piaget, *La psychogenèse des connaissances et sa signification épistémique,* (Piaget et al. 1979, p. 54, French version)). Finally, the primacy of the endogenous process is illustrated by the precedence of development over apprenticeship in the Piagetian program.

Beth formulates the terms of the debate very clearly. When it comes to account for the factors that structure knowledge, the social factors especially are relegated to background: "the principal conclusions which the varied works about child psychology have offered to pedagogy for a few years are thus relative to the very nature of intellectual development. On the one hand, this development is primarily due to the subject's activities and, especially to those directed from the sensory-motor action to the best-interiorized operations; the driving force is constantly an irreducible and spontaneous "operativity". On the other hand, this "operativity" is neither preformed once and for all nor explicable by the only external contributions of experience or social transmission: it is the product of successive constructions and *the principal factor of this constructivism is an equilibration by self-regulations* making it possible to remedy the temporary inconsistencies, solve the problems, and overcome the crises or imbalances by a constant development of new structures that school can ignore or support according to the methods employed" (*Psychologie et pédagogie* (Piaget 1969, pp. 61–62)). See also, for example, the suggested explanation of equilibration involving self-regulation as a formative process of the structures (Piaget and Inhelder 1966, pp. 125–126, French version). Thus, for Piaget, the principal factor, that is to say the truly causal factor in mental development, is an endogenous process of construction of structures. The activity of the environment *(milieu)* is simply disrupting.

Toutefois, on peut toujours se demander laquelle des deux hypothèses est préférable d'un certain point de vue, et je pense que du point de vue du logicien la deuxième hypothèse est préférable. Je ne veux pas dire que la première hypothèse est moins logique, mais seulement que la deuxième s'accorde mieux avec les conceptions générales dont part la logique moderne. Permettez-moi donc de donner une esquisse rapide d'une conception du développement de la pensée qui ne dérive pas d'expériences psychologiques mais qui, pour le logicien, paraît plus ou moins naturelle.

Ce qu'on a coutume d'appeler développement de la pensée est l'apprentissage de l'emploi correct du langage. Ce langage se caractérise par une double structure ; une[35] peut distinguer sa structure matérielle de sa structure formelle.

La structure matérielle consiste dans une hiérarchie de termes et de locutions de plus en plus abstraites, la structure formelle dans le système de liaisons entre les différents éléments dans cette hiérarchie.

L'apprentissage de l'emploi du langage est dominé par la structure matérielle du langage. Avant d'apprendre l'emploi direct du mot « couleur »⟦,⟧ il faut qu'on sache déjà employer correctement les mots « rouge », « bleu », etc. Tout en pénétrant dans la structure formelle[36] du langage, on se familiarise également avec sa structure formelle.

D'après cette conception, le développement progressif de la pensée serait donc dominé exclusivement par la structure interne du langage. L'observation de ce développement ne nous apprendrait donc rien sur le mécanisme interne de la pensée, elle ne pourrait que nous renseigner sur la structure du langage.

Il me semble qu'en grandes lignes cette conception s'accorde assez bien avec vos observations. Prenons comme exemple votre observation que, dans le développement mental, les éléments de la logique des propositions ne se présentent que tardivement. Or, d'après cette conception, c'est ce qu'on devrait attendre. La logique des propositions est l'élément dans la structure formelle du langage qui relie, dans la structure matérielle, l'échelle de la phrase simple à celle des phrases composées. Il faut bien qu'on sait ⟦sic !⟧ employer les phrases simples avant d'apprendre l'emploi des phrases composées.[37]

[35]Read: "on".

[36]Read: "matérielle".

[37]Beth's answer is that the late acquisition of propositional logic illustrates the idea that the progressive development of thought is dominated by the structure of language (here: combining sentences to complex sentences (propositional logic) once we learn to make simple sentences). What Beth contradicts is thesis (i), which he rightly attributes to Piaget. The conclusion to be drawn is that Piaget's observation is not an argument in favor of spontaneous endogenous development (i.e., the existence of an internal thought), but an argument for (ii), i.e., the idea that the structure of language is involved.

We have here a beautiful illustration of a debate of opinions: an interlocutor loses this kind of debate and the other wins if the latter shows that the thesis of the former (late appearance of propositional logic) is in fact an inference of his own thesis (differentiation of language).

Encore une fois, je ne dis pas que l'hypothèse (ii) est vraie ou même pas qu'elle est vraisemblable. Je suis prêt à reconnaître la possibilité de données expérimentales qui l'infirment. Toutefois, je serais content d'avoir votre opinion à cet égard.

Je voudrais également souligner que pour la logique pure la question n'a pas d'importance. La logique présuppose la structure formelle du langage sous forme intégrale. C'est pour cette raison qu'elle peut inverser l'ordre génétique et partir de la logique des propositions en tant que structure primaire.

Voici donc quelques indications provoquées par votre lettre, et qui, peut-être, peuvent servir de point de départ pour la partie (3).

Merci de votre indication sur l'étude de Burger. À présent, je ne m'occupe guère des questions historiques, étant absorbé par l'étude de certaines questions logiques très abstraites concernant le problème de la décision.

Veuillez croire, mon cher collègue, à mes sentiments les plus dévoués.

5. Piaget to Beth[38]

UNIVERSITÉ DE GENÈVE
SCHOLA GENEVENSIS MDLIX

FACULTÉ DES SCIENCES

Genève, le 24 Mai 1951

Cher Monsieur Beth,

C'est à moi de m'excuser de mon retard, (1)° un travail à finir sur la perception.

J'ai trouvé votre importante lettre, en rentrant d'Oxford, avec d'autant plus de plaisir que la question que vous me posez, à propos du point 3, converge en partie avec celle que j'allais vous poser de mon côté quant à la manière d'aborder ce point (3) pour assurer une collaboration fructueuse entre nous.

Mais procédons par ordre

I. Nous sommes donc d'accord sur l'intérêt progressif des points 1, 2 et 3 et sur la nécessité de ne renoncer ni à 2 ni même à 1. Pour ce qui est de votre question (le développement constitue-t-il (a) un développement spontané ou (b) un résultat des actions du milieu, je répondrai que les deux hypothèses

---

[38]Manuscript; 10 pages.

ne sont pas exclusives et que les faits parlent sans cesse en faveur de l'action simultanée de ces deux sortes de facteurs. La difficulté principale est même d'arriver à les dissocier, ce qu'on peut faire en certains cas, mais pas en d'autres.[39]

Partons de l'hypothèse que les structures logiques et mathématiques sont imposées à l'enfant par le milieu. On constate alors que leur acquisition s'effectue selon des stades assez réguliers (dans leur ordre de succession et indépendamment des âges moyens qui peuvent varier). Par exemple, dans le cas de l'espace, certaines notions topologiques précèdent de beaucoup (avant tout enseignement) les notions métriques⟦,⟧ etc. Il faut en conclure que si tout n'est pas assimilé simultanément et que si cette assimilation suit un ordre de succession constant, c'est donc qu'il existe des facteurs de développement spontané conditionnant l'assimilation elle-même ou pourrait⟦,⟧ il est vrai⟦,⟧ expliquer l'ordre constant de la succession par la nécessité de procéder du simple au complexe. Mais les qualités de simplicité ou de complexité sont toujours relatives à une structure mentale (et ce qui est plus simple pour l'enfant coïncide rarement avec ce que nous croyons tel !). L'essentiel est alors l'étude des paliers successifs d'acquisition, étant entendu qu'il y a toujours action du milieu (mais variable : ⟦par ex⟧emple les sourds-muets qui acquièrent les opérations concrètes de classification, de sériation, etc.) mais aussi toujours des éléments de structurations spontanés bien qu'on ne puisse déterminer avec certitude leur nature ni l'étendue de leur action.

III. [sic !] J'en viens alors à la proposition que j'allais vous faire avant de recevoir votre lettre et qui permet précisément d'éviter que nous ayons à prendre position sur des questions comme celles-là. Elle consisterait à :

(1) Prendre comme système de référence la logique formelle sous la forme que vous jugerez adéquate, en tant qu'elle caractérise le mécanisme de pensée des adultes d'un certain niveau et qu'elle présuppose les structures formelles de leur langage, etc.[40]

(2) Caractériser les niveaux antérieurs (dont chacun des paliers génétiques sur lesquels j'aurai les précisions nécessaires) par (a) les éléments déjà atteints, s'il y en a, de la logique décrite en (1) et (b) par ce qui manque encore pour pouvoir l'atteindre intégralement.

[39] Piaget once again proposes his solution, which does not seem unreasonable. Clearly, the fact that Beth is the winner of the debate about a special case (propositional logic), does not imply that hypothesis (ii) is always preferable to hypothesis (i).

[40] The main difficulty seems to be what one understands by logic. For Beth, logic is the formal language system in its most differentiated form. For Piaget, however, logic is the structure built empirically in the mind. Initially, he proposed a hierarchy beginning with the most rudimentary structures from children, with the structures in the minds of cultivated adults, and ending with the expert minds of mathematicians (see below in this letter).

De cette manière, nous pourrions peut-être parvenir à construire un instrument d'analyse indépendant de nos divergences possibles et notamment des grandes questions concernant le processus même de genèse et de développement.

Il est, en effet, à redouter que, sans une telle méthode, nous en serions éternellement aux questions préalables.

Pour prendre un exemple de ces divergences possibles et de la manière dont nous pourrions les surmonter, j'ai pour ma part des doutes sur le rôle primordial du langage aux niveaux antérieurs à 12 ans (logique des propositions). Il y a vers 7–8 ans des opérations que l'enfant sait exécuter au cours de manipulations d'objets et qu'il sait fort mal traduire verbalement. Par exemple, on voit des enfants faire une classification correcte d'objets et ne pas savoir indiquer verbalement les critères qu'ils ont effectivement adoptés (ils en indiquent même d'autres !). En précisant alors ce qui est atteint et ce qui manque par rapport à notre logique de référence, nous ferions action positive et utile. Quant aux questions fondamentales, nous pourrions exposer nos deux thèses ou notre thèse commune en conclusion. ~~Autre exemple le rapport entre le~~

D'une manière générale, toutes nos recherches psychologiques depuis des années, ont précisément eu pour but d'atteindre les opérations même de la pensée réduisant l'élément langage au *minimum.* Au début, c'est-à-dire il y a une trentaine d'années, j'ai cru que pour étudier le développement de la logique de l'enfant il suffisait d'analyser son langage et de s'en tenir à des épreuves verbales. Depuis une vingtaine d'années au contraire nous ne travaillons plus que sur des épreuves portant sur des actions réelles et atteignons ainsi des *opérations* qui, suivant les cas, sont ensuite exprimées verbalement de façon correcte ou incorrecte par les sujets.

Même dans le problème du passage de la logique à classer des relations à celle des propositions, nous procédons d'abord par examen des actions. L'enfant ou l'adolescent reçoit par exemple pour tâche de découvrir une loi physique au moyen d'un dispositif matériel (par exemple la relation des angles dans un jeu de billard ou des relations de couleurs avec quatre ou cinq solutions chimiques).

Or, tandis que les enfants de 7–12 ans se bornent à des classements, sériations, correspondances, etc.⟦,⟧ selon des structures élémentaires, les sujets du niveau de 12–15 ans procèdent ?à ? l'action au moyen d'une combinatoire isomorphe au lattice de la logique des propositions : exclusions, conjonctions et, disjonctions, implications, etc. Bien entendu la différence des deux niveaux se retrouve dans le langage, mais j'aurais beaucoup de peine à admettre que le langage soit le seul facteur essentiel, et encore plus de difficulté à admettre que les recherches n'atteignent pas le mécanisme de la pensée.

Avec la méthode que je me permets de vous proposer nous n'aurions pas à décider dès le départ entre les hypothèses. Nous pourrions en arriver finalement à cette discussion, ou l'éviter. Le problème préalable est en tout cas de formuler sur chaque palier ce qui est atteint et ce qui manque (au point de vue des opérations utilisées et de leurs expressions linguistiques), et de le formuler en un langage logistique adéquat. Nous obtiendrons ainsi un tableau instructif en lui-même et qui pourrait servir aux logiciens comme aux psychologues dans les discussions sur les rapports entre la logique, le langage et la pensée réelle. Aux entretiens de Zurich où j'ai parlé de développement des opérations logiques le R. P. Durbale m'a répondu que mon schéma lui rappelait de près les processus d'équilibrations successives que l'on observe dans l'homéostat d'Ashby. Si nous étions en possession du schéma que je vous propose de construire en commun, de telles comparaisons cybernétiques prendraient peut-être une signification précise, au point de vue des passages d'une structure à une autre.

Mais j'ai aussi une question préalable à vous poser. Dans un article récent, Bernays dit qu'il n'y a une application propre d'inférences logiques que dans les raisonnements de caractères mathématiques.[41] D'autre part, en réponse à ma note préliminaire de Zurich⟦,⟧ le chanoine Feys a répondu que la recherche des relations entre la logique et la pensée réelle ne lui paraît avoir de chance de succès qu'en analysant la pensée des mathématiciens. Si l'affirmation de Bernays était exacte⟦,⟧ cela nous forcerait à situer bien haut le système de référence (1) dont je vous parlais tout à l'heure (p. 3). En ce cas c'est déjà à propos de la logique courante et de la structure formelle du langage usuel qu'il faudrait poser le problème de ce qui manque et de ce qui est atteint par rapport au système de référence choisi. Qu'en pensez-vous ?

Je suis à votre disposition pour toutes autres questions préalables, en particulier sur la manière d'organiser pratiquement notre collaboration à distance, et, en vous remerciant très vivement, je vous prie, cher Monsieur Beth, de croire à mes sentiments très dévoués.

J. Piaget

Post-Scriptum. Bien que ma lettre soit déjà trop longue je m'aperçois que je n'ai pas répondu directement à votre question. Voici donc ma réponse :

(1) Le développement de la pensée n'est pas simplement un apprentissage de l'emploi correct du langage, parce que ce développement est d'abord une coordination progressive des *actions.*
(2) Les actions deviennent des opérations dans la mesure où leur coordination aboutit à un mode de composition réversible. Il y a donc une logique des actions plus élémentaires que la logique verbalisée.
(3) Le langage intervient dans la prise de conscience des actions : cette prise de conscience d'abord très inadéquate aux actions elles-mêmes ne devient réellement adéquate qu'au niveau des opérations propositionnelles (après 12 ans).

La preuve expérimentale de l'indépendance relative du point (2) par rapport au langage est à chercher en particulier dans l'étude de la construction des notions de conservation. Avant 6–7 ans une collection d'objets est considérée par l'enfant comme se modifiant lorsqu'on en change la configuration spatiale (=perceptive).

[41] Bernays (1951).

Par exemple, 10 perles transvasées de A  en B  ne feront plus 10 perles mais >10 ou <10. L'arrivée à la notion de la conservation nécessaire s'effectue grâce à la réversibilité progressive des actions effectuées et des transformations de relations qu'elles engendrent. Je ne dis pas que le langage ne joue pas de rôle, mais c'est un rôle réflexif (prise de conscience) et non pas primaire. On peut ainsi suivre les étapes d'une structuration logique des actions elles-mêmes, d'un côté, et de leur verbalisation, d'un autre côté : l'expérience montre qu'il y a là deux facteurs bien distincts, avec parfois des années de décalage entre l'opération en acte et la même opération en paroles. Par exemple le schéma $(B > A) + (B < C) \rightarrow (A < C)$ est d'une difficulté bien plus grande sur le plan verbal qu'en action, de même l'inclusion elle-même.

J. P.

6. Beth to Piaget[42]

Amsterdam, le 9 juin 1951

Bern. Zweerskade 23/I.

Cher Monsieur Piaget,

J'ai bien reçu votre si intéressante lettre du 24 mai, que je n'ai pas voulu répondre qu'après avoir réfléchi longtemps. Il va de soi que je ne désire point rester inutilement aux questions préalables ; d'autre part, pour qu'un effort commun puisse être fécond, il faut bien qu'on dispose d'un certain fonds de points de vue en commun.

Or vous me proposez comme système de référence la logique formelle sous la forme que je jugerais adéquate, en tant qu'elle caractérise le mécanisme de pensée des adultes d'un certain niveau.

Mais ce que je mets en doute, c'est précisément l'existence, voir la possibilité d'une telle logique formelle : ce qui a fait échouer, pendant des siècles, tout effort à établir une logique formelle dépassant le système d'Aristote, c'est le souci de construire un système de logique formelle capable en même temps de caractériser le mécanisme de la pensée.

Je me permets de faire deux autres observations concernant les idées développées dans votre lettre.

[42]Manuscript in typescript ; 4 pages.

(1) Pour illustrer votre thèse de l'indépendance relative de la pensée par rapport au langage, vous mentionnez le cas des enfants qui effectuent une classification bien qu'étant incapables de le décrire verbalement.
    Je ne crois pas que cet example[43] constitue une réfutation de mon point de vue. En effet, il se peut que ces enfants aient au préalable acquis l'habitude de classifier des objets par voie linguistique, et que l'application de cette opération ne constitue qu'une extension secondaire.
(2) J'avais mentionné la possibilité que l'ordre constant du développement mental tire son origine non pas d'une disposition innée, mais plutôt d'une nécessité dérivant de la structure du langage, du monde extérieur, etc. Vous me répondez que les qualités de simplicité sont toujours relatives.

Cette réponse ne me satisfait pas. Un développement conditionné[e] par une nécessité extérieure ne va pas forcément du simple au complexe.

Il y avait un temps où les enfants apprenaient à un âge fort tendre à parler, lire et écrire le latin, avant de savoir lire leur langage à eux.

C'était sans doute un procédé peu pédagogique, mais non pas impossible à effectuer. Mais il serait impossible d'effectuer ce procédé avec un enfant qui n'a jamais entendu parler, qui, par conséquent ne sait pas encore ce que c'est le langage. Je n'affirme pas que vos thèses sont fausses ; je crois seulement qu'elles sont, sous certains respects, insuffisamment prouvées.

Pour éviter tout malentendu, permettez-moi d'énoncer aussi mes thèses à moi.

(1) La logique ne prétend pas à constituer une description de la pensée ; une telle ambition s'est montrée peu favorable à son développement.
(2) La logique n'a trait qu'à certaines propriétés de certaines langues.
(3) La langue ne constitue pas une description de la pensée, la pensée verbale ne constituant qu'une forme assez spéciale de la pensée.

Les rapports entre la logique et la pensée logique—j'entends par pensée logique la pensée verbale en tant qu'elle vise à ébaucher des raisonnements—ne constituent aucunement une identité de structure entre la logique d'une part et la pensée logique de l'autre. Le raisonnement, résultat final de l'effort de la pensée logique, ne constitue pas un document qui serait intéressant au point de vue psychologique. Pour le psychologue, les notes rapides jetées par le logicien seraient plus instructives ; mais elles ne donnent qu'un reflet inadéquat de ce qui s'est passé.

Ces remarques me mettent en l'état de répondre à vos questions au sujet des paroles de MM. Bernays et Feys, et à votre post-scriptum. Je suis d'accord avec eux que la véritable pensée logique ne se rencontre guère que chez les mathématiciens. Il va de soi que l'analyse de la pensée d'un mathématicien n'est pas une entreprise simple. Mais je crois qu'on peut, d'une façon sommaire, en prévoir le résultat ; voici comment je voudrais le décrire, au moyen de la terminologie employée dans votre post-scriptum que je trouve fort lucide.

[43]Read: exemple.

Résoudre un problème mathématique, c'est en général dessiner un nouveau type d'action moyennant une nouvelle coordination des types d'action déjà disponibles. Il s'agit alors de trouver l'idée-clef permettant d'effectuer cette nouvelle coordination.

Dans cette recherche de l'idée-clef, la pensée est dirigée, canalisée, par des « forces mentales » qui la poussent et la retiennent ; parmi ces forces mentales, il y a : les connaissances mathématiques dont le chercheur dispose, un certain fonds de méthodes de solution, certaines images intuitives d'usage personnel, d'ordinaire très vagues et très variables, la conscience du problème, les conditions imposées par la logique.

En général, ces dernières n'interviennent que tardivement, l'idée-clef étant trouvée et éprouvée, au moment qu'il s'agit de formuler une démonstration en règle.

Cela n'implique pas, comme pensent beaucoup de mathématiciens, que la logique est stérile au point de vue athématique ; en effet, ce n'est que la démonstration en règle qui permet[te] de juger de la portée de l'idée-clef. Parfois l'analyse logique montre que l'idée-clef ne revient qu'à une application plus ou moins ingénieuse d'une méthode déjà connue ; en d'autres cas, l'idée-clef se révèle capable d'applications fort variées et la solution du problème original n'est donc que l'introduction à un développement nouveau en mathématiques.

Il va de soi que cette description du mécanisme de la pensée mathématique est bien sommaire et trop schématique. Mais elle pourra peut-être éclaircir le point de vue de MM. Bernays et Feys qui s'identifie à peu près au mien.

Je suis d'accord que, pour pénétrer dans les niveaux primitifs de la pensée, il faut étudier les actions. Je crois, d'ailleurs, que la pensée en général se réduit à une action intériorisée, la pensée logique dérivant de l'intériorisation de l'action logique, c'est-à-dire l'action qui consiste à prononcer un raisonnement.

Les lois logiques jouent donc, dans la pensée du logicien, le même rôle que les lois de la physique dans la pensée d'un ingénieur. Le dernier doit, en projetant un nouveau type de moteur, tenir compte des lois de la physique, dont sa connaissance constitue une des « forces mentales » qui dirigent et canalisent sa pensée ; toutefois, les lois de la physique ne constituent pas, pour cette raison, une description du mécanisme de sa pensée.

Je crois donc que, parmi les « forces mentales » qui dirigent et canalisent la pensée, il y en qui ne tirent pas leurs origines de l'esprit lui-même, mais qui proviennent des influences extérieures. Il va de soi qu'il faut supposer qu'en outre il y a des « forces mentales » de caractère autochtone. Je pense également que les lois de la logique n'appartiennent pas à ces dernières.

Il me paraît que la difficulté primordiale de la psychologie de la pensée réside dans le fait que ce qui est observé en premier lieu, c'est ce qui provient des influences extérieures. Supposons que nous observons [sic !] un ouvrier très capable et très inventeur, qui est assez cultivé pour nous expliquer pourquoi il fait ce qu'il fait. Ses actions et ses explications nous donneront bien des renseignements, mais il est à craindre qu'il ne pourra pas nous révéler le secret de son ingéniosité.

J'espère que cette lettre puisse contribuer à vous faire comprendre mon point de vue. Il va de soi que je ne veux pas me présenter en psychologue professionnel ; pourtant, il me semble que mes études m'ont permis et même for ?cés ? d'observer certains phénomènes qui intéressent la psychologie de la pensée sous un angle que [sic !] diffère de celui du psychologue mais qui, peut-être, pourrait fournir certains éclaircissements supplémentaires.

Je vous prie, cher Monsieur Piaget, d'agréer l'assurance de mes sentiments respectueux.

7. Piaget to Beth[44]

Ausserberg, le 6 Août 1951

Cher Monsieur Beth,

C'est à moi de m'excuser de mon grand retard, que vous n'avez pas dû comprendre et qui est dû à des causes bien peu intellectuelles. J'ai reçu votre excellente lettre du 9 juin à Paris, pendant la Conférence de l'Unesco où j'étais président de Commission du programme et n'avais plus aucun temps. Je suis revenu à Genève le 10 juillet pour des examens et en suis parti le 13 pour Stockholm où le Congrès de psychologie m'a de nouveau occupé complètement. Après quoi j'étais très fatigué et c'est seulement maintenant que je puis vous répondre après avoir rédigé en hâte une conférence pour le congrès d'Amersfoort.[e]

Laissez-vous dire que votre lettre m'a prodigieusement intéressé et excité. Je crois comprendre assez bien votre point de vue qui me paraît de plus en plus cohérent et s'apparente en somme à celui des sociologues de la pensée. Mais il ne me paraît nullement supprimer mon problème, et c'est ce que je vais à nouveau essayer de vous expliquer.

Pour cela je distinguerai trois sections dans ma réponse : (I) les malentendus⟦,⟧ (II) la question de fond et (III) les méthodes qui nous permettront de collaborer tout en conservant nos points de vue respectifs.

(I) *Malentendus.* Il me paraît y en avoir deux dans votre réponse, dû au fait que je me suis mal exprimé :

(1) Je vous ai écrit que les qualités de simplicité sont toujours relatives non pas comme argument pour justifier l'idée d'un développement spontané, mais comme objection à l'idée que la logique des classes apparaîtrait avant celle des propositions uniquement parce qu'elle serait plus simple. Mais ceci n'a pas d'importance⟦.⟧

---

[44] Manuscript ; 9 pages.

[e] Où je ne puis malheureusement pas aller, entre autres pour raison de fatigue.

(2) Je vous demandais que nous prenions comme système de référence la logique dont deviennent capables les adultes d'un certain niveau en pensant non pas à un stade général d'évolution, mais justement à la pensée mathématique. Je suis d'accord avec vous (et Bernays et Feys) que la véritable pensée logique ne se rencontre guère que chez les mathématiciens. Ceci pourrait donc constituer notre système de référence commun pour déterminer ce qui manque ~~à d'autres niveaux~~ du point de vue logique aux structures de la pensée d'un niveau inférieur à celui-là.

(II) J'en viens maintenant aux *questions de fond.* J'aimerais d'abord vous redire à nouveau que je crois votre point de vue très juste dans ce qu'il affirme (l'apport extérieur) mais seulement incomplet à cause de ce qu'il nie (le développement spontané).

(1) L'apport extérieur est incontournable. L'enfant reçoit du dehors un langage (avec sa structure logique approximative) et un ensemble de connaissance organisée. Sans cet apport social et linguistique, il ne dépasserait peut-être que de peu le niveau du Chimpanzé (intelligence sensori-motrice, perception, etc.) Nous sommes d'accord là-dessus.

Mais le problème psychologique subsiste entièrement : au moyen de quels mécanismes internes l'apport extérieur est-il articulé ? Ce problème se pose à propos des actions (a) du milieu physique (b) du milieu social.

Exemple : le langage lui-même. Un psychologue américain a élevé son enfant avec un petit chimpanzé de même âge. Pourquoi le premier seul a-t-il appris à parler ? C'est que si la *langue* est sociale, la *parole* suppose des conditions psychologiques (fonction symbolique, etc.), dont seule ~~la présence~~ l'intervention permet l'acquisition du langage.

(2) Je reprends maintenant l'exemple de la classification. Bien sûr que le langage comporte des changements qui s'impriment du dehors dans l'esprit de l'enfant. Mais cela suffit-il comme explication ? Ne faut-il pas dire aussi qu'un esprit inapte à toute classification serait incapable d'apprendre un langage ?

Or, puisque vous doutez du fait que je vous ai cité (ce qui est très stimulant),[f] il suffit de chercher ailleurs. Les sourds-muets savent classer avant d'apprendre à parler. Il existe des classements sensori-moteurs avant l'acquisition du langage. D'autre part, les classifications inhérentes au langage ne sont assimilées que peu à peu et dans un certain ordre de succession. Si tout provenait des apports extérieurs, sans instruments internes rendant l'articulation possible, les acquisitions devraient ou bien se faire au hasard (ce qui n'est vrai que très partiellement), ou bien suivre l'ordre du simple au complexe. Mais (c'est ici que ce plaçait ma remarque)

[f]Je ne puis naturellement par lettre⌈s⌉ m'en tenir [(qu']] à des indications trop sommaires. Mais j'ai publié des volumes entiers sur le développement des notions et opérations élémentaires (inclusion, correspondance, nombre, etc.).

la simplicité est relative et ce qui est élémentaire au point de vue génétique ne correspond nullement à ce qui nous paraît simple (après coup).

(3) Bref sans nier en rien l'importance des apports extérieurs (dans mes premiers livres j'expliquais mettre tout le développement psychologique des conduites logiques par des facteurs sociaux et verbaux !) je pense maintenant que le problème génétique est infiniment plus complexe et que toute action comporte toujours à des degrés divers des facteurs sociaux, des facteurs relevant de l'expérience individuelle et des facteurs de maturation héréditaire. Je n'ai pas de preuve générale à vous offrir mais tous les faits étudiés d'un peu près sont conformes à ce schéma.

(4) Mais le dosage des influences externes et internes me paraît au fond assez secondaire pour notre but (surtout qu'il est impossible à faire dans la plupart des cas). Il y a un problème beaucoup plus important et sur ce point je pense que nous sommes beaucoup plus près d'être d'accord que vous le croyez. Ce problème est de savoir si la logique correspond à des activités mentales déterminées et réelles. Sur ce point vous répondez « non » et vous croyez que je réponds « oui ». Or ma réponse est ~~beaucoup~~ plus nuancée et au fond très conciliable avec la vôtre. Je crois que tout système organisé d'activités mentales tend vers certaines formes d'équilibre mobile, qui ne sont jamais atteintes complètement et qui se définissent par l'ensemble des transformations virtuelles compatibles avec les liaisons du système donné. Or, pour moi⟦,⟧ la logique correspond aux formes d'équilibres terminales et non pas à des activités réelles, qui sont toujours incomplètement équilibrées. Autrement dit, loin d'être innée, elle n'est même pas psychologiquement réelle ou actuelle, elle correspond à l'ensemble des possibles et non pas à quelques opérations psychologiquement réalisées au sein de ces ensembles. C'est pourquoi je ne suis nullement hostile à l'idée que seules les formes raffinées de pensée mathématique sont logiques : dans mon langage je dirais que seules elles atteignent un équilibre stable des transformations, équilibre demeurant incomplet dans les formes courantes de pensées verbales et bien plus précaire encore dans l'intelligence préverbale.

Il n'en est pas moins intéressant d'étudier les structurations successives marquant les progrès d'équilibration et de chercher à formuler les approximations successives (et non pas seulement les formes finales) de l'équilibre. Par contre⟦,⟧ il est assez secondaire de vouloir doser la part exacte des apports internes ou extérieurs, car les lois d'équilibre ou de structuration d'ensemble sont générales et s'appliquent aussi bien aux échanges entre individus qu'à la pensée intérieure.

Il est très difficile de détailler par lettre ce point de vue, mais comme la Société de Signifique m'a demandé de traiter un sujet analogue pour la Conférence d'Amersfoort de cet été, je viens de rédiger un papier en pensant surtout à votre lettre et à vous-même, de manière à répondre à vos questions plus complètement que par correspondance. Si vous avez le temps de lire ce manuscrit (26 pages) je demanderai à Kruseman de vous l'envoyer avant son impression. Sinon il sera sans doute imprimé d'ici quelques mois.[45] Dites-moi ce qui vous convient.

(III) Suggestion pour notre collaboration. Je pense que ces échanges de vue préalables auront été fort utiles et qu'il est très fructueux pour traiter notre sujet de partir de positions aussi différentes que les nôtres. Cela nous forcera à nous en tenir le plus objectivement possible aux faits et à ~~écarter toutes~~ nous méfier des interprétations : j'entends par faits le tableau des stades d'évolutions et des structures qui les caractérisent et par interprétations une théorie du développement plutôt qu'une autre.

Outre les parties historiques et terminologiques, que l'on pourra ~~faire après~~ rédiger ensuite (notre terminologie étant à préciser au fur et à mesure des besoins), le problème essentiel serait de déterminer pour chaque grand stade ce qui, dans les structures données et dans leurs formes d'équilibre, correspond partiellement aux structures logiques et ce qui en diffère. Et comme nous sommes d'avance d'accord sur l'existence des différences et sur l'hypothèse que celles-ci l'emportent de beaucoup sur les convergences, c'est l'analyse de ~~celles-ci~~ ces oppositions qui pourrait nous servir de fil conducteur.

On pourrait par exemple suivre un ordre d'analyse régressive et analyser successivement (1) la pensée hypothético-déductive de l'adolescent⟦,⟧ (2) les opérations concrètes de 7 à 12 ans⟦,⟧ (3) la pensée préopératoire de 2 à 7 ans⟦,⟧ (4) le schématisme sensori-moteur.

Je vous donnerai sur chaque période du tableau des principes types de raisonnements, d'opérations ou des solutions de problèmes verbaux et pratiques dont sont capables les sujets, en cherchant à caractériser ces conduites par une structure d'ensemble. Vous seriez juge d'autre part, d'un écart existant entre ces structures et la logique choisie par vous comme système de référence. Nous dresserions ainsi un tableau objectif des structurations successives en référence avec les structures logiques. Ce résultat atteint serait en lui-même extrêmement instructif et nous déciderions alors s'il y a lieu d'aller plus loin ou de s'en tenir là. Aller plus loin pourrait signifier soit une étude commune sur les raisons de l'écart entre la pensée et la logique,[g] soit deux conclusions séparées indiquant nos points de vue respectifs.

Il va de soi que ce sont là de simples suggestions. Si vous en voyez de meilleures j'en serais enchanté. De toutes manières⟦,⟧ je me promets beaucoup d'une collaboration fondée sur notre commun désir d'y voir clair sur une question aussi troublante et fondamentale que les relations entre la pensée et la logique et je pense que nos résultats pourraient être utiles à beaucoup d'esprits préoccupés par le même problème.

---

[45] Piaget, Jean (1954), Les activités mentales en rapport avec les expressions symboliques, logiques et mathématiques. Conférence donnée devant la Société internationale de signifique à la 7e Conférence d'été internationale de linguistique psychologique, Amersfoort/Pays-Bas, 13–18 août 1951.

[g] Écart constant ou écart diminuant d'une période à l'autre ? de ? l'évolution.

Encore un mot avant de terminer cette trop longue lettre. Vous vous rappelez que j'avais préparé une réponse à votre article de *Méthodos* et que je vous l'avais soumise (je l'avais aussi envoyée à M. Feys qui m'avait fait des objections analogues lors des derniers entretiens de Zurich). Or, en rentrant de Paris, j'ai trouvé un mot de M. Bocheński déclarant ma réponse trop longue et me demandant de l'abréger. Comme mon but était plus constructif que polémique, j'ai alors simplement rédigé le petit papier ci-inclus.[46] J'ai en outre dit à Bocheński que je vous le soumets à nouveau et que comme la note en garde du texte est d'ordre personnel et vous engage autant que moi (ou plutôt se réfère à notre correspondance), je la supprimerai naturellement si vous le désirez. Je vous prie donc de me dire si vous le désirez. Je vous prie donc de me dire si vous m'autorisez à la maintenir ou si vous désirez sa suppression[47] ⟦.⟧

Veuillez croire, cher Monsieur Beth, à mes sentiments très cordiaux.

J. Piaget

7'. Piaget's Published Answer to Beth[48]

21. VIII. 51[49]

B 510910d (1° bosse)[50]

À PROPOS D'UN TRAITÉ DE LOGIQUE

Réponse à M. E. W. Beth
JEAN PIAGET
Ch. Sur Rang, 7

Pinchat, Veyrier (Genève, Suisse)

[Reçu le 29 juillet 1951]

En publiant ci-dessous, par désir d'objectivité, une réponse de M/ Beth /.
*(*Methodos, *II, 1950, 6–7, pp. 258–264), nous tenons à rappeler/que l'ouvrage du* /

[46] See next text (7′).

[47] The note was published without further modifications (see *Text* 8 for Beth's positive appreciation, especially of note (2), under the title "À propos d'un traité de logique: réponse à M. E. W. Beth" (Piaget 1951).

[48] Printed proof with handwritten corrections ; 2 pages (see note 32).

[49] Handwritten supplement.

[50] Handwritten supplement.

distingué psychologue genevois porte le titre de Traité de Logique. *C'est en tant que*
é *tel qu'il a provoqué les r/serves du logicien qu'est M. Beth. Nous sommes heureux de constater que l'intention de M. Piaget n'était pas de faire de la logique ; il est donc bien vrai que cette discussion n'aura pas été vaine.*

tude ~~MW C~~ critique que M. Beth a bien voulu consacrer à mon Traité de Logique méritait une réponse détaillée. Je l'ai écrite, mais, comme elle se trouve trop longue pour paraître dans la Section de logique formelle de *Methodos,* je la publierai (ou en publierai la substance) ailleurs, me bornant pour l'instant aux quelques remarques suivantes.

—o
1. Du point de vue de la logique axiomatique auquel se place M. Beth, je c~~a~~mprends parfaitement sa réaction et ses objections, et je les considère comme d'autant plus importantes qu'elles émanent d'un auteur dont les travaux logistiques forcent respect.
2. Je ne crois pas, par contre, que M. Beth ait exactement saisi le but ni les limites de ma recherche, tels qu'ils ressortent des pages v–vi de l'ouvrage (*Avant-Propos*) : fournir un modèle logistique des structures propres aux opérations réelles de la pensée, considérées selon leur processus de formalisation spontanée. D'un tel point de vue, qui n'est pas celui de la logique axiomatique, mais de l'étude des isomorphismes possibles entre les structures formelles et les structures réelles, plusieurs des soi-disant erreurs ou « déviations » signalées par M. Beth s'expliquent aisément.
3. Mais la chose essentielle, pour qui s'intéresse aux rapports des structures logiques et des données de la psychologie de la pensée, n'est pas de peser les —([1]) défauts ou les mérites de cette tentative particulière~~(1)~~ : elle est de trouver une méthode ou un instrument technique de collaboration possible entre le logisticien et le psychologue pour l'étude et la solution du problème que j'ai cherché à soulever.

—ê
4. La seule réponse digne de deux chercheurs honn§tes et également respectueux du vrai que je puisse faire à M. Beth est donc de lui proposer, sincèrement et sérieusement, une telle collaboration. Si les travaux d'un logisticien de sa valeur, et bien informé des choses de la psychologie, ne suffisent pas à constituer l'instrument de travail nécessaire à un psychologue cherchant à comprendre les rapports entre les structures réelles et formelles : et si inversement les essais d'un tel psychologue éprouvant le besoin d'une formulation logistique paraissant dévoués [sic !] de fondement aux yeux de ce logicien, la coopération de ces deux sortes d'esprit doit pouvoir conduire, soit à dégager une solution suffisamment générale du problème posé, soit à montrer l'impossibilité de le résoudre actuellement. Dans les deux cas, la discussion amorcée dans *Methodos* —([2]) n'aura pas été vaine~~(2)~~.

(1) Notons que notre essai a donné lieu également à des réactions bien différentes de celle de M. Beth : voir par exemple l'article de F. Kröner (« Zur Logik von J. Piaget ») (Kröner 1950) et celui de N. Isaacs dans le *British Journal of Psychology* (Isaacs 1951).

(2) Depuis le moment où ma première réponse lui a été communiquée, M. Beth a bien voulu accepter le principe d'une telle collaboration, qui en est aujourd'hui aux échanges de vue prealables sans qu'il soit bien entendu possible d'en préjuger l'issue. Qu'il me soit permis de l'en remercier bien vivement.

8. Beth to Piaget[51]

le 9 Août[52]

Cher Monsieur Piaget,

Votre lettre arriva au moment le plus propice. En effet, hier soir j'avais arrangé les documents qui se rapportent à nos échanges de vue pour me préparer aux discussions au Herzberg organisées par M. Gattegno et auxquelles, si j'ai bien compris, nous participerons tous deux. Je me contente donc de porter à votre attention le plus pressant en ce moment.

(1) [53]La deuxième version de votre réponse pour *Methodos* me paraît excellente à tout point de vue. La note en bas décrit très bien la situation et je vous suis fort reconnaissant de bien avoir voulu l'ajouter à ce texte qui fait, il me semble, autant d'honneur à vous-même qu'à moi.

(2) Je me suis ⟦mis⟧ d'accord avec M. Gattegno de préparer pour les discussions au Herzberg deux exposés sur les sujets suivants :

   (i) Les rapports entre les programmes de mathématiques de l'enseignement supérieur et de l'enseignement secondaire ;

   (ii) La logique et la psychologie dans la recherche des fondements.[54]

   En rédigeant le texte de ce deuxième exposé⟦,⟧ il me serait bien utile de pouvoir consulter le texte de votre article pour *Synthese*.[55] Je vous serais donc fort reconnaissant de bien vouloir demander M. Kruseman de me faire parvenir ce texte. Le temps étant court, je vous proposerais de vous adresser en même temps à M. Kruseman et à M. Vuysje (Corn. Krusemanstraat

[51]Manuscript in typescript ; 2 pages.

[52][1951].

[53]Read: (1).

[54]These lectures, given at the Third International Seminar on the Teaching of Mathematics held in Herzberg (Switzerland) in August 1951, remain unpublished (inventory number 665, Rijksarchief Haarlem, Aug 1951). Nevertheless, as regards Beth's first lecture, there is a related publication, although with a different title: "Réflexions sur l'organisation et la méthode de l'enseignement mathématique" (Beth 1955)

[55]Cf. letter 6, Footnote 45, p. 79.

29/II, Amsterdam-Z.) et de leur dire que je dois partir le 17 Août pour le Volksbildungsheim Herzberg, Asp, (Aargau) en Suisse. Gattegno m'a dit que le deuxième exposé serait mis en ordre que la deuxième semaine de la conférence.

(iii) Je serai bien content de vous voir au Herzberg. Cette rencontre offre une bonne occasion de discuter les différents problèmes qui no⟦u⟧s occupent. Si malheureusement, vous ne pourriez pas être présent, je vous prie de bien vouloir me renseigner. Dans ce cas, il serait peut-être prudent que je passe sous silence nos échanges de vue⟦s⟧ qui se trouvent encore dans une phase préliminaire. Qu'en pensez-vous ?

(iv) Il y a quelques jours, on m'a offert de la part du Gouvernement des États-Unis une bourse d'études qui me permettrait de faire, pendant plusieurs mois, des recherches dans ce pays. Si je peux faire les arrangements qui me permettront d'accepter cette bourse, cela remettrait évidemment pour une année l'exécution de notre projet de collaboration. Mais même si je ne peux pas accepter, ce projet de collaboration pose des questions pratiques assez difficiles (mais non pas insurmontables) que je serais content de pouvoir discuter avec vous.

Veuillez agréer, cher Monsieur Piaget, l'expression de mes sentiments les plus respectueux.

9. Piaget to Beth[56]

Ausserberg (Valais), le 19 Août 1951

Cher Monsieur Beth,—Merci de votre bonne lettre, arrivée malheureusement trop tard pour que j'y réponde à Amsterdam (trois changements d'adresse et pas d'*express* à la montagne !) Kruseman vous enverra mon manuscrit sitôt dactylographié.

Je viens 48 heures au Herzberg, 24 comme promis à Gattegno et 24 pour vous voir et vous entendre (j'espère que votre seconde conférence coïncidera avec mon passage). Je me réjouis fort de parler avec vous et, en attendant ce plaisir, je vous prie de croire en mes sentiments très amicaux.

J. Piaget

[56]Postcard sent on 21.VIII 51.

10. Piaget to Beth[57]

UNIVERSITÉ DE PARIS
FACULTÉ DES LETTRES[58]

Paris, le 3 mai 1953

Mon cher Ami,

Il y a une éternité que je ne vous ai plus écrit et il faut que je vous explique pourquoi.

L'année dernière j'ai eu de nombreux soucis de santé, pour mon père (qui est mort au printemps 1952) et pour moi-même. J'ai été finalement opéré (calculs et prostate) puis ai fait une phlébite qui m'a handicapé jusque récemment.

D'autre part, j'ai été nommé l'été dernier à la Sorbonne (c'est la première fois qu'on confie un enseignement régulier à un étranger depuis le XIIIe siècle, ce qui fait que je n'ai pu refuser). Mais je garde un cours de 3 heures et mes recherches à Genève, ce qui m'oblige à faire chaque semaine le voyage Genève-Paris et retour. En outre, je viens de faire un voyage de conférences aux U.S.A. où je dois retourner en juin.

Tout ceci vous explique ~~que~~ mon silence, ce qui ne signifie en rien que j'aie abandonné notre projet ni oublié nos bonnes conversations du Herzberg.

Entre temps, j'ai publié un petit livre sur les groupes de transformations ~~dans~~ portant sur les 256 opérations ternaires ?… ? : « *Essai sur les transformations logiques* ». L'avez-vous reçu des Presses Universitaires[59] ? Sinon je vous l'enverrai et serai très intéressé de savoir ce que vous en pensez.

De même⟦,⟧ j'ai écrit un petit article dans *Methodos* sur l'application de la log ⟦ique⟧ (en tant qu'algèbre) à la psychologie. Recevez-vous encore *Methodos*[60] ? Sinon je vous l'enverrai aussi.

Enfin l'Université de Manchester va publier en anglais les conférences que j'ai faites en octobre à cette Université sur les relations de l'algèbre logistique et de la psychologie. Je vous les enverrai sitôt parues.[61]

En attendant, mes hommages à Madame Beth s.v.p. et à vous, cher Ami, mon très cordial souvenir.

J. Piaget

---

[57]Manuscript ; 2 pages.

[58]In the margin, Piaget writes. "Université de Paris, Faculté des Lettres": "Mon adresse est toujours Pinchat, Genève (Suisse)"

[59]Cf. Footnote b, p. 58.

[60]Piaget (1952a).

[61] Piaget (1953).

11. Piaget to Beth[62]

UNIVERSITÉ DE GENÈVE
SCHOLA GENEVENSIS MDLIX

FACULTÉ DES SCIENCES

Genève, le 26 janvier 1954

Mon cher Ami,

J'ai été très touché de recevoir vos tirés à part et vous en remercie très vivement. D'autre part, notre ami commun Gattegno, que j'ai vu à Londres l'autre jour, m'a transmis vos amitiés et je vous en remercie beaucoup.

Je vous ai donné de mes nouvelles il y a je crois deux ou trois mois, dans une lettre entrant en quelques détails. L'avez-vous reçue[63] ? Je suis le premier à comprendre que l'on ne répond pas aux lettres quand on a à ce moment précis un travail en train qui vous occupe entièrement. Mais, si vous ne l'avez pas reçue, je vous redonnerai ces nouvelles dans une lettre ultérieure.

Depuis lors, ont paru aux Manchester University Press mes conférences de l'année dernière à l'Université de Manchester, sous le titre « Logic and Psychology ». J'espère que vous les avez reçues, sinon je m'en occuperai.

Monsieur le Professeur E. W. Beth[64]
Bernard Zweerskade
Amsterdam Z.

J'ai le projet, si la chose est possible, de constituer à Genève un petit centre d'épistémologie génétique. Si je trouve le financement nécessaire, j'aimerais organiser quelques recherches et éventuellement un symposium sur les relations entre la logique et la psychologie. Au cas où ce projet aboutirait, je ne manquerai pas de recourir à vous pour la collaboration que vous jugerez opportune.

Mais en attendant, mes cours de Sorbonne me prennent beaucoup de temps et je dois faire encore un séjour à Princeton U.S.A. où l'Institute for Advanced Studies m'a invité à passer quelque temps.

---

[62] Manuscript in typescript ; 2 pages.

[63] This letter is missing.

[64] This address ends the first page of the letter. The second page of the letter begins with the following heading: "le 26 janvier 1954, Monsieur le Professeur E. W. Beth".

En vous priant de transmettre mes meilleurs souvenirs à Madame Beth, je vous prie, mon cher Ami, de croire en mes sentiments très fidèlement dévoués.

Jean Piaget

12. Beth to Piaget[65]

le 28 janvier 1954

Mon cher Ami,

J'ai vraiment fort apprécié vos deux lettres et je vous demande pardon d'avoir tellement tardé à vous répondre. Pour tout dire, j'ai commencé deux ou trois fois, mais j'ai voulu entrer un peu dans le détail de mes activités et pour un rapport détaillé il faut un certain repos et un minimum de temps.

Vous savez que quelques mois après notre rencontre au Herzberg nous avons fait un voyage aux États-Unis, où j'ai travaillé à Berkeley avec Tarski pendant environ six mois ; en rentrant, nous avons en cinq semaines traversé les États-Unis en voiture et en zigzag. Le séjour fut pour nous deux une expérience intéressante et fructueuse, qui était toutefois assombrie par le décès de mon père, survenu en février 1952.

Après notre retour, nous avons été même plus occupés comme [sic !] d'habitude, surtout en raison des recherches excitées par les renseignements que j'avais pu obtenir en Amérique, mais également en vertu de mon rôle, d'ailleurs modeste, dans les préparations du Congrès international de Mathématiques. Vous comprendrez que, par la nature de mon domaine particulier, je suis en relation avec plusieurs organisations scientifiques, ce qui implique une correspondance assez abondante. Je m'occupe à présent de problème de me débarrasser un peu pour trouver le temps nécessaire pour mes activités centrales.

Celles-ci embrassent mes cours de logique et de philosophie des sciences, mes recherches sur certains problèmes métamathématiques, dont j'ai publié les premiers résultats dans les *Proceedings,* mes *Foundations of Mathematics,* dont la moitié environ est rédigé, et la rédaction des *Studies in Logic.*[66]

À l'Université, j'ai avec Heyting un *Institut pour la Recherche des Fondements*, qui assure à nos activités communes ou parallèles un certain degré d'autonomie. J'en suis directeur, puisque Heyting est directeur de l'*Institut Mathématiques* de l'Université, où se trouvent les localités et les possessions de notre Institut à nous.

Je n'ai pas encore vu les différentes publications dont vous parlez. De *Methodos,* je n'ai reçu que les volumes qui contiennent la rubrique de logique mathématique,

---

[65] Manuscript in typescript ; 2 pages.

[66] In fact, Beth was, together with L. E. J. Brouwer and A. Heyting, editor of the series "Studies in Logic and the Foundations of Mathematics", founded on his initiative.

et la série à notre Institut commence par le vol. 5. Mais il va sans dire que j'aurai soin de combler dans le temps ces lacunes qui sont presque inévitables dans une bibliothèque d'origine fort récente.

Votre projet de constituer un centre d'épistémologie génétique et d'organiser un symposium sur les relations entre la logique et la psychologie m'intéresse beaucoup. Comme vous savez, mes étudiants qui se spécialisent en philosophie des sciences viennent de directions divergentes, et j'espère que parmi eux je trouverai quelqu'un qui ait les connaissances psychologiques qu'il faut pour approfondir notre problème et qui puisse venir à Genève pour travailler avec vous.

Comme vous savez peut-être, je viendrai à Paris—probablement en avril ou mai—pour donner suite à une invitation de la Faculté des Sciences à discuter les possibilités d'une collaboration qui sans doute serait bien fructueuse.[67]

Je suis fort content que notre ami Gattegno vous a transmis nos amitiés. Je lui avais promis le texte de mes conférences au Herzberg, mais malheureusement d'autres devoirs urgents sont intervenus et je n'ai pas encore ⟦pu⟧ pouvoir terminer mon manuscrit. Ce sera en tout cas une des premières tâches dont je m'acquitterai.

Voilà donc le rapport que je vous devais. Ma femme me joint [sic !] à vous souhaiter un très fructueux séjour à Princeton et à vous demander de bien vouloir transmettre nos salutations bien cordiales à nos amis là-bas : Church, Gödel, Carnap et Lyndon.

Veuillez croire, mon cher Ami, à nos amitiés bien sincères.

13. Piaget to Beth[68]

UNIVERSITÉ DE GENÈVE
SCHOLA GENEVENSIS MDLIX

FACULTÉ DES SCIENCES

Genève, le 28 mai 1955

Mon cher Ami,

Je crois que c'est à moi de vous écrire et ai bien peur de n'avoir pas répondu encore à la si aimable lettre où vous me donniez amicalement de vos nouvelles en détail.

J'ai en effet été très pris cette année (trois mois à Princeton et mes voyages hebdomadaires Paris-Genève).

---

[67]Cf. Beth (1956).

[68]Manuscript in typescript ; 2 pages.

Je viens de recevoir de la Fondation Rockefeller des fonds pour la création d'un Centre International d'Épistémologie Génétique, avec pour programme pendant les deux premières années l'étude des relations éventuelles entre les structures logiques et les activités du sujet (langage, etc. . .). C'est donc exactement le problème au sujet duquel nous avons commencé à correspondre et sur lequel j'aurais grand besoin de vos lumières et de vos conseils.

Le travail du Centre s'organisera de la manière suivante :

- premièrement, pendant l'année, des recherches de quelques membres résidents. À cet égard, j'espère avoir à demeure pendant les premières années Messieurs W. Mays de Manchester (logique cybernétique), Apostel de Bruxelles (logique) et Mandelbrot de Paris (un spécialiste de la théorie de l'information) ; nous trouverons les psychologues à Genève même. Je crois que Léo Apostel a été votre élève pendant quelques mois et je serais heureux que vous me disiez si vous le considérez comme connaissant suffisamment votre pensée et vos méthodes.
- deuxièmement : à la fin de l'année fin juin ou début juillet, je pense réunir (aux frais du Centre) un symposium d'une dizaine de personnalités au plus, pour discuter le problème choisi ainsi que les résultats obtenus pendant l'année. J'espère très vivement que vous pourrez assister à ce symposium et je me permets dès maintenant de vous y inviter très amicalement.

Vous savez combien votre position si nette et si opposée à tout psychologisme est indispensable à considérer dans un problème tel que le nôtre. J'attache donc un prix exceptionnel à votre collaboration et vous en avez toutes les raisons.

D'autre part, je serai fort heureux, lorsque nous aurons acquis quelques expériences, de pouvoir vous demander pour la seconde année de notre activité, de nous désigner un de vos élèves pour passer un an à Genève.

Enfin, si ce n'est pas abuser de vous, je me permettrai de vous envoyer de temps en temps, de nos papiers ou projets de travaux, pour que vous nous donniez si vous le désirez, votre réaction avec votre netteté habituelle, dont vous savez combien j'apprécie la franchise.

En vous priant de transmettre mon bon souvenir à Madame Beth, je vous prie de croire Cher Ami, à mes sentiments très cordialement et très fidèlement dévoués,

J. Piaget

P. S.[69] Peut-être auriez-vous déjà quelqu'un de libre pour l'année 1955–56. Mais je n'ai plus de finances que pour un jeune assistant (quelques milliers de frs. Suisses) et encore cela n'est pas complètement certain.

[69]This post script is not in typescript.

14. Beth to Piaget[70]

le 3 juin 1955

Monsieur le Professeur Jean Piaget
Faculté des Sciences
Université de
G E N È V E
SUISSE

Mon cher Ami,

Je vous remercie de votre lettre du 28 mai et je tiens tout particulièrement à vous féliciter sans retard d'avoir pu établir votre Centre International d'Épistémologie Génétique qui sans doute vous permettra de diriger des recherches fort importantes.

Il va sans dire que je suis à votre disposition pour vous donner les renseignements ou les conseils dont vous auriez besoin.

Quant à Monsieur Apostel, voici ce que je peux vous dire. Il y a quelques années, il est venu passer quelques semaines (peut-être deux mois) à Amsterdam pour me demander conseil sur une thèse concernant une méthode topologique pour traiter la causalité ; mais je ne me rappelle plus les détails de ce travail que je n'ai jamais vu sous forme imprimée. Depuis je l'ai rencontré plusieurs fois dans des congrès et j'ai vu de sa main deux ou trois articles. À mon avis, M. Apostel n'est pas (encore) un spécialiste en logique⟦,⟧ mais plutôt un mathématicien bien instruit et fort intelligent, avec un grand intérêt pour les questions philosophiques et pour le problème de fondement. Une année chez vous qui lui permet de faire des recherches et d'approfondir ses connaissances portera sans doute des fruits.

J'accepte avec grand plaisir votre invitation d'assister à votre symposium ; la date : fin juin ou début de juillet s'accorde très bien avec notre programme habituel.[71]

Pour ce qui regarde mes élèves, il serait peut-être utile que je vous donne des détails concernant nos programmes d'études. En principe, les études durent six ans, trois ans pour la candidature et trois ans pour l'examen doctoral, qui confère le droit d'enseigner mais non pas le grade de docteur. Ensuite, on cherche une position, parfois comme assistant à l'Université. Les bons étudiants continuent alors leurs études pour présenter, après quelques années, une thèse de doctorat. Tout candidat en sciences (Mathématiques, physique,... n'importe) a le droit de préparer un

[70]Manuscript in typescript ; 2 pages.

[71]Cf. Footnote 5.

examen doctoral avec, comme matière principale, la philosophie et, comme matière secondaire, un ou deux autres domaines (par exemple, mathématiques et physique) qu'il pourra ensuite enseigner. Ce sont les candidats qui font un tel choix qui deviennent mes élèves. Il va de soi qu'ils ont fort besoin de ces trois années (qui deviennent souvent quatre ou cinq), parce qu'ils débutent presque sans formation philosophique (pour la même raison, ceux que ne choisissent la philosophie qu'au titre de la matière secondaire ne vous seraient pas utiles). En moyenne, il n'y a qu'un étudiant par an qui fasse ce choix, ce qui est d'ailleurs naturel.

Pour faire un[e] stage chez vous, il faudrait qu'un étudiant choisisse l'année qui précède ou qui suit son examen doctoral.

Ceci posé, il y aurait en premier lieu deux personnes qui pourraient être prises en considération pour l'année académique 1956–57.

(1) M. F.W.J. Marx, qui a été mon assistant en 1952–53. Il a fait la candidature en psychologie, et prépare un examen doctoral en philosophie avec psychologie et mathématiques. Cette préparation s'est prolongée en raison de lacunes de formation en mathématiques.
(2) S.J. Doorman, qui a été mon assistant en 1953–54 et en 1954–55. Candidature en mathématiques et physique, prépare un examen doctoral en philosophie avec mathématiques.

La matière pour l'examen doctoral en philosophie se compose de : (i) philosophie générale (MM. Pos et Oldewelt) ; (ii) méthodologie d'un ou deux domaines spéciaux (p. ex.⟦,⟧ M. Heyting pour les mathématiques intuitionnistes, M. van Dantzig pour la statistique, etc.) ; (iii) logique mathématique.

Il va de soi que seuls les bons étudiants choisissent la philosophie. Doorman est probablement le plus doué des deux, mais la formation psychologique de Marx (Révesz et Dyker) vous serait peut-être également utile. Pour l'avenir, il y a encore M. Nienhuis, qui sera mon assistant en 1955–56, M. Bolkestein, qui va débuter en Octobre, et M. Staal qui est de la même année que Doorman⟦,⟧ mais qui a interrompu ses études pour accepter une bourse d'études pour Madras et qui reste encore là-bas pendant l'année prochaine.

Je vous remets ci-inclus le résumé d'un travail qui sera publié dans un proche avenir et qui sera de nature à vous intéresser. J'ai trouvé une nouvelle méthode pour établir la logique élémentaire qui s'approche d'avantage à [sic !] notre manière habituelle de raisonner que les formalisations courantes. Elle se rattache directement à l'interprétation des formules⟦,⟧ tandis que dans les systèmes usuels celle-ci n'intervient qu'après coup.

Agréez, Cher Ami, avec les salutations bien cordiales que ma femme demande de vous transmettre, l'expression de mes sentiments dévoués et fidèles.

15. Piaget to Beth[72]

UNIVERSITÉ DE GENÈVE
SCHOLA GENEVENSIS MDLIX

FACULTÉ DES SCIENCES

Genève, le 15 juin 1955

M. Le Professeur E.W. Beth Bernard Zweerskade, 23 1, AMSTERDAM.

Mon cher Ami,

Je vous remercie très vivement de votre aimable réponse, qui m'a été fort utile, et de votre acceptation d'assister à notre premier Symposium du Centre d'Épistémologie Génétique. Je pense que la date en sera la première semaine de juillet 1956.

Si cela vous intéresse, je serai enchanté de vous adresser⟦,⟧ dès qu'ils seront au point⟦,⟧ les plans de travaux de notre Centre, notamment les plans d'activité de M. Apostel et de M. Mandelbrot. Vous savez combien votre avis nous serait utile.

En vous priant de transmettre mes hommages à Madame Beth, je vous prie de croire, mon cher Ami, à mes sentiments très dévoués,

Jean Piaget

References

E. Barth, In the service of human society: formal, informal or anti-logical – the philosophy of the logician Evert Willem Beth (1908–1964). Informal Log. **12**(1), 1–10 (1990)
E. Barth, Beth's philosophical intentions: An introduction. Philos. Sci. **3**(4), 3–30 (1998–1999)
P. Bernays, Logique et science, in *Congrès international de philosophie des sciences*, Paris, 1949, vol. II; Logique (Hermann, Paris, 1951), pp. 1–5
E.W. Beth, *Rede en Aanschouwing in de Wiskunde*. PhD thesis, Rijksuniversiteit Utrecht, Groningen, 1935. P. Noordhoff N.V.
E.W. Beth, De significa van de pasigraphische systemen. Euclides **13**, 145–158 (1936–1937)
E.W. Beth, Getalbegrip en tijdsaanschouwing. Euclides **15**, 190–210 (1938–1939)

[72]Manuscript in typescript; 1 page.

E.W. Beth, Te psychologische argumenten en rischtlijnen voor de vernieuwing van het onderwijs in de wiskunde. Euclides **16**, 1–23 (1939–1940)
E.W. Beth, The evolution of ideas. Hundred years of symbolic logic. A retrospect on the occasion of the Boole-De Morgan century. Dialectica **1**(4), 331–346 (1947)
E.W. Beth, Les relations de la dialectique à la logique. Dialectica **2**(2), 109–119 (1948)
E.W. Beth, *Les Fondements logiques des mathématiques* (Gauthiers-Villars/E. Nauwelaerts, Paris/Louvain, 1950a)
E.W. Beth, À propos d'un "Traité de Logique". Methodos **2**(6/7), 258–264 (1950b)
E.W. Beth, Réflexions sur l'organisation et la méthode de l'enseignement mathématique, in *L'Enseignement des mathématiques*, ed. by J. Piaget, E.W. Beth, J. Dieudonné, A. Lichnerowicz, G. Choquet, C. Gattegno (Delachaux et Niestlé, Neuchâtel, 1955), pp. 35–46
E.W. Beth, *L'Existence en mathématiques. Conférences faites à la Sorbonne au titre des échanges culturels franco-néerlandais du 29 mars au 7 avril 1954* (Gauthiers-Villars/E. Nauwelaerts, Paris/Louvain, 1956)
E.W. Beth, La logique formelle et la pensée naturelle, in *Épistémologie génétique et recherche psychologique par W. E. Beth, W. Mays et J. Piaget*. Etudes d'épistémologie génétique (Presses Universitaires de France, Paris, 1957), pp. 131–134
E.W. Beth, F. Gonseth, À propos des exposés de MM. Ph. Devaux et E. W. Beth. Dialectica **2**(2), 120–125 (1948)
E.W. Beth, J. Piaget, *Épistémologie mathématique et psychologie. Essai sur les relations entre la logique formelle et la pensée réelle* (Presses Universitaires de France, Paris, 1961)
J.M. Bocheński, *Précis de logique mathématique*. Volume 2 of Collection Synthèse (F.G. Kroonder, Bussum, 1949)
A. Burdman, S. Feferman, Logic and methodology, center stage. Philos. Sci. **14**(1), 159–168 (2010)
F. Gonseth, L'épistémologie génétique et la méthodologie dialectique: à propos de l'ouvrage récent de J. Piaget: "Introduction à l'épistémologie génétique". Dialectica **4**(1), 5–20 (1950a)
F. Gonseth, Réponse à M. Piaget. Dialectica **4**(16), 296–304 (1950b)
N. Isaacs, Critical notice. Br. J. Psychol. **42**, 185–188 (1951)
F. Kröner, Zur logik von J Piaget. Dialectica **4**, 49–64 (1950)
J. Piaget, *La Naissane de l'intelligence chez l'enfant* (Delachaux et Niestlé, Paris, 1936)
J. Piaget, Classes, relations et nombres. Archives de psychologie **30** 198–201 (1944–1945)
J. Piaget, *La Psychologie de l'intelligence* (Armand Colin, Paris, 1947)
J. Piaget, Discussion. Dialectica **2**(2), 126–142, 139, (1948)
J. Piaget, *Traité de logique: essai de logistique opératoire* (Armand Colin, Paris, 1949)
J. Piaget, Épistémologie génétique et méthodologie dialectique. Dialectica **4**(4), 287–295 (1950)
J. Piaget, À propos d'un traité de logique: réponse à M. E. W. Beth. Methodos **3**(11), 243–244 (1951)
J. Piaget, La logistique axiomatique ou "pure", la logistique opératoire ou psychologique et les réalités auxquelles elles correspondent. Methodos **4**(13), 72–84 (1952a)
J. Piaget, *Essai sur les transformations des opérations logiques. Les 256 opérations ternaires de la logique bivalente des propositions* (Presses Universitaires de France, Paris, 1952b)
J. Piaget, *Logic and Psychology*, vol. XIX, 1st edn. (Manchester University Press, Manchester, 1953). With an introd. on Piaget's logic by W. Mays (Transl. by W. Mays, A. N. Whitehead)
J. Piaget, Les activités mentales en rapport avec les expressions symboliques, logiques et mathématiques. Synthese **9**(2), 73–90 (1954)
J. Piaget, *Psychologie et pédagogie* (Denoël, Gonthier, Paris, 1969)
J. Piaget, F. Gonseth, Groupements, groupes et latices. Archives de psychologie **31**(121), 65–73 (1946)
J. Piaget, B. Inhelder, *De la logique de l'enfant à la logique de l'adolescent: essai sur la construction des structures opératoires formelles* (Presses Universitaires de France, Paris, 1955) 2nd edition, 1970
J. Piaget, B. Inhelder, *La Psychologie de l'enfant* (Presses Universitaires de France, Paris, 1966) (English translation: *The Psychology of the Child* (Basic Books, New York, 1969))

J. Piaget, E.W. Beth, W. Mays, *Épistémologie génétique et recherche psychologique* (Presses Universitaires de France, Paris, 1957)

J. Piaget, N. Chomsky, M. Piattelli-Palmarini, La psychogenèse des connaissances et sa signification épistémique, in *Théories du langage, théories de l'apprentissage: le débat entre Jean Piaget et Noam Chomsky* (Éditions du Seuil, Paris, 1979) (English translation: *Language and Learning: The Debate between Jean Piaget and Noam Chomsky*, J. Piaget, N. Chomsky, M. Piattelli-Palmarini (Harvard University Press, Cambridge, 1980))

W. Van Orman Quine, On what there is, in *From a Logical Point of View* (Harvard University Press, Cambridge/London, 1953), pp. 1–19

W. Van Orman Quine, Epistemology naturalized, in *Ontological Relativity and Other Essays* (Columbia University Press, New York, 1969), pp. 69–90

Part II
Epistemology, Context, Formalism

Chapter 5
Principles of Knowledge, Belief and Conditional Belief

Guillaume Aucher

5.1 Introduction

Elucidating the nature of the relationship between knowledge and belief is an old issue in epistemology dating back at least to Plato. Two approaches to addressing this problem stand out from the rest. The first consists in providing a *definition* of knowledge, in terms of belief, that would somehow pin down the essential ingredient binding knowledge to belief. The second consists in providing a complete characterization of this relationship in terms of logical *principles* relating these two notions. The accomplishment of either of these two objectives would certainly contribute to solving this problem.

The success of the first approach is hindered by the so-called 'Gettier problem'. Until recently, the view that knowledge could be defined in terms of belief as 'justified true belief' was endorsed by most philosophers. This notion of justification, or "right to be sure" as Ayer called it (1956), was therefore the key element relating knowledge to belief, even though Ayer admitted that determining the general conditions needed to "have the right to be sure" would be too complicated, if at all possible. Gettier's seminal three page paper presents two counterexamples which shatters this classical analysis (Gettier 1963).[1] Following this publication, a

[1]One of these two examples is the following. Suppose that Smith has strong evidence that 'Jones owns a Ford' (1) (for instance, Jones has owned a Ford ever since Smith has known him). Then, because of (1) and by propositional logic, Smith is also justified in believing that 'Jones owns a Ford *or* his friend Brown is in Barcelona' (2), even if Smith has no clue where Brown is at the moment. However it turns out that Jones does not own a Ford and that by pure coincidence Brown is actually in Barcelona. Then, (a) (2) is true, (b) Smith believes (2), and (c) Smith is justified in

G. Aucher (✉)
University of Rennes 1, INRIA Campus de Beaulieu,
263, Avenue du Général Leclerc, Bât 12, 35042 Rennes, France
e-mail: guillaume.aucher@irisa.fr

M. Rebuschi et al. (eds.), *Interdisciplinary Works in Logic, Epistemology, Psychology and Linguistics*, Logic, Argumentation & Reasoning 3,
DOI 10.1007/978-3-319-03044-9_5, © Springer International Publishing Switzerland 2014

large number of other definitions of knowledge were proposed, analyzed and refined in order to determine the additional clause needed to define knowledge in terms of belief. However, no consensus came out of this undertaking and the exact nature of the relationship between knowledge and belief remains to this day elusive (Lycan 2006).

The second approach is related to the method employed by epistemic logicians such as Hintikka or Lenzen to better understand and "explicate" the notions of knowledge and belief. In his seminal book (1962), Hintikka examines the validity of various principles with the help of a logical model based on the Kripke semantics of modal logic. This publication sparked numerous discussions about the inherent properties of these epistemic notions, and a large spectrum of informational attitudes were explored (Lenzen (1978) provides a good overview of that period). Many axioms, viewed as reasoning principles, were proposed and discussed, especially interaction axioms relating the notions of knowledge and belief. This quest for reasoning principles somehow vanished in the 1980s when epistemic logic was taken over by computer scientists to address other problems related to various applications. In the early 1990s, however, new interaction axioms relating knowledge and *conditional* belief were elicited by some researchers in artificial intelligence (Moses and Shoham 1993; Lamarre and Shoham 1994).

To better grasp the relationship binding knowledge to belief, we review and examine in this paper the validity of the different axioms (and inference rules) relating knowledge to belief which have been proposed in the epistemic logic literature. In doing so, we are bound to encounter many of the problems that epistemic logic has had to face in its relatively short (modern) history. This paper is therefore more an exposition than a research paper. However, we will also contribute to this area by providing conditions under which the notion of belief can be formally defined in terms of knowledge, and vice versa. We will also prove that certain convoluted axioms dealing only with the notion of knowledge can be derived from understandable interaction axioms relating knowledge and *conditional* belief.

This paper is organized as follows. In Sect. 5.2, we will briefly describe the role that epistemic logic has played in the development of computer science (and to a lesser extent in philosophy). We will also set the modeling assumptions that will be used in the rest of the paper. Then, in Sect. 5.3, we will delve into our subject matter and review the most common epistemic principles (i.e. principles pertaining to the notion of knowledge) and doxastic principles (i.e., principles pertaining to the notion of belief) occurring in the epistemic logic literature. In Sect. 5.4, we will review the interaction principles relating knowledge to belief on the one hand, and relating knowledge to conditional belief on the other hand. In Sect. 5.5, we provide the logical apparatus needed to formalize our approach. In Sect. 5.6, we will investigate formally under which conditions knowledge can be defined in terms

believing (2). So Smith has a true and justified belief in (2). Intuitively, however, one could not say that Smith knows (2).

of belief, and vice versa. Finally, in Sect. 5.7, we will show that certain convoluted axioms for knowledge can be derived from simpler axioms of interaction between knowledge, belief and conditional belief.

5.2 Prolegomena

5.2.1 Epistemic Logic in Philosophy and Computer Science

Following the publication of Hintikka (1962), philosophers and logicians tried to formulate explicit principles governing expressions of the form "a knows that φ" (subsequently formalized as $K\varphi$) or "a believes that φ" (subsequently formalized as $B\varphi$), where a is a human agent and φ is a proposition. In other words, philosophers sought to determine 'the' logic of knowledge and belief. This quest was grounded in the observation that our intuitions of these epistemic notions comply to some systematic reasoning properties, and was driven by the attempt to better *understand* and *elucidate* them. Lenzen indeed claims, following Hintikka, that the task of epistemic logic consists "(1) in *explicating* the epistemic notions, and (2) in examining the validity of the diverse principles of epistemic logic *given such an explication*" (Lenzen 1978, p. 15). As we will see in the rest of this paper, assessing whether a given principle holds true or not does raise our own awareness of these epistemic notions and reveals to us some of their essential properties.

For many computer scientists, reaching such an understanding (via this kind of conceptual analysis) is not as central as for philosophers, partly because the agents considered in the "applications" of computer science are typically assumed to be non-human. Voorbraak even claims that his notion of objective knowledge "applies to *any* agent which is capable of processing information [and] may very well be a device like a thermostat or a television-receiver" (Voorbraak 1993, p. 55). In computer science, epistemic logic is often viewed as a *formal tool* used to represent uncertainty in different kinds of settings.[2] From this perspective, a specific set of axioms and inference rules for knowledge and belief will apply to a specific applied context. Originally, this interest taken in epistemic logic by computer scientists stemmed from their observation that the notion of knowledge plays a central role in the informal reasoning used especially in the design of distributed protocols. So, in a sense, the logical analysis of epistemic notions carried out by logicians and philosophers provided computer scientists with formal models. These models were 'used' and developed further to address particular issues such as the problem of reaching an agreement in order to coordinate actions in distributed

---

[2]Fagin et al. (1995) and Meyer and van der Hoek (1995) are the standard textbooks in computer science dealing with epistemic logic. Also see the survey Gochet and Gribomont (2006) for a more interdisciplinary approach and Halpern (2003) for a broader account of the different formalisms dealing with the representation of uncertainty.

systems (Halpern and Moses 1990) or the problem of diagnosing electric circuits (Friedman and Halpern 1997), or even problems of computer security (Deschene and Wang 2010). As a result of this shift, the computability properties of various epistemic logics were investigated systematically (Halpern and Moses 1992) and other epistemic notions involving multiple agents were introduced in epistemic logic (Fagin et al. 1995), such as the notion of *distributed knowledge* and *common knowledge* (originally studied by the philosopher Lewis (1969)).

One should note that there is also a discrepancy between the analyses of the notion of knowledge in epistemic logic and in (mainstream) epistemology. As Castañeda already commented soon after the publication of Hintikka (1962), "Hintikka's 'K' ('B') does not seem to correspond to any of the senses of 'know' ('believe') that have been employed or discussed by philosophers. But Hintikka's systems are an excellent source from which we may eventually arrive at a formalization of the philosophers' senses of 'know' and 'believe' " (Castañeda 1964, p. 133). As it turns out, some recent publications bear witness to a revival of the ties between epistemic logic and (mainstream) epistemology (Hendricks and Symons 2006; Hendricks 2005).

5.2.2 *Modeling Assumptions*

If we want to *define* knowledge in terms of belief and give a complete and accurate account of this notion, then we should not limit our analyses to knowledge and belief only. Indeed, other related notions will inevitably play a role, such as the notions of justification, (un)awareness, or even epistemic surprise.[3] In that respect, note that other related mental states such as goal, desire and intention are also necessary if we want to develop logics for rational agents (such as a computer program, a software or a machine) that need to act on their environment so as to reach certain goals (possibly in cooperation with other agents).[4] Nevertheless, if we are only interested in elucidating the nature of the relationship binding knowledge to belief, then it is possible to abstract away from these related notions and identify *principles* relating knowledge and belief only.

[3]The notion of justification is dealt with in the field of justification logic (Artemov and Fitting 2011). Logical models of (un)awareness have been proposed in economics (Heifetz et al. 2006) and artificial intelligence (Fagin and Halpern 1987) with a recent proposal in Halpern and Rêgo (2009). Some models for the notion of epistemic surprise can be found in Aucher (2007) and Lorini and Castelfranchi (2007).

[4]There are a number of logical frameworks that deal with rational agency: Cohen and Levesque's theory of intention (1990), Rao and Georgeff's BDI architecture (Georgeff and Rao 1991; Rao and Georgeff 1991), Meyer et al.'s KARO architecture (van Linder et al. 1998; Meyer et al. 2001), Wooldridge's BDI logic LORA (2000) and Broersen et al.'s BOID architecture (2001).

This said, we have to be a bit more explicit and accurate about the kind of principles we are interested in, and also about the modeling assumptions that we follow. Firstly, these principles have to be interpreted as analytically true relations between the notions of knowledge and belief. This means that we do not take into account the pragmatic conditions of their utterance. Therefore, the fact that I cannot reasonably utter the so-called Moore sentence 'proposition p holds but I do not believe that p', or the fact that from the mere utterance of 'I know that p', the listener can only infer that I believe that p, will not be explained. For an account of these pragmatic issues, the interested reader can consult (Lenzen 2004). Consequently, we depart from the approach developed in (Hintikka 1962), because Hintikka studies what he calls epistemic "statements". According to Hintikka, "a statement is the act of *uttering, writing*, or otherwise *expressing* a declarative sentence. A sentence is the form of words which is uttered or written when a statement is made" (Hintikka 1962, p. 6) (my emphasis). On the other hand, our choice of assumptions is supported by Lenzen's claim that "one may elaborate the meaning of epistemic expressions in a way that is largely independent of [...] the pragmatic conditions of utterability" (Lenzen 2004, p. 17). Secondly, throughout this paper and as it is usually implicitly assumed in epistemic logic, we will follow a perfect external approach. This means that the epistemic state of the agent under consideration is modeled from the point of view of an external modeler who has perfect and complete access to and knowledge of this state.[5] Therefore, the principles pertain to an agent other than the modeler who states them. Finally, as is often the case in epistemic logic, we will be interested only in *propositional knowledge*, that is knowledge *that* something holds, in contrast to non-propositional knowledge, that is, knowledge *of* something (such as the knowledge of an acquaintance or a piece of music), and in contrast to knowledge of how to do something.[6]

5.3 Epistemic and Doxastic Principles

In this section, we will briefly review the most common principles of the logics of knowledge and belief that occur in the literature (spelled out in the form of axioms and inference rules). They have all been commented on and discussed extensively in the philosophical literature, and the interested reader can consult (Lenzen 1978) for more details. That said, there is currently no real consensus in favour of any proposed set of epistemic principles, even among computer scientists.

[5]See Aucher (2010) for more details on the perfect external approach and its connection with the other modeling approaches, namely the internal and the imperfect external approaches.

[6]Gochet (2007) reviews the various attempts to formalize the notion of *knowing how* in artificial intelligence and logic.

5.3.1 Epistemic Principles

Any normal modal logic contains the axiom K and the inference rule Nec. Hintikka's epistemic logic is no exception:

$$(K(\psi \to \varphi) \wedge K\psi) \to K\varphi \tag{K}$$

$$\text{If } \varphi \text{ then } K\varphi \tag{Nec}$$

Axiom K and rule Nec have been attacked ever since the beginning of epistemic logic. They state that the agent knows all tautologies (Nec) and knows all the logical consequences of her knowledge (K). This can indeed be considered as a non-realistic assumption as far as human agents are concerned, but it is also a problem in numerous applications of epistemic logic. In the context of computer security, we may want, for example, to reason about computationally bounded adversaries to determine whether or not they can factor a large composite number (Halpern and Pucella 2002). It is not possible, however, to perform such reasoning if we assume that the adversary's knowledge complies to axiom K and inference rule Nec.[7] This problem, named the "logical omniscience problem", turns out to be one of the main problems in epistemic logic, and numerous and various proposals have been made over the years in order to solve it. It undermines not only the notion of knowledge but also the notion of belief (because, as we will see, this notion also complies with the principles K and Nec). In this context, the notion of awareness plays an important role and it is also relevant to distinguish between *implicit* knowledge/belief and *explicit* knowledge/belief. An agent's implicit knowledge includes the logical consequences of her explicit knowledge (Levesque 1984). We refer the interested reader to Fagin et al. (1995, Chap. 9), Gochet and Gribomont (2006, pp. 157–168) or Halpern and Pucella (2011) for more details on the logical omniscience problem.

Hintikka further claims in (Hintikka 1962) that the logic of knowledge is S4, which is obtained by adding to K and Nec the axioms T and 4:

$$K\varphi \to \varphi \tag{T}$$

$$K\varphi \to KK\varphi \tag{4}$$

These axioms state that if the agent knows a proposition, then this proposition is true (axiom T for Truth), and if the agent knows a proposition, then she knows that she knows it (axiom 4, also known as the "KK-principle"or "KK-thesis"). Axiom T is often considered to be the hallmark of knowledge and has not been subjected

[7] See Deschene and Wang (2010) for a survey of approaches to computer security issues which use epistemic logic.

to any serious attack. In epistemology, axiom 4 tends to be accepted by internalists, but not by externalists (Hemp 2006) (also see Lenzen (1978, Chap. 4)). A persuasive argument against this axiom has been propounded by Williamson (2000, Chap. 5) for the case of *inexact knowledge*, that is, knowledge that obeys a *margin for error principle*. The knowledge that one gains by looking at a distant tree in order to know its height is an example of inexact knowledge. A solution to Williamson's luminosity paradox is proposed by Bonnay and Egré (2008) by resorting to a particular semantics for modal logic called "centered semantics", which validates axiom 4 without requiring the accessibility relation to be transitive. Axiom 4 is nevertheless widely accepted by computer scientists (but also by many philosophers, including Plato, Aristotle, Saint Augustine, Spinoza and Shopenhauer, as Hintikka recalls in (Hintikka 1962)).

A more controversial axiom for the logic of knowledge is axiom 5:

$$\neg K\varphi \rightarrow K\neg K\varphi \tag{5}$$

This axiom states that if the agent does not know a proposition, then she knows that she does not know it. This addition of 5 to S4 yields the logic S5. Most philosophers (including Hintikka) have attacked this axiom, since numerous examples from everyday life seem to invalidate it. For example, assume that a university professor believes (is certain) that one of her colleague's seminars is on Thursday (formally Bp). She is actually wrong because it is on Tuesday ($\neg p$). Therefore, she does not know that her colleague's seminar is on Tuesday ($\neg Kp$). If we assume that axiom 5 is valid then we should conclude that she knows that she does not know that her colleague's seminar is on Tuesday ($K\neg Kp$) (and therefore she also believes that she does not know it: $B\neg Kp$). This is obviously counterintuitive. More generally, axiom 5 is invalidated when the agent has mistaken beliefs which can be due for example to misperceptions, lies or other forms of deception.[8] As it turns out, this axiom is often used by computer scientists because it fits very well with the assumptions they have to make in most of the applied contexts they deal with.

Finally, we examine an axiom which has not drawn much attention in epistemic logic. This axiom plays, however, a central role in the logic of the notion of 'being informed' which has recently been introduced by Floridi (2006).

$$\varphi \rightarrow K\neg K\neg\varphi \tag{B}$$

Axiom B states that if φ is true, then the agent knows that she considers it possible that φ is true. In other words, it cannot be the case that the agent considers it possible

[8]Sakama et al. (2010) and van Ditmarsch et al. (2011) provide two independent logical accounts of the notion of lying and other kinds of deception using epistemic logic (resp. dynamic epistemic logic).

that she knows a false proposition (that is, $\neg(\neg\varphi \land \neg K\neg K\varphi)$). As pointed out by Floridi (2006), the validity of this axiom embeds a 'closed world assumption' similar to the assumption underlying the validity of axiom 5. As a matter of fact, adding axiom B to the logic S4 yields the logic S5. To be more precise, the sets $\{\mathsf{T}, \mathsf{B}, 4\}$ and $\{\mathsf{T}, 5\}$ are logically equivalent. Therefore, if we assume that axioms T and 4 are valid, then axiom B falls prey to the same attack as the one presented in the previous paragraph, since in that case we can derive axiom 5. We may wonder if a similar argument against axiom B holds in the logic KTB, that is, if we drop axiom 4. Wheeler argues that it is indeed the case (Wheeler 2012).[9]

The logic KTB (also known as B or Br or Brouwer's system) has been propounded by Floridi as the logic of the notion of 'being informed'. One of the main differences between the logic of this notion and the standard logic of knowledge is the absence of introspection (which is characterized by axiom 4). Floridi claims that his results "pave the way [...] to the possibility of a non-psychologistic, non-mentalistic and non-anthropomorphic approach to epistemology, which can easily be applied to artificial or synthetic agents such as computers, robots, webbots, companies, and organizations" (Floridi 2006, p. 456). In that respect, his notion of 'being informed' is similar to Voorbraak's notion of objective knowledge, since, as we already mentioned in Sect. 5.2.1, objective knowledge "applies to *any* agent which is capable of processing information [and] may very well be a device like a thermostat or a television-receiver" (Voorbraak 1993, p. 55). The claim that the notion of 'being informed' is an independent cognitive state which cannot be reduced to knowledge or belief has been attacked recently by Wheeler (2012). His attack is based on the argument against axiom B sketched in Footnote 9 (where the notion of knowledge is replaced with the notion of being informed).

5.3.2 *Doxastic Principles*

We have to be careful with the notion of belief, since the term 'belief' refers to different meanings: my belief that it will rain tomorrow is intuitively different from my belief that the Fermat-Wilson theorem is correct. This intuitive semantic difference that anyone can perceive stems from the fact that the doxastic strength of these two beliefs are not on the same 'scale'.

---

[9]Wheeler's argument against axiom B is based on two theorems derivable in the logic KTB. One of them is the following: $K(\varphi \to K\psi) \to (\neg K\neg\varphi \to \psi)$. If φ stands for 'the agent sees some smoke' and ψ stands for 'there is fire', then the consequent of this theorem states that if the agent considers it possible that he sees some smoke (without necessarily being sure of it), then there is fire. This conclusion is obviously counterintuitive.

5.3.2.1 Weak and Strong Belief

Lenzen argues in (Lenzen 1978) that there are two different kinds of belief, which he calls *weak* and *strong* belief (or *conviction*). We will now explain (succintly) the difference between these two types of belief.[10]

Weak Belief

Assume that the agent conjectures an arithmetical theorem φ from a series of examples and particular cases she has examined. The more examples the agent will have checked, the more she will 'believe' that this theorem holds true. We can naturally give a probabilistic semantics to this notion of belief and define a corresponding belief operator as follows:

$$B^r_w\varphi \triangleq Prob(\varphi) > r$$

where r is a real number ranging over the interval [0.5;1[. It is read as 'the agent believes, at least to the degree r, that φ'. The formula $Prob(\varphi)$ represents the subjective probability the agent assigns to the likelihood of φ; the bigger r is, the more the agent 'believes' in φ. It turns out that the reasoning principles validated by this notion of belief do not depend on the value of r. In particular, the principle $(B^r_w\varphi \wedge B^r_w\psi) \rightarrow B^r_w(\varphi \wedge \psi)$ is *not* valid. For $r = 0.5$, this notion of belief is called *weak belief* by Lenzen (1978); we denote it here as $B_w\varphi$ and it stands for 'the agent *w*eakly believes φ' or 'the agent thinks φ more probable than not'. Note that this modal operator is studied from a logical point of view by Herzig (2003). Instead of resorting to probability to represent this continuum of degrees of belief, we could also define a graded belief modality $B^n_w\varphi$, standing for 'the agent *w*eakly believes with degree at most n that φ', where n is a natural number.[11] A semantics for this modality based on Ordinal Conditional Functions (OCF) as introduced (Spohn 1988a) is proposed by Aucher (2004), Laverny and Lang (2005), and van Ditmarsch (2005). However, the intended interpretation of OCF in these papers deviates from Spohn's intended interpretation, resulting in a definition of the graded belief modality which confuses the notions of weak and strong belief. As it turns out, the principle $(B^n\varphi \wedge B^n\psi) \rightarrow B^n(\varphi \wedge \psi)$ *is* valid with this OCF-based semantics, unlike with probabilistic semantics.

---

[10]A relatively more detailed analysis distinguishing weak from strong belief is also presented in Shoham and Leyton-Brown (2009, pp. 414–415). Also see Lenzen (1978).

[11]One should not confuse these graded belief modalities with the graded modalities $M_n\varphi$ found in Fine (1972), de Rijke (2000), and van der Hoek and Meyer (1992). Indeed, the intended interpretation of $M_n\varphi$ is 'there are more than n accessible worlds that verify φ'.

Strong Belief

Now, if the agent comes up with a proof of this arithmetical theorem that she has checked several times, she will still 'believe' in this theorem, but this time with a different strength. Her belief will be a conviction, a certainty:

$$B\varphi \triangleq Prob(\varphi) = 1.$$

That said, her certainty might still be erroneous if there is a mistake in the proof that she did not notice. We will denote this second type of belief with the formula $B\varphi$ and read it as 'the agent strongly believes (is certain) that φ'.[12] Unlike weak belief (defined over a probabilistic semantics), strong belief validates the following axiom:

$$(B\varphi \wedge B\psi) \rightarrow B(\varphi \wedge \psi). \qquad \text{(K')}$$

Note also that, according to probability theory, strong belief entails weak belief:

$$B\varphi \rightarrow B_w\varphi \qquad \text{(BB}_\text{w}\text{1)}$$

and that

$$B_w\varphi \wedge B\psi \rightarrow B_w(\varphi \wedge \psi). \qquad \text{(BB}_\text{w}\text{2)}$$

This notion of strong belief is also sometimes called *plain* belief (Spohn 1988b) or *acceptance* (Gärdenfors 1988).

Remark 5.3.1. The notions of weak and strong belief are often confused in the literature. This may lead to apparent paradoxes such as the lottery paradox (Kyburg 1961). Weak and strong beliefs are indeed intertwined in the formulation of this paradox. Once these two notions are clearly identified and separated, the paradox vanishes. As Lenzen writes, "Consider a fair lottery with n tickets, only one of which is the winning ticket. For each ticket j, the chance of j being the winning ticket then is $\frac{1}{n}$. Thus, any individual a whose subjective expectation accords with the objective probabilities will have to presume [...] that j is not the winning ticket, $B_w\neg p_1 \wedge \ldots \wedge B_w\neg p_n$. But since a knows that one ticket will win, he a fortiori believes (strongly) that one ticket will win, $B(p_1 \vee \ldots \vee p_n)$. Hence his set of believings is neither consistent nor deductively closed." (Lenzen 1978, p. 38) □

[12] The modal operators of weak and strong belief are denoted "$B\varphi$" and "$C\varphi$" respectively in Lenzen (1978).

Conditional Belief

The description of the agent's doxastic state can be enriched if we also consider what the agent *would* believe if she was confronted with new evidence about the current situation. This has led Lamarre and Shoham in (Lamarre and Shoham 1994) to define two operators of conditional belief, $B^{\psi}\varphi$ and $B_w^{\psi}\varphi$.[13] The semantics of these operators of conditional belief is based on the semantics of default statements.

A default statement $\psi \supset \varphi$ can be read in various ways: 'if ψ holds, then typically φ holds' or 'if ψ, then by default φ'. Friedman and Halpern (1997) and Lamarre and Shoham (1994) interpret a default statement $\psi \supset \varphi$ as a conditional belief statement: 'the agent believes φ, given assumption ψ' or more precisely 'if ψ were announced to the agent, she would believe that φ held (before the announcement)'. Given this intended interpretation, the notion of strong belief $B\varphi$ (resp. weak belief) corresponds in this richer setting to the formula $B^{\top}\varphi$ (resp. $B_w^{\top}\varphi$). This epistemic interpretation of a default statement, and hence also of its underlying logical semantics, is meaningful. It is grounded in the relations set up by Makinson and Gärdenfors (1989) between AGM theory of belief change (Alchourrón et al. 1985; Gärdenfors 1988) and default logic. This epistemic interpretation is also supported by the fact that the famous *Ramsey test* basically defines belief revision in terms of default logic. Indeed, the idea of the Ramsey test is that an agent should believe φ after learning ψ if and only if he currently believes that φ would be true if ψ were true (i.e., $\psi \supset \varphi$).

This notion of conditional belief gives rise in turn to a derived doxastic notion called "safe belief" by Baltag and Smets (2006, 2008a,b). A safe belief in φ is expressed by the formula $B^{\neg\varphi}\bot$. This notion corresponds intuitively to a belief which cannot be defeated by any assumption. It is therefore very close to the definition of knowledge as undefeated true belief proposed by Lehrer and Paxson in (1969), the only difference being that their notion of knowledge cannot be defeated by any *true* assumption. Originally introduced for technical reasons by Boutilier (1994) to deal with defeasible reasoning, this operator of safe belief has been reintroduced recently in the context of *dynamic* epistemic logic (van Ditmarsch et al. 2007; van Benthem 2011) together with the notions of "hard" and "soft" information, in order to deal with belief revision (unlike "hard" information, "soft" information is revisable).[14]

Remark 5.3.2. If we added dynamics to our framework, as do Baltag and Smets (2006, 2008a,b), then we would also have formulas of the form $[\psi!]B\varphi$, whose reading would be '*after* the announcement of ψ, the agent believes φ'. This reading is different from the (extended) reading of our formulas $B^{\psi}\varphi$: 'if ψ were announced to the agent, she would believe that φ held *before* the announcement'. The latter

---

[13] These two operators are respectively denoted "$C^{\psi}\varphi$" and "$B^{\psi}\varphi$" in (Lamarre and Shoham 1994).

[14] For more details, see van Benthem (2007, 2011), Baltag and Smets (2006, 2008a,b), and also Pacuit (2014) in this book.

operator is a revision of the agent's beliefs about the state of the world as it was *before* the announcement, and the former is a revision of the state of the world as it is *after* the announcement. Note, however, that this important distinction between *static* belief revision and *dynamic* belief revision collapses in the case of propositional formulas ψ, which most interests us here. □

For the rest of the paper, we will be interested only in the notion of strong belief (certainty) and its conditional version. We will show that convoluted axioms for knowledge such as .3 and .3.2, which can hardly be expressed in terms of intuitive interaction axioms dealing with strong beliefs only, can be expressed in terms of interaction axioms dealing with *conditional* beliefs, which are easier to grasp.

5.3.2.2 Principles of Strong Belief

The logic of (strong) belief is less controversial than the logic of knowledge. It is usually considered to be KD45, which is obtained by adding to the axiom K and inference rule Nec (where the knowledge operator is replaced by the belief operator) to the following axioms D, 4 and 5:

$$B\varphi \to \neg B\neg\varphi \quad \text{(D)}$$

$$B\varphi \to BB\varphi \quad \text{(4)}$$

$$\neg B\varphi \to B\neg B\varphi \quad \text{(5)}$$

Axioms 4 and 5 state that the agent has positive and negative introspection over her own beliefs. Some objections have been raised against Axiom 4 (see Lenzen (1978, Chap. 4) for details). Axiom D states that the agent's beliefs are consistent. In combination with axiom K (where the knowledge operator is replaced by a belief operator), axiom D is in fact equivalent to a simpler axiom D' which conveys, maybe more explicitly, the fact that the agent's beliefs cannot be inconsistent ($B\bot$):

$$\neg B\bot \quad \text{(D')}$$

In all the theories of rational agency developed in artificial intelligence (and in particular in the papers cited in Footnote 4), the logic of belief is KD45. Note that all these agent theories follow the perfect external approach. This is at odds with their intention to implement their theories in machines. In that respect, an internal approach seems to be more appropriate since, in this context, the agent needs to reason from its own internal point of view. For the internal approach, the logic of belief is S5, as proved by Aucher (2010) and Arlo-Costa (1999) (for the notion of *full belief*).[15]

[15]In both philosophy and computer science, there is formalization of the internal point of view. Perhaps one of the dominant formalisms for this is auto-epistemic logic (Moore 1984, 1995).

5.3.2.3 Principles of Conditional Belief

The axioms and inference rules of an axiomatic system called system P form the core of any axiomatic system that deal with non-monotonic reasoning. A generalized version of this system (taken from Friedman and Halpern 1997), which allows us to express boolean combinations of default statements is reproduced below (we omit modus ponens and all the substitution instances of propositional tautologies). We recall that $B^{\psi}\varphi$ reads as 'the agent (strongly) believes φ, given assumption ψ' or more precisely 'if ψ were announced to the agent, she would believe that φ held (before the announcement)'. We leave the reader to find out the natural intuitions underlying these axioms and inference rules.

$$B^{\psi}\psi \tag{C1}$$

$$(B^{\psi}\varphi_1 \wedge B^{\psi}\varphi_2) \rightarrow B^{\psi}(\varphi_1 \wedge \varphi_2) \tag{C2}$$

$$(B^{\psi_1}\varphi \wedge B^{\psi_2}\varphi) \rightarrow B^{\psi_1 \vee \psi_2}\varphi \tag{C3}$$

$$(B^{\psi}\varphi \wedge B^{\psi}\chi) \rightarrow B^{\psi \wedge \varphi}\chi \tag{C4}$$

$$\text{If } \psi \leftrightarrow \psi' \text{ then } B^{\psi}\varphi \leftrightarrow B^{\psi'}\varphi \tag{RC1}$$

$$\text{If } \varphi \rightarrow \varphi' \text{ then } B^{\psi}\varphi \rightarrow B^{\psi}\varphi' \tag{RC2}$$

Note that axiom C2 is an indication that this notion of conditional belief is a generalization of the notion of *strong* belief rather than *weak* belief, since, as we have already noted, $(B\varphi \wedge B\psi) \rightarrow B(\varphi \wedge \psi)$ holds, but $(B_w\varphi \wedge B_w\psi) \rightarrow B_w(\varphi \wedge \psi)$ does not hold in general (at least for the probabilistic semantics of weak belief).

5.4 Principles of Interaction

In this section, we will set out the interaction axioms which have been proposed and discussed in the epistemic logic literature and which connect the notions of belief or conditional belief with the notion of knowledge. We will start by reviewing interaction axioms that deal with strong belief, and then we will consider interaction axioms that deal with *conditional* belief. Note that a classification of certain interaction principles has been proposed by van der Hoek (1993).[16]

In philosophy, there are models of full belief like the one offered by Levi (1997) which is also related to ideas in auto-epistemic logic. See Aucher (2010) for more details on the internal approach and its connection to the other modeling approaches, namely the imperfect and the perfect external approaches.

[16]The classification is as follows. If X, Y, Z are epistemic operators, $X\varphi \rightarrow YZ\varphi$ are called *positive introspection formulas*, $\neg X\varphi \rightarrow Y\neg Z\varphi$ are called *negative introspection formulas*, $XY\varphi \rightarrow Z\varphi$ are called *positive extraspection formulas*, $X\neg Y \rightarrow \neg Z\varphi$ are called *negative extraspection formulas*, and $X(Y\varphi \rightarrow \varphi)$ are called *trust formulas*.

5.4.1 Principles of Interaction with Strong Belief

The following interaction axioms are suggested by Hintikka (1962) and are often encountered in the literature:

$$K\varphi \rightarrow B\varphi \tag{KB1}$$

$$B\varphi \rightarrow KB\varphi \tag{KB2}$$

Axiom KB1 is a cornerstone of epistemic logic. Just as axiom T, it follows from the classical analysis of knowledge of Plato presented in the Theaetethus. It turns out that axiom KB1 is rejected in Voorbraak's logic of objective knowledge, because his notion of knowledge does not necessarily apply to humans, but rather applies in general to any information-processing device. It is adopted by Halpern (1996), but only for propositional formulas φ. Axiom KB2 highlights the fact that the agent has "privileged access" to his doxastic state. If we assume, moreover, that the axioms D, 4, 5 for belief hold, then we can derive the following principle (because in that case $\neg B\varphi \leftrightarrow B\neg B\varphi$ is valid):

$$\neg B\varphi \rightarrow K\neg B\varphi \tag{KB2'}$$

Axiom KB3 below confirms that our notion of belief does correspond to a notion of conviction or certainty. This axiom entails the weaker axiom $B\varphi \rightarrow B_w K\varphi$ (also discussed in Lenzen (1978)).

$$B\varphi \rightarrow BK\varphi \tag{KB3}$$

The underlying intuition of KB3 is that "*to the agent*, the facts of which he is certain appear to be knowledge" (Lamarre and Shoham 1994, p. 415) (my emphasis). This informal analysis of the notion of strong belief is formally confirmed by the fact that the axiom $B(B\varphi \rightarrow \varphi)$ is valid in the KD45 logic of belief, and also by the fact that the axiom $B\varphi \rightarrow \varphi$, which is a key axiom of the notion of knowledge, is an axiom of the *internal* version of epistemic logic (Aucher 2010).

Lenzen also introduces, in (Lenzen 1979), the following interaction axiom:

$$\hat{B}K\varphi \rightarrow B\varphi \tag{KB3'}$$

This can be equivalently rewritten as $\hat{B}\varphi \rightarrow B\hat{K}\varphi$, where $\hat{B}\varphi$ and $\hat{K}\varphi$ are abbreviations of $\neg B\neg\varphi$ and $\neg K\neg\varphi$ respectively. In this form, this states that, if φ is compatible with everything the agent *believes*, then the agent actually believes that it is compatible with everything she *knows* that φ.

Remark 5.4.1. It is difficult to make sense intuitively of the distinction between $\hat{K}\varphi$ and $\hat{B}\varphi$, since they both refer to what the agent considers possible. Hintikka proposes (1962, p. 3), the following reading: the formula $\hat{K}\varphi$ should be read as "it is possible, for all that the agent knows, that φ" or "it is compatible with everything the agent knows that φ"; and the formula $\hat{B}\varphi$ should be read as "it is compatible with everything the agent believes that φ". In view of our modeling assumptions, we can add that the former possibility is ascribed externally by the modeler given her knowledge of the epistemic state of the agent, whereas the latter possibility can be determined internally by the agent herself.

Another interaction axiom also introduced by Lenzen (1978) defines belief in terms of knowledge:

$$B\varphi \leftrightarrow \hat{K}K\varphi \tag{KB4}$$

Although this definition might seem a bit mysterious at first sight, it actually makes perfect sense, as explained in Lenzen (1978). Indeed, the left to right direction $B\varphi \rightarrow \hat{K}K\varphi$ can be rewritten $K\neg K\varphi \rightarrow \neg B\varphi$, that is, $\neg(K\neg K\varphi \wedge B\varphi)$. This first implication states that the agent cannot, at the same time, know that she does not know a proposition and be certain of this very proposition. The right to left direction $\hat{K}K\varphi \rightarrow B\varphi$ can be rewritten $\hat{B}\neg\varphi \rightarrow K\neg K\varphi$. This second implication states that, if the agent considers it possible that φ might be false, then she knows that she does not know φ.

Finally, the last interaction axiom we will consider is in fact a definition of knowledge in terms of belief:

$$K\varphi \leftrightarrow (\varphi \wedge B\varphi) \tag{KB5}$$

It simply states that knowledge is defined as true belief. This definition of knowledge in terms of belief lacks the notion of justification addressed in the field of justification logic (Artemov and Fitting 2011). This definition has also been attacked by philosophers since, according to it, the agent's knowledge could simply be due to some "epistemic luck". Roughly speaking, this means that the agent could believe a proposition which turns out *by chance* to be true, although this belief cannot qualify as knowledge if one considers the whole epistemic context. An explanation of this notion of "epistemic luck" in logical terms is proposed by Halpern et al. (2009a) (but also see Prichard (2004)).

5.4.1.1 The Collapse of Knowledge and Belief

In any logic of knowledge and belief, if we adopt axiom 5 for the notion of knowledge, axiom D for the notion of belief and KB1 as the only interaction axiom, then we end up with counterintuitive properties. First, as noted by Voorbraak, we can derive the theorem $BK\varphi \rightarrow K\varphi$.[17] This theorem entails that "one cannot believe to know a false proposition" (Voorbraak 1993, p. 8). As it turns out, these axioms are adopted in the first logical framework combining modalities of knowledge and belief (Kraus and Lehmann 1986). Moreover, if we add the axiom KB3, we can also prove that $B\varphi \rightarrow K\varphi$. This theorem collapses the distinction between the notions of knowledge and belief.

A systematic approach has been proposed by van der Hoek to avoid this collapse (1993). He showed, thanks to correspondence theory, that any multi-modal logic with both knowledge and belief modalities that includes the set of axioms $\{\mathsf{D}, \mathsf{5}, \mathsf{KB1}, \mathsf{KB3}\}$ entails the theorem $B\varphi \rightarrow K\varphi$. He also showed, however, that for each proper subset of $\{\mathsf{D}, \mathsf{5}, \mathsf{KB1}, \mathsf{KB3}\}$, counter-models can be built which show that none of those sets of axioms entail the collapse of the distinction between knowledge and belief. So we have to drop one principle in $\{\mathsf{D}, \mathsf{5}, \mathsf{KB1}, \mathsf{KB3}\}$. Axioms D and KB3 are hardly controversial given our understanding of the notion of strong belief. In this case we have to drop either KB1 or 5. Voorbraak proposes to drop axiom KB1. His notion of knowledge, which he calls *objective knowledge*, is therefore unusual in so far as it does not require the agent to be aware of its belief state. But, as we have said, he clearly warns that this notion applies to any information-processing device, and not necessarily just to humans. Note that Floridi has similar reservations against axiom KB1 (2006), since his notion of *being informed* shares similar features with Voorbraak's notion of *objective knowledge*. Halpern also proposes (1996) to drop axiom KB1 and to restrict to propositional formulas. This restriction looks a bit ad hoc at first sight. Dropping axiom 5 seems to be the most reasonable choice in light of the discussion about this axiom in Sect. 5.3.1.

By dropping 5, we then only have to investigate the logics between S4 and S5 as possible candidates for a logic of knowledge (S5 excluded), as Lenzen did in (Lenzen 1979).

[17] Here is the proof:

1	$K\varphi \rightarrow B\varphi$	Axiom KB1
2	$K\neg K\varphi \rightarrow B\neg K\varphi$	KB1 : $\neg K\varphi/\varphi$
3	$B\varphi \rightarrow \neg B\neg\varphi$	Axiom D
4	$B\neg\varphi \rightarrow \neg B\varphi$	3, contraposition
5	$B\neg K\varphi \rightarrow \neg BK\varphi$	4 : $K\varphi/\varphi$
6	$\neg K\varphi \rightarrow K\neg K\varphi$	Axiom 5
7	$\neg K\varphi \rightarrow B\neg K\varphi$	6,2, Modus Ponens
8	$\neg K\varphi \rightarrow \neg BK\varphi$	7,5, Modus Ponens
9	$BK\varphi \rightarrow K\varphi$	8, contraposition.

5.4.2 Principles of Interaction with Conditional Belief

The following axioms $\mathsf{KB1}^{\psi}$, $\mathsf{KB2}^{\psi}$ and $\mathsf{KB3}^{\psi}$ are natural conditional versions of the axioms KB1, KB2, KB3: if ψ is replaced by $\top$ in these three axioms correspond to the axioms KB1, KB2, KB3. Axioms $\mathsf{KB1}^{\psi}$ and $\mathsf{KB2}^{\psi}$ are first introduced by Moses and Shoham (1993) and are also adopted by Friedman and Halpern (1997). Axiom $\mathsf{KB3}^{\psi}$ is actually introduced by Lamarre and Shoham (1994) in the form $B^{\psi}\varphi \to B_w^{\psi} K(\psi \to \varphi)$.

$$K\varphi \to B^{\psi}\varphi \qquad (\mathsf{KB1}^{\psi})$$

$$B^{\psi}\varphi \to KB^{\psi}\varphi \qquad (\mathsf{KB2}^{\psi})$$

$$B^{\psi}\varphi \to B^{\psi}K(\psi \to \varphi) \qquad (\mathsf{KB3}^{\psi})$$

Axiom $\mathsf{KB1}^{\psi}$ states that, if the agent knows that φ, then she also believes that φ, and so on under any assumption ψ. Note that $\mathsf{KB1}^{\psi}$ entails the weaker principle $K\varphi \to (\psi \to B^{\psi}\varphi)$, which is tightly connected to the Lehrer and Paxton's definition of knowledge as undefeated true belief (Lehrer and Paxson 1969). Indeed, this derived principle states that if the agent knows that φ (formally $K\varphi$), then her belief in φ cannot be defeated by any *true* information ψ (formally $\psi \to B^{\psi}\varphi$). Note that this very principle entails an even weaker variant of $\mathsf{KB1}^{\psi}$ introduced by Moses and Shoham (1993), namely $K\varphi \to \left(B^{\psi}\varphi \vee K\neg\psi\right)$, i.e., $K\varphi \to \left(\hat{K}\psi \to B^{\psi}\varphi\right)$. Axiom $\mathsf{KB2}^{\psi}$ is a straightforward generalization of KB2. As for $\mathsf{KB3}^{\psi}$ it states that, if the agent believes φ under the assumption that ψ, then, given this very assumption ψ, she also believes that she knows φ conditional on ψ.

The axioms $\mathsf{KB4}^{\psi}$ and $\mathsf{KB5}^{\psi}$ below are also introduced in Lamarre and Shoham (1994):

$$\neg B^{\psi}\varphi \to K(\hat{K}\psi \to \neg B^{\psi}\varphi) \qquad (\mathsf{KB4}^{\psi})$$

$$\hat{K}\psi \to \neg B^{\psi}\bot \qquad (\mathsf{KB5}^{\psi})$$

Axiom $\mathsf{KB4}^{\psi}$ is a conditional version of axiom KB2'. It is introduced by Lamarre and Shoham (1994) in the form $\neg B^{\psi}\varphi \to K(K\neg\psi \vee \neg B^{\psi}\varphi)$. Another possible conditional version of KB2' could have been $\neg B^{\psi}\varphi \to K\neg B^{\psi}\varphi$, and this axiom is indeed adopted by Moses and Shoham (1993). However, "this simpler axiom ignores the possibility of assumptions which are known to be false, and is valid only for the case of $\psi = \top$" (Lamarre and Shoham 1994, p. 420).

Axiom $\mathsf{KB5}^{\psi}$ states that, if ψ is compatible with everything the agents knows, then her beliefs given this assumption cannot be inconsistent. In particular, if ψ holds then the agent's doxastic state given this assumption cannot be inconsistent: $\psi \to \neg B^{\psi}\bot$ (because $\psi \to \hat{K}\psi$ is valid according to axiom T). Axiom $\mathsf{KB5}^{\psi}$

is introduced in Lamarre and Shoham (1994) in the equivalent form $\hat{K}\psi \to \left(B^{\psi}\varphi \to \neg B^{\psi}\neg\varphi\right)$. Together with $\mathsf{KB1}^{\psi}$ and system P, it entails that knowledge is definable in terms of conditional belief. This definition of knowledge actually coincides with the notion of "safe belief" introduced by Baltag and Smets (2008a).

$$K\varphi \triangleq B^{\neg\varphi}\bot \qquad \text{(Def K)}$$

Conversely, some definitions of conditional belief in terms of knowledge have been proposed in the literature. In Moses and Shoham (1993), the following three definitions are introduced:

$$B^{\psi}\varphi \triangleq K(\psi \to \varphi) \qquad \text{(Def1 CB)}$$

$$B^{\psi}\varphi \triangleq K(\psi \to \varphi) \wedge (K\neg\psi \to K\varphi) \qquad \text{(Def2 CB)}$$

$$B^{\psi}\varphi \triangleq K(\psi \to \varphi) \wedge \neg K\neg\psi \qquad \text{(Def3 CB)}$$

The third definition entails the second definition, which itself entails the first definition. However, as one can easily check, none of these three definitions avoids the collapse of the notions of knowledge and belief. Indeed, if we replace ψ with $\top$ in these three definitions, we obtain that $B^{\top}\varphi \leftrightarrow K\varphi$ holds. Hence, if the operator $B^{\top}\varphi$ (i.e., the operator $B\varphi$) is interpreted as a strong belief operator, then these definitions are untenable.

In the spirit of these three definitions, we propose the following weaker interaction axiom which does not collapse the distinction between knowledge and belief:

$$B\neg\psi \to \left(B^{\psi}\varphi \to K\left(\psi \to \varphi\right)\right) \qquad (\mathsf{KB6}^{\psi})$$

If we assume, moreover, that $\mathsf{KB1}^{\psi}$ holds, then this axiom $\mathsf{KB6}^{\psi}$ entails that if the agent (strongly) believes that ψ does not hold, then her beliefs given ψ coincide with her knowledge given ψ, i.e., $B\neg\psi \to (B^{\psi}\varphi \leftrightarrow K(\psi \to \varphi))$. Indeed, given $\mathsf{KB1}^{\psi}$, one can prove that $K(\psi \to \varphi) \to B^{\psi}\varphi$ holds.

Finally, we note that the inference rules (RC1) and (RC2) of system P are translated by Lamarre and Shoham (1994) by the following two interaction axioms. The intuitive meaning of these axioms is clear.

$$K(\psi \leftrightarrow \psi') \to (B^{\psi}\varphi \leftrightarrow B^{\psi'}\varphi)$$

$$K(\varphi \to \varphi') \to (B^{\psi}\varphi \to B^{\psi}\varphi')$$

5.5 Logical Formalization

In this section, we will see the standard formal semantics of knowledge, (strong) belief and (strong) conditional belief. For examples and applications of these semantics in computer science, the interested reader can consult Fagin et al. (1995) or Meyer and van der Hoek (1995). We will also introduce the convoluted axioms .2, .3, .3.2 and .4 (together with the class of frame they define), and we will formally define what a (modal) logic is.

5.5.1 *A Semantics of Knowledge and Strong Belief*

In the rest of this paper, Φ is a set of propositional letters. We define the epistemic-doxastic language $\mathcal{L}_{KB}$ as follows:

$$\mathcal{L}_{KB}: \varphi ::= p \mid \neg\varphi \mid \varphi \wedge \varphi \mid B\varphi \mid K\varphi$$

where p ranges over Φ. The propositional language $\mathcal{L}_0$ is the language $\mathcal{L}_{KB}$ without the knowledge and belief operators K and B. The language $\mathcal{L}_K$ is the language $\mathcal{L}_{KB}$ without the belief operator B, and the language $\mathcal{L}_B$ is the language $\mathcal{L}_{KB}$ without the knowledge operator K. The formula $B\varphi$ reads as 'the agent believes φ' and $K\varphi$ reads as 'the agent knows φ'. Their dual operators $\hat{B}\varphi$ and $\hat{K}\varphi$ are abbreviations of $\neg B\neg\varphi$ and $\neg K\neg\varphi$ respectively.

In epistemic logic, a semantics of the modal operators of belief (B) and knowledge (K) is often provided by means of a Kripke semantics. The first logical framework combining these two operators with a Kripke semantics is proposed by Kraus and Lehmann (1986).

5.5.1.1 Epistemic-Doxastic Model

An *epistemic-doxastic model* $\mathcal{M}$ is a multi-modal Kripke model $\mathcal{M} = (W, R_B, R_K, V)$ where W is a non-empty set of possible worlds, $R_K, R_B \in 2^{W\times W}$ are binary relations over W called *accessibility relations*, and $V : \Phi \to 2^W$ is a mapping called a *valuation* assigning to each propositional letter p of Φ a subset of W. An *epistemic-doxastic frame* $\mathcal{F}$ is an epistemic-doxastic model without valuation. We often denote $\mathcal{R}(w) = \{v \in W \mid w\mathcal{R}v\}$ and $R_B(w) = \{v \in W \mid wR_Bv\}$.

Let $\varphi \in \mathcal{L}_{KB}$, let $\mathcal{M}$ be an epistemic-doxastic model and let $w \in \mathcal{M}$. The satisfaction relation $\mathcal{M}, w \models \varphi$ is defined inductively as follows:

$$\begin{array}{lll}
\mathcal{M}, w \models p & \text{iff} & w \in V(p) \\
\mathcal{M}, w \models \varphi \wedge \varphi' & \text{iff} & \mathcal{M}, w \models \varphi \text{ and } \mathcal{M}, w \models \varphi' \\
\mathcal{M}, w \models \neg\varphi & \text{iff} & \text{not } \mathcal{M}, w \models \varphi \\
\mathcal{M}, w \models B\varphi & \text{iff} & \text{for all } v \in R_B(w), \mathcal{M}, v \models \varphi \\
\mathcal{M}, w \models K\varphi & \text{iff} & \text{for all } v \in \mathcal{R}(w), \mathcal{M}, v \models \varphi.
\end{array}$$

We denote $[\![\varphi]\!]_{\mathcal{M}} = \{w \in \mathcal{M} \mid \mathcal{M}, w \models \varphi\}$. We abusively write $w \in \mathcal{M}$ for $w \in W$. If Γ is a set of formulas of $\mathcal{L}_{KB}$, then we write $\mathcal{M} \models \Gamma$ when for all $\varphi \in \Gamma$ and all $w \in \mathcal{M}$, it holds that $\mathcal{M}, w \models \varphi$. Likewise, if $\mathcal{F} = (W, R_B, R_K)$ is an epistemic-doxastic frame, then we abusively write $w \in \mathcal{F}$ for $w \in W$. If Γ is a set of formulas of $\mathcal{L}_{KB}$, then we write $\mathcal{F} \models \Gamma$ when for all $\varphi \in \Gamma$ and all valuation V, $(\mathcal{F}, V) \models \varphi$, and we say that Γ is *valid in* $\mathcal{F}$.

5.5.2 A Semantics of Knowledge and Conditional Belief

Taking up the work of Friedman and Halpern (2001), we define the syntax of the language $\mathcal{L}_{KB^\psi}$ inductively as follows:

$$\mathcal{L}_{KB^\psi} : \varphi \ ::= \ p \ \mid \ \neg\varphi \ \mid \ \varphi \wedge \varphi \ \mid \ B^\varphi\varphi \ \mid \ K\varphi$$

where p ranges over Φ. The symbol $\top$ is an abbreviation for $p \vee \neg p$, and $B\varphi$ is an abbreviation for $B^\top\varphi$. The language $\mathcal{L}_K$ is $\mathcal{L}_{KB^\psi}$ without the belief operator B^ψ, and the language $\mathcal{L}_{B^\psi}$ is $\mathcal{L}_{KB^\psi}$ without the knowledge operator K.

Numerous semantics have been proposed for default statements, such as preferential structures (Kraus et al. 1990), ϵ-semantics (Adams 1975), possibilistic structures (Dubois and Prade 1991), and κ-ranking (Spohn 1988a,b). They all have in common that they validate the axiomatic system P originally introduced in Kraus et al. (1990). A slightly different version of this system is reproduced in Sect. 5.3.2.3. This remarkable fact is explained in Friedman and Halpern (2001), where a general framework based on *plausibility measures* is proposed. As proved in that paper, plausibility measures generalize all these semantics. We can nevertheless mention that other logical formalisms dealing with conditional beliefs are proposed in the economics literature (Board 2004). These other formalisms have been taken up in the field of *dynamic* epistemic logic (Baltag and Smets 2006, 2008a,b).

We adopt the general framework of plausibility measures to provide a semantics for $\mathcal{L}_{KB^\psi}$. Plausibility spaces and epistemic-plausibility spaces are introduced respectively by Friedman and Halpern (1997, 2001). Because these structures will play a role only in the proofs of the subsequent theorems, their definitions and the truth conditions of the language $\mathcal{L}_{KB^\psi}$ are postponed until the appendix, together with the proofs of all the theorems and propositions in this paper.

5.5.3 Logics of Knowledge, Belief and Conditional Belief

A *(modal) logic* L for a modal language $\mathcal{L}$ is a set of formulas of $\mathcal{L}$ that contains all propositional tautologies and is closed under modus ponens (that is, if $\varphi \in \mathsf{L}$ and $\varphi \rightarrow \psi \in \mathsf{L}$, then $\psi \in \mathsf{L}$) and uniform substitution (that is, if φ belongs to L then so do all of its substitution instances (Blackburn et al. 2001, Definition 1.18)). A modal logic is usually defined by a set of axioms and inference rules. A formula belongs to the modal logic if it can be derived by successively applying (some of) the inference rules to (some of) the axioms. We are interested here in *normal modal logics*. These modal logics contain the formulas $(B(\varphi \rightarrow \psi) \wedge B\varphi) \rightarrow B\psi$ and $(K(\varphi \rightarrow \psi) \wedge K\varphi) \rightarrow K\psi$ (i.e., axiom K), and the inference rules of belief and knowledge necessitation: from $\varphi \in \mathsf{L}$, infer $B\varphi \in \mathsf{L}$, and from $\varphi \in \mathsf{L}$, infer $K\varphi \in \mathsf{L}$ (i.e., inference rule Nec). A modal logic *generated* by a set of axioms Γ is the smallest normal modal logic containing the formulas Γ.

Below, we give a list of properties of the accessibility relations R_B and $\mathcal{R}$ that will be used in the rest of the paper. We also give, below each property, the axiom which *defines* the class of epistemic-doxastic frames that fulfill this property (see Blackburn et al. (2001, Definition 3.2) for a definition of the notion of *definability*). We choose, without any particular reason, to use the knowledge modality to write these conditions (Fig. 5.1).

The logic $(\mathsf{KD45})_B$ is the smallest normal modal logic for $\mathcal{L}_B$ generated by the set of axioms $\{\mathsf{D}, \mathsf{4}, \mathsf{5}\}$. The logic $(\mathsf{P})_{B^\psi}$ is the smallest logic for $\mathcal{L}_{B^\psi}$ containing the axioms $\mathsf{C1}$-$\mathsf{C4}$ and inference rules $\mathsf{RC1}$-$\mathsf{RC2}$ from Sect. 5.3.2.3.[18] For any $\mathsf{x} \in \{.2, .3, .3.2, .4\}$, the logic $(\mathsf{S4.x})_K$ is the smallest normal modal logic for $\mathcal{L}_K$ generated by the set of axioms $\{\mathsf{T}, \mathsf{4}, \mathsf{x}\}$. We have the following relationship between these logics:

$$(\mathsf{S4})_K \subset (\mathsf{S4.2})_K \subset (\mathsf{S4.3})_K \subset (\mathsf{S4.3.2})_K \subset (\mathsf{S4.4})_K \subset (\mathsf{S5})_K$$

If L and L' are two sets of formulas (possibly logics), we denote by $\mathsf{L} + \mathsf{L}'$ the smallest normal modal logic containing L and L'. Note that $\mathsf{L} + \mathsf{L}'$ may be different from $\mathsf{L} \cup \mathsf{L}'$ in general, because $\mathsf{L} \cup \mathsf{L}'$ may not be closed under modus ponens or uniform substitution.

[18] Note that the axiom $(B^\psi(\varphi \rightarrow \varphi') \wedge B^\psi\varphi) \rightarrow B^\psi\varphi'$ and the inference rule from φ infer $B^\psi\varphi$ are both derivable in $(\mathsf{P})_{B^\psi}$. Therefore, $(\mathsf{P})_{B^\psi}$ is also a *normal* modal logic.

serial: D:	$\mathcal{R}(w) \neq \varnothing$ $K\varphi \rightarrow \hat{K}\varphi$
transitive: 4:	If $w' \in \mathcal{R}(w)$ and $w'' \in \mathcal{R}(w')$, then $w'' \in \mathcal{R}(w)$ $K\varphi \rightarrow KK\varphi$
Euclidean: 5:	If $w' \in \mathcal{R}(w)$ and $w'' \in \mathcal{R}(w)$, then $w' \in \mathcal{R}(w'')$ $\neg K\varphi \rightarrow K\neg K\varphi$
reflexive: T:	$w \in \mathcal{R}(w)$ $K\varphi \rightarrow \varphi$
symetric: B:	If $w' \in \mathcal{R}(w)$, then $w \in \mathcal{R}(w')$ $\varphi \rightarrow K\neg K\neg \varphi$
confluent: .2:	If $w' \in \mathcal{R}(w)$ and $w'' \in \mathcal{R}(w)$, then there is v such that $v \in \mathcal{R}(w')$ and $v \in \mathcal{R}(w'')$ $\hat{K}K\varphi \rightarrow K\hat{K}\varphi$
weakly connected .3:	If $w' \in \mathcal{R}(w)$ and $w'' \in \mathcal{R}(w)$, then $w' = w''$ or $w' \in \mathcal{R}(w'')$ or $w'' \in \mathcal{R}(w')$ $\hat{K}\varphi \wedge \hat{K}\psi \rightarrow \hat{K}(\varphi \wedge \psi) \vee \hat{K}(\psi \wedge \hat{K}\varphi) \vee \hat{K}(\varphi \wedge \hat{K}\psi)$
semi-Euclidean: .3.2:	If $w'' \in \mathcal{R}(w)$ and $w \notin \mathcal{R}(w'')$ and $w' \in \mathcal{R}(w)$, then $w'' \in \mathcal{R}(w)$ $(\hat{K}\varphi \wedge \hat{K}K\psi) \rightarrow K(\hat{K}\varphi \vee \psi)$
RI: .4:	If $w'' \in \mathcal{R}(w)$ and $w \neq w''$ and $w' \in \mathcal{R}(w)$, then $w'' \in \mathcal{R}(w')$ $(\varphi \wedge \hat{K}K\varphi) \rightarrow K\varphi$

Fig. 5.1 List of properties of the accessibility relations R_B and $\mathcal{R}$ and corresponding axioms

5.6 Defining Knowledge in Terms of Belief and Vice Versa

The definability of modalities in terms of other modalities is studied from a theoretical point of view by Halpern et al. (2009b). This study is subsequently applied to epistemic logic (Halpern et al. 2009a). Three notions of definability emerge from this work: explicit definability, implicit definability and reducibility. It has been proven that, for modal logic, explicit definability coincides with the conjunction of implicit definability and reducibility (unlike first-order logic, where the notion of explicit definability coincides with implicit definability only). In this paper, we are interested only in the notion of *explicit* definability, which is also used by Lenzen in (1979). Here is its formal definition:

Definition 5.6.1 (Halpern et al. 2009a). Let L be a (modal) logic for $\mathcal{L}_{KB}$ (resp. $\mathcal{L}_{KB^{\psi}}$).

- We say that K is *explicitly defined in* L *by the definition* $Kp \triangleq \delta$, where $\delta \in \mathcal{L}_B$ (resp. $\delta \in \mathcal{L}_{B^{\psi}}$), if $Kp \leftrightarrow \delta \in \mathsf{L}$.
- We say that B (resp. B^{ψ}) is *explicitly defined in* L *by the definition* $Bp \triangleq \delta$, where $\delta \in \mathcal{L}_K$, if $Bp \leftrightarrow \delta \in \mathsf{L}$ (resp. $B^{\psi} p \leftrightarrow \delta \in \mathsf{L}$).

Obviously, putting together an epistemic logic and a doxastic logic, for example $(\mathsf{S4})_K + (\mathsf{KD45})_B$, does not yield a genuine epistemic-doxastic logic since the two notions will not interact. We need to add interaction axioms. In (Halpern et al. 2009a), only the interaction axioms $\mathsf{KB1}$ and $\mathsf{KB2}$ suggested by Hintikka (1962) are considered. In this section, we will also add the interaction axiom $\mathsf{KB3}$, suggested by Lenzen (1978), since this axiom is characteristic of the notion of strong belief, as we explained in Sect. 5.4.1.

5.6.1 Defining Belief in Terms of Knowledge

We will address the problem of defining belief in terms of knowledge from a syntactic perspective and from a semantic perspective.

5.6.1.1 Syntactic Perspective

Lenzen is the first to note that the belief modality can be defined in terms of knowledge if we adopt $\{\mathsf{KB1}, \mathsf{KB2}, \mathsf{KB3}\}$ as interaction axioms:

Theorem 5.6.2 (Lenzen 1979). *The belief modality B is explicitly defined in the logic $\mathsf{L} = (\mathsf{S4})_K + (\mathsf{KD45})_B + \{\mathsf{KB1}, \mathsf{KB2}, \mathsf{KB3}\}$ by the following definition:*

$$B\varphi \triangleq \hat{K}K\varphi \qquad \text{(Def B)}$$

Consequently, the belief modality B is also defined by Def B *in any logic containing* L.

As a consequence of this theorem, the belief modality is also explicitly defined by $B\varphi \triangleq \hat{K}K\varphi$ in the logics $(\mathsf{S4.x})_K + (\mathsf{KD45})_B + \{\mathsf{KB2}, \mathsf{KB1}, \mathsf{KB3}\}$, where x ranges over $\{.2, .3, .3.2, .4\}$. This result is in contrast with Theorem 4.8 of Halpern et al. (2009a), from which it follows that the belief modality can*not* be explicitly defined in the logic $(\mathsf{S4.x})_K + (\mathsf{KD45})_B + \{\mathsf{KB1}, \mathsf{KB2}\}$, and so on for any $\mathsf{x} \in \{.2, .3, .3.2, .4\}$. We see here that the increase in expressivity due to the addition of the interaction axiom KB3 plays an important role in bridging the gap between belief and knowledge. Note that the definition Def B of belief in terms of knowledge corresponds to the interaction axiom KB4, which has already been discussed in Sect. 5.4.1.

5.6.1.2 Semantic Perspective

Given that Theorem 5.6.2 shows that the belief modality B can be defined in terms of the knowledge modality K, we would expect that the belief accessibility relation R_B could also be 'defined' in terms of the knowledge accessibility relation $\mathcal{R}$ in any frame that validates $\mathsf{L} = (\mathsf{S4})_K + (\mathsf{KD45})_B + \{\mathsf{KB1}, \mathsf{KB2}, \mathsf{KB3}\}$. The following result, already pointed out by Stalnaker (2006) (without proof), shows that this is indeed the case:

Theorem 5.6.3. *Let $\mathcal{F}$ be a frame such that $\mathcal{F} \models (\mathsf{S4})_K + (\mathsf{KD45})_B + \{\mathsf{KB1}, \mathsf{KB2}, \mathsf{KB3}\}$. Then, for all $w, v \in \mathcal{F}$, it holds that*

$$wR_Bv \quad \textit{iff} \quad \textit{for all } u \in \mathcal{F}, \ w\mathcal{R}u \textit{ implies } u\mathcal{R}v \qquad (\mathsf{Def}\ \mathsf{R_B})$$

Note that if we are in a world w such that wR_Bw, then the accessibility relation for knowledge $\mathcal{R}$ is Euclidean at w and axiom 5 holds at w. But according to our analysis in Sect. 5.4.1, this also entails that the notions of knowledge and belief collapse into one another (the proof in Footnote 17 can be adapted to this particular setting). Therefore, in the logic $\mathsf{L} = (\mathsf{S4})_K + (\mathsf{KD45})_B + \{\mathsf{KB1}, \mathsf{KB2}, \mathsf{KB3}\}$, the following principle holds:

If *all* the agent's beliefs hold true,
then her beliefs are actually all knowledge.

If it turns out that the agent has a single erroneous belief, then the conclusion of this principle obviously does not hold anymore. This principle is intuitively correct and can be explained informally by the following reasoning. If all my beliefs are correct (true), then the justification of any specific belief φ is also 'correct', since this very justification is based on my own beliefs. Therefore, any specific belief φ is justified and this justification is in a certain sense 'correct'. Consequently, all my beliefs φ turn out in fact to be knowledge.

Note that this principle holds in any logic that extends L. In particular, all the logics considered in the rest of this paper validate this reasonable principle.

5.6.2 *Defining Knowledge in Terms of Belief*

We will address the problem of defining knowledge in terms of belief from a syntactic perspective and from a semantic perspective.

5.6.2.1 Syntactic Perspective

Defining knowledge in terms of belief depends on the logic of knowledge that we deal with. As the following proposition shows, knowledge can be defined in terms of belief if the logic of knowledge is S4.4, but not if the logic of knowledge is S4 and S4.x, where x ranges over $\{.2, .3, .3.2\}$.

Theorem 5.6.4. • *The knowledge modality K is explicitly defined in the logic* $(S4.4)_K + (KD45)_B + \{KB1, KB2, KB3\}$ *by the following definition:*

$$K\varphi \triangleq \varphi \wedge B\varphi \qquad \text{(Def K)}$$

- *The knowledge modality K cannot be explicitly defined in the logics* $(S4.x)_K + (KD45)_B + \{KB1, KB2, KB3\}$ *for any* $x \in \{.2, .3, .3.2\}$.

This result can be contrasted with Theorem 4.1 of Halpern et al. (2009a), from which it follows that the knowledge modality can*not* be explicitly defined in the logic $(S4.4)_K + (KD45)_B + \{KB1, KB2\}$. We see once again that the increase in expressivity due to the addition of the interaction axiom KB3 plays an important role in bridging the gap between belief and knowledge.

5.6.2.2 Semantic Perspective

As a semantic counterpart to Theorem 5.6.4, the knowledge accessibility relation K cannot be 'defined' in a frame that validates the logic $L = (S4)_K + (KD45)_B + \{KB1, KB2, KB3\}$. Therefore, there are, in principle, several possible ways to 'extend' the belief accessibility relation R_B to a knowledge accessibility relation $\mathcal{R}$. Indeed, each interaction axiom *defines* a class of epistemic-doxastic frames (Blackburn et al. 2001, Definition 3.2). This imposes some constraints on the knowledge accessibility relation $\mathcal{R}$, though without determining it completely. We are now going to present these constraints.

The interaction axiom KB1 defines the class of epistemic-doxastic frames $\mathcal{F}$ such that for all $w, v \in \mathcal{F}$,

$$\text{If } wR_Bv \text{ then } w\mathcal{R}v \qquad (5.1)$$

The addition of the interaction axioms KB2 and KB3 to KB1 defines the class F of epistemic-doxastic frames $\mathcal{F}$ such that for all $w, v \in \mathcal{F}$,

$$\text{If } wR_Bw \text{ then } (w\mathcal{R}v \text{ iff } wR_Bv) \tag{5.2}$$

So, we still have to specify the worlds accessible by $\mathcal{R}$ for the worlds w such that it is *not* the case that wR_Bw. Indeed, if wR_Bw, then it holds that $\mathcal{R}(w) = R_B(w)$ according to Eq. 5.2.

In (Stalnaker 2006), Stalnaker introduces four possible extensions of the belief accessibility relation R_B to a knowledge accessibility relations $\mathcal{R}$. These four possible extensions turn out to correspond to our four logics of knowledge: S4.2, S4.3, S4.3.2 and S4.4.

1. The first extension consists in the reflexive closure of the accessibility relation R_B. This is the minimal extension possible and it yields the objectionable definition of knowledge as true belief, whose logic is S4.4.[19]
2. The second extension consists in defining $w\mathcal{R}v$ as ((wR_Bw and wR_Bv) or (not wR_Bw)). This is the maximal extension possible and it yields the logic S4.3.2.[20]
3. The third extension consists in defining knowledge as true belief which cannot be defeated by any true fact. In other words, a fact is known if and only if it is true and it will still be believed after any possible truthful announcement.[21] This yields the logic S4.3.[22] Lehrer and Paxson proposed to add this last condition to the classical notion of knowledge as justified true belief in order to cope with the 'Gettier Problem' (Lehrer and Paxson 1969).
4. The last extension consists in weakening the condition of the third extension. Stalnaker indeed argues in addition that this definition of knowledge as undefeated true belief should not be a sufficient and necessary condition for knowledge, but rather only a sufficient one. This contention gives the last possible extension of the accessibility relation for belief to an accessibility relation for knowledge.

Note that Rott also investigates systematically, but with the help of a 'sphere' semantics, how a number of epistemological accounts of the notion of knowledge

---

[19]That is, S4 plus .4: $(\varphi \wedge \hat{K}K\psi) \rightarrow K(\varphi \vee \psi)$; see Sect. 5.5.3.

[20]That is, S4 plus .3.2: $(\hat{K}\varphi \wedge \hat{K}K\psi) \rightarrow K(\hat{K}\varphi \vee \psi)$; see Sect. 5.5.3.

[21]For this definition to be consistent, we have to add another constraints that Stalnaker does not mention: in this definition, knowledge should only deal with propositional facts belonging to the propositional language $\mathcal{L}_0$. Indeed, assume that the agent believes non-p (formally $B\neg p$). Then clearly the agent knows that she believes non-p by KB2 (formally $KB\neg p$). However, assume that p is actually true. If we apply this definition of knowledge, then, if she learnt that p (which is true), she should still believe that she believes non-p (formally $BB\neg p$), so she should still believe non-p (formally $B\neg p$), which is of course counterintuitive. This restriction on propositional knowledge does not produce a loss of generality because we assume that the agent knows everything about her own beliefs and disbeliefs.

[22]That is, S4 plus .3: $\hat{K}\varphi \wedge \hat{K}\psi \rightarrow \hat{K}(\varphi \wedge \hat{K}\psi) \vee \hat{K}(\varphi \wedge \psi) \vee \hat{K}(\psi \wedge \hat{K}\varphi)$; see Sect. 5.5.3.

(including Nozick's account) convert belief into knowledge (Rott 2004). Like us, he does so not by considering the notion of justification, but by resorting to other properties such as the stability of beliefs, the sensitivity to truth or the strength of belief and of epistemic position.

5.7 A Derivation of Axioms .2, .3, .3.2, .4 from Interaction Axioms

In this section, we show that the convoluted axioms for knowledge .2, .3, .3.2 and .4 can be derived from understandable interaction axioms if we consider the logic $(\mathsf{S4})_K$ for the notion of knowledge and the logic $(\mathsf{KD45})_B$ (or $(\mathsf{P})_{B^\psi}$) for the notion of belief (or conditional belief).

5.7.1 *Derivation of Axiom .2*

Theorem 5.6.2 can be equivalently formulated as $(\mathsf{S4.x})_K + (\mathsf{KD45})_B + \{\mathsf{KB1}, \mathsf{KB2}, \mathsf{KB3}\} = (\mathsf{S4.x})_K + (\mathsf{KD45})_B + \{\mathsf{KB1}, \mathsf{KB2}, \mathsf{KB3}\} + \{B\varphi \leftrightarrow \hat{B}^K K\varphi\}$. Note, however, that Lenzen proved, in (Lenzen 1979), an even stronger result, which is the following[23]:

$$(\mathsf{S4})_K + (\mathsf{KD45})_B + \{\mathsf{KB2}, \mathsf{KB1}, \mathsf{KB3}\} = (\mathsf{S4.2})_K + \{B\varphi \leftrightarrow \hat{B}^K K s\varphi\}$$

This proposition states not only that the belief modality is definable in terms of knowledge, but also that axiom .2 is derivable from the interaction axioms $\{\mathsf{KB2}, \mathsf{KB1}, \mathsf{KB3}\}$ in the logic $(\mathsf{S4})_K + (\mathsf{KD45})_B$, that is:

$$.2 \in (\mathsf{S4})_K + (\mathsf{KD45})_B + \{\mathsf{KB1}, \mathsf{KB2}, \mathsf{KB3}\} \qquad (.2)$$

S4.2 is the logic of knowledge propounded by Lenzen and Stalnaker. It is also the logic of the notion of *justified knowledge* studied by Voorbraak in (Voorbraak 1993).

5.7.2 *Derivation of Axiom .3*

Lenzen does not provide an intuitive characterization of axiom .3 in terms of interaction axioms. In fact, I believe that such a characterization is not possible if

[23]Lenzen uses axiom $\mathsf{KB3}'$ instead of KB3, but one can easily show that the replacement does not invalidate the proposition.

we consider the language $\mathcal{L}_B$ only, and that we need to consider a more expressive language. It turns out that $\mathcal{L}_{KB^\psi}$ is sufficiently expressive to derive .3:

$$.3 \in (\mathsf{S4})_K + (\mathsf{P})_{B^\psi} + \{\mathsf{KB1}^\psi, \mathsf{KB5}^\psi, \mathsf{KB4}^\psi\} \tag{.3}$$

We can recall that $\mathsf{KB1}^\psi$ stands for $K\varphi \to B^\psi\varphi$, $\mathsf{KB5}^\psi$ for $\hat{K}\psi \to \neg B^\psi\bot$ and $\mathsf{KB4}^\psi$ for $\neg B^\psi\varphi \to K(\hat{K}\psi \to \neg B^\psi\varphi)$.

The logic S4.3 is propounded as the logic of knowledge by van der Hoek (1993).

5.7.3 Derivation of Axiom .3.2

With a language without conditional belief operator, Lenzen provides, in (Lenzen 1979), a derivation of .3.2 by resorting to the interaction axiom KB5 below:

$$.3.2 \in (\mathsf{S4})_K + (\mathsf{KD45})_B + \{\mathsf{KB1},\mathsf{KB2},\mathsf{KB3},\mathsf{KB5}\}$$

where

$$(K\varphi \to K\psi) \wedge B(K\varphi \to K\psi) \to K(K\varphi \to K\psi) \tag{KB5}$$

As it turns out, Lenzen proves, in (Lenzen 1979), an even stronger result, which is the following:

$$(\mathsf{S4.3.2})_K + (\mathsf{KD45})_B + \{\mathsf{KB1},\mathsf{KB2},\mathsf{KB3}\} = (\mathsf{S4})_K + (\mathsf{KD45})_B + \{\mathsf{KB1},\mathsf{KB2},\mathsf{KB3},\mathsf{KB5}\}$$

Note that the interaction axiom KB5 is a special instance of the definition of knowledge as true belief, $p \wedge Bp \to Kp$, since p is substituted here by $K\varphi \to K\psi$. Even with this observation, it is still difficult to provide an intuitive reading of this interaction axiom. Instead, we can show that .3.2 is derivable in a logic *with* conditional belief by means of the interaction axioms KB5, which is easier to grasp.

$$.3.2 \in (\mathsf{S4})_K + (\mathsf{P})_{B^\psi} + \{\mathsf{KB1}^\psi, \mathsf{KB5}^\psi, \mathsf{KB4}^\psi, \mathsf{KB6}^\psi\} \tag{.3.2}$$

We can recall that the key interaction axiom $\mathsf{KB6}^\psi$ stands for $B\neg\psi \to (B^\psi\varphi \to K(\psi \to \varphi))$.

5.7.4 Derivation of Axiom .4

Axiom .4 can be seen as a weakening of axiom 5 since it can be rewritten as follows: $p \to (\neg K\varphi \to K\neg K\varphi)$. The logic S4.4 is sometimes called the logic of 'true belief'. This denomination is indeed very appropriate. Lenzen proves, in (Lenzen 1979), the following equation:

$$(\mathsf{S4.4})_K + (\mathsf{KD45})_B + \{\mathsf{KB1},\mathsf{KB2},\mathsf{KB3}\} = (\mathsf{S4})_K + (\mathsf{KD45})_B + \{\mathsf{KB4}\}$$

where we recall that the interaction axiom KB4 is $K\varphi \leftrightarrow \varphi \wedge B\varphi$. From this equation, one can easily derive the following result:

$$.4 \in (\mathsf{S4})_K + (\mathsf{KD45})_B + \{\mathsf{KB1}, \mathsf{KB2}, \mathsf{KB3}, \mathsf{KB5}\} \qquad (.4)$$

Kutschera argues for S4.4 as the logic of knowledge (von Kutschera 1976).

5.8 Concluding Remarks

In this paper, we have reviewed the most prominent principles of logics of knowledge and belief, and the principles relating knowledge, belief and conditional belief to one another. In doing so, we have encountered most of the problems that have beset epistemic logic during its relatively short (modern) history. We have shown that the convoluted axioms .3 and .3.2 for knowledge, which can hardly be understood in terms of interaction axioms dealing with (strong) belief only, can be expressed in terms of interaction axioms dealing with *conditional* beliefs, which are easier to grasp. We have also demonstrated that the addition of the interaction axiom $B\varphi \rightarrow BK\varphi$, which is characteristic of the notion of (strong) belief, plays an important role in bridging the gap between the notions of belief and knowledge.

As we explained in Sect. 5.3.2, the term "belief" has different meanings: my (weak) belief that it will be sunny tomorrow is different from my (strong) belief that the Fermat-Wilson theorem holds true. In this paper, we have only focused on the notion of strong belief. To deal with the notion of weak belief, we could enrich our language either with a probabilistic-doxastic operator $Prob(\varphi) \geq r$ (where r ranges over $]0.5; 1[$), or with a graded belief modality $B^n\varphi$ (where n ranges over $\mathbb{N}$), or simply with a weak belief operator $B_w\varphi$. This latter language actually corresponds to a language introduced by Lenzen in (Lenzen 2004). Its conditionalized version corresponds to the full language of Lamarre and Shoham (1994), which the authors of this paper have completely axiomatized.

Even if our aim was not to argue in favour of a particular logic of knowledge, it is nevertheless clear from our discussion that, on the one hand, logics like S4.2 or S4.3 are better suited to reasoning about the knowledge of agents in the most general kinds of situations; on the other hand, the simple and widely used logic S5 is more appropriate for dealing with particular situations where agents cannot have erroneous beliefs, as we have already argued at the end of Sect. 5.4.1. As a matter of fact, the logic S5 is an enrichment of these logics with extra assumptions (it is actually a superset of them). More work is needed to fully understand the logics between S4 and S5 (exclusive) and in particular to investigate and study their dynamic extensions.

5.9 Plausibility Space and Epistemic-Plausibility Space

5.9.1 Plausibility Space

If W is a non-empty set of possible worlds, then an *algebra over* W is a set of subsets of W closed under union and complementation. In the rest of the paper, D is a non-empty set partially ordered by a relation $\leq$ (so that $\leq$ is reflexive, transitive and anti-symmetric). We further assume that D contains two special elements $\top$ and $\bot$ such that for all $d \in D$, $\bot \leq d \leq \top$. As usual, we define the ordering $<$ by taking $d_1 < d_2$ if and only if $d_1 \leq d_2$ and $d_1 \neq d_2$. A *(qualitative) plausibility space* is a tuple $S = (W, \mathcal{A}, Pl)$ where:

- W is a non-empty set of possible worlds;
- $\mathcal{A}$ is an algebra over W;
- $Pl : \mathcal{A} \to D$ is a function mapping sets of $\mathcal{A}$ into D and satisfying the following conditions:

  A0 $Pl(W) = \top$ and $Pl(\emptyset) = \bot$;

  A1 If $A \subseteq B$, then $Pl(A) \leq Pl(B)$;

  A2 If A, B, and C are pairwise disjoint sets, $Pl(A \cup B) > Pl(C)$, and $Pl(A \cup C) > Pl(B)$, then $Pl(A) > Pl(B \cup C)$;

  A3 If $Pl(A) = Pl(B) = \bot$, then $Pl(A \cup B) = \bot$.

We denote by $\mathcal{S}$ the class of all (qualitative) plausibility spaces.

5.9.2 Epistemic-Plausibility Space and Truth Conditions

An *epistemic-plausibility space* is a tuple $\mathcal{M} = (W, R, V, \mathcal{P})$ where:

- W is a non-empty set of possible worlds;
- $\mathcal{R} \in 2^{W \times W}$ is a binary relation over W called an *accessibility relation*;
- $V : \Phi \to 2^W$ is a function called a *valuation* mapping propositional variables to subsets of W;
- $\mathcal{P} : W \to \mathcal{S}$ is a function called a *plausibility assignment* mapping each world $w \in W$ to a (qualitative) plausibility space $(W_w, \mathcal{A}_w, Pl_w)$ such that $W_w \subseteq W$.

Let $\varphi \in \mathcal{L}_{KB^{\psi}}$, let $\mathcal{M}$ be an epistemic-plausibility space and let $w \in \mathcal{M}$. The satisfaction relation $\mathcal{M}, w \models \varphi$ is defined inductively as follows:

$$\begin{array}{lll}
\mathcal{M}, w \models p & \text{iff} & w \in V(p) \\
\mathcal{M}, w \models \varphi \wedge \varphi' & \text{iff} & \mathcal{M}, w \models \varphi \text{ and } \mathcal{M}, w \models \varphi' \\
\mathcal{M}, w \models \neg\varphi & \text{iff} & \text{not } \mathcal{M}, w \models \varphi \\
\mathcal{M}, w \models B^{\psi}\varphi & \text{iff} & \text{either } Pl_w(\llbracket\psi\rrbracket_w) = \bot \text{ or } Pl_w(\llbracket\psi \wedge \varphi\rrbracket_w) > \\
& & \qquad Pl_w(\llbracket\psi \wedge \neg\varphi\rrbracket_w) \\
\mathcal{M}, w \models K\varphi & \text{iff} & \text{for all } v \in \mathcal{R}(w), \mathcal{M}, v \models \varphi
\end{array}$$

where $\llbracket\varphi\rrbracket_w = \{v \in W_w \mid \mathcal{M}, v \models \varphi\}$. We abusively write $w \in \mathcal{M}$ for $w \in W$, and we also write $\mathcal{M} \models \varphi$ when for all $w \in \mathcal{M}$, $\mathcal{M}, w \models \varphi$. If Γ is a set of formulae (possibly infinite), we write $\mathcal{M} \models \Gamma$ when $\mathcal{M} \models \varphi$ for all $\varphi \in \Gamma$.

5.10 Proofs of Theorems 5.6.3 and 5.6.4

5.10.1 Proof of Theorem 5.6.3

Theorem 5.10.1. *Let $\mathcal{F}$ be a frame such that $\mathcal{F} \models (S4)_K + (KD45)_B + \{KB1, KB2, KB3\}$. Then, for all $w, v \in \mathcal{F}$, it holds that*

$$wR_Bv \textit{ iff for all } u \in \mathcal{F}, w\mathcal{R}u \textit{ implies } u\mathcal{R}v \qquad \text{(Def R}_\text{B})$$

Proof. Let $\mathcal{F} = (W, R_B, R_K)$ be an epistemic-doxastic frame such that $\mathcal{F} \models (\mathsf{S4})_K + (\mathsf{KD45})_B + \{\mathsf{KB1}, \mathsf{KB2}, \mathsf{KB3}\}$. Then, because the axioms T, D, 4 and 5 define, respectively, the properties of reflexivity, seriality, transitivity and Euclideanity, R_B is serial, transitive and Euclidean, and $\mathcal{R}$ is reflexive and transitive. Moreover, by the validity of KB1, $R_B \subseteq \mathcal{R}$. We can now prove that (Def $\mathsf{R_B}$) holds.

- From left to right: assume towards a contradiction that there are $w, v, u \in \mathcal{F}$ such that $v \in R_B(w)$ and $u \in \mathcal{R}(w)$ and not $v \in \mathcal{R}(u)$.

  Let $p \in \Phi$. We define a valuation V over W such that $V(p) = R_B(w)$. Let $\mathcal{M}$ be the epistemic-doxastic model defined by $\mathcal{M} = (\mathcal{F}, V)$. Then, $\mathcal{M}, w \models Bp$. So, $\mathcal{M}, w \models KBp$ by the validity of KB2. Therefore, $\mathcal{M}, u \models Bp$ because $u \in \mathcal{R}(w)$. So, $\mathcal{M}, u \models \hat{B}p$ because R_B is serial. Then, there is $t \in R_B(u)$ such that $\mathcal{M}, t \models p$. That is, there is $t \in R_B(u)$ such that $t \in R_B(w)$, because $V(p) = R_B(w)$. However, by assumption, $v \in R_B(w)$. Therefore, because R_B is Euclidean, $v \in R_B(t)$. So, $t \in R_B(u)$ and $v \in R_B(t)$. Therefore, by the transitivity of R_B, $v \in R_B(u)$. Then, $v \in \mathcal{R}(u)$, because $R_B \subseteq \mathcal{R}$. This is impossible by assumption. We therefore reach a contradiction.

- From right to left: assume towards a contradiction that there are $w, v \in \mathcal{F}$ such that $v \notin R_B(w)$ and for all $u \in \mathcal{F}$, $u \in \mathcal{R}(w)$ implies $v \in \mathcal{R}(u)$.

  Let $p \in \Phi$. We define a valuation V such that $V(p) = R_B(w)$. Let $\mathcal{M}$ be the epistemic-doxastic model defined by $\mathcal{M} = (\mathcal{F}, V)$. Then, $\mathcal{M}, w \models Bp$. Then, $\mathcal{M}, w \models BKp$ by validity of KB3. Because R_B is serial, there is $u \in R_B(w)$ such that $\mathcal{M}, u \models Kp$. Now, because $R_B \subseteq \mathcal{R}$, we also have that $u \in \mathcal{R}(w)$. Then, by assumption $v \in \mathcal{R}(u)$. Therefore, $\mathcal{M}, v \models p$. Then, by the definition of V, we have that $v \in R_B(w)$. This is impossible by assumption. We therefore reach a contradiction.

5.10.2 Proof of Theorem 5.6.4

Theorem 5.10.2. • *The knowledge modality K is explicitly defined in the logic* $(S4.4)_K + (KD45)_B + \{KB1, KB2, KB3\}$ *by* $K\varphi \triangleq \varphi \wedge B\varphi$.
- *The knowledge modality K cannot be explicitly defined in the logics* $(S4.x)_K + (KD45)_B + \{KB1, KB2, KB3\}$ *for any* $x \in \{.2, .3, .3.2\}$.

Proof. The first item in this theorem is owed to Lenzen (1979). We will only prove the second item. The proof method is similar to the proof method for Theorem 4.1 of Halpern et al. (2009a). If K is explicitly defined in $\mathsf{L} = (\mathsf{S4.3.2})_K + (\mathsf{KD45})_B + \{\mathsf{KB1,KB2,KB3}\}$ by $Kp \leftrightarrow \delta$, then for every epistemic-doxastic model $\mathcal{M}$ such that $\mathcal{M} \models \mathsf{L}$, it holds that $[\![Kp]\!]_{\mathcal{M}} = [\![\delta]\!]_{\mathcal{M}}$, and therefore $[\![Kp]\!]_{\mathcal{M}} \in \{[\![\varphi]\!]_{\mathcal{M}} \mid \varphi \in \mathcal{L}_B\}$. We prove the theorem by constructing an epistemic-doxastic model $\mathcal{M}$ such that $\mathcal{M} \models \mathsf{L}$ and such that $[\![Kp]\!]_{\mathcal{M}} \notin \{[\![\varphi]\!]_{\mathcal{M}} \mid \varphi \in \mathcal{L}_B\}$.

Consider the following epistemic-doxastic frame $F = (W, R)$ where $W = \{w_1, w_2, w_3, w_4\}$, $R_B = \{(w_1, w_1), (w_2, w_2), (w_3, w_2), (w_4, w_2)\}$, and $\mathcal{R} = R_B \cup \{(w_3, w_3), (w_4, w_4), (w_3, w_4), (w_4, w_3)\}$. Let $\mathcal{M} = (F, V)$ be the epistemic-doxastic model based on F such that V maps each primitive proposition to $\{w_1, w_2, w_4\}$. Clearly, $\mathcal{M} \models \mathsf{L}$. One can also show by induction on the structure of formulas in $\mathcal{L}_B$ that $\{[\![\varphi]\!]_{\mathcal{M}} \mid \varphi \in \mathcal{L}_B\} = \{\{w_1, w_2, w_4\}, \{w_3\}, \emptyset, W\}$, but $[\![Kp]\!]_{\mathcal{M}} = \{w_1, w_2\}$.

5.11 Proofs of Equations .3 and .3.2

5.11.1 Proof of Equation .3

$$.3 \in (\mathsf{S4})_K + (\mathsf{P})_{B^\psi} + \left\{\mathsf{KB1}^\psi, \mathsf{KB5}^\psi, \mathsf{KB4}^\psi\right\} \qquad (.3)$$

Proof. The proof of Eq. .3 is purely syntactic. Note first that

$$B^{\psi}\bot \leftrightarrow B^{\psi}\neg\psi \in (\mathsf{P})_{B^{\psi}} \tag{5.3}$$

This fact will be used in the following proof:

1	$\hat{K}\varphi \wedge \hat{K}\psi$	Hypothesis
2	$\hat{K}(\varphi \vee \psi)$	1, K
3	$\neg B^{\psi\vee\varphi}\bot$	2, KB5$^{\psi}$
4	$\neg B^{\varphi\vee\psi}\neg(\varphi \vee \psi)$	3, Eq. 5.3
5	$\neg B^{\varphi\vee\psi}(\neg\varphi \wedge \neg\psi)$	4, rewriting
6	$\neg\left(B^{\varphi\vee\psi}\neg\varphi \wedge B^{\varphi\vee\psi}\neg\psi\right)$	5, C2
7	$\neg B^{\varphi\vee\psi}\neg\varphi \vee \neg B^{\varphi\vee\psi}\neg\psi$	rewriting
8	$K\left(\hat{K}(\varphi \vee \psi) \to \neg B^{\varphi\vee\psi}\neg\varphi\right) \vee K\left(\hat{K}(\varphi \vee \psi) \to \neg B^{\varphi\vee\psi}\neg s\psi\right)$	7, KB4$^{\psi}$
9	$K\left(\psi \to \neg B^{\varphi\vee\psi}\neg\varphi\right) \vee K(\varphi \to \neg B^{\varphi\vee\psi}\neg\psi)$	8, T
10	$K\left(\psi \to \hat{K}\varphi\right) \vee K\left(\varphi \to \hat{K}\psi\right)$	9, KB1$^{\psi}$
11	$\hat{K}(\psi \wedge \hat{K}\varphi) \vee \hat{K}(\varphi \wedge \hat{K}\psi)$	1, 10, K
12	$\hat{K}(\psi \wedge \hat{K}\varphi) \vee \hat{K}(\varphi \wedge \hat{K}\psi) \vee \hat{K}(\varphi \wedge \psi)$	11, K

5.11.2 Proof of Equation .3.2

$$.3.2 \in (\mathsf{S4})_K + (\mathsf{P})_{B^{\psi}} + \left\{\mathsf{KB1}^{\psi}, \mathsf{KB5}^{\psi}, \mathsf{KB4}^{\psi}, \mathsf{KB6}^{\psi}\right\} \tag{.3.2}$$

We first prove a lemma:

Lemma 5.11.1. *Let $\mathcal{M}$ be an epistemic-plausibility space. If $\mathcal{M} \models (S4)_K + (P)_{B^{\psi}} + \{KB1^{\psi}, KB4^{\psi}\}$, then $\mathcal{M} \models \left(\hat{K}\psi \to \hat{K}(\psi \wedge K(\psi \to \varphi))\right) \to B^{\psi}\varphi$.*

Proof. Let $w \in \mathcal{M}$ and assume that $\mathcal{M}, w \models \hat{K}\psi \to \hat{K}(\psi \wedge K(\psi \to \varphi))$. Assume towards a contradiction that $\mathcal{M}, w \models \neg B^{\psi}\varphi$. Then, by definition, $Pl_w([\![\psi]\!]_w) \neq \bot$ and $Pl_w([\![\psi \wedge \varphi]\!]_w) \not> Pl_w([\![\psi \wedge \varphi]\!]_w)$. Because $Pl_w([\![\psi]\!]_w) \neq \bot$, it holds that $\mathcal{M}, w \models \neg B^{\psi}\bot$. Now, because $\models B^{\psi}\psi$ by Ref, we have that $\models B^{\psi}\neg\psi \to B^{\psi}\bot$ by axiom C2, i.e., $\models \neg B^{\psi}\bot \to \neg B^{\psi}\neg\psi$. Therefore, $\mathcal{M}, w \models \neg B^{\psi}\neg\psi$. So, by axiom KB1$^{\psi}$, $\mathcal{M}, w \models \hat{K}\psi$. Then, by assumption, $\mathcal{M}, w \models \hat{K}(\psi \wedge K(\psi \to \varphi))$. So, there is $v \in \mathcal{R}(w)$ such that $\mathcal{M}, w \models \psi \wedge K(\psi \to \varphi)$. Therefore, $\mathcal{M}, v \models K(\psi \to \varphi)$, and so $\mathcal{M}, v \models B^{\psi}(\psi \to \varphi)$ by application of axiom KB1$^{\psi}$. Therefore, $\mathcal{M}, w \models B^{\psi}\varphi$ because $\models B^{\psi}\psi$. Now, $\mathcal{M}, w \models \neg B^{\psi}\varphi$, and so $\mathcal{M}, w \models K\left(\hat{K}\psi \to \neg B^{\psi}\varphi\right)$

by axiom $\mathsf{KB4}^{\psi}$. So, $\mathcal{M}, v \models \hat{K}\psi \rightarrow \neg B^{\psi}\varphi$. Since $\mathcal{M}, v \models \psi$, we also have that $\mathcal{M}, v \models \hat{K}\psi$ by axiom T. Therefore, $\mathcal{M}, v \models \neg B^{\psi}\varphi$, which contradicts our previous deduction. So, we reach a contradiction, and then $\mathcal{M}, w \models B^{\psi}\varphi$.

We can now prove Eq. .3.2.

Proof. Let $\mathcal{M}$ be a model and $w \in \mathcal{M}$. Assume that $\mathcal{M} \models (\mathsf{S4})_K + (\mathsf{K})_{B^{\psi}} + \{\mathsf{KB1}^{\psi}, \mathsf{KB5}^{\psi}, \mathsf{KB4}^{\psi}, \mathsf{KB6}^{\psi}\}$.

Then, by Lemma 5.11.1, $\mathcal{M} \models \left(\hat{K}\psi \rightarrow \hat{K}(\psi \wedge K(\psi \rightarrow \varphi))\right) \rightarrow B^{\psi}\varphi$, i.e., $\mathcal{M} \models \neg B^{\psi}\varphi \rightarrow \left(\hat{K} \wedge K\left(\psi \rightarrow \hat{K}(\psi \wedge \neg\varphi)\right)\right)$. Now, because $\mathcal{M} \models \{\mathsf{KB1}^{\psi}, \mathsf{KB6}^{\psi}\}$, it holds that $\mathcal{M} \models B\neg\psi \rightarrow \left(K(\psi \rightarrow \varphi) \leftrightarrow B^{\psi}\varphi\right)$. Therefore, $\mathcal{M} \models B\neg\psi \wedge \hat{K}(\psi \wedge \neg\varphi) \rightarrow \left(\hat{K}\psi \wedge K\left(\psi \rightarrow \hat{K}(\psi \wedge \neg\varphi)\right)\right)$. So,

$$\mathcal{M} \models \left(\hat{K}K\neg\psi \wedge \hat{K}(\psi \wedge \varphi)\right) \rightarrow \hat{K}\psi \wedge K\left(\psi \rightarrow \hat{K}(\psi \wedge \varphi)\right) \tag{5.4}$$

Now, assume that $\mathcal{M}, w \models \hat{K}\varphi \wedge \hat{K}K\neg\psi$. We will show that

$$\mathcal{M}, w \models K\left(\hat{K}\varphi \vee \neg\psi\right) \tag{5.5}$$

1. If $\mathcal{M}, w \models K\neg\psi$, then (5.5) holds.
2. If $\mathcal{M}, w \models \hat{K}\psi$, then, because $\mathcal{M} \models (\mathsf{S4})_K + (\mathsf{K})_{B^{\psi}} + \{\mathsf{KB1}^{\psi}, \mathsf{KB5}^{\psi}, \mathsf{KB4}^{\psi}\}$, it holds that $\mathcal{M} \models .3$ by Eq. .3.

   Now, because $\mathcal{M}, w \models \hat{K}\varphi$ by assumption, by application of .3, it holds that either $\mathcal{M}, w \models \hat{K}(\psi \wedge \hat{K}\varphi)$ or $\mathcal{M}, w \models \hat{K}(\varphi \wedge \hat{K}\psi)$.

   a. If $\mathcal{M}, w \models \hat{K}(\psi \wedge \hat{K}\varphi)$, then by application of (5.4), it holds that
      $\mathcal{M}, w \models \hat{K}\psi \wedge K\left(\psi \rightarrow \hat{K}(\psi \wedge \hat{K}\varphi)\right)$,
      then $\mathcal{M}, w \models K(\psi \rightarrow \hat{K}\hat{K}\varphi)$
      i.e., $\mathcal{M}, w \models K(\psi \rightarrow \hat{K}\varphi)$
      i.e., $\mathcal{M}, w \models K(\neg\psi \vee \hat{K}\varphi)$
   b. If $\mathcal{M}, w \models \hat{K}(\varphi \wedge \hat{K}\psi)$, then, because $\models \hat{K}K\neg\hat{K}\psi \leftrightarrow \hat{K}K\neg\psi$, we have that $\mathcal{M}, w \models \hat{K}K\neg\hat{K}\psi$. Therefore, by application of (5.4), it holds that
      $\mathcal{M}, w \models \hat{K}\hat{K}\psi \wedge K\left(\hat{K}\psi \rightarrow \hat{K}\left(\hat{K}\psi \wedge \varphi\right)\right)$.
      So, $\mathcal{M}, w \models K\left(\hat{K}\psi \rightarrow \hat{K}\varphi\right)$
      i.e., $\mathcal{M}, w \models K(\psi \rightarrow \hat{K}\varphi)$ because $\models \psi \rightarrow \hat{K}\psi$,
      i.e., $\mathcal{M}, w \models K(\neg\psi \vee \hat{K}\varphi)$.

Acknowledgements I thank Manuel Rebuschi and Franck Lihoreau for helpful comments on this paper. I also thank the anonymous English native speaker referee for detailed comments.

References

E. Adams, *The Logic of Conditionals*. Volume 86 of Synthese Library (Springer, Dordrecht, 1975)

C.E. Alchourrón, P. Gärdenfors, D. Makinson, On the logic of theory change: partial meet contraction and revision functions. J. Symb. Log. **50**(2), 510–530 (1985)

H. Arlo-Costa, Qualitative and probabilistic models of full belief, in *Logic Colloquium'98*, Prague, ed. by S. Buss, P. Hajek, P. Pudlak. Lecture Notes on Logic, vol. 13 (1999)

S. Artemov, M. Fitting, Justification logic, in *The Stanford Encyclopedia of Philosophy*, Fall 2012 edn., ed. by E.N. Zalta. http://plato.stanford.edu/archives/fall2012/entries/logic-justification/

G. Aucher, A combined system for update logic and belief revision, in *Proceedings of the PRIMA*, Auckland, ed. by M. Barley, N.K. Kasabov. Volume 3371 of Lecture Notes in Computer Science (Springer, 2004), pp. 1–17

G. Aucher, Interpreting an action from what we perceive and what we expect. J. Appl. Non-Class. Log. **17**(1), 9–38 (2007)

G. Aucher, An internal version of epistemic logic. Studia Logica **1**, 1–22 (2010)

A.J. Ayer, *The Problem of Knowledge* (Penguin books, London, 1956)

A. Baltag, S. Smets, Conditional doxastic models: a qualitative approach to dynamic belief revision. Electron. Notes Theor. Comput. Sci. **165**, 5–21 (2006)

A. Baltag, S. Smets, A qualitative theory of dynamic interactive belief revision, in *Logic and the Foundations of Game and Decision Theory (LOFT 7)*, ed. by G. Bonanno, W. van der Hoek, M.J. Wooldridge. Texts in Logic and Games, vol. 3 (Amsterdam University Press, Amsterdam, 2008a), pp. 9–58

A. Baltag, S. Smets, The logic of conditional doxastic actions, in *New Perspectives on Games and Interaction*, ed. by K.R. Apt, R. van Rooij. Texts on Logic and Games, vol. 4 (Amsterdam University Press, Amsterdam, 2008b). http://www.illc.uva.nl/TLG/index.php%3Fpage=10_1_3_4.html

P. Blackburn, M. de Rijke, Y. Venema, *Modal Logic*. Volume 53 of Cambridge Tracts in Computer Science (Cambridge University Press, Cambridge/New York, 2001)

O. Board, Dynamic interactive epistemology. Games Econ. Behav. **49**, 49–80 (2004)

D. Bonnay, P. Egré, Inexact knowledge with introspection. J. Philos. Log. **38**(2), 179–227 (2008)

C. Boutilier, Conditional logics of normality: a modal approach. Artif. Intell. **68**(1), 87–154 (1994)

J. Broersen, M. Dastani, J. Hulstijn, Z. Huang, L.W.N. van der Torre, The BOID architecture: conflicts between beliefs, obligations, intentions and desires, in *Proceedings of the Fifth International Conference on Autonomous Agents*, Montreal, 2001, pp. 9–16

H.-N. Castañeda, Review of 'knowledge and belief'. J. Symb. Log. **29**, 132–134 (1964)

P. Cohen, H. Levesque, Intention is choice with commitment. Artif. Intell. **42**, 213–261 (1990)

M. de Rijke, A note on graded modal logic. Studia Logica **64**(2), 271–283 (2000)

F. Deschene, Y. Wang, To know or not to know: epistemic approach to security protocol verification. Synthese **177**(Supplement 1), 51–76 (2010)

D. Dubois, H. Prade, Possibilistic logic, preferential model and related issue, in *Proceedings of the 12th International Conference on Artificial Intelligence (IJCAI)*, Sydney (Morgan Kaufman, 1991), pp. 419–425

R. Fagin, J.Y. Halpern, Belief, awareness, and limited reasoning. Artif. Intell. **34**(1), 39–76 (1987)

R. Fagin, J. Halpern, Y. Moses, M. Vardi, *Reasoning About Knowledge* (MIT, Cambridge, 1995)

K. Fine, In so many possible worlds. Notre Dame J. Form. Log. **13**(4), 516–520 (1972)

L. Floridi, The logic of being informed. Logique et Analyse **49**(196), 433–460 (2006)

N. Friedman, J.Y. Halpern, Modeling belief in dynamic systems, Part I: foundations. Artif. Intell. **95**(2), 257–316 (1997)

N. Friedman, J.Y. Halpern, Plausibility measures and default reasoning. J. ACM **48**(4), 648–685 (2001)

P. Gärdenfors, *Knowledge in Flux (Modeling the Dynamics of Epistemic States)* (Bradford/MIT, Cambridge, 1988)

M. Georgeff, A. Rao, Asymmetry thesis and side-effect problems in linear time and branching time intention logics, in *Proceedings of the Twelfth International Joint Conference on Artificial Intelligence (IJCAI-91)*, Sydney, 1991, pp. 498–504

E. Gettier, Is justified true belief knowledge? Analysis **25**, 121–123 (1963)

P. Gochet, *Logique épistémique et philosophie des mathématiques*, chapter Un problème ouvert en épistémologie: la formalisation du savoir-faire. Philosophie des sciences. Vuibert, 2007

P. Gochet, P. Gribomont, Epistemic logic, in *Twentieth Century Modalities*, ed. by D.M. Gabbay, J. Woods. Handbook of the History of Logic, vol. 7 (Elsevier, Amsterdam, 2006), pp. 99–195

J.Y. Halpern, Should knowledge entail belief? J. Philos. Log. **25**(5), 483–494 (1996)

J. Halpern, *Reasoning About Uncertainty* (MIT, Cambridge, 2003)

J. Halpern, Y. Moses, Knowledge and common knowledge in a distributed environment. J. ACM **37**(3), 549–587 (1990)

J. Halpern, Y. Moses, A guide to completeness and complexity for modal logics of knowledge and belief. Artif. Intell. **54**, 311–379 (1992)

J.Y. Halpern, R. Pucella, Modeling adversaries in a logic for security protocol analysis, in *Formal Aspects of Security*, London, ed. by A.E. Abdallah, P. Ryan, S. Schneider. Volume 2629 of Lecture Notes in Computer Science (Springer, 2002), pp. 115–132

J.Y. Halpern, R. Pucella, Dealing with logical omniscience: expressiveness and pragmatics. Artif. Intell. **175**(1), 220–235 (2011)

J.Y. Halpern, L.C. Rêgo, Reasoning about knowledge of unawareness revisited, in *Proceedings of the TARK*, Berkeley, ed. by A. Heifetz, 2009, pp. 166–173

J.Y. Halpern, D. Samet, E. Segev, Defining knowledge in terms of belief: the modal logic perspective. Rev. Symb. Log. **2**, 469–487 (2009a)

J.Y. Halpern, D. Samet, E. Segev, On definability in multimodal logic. Rev. Symb. Log. **2**, 451–468 (2009b)

A. Heifetz, M. Meier, B. Schipper, Interactive unawareness. J. Econ. Theory **130**(1), 78–94 (2006)

D. Hemp, The KK (knowing that one knows) principle, in *The Internet Encyclopedia of Philosophy*, ed. by J. Fieser, B.H. Dowden (J. Fieser, Martin, 2006). http://www.iep.utm.edu/home/about/, Oct 2006

V. Hendricks, *Mainstream and Formal Epistemology* (Cambridge University Press, Cambridge, 2005)

V. Hendricks, J. Symons (eds.), *8 Bridges Between Formal and Mainstream Epistemology*, vol. 128 (Springer, Dordrecht, 2006)

A. Herzig, Modal probability, belief, and actions. Fundamenta Informaticae **57**(2–4), 323–344 (2003)

J. Hintikka, *Knowledge and Belief, an Introduction to the Logic of the Two Notions* (Cornell University Press, Ithaca/London, 1962)

S. Kraus, D. Lehmann, Knowledge, belief and time, in *Automata, Languages and Programming*, ed. by L. Kott. Volume 226 of Lecture Notes in Computer Science (Springer, Berlin/Heidelberg, 1986), pp. 186–195

S. Kraus, D.J. Lehmann, M. Magidor, Nonmonotonic reasoning, preferential models and cumulative logics. Artif. Intell. **44**(1–2), 167–207 (1990)

H.E. Kyburg, *Probability and the Logic of Rational Belief* (Wesleyan University Press, Middletown, 1961)

P. Lamarre, Y. Shoham, Knowledge, certainty, belief, and conditionalisation (abbreviated version), in *Proceedings of the KR*, Bonn, 1994, pp. 415–424

N. Laverny, J. Lang, From knowledge-based programs to graded belief-based programs, Part II: off-line reasoning, in *Proceedings of the IJCAI*, Edinburgh, 2005, pp. 497–502

K. Lehrer, T. Paxson, Knowledge: undefeated justified true belief. J. Philos. **66**, 225–237 (1969)

W. Lenzen, *Recent Work in Epistemic Logic*. Acta Philosophica Fennica, vol. 30 (North Holland, Amsterdam, 1978)

W. Lenzen, Epistemologische Betractungen zu [S4;S5]. Erkenntnis **14**, 33–56 (1979)

W. Lenzen, Knowledge, belief, and subjective probability: outlines of a unified system of epistemic/doxastic logic, in *Knowledge Contributors*, ed. by V.F. Hendricks, K.F. Jørgensen, S.A. Pedersen, J. Symons, D. Dalen, T.A.F. Kuipers, T. Seidenfeld, P. Suppes, J. Woleński. Volume 322 of Synthese Library (Springer, The Netherlands, 2004), pp. 17–31
H. Levesque, A logic of implicit and explicit knowledge, in *Proceedings of the AAAI-84*, Austin, 1984, pp. 198–202
I. Levi, The logic of full belief, in *The Covenant of Reason: Rationality and the Commitments of Thought* (Cambridge University Press, Cambridge/New York, 1997), pp. 40–69
D. Lewis, *Convention, a Philosophical Study* (Harvard University Press, Cambridge, 1969)
E. Lorini, C. Castelfranchi, The cognitive structure of surprise: looking for basic principles. Topoi Int. Rev. Philos. **26**(1), 133–149 (2007)
W. Lycan, On the Gettier problem, in *Epistemology Futures*, ed. by S.C. Hetherington (Oxford University Press, Oxford/New York, 2006), pp. 148–168
D. Makinson, P. Gärdenfors, Relations between the logic of theory change and nonmonotonic logic, in *The Logic of Theory Change*, Konstanz, ed. by A. Fuhrmann, M. Morreau. Volume 465 of Lecture Notes in Computer Science (Springer, 1989), pp. 185–205
J.-J.Ch. Meyer, W. van der Hoek, *Epistemic Logic for AI and Computer Science* (Cambridge University Press, Cambridge, 1995)
J.-J.Ch. Meyer, F. de Boer, R. van Eijk, K. Hindriks, W. van der Hoek, On programming KARO agents. Log. J. IGPL **9**(2), 245–256 (2001)
R.C. Moore, Possible-world semantics for autoepistemic logic, in *Proceedings of the Non-monotonic Reasoning Workshop*, New Paltz, 1984, pp. 344–354
R.C. Moore, *Logic and Representation*. CSLI Lecture Notes (Center for the Study of Language and Information, Stanford, 1995)
Y. Moses, Y. Shoham, Belief as defeasible knowledge. Artif. Intell. **64**, 299–321 (1993)
E. Pacuit, Procedural information and the dynamics of belief, in *Dialogue, Rationality, Formalism*. LEUS (Springer, 2014)
D. Prichard, Epistemic luck. J. Philos. Res. **29**, 193–222 (2004)
A. Rao, M. Georgeff, Modeling rational agents within a BDI-architecture, in *Proceedings of Knowledge Representation and Reasoning (KR & R-91)*, Cambridge, ed. by R. Fikes, E. Sandewall (Morgan Kaufmann, 1991), pp. 473–484
H. Rott, Stability, strength and sensitivity: converting belief into knowledge. Erkenntnis **61**, 469–493 (2004). doi:10.1007/s10670-004-9287-1
C. Sakama, M. Caminada, A. Herzig, A logical account of lying, in *Logics in Artificial Intelligence*, ed. by T. Janhunen, I. Niemelä. Volume 6341 of Lecture Notes in Computer Science (Springer, Berlin/Heidelberg, 2010), pp. 286–299
Y. Shoham, K. Leyton-Brown, *Multiagent Systems: Algorithmic, Game-Theoretic, and Logical Foundations* (Cambridge University Press, Cambridge/New York, 2009)
W. Spohn, Ordinal conditional functions: a dynamic theory of epistemic states, in *Causation in Decision, Belief Change, and Statistics*, vol. 2 (Reidel, Dordrecht, 1988a), pp. 105–134
W. Spohn, A general non-probabilistic theory of inductive reasoning, in *Proceedings of the UAI*, Minneapolis, ed. by R.D. Shachter, T.S. Levitt, L.N. Kanal, J.F. Lemmer (North-Holland, 1988b), pp. 149–158
R. Stalnaker, On logics of knowledge and belief. Philos. Stud. **128**, 169–199 (2006)
J. van Benthem, Dynamic logic for belief revision. J. Appl. Non-Class. Log. **17**(2), 129–155 (2007)
J. van Benthem, *Logical Dynamics of Information and Interaction* (Cambridge University Press, Cambridge/New York, 2011)
W. van der Hoek, Sytems for knowledge and belief. J. Log. Comput. **3**(2), 173–195 (1993)
W. van der Hoek, J.-J.Ch. Meyer, Graded modalities in epistemic logic, in *Proceedings of the LFCS*, Tver, ed. by A. Nerode, M.A. Taitslin. Volume 620 of Lecture Notes in Computer Science (Springer, 1992), pp. 503–514
H. van Ditmarsch, Prolegomena to dynamic logic for belief revision. Synthese **147**, 229–275 (2005)

H. van Ditmarsch, W. van der Hoek, B. Kooi, *Dynamic Epistemic Logic*. Volume 337 of Synthese Library (Springer, Dordrecht, 2007)
H.P. van Ditmarsch, J. van Eijck, F. Sietsma and Y. Wang, On the logic of lying, in: *Games, Actions and Social Software*, ed. by J. van Eijck, R. Verbrugge. LNCS 7010 (Springer, Dordrecht, 2011)
B. van Linder, W. van der Hoek, J.-J.Ch. Meyer, Formalising abilities and opportunities of agents. Fundamenta Informaticae **34**(1–2), 53–101 (1998)
F. von Kutschera, *Einführung in die Intensionale Semantik* (W. de Gruyter, Berlin, 1976)
F. Voorbraak, As Far as I know. Epistemic Logic and Uncertainty. PhD thesis, Utrecht University, 1993
G. Wheeler, Is there a logic of information? J. Exp. Theor. Artif. Intell. (special issue on Inforgs and the Infosphere: Themes from Luciano Floridi's Philosophy of Artificial Intelligence) (2012)
T. Williamson, *Knowledge and Its Limits* (Oxford University Press, Oxford/New York, 2000)
M. Wooldridge, *Reasoning About Rational Agents* (MIT, Cambridge, 2000)

Chapter 6
Procedural Information and the Dynamics of Belief

Eric Pacuit

6.1 Introduction

The point of departure for modern epistemic and doxastic logic is Jaakko Hintikka's seminal book *Knowledge and Belief: An Introduction to the Logic of the Two Notions* (Hintikka 1962).[1] While Hintikka's project sparked some discussion among mainstream epistemologists (especially regarding the "KK Principle": Does knowing something imply that one knows that one knows it?),[2] much of the work on epistemic and doxastic logic was taken over by game theorists (Aumann 1999) and computer scientists (Fagin et al. 1995) in the 1990s.[3] See Bonanno and Battigalli (1999) and Brandenburger (2007) for a survey of epistemic issues that arise in game theory and Fagin et al. (1995) for applications of epistemic logic in computer science.

This focus on different areas of "application" has pushed the analysis beyond the basic epistemic logic of Hintikka (1962) and Aumann (1999) (representing an agent's "hard" information) to "softer" informational attitudes that may be revised. Recent work by epistemic logicians has identified and analyzed a rich repertoire

[1]This important book has recently been reissued and extended with some of Hintikka's latest papers on epistemic logic (Hintikka 2005).

[2]Timothy Williamson (2000, Chap. 5) has a well-known and persuasive argument against this principle, cf. for a discussion of interesting issues for epistemic logic deriving from Williamson's argument (Egré and Bonnay 2009).

[3]Recently, focus has shifted back to Philosophy, with a growing interest in "bridging the gap between formal and mainstream epistemology". Witness the collection of articles (Hendricks 2006) and the book *Mainstream and Formal Epistemology* by Vincent Hendricks (2006).

E. Pacuit (✉)
Tilburg Institute for Logic and Philosophy of Science, Tilburg University,
Warandelaan 2, 5037 AB Tilburg, The Netherlands
e-mail: epacuit@umd.edu

M. Rebuschi et al. (eds.), *Interdisciplinary Works in Logic, Epistemology, Psychology and Linguistics*, Logic, Argumentation & Reasoning 3,
DOI 10.1007/978-3-319-03044-9_6, © Springer International Publishing Switzerland 2014

of *informational attitudes*. Examples that have been subjected to a logical analysis include different flavors of belief, such as "strong" and "safe" belief (van Benthem 2007; Baltag and Smets 2006); "syntactic" notions, such as awareness (Halpern and Rego 2009) and "explicit knowledge" (Ågotnes and Alechina 2007); variants of "knowing how", such as the "constructive" knowledge" of Jamroga and Ågotnes (2007); and, of course, the many different representations of *graded beliefs* found in Artificial Intelligence and Decision and Game Theory (see Halpern (2005), and references therein). The goal of a logical analysis is to see how these different notions of knowledge and belief fit together.

In this paper, I am not interested in these *static* logics of informational attitudes per se. Rather, my focus is on the dynamic operations that change these informational attitudes during a social interaction or rational inquiry. Current *dynamic* logics of belief revision and information update focus on two key aspects of informative actions:

1. The agents' *observational* powers. Agents may perceive the same event differently, and this can be described in terms of what agents do or do not observe. Examples range from *public announcements*, where everyone witnesses the same event, to private communications between two or more agents, with no other agents aware that an event took place.
2. The *type* of change triggered by the event. Agents may differ in precisely how they incorporate new information into their epistemic states. These differences are based, in part, on the agents' perception of the *source* of the information. For example, an agent may consider a particular source of information *infallible* (not allowing for the possibility that the source is mistaken) or merely *trustworthy* (accepting the information as reliable, though allowing for the possibility of a mistake).

One of the goals of this paper is to introduce the key ideas and main definitions that form the foundations of these dynamic logics of interaction and inquiry.

Many of the recent developments in this area have been driven by analyzing *concrete* examples. These range from toy examples, such as the infamous muddy children puzzle, to philosophical quandaries, such as Fitch's Paradox, to everyday examples of social interaction. Different logical systems are then judged, in part, on how well they conform to the analyst's intuitions about the relevant set of examples. But this raises an important methodological issue: Implicit assumptions about what the actors know and believe about the situation being modeled often guide the analyst's intuitions. In many cases, it is crucial to make these underlying assumptions explicit.

The general point is that *how* an agent comes to know or believe that some proposition p is true is as important (or, perhaps, more important) than the fact that the agent knows or believes that p is the case (cf. the discussion in van Benthem (2009, Sect. 2.5)). One lesson to take away is that during a social interaction, the agents' "knowledge" and "beliefs" are both influenced by *and* shaped by the *social* events. The following example taken from Pacuit et al. (2006) illustrates this point.

Suppose that Uma is a physician whose neighbor Sam is ill, and consider the following cases:

Case 1: Uma does not know and has not been informed that Sam is ill. Uma has no obligation (as yet) to treat her neighbor.

Case 2: The neighbor's daughter Ann comes to Uma's house and tells her that Sam is ill. Now Uma does have an obligation to treat Sam or, perhaps, to call for an ambulance or a specialist.

These simple examples highlight the observation that an agent's obligation often depends on what the agent knows, and, indeed, one cannot reasonably be expected to respond to a problem if one is not aware of its existence. This, in turn, creates a secondary obligation on Ann to inform Uma that her father is ill. But these obligations depend on certain (implicit) information that Uma and Ann have about each other. For example, Ann is not under any obligation to tell Uma that her father is ill if she justifiably believes that Uma would not treat her father even if she knew of his illness. Thus, in order for Ann to *know* that she has an obligation to tell Uma about her father's illness, Ann must *know* that "Uma will, in fact, treat her father (in a reasonable amount of time) upon learning of his illness". Furthermore, if Uma has a good reason to believe that Ann always lies about her father being ill, then she is under no obligation to treat Sam. See Pacuit et al. (2006) for a formal treatment of these examples.

Two "types" of information play a role in the above discussion. The first, which might be called "meta-information" (cf. the discussion in Stalnaker (2009)) is information about how "trusted" or "reliable" the sources of the information are. This is particularly important when analyzing how an agent's beliefs change over an extended period of time. For example, rather than taking a stream of contradictory incoming evidence (i.e., the agent receives the information that p, then the information that q, then the information that $\neg p$, then the information that $\neg q$) at face value (and performing the suggested belief revisions), a rational agent may consider the stream itself as evidence that the source is not reliable.[4]

There is much more to say about logical models of trust and reliability, but, in this paper, I am interested in a second "type" of information: **procedural information**. This is information about the underlying *protocol* specifying which events (observations, messages, actions) are available (or permitted) at any given moment. Procedural information is intended to represent the rules or conventions that govern many of our social interactions. For example, in a conversation, it is typically not polite to blurt everything out at the beginning, but, rather, to speak in small chunks. Other natural conversational protocol rules include "do not repeat yourself", "let others speak in turn", and "be honest". Imposing such rules *restricts* the legitimate sequences of possible statements or events.

---

[4]Cf. the very interesting discussion of *higher-order evidence* in the (formal) epistemology literature (Christensen 2010).

A *protocol* describes what the agents "can" or "cannot" do (say, observe) in a social interactive situation or rational inquiry. This leads to *substantive* assumptions about the formal model, such as which actions (observations, messages, utterances) are available (permitted) at any given moment. These assumptions can be roughly categorized according to the different uses of "can":

1. To describe physical, temporal or historical possibilities: A typical example is the assumption that an agent *cannot* receive a message unless another agent sent it earlier. Such assumptions limit the options available to the agents at any given moment.
2. To describe the agents' abilities, or skills: The options available to an agent at any given moment are defined not only by what is "physically possible", but also by the agent's *capacity* to perform various actions. For example, "Ann *can* throw a bulls-eye" typically means that Ann has the ability to (repeatedly) throw a bulls-eye.
3. To describe compliance to some type of norm: The social or conversational[5] norms at play in the interactive situation being modeled (i.e., the "rules of the game") impose further constraints on options available to each agent.

So, a protocol encodes not only which options are *feasible*, but also what is *permissible* for the agents to do or say. Of course, an interesting and important component of a logical analysis of rational agency is to disambiguate these different meanings of "can" (I do not discuss these issues here, see John F. Horty (2001), Dag Elgesem (1997) and Charles B. Cross (1986) for discussions).

A typical assumption is that there is a fixed, global protocol that all the agents have (explicitly or implicitly) agreed to follow (and this is commonly known). This raises an important question: *In what sense do the agents know the protocol?* Formally, the protocol describes which states or histories are "in the model", so the *proposition* expressing that "the protocol is being followed" is the set of *all* elements in the model (i.e., the set W of all possible worlds in the model). Thus, in terms of the agents' *propositional knowledge*, "knowing the protocol" amounts to knowing that "the set of possible states is W", but this just means that the agent knows that "$\top$". Nonetheless, "knowing the protocol" has important practical and pragmatic ramifications on the agents' information.[6] First, the protocol explicitly limits the observations, messages and/or actions available (or permitted) to the agent. Second, the protocol affects how the agents interpret their observations (Parikh and Ramanujam 2003).

This is an exploratory paper focused on ideas and concepts rather than on concrete results. I focus only on dynamic logics of knowledge and belief for a single agent. This is not because I do not find the many-agent situation interesting or important. Quite the opposite: I focus on a single agent only to simplify the exposition and technical details. Section 6.2 is a general introduction to the many

[5]See Parikh and Ramanujam (2003), Sect. 6, for a discussion of Gricean norms in this context.

[6]See Pacuit and Simon (2011), and references therein, for a logic to reasoning about what agents know about a protocol, or plan, that they are executing.

different flavors of dynamic epistemic and doxastic logics for non-specialists. Section 6.3 is an extended discussion of the role that procedural information plays in dynamic logics of belief revision. Finally, I offer some conclusions in Sect. 6.4.

6.2 A Primer on Logics of Informational Change

In this section, I introduce the key logical frameworks that incorporate how a (rational) agent's information changes in response to new information or evidence. This is a well-developed area attempting to balance sophisticated logical analysis with philosophical insight. Of course, I will not be able to do justice to the entire literature here, see van Benthem (2011) and references therein for a broad overview.

6.2.1 Static Models of Hard and Soft Information

The formal models introduced below can be broadly described as "possible worlds models", familiar in much of the philosophical logic literature. Setting aside any conceptual difficulties surrounding the use of these models, the structures I study in this paper are instances of a relational model:

Definition 6.2.1 (Relational Model). Let At be a (finite) set of atomic sentences. A **relational model** (based on At) is a tuple $\langle W, R, V\rangle$ where W is a finite set whose elements are called *possible worlds* or *states*; $R \subseteq W \times W$ is a relation; and $V : \mathsf{At} \to \wp(W)$ is a valuation function mapping atomic propositions to sets of states. □

Elements $p \in \mathsf{At}$ are intended to describe ground facts about the situation being modeled, such as "it is raining" or "the red card is on the table". A nonempty set W is intended to represent the different possible "scenarios" (elements of W are called possible worlds or states). The valuation function V associates with every ground fact the set of situations where that fact holds. Finally, the agent's informational attitude is defined in terms of the relation R. Different properties of R give rise to different types of attitudes. There are two types of attitudes that are important for this paper.

The first is the attitude that is associated with the agent's *hard* information. For lack of a better term (and following standard usage), I call this the agent's *knowledge*. In this case, I assume that R is an equivalence relation (i.e., reflexive, transitive and symmetric) and write '$\sim$' for R. Rather than *directly* representing the agent's *hard information*, the relation $\sim$ describes the "implicit consequences" of this information in terms of an "*epistemic indistinguishability relations*".[7] The idea

[7]The phrasing "epistemic indistinguishability", although common in the epistemic logic literature, is misleading since, as a relation, "indistinguishability" is *not* transitive. A standard example is: A

is that each agent has some "hard information" about the situation being modeled, and agents cannot distinguish between states that agree on this information. I call structures $\langle W, \sim, V\rangle$ an **epistemic model**.

A simple propositional modal language is often used to describe the agent's knowledge at states in an epistemic model. Formally, let $\mathcal{L}_{EL}$ be the (smallest) set of sentences generated by the following grammar:

$$\varphi := p \mid \neg\varphi \mid \varphi \wedge \varphi \mid K\varphi$$

where $p \in \mathsf{At}$ (the set of atomic propositions). The additional propositional connectives ($\rightarrow, \leftrightarrow, \vee$) are defined as usual and the dual of K, denoted L, is defined as follows: $L\varphi := \neg K\neg\varphi$. The intended interpretation of $K\varphi$ is "according to the agent's current (hard) information, φ is true" (again, I can also say that "the agent knows that φ is true"). Given a story or situation we are interested in modeling, each state $w \in W$ of an epistemic model $\mathcal{M} = \langle W, \sim, V\rangle$ represents a possible scenario which can be described in the formal language given above: If $\varphi \in \mathcal{L}_{EL}$, I write $\mathcal{M}, w \models \varphi$ provided φ is a correct description of some aspect of the situation represented by w. This can be made precise as follows:

Definition 6.2.2 (Truth). Let $\mathcal{M} = \langle W, \sim, V\rangle$ be an epistemic model. For each $w \in W$, φ **is true at state** w, denoted $\mathcal{M}, w \models \varphi$, is defined by induction on the structure of φ:

- $\mathcal{M}, w \models p$ iff $w \in V(p)$
- $\mathcal{M}, w \models \neg\varphi$ iff $\mathcal{M}, w \not\models \varphi$
- $\mathcal{M}, w \models \varphi \wedge \psi$ iff $\mathcal{M}, w \models \varphi$ and $\mathcal{M}, w \models \psi$
- $\mathcal{M}, w \models K\varphi$ iff for all $v \in W$, if $w \sim v$ then $\mathcal{M}, v \models \varphi$ $\triangleleft$

The above epistemic models are intended to represent the agent's *hard information* about the situation being modeled. In fact, by using standard techniques from the mathematical theory of modal logic, I can be much more precise about the sense in which these models "represent" the agent's hard information. In particular, *modal correspondence theory* (see Blackburn et al. (2002, Chap. 3)) rigorously relates properties of the relation in an epistemic model with modal formulas (cf. Blackburn et al. 2002, Chap. 3).[8] The following table lists some key formulas in the language $\mathcal{L}_{EL}$ with their corresponding (first-order) property and the relevant underlying assumption.

These properties have generated much discussion among philosophers, computer scientists and logicians. While the logical omniscience assumption (which is valid

cup of coffee with n grains of sugar is indistinguishable from a cup with $n+1$ grains; however, transitivity would imply that a cup with 0 grains of sugar is indistinguishable from a cup with 1,000 grains of sugar. In this context, two states are "epistemicly indistinguishable" for an agent if the agent has the "same information" in both states. This is indeed an equivalence relation.

[8]To be more precise, the key notion here is *frame definability*: A frame is a pair $\langle W, R\rangle$ where W is a nonempty set and R a relation on W. A modal formula is valid on a frame if it is valid in every model based on that frame. It can be shown that some modal formulas have first-order

Assumption	Formula	Property
Logical Omniscience	$K(\varphi \rightarrow \psi) \rightarrow (K\varphi \rightarrow K\psi)$	—
Veridical	$K\varphi \rightarrow \varphi$	Reflexive
Positive Introspection	$K\varphi \rightarrow KK\varphi$	Transitive
Negative Introspection	$\neg K\varphi \rightarrow K\neg K\varphi$	Euclidean

on all models regardless of the properties of the accessibility relation) has generated the most extensive criticisms (cf. Stalnaker 1991) and responses (cf. Fagin et al. 1995, Chap. 9) the two introspection principles have also been the object of intense discussion (cf. Williamson 2000; Egré and Bonnay 2009). These discussions are fundamental to the theory of knowledge and its formalization, but here I take epistemic models for what they are: formal models of hard information, in the sense introduced above.

The theory of belief *revision* started with the seminal paper by Alchourrón et al. (1985). In this paper, I focus on logical models of belief revision. The standard approach is to use a relational model where the relation is a *connected preorder* (reflexive and transitive). Such orders are typically called *plausibility orderings* and are denoted '$\preceq$'. While $\sim$ partitions the set of possible worlds according to the agent's hard information, the ordering $\preceq$ represents the possible worlds that the agent considers more plausible (i.e., it represents the agent's soft information). A **plausibility model** is a relational structure $\mathcal{M} = \langle W, \preceq, V \rangle$. David Lewis (1973) first used these structures as a semantics for *conditionals* (Grove 1988). These structures have been extensively studied by logicians (van Benthem 2007; van Ditmarsch 2005; Baltag and Smets 2006), game theorists (Board 2004), and computer scientists (Boutilier 1992; Lamarre and Shoham 1994).

The richer models allows us to define a variety of (soft) informational attitudes. I first need some additional notation. For $X \subseteq W$, let

$$Min_{\preceq}(X) = \{v \in X \mid v \preceq w \text{ for all } w \in X\}$$

denote the set of minimal elements of X according to $\preceq$. This set is interpreted as the set of worlds the agent considers most plausible.[9] Also, the plausibility relation $\preceq$ can be *lifted* to subsets of W as follows[10]

$$X \preceq Y \text{ iff } x \preceq y \text{ for all } x \in X \text{ and } y \in Y.$$

correspondents P where for any frame $\langle W, R \rangle$, the relation R has property P iff φ is valid on $\langle W, R \rangle$.

[9]It is a convention in this literature that going down according to $\preceq$ corresponds to being *more* plausible. This is just a convention which can be easily changed.

[10]This is only one of many possible choices here, but it is the most natural in this setting (cf. Liu 2008, Chap. 4).

Suppose that $\mathcal{M} = \langle W, \preceq, V \rangle$ is a plausibility model with $w \in W$, and consider the following modalities:

- *Belief*: $\mathcal{M}, w \models B\varphi$ iff for all $v \in Min_{\preceq}(W)$, $\mathcal{M}, v \models \varphi$.
  This is the usual notion of belief that satisfies the standard properties discussed above (e.g., positive and negative introspection).
- *Robust Belief*: $\mathcal{M}, w \models \Box\varphi$ iff for all v, if $v \preceq w$ then $\mathcal{M}, v \models \varphi$.
  Thus, φ is robustly believed if φ is true in *all* states that the agent considers more plausible. This stronger notion of belief has also been called *certainty* by some authors (cf. Shoham and Leyton-Brown 2009, Sect. 13.7).
- *Strong Belief*: $\mathcal{M}, w \models B^s\varphi$ iff there is a $v \in W$ such that $\mathcal{M}, v \models \varphi$ and $\{x \mid \mathcal{M}, x \models \varphi\} \preceq \{x \mid \mathcal{M}, x \models \neg\varphi\}$.
  So, φ is strongly believed provided it is epistemically possible and the agent considers *any* state satisfying φ more plausible than *any* state satisfying $\neg\varphi$. This notion has also been studied in Stalnaker (1994) and Battigalli and Siniscalchi (2002).
- *Knowledge*: $\mathcal{M}, w \models K\varphi$ iff for all $v \in W$, $\mathcal{M}, v \models \varphi$.
  Knowledge is interpreted as a universal modality here. The intuition is that the agent's plausibility ordering ranges over the states that the agent has not ruled out according to her hard information.

The logic of these notions has been extensively studied by Alexandru Baltag and Sonja Smets in a series of articles (Baltag and Smets 2006, 2008a, 2009). The following example illustrates the relationship between these different notions.

Example 6.2.3 (Relationships between the different notions of belief). It is not hard to see that if an agent knows p (Kp is true) then the agent believes p according to all the definitions above (i.e., $Kp \to (Bp \wedge \Box p \wedge B^s p)$ is valid). Furhtermore, both strong belief and robust belief in p implies the agent believes p. What about the relationship between strong belief and robust belief? These two notions of belief are logically independent. Consider the following plausibility model where $w_2 \models \Box p \wedge \neg B^s p$. I draw an arrow from v to w if $w \preceq v$ (to keep the notation down, I do not include all arrows. The remaining arrows can be inferred by transitivity).

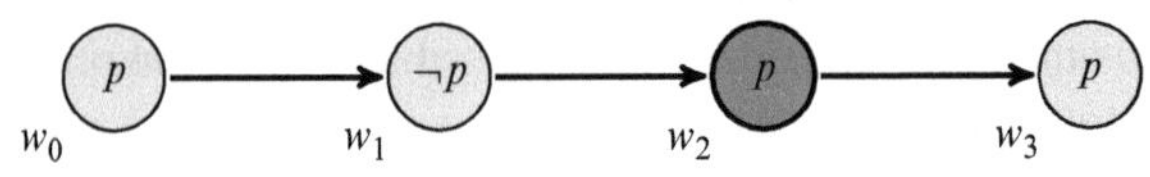

To see that strong belief need not imply robust belief, consider the following variant of the above plausibility model where $w_2 \models B^s p \wedge \neg\Box p$:

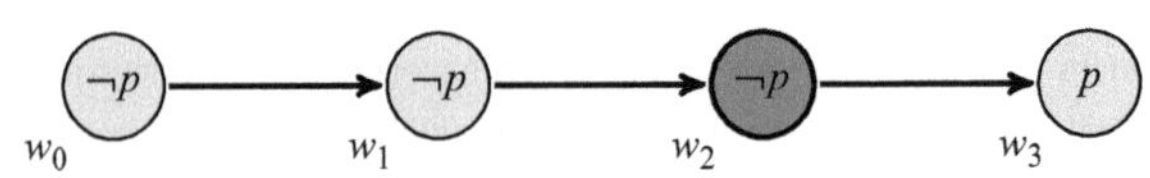

□

As noted above, a crucial feature of these informational attitudes is that they are *defeasible* in light of new evidence. In fact, these attitudes can be characterized in terms of how an agent would change her beliefs in response to certain types of evidence. The notion of *conditional belief* is needed to make this idea precise. Suppose that $\mathcal{M} = \langle W, \preceq, V\rangle$ is a plausibility model and φ and ψ are formulas; then, we say that *the agent believes* φ *given* ψ (or *believes* φ *conditional on* ψ), denoted $B^{\psi\varphi}$, provided

$$\mathcal{M}, w \models B^{\psi\varphi} \text{ iff for all } v \in Min_{\preceq}([\![\psi]\!]_{\mathcal{M}}), \mathcal{M}, v \models \varphi$$

where $[\![\psi]\!]_{\mathcal{M}} = \{w \mid \mathcal{M}, w \models \psi\}$ is the *truth set* of ψ. So, 'B^{ψ}' encodes the agent will believe upon receiving (possibly misleading) evidence that ψ is *true*. Two observations are immediate. First, I can now define belief $B\varphi$ as $B^{\top\varphi}$ (belief in φ given a tautology). Second, unlike beliefs, conditional beliefs may be inconsistent (i.e., $B^{\psi}\bot$ may be true at some state). In such a case, agent i cannot (on pain of inconsistency) revise by ψ, but this will happen only if the agent has hard information that ψ is false. Indeed, $K\neg\varphi$ is logically equivalent to $B^{\varphi}\bot$ (over the class of plausibility models). This suggests the following (dynamic) characterization of an agent's hard information as unrevisable beliefs:

$$\mathcal{M}, w \models K\varphi \text{ iff } \mathcal{M}, w \models B^{\psi}\varphi \text{ for all } \psi.$$

Safe belief and strong belief can be similarly characterized by restricting the admissible evidence:

- $\mathcal{M}, w \models \Box\varphi$ iff $\mathcal{M}, w \models B^{\psi}\varphi$ for all ψ with $\mathcal{M}, w \models \psi$.
  That is, the agent safely believes φ iff she continues to believe φ given any true formula.
- $\mathcal{M}, w \models B^{s}\varphi$ iff $\mathcal{M}, w \models B\varphi$ and $\mathcal{M}, w \models B^{\psi}\varphi$ for all ψ with $\mathcal{M}, w \models \neg K(\psi \to \neg\varphi)$.
  That is, the agent strongly believes φ iff she believes φ and continues to believe φ given any evidence (truthful or not) that is not known to contradict φ.

Baltag and Smets (2009) provide an elegant logical characterization of the above notions. First of all, note that conditional belief (and, hence, belief) and strong belief are *definable* in this language:

- $B^{\varphi\psi} := L\varphi \to L(\varphi \wedge \Box(\varphi \to \psi))$
- $B^{s}\varphi := B\varphi \wedge K(\varphi \to \Box\varphi)$

Thus, we can consider a modal language containing a universal modality (which I have called knowledge) and the usual modality for the plausibility ordering (which I have called robust belief). As discussed above, K satisfies logical omniscience, veracity and both positive and negative introspection. Safe belief, $\Box$, shares all of these properties except negative introspection. Modal correspondence theory can again be used to characterize the remaining properties:

- Knowledge implies safe belief: $K\varphi \to \Box\varphi$
- Connectedness: $K(\varphi \vee \Box\psi) \wedge K(\psi \vee \Box\varphi) \to K\varphi \vee K\psi$

6.2.2 Dynamics of Beliefs

The central issue here is how to incorporate *new* information into an epistemic or plausibility model. At a fixed moment in time, the agents are in some *epistemic state* (which may be described by an epistemic or plausibility model). The question is: How does (the model of) this epistemic state change during the course of some social interaction?

The most basic type of informational change is a so-called *public announcement* (Plaza 1989; Gerbrandy 1999). This is the event where some proposition φ (in the language of $\mathcal{L}_{EL}$) is made *publicly* available. That is, it is completely open and all agents not only observe the event, but also observe everyone else observing the event, and so on ad infinitum (cf. the first aspect of informative actions discussed in the introduction). Furthermore, all agents treat the source as *infallible* (cf. the second aspect of informative actions discussed in the introduction). Thus, the effect of such an event on an epistemic or plausibility model should be clear: *Remove* all states that do not satisfy φ. Formally:

Definition 6.2.4 (Public Announcement). Suppose that $\mathcal{M} = \langle W, R, V\rangle$ is a relational model and φ is a formula (in the language of epistemic logic or conditional beliefs). The model updated by the **public announcement of** φ is the structure $\mathcal{M}^{\varphi} = \langle W^{\varphi}, R^{\varphi}, V^{\varphi}\rangle$ where $W^{\varphi} = \{w \in W \mid \mathcal{M}, w \models \varphi\}$, $R^{\varphi} = R \cap W^{\varphi} \times W^{\varphi}$, and for all atomic propositions p, $V^{\varphi}(p) = V(p) \cap W^{\varphi}$. □

It is not hard to see that if $\mathcal{M}$ is a relational model (i.e., an epistemic or plausibility model), then so is $\mathcal{M}^{\varphi}$. The models $\mathcal{M}$ and $\mathcal{M}^{\varphi}$ describe two different moments in time, with $\mathcal{M}$ describing the current or initial information state of the agent and $\mathcal{M}^{\varphi}$ the information state *after* the information that φ is true has been incorporated in $\mathcal{M}$. This temporal dimension can also be represented in the logical language with modalities of the form $[!\varphi]\psi$. The intended interpretation of $[!\varphi]\psi$ is "ψ is true after the public announcement of φ", and truth is defined as $\mathcal{M}, w \models [!\varphi]\psi$ iff if $\mathcal{M}, w \models \varphi$ then $\mathcal{M}^{\varphi}, w \models \psi$.

For the moment, let us focus on epistemic models and consider the formula $\neg K\psi \wedge [!\varphi]K\psi$: This says that "the agent (currently) does not know ψ, but after the announcement of φ, the agent knows ψ". So, languages with these announcement modalities can describe what is true both before and after the announcement.

A fundamental insight is that there is a strong logical relationship between what is true before and after an announcement in the form of so-called *recursion axioms*:

$$
\begin{array}{lcl}
[!\varphi]p & \leftrightarrow & \varphi \rightarrow p, \text{ where } p \in \mathsf{At} \\
[!\varphi]\neg\psi & \leftrightarrow & \varphi \rightarrow \neg[!\varphi]\psi \\
[!\varphi](\psi \wedge \chi) & \leftrightarrow & [!\varphi]\psi \wedge [!\varphi]\chi \\
[!\varphi]K\varphi & \leftrightarrow & \varphi \rightarrow K(\varphi \rightarrow [!\varphi]\psi)
\end{array}
$$

These recursion axioms can be used to show that the announcement modalities do not add any expressive power to the standard epistemic modal language (without common knowledge).[11] More than that, these recursion axioms provide an insightful syntactic analysis of announcements that complements the semantic analysis: The recursion axioms describe the effect of an announcement in terms of what is true before the announcement.

Now, what is the effect of a public announcement on the agents' soft information? I will start by clarifying the relationship between conditional belief $B^{\varphi}\psi$ and beliefs after a public announcement $[!\varphi]B\psi$. *Prima facie*, the two statements seem to express the same thing; and, in fact, they are equivalent provided that ψ is a *true ground formula* (i.e., does not contain any modal operators). However, the formulas are not equivalent in general: The reader is invited to check that $B^{p}(p \wedge \neg Kp)$ is satisfiable, but $[!p]B(p \wedge \neg Kp)$ is not satisfiable. The situation is nicely summarized as follows: "$B^{\psi}\varphi$ says that if the agent would learn φ, then she would come to believe that ψ was the case (before the learning)... $[!\varphi]B\psi$ says that after learning φ, the agent would come to believe that ψ is the case (in the worlds after the learning)" (Baltag and Smets 2008b, p. 2). Thus, the conditional beliefs *encode* how the agent's beliefs will change in the presence of new information. In particular, conditional beliefs are crucial for a recursion axiom analysis. Note that the above recursion axiom for knowledge is not valid when replacing K with B on plausibility models. We do, however, have the following recursion axioms (valid on the class of plausibility models):

$$
\begin{array}{lcl}
[!\varphi]B\psi & \leftrightarrow & B^{\varphi}[!\varphi]\psi \\
[!\varphi]B_i^{\psi}\chi & \leftrightarrow & (\varphi \rightarrow B_i^{\varphi \wedge [!\varphi]\psi}[!\varphi]\chi)
\end{array}
$$

There are also recursion axioms for robust and strong belief, but I do not discuss them here (see van Benthem (2011) for a discussion).

[11] This is not true for multiagent languages with a common knowledge operator. Nonetheless, a recursion axiom-style analysis is still possible, though the details are beyond the scope of this paper, see van Benthem et al. (2006).

A public announcement is only one type of informative action. It is an action where the agent is certain about *what* is being observed and treats the incoming information as infallible. Other types of informative actions can be defined by varying these these two aspects. In order to model situations where the agent is *misinformed* or *uncertain* about what she is observing, there must be a way to describe this uncertainty. Based on the logical framework introduced in Baltag et al. (1998), the key idea is to model such a complex epistemic event as a relational structure. I will not discuss this approach here (consult van Ditmarsch et al. (2007) for an overview of this approach). In this paper, I am primarily interested in informative actions where the source is trusted, but not necessarily treated as *infallible*.

As is well known from the belief revision literature, there are many ways to transform a plausibility model given some new information (Rott 2006). I do not have the space to survey this entire literature here (see van Benthem (2011) and Baltag and Smets (2009) for modern introductions). Instead, I will sketch some key ideas. The pictures below illustrate different ways that a plausibility model can incorporate φ.

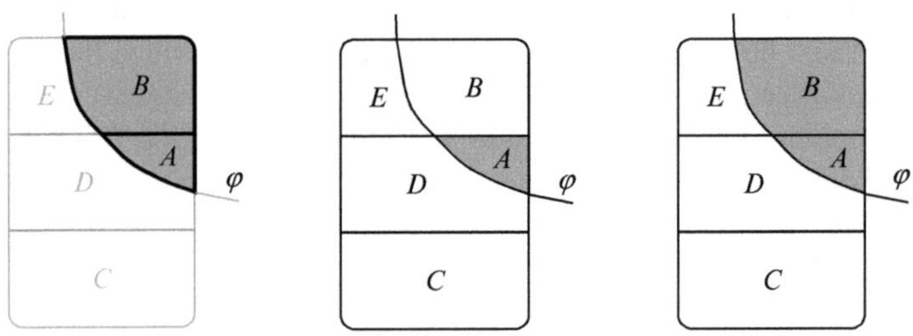

$!(\varphi) : A < B$ $\quad$ $\uparrow(\varphi): A < C < D < B \cup E$ $\quad$ $\Uparrow(\varphi): A < B < C < D < E$

The general approach is to define a way of *transforming* a plausibility model given a formula φ. The operation on the left is the *public announcement* operation discussed above. For the other transformations, while the players do *trust* the source of φ, they do not treat the source as infallible. Perhaps the most ubiquitous policy is *conservative upgrade* ($\uparrow \varphi$), which lets the agent only tentatively accept the incoming information φ by making the best φ-worlds the new minimal set and keeping the old plausibility ordering the same on all other worlds. The operation on the right, *radical upgrade* ($\Uparrow \varphi$), is stronger, moving *all* φ worlds before all the $\neg\varphi$ worlds and otherwise keeping the plausibility ordering the same. I will make use of conservative upgrade in the next section, so I state the formal definition below:

Definition 6.2.5 (Conservative Upgrade). Given a plausibility model $\mathcal{M} = \langle W, \preceq, V \rangle$ and a formula φ, the *radical* upgrade of $\mathcal{M}$ with φ is the model $\mathcal{M}^{\uparrow\varphi} = \langle W^{\uparrow\varphi}, \preceq^{\uparrow\varphi}, V^{\uparrow\varphi} \rangle$ with $W^{\uparrow\varphi} = W$, $V^{\uparrow\varphi} = V$ and $\preceq^{\uparrow\varphi}$ is the smallest relation satisfying:

1. For all $x \in Min_{\preceq}(\llbracket\varphi\rrbracket_{\mathcal{M}})$ and $y \notin Min_{\preceq}(\llbracket\varphi\rrbracket_{\mathcal{M}})$, $x \prec^{\uparrow\varphi} y$;
2. For all $x, y \in Min_{\preceq}(\llbracket\varphi\rrbracket_{\mathcal{M}})$, $x \preceq^{\uparrow\varphi} y$; and
3. For all $x, y \notin Min_{\preceq}(\llbracket\varphi\rrbracket_{\mathcal{M}})$, $x \preceq^{\uparrow\varphi} y$ iff $x \preceq y$. ◁

These dynamic operations satisfy a number of interesting logical principles (van Benthem 2011; Baltag and Smets 2009), but a full discussion is beyond the scope of this paper.

6.3 Making the Protocol Explicit

A number of authors have forcefully argued that the underlying protocol (i.e., the procedural information) is an important component of any analysis of (social) interactive situations and should be explicitly represented in a formal model (cf. Fagin et al. 1995; van Benthem et al. 2009; Parikh and Ramanujam 2003; Hoshi 2009; Wang 2010). Indeed, much of the work over the past 20 years using epistemic logic to reason about distributed algorithms has provided interesting case studies highlighting the interplay between "protocol analysis" and epistemic reasoning (an important example here is the seminal paper by Halpern and Moses (1990) on the "generals problem").

The first observation is that the recursion axioms from Sect. 6.2.2 already illustrate the mixture of factual and *procedural* truth that drives conversations or processes of observation. Consider the formula $\langle\varphi\rangle\top$ (with $\langle\varphi\rangle\psi = \neg[\varphi]\neg\psi$ the dual of $[\varphi]$), which means "φ is *announceable*". It is not hard to see that $\langle\varphi\rangle\top \leftrightarrow \varphi$ is derivable using standard modal reasoning and the above reduction axioms. The left-to-right direction represents a semantic fact about public announcements (only true facts can be announced), but the right-to-left direction represents specific *procedural information*: Every true formula is available for announcement. But this is only one of many different protocols and different assumptions about the protocol is reflected in a logical analysis. Consider the following variations of the reduction axiom for knowledge (van Benthem et al. 2009, Sect. 4):

1. $\langle\varphi\rangle K_i\psi \leftrightarrow \varphi \wedge K_i\langle\varphi\rangle\psi$
2. $\langle\varphi\rangle K_i\psi \leftrightarrow \langle\varphi\rangle\top \wedge K_i(\varphi \rightarrow \langle\varphi\rangle\psi)$
3. $\langle\varphi\rangle K_i\psi \leftrightarrow \langle\varphi\rangle\top \wedge K_i(\langle\varphi\rangle\top \rightarrow \langle\varphi\rangle\psi)$

Each of these axioms represents a different assumption about the underlying protocol and how it affects the agent's knowledge. The first is the above recursion axiom (in dual form) and assumes a specific protocol (which is common knowledge) where all true formulas are always available for announcement. The second (weaker) axiom is valid when there is a fixed protocol that is common knowledge. Finally, the third adds a requirement that the agents must know which formulas are currently available for announcement. Of course, the above three formulas are all *equivalent* given our definition of truth in an epistemic model (Definition 6.2.2) and public announcement (Definition 6.2.4). In order to see a difference, the *protocol information* must be explicitly represented in the model (see van Benthem et al. (2009) for a fuller discussion).

6.3.1 Protocol Information in Dynamic Logics of Belief Revision

The problem of *iterated revision* has been extensively studied (Boutilier 1996; Darwiche and Pearl 1997; Nayak et al. 2003; Stalnaker 2009), and although there are many proposals, there still remain a number of conceptual problems (see Stalnaker (2009) for a discussion). In this section, I focus on one such issue.

The main problem is this: Suppose that the agent receives a sequence of consistent formulas and uses, for example, radical upgrade to adjust her plausibility orderings. Since the information is consistent, no matter what the order in which she incorporates the information, she will always end up with the same beliefs. However, the different orders can lead to very different *conditional* beliefs, and this, in turn, means that there could be drastic differences in the result of incorporating information that contradicts one of the previous pieces of information.

Consider an example that has been extensively discussed in the literature. Suppose that you are in the forest and happen to see a strange-looking animal. You consult your animal guidebook and find a picture that seems to match the animal you see. The guidebook says that the animal is a type of bird, so that is what you conclude: The animal before you is a bird. After looking more closely, you also notice that the animal is red. So, you also update your beliefs with that fact. Now, suppose that an expert (whom you trust) happens to walk by and tells you that the animal is, in fact, not a bird. After incorporating this information into your beliefs (using conservative upgrade), you will no longer believe that the bird is red. Below is the sequence of upgrades (let b denote the proposition "the animal is a bird", $\overline{b}$ the negation of b, r is the proposition "the animal is red" and $\overline{r}$ the negation of r).

Note that in the last model, $\mathcal{M}_3$, the agent does not believe that the bird is red. The problem is that there does not seem to be any justification for why the agent drops her belief that the bird is red. There has been much discussion of this problem in the literature on iterated belief revision. Note that using radical upgrade, the agent would still believe the bird is red in $\mathcal{M}_3$ (as the reader is invited to check). My goal here is not to argue for or against one particular solution to this puzzle (see, for example Nayak et al. (2003, Sect. 5.1)). Rather, I want to highlight some general points about the underlying protocol specifying the order in which propositions are incorporated into the agent's epistemic state. In particular, the following sequence of updates is not problematic:

Of course, if we update the third model $\mathcal{M}_2$ with $\uparrow\overline{r}$, then the agent will drop her belief that b is true, which is equally problematic. This discussion highlights the importance of "procedural information" when reasoning about how an agent's beliefs change over time.

I conclude this section by introducing a logical framework that can reason about an agent's beliefs, and how her beliefs change in response to an explicit protocol describing which formulas (and types of updates) are available to her.

I start by being more precise about the definition of a protocol. A **tree** is a pair $\langle T, \rightarrowtail \rangle$ where T is a (finite) set of moments and $\rightarrowtail \subseteq T \times T$ satisfies the following properties:

- For each $t_1, t_2, t_3 \in T$, if $t_1 \rightarrowtail t_2$ and $t_3 \rightarrowtail t_2$ then $t_1 = t_3$, and
- If $(t_1, \ldots, t_n)$ is a sequence in T with $t_i \rightarrowtail t_{i+1}$ for each $i = 1, \ldots, n-1$, then $t_n \neq t_1$.

If $t_1 \rightarrowtail t_2$, we say t_2 is an immediate successor of t_1. A path p in T starting at node t is a sequence $(t_1, \ldots, t_n)$ where $t_1 = t$, for each $i = 1, \ldots, n-1$, $t_i \rightarrowtail t_{i+1}$. We say a path $p = (t_1, \ldots, t_n)$ is maximal if t_n does not have any immediate successors.

A *protocol* describes the different ways in which an agent can incorporate available information into her beliefs. Formally, a protocol is a labeled tree where the edges are labeled with specific types of belief transformations.

Definition 6.3.1 (Protocol). A **protocol** for a language $\mathcal{L}$ and set of model transformations X is a tuple $\langle T, \rightarrowtail, l \rangle$ where $\langle T, \rightarrowtail \rangle$ is a tree and l assigns to each edge (i.e., pair (t, t') where t' is an immediate successor of t) a symbol $\tau(\varphi)$ where $\tau \in X$ is a model transformation and $\varphi \in \mathcal{L}$ is a formula. □

Let $\mathcal{P} = \langle T, \rightarrowtail, l \rangle$ be a protocol and $\mathcal{M} = \langle W, \preceq, V \rangle$ an initial plausibility model. The plausibility model at instant $t \in T$ is defined as follows by iteratively updating $\mathcal{M}$ according to the (unique) path in T leading to node t. Rather than giving a formal definition, I discuss an example. Consider the following protocol:

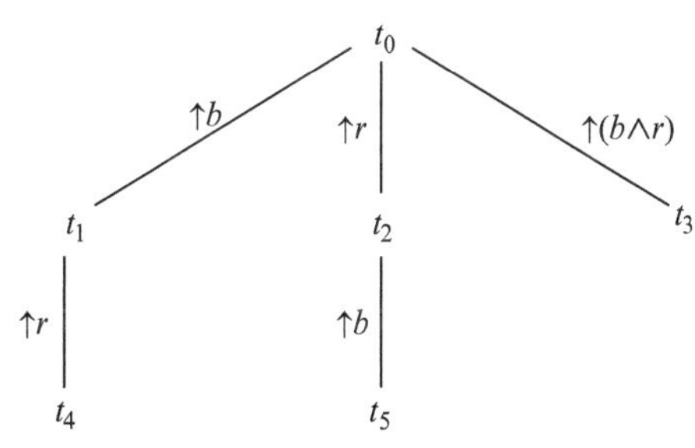

If $\mathcal{M}$ is the initial model in Fig. 6.1 (i.e., $\mathcal{M}_0$), then $\mathcal{M}_{t_4}$ is the model $\mathcal{M}_2$ in Fig. 6.1 and $\mathcal{M}_{t_5}$ is the model $\mathcal{M}_2$ in Fig. 6.2. We are interested in pairs $(\mathcal{M}_t, \mathcal{P})$ where t is a node in $\mathcal{P}$, and $\mathcal{M}_t$ is the model generated from an initial model $\mathcal{M}$ as described above.

The above protocol represents the different ways in which the agent from the previous example can go about incorporating the information that the animal she is looking at is a red bird. Why would a rational agent prefer one path over another in a given protocol? One answer might be that this is part of the description

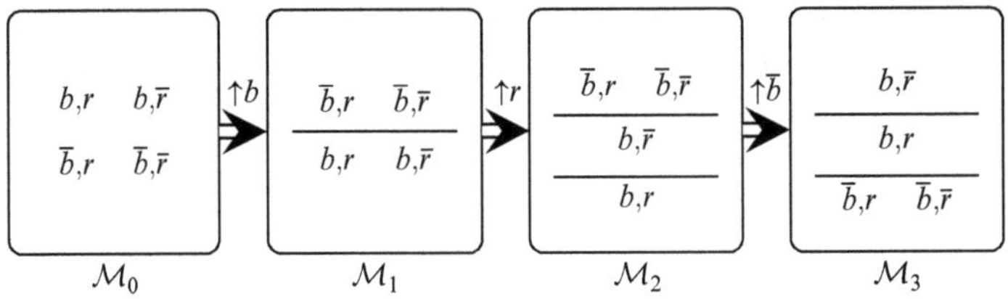

Fig. 6.1 A conservative upgrade sequence

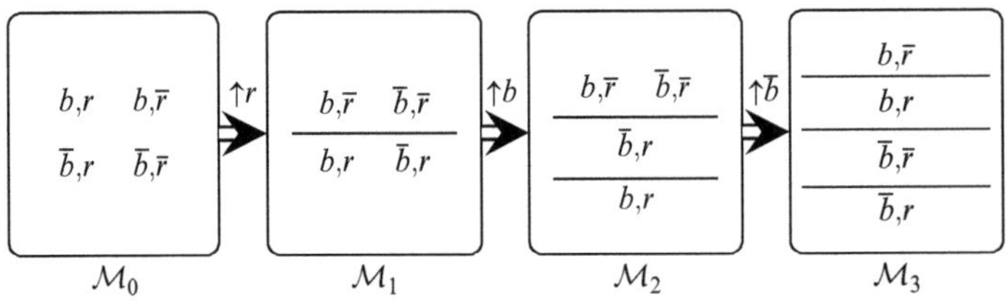

Fig. 6.2 Another conservative upgrade sequence

of the problem (i.e., that Ann first received the information that b and *then* the information that r). But this means that the agent has (implicitly or explicitly) agreed to conform to this specific protocol (a tree with a single branch with the labels $\uparrow b$ and $\uparrow r$), *not* to the protocol displayed above. The branching structure in a protocol represents situations where the agent has not (yet) committed to a particular way of incorporating the received evidence. Now, some beliefs might be *robust* in the sense that every (maximal) path in the protocol leads to a model where the agent has that belief. In the above protocol, all maximal paths lead to models (namely models $\mathcal{M}_{t_3}$, $\mathcal{M}_{t_4}$, and $\mathcal{M}_{t_5}$) where the agent believes that the animal is a red bird.

Of course, the situation becomes more interesting when the agent receives information that contradicts evidence found on some or all of the paths in the current protocol. This is the case when she receives the information that the animal is not a bird (denoted by $\overline{b}$). Rather than asking how the agent should incorporate this information into her current beliefs, we should ask how she should incorporate this information into her current protocol. One response would be to add $\uparrow \overline{b}$ at the end of all paths in the protocol. But other operations make sense. For example, a more cautious response would add an edge labeled by $\uparrow\overline{b}$ only to the node t_5. This analysis raises the following question: What are the natural operations on protocols and rational principles that these operations should conform to?

There are many temporal extensions of our basic doxastic language that one can use to reason about these structures (see Bonanno (2007) and Bonanno (2012); Dégremont (2010) for some examples). A complete account of these different logical systems will be left for future work. Here is one example: Include an operator '$\Diamond$' that quantifies over maximal paths in the protocol. Suppose that $\mathcal{M}$ is an initial plausibility model, $\mathcal{P}$ is a protocol, w is a state in $\mathcal{M}$ and t a moment in $\mathcal{P}$. Interpret formulas at pairs $(\mathcal{M}_t, \mathcal{P}, w)$ where $\mathcal{M}_t$ is defined as above (assuming the initial model is $\mathcal{M}$). The definition of the different informative attitudes (e.g., conditional beliefs) is as it is in Sect. 6.2.1. Here, I give only the definition of the new temporal operator:

- $\mathcal{M}_t, \mathcal{P}, w \models \Diamond\varphi$ provided that there exists a maximal path $p = (t, t_1, \ldots, t_n)$ such that $\mathcal{M}_{t_n}, \mathcal{P}_0, w \models \varphi$, where $\mathcal{P}_0$ is a single node protocol.

Thus, $\Diamond\varphi$ not only "moves time forward", but also "resets" the protocol.[12] Let $\Box$ be the dual of $\Diamond$ (i.e., $\Box\varphi$ is $\neg \Diamond \neg\varphi$). Then, $\Box\varphi$ means that φ is true after every way of updating beliefs consistent with the current protocol. But then we need some way to build up a protocol. One proposal is to reinterpret the dynamic modalities $[\Uparrow\varphi]$ as operations that change the protocol:

- $\mathcal{M}_t, \mathcal{P}, w \models [\uparrow \varphi]\psi$ iff $\mathcal{M}_t, \mathcal{P}^{\uparrow\varphi}, w \models \psi$, where $\mathcal{P}^{\uparrow\varphi}$ is the protocol that incorporates φ.

To make things concrete, suppose that $\mathcal{P}^{\uparrow\varphi}$ is the protocol that adds edges labeled by $\uparrow\varphi$ at *all* of the leave nodes in $\mathcal{P}$. This language can then express precisely what is puzzling about the example discussed in this section:

$$\Box Br \wedge [\uparrow\overline{b}]\neg\Box Br$$

The belief that the animal is red is *robust* in the given protocol, but after incorporating a proposition that is "irrelevant" to r (i.e., $\overline{b}$), this belief is no longer robust. This formula is true given the above protocol and the initial model where all four possible states are equally plausible.

These are only some initial ideas, but they illustrate the richness of the proposed framework. A complete logical analysis will be left for future work.

6.4 Conclusions

Agents are faced with many diverse tasks as they interact with the environment and one another. At certain moments, they must *react* to their (perhaps surprising) observations, while at other moments, they must be *proactive* and choose to perform a specific (informative) action. In interactive and learning situations, there are many (sometimes competing) *sources* for these attitudes: For example, the type of "communicatory event" (public announcement, private announcement); the disposition of the other participants (are the sources of information *trustworthy*?);

---

[12] Of course, one could drop this assumption and assume that the protocol remains fixed. I do not pursue this line of inquiry here.

and other implicit assumptions about procedural information (reducing the number of possible observations). A key aspect of any formal model of a (social) interactive situation or situation of rational inquiry is the way it accounts for the

> ...information about how I learn some of the things I learn, about the sources of my information, or about what I believe about what I believe and don't believe. If the story we tell in an example makes certain information about any of these things relevant, then it needs to be included in a proper model of the story, if it is to play the right role in the evaluation of the abstract principles of the model (Stalnaker 2009, p. 203).

I had two goals in this paper. First and foremost, I surveyed recent dynamic logics of belief revision (see van Benthem (2011) for full coverage of this topic). My second goal was to discuss why it is important to make explicit the underlying assumptions about the procedural information available to the agents in the situation being modeled. I also sketched some initial ideas of a logic for reasoning about this procedural information. There are a number of papers that explore the ideas touched on in this paper in much more detail. The interested readers is invited to consult Hoshi (2009), Wang (2010), van Ditmarsch et al. (2011), Rodenhäuser (2011) and Pacuit and Simon (2011) for more information.

References

T. Ågotnes, N. Alechina, The dynamics of syntactic knowledge. J. Log. Comput. **17**(1), 83–116 (2007)

C.E. Alchourrón, P. Gärdenfors, D. Makinson, On the logic of theory change: partial meet contraction and revision functions. J. Symb. Log. **50**, 510–530 (1985)

R. Aumann, Interactive epistemology I: knowledge. Int. J. Game Theory **28**, 263–300 (1999)

A. Baltag, S. Smets, Conditional doxastic models: a qualitative approach to dynamic belief revision, in *Proceedings of WOLLIC 2006, Electronic Notes in Theoretical Computer Science*, Stanford University, eds. by G. Mints, R. de Queiroz, 2006, Vol. 165, pp. 5–21

A. Baltag, S. Smets, The logic of conditional doxastic actions, in *New Perspectives on Games and Interaction*, eds. by R. van Rooij, K. Apt. Texts in Logic and Games (Amsterdam University Press, Amsterdam, 2008a), pp. 9–31

A. Baltag, S. Smets, A qualitative theory of dynamic interactive belief revision, in *Logic and the Foundation of Game and Decision Theory (LOFT7)*, eds. by G. Bonanno, W. van der Hoek, M. Wooldridge. Texts in Logic and Games (Amsterdam University Press, Amsterdam, 2008b), pp. 13–60

A. Baltag, S. Smets, ESSLLI 2009 course: dynamic logics for interactive belief revision (2009), Slides available online at: http://alexandru.tiddlyspot.com/#[[ESSLLI%2709%20Slides]]

A. Baltag, L. Moss, S. Solecki, The logic of common knowledge, public announcements and private suspicions, in *Proceedings of the 7th Conference on Theoretical Aspects of Rationality and Knowledge (TARK 98)*, Evanston, ed. by I. Gilboa, 1998, Morgan Kaufmann Publishers Inc. San Francisco, CA, USA, pp. 43–56

P. Battigalli, M. Siniscalchi, Strong belief and forward induction reasoning. J. Econ. Theory **105**, 356–391 (2002)

P. Blackburn, M. de Rijke, Y. Venema, *Modal Logic* (Cambridge University Press, Cambridge, 2002)

O. Board, Dynamic interactive epistemology. Games Econ. Behav. **49**, 49–80 (2004)

G. Bonanno, Axiomatic characterization of AGM belief revision in a temporal logic. Artif. Intell. **171**, 144–160 (2007)

G. Bonanno, Belief change in branching time: AGM-consistency and iterated revision. J. Philos. Log. **41**(1), 201–236 (2012). Manuscript

G. Bonanno, P. Battigalli, Recent results on belief, knowledge and the epistemic foundations of game theory. Res. Econ. **53**(2), 149–225 (1999)

C. Boutilier, Conditional Logics for Default Reasoning and Belief Revision. PhD thesis, University of Toronto, 1992

C. Boutilier, Iterated revision and minimal revision of conditional beliefs. J. Philos. Log. **25**, 262–304 (1996)

A. Brandenburger, The power of paradox: some recent developments in interactive epistemology. Int. J. Game Theory **35**, 465–492 (2007)

D. Christensen, Higher-order evidence. Philos. Phenomenol. Res. **81**(1), 185–215 (2010)

C.B. Cross, 'Can' and the logic of ability. Philos. Stud. **50**(1), 53–64 (1986)

A. Darwiche, J. Pearl, On the logic of iterated belief revision. Artif. Intell. **89**, 1–29 (1997)

C. Dégremont, The Temporal Mind. Observations on the Logic of Belief Change in Interactive Systems. PhD thesis, Institute for Logic, Language and Computation. (DS-2010-03, 2010)

P. Egré, B. Bonnay, Inexact knowledge with introspection. J. Philos. Log. **38**(2), 179–228 (2009)

D. Elgesem, The modal logic of agency. Nord. J. Philos. Log. **2**, 1–46 (1997)

R. Fagin, J. Halpern, Y. Moses, M. Vardi, *Reasoning about Knowledge* (MIT, Cambridge, 1995)

J. Gerbrandy, Bisimulations on Planet Kripke. PhD thesis, University of Amsterdam, 1999

A. Grove, Two modellings for theory change. J. Philos. Log. **17**, 157–170 (1988)

J. Halpern, *Reasoning About Uncertainty* (MIT, Cambridge, 2005)

J. Halpern, Y. Moses, Knowledge and common knowledge in a distributed environment. J. ACM **37**(3), 549–587 (1990)

J. Halpern, L. Rego, Reasoning about knowledge of unawareness revisited, in *Proceedings of Theoretical Aspects of Rationality and Knowledge (TARK'09)*, Stanford, ed. by A. Heifetz, 2009

V. Hendricks, Editor, special issue: "8 bridges between formal and mainstream epistemology". Philos. Stud. **128**(1), 1–227, 2006

V. Hendricks, *Mainstream and Formal Epistemology* (Cambridge University Press, Cambridge, 2006)

J. Hintikka, *Knowledge and Belief: An Introduction to the Logic of the Two Notions* (Cornell University Press, Ithaca, 1962)

J. Hintikka, *Knowledge and Belief: An Introduction to the Logic of the Two Notions (with an Introduction by V. Hendricks and J. Symons)* (King's College Publications, London, 2005)

J. Horty, *Agency and Deontic Logic* (Oxford University Press, Oxford/New York, 2001)

T. Hoshi, Epistemic Dynamics and Protocol Information. PhD thesis, Stanford University, 2009

W. Jamroga, T. Ågotnes, Constructive knowledge: what agents can achieve under imperfect information. J. Appl. Non-class. Log. **17**(4), 423–475 (2007)

P. Lamarre, Y. Shoham, Knowledge, certainty, belief and conditionalisation, in *Proceedings of the International Conference on Knowledge Representation and Reasoning*, Bonn, 1994, pp. 415–424

D. Lewis, *Counterfactuals* (Blackwell, Oxford, 1973)

F. Liu, Changing for the better: preference dynamics and agent diversity. PhD thesis, Institute for Logic, Language and Computation (ILLC), 2008

A. Nayak, M. Pagnucco, P. Peppas, Dynamic belief revision operators. Artif. Intell. **146**, 193–228 (2003)

E. Pacuit, S. Simon, Reasoning with protocols under imperfect information. Rev. Symb. Log. **4**, 412–444 (2011)

E. Pacuit, R. Parikh, E. Cogan, The logic of knowledge based obligation. Synthese **149**(2), 311–341 (2006)

R. Parikh, R. Ramanujam, A knowledge based semantics of messages. J. Log Lang. Inf. **12**, 453–467 (2003)

J. Plaza, Logics of public communications, in *Proceedings, 4th International Symposium on Methodologies for Intelligent Systems*, Charlotte, ed. by M.L. Emrich, M.S. Pfeifer, M. Hadzikadic, Z. Ras, 1989, pp. 201–216. (republished as Plaza (2007))

J. Plaza, Logics of public communications. Synthese **158**(2), 165–179 (2007)

B. Rodenhäuser, A logic for extensional protocols, J. Appl. Non-class. Log. **21**(3–4), 477–502 (2011)

H. Rott, Shifting priorities: simple representations for 27 itereated theory change operators, in *Modality Matters: Twenty-Five Essays in Honour of Krister Segerberg*, eds. by H. Lagerlund, S. Lindström, R. Sliwinski, Vol. 53. Uppsala Philosophical Studies, 2006, pp. 359–384

Y. Shoham, K. Leyton-Brown, *Multiagent Systems: Algorithmic, Game-Theoretic, and Logical Foundations* (Cambridge University Press, Cambridge/New York, 2009)

R. Stalnaker, The problem of logical omniscience I. Synthese **89**, 425–440 (1991)

R. Stalnaker, On the evaluation of solution concepts. Theory Decis. **37**(42), 49–73 (1994)

R. Stalnaker, Iterated belief revision. Erkentnis **70**, 189–209 (2009)

J. van Benthem, Dynamic logic for belief revision. J. Appl. Non-class. Log. **17**(2), 129–155 (2007)

J. van Benthem, The information in intuitionistic logic. Synthese **167**, 329–348 (2009)

J. van Benthem, *Logical Dynamics of Information and Interaction* (Cambridge University Press, Cambridge, 2011)

J. van Benthem, J. van Eijck, B. Kooi, Logics of communication and change. Inf. Comput. **204**(11), 1620–1662 (2006)

J. van Benthem, J. Gerbrandy, T. Hoshi, E. Pacuit, Merging frameworks for interaction. J. Philos. Log. **38**(5), 491–526 (2009)

H. van Ditmarsch, Prolegomena to dynamic logic for belief revision. Synth. Knowl. Ration. Action **147**, 229–275 (2005)

H. van Ditmarsch, W. van der Hoek, B.P. Kooi, *Dynamic Epistemic Logic*, Synthese Library (Springer, Dordrecht, 2007)

H. van Ditmarsch, S. Ghosh, R. Verbrugge, Y. Wang, Hidden protocols, in *Proceedings of the 13th Conference on Theoretical Aspects of Rationality and Knowledge (TARK)*, Groningen, ed. by K. Apt (ACM Digital Library, 2011) http://dl.acm.org/citation.cfm?id=645876

Y. Wang, Epistemic Modelling and Protocol Dynamics. PhD thesis, CWI, 2010

T. Williamson, *Knowledge and Its Limits* (Oxford University Press, Oxford, 2000)

Chapter 7
Reasoning About Knowledge in Context

Franck Lihoreau and Manuel Rebuschi

7.1 Introduction

A major goal of post-cartesian epistemology is to respond to radical skepticism, the view that we know (almost) nothing of what we ordinarily take ourselves to know. The argument most commonly associated with this view is the so-called "argument from ignorance". It starts with the premise that we cannot exclude the possibility that we might be in such alternative worlds as those described by Descartes' *Evil Genius* hypothesis or by Putnam's *Brain in a Vat* scenario. The alleged reason for this inability is that these skeptical hypotheses are designed in such a way that if we were in the skeptical worlds they describe, we'd have exactly the same experiences, memories, beliefs, etc., as those that we actually have, so that for all we know, we might be in these worlds of mass(ive) error. From here, the skeptic's reasoning takes us to the conclusion that we do not know any (or most) of the things that we ordinarily take ourselves to know, for instance, that we have hands, that we are sitting at our desk, etc.

The problem is, of course, that this skeptical conclusion goes against our powerful tendency to think that we do know a lot about many things. In the last few decades, emphasis has been put on the importance, in dealing with this problem, of taking (some notion of) context into consideration when thinking about knowledge and knowledge ascription. This shows in the ever-growing number of discussions on

F. Lihoreau (✉)
Faculdade de Ciências Sociais e Humanas, Instituto de Filosofia da Linguagem,
Universidade Nova de Lisboa, Avenida de Berna, 26 – 4° piso, 1069-061 Lisboa, Portugal
e-mail: franck.lihoreau@fcsh.unl.pt

M. Rebuschi
LHSP – Archives H. Poincaré (UMR 7117), MSH Lorraine (USR 3261) CNRS,
Université de Lorraine, 91, avenue de la Libération, BP 454, 54001 Nancy, France
e-mail: manuel.rebuschi@univ-lorraine.fr

M. Rebuschi et al. (eds.), *Interdisciplinary Works in Logic, Epistemology, Psychology and Linguistics*, Logic, Argumentation & Reasoning 3,
DOI 10.1007/978-3-319-03044-9_7, © Springer International Publishing Switzerland 2014

so-called "contextualist" approaches as defended by Cohen (1999, 2000), DeRose (1992, 1995, 1999), Heller (1999a,b), Lewis (1979, 1996) and others, as well as the increasing interest in theories of "subject-sensitive" knowledge ascriptions *à la* Hawthorne (2004) and Stanley (2005), and of "assessment-sensitive" ascriptions following MacFarlane (2005), to mention but a few of the available accounts that have context playing a significant epistemological role.

In Sect. 7.2, we present four major epistemological positions on the problem of skepticism, with a view to showing the importance of (different notions of) context in the recent philosophical discussions on knowledge. In Sect. 7.3, we provide the foundations for a general formal framework based on the technical notion of "contextual models", which will make it possible to capture those epistemological positions using one and the same language and semantics, and to investigate the logical connections they are bound to endorse between knowledge and context. Finally, Sect. 7.4 adds to that "static" formalism a "dynamic" formalization of context based on a simplified version of Discourse Representation Theory, which will allow us to account for the apparent variation over the course of a conversation in the epistemic standards of the participants, and to overcome such difficulties as the logical omniscience problem that usually plagues normal modal logical approaches to knowledge.

In short, our purpose is to provide formal tools for exploring reasoning about knowledge in context in both its static and dynamic aspects.

7.2 Highlights of Informal Epistemology

In this section we briefly describe and illustrate four prominent positions on the problem of skepticism which, through the discussions they have given rise to in the recent philosophical literature on knowledge, have significantly contributed to making context an issue of prime epistemological importance.

7.2.1 Anti-skeptical Invariantism

The first position, *anti-skeptical invariantism* as we will call it, which can also be found in the literature under the name "moderate invariantism" or "radical anti-skepticism", has it that many and perhaps most of our ordinary knowledge claims are literally true. This view is endorsed by ordinary language philosopher Austin (1946),[1] who observes that the epistemic standards that the skeptic has in mind

[1]It is very common in the literature to find this position associated with the name G. E. Moore, and for this reason called "Moorean invariantism". We find it more convenient to refer to Austin instead.

and which require of us the ability to exclude absolutely all possibilities of error, including the most far-fetched ones, are very different from those which govern our everyday knowledge claims and which do not have such stringent requirements. In everyday life, the standards in place are such that as long as we have no reason to think, for example, that we might be brains in vats, we are not required to rule out this possibility to properly count as knowing, say, that we have hands. Then, according to Austin, the only standards that can be legitimate are those that match our ordinary practice of knowledge ascription. This is the case with the standards that prevail in everyday life: we – ordinarily competent speakers – judge many and perhaps most of our everyday knowledge claims to be correct. Not so with the skeptic's standards, which would make it merely impossible to ever use "know" correctly. So, on this view, we do know a lot.

7.2.2 *Skeptical Invariantism*

The next position, *skeptical invariantism*, or simply *skepticism*, takes us in exactly the opposite direction by claiming that most and perhaps all of our ordinary knowledge claims are literally false. This claim is held by Unger who, in Unger (1971) for instance, proposes relating the word "know" to a class of natural language expressions that are systematically used erroneously, yet in a pragmatically correct way, by competent speakers, and which he labels "absolute terms", as their application admits no degree/exception. The predicate "flat" is one such term: (most of) our ordinary flatness ascriptions are literally false since a surface is flat only if it has absolutely no bumps or other irregularities on it, but no real physical surface can meet this condition, even microscopically. Real surfaces are, however, close enough to being flat given our everyday life interests, goals, presuppositions, etc., for those ascriptions to be justifiedly made, pragmatically speaking. Likewise, "know" too is an absolute term: because we cannot rule out all logical possibilities of error, (most of) our ordinary knowledge ascriptions are literally false; yet, we are pragmatically justified in making them in that we are close enough, with respect to our everyday purposes, interests, etc., to satisfying the conditions for a true ascription. In any case, on this view, we know almost nothing.

7.2.3 *Contextualism*

A third position, *contextualism* as it is called, aims at overcoming the apparent conflict between skepticism and anti-skepticism by holding that the truth or falsity of knowledge ascriptions depends on the context in which they are made. It is defended by Lewis (1979, 1996) for instance, who claims that for an ascription of the type "S knows that p" to be true, the possibilities of error that S must be able to rule out are all and only those that are relevant in the context of the ascription, e.g. those attended to by the ascriber. This condition is met when no not-p possibility is contextually relevant. This is the case in everyday contexts for most contingent propositions, e.g. that we have hands, because in these contexts the far-fetched skeptical possibility that we might be handless brains in vats simply is irrelevant, and therefore need not be ruled out. By contrast, in a philosophical context where such skeptical possibilities have been raised and are being attended to, they are relevant and need to be excluded; but we are unable to rule them out. In these contexts it is therefore false that we know that we are not brains in vats and that we have hands. It is true that we know a lot in ordinary contexts, and very little in skeptical contexts. More generally, on the contextualist view, whether or not it is true that one knows something will depend on the focus, interests, stakes, presuppositions, etc., that make up the context of the "attributor", i.e. the person who is attributing/denying knowledge.

7.2.4 Subjectivism

According to *subjectivism* (or *sensitive moderate invariantism,* or *subject-sensitive invariantism* as it is often called), as defended by Hawthorne (2004) or Stanley (2005), such factors as attention, interests, stakes, etc., are considered relevant to the truth of knowledge ascriptions, but only insofar as they make up the context, not of the attributor, but of the "subject", the person who is being attributed/denied knowledge. This is clear from Hawthorne, who insists that the practical importance, for the subject, of being right and not making a mistake is epistemically crucial, since a subject's anxiety can contribute to making certain possibilities of error salient to him, where salience is equated with relevance. These and only these possibilities will have to be ruled out for the subject to truly count as knowing. Thus, one can know more by worrying less. In particular, "the philosopher who worries about being a brain in a vat, etc., will know less than the dullard who doesn't" (Hawthorne 2004, p 167).

The formal framework to be described in the next section will help us understand more precisely where the connections between subjectivism, contextualism, anti-skepticism and skepticism lie.

7.3 Static Formalism

In this section, we first propose a formal framework for reasoning about knowledge in context, and then show how this framework can be used to capture the various epistemological positions described in the previous section.

7.3.1 *The Formal Framework*

We first describe the "epistemic language" we will be using throughout the paper. We then provide a "contextual semantics" for it that allows four possible definitions of truth for epistemic formulas, and we investigate what usual logical properties of knowledge are preserved in our proposed semantics and how.

7.3.1.1 Syntax

Definition 7.3.1 (Epistemic Language). Let $\mathcal{A}t$ be a set of atomic formulas and J a set of agents. The language we will be using is defined by:

$$\varphi := p \mid \neg\varphi \mid \varphi \wedge \varphi \mid K_j\varphi$$

where $p \in \mathcal{A}t$ and $j \in J$.

We use the common definitions of $\vee$, $\rightarrow$, and $\leftrightarrow$ in terms of $\neg$ and $\wedge$. The intended reading of the epistemic operator $K_j\varphi$ is "Agent j knows that φ". As a convention, an *epistemic formula* will be any formula containing at least one occurrence of an epistemic operator, and a *non-epistemic formula* any formula that contains none.

As should be obvious, the epistemic language that we will be using is simply that of standard epistemic logic.

7.3.1.2 Semantics

The semantics, however, will differ from the standard Kripke semantics in that it will include (i) a set $\mathcal{C}$ of *contexts*, and (ii) a function $\mathcal{R}$ of *relevance* determining the worlds that are relevant in each context:

Definition 7.3.2 (Contextual Model). A *contextual model* for the epistemic language is a structure $\mathcal{M} = \langle W, \{\mathcal{K}_j : j \in J\}, \mathcal{C}, \mathcal{R}, V \rangle$ where (i) W is a non-empty set of worlds, (ii) $\mathcal{K}_j \subseteq W \times W$ is a relation of epistemic accessibility (for each $j \in J$), (iii) $\mathcal{C} = \{c_i : i \in I\}$ is a non-empty set of contexts, which may be finite or not, such that $J \subseteq I$, (iv) $\mathcal{R} : \mathcal{C} \rightarrow \wp(W)^W$ is a function of contextual relevance that associates with each context c_i, for each world w, the set of worlds that are relevant in c_i for w, and (v) $V : \mathcal{A}t \rightarrow \wp(W)$ is a valuation associating with each atom p the set of worlds in which p holds.

Remark. A context c_i can be connected with an agent, i.e., when $i \in J$. But nothing prevents us from connecting contexts with groups of agents instead of individual agents, or with conversations, etc. Also, the semantics considered here remains neutral as to the *nature* of contexts. (A possible modelling inspired by Discourse Representation Theory and whereby contexts can evolve through time over the course of several assertions will be described in Sect. 7.4).

The idea, then, is to relativize truth not only to (a model and) a world as in standard Kripke semantics, but also to a context:

Definition 7.3.3 (Truth). Given a contextual model $\mathcal{M} = \langle W, \{\mathcal{K}_j : j \in J\}, \mathcal{C}, \mathcal{R}, V\rangle$, a state $w \in W$, and a formula φ in the epistemic language, we can define $\mathcal{M}, c, w \models \varphi$ in four possible ways, depending on the clause we choose for epistemic formulas, as follows:

(i) $\mathcal{M}, c, w \models p$ iff $w \in V(p)$
(ii) $\mathcal{M}, c, w \models \neg\varphi$ iff $\mathcal{M}, c, w \not\models \varphi$
(iii) $\mathcal{M}, c, w \models \varphi \wedge \psi$ iff $\mathcal{M}, c, w \models \varphi$ and $\mathcal{M}, c, w \models \psi$
(iv) $\mathcal{M}, c_i, w \models K_j\varphi$ iff for every w', if $\mathcal{K}_j ww'$ and $w' \in \mathcal{R}(c_k)(w)$ then $\mathcal{M}, c_l, w' \models \varphi$ with either one of the following options:

1.1. $k = l = i$
1.2. $k = i, l = j$
2.1. $k = j, l = i$
2.2. $k = l = j$

To refer specifically to one of the four resulting definitions, we will subscript $\models$ with the appropriate number: $\mathcal{M}, c, w \models_{1.2} \varphi$, $\mathcal{M}, c, w \models_{2.2} \varphi$, etc. We will sometimes group the notions two-by-two, letting $\models_{-.2}$ refer unspecifically to the $\models_{1.2}$ case or the $\models_{2.2}$ case, for instance; and $\models$ will refer indifferently to any one of the four notions.[2]

7.3.1.3 The Properties of Knowledge in Contextual Models

We may wonder if the following common axioms and inference rules are preserved in our contextual models, and if not, what condition(s) must be imposed on the relevance function in order to restore them?

K $\models (K_j\varphi \wedge K_j(\varphi \rightarrow \psi)) \rightarrow K\psi$
RN If $\models \varphi$ then $\models K_j\varphi$
T $\models K_j\varphi \rightarrow \varphi$
D $\models K_j\varphi \rightarrow \neg K_j\neg\varphi$, or $\models \neg K_j\bot$
4 $\models K_j\varphi \rightarrow K_jK_j\varphi$
5 $\models \neg K_j\varphi \rightarrow K_j\neg K_j\varphi$
B $\models \varphi \rightarrow K_j\neg K_j\neg\varphi$

[2] We mention all four logically possible options here for the sake of exhaustiveness, although we will not examine all of them. To be precise, option 2.1 will not be relevant to our purpose. See Footnote 6.

To answer this question, let us assume the following convention. In a given contextual model, from the relevance function $\mathcal{R}$ and a context c_k, a new accessibility relation R_{c_k} can be defined by:

$$\forall w.\ \forall w'.\ \mathcal{R}_{c_k} ww' \Leftrightarrow w' \in \mathcal{R}(c_k)(w).$$

Then, clause (iv) for epistemic formulas can be rewritten using the intersection $KK_j^k = KK_j \cap \mathcal{R}_{c_k}$ of the two accessibility relations:

(iv') $\mathcal{M}, c_i, w \models K_j\varphi$ iff for all $w' \in W$, if $KK_j^k ww'$ then $\mathcal{M}, c_l, w' \models \varphi$ (with some conditions on k and l)

Let $\mathbb{M}_n$ be the class of all (unrestricted) contextual models for n agents regardless of the specific choice among options (1.1)–(2.2). It is easy to see that the following proposition holds:

Proposition 7.3.4. *Both the axiom (K) and the necessitation rule* (RN) *are valid with respect to* $\mathbb{M}_n$*:*

(K) $\mathbb{M}_n \models (K_j\varphi \wedge K_j(\varphi \rightarrow \psi)) \rightarrow K_j\psi$
(RN) *If* $\mathbb{M}_n \models \varphi$ *then* $\mathbb{M}_n \models K_j\varphi$

Things get more complex when we turn to the additional possible properties. We will give only sufficient conditions for preserving these properties in contextual models. Two cases are to be systematically distinguished:

1. A simple case has to do with the (–.1) definitions, which by (iv') amount to:

   (iv'/–.1) $\mathcal{M}, c_i, w \models_{-.1} K_j\varphi$ iff for all $w' \in W$, if $KK_j^k ww'$ then $\mathcal{M}, c_i, w' \models_{-.1} \varphi$.

   Here, the only role of context c_i is to set the value of k. The definition is strictly equivalent to that of truth in the standard Kripke model $\mathcal{M}' = \langle W, \{KK_j : j \in J\}, V\rangle$ that corresponds with the contextual model $\mathcal{M} = \langle W, \{KK_j : j \in J\}, \mathcal{C}, \mathcal{R}, V\rangle$, for an operator K_j^k with accessibility relation KK_j^k:
   $\mathcal{M}, c_i, w \models_{-.1} K_j\varphi \Leftrightarrow \mathcal{M}', w \models K_j^k\varphi$.
   Intuitively, contextual models will preserve for K_j, the principles corresponding to the properties of KK_j that are preserved by KK_j^k. To be precise:

   Proposition 7.3.5. *The axioms (T), (B), (4), and (5) are (1.1)- and (2.1)-valid in contextual models* $\mathcal{M}$ *whose relations* K_j *and* $\mathcal{R}_{c_k}$ *are all respectively reflexive, symmetric, transitive, and Euclidean:*

(T)	$\mathcal{M} \models_{-.1} K_j\varphi \rightarrow \varphi$	$\Leftrightarrow$	*KK_j is reflexive and $w \in \mathcal{R}(c_k)(w)$ (for all w)*
(B)	$\mathcal{M} \models_{-.1} \varphi \rightarrow K_j\neg K_j\neg\varphi$	$\Leftrightarrow$	*KK_j is symmetric and $w \in \mathcal{R}(c_k)(w') \Rightarrow w' \in \mathcal{R}(c_k)(w)$*
(4)	$\mathcal{M} \models_{-.1} K_j\varphi \rightarrow K_jK_j\varphi$	$\Leftrightarrow$	*KK_j is transitive and $w \in \mathcal{R}(c_k)(w')$ & $w' \in \mathcal{R}(c_k)(w'') \Rightarrow w \in \mathcal{R}(c_k)(w'')$*
(5)	$\mathcal{M} \models_{-.1} \neg K_j\varphi \rightarrow K_j\neg K_j\varphi$	$\Leftrightarrow$	*KK_j is Euclidean and $w \in \mathcal{R}(c_k)(w')$ & $w \in \mathcal{R}(c_k)(w'') \Rightarrow w' \in \mathcal{R}(c_k)(w'')$*

   Making K_j *and* $\mathcal{R}_{c_k}$ *serial is not sufficient to ensure the validity of (D).*

2. The case is more complicated with the (−.2) definitions, which by (iv') again amount to:

   (iv'/–.2) $\mathcal{M}, c_i, w \models_{-.2} K_j\varphi$ iff for all $w' \in W$, if $KK_j^k ww'$ then $\mathcal{M}, c_j, w' \models_{-.2} \varphi$.

   The difficulty here has to do with formulas with embedded modalities, since their truth will depend on several contexts. We illustrate this with axioms (T), (4), and (5):

   Proposition 7.3.6. *Schema (T) is neither (1.2)-valid nor (2.2)-valid in contextual models $\mathcal{M}$ with reflexive K_j and $\mathcal{R}_{c_k}$ relations. Nevertheless, the following instances of (T) hold in these models:*

   - $\mathcal{M}, c_i, w \models_{-.2} K_j\varphi \rightarrow \varphi$, *for φ a non-epistemic formula;*
   - $\mathcal{M}, c_i, w \models_{-.2} K_j\varphi \rightarrow \varphi$ *if* $\mathcal{R}_{c_i} \subseteq \mathcal{R}_{c_j}$, *for φ an epistemic formula in disjunctive normal form with no negated epistemic operator in it;*
   - $\mathcal{M}, c_i, w \models_{-.2} K_j\varphi \rightarrow \varphi$ *if* $\mathcal{R}_{c_i} = \mathcal{R}_{c_j}$, *for φ an epistemic formula in normal disjunctive form with at least one negated epistemic operator.*

   Proposition 7.3.7. *Validity of (4):*

   - *Schema (4) is (2.2)-valid in contextual models $\mathcal{M}$ with reflexive K_j and $\mathcal{R}_{c_k}$ relations;*
   - *Schema (4) is not (1.2)-valid in contextual models $\mathcal{M}$ with transitive K_j and $\mathcal{R}_{c_k}$ relations. Nonetheless, the following instantiation of (4) holds in such models:* $\mathcal{M}, c_i, w \models_{1.2} K_j\varphi \rightarrow K_jK_j\varphi$ *if* $\mathcal{R}_{c_j} \subseteq \mathcal{R}_{c_i}$.

   Proposition 7.3.8. *Validity of (5):*

   - *Schema (5) is (2.2)-valid in contextual models $\mathcal{M}$ with Euclidean K_j and $\mathcal{R}_{c_k}$ relations;*
   - *Schema (5) is not (1.2)-valid in contextual models $\mathcal{M}$ with Euclidean K_j and $\mathcal{R}_{c_k}$ relations. However, in such models the following instantiation of (5) holds:* $\mathcal{M}, c_i, w \models_{1.2} \neg K_j\varphi \rightarrow K_j\neg K_j\varphi$ *if* $\mathcal{R}_{c_j} \subseteq \mathcal{R}_{c_i}$.

We add a final technical remark:

Proposition 7.3.9 (Reduction to Standard Kripke Semantics). *Definition (1.1) with w-constant relevance function $\mathcal{R}$ – i.e. such that for any context c, $\mathcal{R}(c)$ is constant – reduces to a case of standard Kripkean semantics.*

The proofs of the above propositions are in the Appendix.

7.3.2 The Formal Framework Applied

We now give an epistemological interpretation of our formalism and an application of it in capturing, within a unique framework, the various epistemological positions described in Sect. 7.2.

7.3.2.1 Elements of Epistemological Interpretation

Interpreting the $\mathcal{K}_j$-s

We propose to interpret the accessibility relations $\mathcal{K}_j$ in terms of epistemic indiscernibility, i. e., we have $\mathcal{K}_j ww'$ iff agent j cannot tell w from w' on the (sole) basis of what he knows. If φ holds in a $\mathcal{K}_j$-accessible world thus interpreted, then for all j knows, it might be that φ; in other words, it is epistemically possible that φ.

A question that naturally arises is what kind of relation is the epistemic accessibility relation. Here, our answer is that the $\mathcal{K}_j$ are to be construed as equivalence relations – i.e. reflexive, symmetric, and transitive – thus following the common tendency in the logico-epistemic literature.[3] The main epistemological reason for this is that as a general rule, epistemologists grant the skeptic the premiss that their skeptical worlds are epistemically indiscernible from the actual world, i.e., are exactly the same as the actual world with respect to whatever evidence or information we may have; and *being exactly the same as* is an equivalence relation.

Interpreting $\mathcal{R}$

The relevance function $\mathcal{R}$ allows us to capture the idea of epistemic standards and their contextual variability. Indeed, it makes it possible to represent, for a given situation or world, the set of possible worlds that are relevant relative to a context, where the appropriate context (reference context, agent's context, etc.) depends on which definition we select for $\models$. Given a world w, two contexts c, c' can be associated with two sets of contextually relevant worlds, $\mathcal{R}(c)(w)$ and $\mathcal{R}(c')(w)$. When $\mathcal{R}(c)(w) \subseteq \mathcal{R}(c')(w)$, the truth of an epistemic formula relative to c' will be more difficult to obtain than relative to c. So, each context can be understood as determining via $\mathcal{R}$ a certain level of epistemic requirement. The strengthening – resp. the weakening – of epistemic standards will thus translate, in our framework, as an extension – resp. a restriction – of the set of relevant worlds.

Epistemic Accessibility and Contextual Relevance

The set of contextually relevant worlds for an agent j in a world w cannot be strictly included in the set of epistemically possible worlds for j. For j could know that φ, hence having his accessibility relation $\mathcal{K}_j$ restricted to φ-worlds, yet also know that another agent k does not know that φ when some $\neg\varphi$-world is accessible by $\mathcal{K}_k$; this requires that j be able to *consider* some of these $\neg\varphi$-worlds although they are

[3]See for instance the reference handbook (Fagin et al. 1995) on epistemic logic by Fagin et al. Dissenting views do nonetheless exist, as expressed by Hintikka in 1962, and more recently by Stalnaker in 2006.

not accessible to him. So, letting $\mathcal{K}(j)(w) = \{w' : w' \in W \,\&\, \mathcal{K}_j ww'\}$ be the set of worlds that are epistemically accessible to agent j, what we must not have is this: $\mathcal{R}(c_j)(w) \subsetneq \mathcal{K}(j)(w)$.

Interpreting the c_i-s

Crucial to the epistemological use we want to make of our formal framework is the distinction between the subject and the attributor of knowledge. In both cases, however, we are dealing with an agent. In one case, it is the agent i whom knowledge of a proposition φ is being attributed to; in the other case, it is the agent j who attributes knowledge of φ to i. An agent can also attribute knowledge of a proposition to himself in the first person, as in "I know this-or-that". In this case, he is both knowledge attributor and knowing subject.

To account for these various cases in our framework, we adopt the following conventions. In an evaluation of the form $\mathcal{M}, c_i, w \models K_j\varphi$, (i) at the most general level, context c_i will be called the "context of reference", and c_j the "context of agent j"; (ii) for $i \in I$, on the one hand, agent i will be associated with the "attributor" and c_i referred to as "attributor i's context", and on the other hand, agent j will be associated with the "subject" and c_j referred to as "subject j's context"; and (iii) when considering $\mathcal{R}(c_k)(w)$, we shall refer to c_k as the "attributor's context" or as the "subject's context" depending on whether $k = i$ or $k = j$.

7.3.2.2 Epistemological Interpretation of the $\models$-s

We can now consider the various definitions of $\models$ and connect them with the various epistemological positions mentioned earlier. As we will see, one of the major advantages of our formalism is that it shows what answer each of these positions can give to a problem often underestimated in the epistemological literature, viz. that of embedded epistemic operators.

A first observation is that there seems to be no noticeable difference between definition (1.1) and (1.2) as far as their epistemological interpretation is concerned. The former:

$$\mathcal{M}, c_i, w \models_{1.1} K_j\varphi \text{ iff for every } w', \text{ if } \mathcal{K}_j ww' \text{ and } w' \in \mathcal{R}(c_i)(w) \text{ then } \mathcal{M}, c_i, w' \models \varphi$$

says, basically, that I (= attributor) can truly say that you (= subject) know that φ when *I* can truly say, against *my* epistemic standards, that given your evidence, you know that φ; and the latter definition:

$$\mathcal{M}, c_i, w \models_{1.2} K_j\varphi \text{ iff for every } w', \text{ if } \mathcal{K}_j ww' \text{ and } w' \in \mathcal{R}(c_i)(w) \text{ then } \mathcal{M}, c_j, w' \models \varphi$$

says, basically, that I (= attributor) can truly say that you (= subject) know that φ when *you* can truly say, against *my* epistemic standards, that given your evidence, you know that φ. On both definitions, whether a world is relevant or not depends on the attributor's context.

However, an important difference shows up between the two definitions when we turn to formulas with embedded occurrences of epistemic operators, e.g. formulas like $K_1 K_2 \ldots K_m \varphi$.

Definition (1.1) as Invariantism

Regarding embedded epistemic operators, definition (1.1) yields:

$$\mathcal{M}, c_1, w \models_{1.1} K_2 K_3 \varphi \text{ iff for every } w', w'', \text{ if } \mathcal{K}_2 ww', \mathcal{K}_3 w'w'', w' \in \mathcal{R}(c_1)(w) \text{ and } w'' \in \mathcal{R}(c_1)(w'), \text{ then } \mathcal{M}, c_1, w'' \models_{1.1} \varphi.$$

which amounts to saying this: When attributor 1 says that subject 2 knows that subject 3 knows that φ, for 1's attribution to be true, it is always exactly the same standards as 2 that 3 must satisfy, that is to say, those in place in attributor 1's context. We propose to associate this definition with the two (insensitive) invariantist positions distinguished in Sect. 7.2, viz. skepticism and anti-skepticism. Both hold that the standards for making a true knowledge attribution are the same always and everywhere, regardless of who is attributing and who is being attributed knowledge. Simply, the former holds that those standards are too demanding for any such attribution to ever come out true, while the latter says they are lax enough to make (most of our) everyday knowledge attributions true.
The difference can be expressed formally in our framework by putting different constraints on the relevance function $\mathcal{R}$:

- For skepticism, the constraint that $\mathcal{R}(c_i)(w) = W$, for any i and any w. This means that whatever the attributor's context, the corresponding relevance set is always the entire set of all logically possible worlds, including, of course, such far-fetched worlds as those described by the Evil Genius or the Brain in a Vat hypotheses, which cannot be eliminated on the basis of our limited epistemic capabilities. In assuming this constraint, the skeptic make-believes that she is a god, and that people can reason on other people's knowledge only if they are gods themselves. Skeptical epistemic logic is epistemic logic for divine agents.
- For anti-skepticism, the constraint that for any i and any w, $\mathcal{R}(c_i)(w) = W*$, for some proper subset $W*$ of W, seems to be a minimum requirement, which nonetheless makes it less impossible for non-divine epistemic agents like us to truly claim knowledge. At least in some cases, all contextually relevant possibilities of error can be excluded. A further requirement – given here informally as a first approximation – will have to be that $W*$ be a set of epistemically accessible worlds where most propositions we ordinarily think we have knowledge of are true (e.g. that we have hands).

As should be clear, either one of these constraints will ensure that the set of epistemically relevant worlds is constant across contexts, that is, for any w, i, and j, $R(c_i)(w) = R(c_j)(w)$, which justifies applying to them the label "invariantism".[4]

Definition (1.2) as Contextualism

In contrast with definition (1.1), with embedded epistemic operators, definition (1.2) yields:

$$\mathcal{M}, c_1, w \models_{1.2} K_2 K_3 \varphi \text{ iff for every } w', w'', \text{ if } \mathcal{K}_2 ww', \mathcal{K}_3 w'w'', w' \in \mathcal{R}(c_1)(w) \text{ and } w'' \in \mathcal{R}(c_2)(w'), \text{ then } \mathcal{M}, c_3, w'' \models_{1.2} \varphi.$$

This entails that if an attributor 1 says that subject 2 knows that subject 3 knows that φ, for 1's attribution to be true, the standards that 2 must satisfy for 1's attribution to be true will be those in place in 1's context, while those that 3 must satisfy for it to be true that he knows φ will be those in place in subject 2's context, not attributor 1's context; and the two sets of standards might well be different in their requirements. This, in our opinion, is what we may and must expect from the behavior of genuine contextualist agents (who assume themselves to be such): a contextualist agent ought to reason about other agents' knowledge in the light of her own standards, but she also ought to be aware that the other agents do and ought to do the same too. We therefore suggest associating definition (1.2) with (genuine, self-assumed, coherent) contextualism.[5] To capture formally the contextualist idea that the views of the skeptic and the anti-skeptic are not incompatible, we can simply put on $\mathcal{R}$ the softer constraint that $\mathcal{R}(c_i)(w) \subseteq W$, so that when c_i is a philosophical context, $\mathcal{R}$ yields the set of all logically possible worlds, and when it is an everyday context, $\mathcal{R}$ yields a proper subset of those worlds – preferentially with epistemically possible worlds where most of what we ordinarily think we know is true.

Interestingly, identifying contextualism with definition (1.2) in this way shows that contextualism renders a relatively uncontroversial epistemic principle truly problematic, viz. the "veridicality principle" whereby knowledge requires truth. As Proposition 7.3.6 indicates, the formal version of this principle (schema (T) $K\varphi \rightarrow \varphi$) is (1.2)-valid in contextual models with reflexive contextualized

[4]Note in passing that they make the epistemic relevance set constant across *worlds* too, differing in this respect from "non-absolutist", "circumstance-sensitive" forms of invariantism *à la* Dretske or Nozick, not treated here.

[5]Here, some proponents of contextualism might disagree, as they would be willing to maintain that contextualism is true despite most people lacking awareness of this fact, and being semantically blind to the context-dependence of knowledge ascriptions. This is how, for instance, DeRose seems to conceive of the position. In Lihoreau and Rebuschi (2009), we insist on the distinction between these two construals of the contextualist stance and explore their respective bearings on the issue of epistemic factivity.

accessibility relations $\mathcal{K}_i^k$ only when φ is non-epistemic. This restriction of the implication from knowledge to truth to non-epistemic "facts" is totally in line with the spirit of contextualism for which there are no such things as "epistemic facts". "Know" does not relate to things like $knowledge_1, knowledge_2, \ldots$ that would exist objectively. Since one can count as knowing with respect to one attributor, yet as not knowing with respect to another, the contextualist's concept of knowledge cannot be descriptive, but only purely evaluative. So, if knowledge implies truth, it can only be non-epistemic truth. This is a consequence of contextualism that our proposed formal framework makes clearly salient.

Definition (2.2) as Subjectivism

According to Proposition 7.3.6, we get similar restricted veridicality with definition (2.2.):

$$\mathcal{M}, c_i, w \models_{2.2} K_j\varphi \text{ iff for every } w', \text{ if } \mathcal{K}_j ww' \text{ and } w' \in \mathcal{R}(c_j)(w) \text{ then } \mathcal{M}, c_j, w' \models \varphi$$

This definition, however, is very different from the contextualist spirit of definition (1.2), and closer in our opinion to the spirit of subjectivism. What it says is that only the subject, j, matters. When we attribute knowledge of a proposition to a subject, it is the standards in place in his context, not ours, that matter for the truth or falsity of our attribution. His context is also that in which he himself settles on the truth of the proposition whose knowledge we attribute to him. This means that according to this definition (unlike contextualist definition (1.2)), there are epistemic facts: it is the subject's knowledge that varies from context to context, not merely the truth of our attributions of knowledge to him. Depending on what is at stake in his context, a subject can possess, lack, or lose possession of his knowledge. This is in line with the characterization we gave earlier of subjectivism.

Now, although (not) knowing something is an epistemic *fact*, someone A's knowing that someone else B knows something p does not entail that B knows p. For suppose it is true that A knows that B knows p. Then, A must somehow satisfy the standards in place in his own context for knowing that B knows p. Does this mean that B thereby knows p? No, because nothing in subjectivism prohibits A priori that the standards in place in B's context be no more demanding than those in place in A's context. So, if subjectivism is true, veridicality cannot extend to one's knowledge of someone else's knowledge. This is exactly what definition (2.2) says, and constitutes further motivation for associating subjectivism with it.[6]

[6]As mentioned in Footnote 2, for our purposes, we do not need definition (2.1):

$$\mathcal{M}, c_i, w \models_{2.1} K_i\varphi \text{ iff for every } w', \text{ if } \mathcal{K}_j ww' \text{ and } w' \in \mathcal{R}(c_j)(w) \text{ then } \mathcal{M}, c_i, w' \models \varphi$$

which says that I (attributor) can truly say that you (=subject) know that φ when *I* can truly say, against *your* epistemic standards, that given your evidence, you know that φ. It might, however, prove useful if we augmented the non-modal part of the language with indexical expressions in

7.4 Dynamic Formalism

7.4.1 *The Main Idea*

The notion of context in the previous section was left totally unspecified: we simply took it as a point c_i in a set $\mathcal{C}$. In this section we propose a dynamic formalization of this notion, inspired by the semantics of discourse for natural languages.

The semantics of discourse, in particular *Discourse Representation Theory* (DRT), was invented by Kamp (1981) to account for semantic phenomena specifically connected with discourse dynamics (as opposed to sentence dynamics) and not explainable in standard, say Montagovian, analysis: anaphora resolution, donkey sentences, etc.[7] The "dynamic turn" in formal semantics has led to the creation of other formalisms too, like DPL (*Dynamic Predicate Logic*; see Groenendijk and Stokhof (1991)) where the semantic value of an utterance is treated as a program modifying a context.

DRT builds an intermediate representational level between language and model, made of *discourse representation structures* (DRSs). Each DRS constitutes both (i) the context of interpretation and (ii) the update of an already given DRS by this interpretation – yielding a new DRS. What matters here is the idea of introducing a representational level produced by the interpretation, and which contains "syntactic traces" of the various assertions made in a discourse.

7.4.2 *Pseudo-DRT for a Propositional Language*

For our purposes we will not need such a complex formalism as in DRT. We will not need a universe (due to the lack of individual variables) – except if we want to specify features of extralinguistic context like the speaker, the place, etc., and in what follows we will simply dispense with such features. However, we will need and make use of a set of conditions preceded with a label (in the spirit of Geurts and Maier (2003)).

As usual, a DRS (i.e. a context) will be represented by a box. For instance, the DRS produced by the interpretation of the following discourse:

$$\varphi_1;\ \text{if } \varphi_1 \text{ then agent } i \text{ knows that } \varphi_2;\ \text{therefore } i \text{ knows that } \varphi_2$$

order to account for such knowledge ascriptions as "So-and-so knows that I am here" or "I know that you are there".

[7]For an overview, see van Eijk (2005); for a more complete presentation, see Kamp and Reyle (1993).

will be represented by:

$$c = \begin{array}{|c|c|}\hline A & \varphi_1,\ \varphi_1 \to K_i\varphi_2,\ K_i\varphi_2 \\ \hline \end{array}$$

where the label A is meant to indicate that the relevant context was produced by means of a sequence of assertions. (We do not introduce sub-DRSs since in a propositional language the question of accessibility between universes does not arise.)

This context will be interpreted against a "proto-context", that is to say, a set of presuppositions consisting exclusively of literals, i.e. atoms or negations of atoms (of the form "Agent i is not a brain in a vat", or "Agent j's vision is reliable"). This proto-context will be represented by a box labelled with P:

$$c^\star = \begin{array}{|c|c|}\hline P & h_1, h_2, \ldots, h_n \\ \hline \end{array}.$$

Several definitions are in order here.

Definition 7.4.1. A *discourse* in language $\mathcal{L}$ is a finite (ordered) sequence of formulas of $\mathcal{L}$:

$$D = \langle \varphi_1,\ \ldots,\ \varphi_p \rangle$$

Definition 7.4.2. A *(discourse) context* for $\mathcal{L}$ is a pair consisting of a label X and a set Σ of formulas of $\mathcal{L}$: $c = \langle X,\ \Sigma \rangle$. Notation: $\begin{array}{|c|c|}\hline X & \Sigma \\ \hline \end{array}$.

- An *assertion context* is a context labelled with A: $\begin{array}{|c|c|}\hline A & \varphi_1, \ldots, \varphi_m \\ \hline \end{array}$.
- A *proto-context*, or *presupposition context*, is a context labelled with P: $\begin{array}{|c|c|}\hline P & h_1, h_2, \ldots, h_n \\ \hline \end{array}$, each of the formulas h_i being a literal.

To refer to the labels, formulas, and atoms involved in a context, we use the following conventions:

Notation 7.4.3. Writing conventions:

- The label of a context c is written $Lab(c)$ – i.e. $Lab\left(\begin{array}{|c|c|}\hline X & \Sigma \\ \hline \end{array}\right) = X$;
- The set of formulas of a context c is written $Fo(c)$ – i.e. $Fo\left(\begin{array}{|c|c|}\hline X & \Sigma \\ \hline \end{array}\right) = \Sigma$;
- The set of atoms making up the formulas of a context c is written $At(c)$: $At(c) \in \wp(\mathcal{A}t)$.

Definition 7.4.4. The *agglomeration* of a formula φ with a context c, written $c + \varphi$, is a binary function on $\mathcal{C} \times \mathcal{L}$ taking its values in $\mathcal{C}$ and defined as follows:

$$\begin{array}{|c|c|}\hline X & \varphi_1, \ldots, \varphi_l \\ \hline \end{array} + \psi = \begin{array}{|c|c|}\hline X & \varphi_1, \ldots, \varphi_l,\ \psi \\ \hline \end{array}.$$

The foregoing definition entails that if a formula is already in a context, its agglomeration does not modify this context.

Definition 7.4.5. The *representation* of a discourse $D = \langle \varphi_1, \ldots, \varphi_p \rangle$ relative to a context c, $R(c, D)$, is a finite sequence of assertion contexts $\langle c_0, c_1, \ldots, c_p \rangle$ formed by successive agglomeration of the formulas of D, i.e. such that:

- If $c = \boxed{X \mid \varphi_1, \ldots, \varphi_l}$, then $c_0 = \boxed{A \mid \varphi_1, \ldots, \varphi_l}$;
- For each index $i \in \{0, \ldots, p-1\}$, we have: $c_{i+1} = c_i + \varphi_{i+1}$.

Now that we can represent discourses by a set of markers (the formulas of the context) representing the various assertions of a discourse, we must consider the semantic interpretation of contexts.

Definition 7.4.6. The *semantic value* $[\![c]\!]$ of a context c in a Kripke model $\mathcal{M} = \langle W, \mathcal{K}, V \rangle$ is the set of possible worlds compatible with the formulas of c:

$$\text{If } c = \boxed{X \mid \varphi_1, \ldots, \varphi_l}, \text{ then } [\![c]\!] = \{w : w \in W \;\&\; \mathcal{M}, w \models (\varphi_1 \wedge \ldots \wedge \varphi_l)\}.$$

What remains to be done is to introduce a dynamic component at the level of proto-contexts. A proto-context must enable regimentation of the presuppositions of a discourse, that is, of those statements whose truth is not put into question and which are not even made explicit in the discourse context. The discourse itself can make a presupposition explicit or put it into question, and thereby modify the proto-context.

Definition 7.4.7. The *fusion* of two contexts is a partial binary function $\# : \mathcal{C} \times \mathcal{C} \rightarrow \mathcal{C}$ such that, for any pair $\langle c_1, c_2 \rangle$ where $c_1 = \boxed{P \mid h_1, h_2, \ldots, h_n}$ is a proto-context and $c_2 = \boxed{A \mid \varphi_1, \varphi_2, \ldots, \varphi_m}$ is an assertion context:

$$c_1 \# c_2 = \boxed{P \mid h_1, h_2, \ldots, h_n} \# \boxed{A \mid \varphi_1, \varphi_2, \ldots, \varphi_m} = \boxed{P \mid h_{i_1}, h_{i_2}, \ldots, h_{i_k}}$$

with:

- $Fo(c_1 \# c_2) \subseteq Fo(c_1)$;
- $At(c_1) \backslash At(c_1 \# c_2) = At(c_1) \cap At(c_2)$.

In other words, fusion removes from the proto-context all those literals that are atoms or negations of atoms included in the assertion context. Based on this definition, we can then consider a new sequence of contexts resulting from the analysis of a discourse, viz. the sequence of proto-contexts which parallels the representation of the discourse:

Definition 7.4.8. Given a proto-context $c^\star$ and a discourse $D = \langle \varphi_1, \ldots, \varphi_p \rangle$ interpreted relative to an initial context c with representation $R(c, D) = \langle c_0, c_1, \ldots, c_p \rangle$, we build the *history* of proto-context $c^\star$, written $H(c^\star, c, D)$, consisting of a sequence of proto-contexts $\left\langle c_0^\star, c_1^\star, \ldots, c_p^\star \right\rangle$ such that:

- $c_0^\star = c^\star \# c$;
- For every index $i \in \{0, \ldots, p-1\}$, we have: $c_{i+1}^\star = c_i^\star \# c_{i+1}$.

A history of proto-contexts thus explains the progressive modification of the set of presuppositions by removing the literals that are made explicit (or whose negation is made explicit) in the discourse.

We can associate with a history of proto-contexts a (w-constant) *relevance function* such that:

$$\forall w : \mathcal{R}(c_i^\star)(w) = [\![c_i^\star]\!].$$

This function allows the set of contextually relevant worlds to evolve over the course of the interpretation of a discourse.

7.4.3 Application

The static formalism described in Sect. 7.3 runs into a problem faced by all systems of normal modal logic and having to do with the logical omniscience that follows from accepting axiom K – the epistemic closure principle – and the necessitation rule.

The DRT-based semantics just described allows us to overcome these difficulties. The effects of the necessitation rule can indeed be bypassed if we suppose that each assertion modifies the evaluation context. That is to say, although we do have $K\varphi_1$, $K(\varphi_1 \to \varphi_2)$, $K\varphi_2$ relative to a constant context, this is no longer the case when the context evolves over a sequence of assertions.

We propose evaluating $K\varphi_1$ relative to an initial empty context, $c = \begin{array}{|c|c|}\hline A & \quad \\ \hline\end{array}$; we then evaluate the next formula $K(\varphi_1 \to \varphi_2)$ relative to the new context produced by the agglomeration of $K\varphi_1$, viz.: $c_1 = \begin{array}{|c|c|}\hline A & K\varphi_1 \\ \hline\end{array}$. This generates a third context, $c_2 = \begin{array}{|c|c|}\hline A & K\varphi_1,\ K(\varphi_1 \to \varphi_2) \\ \hline\end{array}$, relative to which the conclusion $K\varphi_2$ can be false, depending on the effect of the first two assertions on the history of the initial proto-context.

7.4.3.1 Example

To make things simple, let us assume an epistemic language with only one operator K and a unique relation $\mathcal{K}$. Given a presupposition context containing $h_1 = \neg r$, read as "The agent is not a brain in a vat", the initial proto-context then is: $c^\star = \begin{array}{|c|c|}\hline P & \neg r,\ h_2, \ldots, h_n \\ \hline\end{array}$, and corresponds with ordinary, rather lax epistemic standards, quite unlike those of the skeptic. Let us analyze the following (well-known) piece of discourse:

- φ_1. The agent knows that he has two hands.
- φ_2. If the agent knows that he has two hands then he knows that he is not a brain in a vat.
- φ_3. Therefore, the agent knows that he is not a brain in a vat.

Letting p stand for the atom expressing that the agent has two hands, we get the following discourse: $D = \langle Kp,\ K(p \to \neg r),\ K\neg r\rangle$. To interpret it, we suppose that neither p nor $\neg p$ is part of the initial presuppositions ($p \notin At(c^\star)$). In the following figure, the two sequences generated by D are in two parallel columns:

D	Representation of D	Proto-context history
		$c^\star = \boxed{P \mid \neg r, h_2, \ldots, h_n}$
	$c_0 = c = \boxed{A \mid \ }$	$c_0^\star = \boxed{P \mid \neg r, h_2, \ldots, h_n}$
$\varphi_1.Kp$	$c_1 = \boxed{A \mid Kp}$	$c_1^\star = \boxed{P \mid \neg r, h_2, \ldots, h_n}$
$\varphi_2.K(p \to \neg r)$	$c_2 = \boxed{A \mid Kp, K(p \to \neg r)}$	$c_2^\star = \boxed{P \mid h_2, \ldots, h_n}$
$\varphi_3.K\neg r$	$c_3 = \boxed{A \mid Kp, K(p \to \neg r), K\neg r}$	$c_3^\star = \boxed{P \mid h_2, \ldots, h_n}$

As mentioned above, we can put the history of the proto-context to use to define a relevance function, thereby obtaining a constant function on $c^\star$, $c_0^\star$, and $c_1^\star$, whose co-domain (the relevant worlds) extends from $c_2^\star$:

$$\mathcal{R}(c^\star) = \mathcal{R}(c_0^\star) = \mathcal{R}(c_1^\star) = [\![c^\star]\!] \subsetneq [\![c_2^\star]\!] = \mathcal{R}(c_2^\star) = \mathcal{R}(c_3^\star).$$

Each formula φ_i of D is interpreted against the previous context of the representation, c_{i-1}. Let us suppose that the interpretation of the first two assertions is true in a given world w. Then:

$$\begin{array}{lll} \mathcal{M}, c_0, w \models Kp & \text{i.e.:} & \forall w' \in \mathcal{R}(c_0^\star)(w)(= [\![c^\star]\!]) : \mathcal{K}w, w' \\ & & \Rightarrow \mathcal{M}, c_0, w' \models p \\ \mathcal{M}, c_1, w \models K(p \to \neg r) & \text{i.e.:} & \forall w' \in \mathcal{R}(c_1^\star)(w)(= [\![c^\star]\!]) : \mathcal{K}w, w' \\ & & \Rightarrow \mathcal{M}, c_1, w' \models (p \to \neg r) \end{array}$$

It follows that *relative to* c_1, the formula $K\neg r$ is true in w. But it is relative to c_2 that it is evaluated, whose class of relevant worlds is a proper extension of $[\![c^\star]\!]$:

$$\mathcal{M}, c_2, w \models K\neg r \quad \Leftrightarrow \quad \forall w'' \in \mathcal{R}(c_2^\star)(w)(= [\![c_2^\star]\!]) : \mathcal{K}w, w'' \Rightarrow \mathcal{M}, c_2, w'' \models \neg r.$$

So, for $K\neg\varphi$ to fail to hold in w, all we need is a world that is $\mathcal{K}$-accessible from w, where the agent is a brain in a vat, and which is relevant in context c_2. And in this context, unlike in c_1, there can be one such world, as the following example shows.

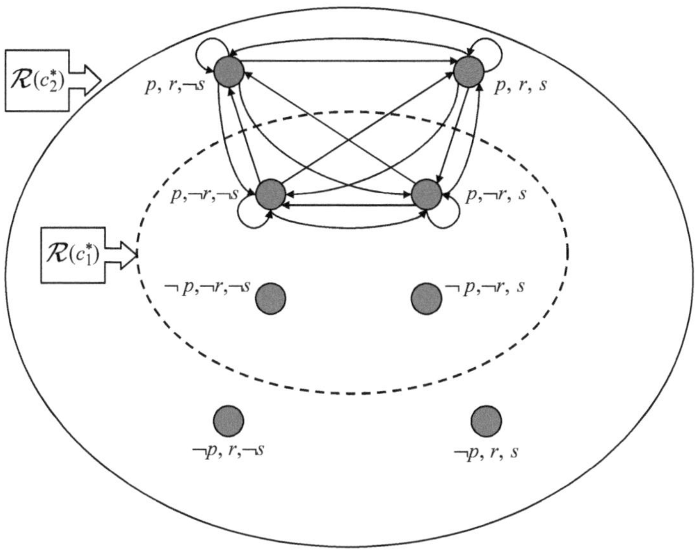

7.4.4 Discourse Contexts and Belief Bases

The dynamic approach just proposed is akin to the well-known AGM model of belief revision proposed in Alchourrón et al. (1985) (for a recent overview, see van Ditmarsch et al. (2008)). We chose not to make use of the latter approach because it is not sensitive enough to the syntax of formulas, and is therefore too *static*.

Belief bases in the AGM model are deductively closed: this results in a level of idealization that is too high to deal with certain epistemological issues (see Hansson (2003)), as we inherit *ipso facto* the problems of logical omniscience. By contrast, the DRT-inspired discourse contexts are finite – and even very limited – sets of formulas: only those formulas that directly represent assertions are introduced in an assertion context. A formula being in a context therefore does not imply that, say, all disjunctions containing that formula are in that context. Unlike belief bases, discourse contexts are not deductively closed.

The set of formulas of a given context c, $Fo(c)$, nonetheless coincides with its deductive closure ($Cn(c)$) *as far as evaluation is concerned.* We can then consider describing agglomeration as an *expansion*, and fusion of a proto-context with an assertion context as a *contraction* of the proto-context.

Belief revision theories could also be of relevance at the level of assertion contexts when a discourse generates an inconsistency that calls for a revision of the DRS. Several connections can therefore be drawn between the approach developed in this paper and the dominant approaches to doxastic dynamics in artificial intelligence.

7.5 Conclusion

In this paper we have laid out the foundations of a formal framework that uses the tools of epistemic logic to advance epistemological analysis.

Epistemologically speaking, the application of our framework to capturing various philosophical positions about knowledge will have to be extended so as to account for two sorts of positions: "assessment-sensitive" positions à la MacFarlane (2005), for whom epistemic standards vary with the context of the person who evaluates a knowledge ascription for truth or falsity; and "circumstance-sensitive" positions as those advanced by Dretske or Nozick, for whom epistemic standards vary not with any context whatsoever, but with the world with respect to which the subject's epistemic position is being evaluated. This is left for future work.

Logically speaking, the very framework of contextual models requires further exploration. Here we have sketched a "deviant" two-dimensional semantics that augments the usual possible world structure with a relevance function. A step further would be to develop a syntax to match those models by introducing context operators of the type $[c_i]$ and $\langle c_i \rangle$, which would make it possible to refer explicitly to context-dependence directly in the object-language.[8] Combining such operators with contextualized epistemic operators would allow us to capture various epistemological positions within the same contextual model, and therefore to account for the logical behavior of, say, a contextualist agent reasoning about the knowledge of a skeptical agent reasoning about an anti-skeptical agent. The contextual model framework could also be extended along further lines, e.g.:

- By exploring different axiom systems (S4, T, etc.) for defining the epistemic operators K_i;
- By adding an *awareness* operator, or a notion of *similarity* between worlds, or any other modification that might block epistemic closure at the "static" level of the framework (as required by positions like Dretske's or Nozick's);
- By adding operators for belief and justification (possibly in the line of Artemov and Nogina (2005));
- By adding appropriate alethic modalities to allow for the treatment of counterfactual epistemic statements like "Had Mary seen Paul at the party, she'd know";
- By adding indexical symbols to the non-modal fragment of the language so as to account for statements like "Mary knows I'm in Paris" or "I know you're there".

This too is left for future work.

Generally speaking, studying how our epistemic language can be modified and enriched should allow us to provide a finer-grained modelling of the various positions that can be found in the epistemological literature within our framework of contextual models.

---

[8]Work in this vein can be found in our paper on "contextual epistemic logic" (Rebuschi and Lihoreau 2008).

Appendix: Proofs

Proposition 7.3.5 *The axioms (T), (B), (4), and (5) are (1.1)- and (2.1)-valid in contextual models $\mathcal{M}$ whose relations K_j and $\mathcal{R}_{c_k}$ are all respectively reflexive, symmetric, transitive, and Euclidean:*

(T)	$\mathcal{M} \models_{-.1} K_j\varphi \to \varphi)$	$\Leftrightarrow$	*KK_j is reflexive and $w \in \mathcal{R}(c_k)(w)$ (for all w)*
(B)	$\mathcal{M} \models_{-.1} \varphi \to K_j\neg K_j\neg\varphi$	$\Leftrightarrow$	*KK_j is symmetric and $w \in \mathcal{R}(c_k)(w')$ $\Rightarrow w' \in \mathcal{R}(c_k)(w)$*
(4)	$\mathcal{M} \models_{-.1} K_j\varphi \to K_jK_j\varphi$	$\Leftrightarrow$	*KK_j is transitive and $w \in \mathcal{R}(c_k)(w')$ & $w' \in \mathcal{R}(c_k)(w'') \Rightarrow w \in \mathcal{R}(c_k)(w'')$*
(5)	$\mathcal{M} \models_{-.1} \neg K_j\varphi \to K_j\neg K_j\varphi$	$\Leftrightarrow$	*KK_j is Euclidean and $w \in \mathcal{R}(c_k)(w')$ & $w \in \mathcal{R}(c_k)(w'') \Rightarrow w' \in \mathcal{R}(c_k)(w'')$*

Making K_j and $\mathcal{R}_{c_k}$ serial is not sufficient to ensure the validity of (D).

Proof.

- Suppose that for any j and k, KK_j and $\mathcal{R}_{c_k}$ are reflexive. Since the intersection of two reflexive relations is itself reflexive, the intersection KK_j^k of KK_j and $\mathcal{R}_{c_k}$ must be reflexive. Therefore, $\mathcal{M}', w \models K_j^k\varphi \to \varphi$, which amounts to $\mathcal{M}, c_i, w \models_{-.1} K_j\varphi \to \varphi$.
- As to axioms (B), (4) and (5), we can likewise simply observe that symmetry, transitivity and Euclideanness are preserved by the intersection of two relations.
- As to axiom (D), however, seriality is not preserved in this way. For instance, the two relations $S = \{\langle a, b\rangle, \langle b, b\rangle\}$ and $T = \{\langle a, b\rangle, \langle b, a\rangle\}$ are both serial, yet their intersection boils down to $\{\langle a, b\rangle\}$.

Proposition 7.3.6. *Schema (T) is neither (1.2)-valid nor (2.2)-valid in contextual models $\mathcal{M}$ with reflexive K_j and $\mathcal{R}_{c_k}$ relations. Nevertheless, the following instances of (T) hold in these models:*

- *$\mathcal{M}, c_i, w \models_{-.2} K_j\varphi \to \varphi$, for φ a non-epistemic formula;*
- *$\mathcal{M}, c_i, w \models_{-.2} K_j\varphi \to \varphi$ if $\mathcal{R}_{c_i} \subseteq \mathcal{R}_{c_j}$, for φ an epistemic formula in disjunctive normal form with no negated epistemic operator in it;*
- *$\mathcal{M}, c_i, w \models_{-.2} K_j\varphi \to \varphi$ if $\mathcal{R}_{c_i} = \mathcal{R}_{c_j}$, for φ an epistemic formula in normal disjunctive form with at least one negated epistemic operator.*

Proof.

- (T) is not (-.2)-valid: Let $\mathcal{M}$ be a contextual model with reflexive relations, c_i a context, and w a world s.t. for any given formula φ, $\mathcal{M}, c_i, w \models_{-.2} K_j\varphi$. Then, for every w' s.t. $KK_j^k ww'$, $\mathcal{M}, c_j, w' \models_{-.2} \varphi$. Since KK_j^k is reflexive, in particular $\mathcal{M}, c_j, w \models_{-.2} \varphi$. This does not imply that $\mathcal{M}, c_i, w \models_{-.2} \varphi$: for instance, if φ is of the form $K_m\psi$, there can be a world w_0 s.t. $\mathcal{R}_{c_i} ww_0$, $\neg\mathcal{R}_{c_j} ww_0$ where ψ is not satisfied.
- Under the same assumptions, take φ to be non-epistemic. Then, from clauses (i)–(iii) for $\models$ in contextual models, the value of φ is independent of context. So, $\mathcal{M}, c_j, w \models_{-.2} \varphi$ entails $\mathcal{M}, c_i, w \models_{-.2} \varphi$. Therefore, (T)'s instantiation with non-epistemic formulas is (-.2)-valid.

- With the same assumptions again, let us further suppose (1) φ to be in normal disjunctive form with no negation of an epistemic operator, and (2) that $\mathcal{R}_{c_i} \subseteq \mathcal{R}_{c_j}$. Then, φ is a disjunction of formulas: $\varphi_h = K_{h_1}\psi_{h_1} \wedge K_{h_m}\psi_{h_m} \wedge \psi_{h_{m+1}} \wedge \ldots \wedge \psi_{h_{m+n}}$, for $\psi_{h_{m+1}}, \ldots, \psi_{h_{m+n}}$ non-epistemic formulas. When $\mathcal{M}, c_j, w \vDash_{-.2} \varphi$, we have two cases:

  1. The truth of $\varphi = \varphi_1 \vee \ldots \vee \varphi_k$ rests on a sub-formula φ_h with no epistemic component. In this case, $\mathcal{M}, c_j, w \vDash_{-.2} \varphi_h$ implies that $\mathcal{M}, c_i, w \vDash_{-.2} \varphi_h$, hence that $\mathcal{M}, c_i, w \vDash_{-.2} \varphi$.
  2. The truth of $\varphi = \varphi_1 \vee \ldots \vee \varphi_k$ rests on a sub-formula φ_h with epistemic components, hence on the truth of the sub-formulas $K_{h_1}\psi_{h_1}, \ldots, K_{h_m}\psi_{h_m}$ of φ_h. Therefore, for each index $e \in \{h_1, \ldots, h_m\}$, we have $\mathcal{M}, c_j, w \vDash_{-.2} K_e\psi_e$; in other words, for all w', if $KK_e^k ww'$ then $\mathcal{M}, c_e, w' \vDash_{-.2} \psi_e$. We (provisionally) distinguish the two (-.2) definitions:

     2.2: $\mathcal{M}, c_j, w \vDash_{2.2} K_e\psi_e$ equates: for all w', if $KK_e^e ww'$ then $\mathcal{M}, c_e, w' \vDash_{2.2} \psi_e$; in other words, the truth condition of $K_e\psi_e$ is independent of context c_j; so, we also have: $\mathcal{M}, c_i, w \vDash_{2.2} K_e\psi_e$.

     1.2: $\mathcal{M}, c_j, w \vDash_{1.2} K_e\psi_e$ equates: for all w', if $KK_e^j ww'$ then $\mathcal{M}, c_e, w' \vDash_{1.2} \psi_e$; here, the truth condition for $K_e\psi_e$ depends on context c_j. But we have assumed that $\mathcal{R}_{c_i} \subseteq \mathcal{R}_{c_j}$, which entails that $\mathcal{R}_{c_i} \cap KK_e \subseteq \mathcal{R}_{c_j} \cap KK_e$, i.e. $KK_e^i \subseteq KK_e^j$. Therefore, for all w', if $KK_e^i ww'$ then $KK_e^j ww'$, hence $\mathcal{M}, c_e, w' \vDash_{1.2} \psi_e$. This amounts to $\mathcal{M}, c_i, w \vDash_{1.2} K_e\psi_e$.

  We have thus shown that for each of the epistemic components $K_e\psi_e$ of φ_h, $\mathcal{M}, c_i, w \vDash_{-.2} K_e\psi_e$; for the non-epistemic components $\psi_{h_{m+1}}, \ldots, \psi_{h_{m+n}}$, truth is independent of context and transposes from c_j to c_j. Hence, we have established that φ_h, $\mathcal{M}, c_i, w \vDash_{-.2} \varphi_h$, and therefore that $\mathcal{M}, c_i, w \vDash_{-.2} \varphi$. Conclusion: we have $\mathcal{M}, c_i, w \vDash_{-.2} K_j\varphi \to \varphi$.
- The case of formulas $\varphi = \varphi_1 \vee \ldots \vee \varphi_k$ whose truth rests on conjunctive components φ_i including sub-formulas of the type $\neg K_e\psi_e$ requires more than the mere inclusion of the sets of contextually relevant worlds. Assuming the identity of these sets guarantees the transition of truth from context to context. The proof is similar to the previous one.

Proposition 7.3.7. *Validity of (4):*

- *Schema (4) is (2.2)-valid in contextual models $\mathcal{M}$ with reflexive K_j and $\mathcal{R}_{c_k}$ relations;*
- *Schema (4) is not (1.2)-valid in contextual models $\mathcal{M}$ with transitive K_j and $\mathcal{R}_{c_k}$ relations. Nonetheless, the following instantiation of (4) holds in such models: $\mathcal{M}, c_i, w \vDash_{1.2} K_j\varphi \to K_jK_j\varphi$ if $\mathcal{R}_{c_j} \subseteq \mathcal{R}_{c_i}$.*

Proof.

(2.2): Let $\mathcal{M}$ be a contextual model with transitive relations, c_i a context, w a world, and φ a formula. We assume that (a) $\mathcal{M}, c_i, w \vDash_{2.2} K_j\varphi$, and, *ad absurdum*, that (b) $\mathcal{M}, c_i, w \not\models_{2.2} K_j K_j \varphi$. From (a), it follows that for any w', if $KK_j^j ww'$ then $\mathcal{M}, c_j, w \models_{2.2} \varphi$. From (b), it follows that there are two worlds w_1, w_2, s.t. $KK_j^j ww_1$, $KK_j^j w_1 w_2$, and (c) $\mathcal{M}, c_j, w_2 \not\models_{2.2} \varphi$. Since the relations are supposed to be transitive, we have $KK_j^j ww_2$; and therefore by (a), we get $\mathcal{M}, c_j, w_2 \models_{2.2} \varphi$, which directly contradicts (c). Conclusion: $\mathcal{M}, c_i, w \models_{2.2} K_j\varphi \to K_j K_j \varphi$.

(1.2): Let $\mathcal{M}$ be a contextual model with transitive relations, c_i and c_j two contexts s.t. $\mathcal{R}_{c_j} \subseteq \mathcal{R}_{c_i}$, w a world, and φ a formula. We assume that (a) $\mathcal{M}, c_i, w \models_{1.2} K_j\varphi$, and *ad absurdum* that (b) $\mathcal{M}, c_i, w \not\models_{1.2} K_j K_j \varphi$. From (a), it follows that for all w', if $KK_j^i ww'$ then $\mathcal{M}, c_j, w \models_{1.2} \varphi$. From (b), it follows that there are two worlds w_1, w_2 s.t. $KK_j^i ww_1$, $KK_j^j w_1 w_2$, and (c) $\mathcal{M}, c_j, w_2 \not\models_{1.2} \varphi$. Since $\mathcal{R}_{c_j} \subseteq \mathcal{R}_{c_i}$, we may infer $KK_j^i w_1 w_2$ from $KK_j^j w_1 w_2$. Now, since the relations are supposed to be transitive, from $KK_j^i ww_1$ and $KK_j^i w_1 w_2$ we may infer $KK_j^i ww_2$; therefore, by (a), we have $\mathcal{M}, c_j, w_2 \models_{1.2} \varphi$, which contradicts (c). Conclusion: $\mathcal{M}, c_i, w \models_{1.2} K_j\varphi \to K_j K_j \varphi$.

Proposition 7.3.8. *Validity of (5):*

- *Schema (5) is (2.2)-valid in contextual models $\mathcal{M}$ with Euclidean K_j and $\mathcal{R}_{c_k}$ relations;*
- *Schema (5) is not (1.2)-valid in contextual models $\mathcal{M}$ with Euclidean K_j and $\mathcal{R}_{c_k}$ relations. However, in such models the following instantiation of (5) holds: $\mathcal{M}, c_i, w \models_{1.2} \neg K_j\varphi \to K_j\neg K_j\varphi$ if $\mathcal{R}_{c_j} \subseteq \mathcal{R}_{c_i}$.*

Proof.
The proof is similar to that of (4). We assume that we have both $\mathcal{M}, c_i, w \models_{-.2} \neg K_j\varphi$ and $\mathcal{M}, c_i, w \models_{-.2} \neg K_j\neg K_j\varphi$, which leads to contradictory requirements on a world w_0, the first assumption requiring that $\mathcal{M}, c_j, w_0 \not\models_{-.2} \varphi$, the second implying that $\mathcal{M}, c_j, w_0 \not\models_{-.2} \varphi$ given the Euclideanness of KK_j^j for (2.2), and that of KK_j^i for (1.2).

Proposition 7.3.9. *Definition (1.1) with w-constant relevance function $\mathcal{R}$, i.e. s.t. for any context c, $\mathcal{R}(c)$ is constant, reduces to a case of standard Kripkean semantics.*

Proof.
Suppose the relevance function $\mathcal{R}$ in a contextual model $\mathcal{M} = \langle W, \{KK_j : j \in I\}, \mathcal{C}, \mathcal{R}, V\rangle$ is w-constant, and consider a particular context c_i. We build a standard Kripke model from $\mathcal{M}$, $\mathcal{M}^{c_i} = \left\langle W^{c_i}, \{KK_j^{c_i} : j \in I\}, \mathcal{C}^{c_i}, \mathcal{R}^{c_i}, V\right\rangle$, where $W^{c_i} = \mathcal{R}(c_i)$, and $KK_j^{c_i}$ is the restriction of KK_j to $\mathcal{R}(c_i)$. Then, for any world $w \in \mathcal{R}(c_i)$:

(i) if α is an atom: $\mathcal{M}, c_i, w \models_{1.1} \alpha \Leftrightarrow w \in V(\alpha) \Leftrightarrow \mathcal{M}^{c_i}, w \models \alpha$

For points (ii) and (iv) below, we accept the recurrence hypothesis: $\mathcal{M}, c_i, w \vDash_{1.1} \varphi \Leftrightarrow \mathcal{M}^{c_i}, w \vDash \varphi$, and for point (iii), the corresponding hypotheses with φ_1 and φ_2.

(ii) $\mathcal{M}, c_i, w \vDash_{1.1} \neg\varphi \Leftrightarrow \mathcal{M}, c_i, w \nvDash_{1.1} \varphi \Leftrightarrow \mathcal{M}^{c_i}, w \nvDash \varphi \Leftrightarrow \mathcal{M}^{c_i}, w \vDash \neg\varphi$

(iii) $\mathcal{M}, c_i, w \vDash_{1.1} \varphi_1 \vee \varphi_2 \Leftrightarrow \mathcal{M}, c_i, w \vDash_{1.1} \varphi_1$ or $\mathcal{M}, c_i, w \vDash_{1.1} \varphi_2 \Leftrightarrow$ $\mathcal{M}^{c_i}, w \vDash \varphi_1$ or $\mathcal{M}^{c_i}, w \vDash \varphi_2 \Leftrightarrow \mathcal{M}^{c_i}, w \vDash \varphi_1 \vee \varphi_2$

(iv) $\mathcal{M}, c_i, w \vDash_{1.1} K_j\varphi \Leftrightarrow$ for all $w' \in W$ s.t. KK_jww', if $w' \in \mathcal{R}(c_i)$ $[= W^{c_i}]$ then $\mathcal{M}, c_i, w' \vDash_{1.1} \varphi \Leftrightarrow$ for all $w' \in W^{c_i}$ s.t. KK_jww', $\mathcal{M}^{c_i}, w' \vDash \varphi \Leftrightarrow$ $\mathcal{M}^{c_i}, w \vDash K_j\varphi$.

References

C.E. Alchourrón, P. Gardenfors, D. Makinson, On the logic of theory change: partial meet contraction and revision functions. J. Symbol. Log. **50**, 510–530 (1985)

S. Artemov, E. Nogina, Introducing justification into epistemic logic. J. Log. Comput. **15**, 1059–1073 (2005)

J. Austin, Other minds. Proc. Aristot. Soc. Suppl. **20**, 148–187 (1946)

S. Cohen, Contextualism, skepticism, and the structure of reasons. Philos. Perspect. **13**, 57–89 (1999)

S. Cohen, Contextualism and skepticism, in *Scepticism: Philosophical Issues*, vol. 10, ed. by E. Sosa, E. Villanueva (Blackwell, Boston, 2000), pp. 94–107

K. DeRose, Contextualism and knowledge attributions. Philos. Phenomenol. Res. **52**, 913–929 (1992)

K. DeRose, Solving the skeptical problem. Philos. Rev. **104**, 1–52 (1995)

K. DeRose, Contextualism: an explanation and defense, in *The Blackwell Guide to Epistemology*, ed. by J. Greco, E. Sosa (Blackwell, Malden, 1999), pp. 187–205

R. Fagin, J. Halpern et al., *Reasoning About Knowledge* (MIT, Cambridge, 1995)

E. Geurts, B. Maier, Layered DRT, ms. (7 Nov 2003)

M. Groenendijk, J. Stokhof, Dynamic predicate logic. Linguist. Philos. **14**, 39–100 (1991)

S.O. Hansson, Ten philosophical problems in belief revision. J. Log. Comput. **13**, 37–49 (2003)

J. Hawthorne, *Knowledge and Lotteries* (Oxford University Press, Oxford, 2004)

M. Heller, Relevant alternatives and closure. Australas. J. Philos. **77**, 196–208 (1999a)

M. Heller, The proper role for contextualism in an anti-luck epistemology. Philos. Perspect. **13**, 115–129 (1999b)

J. Hintikka, *Knowledge and Belief: An Introduction to the Logic of the Two Notions* (Cornell University Press, New York, 1962)

H. Kamp, A theory of truth and semantic representation, in *Formal Methods in the Study of Language*, ed. by J. Stokhof et al. (Matematisch Centrum, Amsterdam, 1981), pp. 277–322

H. Kamp, U. Reyle, *From Discourse to Logic* (Kluwer, Dordrecht, 1993)

D. Lewis, Scorekeeping in a language game. J. Philos. Log. **8**, 339–59 (1979)

D. Lewis, Elusive knowledge. Australas. J. Philos. **74**, 549–567 (1996)

F. Lihoreau, M. Rebuschi, Contextualism and the factivity of knowledge, in *Scientific Knowledge and Common Knowledge*, ed. by D. Lukasiewicz, R. Pouivet (Publishing House Epigram and University of Kazimierz Wielki Press, Bydgoszcz, 2009). pp. 209–224

J. MacFarlane, The assessment sensitivity of knowledge attributions, in *Oxford Studies in Epistemology*, ed. by T. Szabó, J. Hawthorne (Oxford University Press, Oxford, 2005)

M. Rebuschi, F. Lihoreau, Contextual epistemic logic, in *Dialogues, Logics and Other Strange Things*, ed. by C. Degrémont, L. Keiff, H. Rueckert (College Publications, London, 2008), pp. 305–335

R. Stalnaker, On logics of knowledge and belief. Philos. Stud. **128**, 169–199 (2006)

J. Stanley, *Knowledge and Practical Interests* (Oxford University Press, Oxford, 2005)
P. Unger, A defense of scepticism. Philos. Rev. **80**, 198–219 (1971)
H. van Ditmarsch, W. van der Hoek, B. Kooi, *Dynamic Epistemic Logic* (Springer, Dordrecht, 2008)
J. van Eijk, Discourse representation theory, in *Encyclopedia of Language and Linguistics*, 2nd edn. (Elsevier, Boston, 2005)

Chapter 8
The Epistemic Closure Principle and the Assessment Sensitivity of Knowledge Attributions

Tomoyuki Yamada

8.1 Nozick and Contextualists on the Epistemic Closure Principle and the Sceptical Argument Based on It

Philosophers love discussing sceptical arguments. Some of the arguments that have attracted their attention purport to show that we know almost nothing of what we think we know. Such arguments often start with some sceptical possibility in which you would believe, for example, that you are reading this paper in your office in Nancy even if you are not, such as the possibility that you are deceived by Descartes' evil demon, or by a team of super-psychologists who stimulate your brain electrochemically while you are floating in a tank on Alpha Centauri (Nozick 1981, or the movie "The Matrix"), or even the possibility that you are a "disembodied" brain placed in a vat of nutrient fluids which keep you (that is, your brain) alive, and deceived by a super-scientific computer programmed by an evil scientist (Putnam 1981).[1]

If you were in any of these situations, you would have exactly the same experience as you have now, and so, the sceptic argues, you do not know that you are not in such a situation. Then, in the next step, the sceptic reminds you, and

---

[1]The sceptical possibility Nozick discusses seems to be slightly different from the possibility Putnam discusses. Although it is not explicitly stated, it seems that it is you with your whole body, not just your brain, that is kept alive in a tank in Nozick's story. Thus your belief that you have hands is true in Nozick's scenario, while it is false in the brain-in-a-vat scenario. Apart from such small differences, both scenarios are similar in that they are compatible with physicalism. Thus, they stand in contrast with Descartes' scenario, in which the possibility of your being an incorporeal pure thinking thing is raised.

T. Yamada (✉)
Division of Philosophy and Cultural Sciences, Graduate School of Letters, Hokkaido University, Nishi 7, Kita 10, Kita-ku, Sapporo, Hokkaido, 060-0810, Japan
e-mail: yamada@LET.hokudai.ac.jp

M. Rebuschi et al. (eds.), *Interdisciplinary Works in Logic, Epistemology, Psychology and Linguistics*, Logic, Argumentation & Reasoning 3,
DOI 10.1007/978-3-319-03044-9_8, © Springer International Publishing Switzerland 2014

thereby lets you explicitly know, for example, that if you are reading these words in your office in Nancy, you are not floating in a tank on Alpha Centauri. But since you do not know that you are not floating in a tank on Alpha Centauri, the sceptic concludes, you do not know that you are reading these words in your office in Nancy after all.

Let H be the proposition that you are floating in a tank on Alpha Centauri with your brain being stimulated electro-chemically by super-psychologists, and O the proposition that you are reading this paper in your office in Nancy. Then the structure of the above sceptical argument can be schematically depicted as follows:

You do not know that not-H.

But you know that 'O entails not-H'.

Therefore you do not know that O.

The same structure can also be found in sceptical arguments that play on more specific sceptical possibilities, such as the possibility that the animals you see in the pen clearly marked "Zebras" in the city zoo are mules cleverly disguised by the zoo authorities to look like zebras (Dretske 1970). As Dretske (1970, p. 1011) and Nozick (1981, p. 204) have noted, sceptics who argue this way assume something like the following principle:

If S knows that φ and she knows that 'φ entails ψ', then she also knows that ψ.

In logicians' terms, this means that knowledge is closed under known entailment. We refer to this principle as the epistemic closure principle (or ECP for short).[2]

Replacing φ and ψ with O and not-H respectively, ECP can be instantiated, with you as the agent, as:

If you know that O and you know that 'O entails not-H', then you also know that not-H.

ECP thus allows us to derive the conclusion that you know that not-H from the premise that you know that O and the premise that you know that 'O entails not-H'. Given the premise that you know that 'O entails not-H', the possibility of your knowing that O comes to be in conflict with the sceptical possibility of it being the case that H. This and other similar predicaments are sometimes referred to as "sceptical paradoxes" (for example, Cohen 1988, p. 93).

Nozick (1981) argues against this principle from the point of view of his account of knowledge as a belief that tracks the truth. According to his account, an agent S

[2]There are many different formulations of this principle in the literature. Nozick (1981, p. 204) reformulates it as the subjunctive principle: $K(p \prec q)\&Kp \rightarrow Kq$, where we abbreviate 'entails' by '$\prec$' and represent the subjunctive relation by '$\rightarrow$'. We will consider other formulations discussed by Williamson (2000) and Hawthorne (2004), and their weakening proposed by Lawlor (2005) in Sect. 3. For the purpose of discussion in this and the next sections, however, we do not have to worry about the differences in the formulations.

knows that φ if and only if all of the following four conditions are satisfied (Nozick 1981, pp. 172–178):

$$\varphi \text{ is true.} \tag{8.1}$$

$$S \text{ believes that } \varphi . \tag{8.2}$$

$$\text{If } \varphi \text{ were not true, } S \text{ would not believe that } \varphi . \tag{8.3}$$

$$\text{If } \varphi \text{ were true, } S \text{ would believe that } \varphi . \tag{8.4}$$

The subjunctive conditions (8.3) and (8.4) jointly require that in order for S to know that φ, S has "to be someone who would believe it if it were true, and who wouldn't believe it if it were false"; S's belief has to track the truth (Nozick 1981, p. 178).[3]

This account enabled Nozick to deal, in a principled way, not only with the wide variety of examples accumulated in the epistemological literature since Gettier (1963) questioned the traditional account of knowledge as justified true belief, but also with the sceptical arguments that rely on ECP. Generally speaking, an agent S can satisfy one (or both) of the subjunctive conditions (8.3) and (8.4) with respect to φ without satisfying the same condition with respect to ψ even if φ entails ψ and S knows that φ entails ψ. According to Nozick's account, this means that S can know φ without knowing ψ even if S knows that 'φ entails ψ,' and so ECP is false.[4]

Take Condition (8.3). When we think of such a subjunctive, we do not consider all the possible situations in which φ is not true, but only those situations which are as similar as possible to the actual one in other respects. For example, when we think about how the world would have been if Al Gore had won the presidential election in 2000, it would be pointless to think about the situation in which Al Gore had won the election but had been kidnapped soon after the election by extraterrestrial beings who had invaded the earth, although it is a possible situation in which Gore had won the presidential election.

Put in terms of possible worlds accounts of subjunctives, we do not have to take all the not-φ-worlds (worlds in which not-φ holds) into account, but only the not-φ-worlds that are closest to the actual world in applying Condition (8.3) (assuming

---

[3]Nozick (1981) introduces one refinement into Condition (8.4) (Nozick 1981, p. 178), and further "refinements and epicycles" into the whole account (Nozick 1981, pp. 179–196), but we do not have to take them into consideration as they will not affect the point to be discussed in this paper.

[4]Dretske (1970) also argues against ECP. His argument is based on the "relevant alternatives" theory of knowledge, according to which, in order for an agent S to be said to know that φ in a context C, S only needs to be able to exclude the alternatives to φ that are relevant in C. He also introduces a subjunctive condition similar to Nozick's in Dretske (1971), according to which R is a conclusive reason for P if R would not be the case unless P were the case, and S knows that P on the basis of R only if R is a conclusive reason for P. On the relation between Dretske's view and Nozick's, see Nozick (1981, Note 53, pp. 689–690). Stine (1976, Note 1, and pp. 258–259) mentiones the approach in Austin (1946, 1962) as an early discussion making use of the "relevant alternatives" idea, and argues that "relevant alternatives" theorists should not abandon ECP from the Austinian point of view.

that possible worlds are ordered according to some degree of closeness to the actual world). Thus, if you do not believe that O in any not-O-worlds that are closest to the actual world, you will satisfy Condition (8.3) with respect to O. But not-O-worlds that are closest to the actual world only include ordinary worlds that are not much different from the actual one, such as a world in which you are reading a novel (but not this paper) in your office in Nancy, a world in which you are reading this paper in the library of your university (but not in your office), and the like, and you would not believe that O in any such worlds. To be sure, you might believe that O in some not-O-worlds, for example, in a world in which H holds, but such worlds are not among the not-O-worlds closest to the actual world, and so the tracking failures in such remote possible worlds will pose no problem with respect to your knowing that O.[5]

Now what about your belief that not-H? If you do not believe that not-H in any H-worlds (that is, not-not-H-worlds) that are closest to the actual world, then you will satisfy Condition (8.3) with respect to not-H. But you would surely believe that not-H in any H-worlds, and thus fail to satisfy Condition (8.3). Thus, you can satisfy Condition (8.3) with respect to O without satisfying it with respect to not-H although O entails not-H and you know that. Hence you can know that O without knowing that not-H, since no H-worlds seem to be among the not-O-worlds closest to the actual world.

Note that Nozick's goal is not to refute scepticism but "to explain how knowledge is possible, given what the sceptic says that we do accept (for example, that it is logically possible that we are dreaming or are floating in the tank)" Nozick (1981, p. 197). The above result fits well with this goal. If his account is correct, it explains why you can know that you are reading these words in your office in Nancy even if you do not know that you are not floating in a tank on Alpha Centauri with your brain being stimulated. Following Nozick, we will hereafter refer to the not-O-worlds closest to the actual world as "the worlds in the not-O-neighborhood", or even as "the not-O-neighborhood" where there is no danger of confusion. Then, according to his account, you know that O because your belief tracks the truth in any worlds in the not-O-neighborhood and in any worlds in the O-neighborhood; any failures to track the truth in the H-neighborhood are irrelevant to your knowing that O.

If we consider the possibility of your knowing that O in any ordinary situation in everyday life, this explanation seems very natural since it would not seem reasonable to require your belief to track the truth in every possible situation. This kind of "absolute sensitivity" of belief to the truth of what is believed (Nozick 1981, p. 283) does not seem to be needed in everyday life.

[5]Although Nozick himself utilizes possible worlds accounts of subjunctives in explaining the meaning of subjunctives, he explicitly states that he does not mean to endorse any particular possible worlds account, nor is he committed to this type of account. For more on this, see Nozick (1981, pp. 173–174, and Note 8, pp. 680–681).

It seems, however, that there is something not fully comfortable about the way Nozick's account works in constructing a counter-example to ECP. Since ECP is of the form:

$$\text{If } A \text{ and } B\text{, then } C, \quad (8.5)$$

a counter-example to ECP has to be a context in which both A and B are true but C is false. As applied to our example, A, B, and C should be read as

$$\text{You know that } O, \quad (8.6)$$

$$\text{You know that `}O \text{ entails not-}H\text{', and} \quad (8.7)$$

$$\text{You know that not-}H. \quad (8.8)$$

in this order. In order to have a suitable counter-example, it is not enough to have an example in which (8.6) and (8.7) are true in a context C_1 and (8.8) is false in a context C_2, unless C_1 is identical with C_2. Let C_S be the context of the sceptical argument we have been discussing. Then, in order to show that C_S is a counter-example to ECP, we need to show, assuming (8.7) is true in C_S, that (8.6) is true in C_S while (8.8) is false in C_S.

Now, according to Nozick's account, in order for (8.6) to be true in C_S, your belief only has to track the truth in the not-O-neighborhood and the O-neighborhood, and thus any tracking failure in the not-not-H-neighborhood is irrelevant to the truth of (8.6) in C_S, since we can safely assume that no worlds in the not-not-H-neighborhood (that is, the H-neighborhood) are in the not-O-neighborhood. Thus Nozick's account allows us to ignore any tracking failures in the H-neighborhood in assessing the truth value of (8.6) in C_S, and thereby predicts that (8.6) is true in C_S. But C_S is the very context in which the sceptical possibility of tracking failures in the H-neighborhood is explicitly discussed by the sceptic. Moreover, the tracking failures of your belief that not-H in the H-neighborhood is relevant for the falsity of (8.8) in C_S. How can we ignore the tracking failures of your belief that O in the H-neighborhood in assessing the truth value of (8.6) in C_S?

As contextualists have emphasized, people tend to find it implausible to say that we know that O once we have admitted that we do not know that not-H. According to contextualists, this can be understood as follows: epistemic standards have been raised extremely high by a sceptical challenge in C_S, and people tend to find (8.6) implausible according to the raised standards. Nozick's account allows us to ignore tracking failures in the H-neighborhood in the assessment of the truth value of the claim that you know that O in C_S, but it does so because it does not care about the context; it is not sensitive to the fact that the sceptical possibility of such a failure has been mentioned in the very same context C_S. Although it is sensitive to the content, O, of the knowledge which the claim that you know that O attributes to you, it is not sensitive to the change the sceptic has brought about in mentioning the sceptical possibility.[6]

According to contextualists, however, this does not mean that (8.6) is simply false. Proposition (8.6) is false in C_S because the epistemic standards have been raised unusually high, but it can be true in any ordinary context where the epistemic standards in play are relatively low. Thus, contextualists assert that the kind of sceptical arguments we have considered, even if they are successful, do not show our ordinary knowledge claims to be false (for example, see DeRose 1995, pp. 37–38).

Contextualism, it seems, can shed light on the uncomfortableness we felt above about Nozick's account. Although Nozick's account requires the same conditions for knowing that *O* in every context, epistemic standards can vary with context. But exactly in what way our knowledge attributions are context-sensitive is a question that requires careful and systematic examination. In the next section, we will take MacFarlane's discussion of assessment sensitivity of knowledge attributions into consideration.

8.2 Assessment Sensitivity

MacFarlane's account of the semantics of "know", which he calls "relativism", is introduced as a view that can explain the three facts about the use of "know" that jointly exclude all three standard views, namely strict invariantism, sensitive invariantism, and contextualism. The three facts in question are illustrated by an example of a man, say Sam, as follows:

Fact 1 Sam is at work but happy to say that he knows his car is parked in his driveway. He will admit that he does not know this, however, if someone asks him how he knows that his car has not been stolen (MacFarlane 2005, pp. 200–201).

Fact 2 When he concedes, he will not say that he "did know two minutes ago, before the bothersome question raised the standards". He will say that he did not know it then either (MacFarlane 2005, p. 202).

Fact 3 When the standards have been raised, he will also say that his earlier assertion of "I know that my car is parked in the driveway" was false, and if challenged, he will retract his earlier assertion. He will not say "What I asserted was merely that I met the standard for 'knowing' that was in place when I was making the claim" (MacFarlane 2005, pp. 202–203).

[6]This does not mean that Nozick's subjunctive account cannot be made compatible with such changes. For example, there are attempts by DeRose (1995) and Heller (1999) to incorporate Nozickean subjunctive conditions into contextualist accounts of knowledge. One interesting fact about their attempts is that they take opposite attitudes toward ECP. DeRose endorses ECP (1995, pp. 32–33), but Heller rejects it (1999, p. 207). Heller's treatment of ECP, though equipped with the contextually variable set of relevant worlds, seems basically similar to Nozick's.

As regards Fact 1, it does not seem right to say that Sam was speaking non-literally on either occasion, nor does it seem right to say that he made a mistake. Thus the epistemic standards he had to meet in order to count as "knowing" must have changed. This excludes strict invariantism as strict invariantists hold that the standards are fixed.[7]

Fact 2 shows that Sam used the raised standards in play in the current context in deciding whether he had known that his car had been parked in his driveway before; he did not use the standards that had been in play before. This excludes sensitive invariantism, according to which the standards vary with the circumstance of evaluation in the sense of Kaplan (1989). As the circumstance of evaluation relevant here is the circumstance before the bothersome question raised the standards, the standards in play there are the lower standards, but whether he had known his car had been parked in his driveway then was decided according to the raised standards of the current context.

Fact 3 shows that Sam used the standards in play in the current context even in assessing the truth and falsity of his earlier assertion; it excludes contextualism, according to which the standards vary with the context of use. As the assertion evaluated here is his earlier assertion, the standards in play in its context of use are the lower standards, but they were not used here.

Thus, taken at face value, these facts jointly exclude all three standard views (MacFarlane 2005, p. 204).[8] Relativism is introduced at this point by finding new conceptual room for yet another dimension of variability (MacFarlane 2005, p. 217). Unlike strict invariantists, relativists hold that epistemic standards are not fixed. Unlike contextualists and sensitive invariantists, relativists hold that the "epistemic standards relevant for determining the extension of 'know' are not those in play at the context of use or those in play at the circumstance of evaluation, but those in play at the context of assessment" (MacFarlane 2005, p. 217).[9] According to MacFarlane, a context of assessment is "a situation in which a (past, present, or future, actual or merely possible) use of a sentence might be assessed for truth or falsity" (MacFarlane 2005, p. 217).

How this notion of the context of assessment works in analyzing our practices of knowledge attribution can be illustrated by using the above example. When Sam claimed that he knew that his car was parked in his driveway (Fact 1), the truth or falsity of his claim was assessed according to the standard in play in that situation. Here, the context of assessment is identical to the context of use. When the standards

---

[7]Note that this excludes Nozick's subjunctive account as it is a form of invariantism.

[8]As these facts are facts about the use of knowledge-attributing sentences, they can directly tell us only under what conditions people find it reasonable to use such sentences, as we have learned from Grice (1989) and Searle (1969). Thus MacFarlane has made an extensive examination of the possibilities of arguing that one of these facts is a misleading guide to the semantics of "know", and concluded that all of them are implausible. For more on this, see MacFarlane (2005, pp. 204–217).

[9]As this quotation shows, MacFarlane uses "at" in the construction "the standard in play at the context of so-and-so", but we have used, and will continue using, "in" in place of "at" in the informal discussions in this paper.

were raised by the bothersome question, Sam conceded that he did not know that his car was parked in his driveway (Fact 1). The truth value of his concession, which was made in the current context, was assessed according to the raised standards in play in the current context. Here again, the context of assessment is identical to the context of use.

When Sam admitted that he had not known that his car had been parked in his driveway 2 min before (Fact 2), the truth value of his admission made in the current context was assessed with respect to the circumstance before the standards had been raised, but was assessed according to the raised standards in play in the current situation. Here again, the context of assessment is identical to the context of use, though it is distinct from the circumstance of evaluation.

And finally, when Sam admitted that his earlier knowledge claim was false (Fact 3), the claim assessed was the claim made before the standards had been raised, but the standards according to which this claim was assessed were the higher standards in play in his current situation. Here, the context of assessment is distinct from the context of use.[10]

Note that relativism and contextualism give different verdicts on the truth value of knowledge attributions only when the context of assessment is distinct from the context of use. This guarantees that the verdicts they give to knowledge attributions made in the current context will be the same.

Now, let's go back to the context C_S of the sceptical argument discussed in Sect. 8.1, and examine what relativists can say about it. According to relativism, the truth or falsity of the claim that you know that O and that of the claim that you know that not-H should be assessed according to the standards in play in the current context of assessment. Since the current context of assessment is the context of the sceptical argument C_S, the appropriate standards are the standards in play in C_S. But, just as the standards were raised by the bothersome question about the possibility of car theft in the above example, the standards in our sceptical argument have already been raised by the sceptic's challenge. We have to use the raised standards in C_S not only in assessing the truth value of the claim that you know that not-H but also in assessing the truth value of the claim that you know that O.

Thus, relativism enables us to understand the uncomfortableness mentioned above regarding the way Nozick's account works in constructing a counter-example to ECP in exactly the same way as contextualism does. The difference between these two theories will be found elsewhere, namely in the verdicts they give regarding our ordinary knowledge claims. According to contextualism, the standards relevant to determining the truth value of our ordinary knowledge claims are the standards in play in the context of use. Since the context of use of our knowledge claims made in the ordinary context is just that ordinary context, the standards in play

[10]Note that MacFarlane leaves it completely open "how an epistemic standard might be specified, and what features determine which epistemic standard is relevant in a given context or circumstance" (MacFarlane 2005, p. 199). Moreover, although he talks of "high" and "low" standards, he wishes "to leave it open whether standards vary on a linear scale ··· or in a more complex and qualitative way, as on 'relevant alternatives' theories" (MacFarlane 2005, p. 199).

there are the relatively low ordinary standards, and the claim that you know that O made in the ordinary context, for example, will be said to be true even if it is assessed in the context of a sceptical argument such as C_S. According to relativism, however, the relevant standards are those in play in the current context of assessment, and the current context of assessment will be distinct from the context of use if the knowledge attributions whose truth value are to be assessed are made in a context other than the current context. Thus, if the claim that you know that O is made in an ordinary context and its truth or falsity is assessed in that context, it will be said to be true. But in the context of our sceptical argument C_S, not only the truth value of the attributions made in C_S, but also the truth value of the attributions made in any ordinary context will be assessed according to the raised standards in play in C_S. Hence our ordinary knowledge claims made in ordinary context, such as the claim that you know that O, might be said to be false in C_S.

Although this result might make relativism look less appealing than contextualism, it is not contextualism but relativism that is in accordance with our practices of knowledge attribution as we have seen in Fact 3. As Fact 3 excludes contextualism, we will think of relativism as a successor to contextualism, and examine what relativists can, and should, say about our knowledge attributions. As may be expected, relativists can say, mutatis mutandis, almost everything contextualists want to say.

Another thing we need to note here is the fact that we will not have a counterexample to ECP in the context of sceptical arguments. In any context in which the standards in play have been raised so high that we have to admit that we do not know that such-and-such sceptical hypothesis is false, we will also have to admit that we do not know any ordinary thing that entails the negation of the very sceptical hypothesis.

But does this mean that we should accept ECP as true? The answer to this question is not yet settled by our considerations so far since there can be other independent reasons for rejecting ECP. Moreover, we have to take other formulations of the epistemic closure principle into consideration. In the next section, we will examine Lawlor's argument for the weakening of the epistemic closure principle.

8.3 Weakening ECP

As Lawlor notes (2005, pp. 30–31), many philosophers assert that something like ECP must be true on the grounds that it expresses an intuitive and uncontroversial claim about the epistemic value of deduction, a claim to the effect that knowledge can be extended by deduction. For example, Williamson calls the principle:

> "knowing $p_1, \ldots, p_n$, competently deducing q, and thereby coming to believe q is in general a way of coming to know q"

"intuitive closure", and remarks (Williamson 2000, pp. 117–118):

> If we reject it, in what circumstance can we gain knowledge by deduction?

Note that this closure principle, unlike ECP, mentions the act of "competently deducing q." As Hawthorne (2004, p. 32) notes, even if "at t, I know that p and know that p entails q, I may still have to *do* something—namely perform a deductive inference—in order to know that q." Thus, Williamson's formulation is better suited for expressing the above idea of the epistemic value of deduction than ECP in this respect.

Hawthorne (2004, pp. 33–34) proposes the following pair of improved formulations of this principle:

> Multi-Premise Closure (MPC): Necessarily, if S knows $p_1, \ldots, p_n$, competently deduces q, and thereby comes to believe q, while retaining knowledge of $p_1, \ldots, p_n$ throughout, then S knows q.
> Single-Premise Closure (SPC): Necessarily, if S knows p, competently deduces q, and thereby comes to believe q, while retaining knowledge of p throughout, then S knows q.

The added conditions are designed to deal with the possibility of S's knowledge of the premise(s) being destroyed by misleading counter-evidence while a long deduction is performed.

Lawlor admits that the claim that knowledge can be gained through deduction is unobjectionable, but doubts whether "closure principles express such unobjectionable claims" (Lawlor 2005, p. 31). The exact form of the closure principle Lawlor focuses on is shown here:

> Intuitive Closure (IC): Necessarily, if S knows p, competently deduces q from p, and thereby comes to believe q, then S knows q.

Lawlor argues against this principle on the grounds that "*being justified sufficiently to count as knowing* is a complex matter" (italics in original). Suppose a person, say Edward, has deduced q from the known premise p. He might nonetheless have antecedent beliefs that seem to him to provide evidence *against* q. About such a person, Lawlor remarks[11]:

> Until these antecedent beliefs themselves are thrown over, the conclusion he has drawn is one he is not sufficiently justified in for his belief to count as knowledge (Lawlor 2005, p. 34).[12]

After examining various possible responses from the defender of closure, she offers the following weaker principle as "a principle that does all the defender of closure wants" (Lawlor 2005, p. 39):

> Modified Intuitive Closure (IC*): Necessarily, if S knows p, competently deduces q from p, and thereby comes to believe q, and nothing stands in the way of S's belief in q having the level of justification sufficient for knowing q, then S knows q.

---

[11] Exactly speaking, her example does not seem to be an example of a single premise case as it is the case in which Edward deduced that a particular homeopathic cure will very likely not work from what he has learned from chemistry class. But the presumed complexity of what he has learned from chemistry class does not affect the point Lawlor seeks to make.

[12] Lawlor claims that these antecedent beliefs only speak directly against the conclusion, and that Hawthorne's additional condition in SPC cannot deal with them (Lawlor 2005, p. 35).

Note that IC* has the form of a closure principle. It states that knowledge is closed under deduction provided that certain restrictions are met. Assuming that knowledge "requires something like justified true belief", and that "there is some level of justification below which one's belief does not count as knowledge" (Lawlor 2005, p. 34), Lawlor asserts that IC* expresses the intuitive claim that *knowledge can be gained through deduction* (Lawlor 2005, p. 39).

Now, what will happen if we replace ECP with IC* in our sceptical argument? The restrictions incorporated in IC* block the derivation of the sceptical conclusion that you do not know O from the premise that you do not know not-H. As Lawlor notes in her discussion of a different but similar example (Lawlor 2005, p. 41), something stands in the way of your simply knowing, on having made the deduction, that not-H, namely, the acknowledgment that for all you know it might be the case that H. Thus, the claim that you know that O and the claim that you have competently deduced that not-H from the premise that O do not jointly entail the claim that you know that not-H, hence the claim that you do not know that not-H does not entail the claim that you do not know that O.

Does this mean that the sceptics are refuted? The answer to this question is no. As Lawlor notes (2005, p. 47), sceptical arguments can be constructed without relying on a stronger closure principle such as ECP or IC. We will examine one such argument in the next section.

8.4 Another Sceptical Argument

Let us look at the sceptical argument constructed by Brueckner (1994, p. 833). As applied to our example, it goes as follows:

If your evidence for believing that O does not favor O over H, then you lack justification for believing that O. (8.9)

Your evidence for believing that O does not favor O over H. (8.10)

You lack justification for believing that O. (8.11)

You do not know that O. (8.12)

Instead of ECP, this argument is supported by the following principle (Brueckner 1994, p. 830):

Underdetermination Principle (UP): If S's evidence for believing that φ does not favor φ over some incompatible hypothesis ψ, then S lacks justification for believing that φ.

Proposition (8.9) is an instance of UP, and (8.11) is derived from (8.9) and (8.10). Proposition (8.12) is derived from (8.11), and (8.10) comes from H itself, namely, the sceptical hypothesis that you are floating in a tank on Alpha Centauri with your brain being stimulated. If you were in that state, you would have exactly the same experience as you have. So, your evidence does not favor O over H.

Note that the step from (8.11) to (8.12) can be bypassed if we modify UP as a condition on knowledge as follows:

Modified Underdetermination Principle (UP*): If S's evidence for believing that φ does not favor φ over some incompatible hypothesis ψ, then S does not know that φ.

UP* leaves it open whether or not we have to satisfy such a strong condition in order to count as having justification for believing that φ. As we do not have to take a stand on this issue here, we will adopt this modification.

Note also that relativists would not accept UP* in this form as it is not sensitive to the variability of epistemic standards. In order to make UP* sensitive, however, we need to say more about how epistemic standards vary than just to say they become higher or lower. As MacFarlane's minimal account of epistemic standards is compatible with "relevant alternatives" theories (RAT for short), we will modify UP* in terms of the changes in the range of relevant alternatives. In doing so, we also need to avoid putting it in evidentialist terms, as RAT needs not be an internalist theory. Our proposal is as follows:

Sensitive Modified Underdetermination Principle (SUP*): If S believes that φ but is not in a position to rule out some assessment-relevant alternative hypothesis ψ, then S does not know that φ.
Assessment-Relevance (AR): A hypothesis is assessment-relevant iff it is held to be relevant according to the standards in play in the current context of assessment.

We can then rewrite the argument as follows:

If you believe that O but are not in a position to rule out the assessment-relevant alternative hypothesis H, then you do not know that O. (8.13)

You believe that O but are not in a position to rule out the assessment-relevant alternative hypothesis H. (8.14)

You do not know that O. (8.15)

Something like this argument seems to be implicitly appealed to when we talk about a context in which the epistemic standards have been raised so high that no one is able to live up to them. In such a context, a sceptical challenge raises the standards so that the sceptical hypothesis comes to be assessment-relevant. Thus, when a sceptical possibility that H is raised, we tend to find it implausible to say that we know that O once we admit that we do not know that not-H. Since to admit that we do not know that not-H is just to admit that for all we know it might be the case that H, we thereby admit that we are not in a position to rule out the hypothesis H.

Note that relativists can offer an obvious general solution to the predicaments brought about by arguments of this form. According to relativism, we can admit the sceptical conclusions without abandoning the possibility of knowledge. In contexts in which the epistemic standards are raised very high by sceptical challenges like this, we should perhaps admit that our knowledge attributions turn out false, but in ordinary contexts in which the standards in play are relatively low, our mundane knowledge claims will be true.

This solution closely resembles the solution to the sceptical paradox offered by contextualists. The only difference lies in the verdicts they deliver with regards to ordinary knowledge claims made in an ordinary context. According to relativism, such claims can be true if assessed in the ordinary context in which they are made, but might be said to have been false afterwards if a sceptical possibility is raised, whereas according to contextualism, they can remain true if they are true in the context in which they are made. As we have seen, relativism is in accordance with our practices of knowledge attribution in this respect.

Lawlor (2005, pp. 47–48) advises contextualists to live without strong closure and to abandon the claim that they can handle the sceptical paradox neatly on the grounds that we no longer face the sceptical paradox. As we have just seen, however, we still face another epistemic predicament. The fact that the relativist solution to this predicament leaves open the possibility that we might be forced to retract our mundane knowledge attributions in a dialogue with a sceptic might considerably lessen its appeal, but the fact that it is available seems to be worth noting nonetheless. Moreover, we can at least say that we should not dismiss it unless we have other more attractive general solutions.[13]

8.5 Epistemic Closure Principles Again

Let us go back to Lawlor's treatment of the sceptical paradox. As we have seen, the claim that you know that O and the claim that you have competently deduced that not-H from the premise that O do not jointly entail the claim that you know that not-H, because something stands in the way of your simply knowing, on having made the deduction, that not-H. But what stands in the way here is the acknowledgment that, for all you know, it might be the case that H, and this acknowledgment means that you are not able to rule out the assessment-relevant alternative hypothesis that H in this context. Combined with SUP*, this undermines the claim that you know that O. Although one route to the conclusion that you do not know that O has been blocked by replacing ECP or IC with IC*, another route is opened by SUP*. This precludes the possibility of finding a counter-example to IC in this context.

Thus, the only available example which might possibly be a counter-example to the strong closure principles like IC is the example Lawlor uses to motivate the weakening of IC, where the antecedent beliefs that stand in the way of Edward's knowing that q are expected to be abandoned sooner or later. Since Edward will come to know that q when the relevant antecedent beliefs are abandoned, a counter-example can be found only by focusing on "what Edward knows immediately upon his having made his inference" (Lawlor 2005, p. 33).

---

[13] In particular cases, specific solutions may be available. For example, in the case of the disguised mule hypothesis, you might be able to rule out the hypothesis if paint remover is available, or you are so familiar with mules that you can tell the animals you see are not mules (see Stine 1976, pp. 251–252; DeRose 1995, pp. 11–12, 25).

Now the fact that Edward needs a period of reflection to feel certain in his new belief is reminiscent of the distinction between an idealized notion of knowledge and a more realistic notion of human knowledge sometimes mentioned in discussing the so-called problem of logical omniscience. The following formal analogue of the epistemic closure principle holds in any Kripke model of the multi-agent variant of standard epistemic logic.[14]

$$K_a\varphi \wedge K_a(\varphi \rightarrow \psi) \rightarrow K_a\psi. \tag{8.16}$$

The fact that this and several other principles hold in any such Kripke model is sometimes referred to as the problem of logical omniscience, since these principles treat the agents as perfect logical reasoners who know all validities as well as all the consequences of what they know and are free of internal inconsistency.[15] As the properties captured by the formulas in question do not generally hold for human beings, it is sometimes said that they characterize an idealized notion of knowledge, and some logicians and philosophers have suggested that we should develop logics of knowledge and belief free of the problem of logical omniscience.[16]

In this regard, not only Lawlor's IC* but also Williamson's intuitive closure and Hawthorne's MPC and SPC are all designed to be more realistic formulations of closure. Relativists may still complain, however, that they are not sensitive to the variability of epistemic standards. An obvious solution for relativists here is to relativize them to the epistemic standards in the current context of assessment. In doing so, however, we have to take into consideration the possibility of shifts in epistemic standards taking place during the process of deduction. Our first approximation of Sensitive IC* is as follows:

> Sensitive IC* (SIC*): Necessarily, if S knows that p as assessed by the epistemic standard e_{C_A} of the current context of assessment C_A, competently deduces q from p, and thereby comes to believe that q, and nothing stands in the way of S's belief that q counting as knowing that q as assessed by e_{C_A}, then S knows that q in C_A.

Note that we have bypassed the talk about "having the level of justification sufficient for knowing" here, as we did in SUP*.

8.6 Making Sense of Assessment Sensitivity

As MacFarlane has pointed out, the facts about the use of "know" favor relativism over strict invariantism, sensitive invariantism, and contextualism. If we accept the assessment sensitivity of knowledge attributions, however, we have to take the

[14] Here "$\rightarrow$" stands for material implication, not the subjunctive relation.

[15] There is one exception. The formula $\neg(K_a\varphi \wedge K_a\neg\varphi)$ only holds in serial models. For more on this and other relevant principles, see van Ditmarsh et al. (2007, pp. 22–23).

[16] Parikh (2008) proposes an interesting treatment of belief and knowledge free of the problem of logical omniscience.

epistemic standards in play in the context of assessment into consideration in developing a systematic account of the semantics of knowledge-attributing utterances. MacFarlane proposes the following definition (MacFarlane 2005, p. 222):

> A sentence S is true at a context of use C_U and context of assessment C_A just in case for some proposition p,
>
> 1. S expresses p at C_U and C_A, and
> 2. p is true when evaluated at the circumstance determined by C_U and C_A.

This schematic definition can in fact express many different definitions, as there are many different ways of specifying how C_U and C_A work in determining which proposition is expressed and in determining how that proposition is to be evaluated. According to the version of relativism MacFarlane proposes, C_A does no substantive work in determining which proposition is expressed, and so it is an idle wheel in (1). But the circumstance determined by C_U and C_A in (2) is the tuple $\langle w, t, e \rangle$, where w and t are the world and the time of C_U respectively, and e is the epistemic standards in play at C_A. C_A thus plays a substantive role in (2).

As MacFarlane leaves it completely open how epistemic standards might be specified, we have incorporated the notion of "relevant alternatives" in the formulation of SUP*. As relativists seem to be able to say, mutatis mutandis, almost everything contextualists want to say, and most "relevant alternatives" theorists are contextualists, relativists may hope to incorporate more insights from them.

One interesting possibility for further research here is suggested by the talk of "the bothersome question" as the factor which raises the standards. The effects of various utterances that raise the epistemic standards may be studied in the style of the systems of dynamic epistemic logic developed since Plaza (1989) and Gerbrandy and Groeneveld (1997). In these systems, various kinds of information transmissions are modeled as events that update epistemic states of agents.[17] More recently, inspired by these developments, illocutionary acts of commanding and promising have been modeled as two types of events that update deontic statuses of alternative courses of action in Dynamified Deontic Logic (Yamada 2007a,b, 2008a). Illocutionary acts of asserting, conceding, and withdrawing one's own assertions or concessions have been modeled as events that update propositional commitments that agents bear in Dynamic Logic of Propositional Commitment (Yamada 2012). The same strategy is also applied in developing dynamic logics that deal with speech acts that affect preferences of agents in van Benthem and Fenrong Liu (2007), Liu (2008), and Yamada (2008b). It seems that the strategy adopted in these developments can be applied to modeling certain questions and assertions as events that shift the epistemic standards.

[17] van Ditmarsh et al. (2007) is a state-of-the-art textbook of Dynamic Epistemic Logic, which includes a succinct description of its developments.

The treatment of context shifts that change the relevant alternatives, introduced in Holliday (2010), is of much interest in this regard.[18] Although his system does not directly deal with questions or assertions, it shows how changes in epistemic standards can be characterized. He formalizes two versions of RAT, namely the versions developed by Dretske (1981) and Lewis (1996), within one logical system called RA, and shows that Lewis' version is naturally understood in terms of dynamic operations that change what is relevant by extending RA into a dynamic theory RA^+. The language of RA^+ has a formula of the form $[+\varphi]\psi$, which is read as "after the issue of (whether or not) φ is raised, ψ is the case" (Holliday 2010, p. 12). The models for this logic include a total preorder $\preceq$. It is used as the order of relevance. The formula of the form $[+\varphi]\psi$ is defined to be true in a model M at a world w if and only if ψ is true in the updated model $M_{+\varphi}$ at w, and the updated model $M_{+\varphi}$ is obtained by replacing the relevance order $\preceq$ of M with the updated order $\preceq^{+\varphi}$.[19] The updated order $\preceq^{+\varphi}$ is obtained by (i) making the most relevant φ-worlds and the most relevant not-φ-worlds equally relevant and most relevant overall, but (ii) otherwise keeping the old ordering unchanged.

On the basis of these definitions, the following results are established (Holliday 2010, pp. 13–14):

$$\text{The formula } K_l\varphi \to (K_l(\varphi \to \psi) \to k_l\psi) \text{ is valid.} \tag{8.17}$$

$$\text{The formula } K_l\varphi \to [+\psi](K_l(\varphi \to \psi) \to k_l\psi) \text{ is not valid.} \tag{8.18}$$

K_l here stands for knowledge as explained by Lewis. Proposition (8.17) shows that K_l is closed under known implication with respect to a fixed context, while (8.18) shows that it is not closed under known implication across context changes.

From the point of view of relativism, these results raise an interesting question. Proposition (8.18) means that there is a model M and a world w such that $K_l\varphi$ is true but $[+\psi](K_l(\varphi \to \psi) \to k_l\psi)$ is false in M at w. This in turn means that $K_l\varphi$ is true in M at w but $K_l(\varphi \to \psi) \to k_l\psi$ is false in $M_{+\varphi}$ at w. Proposition (8.17) means, however, that $K_l\varphi$ cannot be true in $M_{+\varphi}$ at w if $K_l(\varphi \to \psi) \to k_l\psi$ is false in $M_{+\varphi}$ at w. Thus, $K_l\varphi$ is true in M at w but false in $M_{+\varphi}$ at w. Note that $\preceq$ and $\preceq^{+\varphi}$ represent the epistemic standards as they determine which worlds are most relevant. Thus, if $K_l\varphi$ is evaluated in M at w, it is evaluated as true according to the standard $\preceq$, which is in play in the current context of assessment (M, w), and if it is evaluated in $M_{+\varphi}$ at w, it is evaluated as false according to the standard $\preceq^{+\varphi}$, which is in play in the current context of assessment $(M_{+\varphi}, w)$.

[18] An extended and thoroughly rewritten version of Holliday (2010) is now available as Holliday (2012), but our discussion of his ideas in this chapter is based on Holliday (2010).

[19] Although we usually say that a formula φ is true in a possible world w, we also say that φ is true at w in a model M when we explicitly refer to models and worlds.

This seems compatible not only with contextualism but also with relativism, since these two theories give different verdicts only when the context of use and the context of assessment are distinct. So we need to ask: can there be a way of distinguishing the context of use from the context of assessment in RA^+?

Take a knowledge-attributing sentence S from a natural language, and suppose that it is used to express the proposition that a knows that φ in a context C_1. Suppose also that it is evaluated as true in C_1. What will happen if the epistemic standards are raised? The proposition that a knows that φ might turn out to be false if assessed by the raised standards in the current context C_2. Here, we can speak of C_1 as the context of use and C_2 as the context of assessment, since C_1 is the context in which S was used to express the proposition that a knows that φ and C_2 is the current context in which the truth and falsity of that proposition is assessed.

In the case of the language of RA^+, however, the notion of the context of use seems to have no place, as no formulas are used in a context in the sense in which natural language sentences are used. In this sense, RA^+ cannot discriminate between contextualism and relativism.

Note, however, that the situation can be changed if we combine a multi-agent variant of RA^+ (call it MRA^+) with the dynamic logic of propositional commitments DMPCL developed in Yamada (2012). It then becomes possible to make sense of assessment sensitivity. For the sake of discussion, let us assume, informally, that a simple fusion of DMPCL and MRA^+ is given. Then, in the language of this combined system, we have a formula of the form $[assert_a \eta]\theta$, which means that after an agent a's act of asserting that η, θ holds. The formula of this form is defined to be true at w in M iff the formula of the form θ holds at w in the updated model $M_{assert_a \eta}$. Suppose you have asserted that you know that p at a world w in a model M of the combined system. Let a represent you, and let K_l^a stand for Lewisean knowledge of the agent a. Then, your act of asserting that you know that p can be represented as $assert_a K_l^a p$, and according to DMPCL part of the combined system, a formula of the form $[a\text{-}commt]_a K_l^a p$, which means that you have an assertoric commitment to $K_l^a p$, holds at w in the updated model $M_{assert_a K_l^a p}$. Then update that model further with $[+q]$. If this makes $K_l^a p$ false at w in the resulting model $(M_{assert_a K_l^a p})_{+q}$, both $[a\text{-}commt]_a K_l^a p$ and $\neg K_l^a p$ hold at w in this model. This is exactly the kind of situation captured in Fact 3. You are committed to the claim that you know that p, but that claim is assessed as false. In such a situation, you would surely wish to withdraw your earlier knowledge claim. Thus, there is a possibility of making sense of assessment sensitivity if we take seriously the normative consequences of acts of making knowledge claims.

This seems to be in accordance with MacFarlane's notion of assertoric commitments captured in the following principle:

> *Assertoric Commitment (Dual Contexts)*: In asserting that p at a context C_U, one commits oneself to providing adequate grounds for the truth of p (relative to C_U *and one's current context of assessment*), in response to any appropriate challenge, or (when appropriate) to deferring this responsibility to another asserter on whose testimony one is relying. One can be released from this commitment only by withdrawing the assertion (MacFarlane 2005, p. 229).

Exactly how DMPCL and MRA^+ should be combined, however, is a question that requires substantial further work.[20]

References

J.L. Austin, Other minds, in *Proceedings of the Aristotelian Society, Supplementary Volume*, vol. 20 (Williams and Norgate, London, 1946), pp. 148–187

J.L. Austin, *Sense and Sensibilia* (Clarendon, Oxford, 1962). Reconstructed from the manuscript notes by G.J. Warnock.

A. Brueckner, The structure of the skeptical argument. Philos. Phenomenol. Res. **54**(4), 827–835 (1994)

S. Cohen, How to be a fallibilist. Philos. Perspect. **2**, 91–123 (1988)

K. DeRose, Solving the skeptical problem. Philos. Rev. **104**(1), 1–52 (1995)

F.I. Dretske, Epistemic operators. J. Philos. **67**(24), 1007–1023 (1970)

F.I. Dretske, Conclusive reasons. Australas. J. Philos. **49**(1), 1–22 (1971)

F.I. Dretske, The pragmatic dimensions of knowledge. Philos. Stud. **40**, 363–378 (1981)

J. Gerbrandy, W. Groeneveld, Reasoning about information change. J. Log., Lang. Inf. **6**(2), 147–169 (1997)

E. Gettier, Is justified true belief knowledge? Analysis **23**, 121–123 (1963)

P. Grice, *Studies in the Ways of Words* (Harvard University Press, Cambridge, 1989)

J. Hawthorne, *Knowledge and Lotteries* (Clarendon, Oxford, 2004)

M. Heller, Relevant alternatives and closure. Australas. J. Philos. **77**(2), 196–208 (1999)

W.H. Holliday, Epistemic logic and relevant alternatives, in *Proceedings of the 15th Student Session of the European Summer School in Logic, Language, and Information*, Copenhagen, 2010, ed. by M. Slavkovik, pp. 4–16. An extended and thoroughly rewritten version of this paper is published as W. H. Holliday, Epistemic logic, relevant alternatives, and the dynamics of context, in *New Directions in Logic, Language and Computation: ESSLLI 2010 and ESSLLI 2011 Student Sessions*, eds. by D. Lassiter, M. Slavkovic. Selected papers, volume 7415 of Lecture notes in computer science (Springer, Heidelberg/Dordrecht/London/New York, 2012), pp. 109–129

D. Kaplan, Demonstratives: an essay on the semantics, logic, metaphysics, and epistemology of demonstratives and other indexicals, in *Themes from Kaplan*, eds. by J. Almog, J. Perry, H. Wettstein (Oxford University Press, Oxford, 1989), pp. 481–566

K. Lawlor, Living without closure. Grazer Philosophische Studien **69**, 25–49 (2005)

D. Lewis, Elusive knowledge. Australas. J. Philos. **74**(4), 549–567 (1996)

F. Liu, *Changing for the Better: Preference Dynamics and Agent Diversity*. PhD thesis, University of Amsterdam, 2008. ILLC Dissertation Series DS-2008-02

J. MacFarlane, The assessment sensitivity of knowledge attributions, in *Oxford Studies in Epistemology*, vol. 1, eds. by T.S. Gendler, J. Hawthorne (Clarendon, Oxford, 2005), pp. 197–233

R. Nozick, *Philosophical Explanations* (Harvard University Press, Cambridge, 1981)

R. Parikh, Sentences, propositions and logical ominiscience, or what does deduction tell us. Rev. Symb. Log. **1**, 459–476 (2008)

[20]In the above discussion, we consider a simple fusion of DMPCL and MRA^+. It seems, however, that your act of asserting that you know that φ may have the effect of raising the issue of whether or not it is the case that φ. Such an effect cannot be captured by merely building a simple fusion of DMPCL and MRA^+.

J.A. Plaza, Logics of public communications, in *Proceedings of the 4th International Symposium on Methodologies for Intelligent Systems*, Charlotte, 1989, eds. by M.L. Emrich, M.S. Pfeifer, M. Hadzikadic, W. Ras, pp. 201–216. Reprinted in Synthese, 158, 165–179 (2007)

H. Putnam, *Reason, Truth and History*, (Cambridge University Press, Cambridge, 1981)

J. Searle, *Speech Acts* (Cambridge University Press, Cambridge, 1969)

G.C. Stine, Skepticism, relevant alternatives, and deductive closure. Philos. Stud. **29**(4), 249–261 (1976)

J. van Benthem, Fenrong Liu, Dynamic logic of preference upgrade. J. Appl. Non-Class. Log. **17**(2), 157–182 (2007)

H. van Ditmarsh, W. van der Hoek, B. Kooi, *Dynamic Epistemic Logic, volume 337 of Synthese Library* (Springer, Dordrecht, 2007)

T. Williamson, *Knowledge and its Limits* (Oxford University Press, Oxford, 2000)

T. Yamada, Acts of commanding and changing obligations, in *Computational Logic in Multi-Agent Systems*, eds. by K. Inoue, K. Sato, F. Toni. 7th International Workshop, CLIMA VII, Hakodate, May 2006. Revised selected and invited papers, volume 4371 of Lecture notes in artificial intelligence (Springer, Berlin/Heidelberg/New York, 2007a), pp. 1–19

T. Yamada, Logical dynamics of commands and obligations, in *New Frontiers in Artificial Intelligence, JSAI 2006 Conference and Workshops*, eds. by T. Washio, K. Satoh, H. Takeda, A. Inokuchi, Tokyo, June 2006. Revised selected papers, volume 4384 of Lecture notes in artificial intelligence (Springer, Berlin/Heidelberg/New York, 2007b), pp. 133–146

T. Yamada, Acts of promising in dynamified deontic logic, in *New Frontiers in Artificial Intelligence, JSAI 2007 Conference and Workshops*, eds. by K. Sato, A. Inokuchi, K. Nagao, T. Kawamura, Miyazaki, June 18-22, 2007. Revised Selected Papers, volume 4914 of Lecture notes in artificial intelligence (Springer, Berlin/Heidelberg/New York, 2008a), pp. 95–108

T. Yamada, Logical dynamics of some speech acts that affect obligations and preferences. Synthese **165**(2), 295–315 (2008b)

T. Yamada, Dynamic logic of propositional commitments, in *Between Logic and Reality: Modeling Inference, Action, and Understanding*, eds. by M. Trobok, N. Miščvić, B. Žarnić (Springer, Dordrecht/Heidelberg/London/New York, 2012), pp. 183–200

Part III
Reasoning in Interactive Context

Chapter 9
From Dialogue to Calculation

Martine Batt and Alain Trognon

9.1 Introduction

All gregarious animals use direct interaction as a natural medium of communication. The human species is no exception, other than the fact that human interaction is supplemented with *talk*, i.e., *talk-in-interaction* as Schegloff (1991) so nicely put it, its natural medium.

Today, this conclusion is no longer a thesis in the strict sense, but a truism (Trognon and Batt 2010; Trognon and Bromberg 2007). The neurosciences have recently taught us that interaction is not only "around" us but is also "in" us, reflected in the organization of our brain (Pellegrino et al. 1992; Jeannerot 2002). The psychology of development tells us that newborns start very early to interact with their caretakers by means of proto-conversations, which already have the basic property of all conversation, sequentiality (Trevarthen 1994; Tomasello 2004). It is thus legitimate to conclude, along with Garfinkel (1990, pp. 26–27), that: "every topic of logic, order, reason, meaning, and method is to be discovered and is discoverable, and is respecified and respecifiable only as locally produced, naturally accountable phenomena of order. The phenomena are immortal, ordinary society's commonplace, vulgar, familiar, unavoidable, irremediable and uninteresting 'work of the street' ". Consequently, from a more psychological viewpoint we should assert that "the cognitive subject is not a monad: [that] he interacts continuously with his environment, and in particular with other subjects [. . .] and [that] above all, this interaction brings language into play [. . .] [and that] accounting for this kind of interaction, and notably verbal interaction, which is no doubt its most

M. Batt (✉) • A. Trognon
Laboratoire de Psychologie de l'Interaction et des Relations Intersubjectives (InterPsy – EA 4432), Université de Lorraine, Campus Lettres et Sciences Humaines, 3, Place Godefroy de Bouillon, 54015 Nancy, France
e-mail: martine.batt@univ-lorraine.fr; alain.trognon@univ-lorraine.fr

M. Rebuschi et al. (eds.), *Interdisciplinary Works in Logic, Epistemology, Psychology and Linguistics*, Logic, Argumentation & Reasoning 3,
DOI 10.1007/978-3-319-03044-9_9, © Springer International Publishing Switzerland 2014

elaborate form, constitutes an essential challenge for cognitive psychology (...), to which it must rise" (Caron 1997, p. 233). Today's researchers in psychology should therefore quickly concentrate their efforts on designing devices for observing and analyzing the psychological "faculties" that ground the interactional natural context of accomplishment, so that a "concrete psychology" can emerge, i.e., one that Politzer would have called a *veritable* psychology of memory, language, reasoning, affectivity, and so on.

Developmental social psychology has undeniably met this challenge in terms of data production, through its invention of an experimentation scheme capable of testing the conjecture that individuals improve their "faculties" when they use them in interaction. Thanks to this three-part scheme—pre-test, control group working in an individual setting *vs* experimental group working in an interaction setting, immediate and deferred post-tests.[1] now a must in this type of study—it has been proven that interaction is an irrefutable accelerator of acquisition. Learning is achieved via a variety of processes, the most well-known of which is sociocognitive conflict, Doise (1985), Doise and Mugny (1981), Light and Perret-Clermont (1989), Mugny (1985), Perret-Clermont (1979), and Perret-Clermont and Brossard (1988).[2] However, comparable progress has not been made in matters of data analysis, for as Wertsch and Sammarco (1988, p. 411) noted, the very fact of possessing a great deal of data proving the beneficial role of interaction in learning "still does not solve the problem of what mechanisms are responsible for the transition between interpsychological functioning and intrapsychological functioning."

To solve this problem, it seems that two conditions must be satisfied. First of all, the experimental data must be enhanced by linking the results obtained by each experimental dyad, to the interrelations (e.g., discussions) generated in the course of the interaction, that is, by associating the processes involved, to the product of those processes, the microgeneses. Issues that were impossible to approach in the first half of the twentieth century can now be addressed, and it is surprising that recording and analyzing experimental data produced in interaction situations has not become a common practice in research dealing with interactive contexts. Clearly, performance data is not fine-grained enough to approach the intricacy of the mechanisms that produce it. "In the notion of microgenesis, we find the idea of working in a time scale that differs from that of macrogenesis, but especially the idea that cognitive behavior is analyzed in its utmost detail and in all of its natural complexity. The study of microgeneses points out the characteristics of the interactive process taking place between the subject [his/her partner] and the object, which Piaget analyzed all too globally. It uncovers the coordination and potential integration of the subject's [and his/her partner's] successive solutions and partial models" (Inhelder and de Caprona

[1] See example in Trognon et al. (2008).

[2] See Footnote 1, Laux et al. (2008), and more generally Trognon et al. (2006).

1992, p. 24, passages in brackets added by the present authors)[3]. Secondly, we need to devise a language that formalizes in detail the constituting role of interlocution in the reasoning process.

The principle goal of the present article is to describe such a language, not abstractly but by illustrating how it is used to explore the microgeneses underlying the discovery of the solution to an arithmetic problem by two boys conversing for this purpose. We will work from a corpus taken from a recording of a dyad belonging to the experimental group of an experiment demonstrating that dyads are better than single subjects at solving this problem. By examining this interactive (dialogized) problem-solving situation, we will show how using this language allows us (i) to propose a formal description of the natural unfolding of an interaction process that leads to the discovery of the solution, by identifying above all the nodal components of the solving process, and (ii) thanks to our formal approach, to grasp the moment when an understanding irrupts, a moment that experimental psychology research on the learning of division has described as the initial step in the acquisition of this elementary operation.

9.2 The Sequence

The interaction we are going to examine comes from an experiment comparing children working alone or in dyads (Säljö and Wyndhamn 1990) as they solved multiplication and division problems. The exchange selected was taken from a recording of two children working on a typical school arithmetic problem, which they were solving out loud. The problem could not be done without performing a division. The present study falls in line with two earlier studies devoted to the same interaction (Trognon et al. 1999; Trognon and Batt 2007). The children, John and Mark, were both 10 years old. They were in fifth grade at an elementary school and had been taught division in school. The problem was: *A store owner has 672 videotapes to put on display. He can put 32 on one shelf. Knowing that each of his display racks has 7 shelves, how many racks does he need to display the tapes?* Hereafter, J (John) and M (Mark) will be used to stand for the children. The speaking turns are numbered in succession and the remarks of the experimenter are shown in parentheses.

---

[3]This is what we did in Schwarz et al. (2008), Trognon et al. (2006, 2008), Laux et al. (2008), and Sorsana and Trognon (2011).

[...]	
25M:	(he is reading the problem statement) "how many"
26J:	"shelves" "shelves does he need to display the tapes?"
7M:	shelves I mean racks there are 7 of them you can put 32 on one
28J:	there are 7 levels
29M:	so 32... 32 yeah well you have to...
30J:	have to divide by 32? (he looks at him)
31M:	or maybe times too... because 32 times how many
32J:	unless we get 32 each time
33M:	wait
34J:	7 times 32... 14 (he calculates) hmm!... possible per shelf you can put in 200 ... 224 so all you have to do is take away 224 each time
35M:	per shelf... 32 oh yeah 224... well 600
36J:	224 yeah! per RACK (stressed)
37M:	oh yes well do it on the scratch paper
38J:	yeah
39M:	672 minus 224 minus 224 minus 224 (...)
40J:	(speaking softly) 672 ... minus 224
41M:	have to take
42J:	there!
43M:	have to take, have to take 6 (sigh) this is tough
44J:	four that's it! then there you can still put in two because it's 224, there you can put in two more, so that means he needs three of them
45M:	but if... but...
46J:	yes!?
47M:	try to put in two ... you put... well do like this... wait I'll do it...
48J:	there we already took away one of them
49M:	224
50J:	224 yeah
51M:	well we need three of them minus 224
52J:	so we do like this... you put 672
53M:	yeah!
54J:	72 minus 224 minus 224 minus 224 equals... uh there so that makes 0 (whispers) 224 is equal... don't you want to put any spaces?
55M:	uh! one more time there are
56J:	then so that makes 0 ... so uh 3 shelves... uh 3 ... racks
57M:	(whispers) uh! what do we have to write down to write down three shelves?
58J:	well ... we put... he needs 3 shelves!
59M:	3!?
60J:	3!
61M:	3 racks
62J:	3 racks! well 3 racks we have to put because that makes
63M:	r-a-c-k-s (he is writing)
64J:	racks?
65M:	racks (corrects spelling)
66J:	you forgot the c

(continued)

(continued)

67M:	rac
69J:	rack no it's here the c
70M:	oh! yeah I forgot the r
	(J and M smile)
71J:	yes there's a c and there's no r
72M:	(whispers) … ck done!
	(the children then copy it over neatly, writing down 672 − 224 − 224 − 224 = 0. 3 racks)

9.3 The Problem of Ambiguity

The recording includes 72 speaking turns for 147 utterances. Among these, 31 speaking turns (52 utterances) were necessary to solve the problem, i.e., about half of the turns and a third of the utterances. We will not deduce, however, that speaking turns and utterances not directly related to solving the problem are *cognitively* useless. For example, a lexical ambiguity concerning the term "*shelf*" runs throughout the recording. The children attempt several times to reduce this ambiguity via various means: requests for information from the experimenter (5J-8E),[4] mutual checking of the other's utterances (27M-28J, 34J-35M-36J-37M, 57M-58J-59M-60J-61M-62J[5]), and self-checking (56J). The ambiguity reappears several times, however, leading to confusions in the formulation of the problem (26J, 27M, 28J) and its solution (56J, 57M-…-62J), as if, *upon each step forward in their reasoning* process, and practically all the way to the end, the children had to repeatedly make sure what the terms they were using referred to.

9.4 Analysis of the Relations Woven into the Interaction

In the course of this exchange, the floor is shared equally by the two children. Between 25M and 29M, the children reformulate together the elements of the problem needed to solve it. In 29M, after having reasserted an internal dialogue move *(yeah),* where an overall line of reasoning is connected up *(so),* Mark introduces a deduction in the deontic modality *(have to),* meaning by this that the solution he plans to state is the only one to consider (Gardies 1979). He does not divulge his idea; it is John who, in 30J, finishes his proposal, without pushing it,

[4]J, who brings up this difficulty, states the two interpretations of "shelf", defined as a piece of furniture and as part of a piece of furniture. He is given a satisfactory definition (based on the French word "*tablard*", meaning a shelf in a piece of furniture), which he fully appropriates using a gesture. But this is not enough to make the difficulty disappear.

[5]In 34J-35M-36J-37M, 36J (self-)corrects 34J and (other-)corrects 35M. In 57M-58J-59M-60J-61M-62J, it is 59M that (self-)corrects 57M and (other-)corrects 58J.

by asking instead for confirmation from his partner in the syntactic (interrogative form) and prosodic (rising intonation) registers. This tempered discursive behavior influences Mark who, on his turn in 31M, uses the ontic modality *(maybe)* to propose an alternative *(or)* at the same time as he partially validates John's idea *(too)*. In 32J, John adds a restriction *(unless)*. In 33M, Mark interrupts him, orders him to stop his reasoning *(wait)*. John does not comply. A clearer picture of the relationship between the two children emerges in 37M2, 38J, 39M, 40J. This short sequence contains a request (37M2, (...), 39M) expressed as an imperative utterance *(do it on the scratch paper)*, followed by its satisfaction (40J). It all appears as if Mark has some sort of control over John, since both directive acts in the sequence were uttered by Mark and directed at John. An analysis of the modalities used here seems to show that John's moderated discursive behavior helps the two children work together. We find no traces of conflict between the children, who adopt a collaborative attitude: they correct each other when they make mistakes (as in 36J) and they sometimes use wording aimed at saving face for the other person (as in 30J, 31M, 32J). This sequence is indeed a case of joint problem solving via direct collaborative interaction.

9.5 Cognitive Contributions of Each Child

We can see that, before 34J, the children each ask themselves a categorical question[6] that is the same on the surface: How many shelves are there? But their questions do not refer back to the same referent. The desideratum of John's question corresponds to the total number of shelves needed to display 672 tapes (nS): "*How many shelves does he need to display the tapes?*" The desideratum of Mark's question, on the other hand, must be deduced from the conclusive answer he himself gives: "*How many shelves are there? There are 7 levels*". Mark is thus interested in the number of shelves per rack (nS/R). Note their convergence in positing (as a premise in their respective lines of reasoning) that there are 7 shelves per rack. Note also their divergence—relative, however, since as stated above in our analysis, Mark does not refute John's choice—about what operation to perform: multiplication for Mark, division for John. We therefore know what cognitive processes were carried out by each child before 34J. John's more or less explicit reasoning seems to be: *How many shelves does he need to display the tapes? Knowing that there are 672 tapes to display and knowing that he can display 32 per shelf, he has to have* $672/32 = 21$ *shelves to complete his task. Mark's reasoning seems to be: Knowing that there are 7 shelves per rack and that you can put 32 tapes on each shelf, then*

[6]We will refer here to J. Hintikka's work (Hintikka 1976, 1981). For Hintikka, whether a question is categorical, i.e., a question whose "desideratum instantiates a value of a quantified variable" (Hintikka 1976, p. 60), or propositional, i.e., a question whose "desideratum refers to a proposition" (Hintikka 1976, p. 60), a question is always a request for information.

Table 9.1 Reasoning process of each child before 34J

MARK	JOHN
25M-27M1: how many shelves are there? nS?	26J: how many shelves does he need to display the tapes 672t = nS?
27M2: there are 7 of them (meaning 7 per rack) 7S = *1R*	28J: there are 7 levels (meaning 7 per rack) 7S = *1R*
27M3: you can put 32 on one *(understood to mean one shelf)* 32t = 1S	30J: have to divide by 32?
31M: or maybe times too	
Possible complete lines of reasoning	
Possible reasoning starting from a multiplication operation	Possible reasoning starting from a division operation
32t × 7S = 224t	3R
3R 224t/R) 672t	3R 7S/R) 21S 32t) 672t

there are 7 times 32 tapes per rack. If we follow each child's reasoning until it ends, we get two different routes leading to the conclusive answer to the categorical question asked by the experimenter. This process is shown in Table 9.1, where t stands for tape, S for the set "shelves", R for the set "racks", and D for the set "the whole videotape display" (see Table 9.1).

In truth, the divergence between John and Mark about what should be the first step in solving the problem came before the sequence we are examining here (Trognon et al. 1999).

(Mark reads the problem statement out loud)
1J: Oh you have to divide
2M: maybe not
3J: almost
(…)
16J: wait… you divide by 32
(Silence. They both look at the problem statement on the sheet of paper).

Immediately apparent in this short excerpt is that John plans to use division and that Mark hesitates, although without being capable of making another proposal or objecting. With respect to this situation, the sequence we are studying contains several new elements. While John sticks to his point of view, Mark now has an idea of his own.

9.6 Choosing a Method

We can see, however, that the children do not follow through with their respective lines of reasoning. John seems to "jump" from his own to incorporate Mark's way. We attempted to discover the mechanism underlying this interaction phenomenon.

The inferential path that undoubtedly led John, in 30J, to set forth the idea of dividing 672t by 32t can be described as follows. If we consider that John understood, from the equality (32 tapes = 1 shelf), that one can deduce the equality $(n \times 32\ tapes = n \times 1\ shelf)$—which is something that fifth-grade children normally know—then he can deduce, from the information contained in the problem statement, that a display of 672 tapes is equivalent to several times the display of one shelf of tapes, that is, $n \times 32\ tapes$. So, while n was inaccessible to John in 30J, in 32J when he says "*we get 32 each time*", it seems as if he understands that this number of "*times* it takes to get 32" is the result of the division (672t/32t). Moreover, as he says a few speaking turns later (34J), this is in fact how he seems to conceptualize the division operation. Now at the point when John expresses how he progresses in his reasoning to discover the total number of shelves $(n \times 32t)$ needed to display 672 tapes, Mark asks him this categorical question: "*32 times how many?*" (31M). What is available at that instant in the conversation and in the utterances that John has in memory, is precisely "7 shelves per rack". We can see that John replies "7" and immediately afterwards, in 34J4, "*all you have to do is take away 224 each time*". Uttered by John, this statement in 34J4 seems to reinforce the claim that John had gone through the complete line of reasoning by 34J1, and that by replying 7, and thus by putting 7 and 32 side by side, he is visualizing an entire rack. If so, John had gone from reasoning that $nS = 21$, to reasoning that n becomes $((nSperR) \times nR) = (7 \times 3)$. The noticeable thing in this passage is that John's acceptance of the approach initiated by Mark is a relevant move in the solving approach that John himself had initiated: discover the number of shelves. John's reasoning at the start was based on the set of *all* shelves $(nS = 21)$. Thanks to Mark's question, he proceeds to break down his initial operation: he reasons first about how many shelves there are in a rack, and then *(so all you have to do)* deploys the second part of his reasoning $(nrD \times (7sR \times 32tS))$.

9.7 Cognitive Discovery

John's cognitive discovery (Laughlin et al. 2006) is distributed over two speaking turns (34 and 44), each constituting a part of the solution. This reasoning framework (between 34J and 44J) goes through central utterance 39M.

Once the number of tapes contained in a rack is determined (34Jef-35Me-36Ja) and the erroneous reference corrected and then called the same thing by both children (35Ma-36Jbc-37Ma), Mark suggests that John write down what they agreed

34J	a-b-c-d-:	7 times 32... 14 (he calculates) hmm!... possible
	e-f-:	per shelf you can put in 200... 224
	g:	so all you have to do is take away 224 each time
35M	a-b-c-d-e-f:	per shelf... 32 oh yeah 224... well 600
36J	a-b-c:	224 yeah! per RACK (stressed)
37M	a-b:	oh yes well do it on the scratch paper
38J:		yeah
39M:		672 minus 224 minus 224 minus 224 (...)
40J:		(speaking softly) 672 ... minus 224
41M:		have to take
42J:		there!
43M	a-b-c-d:	have to take, have to take 6 (sigh) this is tough
44J	a-b-c-:	four that's it! then there you can still put in two
	d-:	because it's 224, there you can put in two more
	e:	so that means he needs three of them
45M	a-b:	but if... but...
46J:		yes!?
47M	a-b-:	try to put in two ... you put...
	c-:	well do like this...
	d-e:	wait I'll do it...
48J:		there we already took away one of them
49M:		224
50J:		224 yeah
51M:		well we need three of them minus 224

on the scratch paper. 39M *("672 minus 224 minus 224 minus 224")* operationalizes 34Jg. This takes them from John's proposal in 34Jg *("so all you have to do is take away 224 each time")* to Mark's application of it in 39M *("672 minus 224 minus 224 minus 224")*, so that **what is to be taken away** "each time" becomes a series of three subtractions of 224 from 672. From there, the solution is inferable[7] by both children. Their respective lines of reasoning converge. While Mark had proposed (in 39M) to obtain subtotals reiteratively by doing a series of three subtractions until they arrive at zero (i.e., the total number of tapes displayed), John obtains subtotals reiteratively by carrying out a series of three additions of 224 until he obtains the whole set of 672 tapes (44Jd: "*because it's 224, there you can put in two more*"). In both cases Mark's initial idea is accepted, since 224 (i.e., $7 \times 32 =$ the number of tapes in a rack) is the starting point for the arithmetic operations carried out. More generally, then, intercomprehension[8] in this passage was obtained by a progression through a gradual enrichment process typical of dialogue, which can be represented from the formal standpoint.

[7] In Sorsana and Trognon (1989) sense of the term.

[8] See Trognon and Brassac (1992), Trognon and Saint-Dizier (1999), Trognon (2002), and Trognon and Batt (2010).

9.8 Formal Presentation of Intercomprehension

An axiomatic formalization *à la* Hilbert of the joint solving process, expressed in the four or five utterances composing the fertile moment, might be as follows, where S stands for the set of "shelves", R the set of "racks", D the "whole videotape display", and T "a tape". $T/S = 32$ (the number of tapes in S is equal to 32), $S/R = 7$ (the number of shelves in R is equal to 7), $T/D = 672$ (the number of tapes in the whole display is equal to 672).

1	T/S	32	Premise	
2	S/R	7	Premise	
3	T/D	672	Premise	
4	T/R	T/S × S/R	Algebraic truth	
5	T/R	32 × S/R	=Elim-1,4	Desideratum of Mark's question in 31M
6	T/R	32 × 7	=Elim-2,5	John's implicit reply to Mark in 34J
7	32 × 7	224	Arithmetic	Multiplication done by John in 34J
8	T/R	224	=Elim-6,7	
9	T/R	T/R × R/D	Algebraic truth	
10	T/D	224 × R/D	=Elim-8,9	
11	672	224 × R/D	=Elim-3,10	
12	672	224 × 3	Arithmetic	Division done by John in 54J
13	R/D	3	=Elim-11,12	Solution to the problem

The numbers in the first column refer to the steps in the children's reasoning process. Each step has a corresponding formula. The formulas are propositions. Their content is given in the second column. The third column defines the conceptual status of the formulas. Some are premises given in the problem statement. Others are deductions, e.g., the formulas produced after applying the rules of elimination (5, 6, 8, 10, 11, 13). Still others represent mathematical knowledge. There is what we call "arithmetic" knowledge, which is knowledge related to *how to do operations.* It is quite clear from our corpus that the children know how to add, subtract, and multiply, but we cannot be sure at all that the same holds true for division. In any case, John's first "*inspirations about division*" (1Jb, 16Jb, 18Jb) seem more like "reflex" utterances triggered by the situation than thought-out affirmations. When he produces these utterances, John doesn't seem to be able to explain what he's doing (not even to himself). Besides, he will quickly drop this line of thinking to take up on Mark's proposal to use multiplication. The fourth column labels the different formulas in terms of their role in the interlocution. Line 5 is the desideratum of the question asked by Mark in 31M. Line 6 is John's implicit answer to this question. Line 7 represents the calculation that John does more or less in his head, or more exactly, within a thought that rises to the surface in his remark 34J as: "7 times 32" (John satisfies Mark's request by saying how many times), "... 14" (he states the result of the multiplication of 2 by 7), "hmm!" (he considers this result), "... possible" (he expresses his propositional attitude toward the result), "per shelf you

Table 9.2 Natural deduction describing the joint production of the solution

	Formulas	Rules	John	Mark
1	T/S = 32	Premise		
2	S/R = 7	Premise		
3	T/D = 672	Premise		
4	R/D = a	Desideratum of the question		
5	32 × 7 = 224	Arithmetic knowledge	34Ja-b	
6	T/S ×7 = 224	Elim-5,1		
7	T/S × S/R = 224	Elim-6,2		
8	T/S × S/R = T/R	John's discovery	34Je-f	
9	T/R = 224	Elim-7,8	34Jf	35Me
10	[T/R = 224]? [T/D − (R/D × 224) = 0]	Introd-implic: John's solution		
11	[T/D − (R/D × 224)] = 0	Elim-9,10 = solution	34Jg 36Ja-b	
12	[672 − (R/D × 224)] = 0	Elim-11,3		
13	[− (R/D × 224)] = [(− 224 − (224 − (224)))]	Introd (by Mark) Elim-11,12		51M
14	[672 − (224 − (224 − (224)))] = 0	Elim-12-13		39M
15	{672 − [224 + (2 × (− 224))]} = 0	Equality 14	44Ja-c, 44Jd	
16	[224 + (2 × (− 224))] = [3 × (−224)]	Arithmetic	44Je	
17	{672 − [3 × (− 224)]} = 0	Elim-15-16		51M
18	{672 − (224 − (224 − (224)))} = 0	Reit-14	52Jb-56Jc	
19	3 × (−224) = − 3 × (224)	Elim-17,18		
20	[672 − 3 × (224)] = 0	Elim-17,19		
21	[672 − (3 × (224))] = [672 − (R/D × 224)]	Elim-12,20		
22	R/D = 3	Equality-21	56Jb-c	
23	R/D = 3	Reit-22		61M

The expression on line 17 is arithmetically incorrect, which is why it is shown in quotes. Given that the error is inconsequential, we have written it as such because that's how Mark stated it and because it takes the children farther away from an interpretation of 3 as the number of racks needed for the display

can put in 200 of them (=tapes)" (again confusing "shelf" and "rack", he states T/R or 224), and "so all you have to do is take away 224 each time" (John proposes a procedure for finding R/D).

Compared to the actual unfolding of the children's discourse, the axiomatic formalization seems extremely far-removed. On one side, we have a rigorous reasoning process going from relations between classes (T/S tapes per shelf, T/R tapes per rack, T/D tapes in the whole display, S/R, S/D, and R/D) to their cardinal numbers (32, 224, 672, 7, 21, and 3, respectively); on the other side, we see the children trying out different operations on the numbers as they attempt to make sense out of them, in such a way that *the algebraic truths needed to solve the problem, which are merely stated in the axiomatic model are, on the contrary, truly discovered by the children as they interpret their operations.* A natural deduction that could accompany the distribution of the children's joint reasoning would look something like this (see Table 9.2).

This natural deduction calls for a certain number of remarks. Firstly, not all of the formulas are explicit utterances produced by the children. Those that are, have their discursive counterparts in columns 4 and 5; those that are not, can be considered to have been thought or else the explicit formulas could not have been. For example, it is hard to imagine how 9 could have been uttered without having gone through the manipulations that produced 9 from 5, which, moreover, doesn't mean that this is the only path leading from 5 to 9. Secondly, when a formula shows through the discourse, it is rarely in a literal form. For instance, "so all you have to do is take away 224 each time" (in 34Jg) is certainly not formula 11. The latter is but one formalization among others of the former, its "accuracy" remaining to be discussed. It is the ambiguity of 36Ja-b-c that caused us to lean toward $[T/D - (R/D \times 224)] = 0$. Indeed, 36J could mean "there are 224 tapes in a rack", in which case it would be a self-correction of 34Je-f. Or it could mean "we take away 224 per rack", which would correspond to something like "every time we put a set of 224 tapes in, we use one rack."

More generally, the reasoning brought to bear in a discourse—here, a conversation—can never be totally separated from the discourse itself. The excerpt we are studying provides another example of this. Consider the following utterances taken from the interval (39M, 51M):

44Je:	*so that means* ***he needs three of them***
(…)	
48J:	***there we already took away one of them***
49M:	224
50J:	*224 yeah*
51M:	***well we need three of them minus 224***

44Je acts as an acceptance, even a demonstration, of 39M. But couldn't this conclusion equally well be a sort of answer to the question raised in the problem (formula 4 of the natural deduction)? This question is: "How many racks does he (the seller) need to display the tapes?" To what "*he*" does utterance 44Je refer if it's not the seller mentioned in the problem statement? Let us assume that this hypothesis is validated. So the "*of them*", which in a proximal context would mean "–224", could also mean *racks* in a distal context, which is more consistent with the interpretation that "*he*" means "the seller". *It all seems as if 44Je* were a condensed version of J's current inference, and is the answer to the problem constituted by that same inference. If such a condensed version it is, *then the discourse precedes the calculation.* Now if we put 44Je next to 48J, our hypothesis could even be taken as a kind of symptom. When John produces this utterance (as if he were a teacher), he is making another remark about what 39M was supposed to accomplish in writing. John has just written "–224" and asks Mark to write down two more –224's. At this point, we would expect him to say something like "*we already took away* ***one*** [using the masculine form "*un*" to refer to "one" set of 224 tapes] *of them [i.e., of the three* ***–224's****]*". But instead, he uses "*une*", the feminine form of "one" (was he thinking of "*une bibliothèque*", translated here as "rack"?). What we are seeing here is a sort of *repetition*: the correspondence between the rack on one hand, and the number of tapes a rack can display on the other, *shows up again in the speech*—by way of this little "slip" in gender—before being formulated arithmetically. Mark perceives this, since he introduces a subordinate clarifying exchange (49M, 50J) that allows him to deduce 51M from 39M and thereby erase all traces of this other interpretation that comes through in John's discourse. The answer to the problem will not have emerged from the dialogue this time, but will have been present in the anaphoric mechanisms of the discourse (to the point of interfering somewhat with Mark's discourse), with 51M still referring to what the seller needs.

In fact, a second round of explanations on John's part is required before the exact meaning of the number 3 is grasped by the children. John goes back through his step-by-step rundown of the writing assigned to Mark. The propositional content of this second round extends from 52Jb to 56Jc. We have charted this process below as it unfolded in the discourse.

Propositional content	John's utterances	Mark's utterances
672	52Jb	
$-224-224-224=$	54Ja	
0	54Jc	
0	56Ja	
so 3 shelves	56jb	
3 ... racks	56Jc	61M

9.9 Conclusion: On the Merits of Conducting a Microgenetic Analysis Using Interlocutory Logic

Using an appropriate approach (interlocutory logic) to analyze the children's reasoning process, as dialogized by means of natural language, we were able to detect a stumbling block in their joint reflection about division. But there are other lessons to be learned from our study.

The discussion recorded here seems to us to be a nice example of "theorem in act" (to borrow a term coined by Vergnaud (1994) and Trognon et al. (2007)), for via this discussion, the children jointly enact the theorem of "division into N parts". In the second part of the solving process, where $[672-(3(224))=0]$ is calculated, they do in fact write down a formula that is equal to $[672/224=3]$. What's more, they do indeed produce an utterance containing the answer to the question asked in the problem: 3 racks. However, we will not have failed to notice that *what they write down on the scratch paper is not a division.* By telling us something about the children's epistemological attitudes toward division, does the microgenesis we have uncovered here allow us to come up with an explanation?

The literature (see Bideaud et al. 2004, pp. 265–275) distinguishes several types of division problems. In partition division *(How many pieces of candy will each child get if 12 pieces are divided up between 3 children?),* one is asked to divide up (quotient) a certain quantity into a given number of parts (divisor). In fraction division *(How many tables do you need to seat 12 children if there are 3 children per table?),* one has to find the number of groups (quotient) needed to solve the problem. From the developmental point of view, children understand partition division before fraction division. The problem posed to John and Mark belongs to the second category. "In *fraction* division, the number of groups to make is known from the start, so the terms of the division are expressed directly as a ratio or fraction (for example: 36/3). In this case, understanding the operation to carry out requires the children to see the division as a repeated subtraction. Division can then be understood as the reverse operation of multiplication (itself a repeated addition). [...] Learning how to divide large numbers, which begins in fourth grade in [French] elementary school (age 9–10), is based on *fraction* division. Although partition division is more "intuitive" [...], the acquisition of *fraction* division is necessary for building the logical relations between the terms of a division" (Bideaud et al. 2004, p. 272). Relating the microgenesis of the solution found jointly by Mark and John in this situation, we can say that the children clearly had access to some of the fundamental properties of division, e.g., a representation of division in terms of an iterated subtraction, as we noted above. It remains to be seen whether the fact that the children possessed this representation suffices to assert that they had mastered the concept of division. The answer to this question seems to be "no", since the children's interlocutory behavior did not manifest any references to fraction division as a finished form of appropriation of the arithmetic concept. However, given that the children were pretty good at manipulating one of the two critical properties of fraction division (the sum of the subtracted amounts), it seems legitimate to think that the property they had not yet grasped (the meaning of the fraction) lies in their zone of proximal development. If this is true, then clever experimenters should be able to invent an experimental device capable of distinguishing a full appropriation of fraction division, from a "halfway" appropriation, precisely the one achieved by John and Mark. It would be perfect if a research team combining experimenters and practitioners of the acquisition of arithmetic operations could be set up, in view of tackling this difficult question. Nonetheless, we will already be quite satisfied if we have been able to show that a microgenetic analysis based on interlocutory logic can suggest precise experimental hypotheses relevant to the psychology of learning.

References

J. Bideaud, H. Lehalle, B. Vilette, *La conquête du nombre et ses chemins chez l'enfant* (Presses Universitaires du Septentrion, Villeneuve d'Ascq, 2004)

J. Caron, Psychologie cognitive et interactions conversationnelles, in *Conversation, interaction et fonctionnement cognitif*, ed. by J. Bernicot, A. Trognon, J. Caron-Pargue (Presses Universitaires de Nancy, Nancy, 1997), pp. 221–238

L. Di Pellegrino, L. Fadiga, V. Fogassi, Gallese, G. Rizzolatti, Understanding motor events: a neurophysiological study. Exp. Brain Res. **91**, 176–180 (1992)
W. Doise, Le développement social de l'intelligence: aperçu historique, in *Psychologie sociale du développement cognitif*, ed. by G. Mugny (Peter Lang, Berne, 1985), pp. 39–57
W. Doise, G. Mugny, *Le développement social de l'intelligence* (Delachaux et Niestlé, Lausanne, 1981)
J.-L. Gardies, *Essai sur la logique des modalités* (Presses Universitaires de France, Paris, 1979)
H. Garfinkel, The curious seriousness of professional sociology, in *Les formes de la conversation*, ed. by B. Conein, M. de Fornel, L. Quéré (CNET, Paris, 1990), pp. 145–161
J. Hintikka, *The Semantics of Questions and the Questions of Semantics: Case Studies in the Interrelations of Logic, Semantics, and Syntax*. Volume 28 of Acta Philosophica Fennica (North-Holland, Amsterdam, 1976)
J. Hintikka, Questions de réponses et bien d'autres questions encore. Langue Française **52**, 56–69 (1981)
B. Inhelder, D. de Caprona, Vers le constructivisme psychologique: structures? Procédures? Les deux indissociables, in *Le Cheminement des découvertes de l'enfant*, ed. by B. Inhelder, G. Cellérier, E. Ackermann, A. Blanchet, D. De Caprona, J.-J. Ducret, M. Saada-Robert (Delachaux et Niestlé, Neuchâtel, 1992), pp. 19–50
M. Jeannerot, *Le Cerveau intime* (Odile Jacob, Paris, 2002)
P.R. Laughlin, E.C. Hatch, J.S. Silver, L. Boh, Groups perform better than the best individuals on letters-to-numbers problems: effects of group size. J. Personal. Soc. Psychol. **90**(4), 644–651 (2006)
J. Laux, A. Trognon, M. Batt, Une approche expérimentale et micro génétique de la tâche de sélection de Wason réalisée par des dyades pratiquant un dialogue coopératif. Psychologie Française **53**, 375–397 (2008)
P. Light, A.-N. Perret-Clermont, Social context effect in learning and testeing, in *Cognition and Social Worlds*, ed. by A. Gellatly, D. Rogers, J.A. Svoboda (Oxford University Press, New York, 1989), pp. 99–112
G. Mugny, La psychologie sociale génétique. Une discipline en développement, in *Psychologie sociale du développement cognitif*, ed. by G. Mugny (Peter Lang, Berne, 1985), pp. 15–39
A.-N. Perret-Clermont, *La Construction de l'intelligence dans l'interaction sociale* (Peter Lang, Berne, 1979)
A.-N. Perret-Clermont, A. Brossard, L'intrication des processus cognitifs et sociaux dans les interactions, in *Relations interpersonnelles et développement des savoirs*, ed. by R. Hinde, A.-N. Perret-Clermont, J. Stevenson-Hinde (Delval, Berne, 1988), pp. 441–465
R. Säljö, J. Wyndhamn, Problem-solving, academic performance and situated reasoning a study of joint cognitive activity in formal setting. Br. J. Educ. Psychol. **60**, 245–254 (1990)
E.A. Schegloff, Conversation analysis and socially shared cognition, in *Perspectives on Socially Shared Cognition*, ed. by L.B. Resnick, J.M. Levine, S.D. Teasley (American Psychological Association, Washington, DC, 1991), pp. 150–170
B. Schwarz, A.-N. Perret-Clermont, A. Trognon, P. Marro, Emergent learning in successive activities: learning in interaction in a laboratory context. Pragmat. Cognit. **16**(1), 57–87 (2008)
C. Sorsana, A. Trognon, Contextual determination of human thinking: about some conceptual and methodological obstacles in psychology studies. Human Dev. **54**(4), 204–233 (2011)
D. Sperber, D. Wilson, *La Pertinence* (Éditions de Minuit, Paris, 1989)
M. Tomasello, *Aux origines de la cognition humaine* (Retz, Paris, 2004). Édition originale, 1999
C. Trevarthen, The self born in intersubjectivity: an infant commumnicating, in *The Perceived Self: Ecological and Interpersonal Sources of Self-Knowledge*, ed. by U. Neisser (Cambridge University Press, Cambridge, 1994), pp. 121–173
A. Trognon, Speech acts and the logic of mutual understanding, in *Essays in Speech Acts Theory*, ed. by D. Vanderveken, S. Kubo (John Benjamins and sons, Amsterdam, 2002), pp. 121–133
A. Trognon, M. Batt, Comment conduire l'examen d'un fragment d'interlocution au moyen de la logique interlocutoire? in *Enseigner dans l'interaction*, ed. by A. Specogna (Presses Universitaires de Nancy, Nancy, 2007), pp. 13–33

A. Trognon, M. Batt, Interlocutory logic: a unified framework for studying conversation interaction. in *New Adventures in Language and Interaction*, ed. by J. Streek (Benjamins, Bruxelles, 2010), pp. 9–40

A. Trognon, C. Brassac, L'enchaînement conversationnel. Chiers de linguistique française **13**, 76–106 (1992)

A. Trognon, M. Bromberg, L'interaction sociale, in *Psychologie sociale et ressources humaines*, ed. by S. Ionescu, A. Blanchet, A. Trognon, M. Bromberg. Nouveau cours de psychologie (Presses universitaires de France, Paris, 2007), pp. 63–94

A. Trognon, V. Saint-Dizier, L'organisation conversationnelle des malentendus: Le cas d'un dialogue tutoriel. J. Pragmat. **31**, 787–815 (1999)

A. Trognon, V. Saint-Dizier, M. Grossen, Résolution conjointe d'un problème arithmétique, in *Apprendre dans l'interaction*, ed. by M. Gilly, J.-P. Roux, A. Trognon (Presses Universitaires de Nancy/Publications de l'Université de Provence, Nancy/Aix-en-Provence, 1999), pp. 121–141

A. Trognon, M. Batt, A.-N. Perret-Clermont, P. Marro, Logique interlocutoire de la résolution d'un problème d'arithmétique au sein d'une dyade. Psychologie Française **51**, 171–187 (2006)

A. Trognon, C. Sorsana, M. Batt, D. Longin, Comment identifie-t-on un théorème-en-acte en logique interlocutoire? in *Activité humaine et conceptualisation. Questions à Gérard Vergnaud*, ed. by M. Merri (Presses Universitaires du Mirail, Toulouse, 2007), pp. 763–782

A. Trognon, C. Sorsana, M. Batt, D. Longin, Peer interaction and problem solving. One example of a logical-discursive analysis of a process of joint decision making. Eur. J. Dev. Psychol. **5**(5), 623–643 (2008)

G. Vergnaud, Le raisonnement en physique et en mathématiques. Psychologie Française **39**(2), 153–160 (1994)

J. Wertsch, J. Sammarco, Précurseurs sociaux du fonctionnement cognitif individuel: le problème des unités d'analyse, in *Relations interpersonnelles et développement des savoirs*, ed. by R. Hinde, A.-N. Perret-Clermont, J. Stevenson-Hinde (Delval, Berne, 1988), pp. 395–415

Chapter 10
Dialogue of Rationalities: A Case Study

Marcelo Dascal

10.1 Introduction

The title "Dialogue of Rationalities" given to this chapter is provoking and deliberately chosen. On the provoking side, it stimulates further reflection on a number of entrenched beliefs. Contrary to the widespread belief that reason and rationality are essentially universal and largely uniform across individuals and cultures, this title presupposes that there are substantially different kinds of rationality. Contrary to the contention that a *sine qua non* condition for any dialogue is the sharing between the interlocutors of a conceptual framework, this title implies that, were this indeed a necessary condition, a dialogue between different *rationalities,* which certainly involve significant conceptual differences, would be impossible. In light of the above, the title's combination of 'dialogue' and 'rationalities' (in the plural) calls into question the a priori argument according to which the very notion of differing rationalities is unintelligible since an understanding of it can only be achieved with the cognitive tools of one or the other of the rationalities in question, which in principle are unable to grasp the differences radical enough to count as differences of rationality.

The purpose of this chapter is to explore the consequences of these daring challenges to common wisdom regarding rationality and dialogue. I will undertake to show that none of the above-mentioned alleged features and conditions of rationality and dialogue is in fact a necessary property of these concepts or of the phenomena to which they apply. This will open—at least—the conceptual possibility of a dialogue of cultures or individuals based on the mutual acknowledgment of each other's profound differences at levels as profound as that of rationality. Hopefully,

M. Dascal (✉)
Philosophy Department, Tel-Aviv University, Ramat Aviv, 69978 Tel-Aviv, Israel
e-mail: marcelodascal@gmail.com

M. Rebuschi et al. (eds.), *Interdisciplinary Works in Logic, Epistemology, Psychology and Linguistics*, Logic, Argumentation & Reasoning 3,
DOI 10.1007/978-3-319-03044-9_10, © Springer International Publishing Switzerland 2014

this acknowledgment will pave the way for new modalities of inter-cultural and inter-personal relations, well beyond the touristic, instrumental, and conflictive ones that seem to prevail today.

My strategy consists in describing a case in which different kinds of rationality not only co-exist but also do not exclude each other or attempt to render the other acceptable or intelligible only in one's own terms. Furthermore, it will become apparent that the differences between the kinds of rationality in the case examined are such that they can cooperate with each other in a sort of division of labor that proves to be necessary for epistemic reasons not devoid of metaphysical grounding.

The case study is that of a well-known and important philosopher, Gottfried Wilhelm Leibniz. His particular relevance lies in the fact that the historiography of philosophy classifies him as one of the "rationalists"—perhaps *the* rationalist *par excellence.* Nevertheless, his rationalism has generally been interpreted as monolithic rather than multifaceted, including a fundamental distinction between two kinds of rationality. I believe that I have recently been able to demonstrate the existence of these two types in Leibniz's thought and activities, as well as their deep differences, necessity, roles, grounds, and cooperative interaction.[1] This proves and illustrates the possibility of a dialogue of rationalities. I will summarize the rather unknown and surprising twofold nature of Leibniz's rationalism and suggest how it may be relevant and useful for some of our urgent philosophical and practical needs now and in the future.

10.2 Hard Rationality and Soft Rationality

In a series of publications appearing over the last decade, I argued that, in addition to the "hard" rationality for which Leibniz's rationalism is best known, it was imperative to acknowledge the existence and centrality in his work—theoretical as well as practical—of another, quite different kind of rationality, which I proposed to call 'soft'. Not unexpectedly, in spite of the wealth of textual evidence presented, my innovative proposal was questioned by some Leibniz scholars and supported by others, giving rise to an interesting and productive debate.[2] Instead of engaging directly in this debate here, I will instead focus on an important domain of Leibniz's work in which the hard-soft distinction is at once sharp and dialogical, thus offering a good example of a dialogue of rationalities.

---

[1] See, respectively, Dascal (2003, 2004b, 2001, 2005a, 2008a), as well as the Introductory Essay and the texts in Leibniz (2006).

[2] Consult, for example, some of the chapters of the collective volume *Leibniz: What Kind of Rationalist?* This volume is based on the papers presented at an international conference of Leibniz scholars under the same title, held in Tel Aviv and Jerusalem in 2005. It was published in 2008 and chosen by the international Leibniz Gesellschaft as its annual gift for its members.

Before entering into the description and analysis of this example, let us briefly characterize in what sense I am using the notions of hard and soft rationality:

Hard Rationality

By 'hard' rationality I understand a conception of rationality modeled fundamentally on standard logic and the application thereof.

Under this conception, certainty is the principal aim and sign of knowledge, while inconsistency is the paradigm of irrationality. Mathematics is the most successful implementation of this ideal of rationality and its model. Hard rationality privileges what it takes to be the reasons for mathematics' success.

The conditions of rational thinking and practice, according to hard rationality, comprise: uncompromising obedience to the principle of contradiction; precise definitions formulated in terms of necessary and sufficient conditions; deductive argumentation that ensures the truth and certainty of conclusions; formalization; quantification; computability; axiomatic systems; and similar devices.

Soft Rationality

By 'soft' rationality I understand a conception of rationality that seeks to account for and develop the means to cope with the host of situations—theoretical as well as practical—in which uncertainty and imprecision are the rule.

It rejects the identification as 'irrational' of all that falls short of the standards of hard rationality, and deals with the vast area of the 'reasonable', which lies between the two.

Soft rationality is best represented as a scale on which reasons in favor and against are weighed. But to weigh reasons is not to compute them. The weights of reasons are context-dependent and not precisely quantifiable. Therefore, weighing them does not yield results whose negation would imply contradiction. The balance of reason, unlike deduction, "inclines without necessitating," as Leibniz puts it. But proper weighing provides rational guidance in deliberating.

Soft rationality's logic is non-monotonic rather than deductive. It is the logic of presumptions that justifies without proving, of heuristics for problem-solving and hypothesis generation, of pragmatic interpretation, of negotiation, of exercising judgment, and of countless other procedures we use in our daily lives.

10.3 Leibniz's Dialectic: Hard *cum* Soft

In the vast territory of rationality, Leibniz's "art of controversies", the core of his *sui generis* dialectic, occupies a peculiar position. He conceives it sometimes as a calculus that decides rigorously and unquestionably which of the opposed positions in a controversy is true, and sometimes as a negotiation strategy leading to a conciliation of the adversaries' positions. While the former is a typical hard rationality approach, the latter is typically soft in nature.

Elsewhere I have shown *in extenso* Leibniz's concern for developing both of these procedures as well as for applying each of them in the appropriate circumstances (see Leibniz 2006, Dascal 2008a, and Dascal and Firt 2010). Obviously, I cannot rehash here the detailed evidence, analysis, and arguments supporting this claim. Instead, I will have to content myself with some highlights.

Let me start by noting that the evidence underscores the sharp contrast in method—hence, in rationality—implied by the two ways of handling controversies. Whereas the 'hard' way presumes that the opposition between the contenders amounts to a logical contradiction, the 'soft' way allows for a non-dichotomous reading of the opposed positions, so that they do not necessarily exclude each other (see Dascal 2008b). Unlike the former, therefore, the latter need not be resolved by the total elimination of one position, thus permitting some form of conciliation. But Leibniz does not abandon either the 'hard' way or the 'soft' way. Their concomitance throughout his intellectual career may indeed seem paradoxical and requires some explanation.

The explanation, if one pays attention to the relations between the two branches of Leibniz's dialectic, is in fact relatively simple. Their coexistence turns out not to be a passive juxtaposition. It involves them working together in a sort of division of labor necessary for the encompassing rationalism sought by Leibniz, which neither the one nor the other can provide alone. Let us consider a very important example of how this is achieved by Leibniz.

The "Preliminary Discourse on the Conformity of Faith and Reason", which opens Leibniz's *Essais de Theodicée,* undertakes the difficult task of establishing a common ground between two key domains of Leibniz's thought, perceived already in his time as antagonistic. I want to call attention to the fact that this task is performed by showing how hard and soft dialectic can and must work together in a non-reductive, complementary way. A close look at a few paragraphs of the Discourse should suffice here as a reminder of this important fact.[3]

In Sect. 30, he claims that good definitions and basic logic alone would be sufficient for determining precisely the borderline between reason and faith, thus resolving once and for all the debate over their respective territories:

> There wouldn't be anything as easy as to terminate the disputes about the rights of faith and reason if men wanted to make use of the most vulgar rules of logic and to reason with the minimum of attention. Instead, they get mixed up by oblique and ambiguous expressions (Leibniz 1965, p. 68).

In Sect. 31 he continues this line of argument, stressing the sufficiency of standard logic for tackling issues that can be solved through necessary inferences. This logic, however, is insufficient for "important deliberations" on matters that need a logic which "goes beyond", capable of performing such soft reasoning tasks as estimating probabilities:

[3]The following quotes are my translations of the French original in Leibniz (1965).

> Precision causes us discomfort and rules seem to us childish. This is why vulgar logic (which more or less suffices, however, for the examination of reasonings addressed towards certainty) is left for pupils; and we haven't even noticed those rules that must govern the weight of probabilities, which would be so needed in important deliberations. The source of most of our mistakes lies in the disregard or imperfection of the art of thinking, for there is nothing more imperfect than our Logic, when one goes beyond necessary inferences; and the best philosophers of our time... are very far from having indicated the appropriate means for helping this faculty of *weighing the estimations* of truth and falsity (Leibniz 1965, p. 68).

Such an extension of logic to also cover non-necessary inferences is a *sine qua non* for deliberation on important matters, especially those discussed in "human tribunals, which are not always able to reach the truth, being often forced to rely upon clues and *verisimilitudes,* and above all upon *presumptions or prejudgments*" (Leibniz 1965, p. 69). Yet, although soft considerations of this kind are also needed to discuss metaphysical and theological issues such as whether God is an accomplice of the evil he allows for in the world he created, they cannot be automatically transferred to this more complex and subtle domain without further refinement—which Leibniz provides in Sect. 33. Here, he points out that in addition to legitimizing the use of presumptions, a proper dialectic use must also take into account that they are not equal in "strength", and that the possibility of finding reasons against them is not equally accessible for all presumptions. These nuances are what ultimately rescues God from the charge of complicity mentioned above. They also illustrate how sophisticated the logic and dialectic of soft rationality may have to be in order to be able to deliver its share in the division of labor.

But the need for a division of dialectical labor goes deeper. Its source lies in the great metaphysical divide between the necessary and the contingent, which is essential not only to Leibniz's ontology, but also to his accounts of creation, of liberty, of truth and rationality, and for epistemology and logic. It is also essential to his practice and theory of dialectic. In terms of praxis, it is thanks to this divide that Leibniz can successfully refute the accusations of Spinozism (i.e., determinism) often leveled against him; furthermore, it is by resorting to the distinction between the two branches of dialectic that he can keep at bay the skeptics' and rationalist theologians' attacks against his way of reconciling reason and faith. In terms of theory, besides the fact that it provides the foundation for the distinction between soft and hard dialectic, the necessary/contingent divide provides also the basis for their co-habitation and division of labor. It is worth taking a look, however brief, at this Leibnizian *tour de force.*

Let us start by recalling the dividing points. First, two separate realms correspond to the necessary vs. contingent divide: the set of all possible worlds vs. the one existing actual world. Second, there are two kinds of truth: the truths of reason and the truths of fact (*Monadology* Sects. 33, 34). Third, there exist two great principles upon which reasoning is based: the Principle of Contradiction and the Principle of Sufficient Reason (Sects. 31, 32). Fourth, there are two logics: "*Just as the mathematicians have excelled above the other mortals, in the logic, i.e., the art of reason, of the necessary, so too the jurists did in the logic of the contingent*".[4] And fifth, the split these distinctions build up seems so sharp that dialectic cannot escape it. This raises doubts about the possibility of a cooperative division of labor between its two branches.

However, in spite of the sharpness of the divide, it would be a mistake to think the two sides do not share a significant number of features. First, although contingent and necessary truths differ in kind, they must share a concept of truth, just as God and His creatures, being both existent, however different, must share a concept of existence ("De Contingentia", in Leibniz 1948, p. 303). Second, although the Principle of Contradiction's (PC) jurisdiction is over necessary truths and cannot account for contingent ones—otherwise they would all be necessary (Leibniz 1948, p. 303)—and although without the Principle of Sufficient Reason (PSR) "there would be no principle of truth in contingent things" (Leibniz 1948, p. 305), both principles in fact apply to both realms. The contingent realm cannot contain true propositions that violate the PC, for they would be impossible and therefore necessarily false; furthermore, since the actual world is also a possible world, those truths—the necessary ones—that are true in all possible worlds are also true in it. The PSR, on the other hand, posits that every true proposition must have a reason—and this is precisely the concept of truth shared by necessary and contingent truths. The PSR is "one of the first principles of all human reasoning and after the principle of contradiction it has the greatest use in all the sciences" ("Introduction to a Secret Encyclopedia", in Leibniz 2006, p. 222). Third, the difference lies in that a reason for the former is a demonstration that 'necessitates', whereas a reason for the latter merely 'inclines' ("De Contingentia", in Leibniz 1948, p. 303). This is what the difference between the "two logics"—the mathematician's and the jurist's—amounts to: a different kind of 'validity' of their inferences.

We are thus back to the hard/soft rationality divide, which identifies the *modus operandi* of these two kinds of rationality as that which basically characterizes each of them. The impressive metaphysical, epistemological, and logical aura they have acquired in this last leg of our corresponding dialectic tour no doubt deepens the significance of the divide, as confirmed by Leibniz's tracing it back to God's own decision:

> ... just as God himself decided never to act unless he has true reasons of knowledge, he created rational creatures so that they never act unless they have prevalent or inclining reasons (Leibniz 1948, p. 305).

Nevertheless, as we have observed, the deeper philosophical ground from which this two-pronged dialectic is now seen to flow does not broaden the gap between its soft and hard horns. Rather, it explains why they must both be substantially different and capable of cooperating to cover that deepened and broadened foundation.

---

[4]Gottfried the Truthful of Lublin, "Towards a Balance of Law concerning the Degrees of Proofs and Probabilities". In Leibniz (2006, p. 36). Italics in the original. Immediately following this statement, the text contains a typically soft list of dialectic tools that can be learned from jurists as "logicians of the contingent".

The dialogue and cooperation between the two kinds of rationality exemplified by Leibniz's dialectic, as seen in this example, take place against a clear background of sharp methodological, logical, epistemic, and ontological differences. It is precisely thanks to the acknowledgement by each of them of the differential value of the other that the two rationalities can be partners in a fruitful dialogue without having to sacrifice their identities.

10.4 Theory and Practice: A Two-Pronged Dialogue of Rationalities?

The distinction between different kinds of rationality is of course commonplace in the history of ideas. Perhaps the most generally accepted division is that between practical and theoretical rationality. Nevertheless, this has rarely led to a radical polarization justifying talk of different *rationalities,* of the sort discussed above. Even those who argue that there are unbridgeable gaps between reasoning and acting (e.g., Searle 2001), do not split rationality into theoretical and practical. Leibniz himself, who accepts the theory vs. praxis distinction, recommends not exaggerating the distance between them, pointing out that a worker who is a master in what he does and knows the reasons for doing it "possesses the theory of his art", whereas a "half-scientist full of imaginary science" designs machines and buildings that cannot work "because he lacks the required theory". He also warns that one should be very careful in practical undertakings but should also avoid trusting "reason alone", and concludes that "it is important to have experience or to consult those who have it" (Leibniz 1999, pp. 712–713).

Kant, who also endorses the practical vs. theoretical distinction, goes a step further in unifying practical and theoretical reason in his well-known essay on the absurdity of the saying that something may be true in theory but not in practice, as well as in the Preface to *Grundlegung der Metaphysik der Sitten,* where he argues that this unity is an inevitable consequence of the fact that there can be only one Reason.[5]

There is an ample variety of 'practical reasoning', as well as a variety of combinations of these particular kinds of reasoning with other types of reasoning that are based on logical, mathematical, axiomatic, or other forms of 'hard' rationality (Milgram 2001), such combinations, in so far as they are not reductionist and do not claim for the predominance of one of its components over the other, can be conceived as similar to Leibniz's two-pronged dialectic discussed in Sect. 10.3. Paul Thagard, for instance, offers "a synthesis and partial reconciliation of intuition and calculation models of decision making" (Thagard 2001, p. 356). In his first year courses designed to improve the students' reasoning, however, he faces students

[5]On Kant's role in the history of the efforts to ensure a privileged position for Reason, see Dascal (1990).

"that trust their 'gut feelings' more than they trust the analytical methods that require a systematic and mathematical comparative assessment of competing actions that satisfy multiple criteria" (Thagard 2001, p. 355). The textbooks he uses, he admits, are designed to "encourage people to avoid the of intuition and instead to base their judgments and decisions on reasoning strategies that are less likely to lead to common errors in reasoning" (Thagard 2001, p. 355). This approach clearly subordinates decision making to calculation rather than to intuition, emotion, coherence or other elements Thagard combines in his practical reasoning theory of decision making: "Understanding decision making in terms of emotional coherence enables us to appreciate the merits of both intuition and calculation as contributors to effective practical reasoning" (Thagard 2001, p. 356). Although the predominance of the 'hard rationality' over the 'soft rationality' components of decision making is clear in some of his statements, he also stresses that his aim is "a model of decision making that is both natural and effective" (Thagard 2001, p. 369), and concludes that both kinds of rationality fit each other and can work together without any problem: "Reason and emotion need not be in conflict with each other if the emotional judgment that arises from a coherence assessment takes into account the relevant actions and goals and the relations between them. The procedure I recommend, informal intuition, shows how decisions can be both intuitive and reasonable" (Thagard 2001, p. 369). It is obvious that, whatever the preponderance of any of the two kinds of rationality, the fact (or assumption) that they can both take part simultaneously in a decision illustrates a dialogue of rationalities.

Other theories of decision making, especially that of Festinger, who has introduced the notion of "cognitive dissonance" in order to account for the process of deliberation as being a decision in favor or against one set of reasons or the opposite set of reasons. This 'balance of reasons' approach to decision making thus attributes a primary weight to the comparative (i.e., calculative) role of a 'hard rationality' measure of reasons, which can hardly be matched by its 'soft rationality' counterpart (see Dascal 2005a,b, pp. 41–43; Festinger 1964). Nevertheless, the followers of Festinger's Cognitive Dissonance Theory acknowledge that the 'weaker' reasons in the decision are kept in the decider's active memory and thereby can recover their 'strength' and triumph over the 'weightier' reasons in an alternative deliberation, the two sets of reasons in fact are also capable of a dialogue of rationalities.

10.5 Conclusion

Having discussed so far the possibility and eventual consequences of dialogical interchanges of different rationalities between human beings and cultures, it is convenient to conclude this article by considering the possibilities and consequences of similar interchanges between human minds and artifacts.

The Artificial Intelligence project was launched by the joint marvel of researchers with both the human cognitive capacity and the machine's potential to emulate, improve, and eventually surpass it. Nothing of the sort could be imagined or dreamt by Rene' Descartes, for whom a category abyss separated mind and machine. Since both mind and machine evolved much ever since both appeared in human evolution, and powerfully influenced each other's cognitive powers and beliefs, an at least provisional assessment of their evolution is in order.

Nowadays, the drive to make machines capable of imitating and eventually overtaking the mind seems to have been inverted: dazzled by the marvels of the ever more impressive cognitive capacity of daily marketed gadgets, it is the natural mind that aspires to emulate these devices and incorporate or 'embody' them, thereby 'extending' and 'supersizing' itself. Reflecting on this peculiar, circular evolution of the relation between model and modeled, we should inquire about its consequences. We should ask whether, by modeling our cognitive capability and performance on a limited set of cognitive features selected for implementation in artifacts, next to the cognitive gains undoubtedly achieved thereby, there aren't also unfathomable losses due to overlooking the immense potential of cognitive means of the natural mind that, though not selected for creating its artificial counterparts, evolved naturally and continue to prove their so far incomparable success.[6]

In the context of this paper, we should ask how the emergent hyphenated mind-machine and machine-mind concepts that the processes of mutual emulation and mutual utilization have created can contribute to the topic we have been discussing: dialogues of rationalities. Do they engender a new, unified rationality, capable of bypassing any dialogical problem between humans and their present and future technological counterparts? Or do they perhaps compound such problems by creating two (or more) profoundly different cultures with their respective rationalities, since the emulation in either direction is necessarily highly selective, being shaped by the capabilities of the emulator?

I have no ready-made answers to these questions, of course. But, by way of connecting this concluding section with all the preceding talk on soft and hard rationality and on two-pronged dialectic or dialogue, let me point out that in the case of natural language, it is the 'soft' cognitive resources inherent therein that technological emulations have yet to succeed in imitating, possibly because of the inherent limitations of the artificial languages in terms of which these emulations are produced (see Dascal 2004a and Dresner and Dascal 2001).

References

M. Dascal, La arrogancia de la razón. Isegoría **2**, 75–103 (1990)

M. Dascal, Leibniz and epistemological diversity, in *Unitá e Molteplicità nel Pensiero Filosofico e Scientifico di Leibniz*, ed. by A. Lamarra, R. Palaia (Leo Olschki, Firenze, 2000), pp. 15–37

M. Dascal, Nihil sine ratione → blandior ratio, in *Nihil sine ratione (VII. Internationaler Leibniz Kongress)*, ed. by H. Poser (Leibniz Gesellschaft, Berlin, 2001), pp. 276–280

---

[6]Cognitive variation, individual and collective, is of course one of the cognitive assets of the natural mind. See Lloyd (2007) and Dascal (2000, 2009).

M. Dascal, Ex pluribus unum? Patterns in 522+ Texts of Leibniz's Sämtliche Schriften und Briefe VI, 4. Leibniz Rev. **13**, 105–154 (2003)

M. Dascal, Language as a cognitive technology, in *Cognition and Technology: Co-existence, Convergence, and Co-evolution*, ed. by B. Gorayska, J.L. Mey (John Benjamins, Amsterdam, 2004a), pp. 37–62

M. Dascal, *Alter et etiam*: rejoinder to Schepers. Leibniz Rev. **14**, 137–151 (2004b)

M. Dascal, The balance of reason, in *Logic, Thought, and Action*, ed. by D. Vanderveken (Springer, Dordrecht, 2005a), pp. 27–47

M. Dascal, Debating with myself and debating with others, in *Controversies and Subjectivity*, ed. by P. Barrotta, M. Dascal (John Benjamins, Amsterdam/Philadelphia, 2005b)

M. Dascal, Leibniz's two-pronged dialectic, in *Leibniz: What Kind of Rationalist?* ed. by M. Dascal (Springer, Dordrecht, 2008a), pp. 37–72

M. Dascal, Dichotomies and types of debate, in *Controversy and Confrontation: Relating Controversy Analysis with Argumentation Theory*, ed. by F. van Eemeren, B. Garssen (John Benjamins, Amsterdam, 2008b) pp. 27–49

M. Dascal, Mental diversity and unity: a pragmatic approach to the debate. Pragmat. Cognit. **17**(2), 403–420 (2009)

M. Dascal, E. Firt, Leibniz's conciliatory approaches in scientific controversies, in *The Practice of Reason: Leibniz and His Controversies*, ed. by M. Dascal (John Benjamins, Amsterdam, 2010), pp. 137–167

E. Dresner, M. Dascal, Semantics, pragmatics, and the digital information age. Stud. Commun. Sci. **1**(2), 1–22 (2001)

L. Festinger (ed.), *Conflicts, Decision, and Dissonance* (Tavistok, London, 1964)

G.W. Leibniz, in *G.W. Leibniz: Textes Inédits*, ed. by G. Grua (Presses Universitaires de France, Paris, 1948)

G.W. Leibniz, Essais de théodicée, in *Die philosophischen Schriften von G.W. Leibniz*, ed. by C.I. Gerhardt (Georg Olms, Hildesheim, 1965)

G.W. Leibniz, *Sämtliche Schriften und Briefe*, vol. 4, Series IV (Akademie Verlag, Berlin, 1999)

G.W. Leibniz, *G.W. Leibniz: The Art of Controversies* (Springer, Dordrecht, 2006). Compiled, translated, annotated, and edited by M. Dascal with the cooperation of Q. Racionero and A. Cardoso

G.E.R. Lloyd, *Cognitive Variations: Reflections on the Unity and Diversity of the Human Mind* (Oxford University Press, Oxford, 2007)

E. Milgram (ed.), *Varieties of Practical Reasoning* (MIT, Cambridge, 2001)

J.R. Searle, *Rationality in Action* (MIT, Cambridge, 2001)

P. Thagard, How to make decisions: Coherence, emotion, and practical inference, in *Varieties of Practical Reasoning*, ed. by E. Milgram (MIT, Cambridge, 2001)

Chapter 11
Pragmatics of Veridicity

Denis Vernant

11.1 Veridictional Acts

Austin inaugurated his philosophy of ordinary language by denouncing the "descriptive fallacy" of philosophers and logicians who, in reducing all utterances to propositions, tackle only the descriptive, *constative use of ordinary language*. Thereafter, pragmatics began to emphasize the action-related or "performative" dimension of the social use of natural language.[1] But the time has now come to look in return at *veridictional acts* in their systematicity, for they all bring to play the speaker's attitude about the truth of what he/she is saying (For a statified definition of veridicity, cf. Vernant 2008a). It is therefore important to start by characterizing these acts.

11.1.1 Assertion

As logicians have shown, *assertion* is, conceptually, the most prevalent type of veridictional act.[2] Pragmatics defines it as the act by which a speaker makes a commitment about the truth of what he/she is saying to his/her addressee. This act manifests an *explicit commitment,* which can take on a variable degreeof force

[1]The acts in question are directives, commissives, and declaratives; see Vernant (1997, Chap. III).
[2]See my article, Vernant (2005a, Chap. XIII, pp. 267–288).

D. Vernant (✉)
Département de philosophie – ARSH, Université Pierre-Mendes-France,
1281, avenue centrale, 38040 Grenoble, France
e-mail: Denis.Vernant@upmf-grenoble.fr

M. Rebuschi et al. (eds.), *Interdisciplinary Works in Logic, Epistemology, Psychology and Linguistics*, Logic, Argumentation & Reasoning 3,
DOI 10.1007/978-3-319-03044-9_11, © Springer International Publishing Switzerland 2014

depending on whether it is a simple assertion or a declaration made under oath, etc., or even on whether the assertion is *metadiscursively doubled* by the expression "I assert that...".[3]

11.1.2 Denial

Assertion presupposes an act of *acceptance* of the propositional content of what is being said by the speaker. This act has a strictly pragmatic counterpart, which is the act of *refusal* of that same content via the expression of a *denial.* All too often confounded with simple negation, of which it often shares its surface linguistic form, it was first defined logically back in the 1930s by Lukasiewicz[4] and psychoanalytically by Freud in his famous article on *Verneinung* (Freud 1985). I will characterize *denial* as the speech act by which a speaker expresses his/her *refusal* of what he/she is saying.[5]

11.1.3 Consideration

Assertion and its opposite, denial, are two acts by which the speaker *expresses a commitment,* whether positive or negative, about what he/she is saying to the addressee. However, the speaker also has the possibility of *not* committing and thus settling for simply considering the informative content of what he/she is saying. This is what Frege called *das Fassen des Gedankens* (Frege 1971). Consideration—borrowing the term used by Russell—is a cognitively fundamental operation since it conditions not only the reported speech procedures of natural language and artistic languages, but also the use of apagogical methods of hypothetical reasoning in the formal sciences (Vernant 2008b). *Consideration,* then, grants the speaker some distance from what he/she is saying, in such a way that the question of the speaker's veridictional commitment gets sidestepped.

---

[3]On the pragmatic role of what I call *expositives,* see Vernant (2005b). I will come back later to the iteration of assertions; see Sect. 11.2.2 below.

[4]See my article (Vernant 2006).

[5]D. Vanderveken's illocutionary logic introduces illocutionary denial for *all* types illocutionary acts; see Searle and Vanderveken (1985, pp. 74, 152–155). Here, I will deliberately confine my analysis solely to Denial as a veridictional operator opposing Assertion. One can thus consider my veridictional pragmatics as part of general illocutionary logic. This is why I will use its operators whenever possible. But I will make use of a system (equivalent to modal system T) that is less powerful than the one ($S5$) employed by illocutionary logic ($T \subset S5$).

11.1.4 Estimation

In the same way as assertion possesses an opposite, namely denial, simple consideration has an opposing operation which—for lack of a better term—I will call *estimation*,[6] that is to say, the fact, for the speaker, of making a commitment about what he/she is saying, whether it be positively or negatively. Psychologically and cognitively, consideration and estimation are indeed two opposing attitudes that require a choice on the speaker's part.

11.2 The Opposition-Based Structure of Veridictional Acts

The reader will have understood that veridictional acts are organized according to an opposition-based structure. Before describing this structure, let us first clearly separate the different levels of opposition. As early as 1904, Russell had already clearly distinguished the opposition between truth and falsity, underlain by the metalogical principle of bivalence; the opposition between the logical operations "affirmation" and "negation"; and the opposition between the psychological attitudes "belief" and "disbelief":

> Given a proposition p, there is first its truth and its falsity.../...
>
> Next there is the opposition of p and not-p.../...
>
> Thirdly, there is the subjective opposition of yes and no, which is that of belief or disbelief: either p or not-p can be believed or disbelieved: whether true or false, this is the opposition that specifically characterizes judgment and is absent in assumption (Russell 1973, p. 56).

That left only the opposition between the strictly pragmatic operations of assertion and denial, which involves combining the logical operators that bear on propositional content with the pragmatic operations that characterize the speaker's attitude toward the truth of his/her utterance. Say we have at our disposal two logical operators that bear on propositional content, Affirmation and Negation; we still have to introduce the four pragmatic operations that determine the veridictional acts discerned above: Assertion, Denial, Estimation, and Consideration. If we acknowledge that Assertion and Denial are Estimation attitudes that oppose simple Consideration, then we can depict the combination of the *four pragmatic operators of veridicity* using the following binary tree (see next page):

However, one must not be misled by this dichotomous presentation. Although truth-function oppositions abide by standard logic, governed by the principle of excluded middle, the same does not hold true at the pragmatic level: Assertion is opposed not only to Denial, but also to the *third position* of simple Consideration,

[6] I use this term to refer to "expressing an opinion about". It is closely tied to judgment, but in natural language, its "expressive" dimension remains implicit.

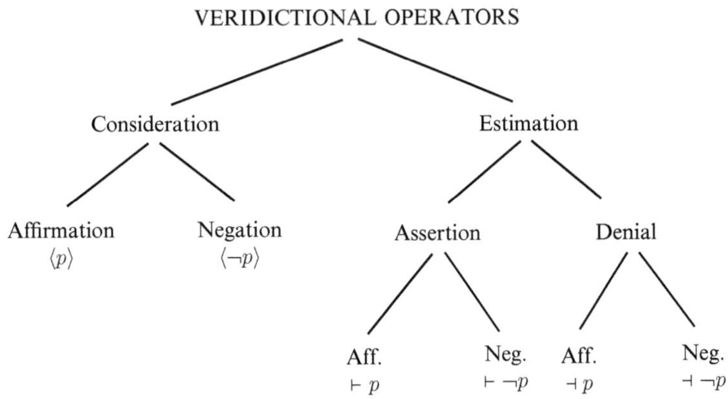

i.e., *suspension* of any decision.[7] The *pragmatics of veridicity* thus presupposes greater flexibility than strict propositional negation in accounting for the speaker's veridictional attitudes toward the informative content of his/her utterance.

11.2.1 Relations Between Veridictional Operators

If, for simplicity's sake, we use letters of the alphabet to stand for veridictional acts, veridictional pragmatics will include the following operators:

A	=	Asserting
C	=	Considering
D	=	Denying
E	=	Estimating

Relations between these veridictional operators can be depicted by the following alternative hexagon:

While relying on the theorems of my *alternative axiomatic system*,[8] let me simply recall a few of the most significant logical relations:

[7] Ockham had already made the distinction between judgment (assent or dissent) and simple apprehension, which he named *neutral proposition*: "Someone can apprehend a proposition and yet not give it one's assent or dissent, as is patent with neutral propositions", De Ockham (1979, I, prol. qu. 1, p. 16). Recall also that in the traditional *disputatio,* three attitudes were possible: *concedo, nego, dubito.*

[8] The reader will find my axiomatization of the relations between the veridictional operators in the Appendix of my Vernant (2009).

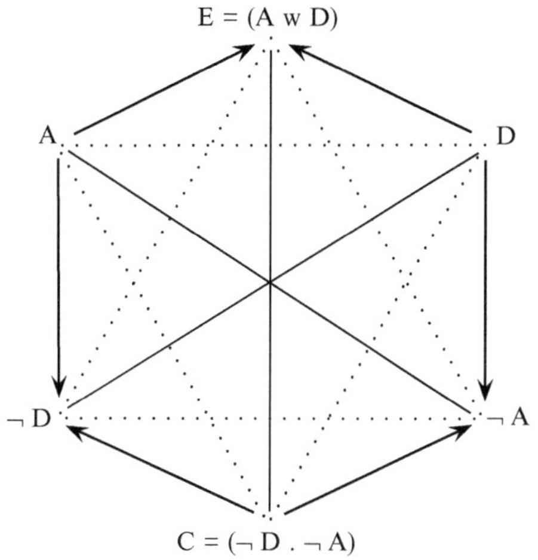

1. The two primitive operators, Assertion and Denial, are opposites, that is to say, incompatible: $A\mathbf{P}|D\mathbf{P}$ (T2).
2. *Non-contradiction* is obeyed by *suspensive* negation of acts: $\neg(A\mathbf{P}\&\neg A\mathbf{P})$ (T29) and $\neg(D\mathbf{P}\&\neg D\mathbf{P})$ (T30), but also by *exclusive* negation: $\neg(A\mathbf{P}\&D\mathbf{P})$ (T3).
3. By contrast, the *excluded middle* no longer holds for A and D, because it is quite possible to not choose between Asserting and Denying by adopting the *neutral position,* which is Consideration (T35).[9]
4. *Double negation* no longer holds for these same acts: not Denying **P** is not equivalent to Asserting **P**. It is indeed always possible to adopt the neutral position of Consideration, and thus: $\neg A\mathbf{P}$. By subalternation, we get $A\mathbf{P} \rhd \neg D\mathbf{P}$ (AX), but not its converse, thus: $\neg(A\mathbf{P} \approx \neg D\mathbf{P})$.[10] And likewise, by subalternation, we get $D\mathbf{P} \rhd \neg A\mathbf{P}$ (T1), but not its converse, thus: $\neg(D\mathbf{P} \approx \neg A\mathbf{P})$.

   The law of *double negation* does apply however to *suspensive* negation, denoted $\neg$. For example, we have: $\neg\neg A\mathbf{P} \approx A\mathbf{P}$ (T38) and $\neg\neg D\mathbf{P} \approx D\mathbf{P}$ (T40).[11]
5. *Bivalence* is preserved insofar as all propositions are either true or false: $\delta : \mathbf{P} \Rightarrow \{T, F\}$. Hence, *when one is making a decision* about a given proposition,

[9] We get the excluded quarter: $(A \vee D \vee C)$.

[10] $\rhd$ is the symbol for illocutionary *commitment* between two acts; see Searle and Vanderveken (1985, Chap. IV, p. 81): "$A_1 \rhd A_2$ iff it is not possible for the speaker to realize A_1 without being committed to A_2". This relation is reflexive, non-anti-symmetric, and transitive; see p. 141. $\approx$ is the symbol for *congruence* of two illocutionary acts; see Searle and Vanderveken (1985, Chap. IV, p. 82): "Two illocutionary acts are *congruent* iff each one commits the speaker to the other". This equivalence relation is definable: $A_1 \approx A_2$ iff $A_1 \rhd A_2$ and $A_2 \rhd A_1$ (where A is any illocutionary act).

[11] It does not hold for *exclusive* negation, which means we do not have $A\mathbf{P} \rhd DD\mathbf{P}$.

it is not possible to not decide the opposite about the proposition that has the opposite truth value. So we have $AP \rhd D \sim P$ (ET6) and $DP \rhd A \sim P$ (ET7). This is a particular case where the veridictional operators bear on propositions that are mutually *exclusive*: $\mathbf{R}|\mathbf{S}$ (see the exclusivity theorems of our axiomatic system, ET1 to ET11).

11.2.2 Syntactic Presentation

Without formalizing the rules for building the formulas of the veridictional language, note simply that every formula is of the type: $F(£)$, where £ denotes the set of well-formed formulas of standard logical calculus $\{P, Q, R, S, \ldots\}$ built from the atomic propositions p, q, etc. by means of the standard connectors $\{\sim, \circ, \vee, \rightarrow, |, etc.\}$, and where F belongs to the set of all formulas built from the veridictional operators $\mathbb{V} = \{A, C, D, E\}$ and the set of all connectives bearing on illocutionary acts $\{\neg, \&, w, |, \rhd, \approx\}$.

We can present our veridictional pragmatics as a particular interpretation, a model, of our *bipolar* axiomatic system[12] of veridicity. Let me recall and comment upon its basic elements:

PRIMITIVE IDEAS:		
	Assertion:	$\vdash \mathbf{P}$
	Denial:	$\dashv \mathbf{P}$
DEFINITIONS:		
	Negation of Assertion:	$\nvdash \mathbf{P} =_{Df} \neg \vdash \mathbf{P}$
	Negation of Denial:	$\not\dashv \mathbf{P} =_{Df} \neg \dashv \mathbf{P}$
	Estimation:	$\dashv\vdash \mathbf{P} =_{Df} (\vdash \mathbf{P}\, w \dashv \mathbf{P})$
	Consideration:	$\langle \mathbf{P} \rangle =_{Df} (\nvdash \mathbf{P}\, \&\, \not\dashv \mathbf{P})$
AXIOMS:		
	Axiom of Assertability:	$AX_1 : \vdash \mathbf{P} \rhd \mathbf{P}$

The kind of assertion in question here is not logical assertion, but rather *pragmatic* assertion per se. What is at stake is not the validity of **P**, but its veridicity.[13] This *axiom of assertability* merely states that in asserting **P**, the speaker

[12]This axiomatic system includes axioms for proving theorems and *counter-axioms* for proving *counter-theorems*. Regarding this bipolarity, see Vernant (2010a).

[13]Of course, pragmatic assertion is the illocutionary act of a given speaker, which does not imply the truth, and *all the less so*, the validity of the proposition in question. It is not to be confused with logical assertion (demonstration) as defined by Russell and Frege, nor with what can be regarded as *established*, i.e., proven. This latter interpretation is the one that Jean de La Harpe adopted in (1950, pp. 26–31).

commits to the truth of **P**: $(AP \rightarrow P)$. This in no way means that **P** is true, but that **P** is *held to be true* in the discursive world proposed by the speaker.[14]

Principle of assertion[15]	$AX2:$	$[\vdash (\mathbf{P} \rightarrow \mathbf{Q}) \,\&\, \vdash \mathbf{P}] \triangleright \vdash \mathbf{Q}$
COUNTER-AXIOM:		
Counter-axiom of negation:	$CAX1$	$\dashv (\neg AP \rightarrow \neg P)$

This axiomatic system[16] allows one to prove all of the component relations of the alternative hexagon, as well as all relations that are excluded. For some pragmatically significant examples, simply consider the case of assertion iteration. With this axiomatic system, it is easy to prove left-to-right implication. One obtains General Theorem 11 from Axiom 1 by simple substitution:

GT11	$\vdash (AAP \rightarrow AP)$	
	$1\ AP \rightarrow P$	$AX1$
	$2\ AAP \rightarrow AP$	Sub. P/AP

In contrast, to prove *Counter-Theorem* 1, which brings right-to-left implication into play, it is useful to first prove General Theorem 8, contraposition:

GT8	$\vdash [(AP \rightarrow AQ) \equiv (\neg AQ \rightarrow \neg AP)]$	
	$(P \rightarrow Q) \equiv (\neg Q \rightarrow \neg P)$	Tautology
	$(AP \rightarrow AQ) \equiv (\neg AQ \rightarrow \neg AP)$	Sub. $P/AP; Q/AQ$.

General Counter-Theorem 1 is then obtained as follows:

GCT1	$\dashv (AP \rightarrow AAP)$	
1	$\dashv (\neg AP \rightarrow \neg P)$	CAX1
2	$\vdash [(AP \rightarrow AQ) \equiv (\neg AQ \rightarrow \neg AP)]$	GT8
3	$\vdash [(AP \rightarrow AAP) \equiv (\neg AAP \rightarrow \neg AP)]$	2, CSub. Q/AP
4	$\dashv (\neg AAP \rightarrow \neg AP)$	1, CSub P/AP
5	$\vdash \{[(AP \rightarrow AAP) \rightarrow (\neg AAP \rightarrow \neg AP)] \circ$ $[(\neg AAP \rightarrow \neg AP) \rightarrow (AP \rightarrow AAP)]\}$	3, Df. biconditional
6	$\vdash [(AP \rightarrow AAP) \rightarrow (\neg AAP \rightarrow \neg AP)]$	5, Elim. conjunction
7	$\dashv (AP \rightarrow AAP)$	6, 4 CR1 is the counter-rule of detachement.

[14]This corresponds to what Karl Otto Apel called "pretension to truth" (Apel 1994, p. 46).

[15]Here we find Russell's "Principle of assertion" (see our article "The Limits of a Logical Treatment of Assertion"). Unlike epistemic logic, which poses the question of omniscience $[K\mathbf{P}\&(\mathbf{P} \rightarrow \mathbf{Q})] \rightarrow K\mathbf{Q}$, there is no risk of omnidiction here since we do not have to assert all of the consequences of our assertions: $\neg\{[\vdash \mathbf{P}\&(\mathbf{P} \rightarrow \mathbf{Q})] \triangleright \vdash \mathbf{Q}\}$.

[16]To simplify my presentation, I will not bring to bear the rules and counter-rules of transformation.

This logically demonstrates that there is no equivalence between assertion and its iteration. We know that such an equivalence is only possible in a formal system as powerful as modal system $S4$ and not in a system as weak as T (Hugues and Cresswell 1968, pp. 43–44).

Such a result is therefore not at all logically surprising or notable. However, it is of critical pragmatic interest in that it takes a stand on the interpretation of assertion iteration. From a strictly pragmatic point of view, it is wise indeed not to confuse or liken assertion and its iteration. Ap symbolizes the assertion of p by a speaker.[17] The speaker commits to the truth of the content of proposition p. This is the case, for example, when the speaker says: "It's raining." In contrast, AAp denotes the operation whose rhetorical effect is to *reinforce* the strength of the initial assertion. In natural language, this is expressed by the fact that the speaker in the above example says something like: "I maintain that it's raining". Pragmatically, the two acts are manifestly different, the first being a simple *assertion,* true or false, the second, an act of a metadiscursive nature—precisely, an *expositive*—which, as such, cannot be untrue by virtue of the sheer fact that it was produced:

> The sentence "It is the case that I maintain that it's raining" clearly has a different truth value than that of the sentence "It's raining" (the former can be true without the latter also being so). (Apel 1994, p. 43)

If we acknowledge this conceptual distinction,[18] we can understand why implication can hold true from left to right, for if one asserts a proposition, one cannot *not* assert it because the metadiscursive commitment is stronger than the simple assertion. In contrast, a simple assertion does not necessarily involve a stronger commitment, from which we can see that the fact of *rejecting* the right-to-left implication renders explicit an entire thematization and conceptualization of a pragmatic nature.[19]

11.2.3 Semantic Presentation

One can develop a *semantics* for interpreting and evaluating the propositions of this veridictional pragmatics. To do so, it is useful to complete these propositions by indicating the speaker who assumes the veridictional act. Accordingly, we use $\vdash_a$ **P** to denote the fact that Speaker a assumes the assertion of **P**. The system

---

[17]As we shall see in the next section, a more sophisticated formalization that incorporates the speaker is possible; it gives us $A_a p$.

[18]Unlike Searle, who ignores the specificity of metadiscursives and unduly classifies "I assert that it's raining" among the assertives; see Searle (1982, p. 61).

[19]Daniel Vanderveken, who formalized Searle's theory, relies on a system equivalent to modal system $S5$; see Vanderveken (1990).

is interpreted *in the first person* as the set of veridictional acts of Assertion, Denial, Estimation, and Consideration of a given speaker. We then evaluate the veridictional act on the *discursive world*[20] that Speaker a proposes by means of his/her various veridictional acts, with world W_a being accessible from initial world W_0. These acts can then be interpreted as follows:

$\vdash_a \mathbf{P}$	Expresses adherence to the truth of **P** in *any* world proposed by a accessible from W_0
$\vdash_a \sim\mathbf{P}$	Expresses adherence to the falsity of **P** in *any* world proposed by a accessible from W_0
$\dashv_a \mathbf{P}$	Expresses refusal of the truth of **P** in *any* world proposed by a accessible from W_0
$\dashv_a \sim\mathbf{P}$	Expresses refusal of the falsity of **P** in *any* world proposed by a accessible from W_0
$\nvdash_a \mathbf{P}$	Expresses abstention of adherence to the truth of **P** in *at least one* world proposed by a accessible from W_0
$\not\dashv_a \mathbf{P}$	Expresses abstention of refusal of the truth of **P** in *at least one* world proposed by a accessible from W_0[21]

Using the semantic table method derived from Kripke,[22] we can write down the veridictional acts in the representation of the discursive world proposed by Speaker a while distinguishing what is asserted from what is not asserted, and within the not-asserted, what is denied from what is not denied. By virtue of Laws ET6 and ET7 recalled above, whenever two incompatible expressions are involved, we will indicate what is asserted by the speaker and what commits him/her to the corresponding denial, and *vice versa.* Proofs will be *by reductio ad absurdum*: in initial world W_0, we will put the presumably false propositions in the right column, and the presumably true ones in the left column. First, we will write the formula to be evaluated at the top of the right column. Then we will analyze the formulas by assigning them to the right or left column according to the rules of the propositional operators, and we will process the elementary formulas obtained by writing down the concerned propositions in the *world proposed by the speaker* that

[20]Here, any illocutionary act is a *proposal* made by the speaker to the addressee, a proposal that must be negotiated to give rise to a jointly assumed "*interact*"; see Vernant (1997, Chap. VIII) and Vernant (2009, Chap. X, Sect. 4.1.1).

[21]Formally, a *Model* is any triplet $< W, S, V >$ in which W is a proposed set of discursive worlds $W_0, W_1, \ldots$; R is the accessibility relation, which is reflexive $(x)(xRx)$ and thus serial $(x)Ez(xRz)$; and V is the function that attributes the values $\{1, 0\}$. $V(A)$ thus reads as follows: For all **P** and W_i, $V(A\mathbf{P}, W_i) = 1$ if for *all* W_j such that $W_i RW_j$, $V(\mathbf{P}, W_j) = 1$, else $V(A\mathbf{P}, W_i) = 0$. Likewise, $V(I)$ reads: for all **P** and W_i, $V(I\mathbf{P}, W_i) = 1$ if for *at least one* W_j such that $W_i RW_j$, $V(\mathbf{P}, W_j) = 1$, else $V(I\mathbf{P}, W_i) = 0$.

[22]See Kripke (1963). The presentation used here is from Jean-Louis Gardies, Gardies (1979, pp. 58 *sq*.).

is accessible from the initial world. An asserted proposition will be in the assertion-of-W_a box, a denied proposition will be in the Denial sub-box, and so on. When the initial formula is valid, we discover a *contradiction* in the world proposed by Speaker a.

Let us consider the formula: $\vdash_a p \rhd \neg \dashv_a p$

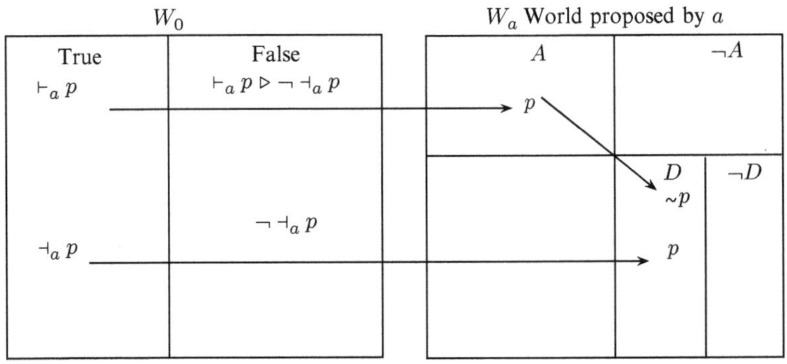

By *reductio ad absurdum,* we begin by writing the formula to be tested in W_0's False box (on the right). To falsify the commitment proposed, it suffices that its antecedent be true and its consequent, false. We then write the antecedent in the True box on the left. Presumably true, $\vdash_a p$ means that p is to be written in the assertion box (A) of Speaker a's proposed world. Applying Russell's Law leads us to write its opposite $\sim p$ in the opposite sub-box, Denial (D). The last step is to write the consequent in the right box of W_0. Whereas $\neg \dashv_a p$ must be false, $\dashv_a p$, presumably true, moves to the right box. This allows us to write p in the Denial sub-box of W_a. We then see that there is a contradiction, since the Denial box authorizes both p and $\sim p$ in W_a. The initial formula is thus proven (it corresponds to axiom AX of our alternative axiomatic system).

Similarly, let us consider the converse: $\neg \dashv_a p \rhd \vdash_a p$

The presumably false formula is put in the right box of W_0. Then its antecedent is put on the left, which allows us to write p in W_a's not-Denied sub-box. The next step is to put the consequent in W_0's right box, from which we can write p in W_a's not-Asserted box. This time, there is no contradiction, p is both not asserted and not denied. The formula is therefore invalid.[23]

[23] The counter-position corresponds to the formula $\neg A \rightarrow E$, which is not included in our axiomatic system since it is equivalent to the *inclusive* disjunction: $A \vee E$.

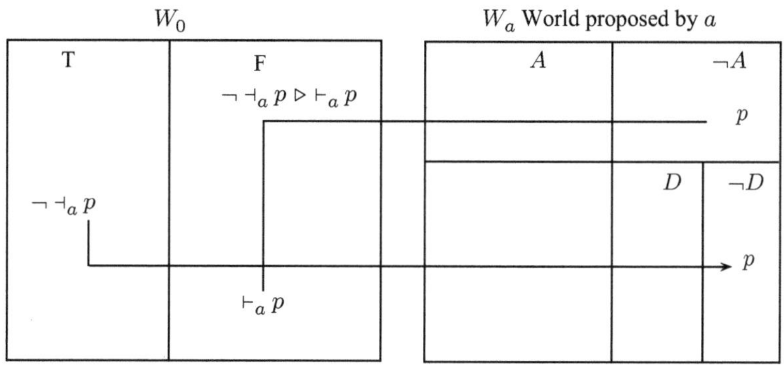

Similarly, it is easy to show that $\vdash_a p \vee \dashv_a p$ is not valid:

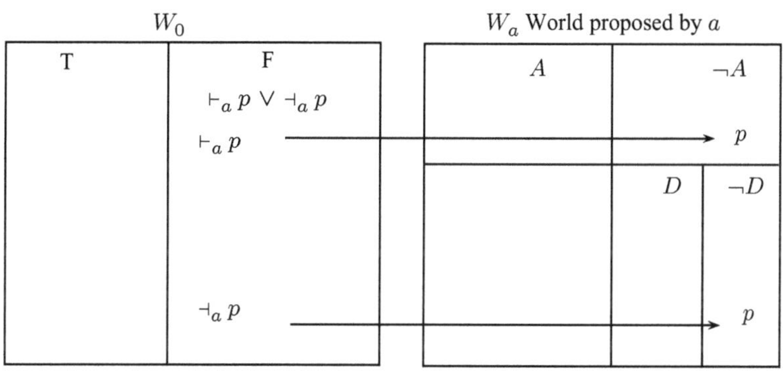

To assume that the disjunction is false, one must assume that each of the disjuncts is false; so they are written in the left box of W_0. The falsity of $\vdash_a p$ causes us to write p in the not-Asserted box of W_a; likewise, the falsity of $\vdash_a p$ requires that we write p in the not-Denied sub-box of W_a. We can easily see that the initial formula is not contradictory and that there exists a third position between assertion and Denial, namely Consideration, as a *suspensive* conjunction of the not-Asserted and the not-Denied.

11.2.3.1 Multi-agent Extension

One can extend the veridictional language to build a *multi-agent, veridictional pragmatics.* It allows us to express the combination of veridictional actions taken by different agents about a given proposition such as $\mathbb{V}_a \mathbb{V}_b \mathbf{P}$, where, for example, $A_a D_b p$ stands for "Agent a asserts that Agent b denies p".[24] Now we can evaluate

[24]For greater clarity, I again use letters of the alphabet to symbolize veridictional acts.

formulas of this type by making the world the second agent proposed, W_{ab}, *subordinate to* the one the first agent proposed, W_a. The subordinate world will not represent what the second agent said, but what the first agent *said that the second agent, b, said.*

The formula to be evaluated here is: $D_a A_b p \triangleright \neg A_a D_b \sim p$.

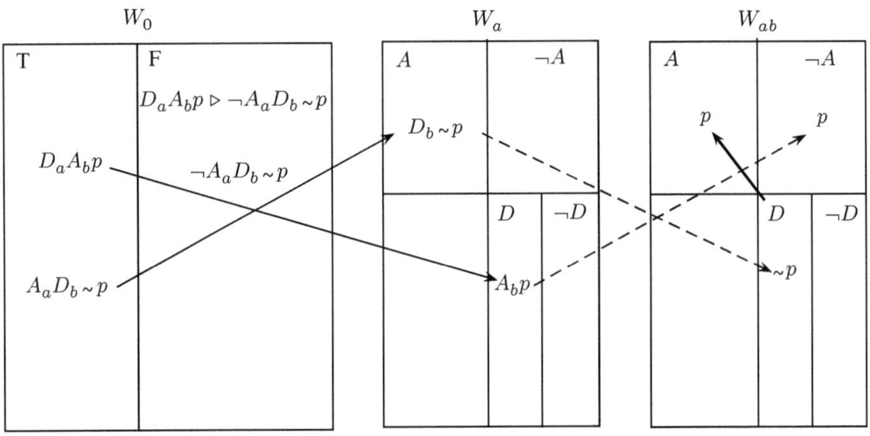

This formula is written in the part right of W_0. The antecedent $D_a A_b p$ is then moved to the left part. This leads us to write $A_b p$ in sub-box D of W_a and thus, p in the $\neg A$ box of W_{ab}. This leaves the consequent $\neg A_a D_b \sim P$, which we put in the right part of W_0. Given that it is preceded by a negation, its affirmative converse moves to the left. So $A_a D_b \sim p$ leads us to write $D_b \sim p$ in box A of W_a and thus $\sim p$ in sub-box D of W_{ab}. Now by virtue of Russell's Law, p must be written in box A of the same world. We can see a contradiction in this world since p cannot be both asserted and not asserted. Because negation of the formula is not possible, this formula is valid.

Likewise, we can symbolize the conjunction of actions of agents about different propositions, such as $\mathbb{V}_a\mathbf{P}\&\mathbb{V}_b\mathbf{Q}$. This construction authorizes the formalization of the veridictional Agreement of two (or more) agents about the same proposition. Here, we have:

Agreement:	$\mathbb{V}_a\mathbf{P}$	&	$\mathbb{V}_b\mathbf{P}$	iff	$\mathbb{V}_a\mathbf{P} \approx \mathbb{V}_b\mathbf{P}$	
Disagreement:	$\mathbb{V}_a\mathbf{P}$	&	$\mathbb{V}_b\mathbf{P}$	iff	$\neg(\mathbb{V}_a\mathbf{P} \approx \mathbb{V}_b\mathbf{P})$ &	$\neg(\mathbb{V}_a\mathbf{P}\vert\mathbb{V}_b\mathbf{P})$
Opposition:	$\mathbb{V}_A\mathbf{P}$	&	$\mathbb{V}_B\mathbf{P}$	iff	$\mathbb{V}_A\mathbf{P}\vert\mathbb{V}_B\mathbf{P}$	

There will be *agreement* if the two agents assert the same proposition (or two propositions that they acknowledge to be equivalent), for example, $\vdash_a \mathbf{P}\& \vdash_b \mathbf{P}$, and *opposition* if they take incompatible stances, such as: $\vdash_a \mathbf{P}\& \dashv_b \mathbf{P}$.

This type of operator provides the link between the present pragmatic dimension of veridicity and the strictly dialogical one developed in our *Dialogical Logic of Veridicity,* aimed at handling relations of agreement, disagreement, and opposition between agents about a given proposition.

11.3 Doxastic Correlates of Veridictional Acts

Like any formal system, an axiomatic system can receive several different *models.* Accordingly, our pragmatic theorization of veridictional acts can serve as a model of our bipolar axiomatic system. But other models are conceivable. Our axiomatic system provides a *formal structure* that holds not only for veridictional speech acts, but also for states of mind, the belief attitudes associated with them. This gives us the following hexagon, which expresses the logical relations between the *doxastic correlates*[25] of veridictional acts:

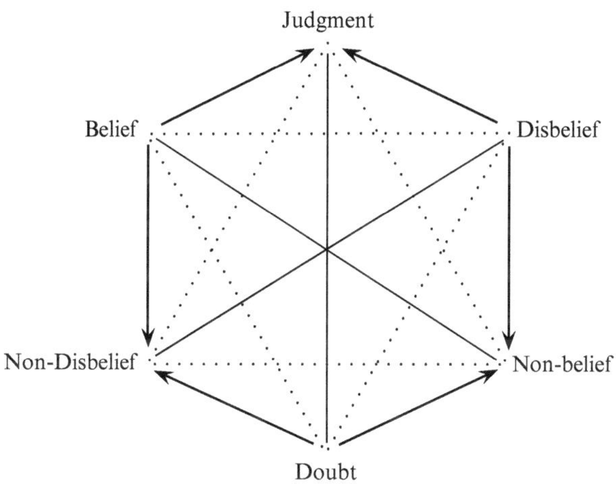

A *judgment,* which is a veridictional commitment expressed by an Assertion or a Denial, rests on an attitude of either Belief or Disbelief and corresponds to the act of Estimation. *Doubt,* as a mental state, corresponds to the neutral, suspensive position of simple Consideration, i.e., both non-belief and non-disbelief.

The theory of veridictional acts and the theory of mental states thus turn out to be two isomorphic models of one and the same axiomatic architecture. Just as it did for speech acts, this formal architecture enables one to clarify and systematize the

[25]The strictly *epistemic* dimension can only intervene in the framework of our *Dialogical Logic of Veridicity,* Vernant (2010b) which accounts for agreement (or disagreement) about the truth in question. Knowledge is necessarily dialogically mutualized.

theory of mental acts. To illustrate with a single example, it establishes logically that one should not—contrary to what is all too often done—confuse disbelief, which is a question of denial, with non-belief, which depends on non-assertion.[26]

11.4 Conclusion

The analysis I have just proposed is first and foremost a *logical* analysis, in that it draws from the age-old "square of opposition" to precisely define the relations between the various possible veridictional acts: Assertion, Non-Assertion, Denial, Non-Denial, Estimation, and Consideration. Although I have chosen to propose an *alternative* to the hexagon of opposition in order to account for the *incompatibility* between Assertion and Denial, the laws of standard propositional calculus are assumptions therein. Accordingly, the theorems of that calculus as well as those of the proposed axiomatic system can be asserted by applying rule R1 of the alternative axiomatic system.[27]

The logical dimension is thus patent. But it must not conceal the strictly *pragmatic* dimension. This means recognizing the difference—which I have never stopped stressing—between logical assertion as a formal, anonymous deduction procedure, and pragmatic assertion as an act of a particular speaker. In other words, one must acknowledge the difference between logical, formal, anonymous truth, and veridicity as an act of a speaker who commits personally to the truth of what he/she is saying. Hence, the axiom of veridicity says nothing about the truth of what is said by the speaker.

In any case, this pragmatics of veridicity does not claim to answer the ancient question of the truth, which requires a *praxiological* type of approach, one that relates the saying to the doing, the words of speakers to the worlds in which those speakers act.[28]

Moreover, the question of veridicity itself is not for as much answered by this logico-pragmatic analysis. As it is described above, my pragmatic logic of veridicity only deals with the acts of a single speaker or with the compared attitudes of two speakers (agreement, opposition, disagreement). As such, the analysis remains *abstract,* for it does not address the fundamentally *dialogical* dimension of discourse. Speech acts are not definable monologically. For example, assertion could never be reduced to the formal schema $A_a p$, but only to $A_{ab} p$ insofar as this formula alone expresses the speaker's commitment to the truth of p *relative to* an addressee b.[29] What's more, these acts only become meaningful in the context of a dialogue

[26]On this crucial distinction, see Vernant (2009, Chaps. I and VII).

[27]See $R1 :\vdash \mathbf{P} \Rightarrow \vdash A\mathbf{P}$, where $\vdash$ is the *metalogical* symbol for deduction and A, that of the act of assertion.

[28]This praxiological dimension is analyzed in Vernant (2009, Chap. XI).

[29]See Vernant (1997, Chap. IV).

wherein they are the outcome of a negotiation process between the interlocutors aimed at their being assumed as *interacts*.[30] Last but not least, these interacts do not take on a *dialogical function* unless they serve as *moves* in the "language game" in which the argumentative exchange that ensures or does not ensure veridictional agreement is being played.[31]

The purpose of the above analysis, then, was solely to rigorously, i.e., logically, define the possible relations between the veridictional acts that characterize a speaker's pragmatic attitude toward what he/she acknowledges, refuses, or simply considers.

In fine, one can also wonder from a zetetic standpoint whether this formalization—leading to a pragmatics of veridictional acts extended to their doxastic correlates—might apply, *cum grano salis,* not to "constative" acts this time, which bring into play the information transmitted between the speaker and the addressee, but strictly to acts of the "performative" type, which introduce purely actional rapports between a speaker and an addressee facing a to-be-solved problem, in a particular situation. I will leave this question unanswered for now.

References

K.O. Apel, *Le Logos propre au langage humain* (Éditions de L'Éclat, Combas, 1994). Translated by M. Charrière & J.-P. Cometti

J. de La Harpe, *La Logique de l'assertion pure* (Presses Universitaires de France, Paris, 1950)

G. De Ockham, *Scriptum in librum primum Sententiarum, Ordinatio, Prologus et distinctio prima* (St Bonaventure, New York, 1979)

G. Frege, Recherches logiques, I – La pensée, II – La négation, in *Écrits logiques et philosophiques* (Seuil, Paris, 1971), pp. 170–213

S. Freud, *Résultats, idées, problèmes*, chapter La négation (Presses Universitaires de France, Paris, 1985), pp. 135–139. (Original text in: *Imago,* 11(3), 1925, 217–221)

J.-L. Gardies, *Essai sur la logique des modalités* (Presses Universitaires de France, Paris, 1979)

G.E. Hugues, M. J. Cresswell, *An Introduction to Modal Logic* (Methuen & Co, London, 1968)

S. Kripke, Semantical analysis of modal logic I. Normal propositional Calculi. Zeitschrift für mathematische Logik und Grundlagen der Mathematik, **9**, 67–96 (1963)

B. Russell, Meinong's theory of complexes and assumptions, in *Essays in Analysis*, ed. by D. Lackey (Allen & Unwin, London, 1973)

J.R. Searle, *Sens et expression, Études de théorie des actes du langage*. Le sens commun (Éditions de Minuit, Paris, 1982). Traduit de l'anglais (États-Unis) et préfacé par Joëlle Proust

J.R. Searle, D. Vanderveken, *Foundations of Illocutionary Logic* (Cambridge University Press, Cambridge, 1985)

D. Vanderveken, *Meaning and Speech Acts – vol. 1, Principles of Language Use, vol. 2, Formal Semantics of Success and Satisfaction* (Cambridge University Press, Cambridge, 1990)

D. Vernant, *Du discours à l'action* (Presses Universitaires de France, Paris, 1997)

D. Vernant, The limits of a logical treatment of assertion, in *Logic, Thought and Action*, ed. by D. Vanderveken (Springer, Dordrecht, 2005a)

[30]See Vernant (1997, Chap. VIII) and Vernant (2009, Chap. X, Sect. 4.1.1.1).

[31]By themselves, assertions are pure abstractions. An assertion assumes a particular function in a dialogue only as a response, a reply, an inquiry, a questioning, etc. See Vernant (2009, Chap. IX).

D. Vernant, Pour une analyse pragmatique de l'acte de citer: les métadiscursifs, in *Citer l'autre*, ed. by A. Wall, M.-D. Popelard (Presses de la Sorbonne Nouvelle, Paris, 2005b), pp. 179–194

D. Vernant, La genèse logique de la dénégation, in *Philosophie et logique en Pologne 1918–1939*, ed. by R. Pouivet, M. Rebuschi. Analyse et Philosophie (Vrin, Paris, 2006), pp. 151–178

D. Vernant, Définition stratifiée de la véridicité, in *Définition, Rôles et fonctions en logique et en mathématiques*, ed. by P. Joray, D. Miéville (Université de Neuchâtel, Neuchâtel, 2008a), pp. 205–237

D. Vernant, L'argumentation par l'absurde: l'opération pragmatique de considération, in *La Logique et les normes, Hommage à J.-L. Gardies*, Number 25 in Recherches sur la philosophie et la langage (Vrin, Paris, 2008b), pp. 73–90

D. Vernant, *Discours et Vérité* (Vrin, Paris, 2009)

D. Vernant, Sur la bipolarité des concepts, des théories et des axiomatiques, in *Construction, Festschrift für Gerhard Heinzmann*, Tributes, ed. by P.-E. Bour, M. Rebuschi, L. Rollet (College Publications, London, 2010a), pp. 667–681

D. Vernant, The dialogical logic of veridicity, in *Logical Properties of Dialogues*, ed. by A. Trognon, M. Batt, J. Caelen, D. Vernant (Presses Universitaires de Nancy, 2010b)

Part IV
Conversation, Pathology, Formalization

Chapter 12
Modeling the Dynamic Effects of Discourse: Principles and Frameworks

Maxime Amblard and Sylvain Pogodalla

12.1 Introduction

In the study of the meaning of natural language expressions, the sentence level provides a natural entry point. Its relevance depends, of course, on the focus we want to put on meaning: as related to thought, to communication, to truth, etc. In this paper, we concentrate on the model theoretic view of meaning, in particular *via* first-order logic representation. This view is commonly referred to as Montague semantics because of Richard Montague's influential work, but is not limited there to.[1] It naturally brings in inference capabilities that, for instance, allows us to discuss the consequences that are true of a world a sentence describes.

In relating natural language utterances to logical representations, a key feature associated with this view is the compositionality principle. This principle basically states that the meaning of a sentence derives from the meaning of its parts and how they combine syntactically. However, some of these parts can only take on meaning with respect to previously uttered sentences. Typical examples of such parts are pronouns. But they are not the only ones.

In Sect. 12.2 we will present phenomena that illustrate the challenges posed by discourse to truth-conditional semantics and compositionality. We will show in Sect. 12.2.1 that proposals to address these challenges rely on the additional device of *contexts* and on the way sentences can access and modify these contexts. This capability is usually referred to as the *context change potential* of a sentence. Depending on the phenomenon, contexts need to represent different kinds of

[1]For an historical and epistemological perspective, see Partee and Hendriks (1997).

M. Amblard (✉) • S. Pogodalla
LORIA, UMR 7503, Université de Lorraine, CNRS, Inria, Campus Scientifique, F-54506 Vandœuvre-lès-Nancy, France
e-mail: maxime.amblard@loria.fr; sylvain.pogodalla@inria.fr

M. Rebuschi et al. (eds.), *Interdisciplinary Works in Logic, Epistemology, Psychology and Linguistics*, Logic, Argumentation & Reasoning 3,
DOI 10.1007/978-3-319-03044-9_12, © Springer International Publishing Switzerland 2014

information: propositions, discourse referents, and variations on these elements. We will also show in Sect. 12.2.2 that taking into account the rhetorical structure of discourse leads to even richer structuring of the context.

We will then devote Sect. 12.3 to the presentation of frameworks that have been designed to model these phenomena. We will also concentrate on formalisms that give an account of the dynamics of discourse in Sect. 12.3.1. We will introduce the well-established formalisms of Discourse Representation Theory (DRT) (Kamp 1981; Kamp and Reyle 1993) in Sect. 12.3.1.2, Dynamic Predicate Logic (DPL) (Groenendijk and Stokhof 1991) in Sect. 12.3.1.3, and the more recently developed approach based on continuation semantics (de Groote 2006) in Sect. 12.3.1.4. Finally, we will introduce Segmented Discourse Representation Theory (SDRT) (Asher and Lascarides 2003), which combines the effects of dynamics and discourse structure.

12.2 Dynamics and Coherence in Discourse: Principles

12.2.1 Dynamics

We have been discussing, at a rather general level, some phenomena that stress a desirable distinction between the semantic content of a single sentence and the content of that sentence when it is uttered in a larger text or discourse. While this provides a general idea of the notion of dynamics which underlies the content of a discourse, we can be more precise. The dynamic feature of a discourse representation appears in the requirement of a notion of *context* in the discourse modeling.

This notion of context is a key feature in the various approaches to discourse modeling. A context stores the elements that have been used so far and are used in sentences to assert things about the world. But sentences can, in turn, access and modify the context and make it ready for the next sentence. Actually, much more than simple texts can modify the context as it is used in a discourse. For instance, finger-pointing at an object can make it salient in a discourse and referable to just as if it had been introduced using a linguistic expression.

The following sections will be devoted to the presentation of a range of phenomena that have been considered in the literature. We defer the formalization of context and its use to Sect. 12.3.1. Using various examples, we will describe what kind of information is relevant to describing context.

12.2.1.1 Presupposition

Presupposition corresponds to the fact that when some expressions are uttered, even if no other clue appears in the preceding discourse (for instance when it is the first sentence in a discourse), the listener may infer certain information that is not explicitly stated. It is even the case that if this information was previously denied, the whole discourse becomes infelicitous. Example (12.1a) is such a sentence, and (12.1b) states the implicit information, the so-called *presupposition*. This presupposition corresponds to the hypothesis the listener will assume, even if he or she has no further evidence for it. The presupposition is said to be *accommodated* and can be used to infer (12.2). Otherwise, if it were false, as in discourse (12.3) where it is linguistically and explicitly denied, this part of the discourse would become infelicitous.

(12.1) a. John stopped smoking.

b. *(Presupposed: John used to smoke)*

(12.2) Someone used to smoke.

(12.3) a. John never smoked.

b. *John stopped smoking.

This intuitively describes a property of the context: it can be updated with non-explicitly-uttered content and it has an effect on the semantic value of the explicitly uttered content.

Expressions enabling this kind of behavior are called *presupposition triggers*. There is a wide range of them, including, for instance (taken from Beaver 1997, 2001):

- Change of state verbs (*stop*, *begin*, etc.);
- Definite description (*the man*, proper nouns, possessives, etc.);
- Factive verbs (*know*, *regret*, etc.);
- Iterative adverbs (*again*, *too*, *in return*, etc.);
- Counterfactual conditionals (*If I had known, then I would not have come*) that presuppose the falsity of the *if* clause.

One way to characterize presupposition is to rely on the robustness of its effects on embedding in complex structures. For instance, both (12.4a) and (12.5a) entail (12.6). However, while (12.4b), which negates (12.4a), still entails (12.6), this is not the case for (12.5b).

(12.4) a. John regrets that Mary left.

b. John does not regret that Mary left.

(12.5) a. Mary left.

b. Mary did not leave.

(12.6) Someone left.

This means that presupposed content embedded under negation can escape this embedding and become a presupposition for the whole sentence. To test whether a clause has presupposed content, it is thus possible to embed it under a negation and check whether this presupposed content is still available. This is called the *embedding under negation test*. More generally, such differences in behavior between asserted and presupposed content can be used to test and identify the presupposed content of an utterance. The way the presupposed content can escape the complex clause it is embedded in is called *projection*. The issue then arises of predicting the presuppositions of a complex clause from the presuppositions of its subclauses. This is the *projection problem*. As Beaver (1997) states,

> (…) the projection problem fits quite naturally into a larger Fregean picture of how language should be analyzed. The projection problem for presupposition is the task of stating and explaining the presuppositions of complex sentences in terms of the presuppositions of their parts.

This makes the projection problem fall within the scope of *compositionality*.

In addition to the embedding under negation test, other constructions, for instance the ones exemplified in (12.7), still imply (12.2) (and even (12.1b)) and may be used to study what is projected, when, and where.

(12.7) a. If John stopped smoking, then he feels healthier

b. Did John stop smoking?

c. Maybe John stopped smoking

d. Peter knows that John stopped smoking

Without discussing the details of the different formalizations of this phenomenon, we would like to stress that the actual definition of the context and meaning of a sentence are at stake here. Each phenomenon is studied with respect to the minimal structure and minimal content of the context that permits its modeling. For Karttunen (1974), the context C of a sentence is the set of sentences that are presupposed. The (local) context of each subclause is computed from the syntactic structure in which it occurs and from the context of the clause.

For instance, if we assume a context C for (12.7a), the antecedent of the condition, the subclause S *John stopped smoking*, also has C as local context. The consequent subclause *he feels healthier* has C *and* S in its local context.

For a sentence to be uttered felicitously, its context and the local context of its subclauses must all entail the presupposition they trigger. So, the context of (12.7a) should at least entail that *John used to smoke*. To see why the antecedent is added to the local context of the consequent, we can contrast (12.8a) and (12.8b), where the presupposition *John stopped smoking* is triggered in the consequent by the factive verb *regrets*. In (12.8a), because the antecedent is added to the local context of the consequent, it trivially entails the presupposition. This is true whatever the context of the whole sentence may be the *if… then* construction can filter presuppositions. They are *locally* accommodated.

On the other hand, (12.8b) cannot provide such an entailment because, whatever the context of the sentence, the addition of the antecedent to the local context of the consequent raises a contradiction. Hence it is considered infelicitous.

(12.8) a. If John stopped smoking, then he regrets he stopped smoking

b. *If John didn't stop smoking, then he regrets he stopped smoking

This gives us a first example of what the context can contain, and how it can be updated. Here, the context basically records a set of propositions possibly extended with the asserted content of subclauses. Karttunen (1974) uses such a context only to predict the felicity of a assertion. The truth conditions of each sentence do not interact with their context. But examples such as (12.3) show that the asserted content of a sentence somehow restricts the possible contexts that are available to assess the felicity of a subsequent sentence. If, at the beginning of the discourse, any model is available, as soon as (12.3a) is uttered, only models that can satisfy its asserted content will be considered. Since such a model cannot entail the presupposed content of (12.3b), this sentence becomes infelicitous.

According to Gazdar (1979), the lack of interaction between truth-conditional content, presupposed context, and the way some lexical items may have presuppositions accommodated by Karttunen (1974), prevents the latter from providing explanatory content to a presupposition. Heim (1983b) proposes another account of presupposition that more closely combines those different aspects. Interestingly enough, this approach introduces the *context change potential* of a sentence, in terms of which the truth of a sentence is defined: "the truth-condionnal aspect of the meaning of any expression is predictable on the basis of its context change potential". This compositional treatment makes it explicit how the evaluation of a complex clause in context relies on modification of the context by the subclauses.

12.2.1.2 Context Update

In order to take into account these interactions between the context against which presuppositions are evaluated and the asserted content of a sentence as proposed by Heim (1983b) and Muskens et al. (1997) introduce the following notations: $\langle S \rangle$ denotes the possibilities (represented by a set of valuations, for instance) that are compatible with the asserted content of S. Then, when two sentences combine, we have $\lceil S_1.S_2 \rceil = \lceil S_1 \rceil \cap \lceil S_2 \rceil$. It is easy to see that, for a sequence of sentences $S_1, S_2, \ldots, S_n$, $\lceil S_1.S_2.\ldots.S_n \rceil = \lceil S_1 \rceil \cap \lceil S_2 \rceil \cap \cdots \cap \lceil S_n \rceil$.

Muskens et al. (1997) also define the *context change potential* $\|S\|$ of a sentence S as a function from context to context: $\|S\| = \lambda C.C \cap \lceil S \rceil$. This operator specifies how the possibilities compatible with a sentence S combine with the context against which the presuppositions are tested.

Then, if a sentence S_1 is processed with context C, the context in which a subsequent sentence S_2 has to be processed is not the same C, but rather C restricted by $\lceil S_1 \rceil$, that is $C \cap \lceil S_1 \rceil = \|S_1\|$. This leads to a typical feature of discourse dynamics, where the effects of combining sentences in a discourse are described by function composition as shown in (12.9).

$$\begin{aligned} \|S_1.S_2\| &= \lambda C.\|S_2\|(\|S_1\|(C)) \\ &= S_2 \circ S_1 \end{aligned} \tag{12.9}$$

Following Heim (1983b), this operator allows Muskens et al. (1997) to propose a dynamic version of the logical connectives ($\bar{\wedge}$, $\bar{\neg}$, $\bar{\Rightarrow}$) and a connective / such that φ/ψ means that φ is the presupposition of ψ. These connectives are defined in (12.10). The definition of / in (12.10c) means that when a sentence ψ that triggers presupposition φ is uttered in a context C, if φ is implied by C (that is does not restrict C), then $\|\psi\|(C)$ can be evaluated. Otherwise, the result is undefined. Of course, when applied to an undefined result, $\|\psi\|$ is also undefined. Equation (12.10a) stipulates that when φ is negated, whatever satisfies φ should be removed from the context. Equation (12.10b) stipulates the same function composition as (12.9).

$$\|\bar{\neg}\varphi\| = \lambda C.C \setminus \|\varphi\|(C) \tag{12.10a}$$

$$\|\varphi \mathbin{\bar{\wedge}} \psi\| = \lambda C.\|\psi\|(\|\varphi\|(C)) \tag{12.10b}$$

$$\|\varphi/\psi\| = \lambda C.\text{if } \|\varphi\|(C) = C \text{ then } \|\psi\|(C) \text{ else undefined} \tag{12.10c}$$

In this approach, the context is modeled by a set of valuations rather than by a set of propositions. Each of the formalizations is then evaluated with respect to these valuations. This gives us another modeling of context.

While function composition here explicitly marks the dynamic nature of the connectives, Muskens et al. (1997) point out that the connectives of (12.10) are not intrinsically dynamic. They provide an equivalent interpretation where the context change potential of a clause in a context does not require evaluation of the context change potential of subclauses in any other context. This gives rise to the characterization of an operator F as static: there exists a P such that $F(C) = C \cap P$ for all contexts C.

An example of an actual dynamic operator is given with the epistemic modal *might* of Update Semantics (Veltman 1996). This operator accounts for example (12.11). Discourse (12.11a) is felicitous because, intuitively, the modal leaves open whether or not it is sunny in the set of possibilities. As a result, all possibilities are available in evaluating the second part which, in turn, reduces the set of possibilities to those where it is not sunny.

On the other hand, the first sentence in (12.11b) restricts the possibilities to those where it is not sunny. There is no possibility left where it might be sunny.

(12.11) a. It might be sunny. It is not sunny.

b. It is not sunny. *It might be sunny.

Equation (12.12) gives the interpretation of a sentence of the form $\Diamond\varphi$.

$$\| \Diamond \varphi\| = \lambda C. \text{ if } \|\varphi\|(C) \cap C \neq \emptyset \text{ then } C \text{ else } \emptyset \tag{12.12}$$

We can show that $\| \Diamond$ **sunny**$\|$ is not static. Let us assume it is static. Then there is a P such that $\| \Diamond$ **sunny**$\|(C) = C \cap P$ for any C. Let us choose C such that it is true of all its possibilities that $\neg$**sunny** holds, then $\|$**sunny**$\|(C) \cap C = \emptyset = C \cap P$. Hence in none of the possibilities of P, $\neg$**sunny** holds. This means that, in all possibilities P, **sunny** holds. So, for any C that contains both possibilities, $\| \Diamond \varphi\|(C) \subsetneq C$. This contradicts with $\| \Diamond \varphi\|(C) = C$ according to (12.12). So $\| \Diamond \varphi\|$ is not static.

12.2.1.3 Anaphora

An anaphora is a specific linguistic expression whose interpretation is a reference. For example, in (12.13a), *him* is an anaphora because it is coreferential with the subject, *Carlotta's dog*. The most common anaphoras are pronouns, which refer to their antecedents, but anaphoras can also be nominal phrases or adverbial phrases. They play a crucial role in maintaining the coherence of a discourse. The study of these phenomena is relevant to various fields, at least including linguistics, as in Binding Theory of Generative Theory; Computational Linguistics with the question of how to pick up the right referent; Cognitive Sciences as indicators of how humans process natural language.

(12.13) a. Carlotta's dog thinks that John loves him.

b. John parks his car.

c. Every man thinks of his mother.

In a simple anaphora as in (12.13b), *his* picks up its interpretation in the local context, which co-refers to John. Anaphoras can also deal with quantification, as in (12.13c). The semantics of such anaphoras consists in the semantic interpretation of the referent element or the variable bound by the quantifier. Note that when the referential element come first, it is anaphora. Otherwise, when it is after, this is called cataphora.

The use of anaphora can be more complex than in the previous examples, where the reference is intra-sentential. In a discourse, the anaphora must be resolved extra-sententially in a set of discourse referents. This increases ambiguity because many discourse referents are introduced. Morpho-syntactic features are not sufficient to distinguish the referent, but syntactic and/or rhetorical relations should help to resolve this problem.

One way to resolve an anaphora is to deal with the quantified antecedent. Examples proposed by Evans (1980) in defining e-pronouns may help us discuss the relations between anaphoras and quantified expressions.

(12.14) a. Few professors came to the party. They had a good time.

b. Every professor came to the party. * He had a good time.

The interpretation of discourse (12.14a) relies on the conjunction of the two sentences, entailing that *they* refer to a subset of professors, albeit *few* of them. But, in a more realistic interpretation, *they* should refer to all the *few* professors who attended the party. Anaphoras can refer to more than the quantified expressions which trigger references to more general sets of entities. But the reverse is not true, as shown in (12.14b), where reference to a specific entity in the set defined by the quantified expression is not acceptable. Another classic problem in resolving anaphoras is that of donkey sentences. We will precisely define this in Sect. 12.3.1.1, where we address the limits of Montague's approach.

Anaphoras can also be of another type, as in definite noun phrase anaphoras where the antecedent is referred to a definite noun phrase representing either the same concept or a semantically close one or one-anaphora, where the anaphoric expression is provided by a *one*-noun phrase.

12.2.1.4 Modal Subordination

Although maintaining a list of discourse referents in context seems adequate in the cases in the previous section, there are other cases where the context needs to be somewhat extended. Modal subordination is such a case. It has been studied in particular with respect to its interaction with anaphora resolution and accessibility. While presupposition requires the context to store a set of propositions, and anaphora a set of discourse referents, modal subordination requires both.

Classical examples of anaphoric links between pronouns and their antecedents across modalities are given in (12.15) from Sells (1985) and in (12.16) from Roberts (1989). In these two examples, the second clause contains a linguistic expression (quantifier, mood operator, adverb, etc.) that makes the sentence dependent on the previous one. Here, the anaphoric pronouns would refer to a discourse referent that is under the scope of a modal. This implies that a subpart of the discourse is potentially defined in a possible world. The use of the present tense in the last sentence induces the interpretation outside the potential described world. We see in (12.15) that indefinites introduced in the antecedent can be retrieved in the modally subordinated sentence as well. However, this fails in the other case (12.15b).

(12.15) If John bought a book$_i$, he'll be reading it$_i$ by now.

a. It$_i$'ll be a murder mystery.

b. * It$_i$ is a murder mystery.

(12.16) If Edna forgets to fill the birdfeeder, she will feel very bad.

a. They will get hungry.

In the interpretation of (12.15a), the modal force in the consequent and the modally subordinated sentence are the same. This is not the case in (12.17): (12.17a) introduces a *modal base*, i.e. a description of the possibility that is involved; then (12.17b) is evaluated relative to this modal base. The context should therefore be updated.

(12.17) a. A thief might break into the house.

b. He would take the silver.

Similarly, (12.18a) shows that discourse referents introduced in the factual world are accessible to pronouns introduced in a modal clause. The reverse is not true, as (12.18b) shows. This contrast suggests that, in addition to keeping track of the modal base, the context should distinguish between two sets of discourse referents: one for discourse referents introduced in factual clauses and available for any reference; one for discourse referents introduced in modal clauses that are only available to reference under modalities.

(12.18) a. A thief has broken into the house. He might take the silver.

b. A thief might break into the house. *He will take the silver.

Modal subordination also interacts with negation. Generally, negation blocks the accessibility of entities under its scope from parts of the discourse that are outside its scope, as (12.19a) shows. But it becomes possible to refer to them through the modal, as in (12.19b).

(12.19) John didn't buy a mystery novel.

a. *It is *War and Peace*.

b. He would be reading it by now.

In (12.19a), *It* could not refer to the novel which is under the scope of the negation and therefore does not exist. In (12.19b), *would* corresponds to the consequent of a counterfactual conditional. It could be interpreted as *If John had bought a mystery novel, then he would be reading it by now*. The second possible interpretation is simply that there is no mystery novel, as expressed in the first part of (12.20).

(12.20)
$$\neg(\exists x\ \mathbf{novel}(x) \wedge \mathbf{buy}(\mathbf{John}, x)) \wedge (\exists y\ \mathbf{novel}(y) \wedge \mathbf{buy}(\mathbf{John}, y) \Longrightarrow \mathbf{read}(\mathbf{John}, y))$$

If modal subordination is related to conjunction, it is also related to disjunction, as in example (12.21), attributed by Roberts (1989) to Barbara Partee.

(12.21) Either there is no bathroom in this house, or it is/must be in a strange place.

The standard interpretation of (12.21) fails to capture the semantics because the bathroom is introduced in the scope of the negation, and then is not accessible. The use of the modal *must* allows the sentence to be interpreted as if the two disjuncts belonged together. The negation is not copied, as it is not part of a condition applied to a referent. Consequently, the disjunction is felicitous.

Roberts (1989) also introduced generalized subordinations in discourse: see example (12.22a). Here, the interpretation of (12.22b) and (12.22c) is possible only with (12.22a) and the restriction of the interpretation of adverbs (*always* and *usually*).

(12.22) a. Harvey courts a girl$_i$ at every convention.
b. She$_i$ always comes to the banquet with him.
c. The girl$_i$ is usually very pretty.

12.2.2 Coherence and Discourse Structure

We have illustrated the phenomena discussed so far by providing a very linear structure for the discourse. Equation (12.9) stresses a single composition mode for sentences. However, it is well known by linguists as by school teachers that texts need to be structured in order to be coherent and understandable. Keeping in mind the objective of understanding the meaning of a complex discourse, we must conclude that this structure is to be taken into account.

As when building a semantic representation of a sentence out of its syntactic structure, we need to be able to find out the underlying structure of a discourse in order to give it meaning. While syntactic theorists now more or less agree on the possible syntactic structures (mainly constituency trees or dependency graphs), there is no such consensus for discourse structure. Marcu (2000) lists the questions that an adequate account of text structure should answer. They include:

- What is the abstract structure of texts? What are the constraints that characterize this structure?
- What are the elementary units of texts?
- What are the relations that could hold between two textual units?
- Is there any correlation between these relations and the concrete realization of texts?

In most theories, the abstract structure is not linear, but hierarchical. This hierarchy arises from a distinction between two kinds of discourse relations: *coordinating* relations and *subordinating* relations. These notions reflect the different roles of a discourse unit: either to expand upon the discourse, or to make it more

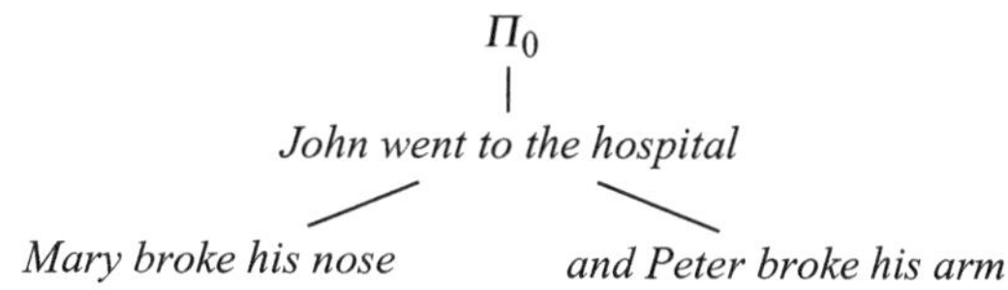

Fig. 12.1 Discourse structure for (12.23)

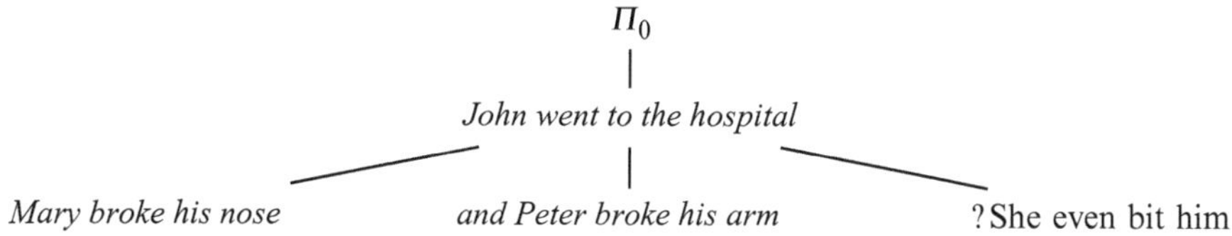

Fig. 12.2 Discourse structure for (12.23–12.25)

precise by providing examples, explanations, etc. In Rhetorical Structure Theory (RST) (Mann and Thompson 1988), *rhetorical relations* hold between two non-overlapping elementary units. One member of a given relation is called the *nucleus* and the other the *satellite*. An example would be the ***Elaboration*** relation that holds between (12.23a) and (12.23b), while a ***Narration*** relation holds between (12.23b) and (12.23c). Figure 12.1 shows the associated hierarchy structure.

(12.23) a. John went to the hospital.

b. Mary broke his nose,

c. and Peter broke his arm.

Characterizing rhetorical relations and discourse units is a difficult task. Some theories favor intention-based approaches (Grosz and Sidner 1986; Mann and Thompson 1988) taking into account communication goals, while others (Polanyi 1988; Asher and Lascarides 2003) favor semantics-based approaches using state or event description.

An important question for discourse relations is how to infer them: what they are and what they link. RST and Segmented Discourse Representation Theory (SDRT) (Asher and Lascarides 2003) provide different solutions. An adequate instantiation of the context should contain the relevant data to help pick the right relation. In giving a precise description of how to build a Segmented DRS (SDRS), Asher and Lascarides (2003) also suggest the elements that should be put into context.

An important element is probably the structure built so far, or at least the *accessible* attachment points. It has been observed, for instance, that a new discourse relation cannot attach just anywhere in the hierarchy, but rather only on the *right frontier* (if the structure is a tree, this corresponds to the nodes on the path from the root to the rightmost leaf). For instance, if (12.23) is followed by one of (12.24), which elaborate on John's injuries, (12.24) can only attach either to (12.23a) (as whith (12.24b) for instance) or to (12.23c) (as for (12.24a)). It cannot attach to (12.23b). In any case, the *it* of (12.24a) cannot refer to John's nose.

(12.24) a. It was even bleeding.

b. He was bleeding.

This *right frontier constraint* seems to be quite strong in attachment points for discourse relations. It also seems to apply to a certain extent to anaphoras. This would explain why extending (12.23) with (12.25) to get the structure of Fig. 12.2 seems wrong (Busquets et al. 2001). Different anaphoras however behave differently with respect to this constraint. For instance, pronouns seem to follow it rather strictly, while definite descriptions do not (Asher 2008). This suggests a model of saliency that is related to discourse structure. Cristea et al. (2000) also shows how anaphora resolution is improved by taking into account the hierarchical structure of texts.

(12.25) She even bit him.

Other inputs for inferring discourse relations of course include lexicalization. Words such as *then*, *because*, etc. strongly suggest what relation is involved. But relations are not necessarily lexicalized as in (12.26). Much has to be considered in order to infer the correct (***Consequence***) relation, including the preceding topic, temporal relations between events, inferences based on background knowledge, etc.

(12.26) John fell. Mary pushed him.

This shows that the context can contain a lot of heterogeneous information. Models and theories of context should be able to provide a way to capture this diversity.

12.3 Frameworks

In this section, we will introduce the formal devices that have been designed to model the phenomena described in the previous sections. With regards to expressing discourse dynamics, we limit ourselves to three frameworks: Discourse Representation Theory (Sect. 12.3.1.2), Dynamic Predicate Logic (Sect. 12.3.1.3), and continuation semantics for discourse (Sect. 12.3.1.4). We will then introduce Segmented Discourse Representation Theory, which adds an account of discourse structures to the dynamic semantics (Sect. 12.3.2).

This first section is devoted to illustrating the limits of standard (static) Montague's semantics in discourse phenomena.

12.3.1 Dynamic Effects

This section aims to describe formal accounts of the phenomena characterized in Sect. 12.2.1. We will rely on well-established formalisms and on associated models linking natural language expressions and their representations. As emphasized above, much effort is dedicated to populating the context and describing how expressions contribute to it compositionally.

Let us first recall some of the shortcomings of Montague's sentence semantics (Montague 1970a,b) as regards intrasentential and intersentential anaphora.

12.3.1.1 Limits of Montague Semantics

The most frequent examples of problems with anaphoric links are so-called *donkey sentences*, as illustrated, familiarly, by Geach (1962). Let us first look at (12.27), presented with its expected semantic representation.

(12.27) If John owns a donkey, he is rich.

$$(\exists x.\mathbf{donkey}(x) \wedge \mathbf{owns}(\mathbf{John}, x)) \implies \mathbf{rich}(\mathbf{John})$$

(12.28) If John owns a donkey, he beats it.

According to the compositionality principle, the expected meaning of (12.28), because its syntactic structure is similar to that of (12.27), is:

$$(\exists x.\mathbf{donkey}(x) \wedge \mathbf{owns}(\mathbf{John}, x)) \implies \mathbf{beats}(\mathbf{John}, x)$$

In the second formula, however the second occurrence of x is *free*. It is *outside* the scope of the existential quantifier. Moreover, instead of an existential quantification, typically introduced by the indefinite article, we expect to have a *universal* quantification that claims something about all the donkeys John owns:

$$(\forall x.(\mathbf{donkey}(x) \wedge \mathbf{owns}(\mathbf{John}, x)) \implies \mathbf{beats}(\mathbf{John}, x))$$

Such examples outline issues both with the composition of the meaning of the clauses (the variable is not bound) and with the lexical semantics (since the indefinite seems to be associated on the one hand with an existential quantifier and on the other hand with a universal quantifier).

Another kind of problem related to pronoun interpretation is exemplified in (12.29) and (12.30). The discourse in (12.29) is felicitous since an antecedent is available to interpret the pronoun in (12.29b). On the other hand, (12.30b) is infelicitous when uttered in the context of (12.30a). The question here is how the negation compositionally affects the contribution of the indefinite such that there is no further possible reference to the variable it introduces. Such observations have given rise to accessibility constraints on discourse antecedents.

(12.29) a. John owns a donkey.

b. It is grey.

(12.30) a. John doesn't own a donkey.

b. *It is grey.

To deal with these phenomena, contexts must now keep track of *discourse referents*. Basically, indefinite noun phrases such as *a donkey* are considered as putting a new item into the context. If correctly recorded, this item can later be accessed by pronouns. The following sections describe different approaches to implementing this intuition. We will then introduce the interpretation given in Muskens (1991) and Muskens et al. (1997) as an execution of programs that change machine states. The control on this execution can be described with continuations, as in functional programming. This view was first expressed by de Groote (2006).

12.3.1.2 Discourse Representation Semantics

Discourse Representation Theory (DRT) is a formalism introduced and developed by Kamp (1981) and Kamp and Reyle (1993). As exemplified above, the key idea is to provide a context where discourse referents can be stored and accessed. A sentence is interpreted in this context and, in turn, can also *update* it by adding new discourse referents. This formalism shares many features with the independent formalism of File Semantics proposed by Heim (1982, 1983a). It is worth noting that, according to Kamp (2005), though DRT has been proposed to overcome the limits of semantic modeling when moving from single sentences to longer texts, the first phenomena under consideration were related to time and ways of expressing the difference between the French imperfect and preterit. Only afterwards was it found to be useful for dealing with donkey sentences.

(12.31) a. A man entered.

b. He smiled.

(12.32) $\exists x.\mathbf{man}(x) \wedge \mathbf{entered}(x) \wedge \mathbf{smiled}(x)$

Formula (12.32) shows the expected semantics for this discourse (12.31). This results from a representation of (12.31a) in an empty context. Because of the existential, (12.31a) contains, it updates the context with a new discourse referent x. In addition, the formula keeps track of the properties this discourse referent satisfies: **man**(x) and **entered**(x). In DRT, this representation is called a *Discourse Representation Structure (DRS)*. It consists of an *universe* that contains the discourse referents and a list of *conditions*. It is often represented with boxes, as in (12.33).

$$\begin{array}{|l|}\hline x \\ \hline \mathbf{man}(x) \\ \mathbf{entered}(x) \\ \hline \end{array} \tag{12.33}$$

The contribution of (12.31b) in (12.34) looks quite similar. An additional condition, called *link*, states that the new entity should refer to some (yet to be determined) other discourse referent.

$$\begin{array}{|l|}\hline y \\ \hline \mathbf{smiled}(y) \\ y = ? \\ \hline \end{array} \tag{12.34}$$

The two DRSs then merge into a new one. The way two DRSs merge depends much on the syntactic rule that combines the two expressions they correspond to. In the case of adding a new sentence to a discourse, the operation is quite simple and consists in joining the universes and conditions. The '?' in the link is instantiated with a discourse referent that is *accessible* from the position that the pronoun occupies. We will say more about accessibility later. For the moment, it is enough to state that the discourse referents in the universe of a DRS are all accessible to the conditions the DRS contains. This finally gives us the DRS of (12.35).

$$\begin{array}{|l|}\hline x\ y \\ \hline \mathbf{man}(x) \\ \mathbf{entered}(x) \\ \mathbf{smiled}(y) \\ y = x \\ \hline \end{array} \tag{12.35}$$

Remark 12.3.1. Note that the combination of the two DRSs is safe as long as their universes do not intersect. Because the variables are technically not bound, without

α-conversion,[2] defining the merge operation becomes quite complex. The semantics of DRSs and of the merge operation need to be carefully adapted in order to avoid the so-called *destructive assignment problem.* van Eijck and Kamp (1997) provide a detailed discussion of this topic. □

Remark 12.3.2. Linking a pronoun to its antecedent is allowed only when the latter belongs to the accessible discourse referents of the former. We will make this notion explicit later on, but it is important to note that *it does not resolve the anaphora.* In a sentence like (12.36), the two discourse referents introduced by the first sentence for *John* and *Mary* are both equally accessible to the two pronouns in the second sentence. A resolution algorithm must choose which of all the accessible discourse referents is the most suitable. Such an algorithm typically relies on morphosyntactic information (gender, case, etc. depending on the language), or on background knowledge, as in (12.37). Since there is no distinction in French between pronouns referring to human and non-human entities, both *Jean* and *l'âne* are accessible to *il* and *le*.

(12.36) John met Mary. He smiled at her.

(12.37)	Jean	possède	un	âne.	Il	le	bat.
	John	owns	a	donkey.	PRO-nom	PRO-acc	beats.

John owns a donkey. He/It beats it/him.

□

Definition 12.3.3 (DRSs in van Eijck and Kamp (1997)). Let V be a set of variables, C a set of constants and P a set of predicates. The *terms* T, the *conditions* K, and the *DRSs* D are defined by:

Terms $T ::= V | C$

Conditions $K ::= \top | P(T, T, \ldots, T) | V = T | V \neq T | \neg D$

DRSs $D ::= \begin{array}{|l|}\hline V\ V\ \ldots\ V \\ \hline K \\ K \\ \vdots \\ K \\ \hline \end{array}$

[2]The operation that allows bound variable renaming in λ-terms and logical formulas.

To save space, we sometime write a DRS D with universe $\{x_1, \ldots, x_n\}$ and conditions $\{K_1, \ldots, K_m\}$) as $D = (\{x_1, \ldots, x_n\}, \{K_1, \ldots, K_m\})$. For two DRSs $D_1 = (\{x_1, \ldots, x_n\}, \{K_1, \ldots, K_m\})$ and D_2, we also define

$$D_1 \implies D_2 \triangleq \neg(\{x_1, \ldots, x_n\}, \{K_1, \ldots, K_m \neg D_2\})$$

□

The condition $V \neq T$ corresponds to the modeling of sentences like (12.38a) to get (12.38b) (from van Eijck and Kamp 1997).

(12.38) a. A man walked in. Another man followed him.

b.
$$\begin{array}{|l|}\hline x \\ \hline \textbf{man}(x) \\ \textbf{walked\_in}(x) \\ \hline \end{array} \cdot \begin{array}{|l|}\hline y\ z \\ \hline \textbf{man}(y) \\ y \neq ? \\ z = ? \\ \textbf{followed}(y, z) \\ \hline \end{array} = \begin{array}{|l|}\hline x\ y\ z \\ \hline \textbf{man}(x) \\ \textbf{walked\_in}(x) \\ \textbf{man}(y) \\ y \neq x \\ z = x \\ \textbf{followed}(y, z) \\ \hline \end{array}$$

Definition 12.3.4 (Subordination and Accessibility). Let K_1 and K_2 be DRSs. K_1 *subordinates* K_2 if:

- $\neg K_2$ is a condition of K_1
- Or there exists K_3 such that K_1 subordinates K_3 and K_3 subordinates K_2.

The discourse referents of K_1 are *accessible* from K_2 if:

- $K_1 = K_2$
- Or K_1 subordinates K_2

□

This definition of accessibility explains the contrast between (12.29b) and (12.30b). The former builds the DRS of (12.39), while the latter builds the DRS of (12.40). In (12.39), all the discourse referents in the universe are accessible for linking; therefore the pronoun can find an antecedent. But in (12.40), K_1 does not subordinate K_0 (while K_0 subordinates K_1); hence the discourse referents of K_1 cannot be accessed from K_0. The pronoun *it* therefore cannot find an antecedent.[3]

[3] We do not discuss here the status of discourse referents for proper nouns. They usually are considered as belonging to the universe of the topmost DRS and are therefore always accessible.

(12.39)
$$\begin{array}{|l|}\hline \mathbf{j}\ y\ t \\ \hline \mathbf{owns}(\mathbf{j},x) \\ \mathbf{donkey}(x) \\ t=? \\ \mathbf{grey}(t) \\ \hline \end{array}$$

(12.40)
$$K_0 : \begin{array}{|l|}\hline \mathbf{j}\ t \\ \hline \neg K_1 : \begin{array}{|l|}\hline x \\ \hline \mathbf{owns}(\mathbf{j},x) \\ \mathbf{donkey}(x) \\ \hline \end{array} \\ t=? \\ \mathbf{grey}(t) \\ \hline \end{array}$$

The last example we will deal with in this section is (12.28), repeated below. For the syntactic structure *if* s_1, s_2 we associate the DRS $(p, K_1 \implies K_2)$, where K_i is the DRS associated with s_i, $i \in \{1,2\}$, and from which p, the set of discourse referents introduced by proper names, has been removed. So the DRS associated with (12.28) is described in (12.42a). Because K_2 is subordinated both by K_1 and K_0, both the discourse referents $\mathbf{j}$ in the universe of K_0 and x in the universe of K_1 are accessible to K_2. Thus, the links can be instantiated so as to result in the DRS of (12.42b). This also shows that any continuation of the discourse will be subordinated neither by K_1 nor by K_2, wherefore none of the discourse referents they introduce will remain accessible (except for the proper names, as already mentioned). This explains why (12.41) is infelicitous.

(12.28) If John owns a donkey, he beats it.

(12.41) a. If John owns a donkey, he beats it.

b. *It suffers.

(12.42) a.

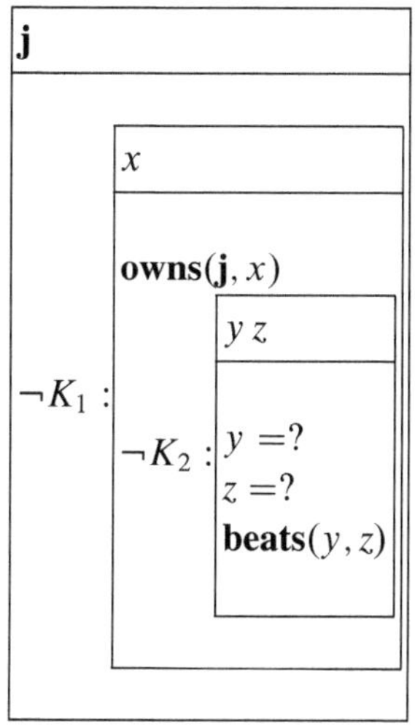

=

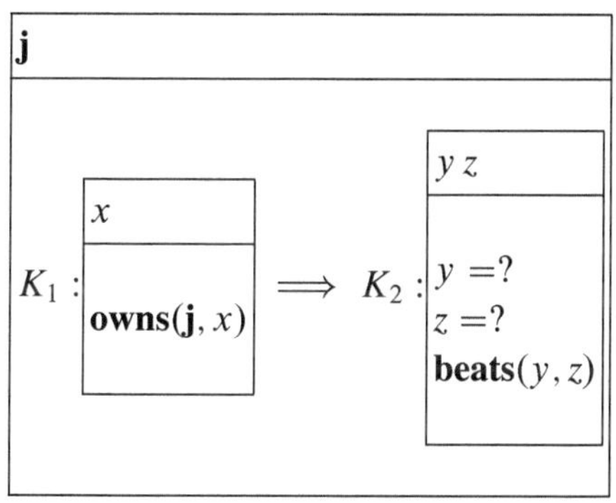

b.

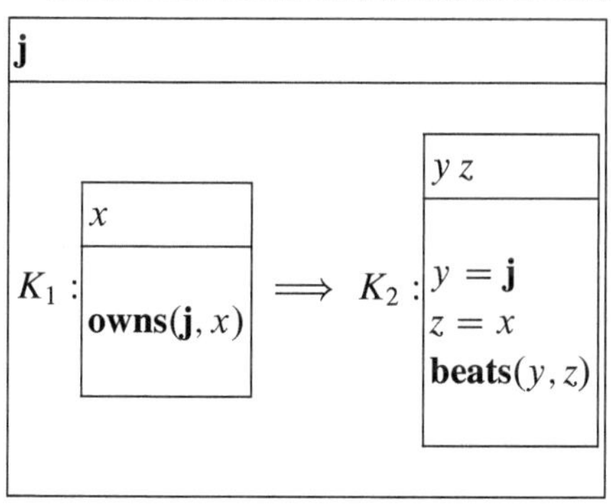

So far we have only described what can be considered as the *formulas* of DRT. We also need to explain how they are interpreted. In particular, DRSs can be provided a truth definition. Such a definition may place more or less emphasis on its *relational* nature. In all cases, it relies on *assignments*.

Definition 12.3.5 (Models and assignments). A *first order model* $\mathcal{M} = \langle M, I \rangle$ has a non-empty domain M and an interpretation function that maps n-ary predicate names (the relation symbols used in DRS conditions) to n-ary relations on M.[4]

An *assignment* s for $\mathcal{M} = \langle M, I \rangle$ is a mapping from a set of variables to elements of M. G is the set of all assignment functions.

Let h and g be assignments and x a variable. Let us say that $h[x]g$ if and only if for all $y \neq x$, $h(y) = g(y)$ (h and g differ at most in the value they assign to x). □

An assignment basically describes a *state* when stipulating what actual values should be used in performing a computation. For instance, computing y = x + 1 does not yield the same result for y when the current state is such that x is assigned 1 (usually noted in programming language x := 1) as if x is assigned 2 (x := 2).

Although several interpretation of DRSs have been given (see van Eijck and Kamp (1997) for instance), they are equivalent in some sense. In particular, as Groenendijk and Stokhof (1991) show, DRSs can be translated into Dynamic Predicate Logic (DPL) formulas such that DRS interpretations can be derived directly from the semantics of DPL formulas.[5] We will present DPL and its semantics in the next section.

Much work based on DRT has been proposed to account for various phenomena. In addition to the aforementioned references, a good introduction in French is given by Corblin (2002). For an account of presupposition within this framework, the reader can refer to van der Sandt (1992) and Geurts (1999). For modal subordination, we can mention (Roberts 1989; Frank and Kamp 1997; Frank 1997; Geurts 1999).

12.3.1.3 Dynamic Predicate Logic

Given the semantics of (12.28), repeated below, and its possible interpretations:

- Strictly following the compositionality principle in (12.43a)
- Actually expected, respecting first order logic syntax and semantics in (12.43b),

it is argued by Groenendijk and Stokhof (1991) that DRSs actually mimic what is observed in (12.43b), in particular with respect to the different parts from which this formula is built and to the scope of the quantifier. This has been considered a weakness regarding adherence to the compositionality principle.[6] The alternative that is provided is *to propose another semantics* so that the formula (12.43a) can represent the meaning of (12.28) and come out with the same truth conditions as expressed in FOL formulas (12.43b).

---

[4]0-ary relations are constants.

[5]For an epistemological view of the evolution of DRS interpretation, see Kamp (2005).

[6]Subsequent work addressed this criticism and showed that DRT could be expressed compositionally, for instance in Muskens (1996) and Amsili and Bras (1998).

(12.28) If John owns a donkey, he beats it.

(12.43) a. $(\exists x.\mathbf{donkey}(x) \wedge \mathbf{owns}(\mathbf{John}, x)) \implies \mathbf{beats}(\mathbf{John}, x)$

b. $(\forall x.(\mathbf{donkey}(x) \wedge \mathbf{owns}(\mathbf{John}, x)) \implies \mathbf{beats}(\mathbf{John}, x))$

Groenendijk and Stokhof (1991) stress that the approach it provided here is inspired by programming languages:

> In this paper we give an alternative account of the phenomena (...) by replacing the standard semantics of the language of first-order predicate logic by a dynamic semantics, which is inspired by systems of dynamic logic as they are used in the denotational semantics of programming languages.

We will elaborate on this comparison at the end of this section. But it is worth noting that the interpretation of a program can be regarded as a relation between an assignment (the input state) and another assignment (the output state) that assign possibly different values to a variable in the input and the output.

Definition

The intuition behind this relational semantics is as follows: starting with an arbitrary assignment g that assigns variables to constants in the model, the meaning of a sentence S specifies the conditions on h, another assignment, such that h can be viewed as one of the possible outputs of $[\![S]\!](g)$. Typically, a sentence that introduces a condition $P(x)$ in DRT will require that $h = g$ and that the interpretation of P holds for the constant that g interprets x as (item 1 of Definition 12.3.6). If the sentence also introduces the discourse referent x, it is interpreted as: whatever the input assignment g was, the new assignment may differ from g only on the value it assigns to x (item 7 of Definition 12.3.6), in particular because this value must now satisfy certain conditions introduced by the sentence or by the remainder of the discourse.

Definition 12.3.6 (DPL syntax and semantics). The syntax of DPL is standard first order logic syntax with equality. In order to differentiate between "dynamic" logical connectives and "static" ones, we use the following notation:

- $\equiv$ for dynamic equality
- $\overline{\wedge}$ for dynamic conjunction
- $\underline{\vee}$ for dynamic disjunction
- $\Rrightarrow$ for dynamic implication
- $\overline{\exists}$ for dynamic existential quantification
- $\overline{\forall}$ for dynamic universal quantification

Table 12.1 Example model $\mathcal{M}$

	John	**Bill**	**Mary**
man	$\top$	$\top$	
entered	$\top$	$\top$	$\top$
smiled	$\top$		$\top$

Let $\mathcal{M} = \langle M, I \rangle$ be a model and g be an assignment. We define $[\![t]\!]_g^{\mathcal{M}} = g(t)$ if t is a variable and $[\![t]\!]_g^{\mathcal{M}} = I(t)$ if t is a constant.

The interpretation function $[\![\cdot]\!]^{\mathcal{M}} \subset G \times G$ (namely $[\![\cdot]\!]^{\mathcal{M}}$ is a relation between assignment functions) is then defined as:

1. $[\![Rt_1 \ldots t_n]\!]^{\mathcal{M}} = \{\langle g, h\rangle | h = g \wedge I(R)\langle [\![t_1]\!]_h, \ldots, [\![t_n]\!]_h^{\mathcal{M}}\rangle\}$
2. $[\![t_1 \equiv t_2]\!]^{\mathcal{M}} = \{\langle g, h\rangle | h = g \wedge [\![t_1]\!]^{\mathcal{M}} = [\![t_2]\!]^{\mathcal{M}}\}$
3. $[\![\bar{\neg}\varphi]\!]^{\mathcal{M}} = \{\langle g, h\rangle | h = g \wedge \neg\exists k.\langle h, k\rangle \in [\![\varphi]\!]^{\mathcal{M}}\}$
4. $[\![\varphi \bar{\wedge} \psi]\!]^{\mathcal{M}} = \{\langle g, h\rangle | \exists k.\langle g, k\rangle \in [\![\varphi]\!]^{\mathcal{M}} \wedge \langle k, h\rangle \in [\![\psi]\!]^{\mathcal{M}}\}$
5. $[\![\varphi \bar{\Rightarrow} \psi]\!]^{\mathcal{M}} = \{\langle g, h\rangle | h = g \wedge \forall k.\langle h, k\rangle \in [\![\varphi]\!]^{\mathcal{M}} \implies \exists j.\langle k, j\rangle \in [\![\psi]\!]^{\mathcal{M}}\}$
6. $[\![\varphi \bar{\vee} \psi]\!]^{\mathcal{M}} = \{\langle g, h\rangle | h = g \wedge \exists k.\langle h, k\rangle \in [\![\varphi]\!]^{\mathcal{M}} \vee \langle h, k\rangle \in [\![\psi]\!]^{\mathcal{M}}\}$
7. $[\![\bar{\exists} x.\varphi]\!]^{\mathcal{M}} = \{\langle g, h\rangle | \exists k.k[x]g \wedge \langle k, h\rangle \in [\![\varphi]\!]^{\mathcal{M}}\}$
8. $[\![\bar{\forall} x.\varphi]\!]^{\mathcal{M}} = \{\langle g, h\rangle | h = g \wedge \forall k.k[x]h \implies \exists j.\langle k, j\rangle \in [\![\varphi]\!]^{\mathcal{M}}\}$

Examples

We can now check the effect of this semantics on the previous examples. Let us start with example (12.31), repeated below, together with the first order logic formula representing its meaning in a strictly compositional way, as in (12.44).

(12.31) A man entered. He smiled.

(12.44) $(\bar{\exists} x.\mathbf{man}(x) \bar{\wedge} \mathbf{entered}(x)) \bar{\wedge} \mathbf{smiled}(x)$

Let us assume a very simple model with three entities and their properties, as described in Table 12.1. By definition,

$$\begin{aligned}
[\![\mathbf{man}(x)]\!]^{\mathcal{M}} &= \{\langle g, h\rangle | g = h \wedge \mathbf{man}(g(x))\} \\
&= \{\langle g, g\rangle | \mathbf{man}(g(x))\} \\
[\![\mathbf{entered}(x)]\!]^{\mathcal{M}} &= \{\langle h, k\rangle | h = k \wedge \mathbf{entered}(h(x))\} \\
&= \{\langle h, h\rangle | \mathbf{entered}(h(x))\}
\end{aligned}$$

So,[7]

$$[\![\mathbf{man}(x) \mathbin{\bar{\wedge}} \mathbf{entered}(x)]\!]$$

$$\begin{aligned}
&= \{\langle g,h\rangle | \exists k.\langle g,k\rangle \in [\![\mathbf{man}(x)]\!] \wedge \langle k,h\rangle \in [\![\mathbf{entered}(x)]\!]\} \\
&= \{\langle g,h\rangle | \exists k.k = g \wedge \mathbf{man}(g(x)) \wedge h = k \wedge \mathbf{entered}(k(x))\} \\
&= \{\langle g,h\rangle | h = g \wedge \mathbf{man}(g(x)) \wedge \mathbf{entered}(g(x))\} \\
&= \{\langle g,g\rangle | \mathbf{man}(g(x)) \wedge \mathbf{entered}(g(x))\}
\end{aligned}$$

And

$$[\![\bar{\exists} x.\mathbf{man}(x) \mathbin{\bar{\wedge}} \mathbf{entered}(x)]\!]$$

$$\begin{aligned}
&= \{\langle g,h\rangle | \exists k.k[x]g \wedge \langle k,h\rangle \in [\![\mathbf{man}(x) \wedge \mathbf{entered}(x)]\!]\} \\
&= \{\langle g,h\rangle | \exists k.k[x]g \wedge k = h \wedge \mathbf{man}(k(x)) \wedge \mathbf{entered}(k(x))\} \\
&= \{\langle g,h\rangle | h[x]g \wedge \mathbf{man}(h(x)) \wedge \mathbf{entered}(h(x))\}
\end{aligned}$$

So, $\langle g,h\rangle \in [\![\bar{\exists} x.\mathbf{man}(x) \mathbin{\bar{\wedge}} \mathbf{entered}(x)]\!]$ requires:

- g and h can only differ in the value they assign to x;
- $\mathbf{man}(h(x))$ and $\mathbf{entered}(h(x))$ must hold.

There is no other requirement on g. With respect to the toy model in Table 12.1, all assignments h must then assign x either to **John** or to **Bill**. This is the condition on the possible output state after processing the first sentence in (12.31).

The second sentence provides for the following interpretation:

$$[\![\mathbf{smiled}(x)]\!] = \{\langle g,h\rangle | h = g \wedge \mathbf{smiled}(h(x))\}$$

For $\langle g,h\rangle \in [\![\mathbf{smiled}(x)]\!]$ in the model described by Table 12.1, this then requires that $g = h$ and either $g(x) = \mathbf{John}$ or $g(x) = \mathbf{Mary}$.

Remark 12.3.7. Since we are considering assignment functions, it make sense to talk about $h(X)$. But the only requirement so far is that **smiled** is true of x. The important thing is that the representation is ready to combine with sentences that put additional conditions on x. □

Putting the two sentences together with the conjunction yields:

$$\begin{aligned}
&[\![(\bar{\exists} x.\mathbf{man}(x) \mathbin{\bar{\wedge}} \mathbf{entered}(x)) \mathbin{\bar{\wedge}} \mathbf{smiled}(x)]\!] \\
&= \{\langle g,h\rangle | \exists k.\langle g,k\rangle \in [\![\exists x.\mathbf{man}(x) \wedge \mathbf{entered}(x)]\!] \wedge \langle k,h\rangle \in [\![\mathbf{smiled}(x)]\!]\} \\
&= \{\langle g,h\rangle | \exists k.k[x]g \wedge \mathbf{man}(k(x)) \wedge \mathbf{entered}(k(x)) \wedge h = k \wedge \mathbf{smiled}(h(x))\} \\
&= \{\langle g,h\rangle | h[x]g \wedge \mathbf{man}(h(x)) \wedge \mathbf{entered}(h(x)) \wedge \mathbf{smiled}(h(x))\}
\end{aligned} \tag{12.45}$$

[7]From now on, we omit the $\mathcal{M}$ superscript since the model is implicitly known. We thus note $[\![\cdot]\!]$ instead of $[\![\cdot]\!]^{\mathcal{M}}$.

This means that whatever the input state, the output state can only differ in the value it assigns to x, but the output state must make true of x the conditions **man**, **entered** and **smiled**. Specifically, the assignment h such that $h(x) =$ **Mary** and which is a possible input and output state for *He smiles* is ruled out in the conjunction (which is a composition of relations) because it cannot be an output state of *A man entered.*

Comments

The following so-called donkey equivalences (Dekker 2011) hold:

$$(\bar{\exists} x.\varphi) \mathbin{\bar{\wedge}} \psi \cong (\bar{\exists} x.\varphi \wedge \psi) \tag{12.46}$$

$$(\bar{\exists} x.\varphi) \Rrightarrow \psi \cong (\bar{\forall} x.\varphi \Rrightarrow \psi) \tag{12.47}$$

We used (12.46) above to show that *he smiled* gets the correct interpretation, with the existential "dynamically extending its scope" over the **smiled** predicate.

Similarly, (12.47) explains why sentence (12.28), repeated below, correctly gets a universal quantification over the individuals that are donkeys.

(12.28) If John owns a donkey, he beats it.

Dynamic logic has been used to account for anaphora (Groenendijk and Stokhof 1991), presupposition (Beaver 1997, 2001), update semantics (Veltman 1996), modal subordination (Stone and Hardt 1997; van Rooij 2005; Ogata 2006; Asher and McCready 2007), etc.

The scope theorem stated in (12.46) makes the logic at hard quite different from the usual first order logic. Moreover, it also suffers from the destructive assignment problem. This problem can be viewed as equivalent to that seer in imperative programming languages. Basically, it involves the fact that an assignment x := 2 in a program hides previous assignments (for instance x:= 1). Suggestions using states to remedy this, such as Dekker's Predicate Logic with Anaphora (PLA) (Dekker 1994), have been made.

Groenendijk and Stokhof (1991) have already mentioned the parallel between computer programs and the way such programs modify machine states to design DPL. This parallelism has been further explored, as in Muskens (1991) and Muskens et al. (1997) or van Eijck and Visser (2010).

The following sections present another approach to dynamics that was also inspired by computer science. Interestingly, it moves us into the paradigm of functional programming languages and the way control is modeled in this setting by means of so-called *continuation*. This provides a way to escape the drawbacks inherited from imperative programming.

```
Function  f(x) ;
begin
return (x+1)
end ;
```

```
Function  f(x) ;
begin
z : =3 ;
return (x+1)
end ;
```

Fig. 12.3 A function with no side effect   A function with side effects

12.3.1.4 Continuation Semantics

In mathematics, a function accepts parameters and returns a value. In imperative programming, using states allows for the implementation of *side effects*. These are effects or changes of states that are not rendered in the return value of a function. For instance, an assignment such as x:=2 can occur in any function, no matter the actual output, and change the states. It is thus possible to add a statement changing the assignment in any function. Assume, for instance, a function that adds 1 to its input. Translating the standard mathematical definition into a programming language would produce the definition on the left in Fig. 12.3. But nothing prevents mixing the intended meaning of this function with some other "hidden" change. In the program on the right in Fig. 12.3, the function f has the side effect of assigning 3 to z.

Functional programming involves function evaluation, just as in mathematics. It is a programming paradigm that avoids states and side effects. It also makes functions first-class citizens, i.e. functions are considered just like any other values and can be parameters as well. A very important notion that comes with this paradigm is that of type systems and type theory. Functional programming as elaboration on λ-calculus and type theory has existed in formal semantics at least since (Montague 1970a,b).[8] In extensional Montague semantics, we usually consider the set of atomic types to be $\{e, t\}$, respectively denoting entities and truth values. In intensional Montague semantics, we usually consider the set of atomic types to be $\{e, t, s\}$, following Gallin (1975), where s denotes possible worlds. In the continuation semantics approach, we use additional atomic types. But let us first illustrate what a continuation is. We assume the type $\mathbb{N}$ of integers. We are considering functions of type $\mathbb{N} \rightarrow \mathbb{N}$. $f = \lambda x.x + 1$ is such a function: it takes an integer as parameter and returns an integer.

It is not possible to describe all the computations in which the result of f will be used. However, we can abstract over them because we know they will take an integer (the result of some $f(x)$) as parameter. And, if we consider only computations that in turn produce integers, the type of these abstractions over computations is then $(\mathbb{N} \rightarrow \mathbb{N})$. We can thus systematically change f into $\overline{f}$ of type $\mathbb{N} \rightarrow (\mathbb{N} \rightarrow \mathbb{N}) \rightarrow \mathbb{N}$ with an additional parameter of type $(\mathbb{N} \rightarrow \mathbb{N})$. This parameter is the *continuation* of the computation in which the result $f(x)$ is involved.

---

[8] We are talking about the standard notions of simply-typed λ-calculus with β-conversion. For an introduction to these concepts, see Carpenter (1997).

Let us now assume that we have two functions, f and g, of type $\mathbb{N} \to \mathbb{N}$. Composing them with the function composition $g \circ f = \lambda x.g(f(x))$ is a standard operation. Can we relate that to some operation on $\overline{f}$ and $\overline{g}$? First, according to the definition of $\overline{\cdot}$, $\overline{g \circ f} = \lambda x\, k.k(g(f\, x))$. Then, if we consider $g \circ f$ applied to x in some continuation k, we can also say that g and k are in the continuation of f.[9] So $\overline{f}$ is applied to x and to some continuation k'. k' is such that when applied to some value x', the result of $g\, x'$ is given to the continuation k. This means that what is evaluated is $\overline{g}\, x'\, k$.

We now have:

$$\begin{aligned}
\overline{g} \,\overline{\circ}\, \overline{f} &= \lambda x\, k.\overline{f}\, x\, (\lambda x'.\overline{g}\, x'\, k) \\
&= \lambda x\, k.\overline{f}\, x\, (\lambda x'.(\lambda x''\, k''.k''(g\, x''))\, x'\, k) \\
&\to_\beta \lambda x\, k.\overline{f}\, x\, (\lambda x'.(k(g\, x'))) \\
&= \lambda x\, k.(\lambda x''\, k'.k'(f\, x''))\, x\, (\lambda x'.(k(g\, x'))) \\
&\to_\beta \lambda x\, k.(\lambda x'.(k(g\, x')))(f\, x) \\
&\to_\beta \lambda x\, k.k(g(f\, x)) \\
&= \overline{g \circ f}
\end{aligned}$$

Continuation semantics for discourse, introduced by de Groote (2006), uses a similar approach, except that we have the usual semantic types e and t, while on the other hand the sentences (the f functions) will have as parameters an additional type γ for the *environment*. In a static approach, the type associated with sentences would take an environment and return a truth value (type $\gamma \to t$). Since we want to have the dynamic counterpart with continuations, they will be interpreted with type $\gamma \to (\gamma \to t) \to t$. de Groote (2006) calls the first parameter of type γ of a sentence the *left context*. This corresponds to the context made from the sentences preceding the current sentence. The second parameter, the continuation of type $(\gamma \to t)$, is called the *right context*, that is the context made from the sentences following the current one: the remaining discourse. Let us have a look at an example with discourse (12.31), repeated below. Sentences are enriched with their continuation semantics.

(12.31) a. A man entered.

$\lambda e\, k.\exists x.(\mathbf{man}(x)) \wedge (\mathbf{entered}(x)) \wedge (k(x :: e))$

b. He smiled.

$\lambda e\, k.(\mathbf{smiled}(\mathtt{sel}\ e)) \wedge (k\, e)$

[9] The *application* of functions to parameters is left associative. We use the following notations: $f(x) = f\, x$ and $(\ldots((f\, x_1)\, x_2)\ldots x_n) = f\, x_1\, x_2 \ldots x_n$ when f takes n parameters and is of type $\alpha_1 \to \alpha_2 \to \ldots \to \alpha_n \to \alpha$ and every x_i is of type α_i.

These semantic recipes make use of two additional operators:

- The :: (update) operator, of type $e \to \gamma \to \gamma$ that inserts entities into the context;
- The `sel` operator, of type $\gamma \to e$, which selects and retrieves an entity from a context.

Just as in DRT, the `sel` operator is meant to implement an anaphora resolution algorithm. It should thus be fed with additional data such as morphosyntactic information. But we need not go into further details here.

Remark 12.3.8. In the semantics of (12.31a), it should be noted that the variable x over which it is quantified is added to the context which is given to the continuation. Similarly, this continuation *is in the scope* of the existential quantifier.

This is how indefinites extend their scope to the remaining part of the discourse.□

We can also provide a way to combine sentences using $\bar{\circ}$, the dynamic version of (12.9) from Sect. 12.2.1.2:

$$\begin{aligned}[\![S_1.S_2]\!] &= [\![S_2]\!]\bar{\circ}[\![S_1]\!] \\ &= \lambda e\, k.[\![S_1]\!]\, e\, (\lambda e'.[\![S_2]\!]\, e'\, k)\end{aligned} \tag{12.48}$$

So, the semantics of (12.31) is:

$$\begin{aligned}[\![(12.31a).(12.31b)]\!] &= \lambda e\, k.[\![(12.31a)]\!]\, e\, (\lambda e'.[\![(12.31b)]\!]) \\ &= \lambda e\, k.[\![(12.31a)]\!]\, e\, (\lambda e'.(\lambda e\, k.(\mathbf{smiled}(\mathtt{sel}\ e)) \wedge (k\ e))\, e'\, k) \\ &= \lambda e\, k.[\![(12.31a)]\!]\, e\, (\lambda e'.(\mathbf{smiled}(\mathtt{sel}\ e')) \wedge (k\ e')) \\ &= \lambda e\, k.(\lambda e\, k.\exists x.(\mathbf{man}(x)) \wedge (\mathbf{entered}(x)) \wedge (k(x :: e))) \\ &\qquad\qquad e\, (\lambda e'.\mathbf{smiled}(\mathtt{sel}\ e') \wedge (k\ e')) \\ &= \lambda e\, k.\exists x.(\mathbf{man}(x)) \wedge (\mathbf{entered}(x)) \\ &\qquad\qquad \wedge (\lambda e'.(\mathbf{smiled}(\mathtt{sel}\ e')) \wedge (k\ e'))(x :: e)) \\ &= \lambda e\, k.\exists x.(\mathbf{man}(x)) \wedge (\mathbf{entered}(x)) \\ &\qquad\qquad \wedge ((\mathbf{smiled}(\mathtt{sel}\ (x :: e))) \wedge (k\ (x :: e)))\end{aligned}$$

We now see that the `sel` operator has to select an entity from the environment $x :: e$. So x is indeed available, and the formulas can be given the standard semantics.

This approach combines very well with Montague's semantics principle and type homomorphism. In (extensional) Montague semantics, the interpretation of the syntactic type of sentence S is interpreted by t. All other interpretations for noun phrases (*NP*) or nouns (*N*) follow:

$$\begin{aligned}
[\![S]\!] &= t \\
[\![NP]\!] &= (e \rightarrow [\![S]\!]) \rightarrow [\![S]\!] \\
[\![N]\!] &= e \rightarrow [\![S]\!]
\end{aligned}$$

These interpretation still hold, except that $[\![S]\!]$ is now $\Omega = \gamma \rightarrow (\gamma \rightarrow t) \rightarrow t$.

$$\begin{aligned}
[\![S]\!] &= \Omega \\
[\![NP]\!] &= (e \rightarrow [\![S]\!]) \rightarrow [\![S]\!] \\
[\![N]\!] &= e \rightarrow [\![S]\!]
\end{aligned}$$

Moreover, by means of a definition of dynamic connectives, standard lexical semantics derives a dynamic version:

$$\begin{aligned}
P \,\overline{\wedge}\, Q &= \lambda e\, k. P\, e\, (\lambda e'. Q\, e'\, k) \\
\overline{\neg} P &= \lambda e\, k. (\neg P\, e (\lambda e'. \top)) \wedge (k\, e) \\
\overline{\exists} x. P &= \lambda e\, k. \exists x. P\, x\, (x :: e)\, k
\end{aligned}$$

The other connectives result from the application of the de Morgan laws. Furthermore, by translating a simple proposition such as $\mathbf{man}(x)$ into a dynamic one $\lambda ek.(\mathbf{man}(x)) \wedge (k\, e)$, we can give the dynamic lexicon that was used to analyze (12.31):

$$\begin{aligned}
[\![man]\!] &= \overline{\lambda x. \mathbf{man}(x)} \\
&= \lambda x. \lambda e\, k. (\mathbf{man}(x)) \wedge (k\, e) \\
[\![a]\!] &= \lambda P\, Q. \overline{\exists} x. (P\, x) \,\overline{\wedge}\, (Q\, x) \\
&= \lambda P\, Q. \lambda e\, k. \exists x. (P\, x\, (x :: e)\, k) \wedge (Q\, x\, (x :: e)\, k) \\
[\![entered]\!] &= \overline{\lambda s. s (\lambda x. \mathbf{entered}(x))} \\
&= \lambda s. \lambda e\, k. s (\lambda x. (\mathbf{entered}(x)) \wedge (k\, e)) \\
[\![smiled]\!] &= \overline{\lambda s. s (\lambda x. \mathbf{smiled}(x))} \\
&= \lambda s. \lambda e\, k. s (\lambda x. (\mathbf{smiled}(x)) \wedge (k\, e)) \\
[\![he]\!] &= \lambda P. \lambda e\, k. P\, (\mathtt{sel}\; e)\, e\, k
\end{aligned}$$

For further explanations on how to automatically derive a dynamic lexicon from a static one, we refer the reader to de Groote (2010) and Lebedeva (2012).

Remark 12.3.9. There are several points to stress:

- $[\![he]\!]$ is not derived from a static semantics. This simply means that it has no counterpart in a static semantics and is only made available when moving to the dynamic interpretation;
- Looking at $\bar{\neg}P$, note that $\neg P$ is fed with the *trivial* continuation. This means that $\neg P$ is completely evaluated within that context. Then, the remainder of the discourse, represented by k, is *not* in the scope of the negation. Moreover, it is fed with the same context as P. This means that whatever discourse referent P introduces, it will not be passed to k. This corresponds to the accessibility constraint as expressed in DRT.

□

de Groote (2006) presents the basics on continuation semantics for discourse and anaphora. Martin and Pollard (2010, 2012) present an elaboration on this basis and also deal with presupposition, as do Philippe de Groote and Lebedeva (2010) and Lebedeva (2012). Asher and Pogodalla (2010) give an account of modal subordination using continuation semantics. They also provide in Asher and Pogodalla (2011) a continuation semantics for SDRT. All these accounts stress that the continuation semantics for discourse is quite flexible with respect to what should be put into the context. This may be entities as well as properties, order relations, etc.

12.3.2 Discourse Structure

In the following, we focus on Segmented Discourse Representation Theory (SDRT), which is an extension of DRT introduced by Asher and Lascarides (2003). This is a dynamic representational theory of discourse that proposes to model the links between the semantic content of a sentence and the general structure of the discourse. Although in this short presentation we have linked SDRT to DRT, SDRT has either DRT, DPL or Continuation Semantics as its model theoretic. Thus the interpretation of rhetorical structures occurs at different levels (depending of the model). Left contexts postulated by SDRT are quite different from those needed to reproduce DRT or DPL in Continuation Semantics.

Rhetorical relations in discourse are needed for discourse semantics. Asher and Lascarides (2003) propose two examples to justify this assertion.

(12.49) a. π_1: John had a great evening last night.

b. π_2: He had a fantastic meal.

c. π_3: He ate salmon.

d. π_4: He devoured lots of cheese.

e. π_5: He won a dancing competition.

f. * It was a beautiful pink.

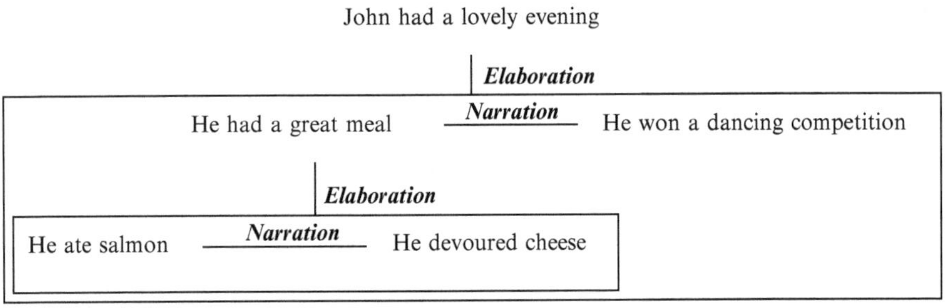

Fig. 12.4 Rhetorical representation of discourse (12.49)

From a semantic perspective, discourse (12.49) does not contain any expressions which block accessibility. Therefore the pronominal anaphora in the last sentence should be resolved in the discourse. DRT over-generates by accepting the last sentence. Only an analysis relying on discourse structure allows us to explain the non-accessibility of the referent, here *salmon*.

The rhetorical relation between the first two sentences is a kind of ***Elaboration***, which means that the second sentence gives details about the first one: ***Elaboration***(π_1, π_2). On the other hand, the relation between π_3 and π_4 is a kind of ***Narration***. π_4 is a temporal progression of π_3. According to Asher (1993), ***Elaboration*** induces a subordination, whereas ***Narration*** induces coordination. Figure 12.4 shows the corresponding hierarchical structure.

A second argument for rhetorical relations given by Asher and Lascarides (2003) is about temporal structure. In (12.50a), the sentence order reflects the temporal one, whereas in (12.50b) it does not. But both have the same tense and aspectual classes. Only the rhetorical relations differ: (12.50a) is a ***Narration*** whereas (12.50b) is an ***Elaboration***.

(12.50) a. John fell. Mary helped him up.

b. John fell. Mary pushed him.

One interesting feature of SDRT is the computational perspective of its definitions, which allows one to propose algorithms that produce representations. The task when using SDRT is to define rules (and then semantic targets) to trigger the use of rhetorical relations. An SDRS is a formal representation of a discourse structure, which can be a DRS, a rhetorical relation, or a boolean combination of the two.

This process can be divided into three steps: first, associate a DRS with the assertion; next, determine the open attachment sites (following the right frontier constraint, defined in the following); then, perform the update of the structure with the new information.

Note that we do not define the argument of the rhetorical relation. In Asher (1993) the relation is proposed over a proposition, whereas in Asher and Lascarides (2003) they are over labels which contain propositions. The difference between the two versions is that, in the second, rhetorical relations occur over coherent subparts of the discourse and are included in a label.

Although we will not explain all the details of the building steps, let us briefly explain the SDRS of (12.49). The discourse starts with a sentence π_1; then it is elaborated with π_2. The meal needs to be elaborated on with π_3 and π_4, with is a narration relation. Then the process introduces an abstract view of $\boldsymbol{Narration}(\pi_3, \pi_4)$ and reifies it with π_7. Finally, π_5 rises up in the structure to the π_2 label as a ***Narration***. Then the process introduces an abstract view of $\boldsymbol{Narration}(\pi_2, \pi_5)$ and reifies it with π_6. This is represented using a set of labels: $A = \{\pi_0, \pi_1, \pi_2, \pi_3, \pi_4, \pi_5, \pi_6, \pi_7\}$. The last sentence that occurs in the input representation is π_5. For each label, we give the representation following the SDRT definition. We introduce a function which associates either a DRS or rhetorical relations (or a logical combination of the two) with the full structure F, which is such that:

$$\begin{array}{ll} F(\pi_1) = K_{\pi_1} & F(\pi_0) \;\; = \boldsymbol{Elaboration}(\pi_1, \pi_6) \\ F(\pi_2) = K_{\pi_2} & F(\pi_6) \;\; = \boldsymbol{Narration}(\pi_2, \pi_5) \wedge \boldsymbol{Elaboration}(\pi_2, \pi_7) \\ F(\pi_3) = K_{\pi_3} & F(\pi_7) \;\; = \boldsymbol{Narration}(\pi_3, \pi_4) \\ F(\pi_4) = K_{\pi_4} & LAST = \pi_5 \\ F(\pi_5) = K_{\pi_5} & \end{array}$$

A more readable way to present these relations would be graphically as Fig. 12.5 shows. We assume that the representation of the discourse is at this step when the last sentence introduces the impossible anaphora.

If we want to add the next sentence of the discourse, (12.49f), to the representation, we need to chose where this sentence must be attached. The Right Frontier Constraint (RFC) enables us to restrict the potential options. Intuitively, this constraint assumes that the last sentence is a possible location, as well as any nodes that subordinate it. This follows the right border of the representation. In the example, we could attache (12.49f) to π_5, π_6, or π_1. The main consequence of this is that the set of accessible discourse referents that the process could use to resolve anaphora is now in this frontier. Thus, *it* cannot refer to the *salmon*. The use of the rhetorical structure limits the over-generation that we discussed previously.

From an SDRS, it is easily possible to derive a logical form based on algorithms developed for DRT. We can then build logical representations of discourse. A major challenge for such frameworks, but also for all those that deal with the semantic-pragmatic interface, lies in defining the process that automatically identifies the rhetorical relations. Even if we find evidence in syntax and semantics, generally with aspectual informations and adverbs, it is still a problem to define them well. We need to encode knowledge in order to infer rhetorical relations, which contain (at least) compositional and lexical semantics, world knowledge, and cognitive states. The logical design of SDRT leads us to believe that this framework could derive part of such information.

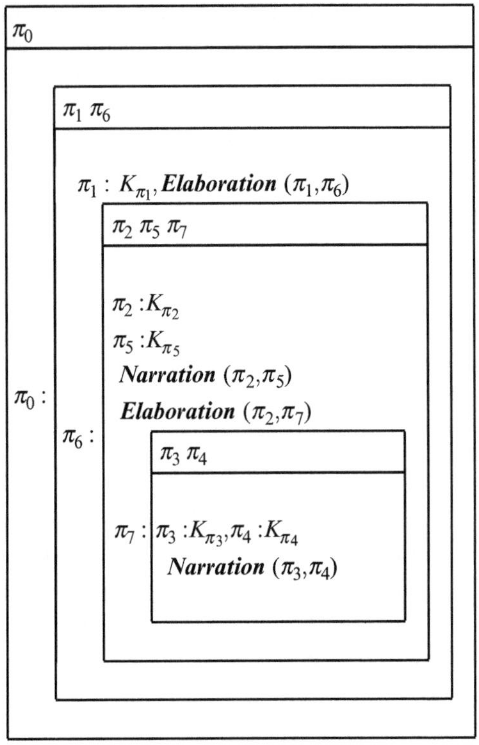

Fig. 12.5 Graphical representation of discourse (12.49)

12.4 Conclusion

We have shown that moving from single sentences to larger texts and discourses leads us to consider specific phenomena. These phenomena share a perspective on sentence behavior within a discourse. In addition to stating facts about the world, sentences need to access and update contexts where enough information is stored in order to correctly interpret the elements of the sentence in particular pronouns. Depending on the phenomenon, the context should minimally consist of:

- A set of propositions or valuations for presupposition;
- A set of discourse referents for declarative discourse;
- Two sets of discourse referents and one of propositions for modal subordination;
- A great deal of additional information (discourse unit referents, discourse structure, topic, etc.) for rhetorical structure inference.

We have presented several important frameworks to account for these phenomena, with their specificities. It is worth stressing that these frameworks have been evolving from rather specific tools, such as DRSs, into somewhat more standard (but not completely) logical tools with DPL and PLA, and to even more standard ones with continuation semantics for discourse. There is an interesting parallelism here with the evolution of programming language theory in computer science, our acknowledged inspiration. At the same time, this comes back to Montague's treatment of noun phrases, where type raising is indeed a continuation passing style (CPS) treatment of entities.

The rationality of these frameworks shows through in their ability to model phenomena in natural language. Computational linguistics offers an interesting testbed, and some have been implemented on a rather large scale, for instance by Bos (2003, 2008), and Marcu (2000). These frameworks also provide ways to analyze natural language usage. Rebuschi et al. (2012, 2014) present SDRT analysis in a pathological context. The claim is that such a specific use of natural language should break down the formal properties expressed by the framework. An interesting point, which is valid at both the cognitive and formal levels, is that schizophrenic interlocutors break at least the right frontier constraint. This suggests that the breaking of right frontier constraint captures a pathological phenomenon. It should thus have cognitive significance. The identification of a pathological use of formal frameworks also opens new perspectives for such approaches.

The frameworks we have discussed make no special assumptions about the syntactic structures from which meaning is derived. In the terminology of Jackendoff (2002), they also present themselves as *generative systems*. This means they have their own rules of well-formedness for building acceptable structures. The fact that not all of them actually correspond to natural language expressions is expressed in the specification of the syntax-semantics interface. The relation this interface defines indeed considers only a subset of all possible semantic forms. An interesting question is how this model can distribute a cognitive model over various elements: syntax, the syntax-semantics interface, and semantics (or pragmatics). Morrill (2000) proposes a model of incremental processing and acceptability for type-theoretical syntax. Could we derive a similar model for semantic processing, in particular for generating expressions from semantic representations?

With respect to representation construction, formalisms provide a large part of systematic process. But they also provide links external to the linguistic process. These links are mainly in the anaphora resolution part, i.e. in the `sel` operator, and the inference of rhetorical relations. For these operations, there is a lot of freedom with respect to the structure of the context and to the processes that operate on it. Their computational complexity may be associated with cognitive capacities or otherwise defined preferences. This is probably reflected in recent work on text summarization and text simplification (Marcu 1997; Clarke and Lapata 2010) with a view to deciding, according to the structure of the discourse, which parts are regarded as more or less important than other ones and should be kept. More generally, these computations, possibly inspired by cognitive models, could be the place to go to reduce the gap between the theoretical ambiguity of semantic models and the generally disambiguated readings people make.

References

P. Amsili, M. Bras, DRT et compositionnalité. T.A.L. **39**(1), 131–160 (1998)

N. Asher, *Reference to Abstract Objects in Discourse.* Studies in Linguistics and Philosophy (Kluwer Academic/Springer, The Netherland, 1993)

N. Asher, Troubles on the right frontier, in *Proceedings of Constraints in Discourse (CID 2005)*, Dortmund, ed. by P. Kühnlein, A. Benz. Volume 172 of Pragmatics & Beyond New Series (John Benjamins Publishing, 2008), pp. 29–52. http://www.benjamins.com/cgi-bin/t_bookview.cgi?bookid=P%26bns%20172

N. Asher, A. Lascarides, *Logics of Conversation.* Studies in Natural Language Processing (Cambridge University Press, Cambridge/New York, 2003)

N. Asher, E. McCready, Were, would, might and a compositional account of counterfactuals. J. Semant. **24**(2), 93–129 (2007)

N. Asher, S. Pogodalla, A montagovian treatment of modal subordination, in *Proceedings of Semantics and Linguistic Theory (SALT) 20*, Vancouver, ed. by N. Li, D. Lutz (Linguistic Society of America, *e*Language, 2010), pp. 387–405. http://elanguage.net/journals/index.php/salt/article/view/20.387.

N. Asher, S. Pogodalla, SDRT and continuation semantics, in *New Frontiers in Artificial Intelligence JSAI-isAI 2010 Workshops, LENLS, JURISIN, AMBN, ISS*, Tokyo, 18–19 Nov 2010, Revised Selected Papers, ed. by T. Onada, D. Bekki, E. McCready. Volume 6797 of Lecture Notes in Computer Science (Springer, 2011), pp. 3–15

D.I. Beaver, Presupposition, in van Benthem and ter Meulen (1997), chapter 17 (1997), pp. 939–1008

D.I. Beaver, *Presupposition and Assertion in Dynamic Semantics.* Studies in Logic, Language, and Information (CSLI Publications, Stanford, 2001)

J. Bos, Implementing the binding and accommodation theory for anaphora resolution and presupposition projection. Comput. Linguist. **29**(2), 179–210 (2003)

J. Bos, Wide-coverage semantic analysis with boxer, in *Semantics in Text Processing. STEP 2008 Conference Proceedings*, Venice, ed. by J. Bos, R. Delmonte Research in Computational Semantics (College Publications, 2008), pp. 277–286

J. Busquets, L. Vieu, N. Asher, La SDRT : une approche de la cohérence du discours dans la tradition de la sémantique dynamique. Verbum, **23**(1), 73–101 (2001)

B. Carpenter, *Type–Logical Semantics. Language, Speech and Communication* (MIT Press, Cambridge, 1997)

J. Clarke, M. Lapata, Discourse constraints for document compression. Computational Linguistics **36**(3), 411–441 (2010)

F. Corblin, *Représentation du discours et sémantique formelle.* Linguistique nouvelle (Presses Universitaires de France, Paris, 2002)

D. Cristea, N. Ide, D. Marcu, V. Tablan, Discourse structure and co-reference: an empirical study, in *Proceedings of the 18th International Conference on Computational Linguistics COLING'2000*, Saarbrücken, 2000

P. de Groote, Towards a montagovian account of dynamics, in *Proceedings of Semantics and Linguistic Theory (SALT) 16*, Tokyo, 2006, ed. by M. Gibson, J. Howell. http://elanguage.net/journals/index.php/salt/article/view/16.1/1791

P. de Groote, Dynamic semantics and discourse, in *Lectures at the International Conference on Semantics and Formal Modelling, JSM'10*, Nancy, 2010. http://jsm.loria.fr/jsm10/documents/lectures/degroote.pdf

P. de Groote, E. Lebedeva, Presupposition accomodation as exception handling, in *Proceedings of the Special Interest Group on Discourse and Dialogue SIGDIAL*, Tokyo, 2010

P. Dekker, Predicate logic with anaphora, in *Proceedings of the Fourth Semantics and Linguistic Theory Conference (SALT)*, Rochester, ed. by L. Santelmann, M. Harvey (DMLL Publications/Cornell University, 1994). http://elanguage.net/journals/salt/article/view/4.79/1569

P. Dekker, Dynamic semantics, in *Semantics: An International Handbook of Natural Language Meaning*, Volume 1, chapter 38, ed. by C. Maienborn, K. von Heusinger, P. Portner (De Gruyter Mouton, Berlin/New York, 2011), pp. 923–945

G. Evans, Pronouns? Linguist. Inq. **11**(2), 337–362 (1980)

A. Frank, *Context Dependence in Modal Constructions*. PhD thesis, Stuttgart University, 1997. 411 pages, Published in 'Arbeitspapiere des Sonderforschungsbereichs 340', 'Sprachtheoretische Grundlagen für die Computerlinguistik, Nr. 91'

A. Frank, H. Kamp, On context dependence in modal constructions, in *Proceedings of SALT VII*, Stanford (CLC Publications and Cornell University, 1997). http://www.cl.uni-heidelberg.de/~frank/papers/salt-online.pdf

D. Gallin, *Intensional and Higher-Order Modal Logic*. North-Holland Mathematics Studies (North-Holland, Amsterdam, 1975)

G. Gazdar, *Pragmatics: Implicature, Presupposition, and Logical Form* (Academic Press, New York, 1979)

P. Geach, *Reference and Generality: An Examination of Some Medieval and Modern Theories* (Cornell University Press, Ithaca, 1962)

B. Geurts, *Presuppositions and Pronouns*. Current Research in the Semantics/Pragmatics Interface (Elsevier, Amsterdam/New York, 1999)

J. Groenendijk, M. Stokhof, Dynamic predicate logic. Linguistics and Philosophy **14**(1), 39–100 (1991)

B.J. Grosz, C.L. Sidner, Attention, intentions, and the structure of discourse. Computational Linguistics **12**(3), 175–204 (1986)

I. Heim, *The Semantics of Definite and Indefinite Noun Phrases*. PhD thesis, University of Massachussetts, Amherst, 1982

I. Heim, File change semantics and the familiarity theory of definiteness, in *Meaning, Use and the Interpretation of Language*, ed. by R. Bäuerle, C. Schwarze, A. von Stechows (Walter de Gruyter & Co, Berlin/New York, 1983a), pp. 164–190 Reprinted in Portner and Partee (2002)

I. Heim, On the projection problem for presuppositions, in *Proceedings of the West Coast Conference on Formal Linguistics*, Stanford, CA, 1983b

R. Jackendoff, *Foundations of Language: Brain, Meaning, Grammar, Evolution* (Oxford University Press, Oxford/New York, 2002)

H. Kamp, A theory of truth and semantic representation, in *Formal Methods in the Study of Language*, ed. by J.A. Groenendijk, T. Janssen, M. Stokhof (Foris, Dordrecht, 1981)

H. Kamp, Théorie des représentations du discours et sémantique dynamique : traitements représentationnels et non représentationnels de l'anaphore, in *Interpréter en contexte*. Cognition et Traitement de l'Information, ed. by F. Corblin, C. Gardent, chapter 4 (Hermes, Lavoisier, 2005), pp. 145–178

H. Kamp, U. Reyle, *From Discourse to Logic* (Kluwer, Dordrecht/Boston, 1993)

L. Karttunen, Presupposition and linguistic context. Theor. Linguist. **1**, 181–194 (1974). Available at http://www2.parc.com/istl/members/karttune/publications/archive/presupplingcontext.pdf

E. Lebedeva, *Expression de la dynamique du discours à l'aide de continuations*. PhD thesis, Université de Lorraine, 2012. In English

W.C. Mann, S.A. Thompson, Rhetorical structure theory: toward a functional theory of text organization. Text **8**(3), 243–281 (1988)

D. Marcu, From discourse structures to text summaries, in *Proceedings of the ACL'97/EACL'97 Workshop on Intelligent Scalable Text Summarization*, Madrid, 1997

D. Marcu, *The Theory and Practice of Discourse Parsing and Summarization* (MIT Press, Cambridge, 2000)

S. Martin, C. Pollard, A higher-order theory of presupposition. Studia Logica **100**(4), 727–751 (2012)

S. Martin, C. Pollard, Hyperintensional dynamic semantics: analyzing definiteness with enriched contexts, in *Proceedings of Formal Grammar (FG) 15*, Copenhagen, 2010. Volume 7395 of Lecture Notes in Computer Science (Springer, 2012), pp. 114–129

R. Montague, English as a formal language, in *Linguaggi nella Società e nella Tecnica*, ed. by B. Visentini et al. (Edizioni di Comunità, Milan, 1970a), pp. 189–224
R. Montague, Universal grammar. Theoria **36**, 373–398 (1970b)
G.V. Morrill, Incremental processing and acceptability. Comput. Linguist. **26**(3), 319–338 (2000)
R. Muskens, Anaphora and the logic of change, in *Logics in AI, Proceedings of JELIA'90*, Amsterdam, ed. by J. van Eijck. Volume 478 of Lecture Notes in Computer Science (Springer, Berlin, 1991), pp. 412–427
R. Muskens, Combining Montague semantics and discourse representation. Linguistics and Philosophy **19**(2), 143–186 (1996)
R. Muskens, J. van Benthem, A. Visser, Dynamics, in van Benthem and ter Meulen (1997), chapter 10 (1997), pp. 587–647
N. Ogata, A dynamic semantics of modal subordination, in *New Frontiers in Artificial Intelligence, Joint JSAI 2005 Workshops*. Volume 4012 of Lecture Notes in Computer Science (Springer, Tokoyo, Japan, 2006), pp. 149–156
B.H. Partee, H.L.W. Hendriks, Montague grammar. in van Benthem and ter Meulen (1997), chapter 1 (1997)
L. Polanyi, A formal model of the structure of discourse. Journal of Pragmatics **12**, 601–638 (1988)
P. Portner, B.H. Partee (eds.), *Formal Semantics: The Essential Readings* (Blackwell, Oxford, 2002)
M. Rebuschi, M. Amblard, M. Musiol, Using sdrt to analyze pathological conversations (2014)
M. Rebuschi, M. Amblard, M. Musiol, Schizophrénie, logicité et compréhension en première 779 personne. *L'Evolution psychiatrique* **78**(1), 127–141 (2013)
C. Roberts, Modal subordination and pronominal anaphora in discourse. Linguist. Philos. **12**(6), 683–721 (1989). Available at http://www.ling.ohio-state.edu/~croberts/modalsub89.pdf
P. Sells, Restrictive and non-restrictive modification. Report N CSLI-85-28, 1985
M. Stone, D. Hardt, Dynamic discourse referents for tense and modals, in *Proceedings of IWCS 2*, Tilburg, 1997
J. van Benthem, A. ter Meulen (eds.), *Handbook of Logic and language* (MIT Press, Cambridge, 1997)
R. van der Sandt, Presupposition projection as anaphora resolution. J. Semant. **9**(4), 333–378 (1992)
J. van Eijck, H. Kamp, Representing discourse in context, in van Benthem and ter Meulen (1997) (1997), pp. 179–237
J. van Eijck, A. Visser, Dynamic semantics, in *The Stanford Encyclopedia of Philosophy*, Fall 2010 edition, ed. by E.N. Zalta (The Metaphysics Research Lab, Center for the Study of Language and Information, Stanford University, Stanford, 2010)
R. van Rooij, A modal analysis of presupposition and modal subordination. Journal of Semantics **22**(3), 281–305 (2005)
F. Veltman, Defaults in update semantics. Journal of Philosophy and Logic **25**(3), 221–261 (1996)

Chapter 13
Dialogue Analysis: Pragmatic and Rhetorical Aspects

Jean Caelen and Anne Xuereb

13.1 Introduction

This article describes a set of analytical tools for dialogue, focused on the pragmatic and rhetorical aspects that we consider fundamental to a dialogue hermeneutic. We begin by reviewing the necessary theoretical background for our purposes, then describe the analytical tools and apply them to a case of dialogue to illustrate their richness and scope. Of course these tools can always be paired with others for a more focused analysis.

We start with the assumption that agents interacting in a dialogue share their representation of the world, and that this representation is influenced by their action on it through the dialogue: it is pragmatics that accounts for this level of articulation between language and action. We present our model of pragmatic analysis in terms of three levels:

- Action supported by the dialogue
    - Thematic structure of the task
    - Goals of the task
- Dynamic advancement of the dialogue
    - Dialogue goals and acts
    - Strategies
- Articulation of pragmatics in the dialogue
    - Rhetorical relations
    - Structuring role of the topic

J. Caelen (✉) • A. Xuereb
Laboratoire d'Informatique de Grenoble (UMR 5217), Domaine universitaire, 220 rue de la Chimie, 38041 Grenoble Cedex 9, France
e-mail: jean.caelen@imag.fr; anne.xuereb@gmail.com

M. Rebuschi et al. (eds.), *Interdisciplinary Works in Logic, Epistemology, Psychology and Linguistics*, Logic, Argumentation & Reasoning 3,
DOI 10.1007/978-3-319-03044-9_13, © Springer International Publishing Switzerland 2014

In this article, we are especially interested in the dynamic advancement of dialogue and the articulation of pragmatics, levels which are of most interest in our approach to dialogue. The level of action will not be addressed here, as it essentially leads to a cognitive analysis of the task, which is beyond the scope of this article.

13.2 Dialogue Goals and Strategies

Dialogue is generally considered to be a conversational game embedded in an action framework (Vernant 1997). The participants are engaged in a dialogue with the intention of achieving several goals. Every dialogue has an interactional side and an interlocutionary side, to which a third level is added, that of the knowledge constructed or exchanged in the course of the dialogue. The role of this newly-built shared knowledge is to fuel either the interlocutory side or the interactional side. The action that is undertaken, and which must both achieve and satisfy its goals, is a combined action—it develops simultaneously in the world and between the participants: this also means that, during the dialogue, the participants must agree on the conditions for achieving these goals (i.e., who does what and how). The goals of the dialogue are thus subordinated to the goals of the combined action, which itself remains in the background of the dialogue. In this context, dialogue strategies are ways of conducting the dialogue as an activity of goal resolution (Caelen 2003).

Thus, to put it more simply, there are many kinds of action in the dialogue: those that are part of the framework of the conversational game itself, and those that relate to the background (world knowledge, etc.). We must therefore distinguish the dialogue goal, which is in the background (and which depends on the situation in the world of the task, social roles, etc.) from the conversational goal which is in the foreground, and which is necessarily shared since it relates to the type of dialogue being engaged in (if this goal is not shared, there is misunderstanding about the type of dialogue). For example, a salary negotiation implies both an external goal in the world (i.e., to obtain a raise for the employee, and to limit it for the employer) and a conversational goal, which is to conduct a true negotiation in the correct or socially acceptable form. Thus, the conversational goal can be satisfied without the ultimate goal necessarily being satisfied (the negotiation can proceed according to the rules—one could say by saving face, following Goffman—without the raise being obtained). The success of this dialogue in game theory would be measured by the difference between the salary increase that was obtained and that which was expected at the start of the dialogue. But this type of success does not arise from the dialogue analysis that we intend to perform in the following; rather, we would measure the gap between the conversational goal reached and that which would be expected in similar cases. In other words, we would like to know whether the conversational goal is met and how. To summarize our vision: the dialogue is presented as a game in which each speaker is trying to meet a goal while best adjusting to another goal—the conversational goal—in which he is engaged

(Caelen and Xuereb 2007). These two "games" are interwoven, making it necessary to sort them out in order to analyze them; we note that sometimes the dialogue goal and the conversational goal are one and the same when the dialogue is an end in itself. This will be the case in the example detailed in the article, which will show both the advantages and the limitations of our approach.

At the start of a dialogue, each conversation partner arrives with his or her own goals and knowledge in the context of a certain state of the world. We define the following terms to be used for the remainder of the article:

Initial goal of the dialogue: the state of the world or the mental state that one of the two speakers wishes to achieve a priori, either for himself (obtain information or directions, acquire knowledge, change the state of the world) or for his partner (share information, allow him to do something, give him advice, etc.).

Conversational goal: goal related to the type of strategy applied in the dialogue in order to reach its ends: convincing, dissuading, making an agreement, sharing, etc.

In what follows, we will use the term *goal* indiscriminately to refer to either a dialogue goal or a conversational goal. While this does not facilitate comprehension, it allows for generalization of the reasoning and encompasses both types of goals in the same formalism.

Exchange: a sequence of turns in speech during which a goal is maintained. The beginning of an exchange is marked by the appearance of a new goal; this goal may be transformed in the course of the exchange (for example, it can be clarified or broken down into sub-goals) and becomes an irreducible final goal upon which the exchange ends in a success or a failure. The successful outcome is one that obeys the double condition of being an *achieved goal* and a *satisfied goal* (Searle and Vanderveken 1985; Vanderveken 1997). An exchange, meanwhile, develops along two axes: the *managing* axis and the *incident* axis (Luzzati 1989).

Goal of the exchange: the goal that is kept in play during the exchange

Final goal: the state of the world or of the situation at the end of the exchange (it always ends, at least by the agreement of the two participants on the fact that there is a failure when there is one, e.g., "the unions and the employers separated with an admission of failure"). The final goal is not always predictable from the start.

Incidence (Luzzati 1989): an exchange whose effect is to challenge the dialogue goal or put it on hold (by change of subject, clarification request, request for details, etc.), but which does not challenge the conversational goal. The dialogue generally continues on this incident axis before coming back to the principal axis of the exchange. There may be several levels of incidence.

Dialogue: a dialogue is a sequence of *exchanges* and *incidences*. Several goals may be treated in the course of a dialogue.

Dialogue strategy: the way of managing turn-taking between interlocutors in order to guide an *exchange* or an *incidence*. The strategy should choose the best *direction of fit* for the goals at a given moment.

Table 13.1 Summary of properties of the strategies from the point of view of the hearer (H) in relation to the speaker (S)

Strategies	Non-inferential			Inferential	
Properties	Reactive	Directive	Constructive	Negotiation	Cooperation
Initiative	S	H	Mixed	Mixed	Mixed
Fit	g_S	g_H	Other	No	Reciprocal
Conv. goal	Maintenance	Maintenance	Detour	Maintenance	Maintenance
Concession	Max.	Min.	N/A	Min.	Max.
Role of H	Passive	Active	Neutral	Active	Active

Direction of fit: There are five possible directions of fit for goals, which lead to five types of strategies, presented from the perspective of the hearer H in a dialogue with the speaker S:

- H abandons his goal in favor of that of S (reactive strategy); in other words, H adjusts his goal toward S's goal (abbreviated as $g_H \rightarrow g_S$)
- H imposes his goal at the expense of S's goal (directive strategy); that is, he forces S to adopt his goal (abbreviated as $g_H \leftarrow g_S$)
- H and S each keep their goals (negotiative strategy); in other words, they do not attempt to adjust their goals a priori (abbreviated as $g_H \leftarrow g' \rightarrow g_S$) even if a compromise ($g'$) is found by the end of the negotiation.
- H and S each take into consideration the other's goal (cooperative strategy); that is, they try to adjust their goals to one another (abbreviated as $g_H \leftrightarrow g_S$)
- H and S both abandon their goals in favor of a third goal (constructive strategy) by taking a constructive detour (abbreviated as $g_H \rightarrow g' \leftarrow g_S$)

We adopt the following notational conventions:

- g_S: initial goal of speaker S,
- g_H: initial goal of the hearer H,
- g_f: final goal of the exchange,
- g_c: conversational goal, assumed to be shared by H and S.

We can thus define the following types of strategies according to the directions of fit described above (in the following, we continue to take the point of view of the hearer H, See Table 13.1).

13.2.1 Non-inferential Strategies

These strategies are called non-inferential insofar as the one who pursues them does not try to find a shared goal with his partner and therefore does not necessarily have to infer his goal.

13.2.1.1 Reactive Strategy

This strategy consists in delegating the initiative to S, either by getting him to take on H's goal (in the case of asking for help or assistance) or by adopting his goal (in the case of the helper or servant). The course of the dialogue then develops:

- By maintaining the goal of the exchange, but without taking the initiative,
- By abandoning his own goal or by making it dependent on g_H.

H is passive and S is active. This results in H opening up all of the types of strategies to his interlocutor S. The direction of fit is therefore $g_H \rightarrow g_S$.

13.2.1.2 Directive Strategy

This strategy consists in holding the initiative in order to guide the dialogue:

- By maintaining the goal of the exchange and holding the initiative,
- By imposing his own goal g_H (therefore trying to make $g_f = g_H$),
- By perhaps ignoring the goal of the speaker g_S, which is somehow considered not to exist.

This results in imposing a reactive or negotiated response on S, and thus limiting his available strategies. H is active and S becomes passive. The direction of fit is then $g_H \leftarrow g_S$.

13.2.1.3 Constructive (or Detour) Strategy

This strategy consists in temporarily displacing the current goal in order to trigger a detour (assumed to be constructive) which is not necessarily an incidence—for example, to point out an oversight or error, make a citation, restate a piece of old information, an experience, etc.:

- The current goal is put on hold, as well as the initial goals,
- A new goal g' is established,
- The initiative may be shared.

The direction of fit is then $g_H \rightarrow g' \leftarrow g_S$. In contrast to an incidence, a detour does not necessarily lead back to the initial exchange, and can put the conversation on hold or lead to another detour.

13.2.2 *Inferential Strategies*

These strategies are called inferential insofar as they require both partners to have a precise knowledge of their respective goals.

13.2.2.1 Cooperative Strategy

This strategy consists in taking into account the goal of one's interlocutor by proposing one or more solutions which lead both to achieve their goals, if they are not incompatible:

- This leads to the unfolding of a complex process—evaluating the situation, presenting an explanation and possibly relevant examples, support, or arguments, and offering a fixed choice (cognitively easier for decision-making), maximizing the concession space,
- By a process of searching for an optimum within a space of possibilities,
- By accompanying the partner to a solution,
- By expanding the conversational goal if necessary.

This results in opening all types of strategies to one's interlocutor. The direction of fit is $g_H \leftrightarrow g_S$.

13.2.2.2 Negotiative Strategy

Negotiation may occur in a situation where the goals are incompatible and (where) the participants want to minimize concessions. The negotiation proceeds according to a fairly standard pattern, by sequences of argumentation (argument/rebuttal) with a proposed sub-optimal solution until the partners reach either convergence or admission of failure. The local tactic is to:

- Try to impose one's goal or accept a compromise,
- Maintain the conversational goal,
- Push the negotiation as far as possible until reaching an acceptable goal g'.

This results in keeping one's interlocutor confined to this strategy. The direction of fit is then $g_H \leftarrow g' \rightarrow g_S$.

13.3 Speech Acts

The theory of speech acts is well known: each speech act is defined in terms of its illocutionary force F and its propositional content p, using the formalism of Searle and Vanderveken (1985). Thus every linguistic or physical action is expressed in the form of Fp.

The dialogue interaction moves forward with help from acts that have the general form Fp = illocutionary force + propositional content (Vanderveken 1990): an act has both preparatory conditions and effects. We will retain our own taxonomy of acts, as it is compatible with the notion of goal defined above: F^A, F^{FA}, F^{FK}, F^K, F^R, F^P. Certain acts are action-oriented (F^A = *perform an action*, F^{FA} = *cause to perform an action*) that is to say, the expected effect in the world (events, facts, accomplishment of a task). Other acts are epistemically oriented (F^K = *inform/cause to know*, F^{FK} = *cause to inform*), that is, they have an effect in the discourse or on (shared or private) knowledge. Finally, other acts are deontically oriented (F^R = *require/cause to have to*, F^P = *allow/cause to be able to*), that is, they create obligations (requirements) or offer choices (possibilities) for further dialogue. Such deontic acts regulate the interaction and can even change the rules of the game.

The table below summarizes these concepts: actions, in the left column, involve speakers A and/or B when they perform them, within a certain orientation, and have their source in the background and the private knowledge of each speaker (K_A denotes A's knowledge and K_B denotes B's knowledge). Their effects apply to a change in mutual knowledge K_{AB}, to plans and goals (development of plans and goals) and the world.

Acts	Involvement	Orientation	Background	Effects
$F^{FK}P$	A, B	Epistemic	World, K_A	K_{AB}
$F^K p$	A	Epistemic	World, K_B	K_{AB}
$F^P p$	A	Deontic	B	Plan
$F^R p$	B	Deontic	B	Goal
$F^{FA} p$	A, B	Action	Goal	World, K_{AB}
$F^A p$	A	Action	Goal	World, K_{AB}

We use the term *retort* for the category of acts that deny the interlocutor the right or ability to perform an action (strong challenges, questioning of roles, etc.). They are of the form "A does not accept that $F_B p$" or "A denies B the act $F_B p$", such as "What right do you have to ask me that?" or "Why should I answer you?", "You don't have the right to impose that on me", etc. A retort is denoted as $\neg Fp$ (to be distinguished from negations, which are of the form $F\neg p$).

The goal of a retort is to create a rupture in the convergence of the dialogue by challenging a conversational goal. It closes the current dialog and moves it to another area (the attack, interruption, evasion, etc.). It becomes impossible at this time for the interlocutor not to respond to this retort, especially if the challenge is accompanied by a personal attack. Retorts are possible following a F^{FK}, F^K, F^{FA}, F^A depending on the social relationship between interlocutors, but have no meaning after F^R and F^P, since in the case of F^R it is a social obligation that cannot be discussed, and in the case of F^P there is a free choice left to the speaker, which is not natural to challenge.

13.4 The Pragmatics of Dialogue

Semantics is not enough to model the interpretation of an utterance (especially due to the presence of phenomena such as coreference, indexicals, ellipses, and implicit elements in the discourse such as presuppositions and implicatures). Dialogue is constructed in action and interaction, and its interpretation requires anchoring the utterance in its actional context: this is the pragmatic level. After reviewing the definitions of presuppositions and implicatures, and that of *topos* in the work of Ducrot, we briefly describe SDRT.

13.4.1 Presuppositions and Implicatures

- **Presuppositions** are pre-propositions, implicit engagements of the interlocutors who share common knowledge. They can be indexically marked, for example for the verb *drink, drink(x)* generally presupposes *liquid(x),* but in the case of definite descriptions like *the king of France is bald,* the constraint holds over the existence of the subject referent.
- **Implicatures** are post-propositions. They are the results of inferences that a hearer is likely to make based on an utterance. They are calculated based on what is said or what is conventionally implicated. For Grice (1975), implicatures—called conversational—arise from the cooperative principle in which what is said is relevant (the principle of economy of speech).

13.4.2 Topos in the Work of Ducrot

For Ducrot (1984), argumentation (which, for him, structures the text or the discourse) depends on the synthesis of three components: the *topical*, the *logical*, and the *encyclopedic*. These three elements are not always easily separable. For Anscombre and Ducrot, *topos* is "the guarantor that authorizes the passage from the argument A to the conclusion C" (Anscombre and Ducrot 1983). It is a general principle underlying a sequence of argumentation presented within a discourse. The *topical* component is the set of *topoi* or arguments that shape the discourse. The *topoi* are common beliefs that lead to results in the form of predicates; they contain rules or principles of inference which, starting from one or more singular facts and a generic hypothesis about reality, allow one to conclude the existence of another singular fact. The *encyclopedic* component is inseparable from the *topical* and *logical* components. It specifies world knowledge, the referential and cultural knowledge shared by the interlocutors. In a way, the concept of *topos* in Ducrot's work generalizes over both implicature and presupposition. Thus, for example, to

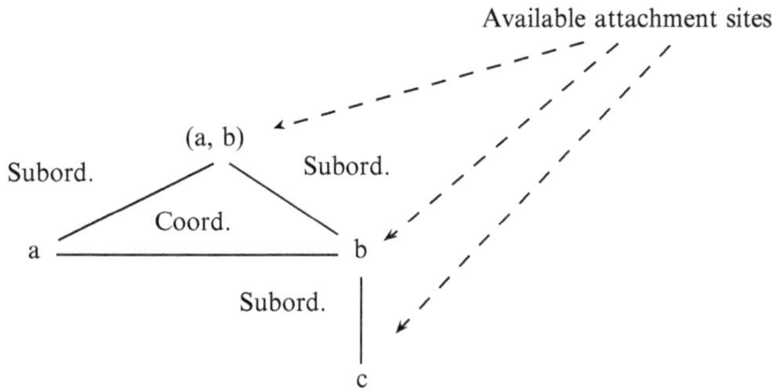

Fig. 13.1 Discourse structure and available attachment sites

say "Peter worked all day" is to produce the *topos* $\exists x : Peter(x) \wedge tired(x)$. The meaning of the verb *work* produces an aggregate of *topoi* from which the arguments are woven and the discourse is constructed.

13.4.3 SDRT

SDRT (Segmented Discourse Representation Theory) is a formal theory of the semantic-pragmatic interface. Bringing together the contributions of discourse analysis for the formalization of the structure of discourse, and dynamic semantics for the interpretation of utterances, it offers a model of discourse coherence based on linguistic and pragmatic knowledge. It extends DRT (Discourse Representation Theory) by adding a logical link between discourse segments. In SDRT, discourse analysis supplies a complex structure where discourse representation structures (DRS) are connected by discourse relations to form "Segmented Discourse Representation Structures" or SDRS (Asher and Lascarides 2003). In this hierarchical structure, relations are of the coordinating type (precedence relation, simple continuation of discourse) or the subordinating type (dominance relations such as Elaboration, Precision). On a graph, subordinating relations are shown with vertical lines, and coordinating relations with horizontal lines. This structure constrains the available attachment sites for a new discourse segment: it can only be attached at available attachment site. In terms of the representation conventions, these available attachment points are called the "the right frontier of discourse" as shown in Fig. 13.1.

In formal terms, an SDRS is a pair $< U, Cond >$, where

- U is a set of discourse referents of speech acts (DRS or SDRS labels π),
- $Cond$ is a set of conditions on the members of U. These are of the form:
  - $\pi : K$, where K is a DRS or an SDRS,
  - $R(\pi_1, \pi_2)$, where R is a discourse relation (rhetorical relation).

An utterance is therefore represented by a formula $\pi : K$, where π is the reference of the speech act (the label), and K is the formula for the act's discourse content. K is either a DRS formula, for simple constituents, or an SDRS formula, for complex constituents. The SDRS is thus a recursive structure.

13.4.3.1 Construction of the Logical Structure of Discourse

SDRT is based on the assumption of discourse coherence: in the SDRS, any constituent except the first utterance must be attached with a rhetorical relation to a constituent present in the context. The hierarchical structure of the SDRS introduces a level of constraint for accessing antecedents of anaphoric conditions: access is only possible for the referents of constituents that dominate the current component or those of the constituent immediately to the left. The discourse structure is updated by an incremental process:

- Construction of the DRS of the current sentence;
- Integration of this segment into the context of the previously constructed SDRS, by:
  - Deciding which discourse referent can be an attachment site,
  - Inferring the discourse relation which links the new DRS to an available attachment site,
  - Updating the resulting SDRS: resolving the sub-specifications, introducing new complex segments.

In case of ambiguity in the attachment site, the principle of Maximize Discourse Coherence allows a choice of the most relevant interpretation. The option with highest coherence is selected by maximizing the number of connections between discourse constituents, with emphasis on rhetorical relations that have the greatest cohesive power, by promoting the resolution of sub-specifications.

13.4.3.2 Rhetorical Relations

The types of rhetorical relations used in SDRT originate in RST (Rhetorical Structure Theory), Mann and Thompson (1988) and the work of Grosz and Sidner (1986). However, their number is reduced in SDRT, which uses discourse relations in terms of their semantic contribution. As such, the relation Elaboration, for example, has a temporal effect: the main event of the elaborating utterance is a part of the main event of the already elaborated event. The complete list of relations is not fixed, but instead should be defined on semantic criteria in terms of the modeled world. The relations described in SDRT the narrative discourse are: Narration, Background, Elaboration, Continuation, Topic, Result, Explanation, Consequence, Contrast and Parallel.

The calculation of rhetorical relations involves the current context (the current SDRS) and the semantics of the statement to be attached, as well as general pragmatic principles and (real-world) knowledge of the domain. SDRT is based on two distinct logical components: *glue logic* for pragmatic reasoning, and the *logic of information content,* for reasoning over the semantics. For each rhetorical relation that is described, the inference rules involve two groups of axioms: the triggering rules and the semantic effects. The triggering rules specify the linguistic clues that allow the speaker to signal the rhetorical relation between two propositions. They depend on the presence of lexical markers; for example, the French lexical marker *car* ('for') indicates a relation of *explanation*, while *puis* ('then') or *ensuite* ('afterwards') are clues for the relation of *narration*. The triggering rules can involve syntactic data: the relation *contrast* (π_1, π_2) is triggered by an isomorphism of structure together with a thematic contrast between the utterances $K\pi_1$ and $K\pi_2$. Semantic effects, on the other hand, specify the semantic contribution of the relationship, and serve to enrich the propositional content of SDRS. The semantic effect of *Narration*(π_1, π_2) is that the main event of π_1 precedes the main event of π_2. The relationship $background(\pi_1, \pi_2)$ semantic result of requiring the main event of π_1 to temporally overlap that of π_2.

After the insertion of a constituent, the structure is updated. Coordinated relations, such as *narration* or *continuation*, require the introduction of a *topic* constituent which subsumes the underlying coordinated constituents. This is a complex constituent whose function is to generalize the information of attached constituents. For subordinating relations, the *topic* constituent is implicit, and is composed of a subordinated constituent.

13.4.4 Dialogue SDRT

SDRT has been shown to be a productive theoretical framework. We complete its description to account for the relations involved in acts of questioning. A question is formalized by the set of propositions in the world that constitute direct responses. An indirect response is a response that allows the hearer to infer the direct answer. The formalization of questioning involves the cognitive states of the dialogue partners, using operators over their beliefs and intentions. Extended SDRT includes the relations *Question-Answer-Pair* (QAP), *Partial Answer Question Pair* $(PQAP)$, *Indirect Question Answer Pair* $(IQAP)$, *Plan-Elaboration, Question Elaboration, and Acknowledgment.* SDRT exploits the fact that questions may be modified or contradicted later in the dialogue. Question-Answer relations are necessarily subordinated, and the *question* node remains available to other attachments even after the first answer (Prévot 2004). The update of the structure after the attachment of *question-answer* relations triggers the insertion of a topic constituent, which then receives the result of the application of the *answer* segment on the *question* segment. For example, the following dialogue

π_2: Where is room C?
π_3: At the end of the hall.
is represented by the schema seen here.

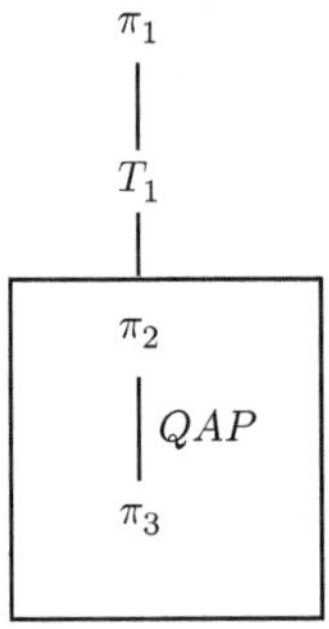

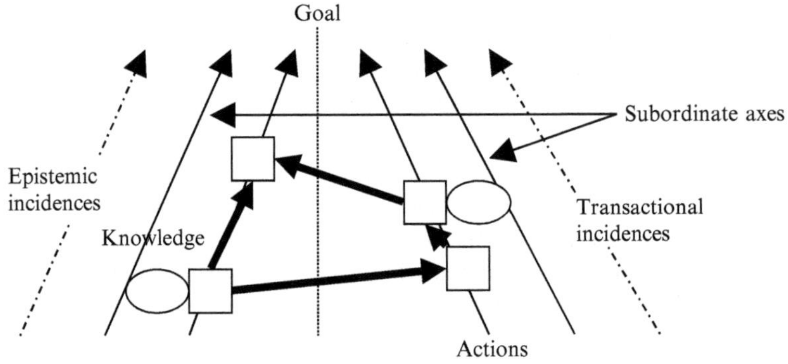

Fig. 13.2 The advancement of dialogue tales place along six axes: the main and subordinate actions, the main and subordinate knowledge, and the transactional and epistemic incidences

The answer π_3 is attached to the question π_2 by a relation QAP. The topic constituent T1 receives the information established by the combination of the question π_2 and the answer π_3. The established information then becomes available for an anaphoric reference in the dialogue that follows.

As we have seen in Sect. 13.2, dialogue is a conversational game embedded in an actional framework. The participants exchange knowledge in order to guide their joint action. The representation of the dialogue should contain more pragmatic information than what can come directly from the utterances, their presuppositions and implicatures, or Ducrot's *topoi*. It must integrate the dialogue context itself (see Fig. 13.2). Thus, the interaction develops on two levels: (a) communicative and (b) transactional. The communicative level is composed of the epistemic level and the deontic level (i.e., the *what to do* and *how to do it*). The deontic level articulates the epistemic level (the necessary knowledge and preparatory conditions for the *doing*) and the transactional level (the *doing together*). It sets up local tactics for moving from one level to another or for avoiding the problem (an *escape*). This is a level of internal regulation of the dialogue by the participants themselves. There is also a control level, external but implicit, about respecting the rules of the dialogue game:

the game ends if someone violates one of these rules. The effect of an action is twofold: on one hand the effect is on the world in the form of facts, and on the other, the effect is on shared knowledge.

A dialogue consists of interventions proceeding from turn-taking in speech. These interventions are formed of sequences of monologue or dialogue. Rhetorical relations of the monologic type are relations linking two acts of a single speaker, either in a single turn of speech or not, which are in relation (i.e., attached in the sense of SDRT) and which structure the discourse of this speaker in the situation of the present dialogue (i.e., here and now). They are of the same nature as in a narrative discourse. Rhetorical relations of the dialogic type, on the other hand, are relations linking two acts (by speaker A, then speaker B) which are in relation (i.e., attached in the sense of SDRT) and which structure the dialogue. They are of the form $Rd = (F_A p, F_B q)$—being in relation does not necessarily mean being consecutive.

Just below we give the list of rhetorical relations that we have retained as relevant to a pragmatic perspective on dialogue. The definitions and the scope of these relations will take on meaning progressively, following examples given and the complete demonstration.

13.4.4.1 Families of Rhetorical Relations in Dialogue

If we consider the different levels of dialogue diagrammed above, we can identify the following families of relations:

1. **The epistemic axis and its subordinate**
   - **Question-answer pairs** (QAP): In a Question-Answer Pair, the response P is meant to provide information relative to the question Q; in this category, we also distinguish $PQAP$ (Partial QAP) and $IQAP$ (Indirect QAP). These questions and answers are relevant to the main (or managing) axis of the dialogue and work together to advance it.
   - **Question Subordination** ($Q-Sub$): Question Subordination involves clarification requests about shared knowledge. These requests are in the background knowledge of the participants (and not on the level of discourse like the QAP). This class includes clarification requests, corrections, reformulations, etc. They are represented as $Q - Sub$:clarification, $Q - Sub$:correction, etc.
   - **Elaborations of knowledge** ($Elab$): Elaborations are the contributions of mutual knowledge built during the dialogue game. These contributions can be made in many ways, both on the managing axis (constructive questions ($Elab_q$) and assertions, for example) and on the subordinate axis—in this case these are the clarifications, corrections, reformulations, etc., which are necessary for the speakers to understand each other. They are represented as $Elab$:clarification, $Elab$:correction, etc.

2. **The action axis and its subordinate**
   - **Request Answer Pair** (RAP): A delegation or request for action followed by concrete action(s) aimed at resolving the current goal. The action-answer can also be indicated as partial ($PRAP$) or indirect ($IRAP$). These relations are to the transactional level what the QAP are to the epistemic level,
   - **Plan Elaboration** ($P-Elab$): Contribution to the formation of a joint plan—this plan becomes the action framework in which the actors achieve resolution of the goal,
   - **Question elaboration** ($Q - Elab$): Contribution to the formation of a plan by a question,
   - **Request elaboration** ($R - Elab$): Action Elaboration—contribution to the formation of a goal—or to the clarification of this goal if it is already established. This transaction over the goal is on the subordinate axis.
3. **The divergents axes: incidences et retorts**
   - **Incidences (I)**: Acts which break the current topic by introducing a new topic. We distinguish incidences with a return the managing topic, or detour, from the incidences without a return to the topic (insults, for example). Detours are generally constructive acts, but indirectly and not immediately for the dialogue background,
   - **Retorts (R)**: These acts behave like closing coordinations. Indeed, one may only follow with an answer to the retort or an escape (opening of a new topic). Retorts do, however, allow changes in the rules of the dialogue, regulating turn-taking and exchanges, and challenging of roles. Their effect is to modify the actors' commitments. These are deontics that bear on the rules governing the coordination of actions in the dialogue game (elaboration of tactics), since the rules are implicitly given at the start and can not be negotiated in this way.
4. **Continuations (C)**: Acts that continue the discourse within the same topic. A subtype of continuations is acquiescences or agreements (*acquiescements*) (Prévot 2004), whose role is either to maintain the thread of dialogue (e.g., *hmm, yeah,* etc.) or to close a series of utterances under a single topic.

13.4.4.2 The Topic Constituent

In order to strengthen the role of pragmatics in the formalization of questioning, we extend the role of the topic constituent into not only a structural element of the dialogue, but also the repository of pragmatic representations being calculated (Xuereb and Caelen 2005). The topic is a complex constituent which is explicitly introduced, and which subsumes the underlying coordinated constituents. This is where the sub-specifications are resolved. During the SDRS update, the set of referents and predicates established in the underlying substructure is merged into the topic, after the presuppositions and implicatures are integrated. The global SDRS is thus built up in the course of the dialogue through the progressive establishment of higher and higher topic levels (union of the coordinated elements, merging of subordinate elements), continuing up to the dominant topic, which consists of the set of all information established by the participants. Presuppositions are integrated in the form of discourse relations added to the context. The topic node is where any corrections are made (challenges, corrections, withdrawals, etc.). It also represents a unit of shared knowledge: in the course of advancing the dialogue, common knowledge is co-constructed by the participants. The branching structure of topics is where the information which is shared and accepted by both interlocutors is instantiated.

13.5 Construction of Dialogue SDRS

13.5.1 Inference of Rhetorical Relations

The inference of rhetorical relations involves the illocutionary force of speech acts and its propositional content. We focus on the pragmatic effects of the dialogue structure and we consider semantic representations of utterances to be given. We will use the predicate *Answer* to denote the resolving answer to a question. An answer is considered 'resolving' if it provides the elements to achieve the underlying action in the world of the task. The answer is direct if it provides all the elements necessary to achieve this action, and indirect if inferences are still needed to provide all the elements necessary to achieve it. An answer is considered partial if it provides some of the elements necessary (it reduces the range of possible answers). We take into account the presuppostions, knowledge shared, and the world of the task. We now briefly detail the inferences put into practice in all dialogue-based rhetorical relations, organized into five groups.

13.5.1.1 Question-Answer Pairs: $QAP, PQAP, IQAP$

For these three relations, the first act of the pair always has an illocutionary force F^{FK}; a question may be answered with an assertion or an action:

$F_A^{FK} \rightarrow F_B^K or F_A^{FK} \rightarrow F_B^A$.
QAP(p, q): *Question-Answer Pair* (i.e., complete answer) Answer(p, q)
Both polarity questions and wh-questions are included in QAP.
PQAP(p, q) : *Partial Question-Answer Pair* (i.e., partial answer)
$q \subset r \wedge Answer(p, r)$
IQAP(p, q): *Indirect Question-Answer Pair* (i.e., indirect answer)
$q \Rightarrow r \wedge Answer(p, r)$

13.5.1.2 Subordinate Questions: $Q - Sub$

These are follow-ups to dependent questions, each of which may be answered (subordination leaves each *question* node open). The semantics for this relation is refined by distinguishing:

Q-Sub:clarification(p, q): question about part of p
Q-Sub:incidence(p, q): question unrelated to the contents of p (nor any sub-part of p, and is also not an elaboration), but staying within the same theme. In this case it is a *detour* and not an *escape*.

13.5.1.3 Knowledge Elaboration: $Elab$:Clarification, $Elab$:Correction

The relation **Elaboration**(p, q) involves a whole/part relation between the main elements of K_p and K_q. We then refine this relation with the following distinctions:

$\mathbf{Elab_q(p, q)}$: q is an elaborating question about the contents of p (question about a detail of p)[1]
Elab : $\mathbf{Explanation(p, q)}$: there is a semantic relation of explanation between p and q. This semantic relation may be expressed by specific lexical markers (*for, since, because,* etc.).
Elab : $\mathbf{Correction(p, q)}$: q contributes a correction of the semantics, by substituting a part of p.
Elab : $\mathbf{Clarification(p, q)}$: q contributes a clarification or further detail about the contents of p, without adding information or modifying p.

13.5.1.4 Delegations or Requests for Action: RAP, $PRAP$, $IRAP$

These relations formalize questions on the level of action. The first act of the pair is always request for action F_{FA} or an offer of action F_P. The hearer may answer it either with an action or with a contribution of information in order to prepare the action: $F_A^{FA} \leftarrow F_B^A ou F_A^{FA} \leftarrow F_B^K; F_A^P \leftarrow F_B^A ou F_A^P \leftarrow F_B^K$

$\mathbf{RAP(p, q)}$ *Request-Answer Pair*
$Answer(p, q)$
$\mathbf{PRAP(p, q)}$ *Partial Request-Answer Pair*
$q \subset r \wedge RAP(p, r)$
$\mathbf{IRAP(p, q)}$ *Indirect Request-Answer Pair*
$q \Rightarrow r \wedge RAP(p, r)$

---

[1] Unlike Asher and Lascarides (2003), we do not distinguish elaborations characterized by a request. Here, $Elab_q$ includes $Elab_r$ as defined in Asher and Lascarides (2003).

13.5.1.5 Relations Linked to Planning

The relations $Q - Elab$, $P - Elab$, $R - Elab$ involve a level of planning or transaction, formalized with the following elements:

- The goal g associated with A's utterance p,
- The answer p' to p that A expects,
- The plan a to be implemented in order to achieve the goal g,
- The shared knowledge of A and B, K_{AB}, and B's private knowledge, K_B.

The speaker A seeks knowledge p' of the type "plan" (that is, *how to do*) from which he may reach a situation where he can infer that, by following through on the plan a implicit in p', he will reach his initial goal g. This plan may not be inferred by the shared knowledge of A and B before the response of B (Prévot 2004). In what follows, we use the predicate Executable(p) which denotes an executable action p.

We distinguish:

$\mathbf{Q - Elab(p, q)}$ *Question Elaboration*
$Answer(q, p') \wedge p'$ supplies a plan a (or a sub-plan) which participates in the resolution of the goal g associated with p.
$\mathbf{R - Elab(p, q)}$ *Request Elaboration*
g is the goal implicit in p, $Executable(q) \wedge F_A^A(q)$ participates in achievement(g). The execution of the answer q supplies A with a goal that he must achieve in order to achieve b.
$\mathbf{Plan - Elab(p, q)}$ *Plan Elaboration*
q constitutes an element of the plan a necessary to achieve the goal associated with p. q is an assertion.

For these three relations, Asher and Lascarides (2003) bring in the cognitive level and the modeling of goals, plans, beliefs and intentions of the speakers. In the context of the completed dialogue, it is best to avoid modeling intentions and beliefs. These relationships are inferred from real-world knowledge of the task, specific to the domain of application and purpose of the current activity.

13.5.1.6 Continuation C

is a coordinating relation. In its dialogue form, when it links the pairs in $QAPs$, it represents the linking of Q/A coordinates, that is, Q_i/A_i sequences and not $Q_1 \ldots Q_i/A_1 \ldots A_i$ sequences. In its monologue form, it links acts of the same type in succession on the same theme (e.g., enumeration of a list). This relationship requires the introduction of a topic which subsumes the coordinated constituents.

13.5.2 Pragmatic Effects: Construction of the Structure

Each rhetorical relation has a specific effect on the SDRS, in particular via its influence on the structure of the topic.

- $QAPs$ and $RAPs$ introduce a *Topic Question.* This topic will receive the result of the application of answer segment to the question segment (Prévot 2004). Thus the sets of coordinated questions and answers link respective QAP pairs under a single *Topic Question.* In the case of linked answers, the dominant topic question will contain the union of assertions obtained by applying the answers to their respective questions,
- $Elabs$ (Elab_q, $Elab$:correction, $Elab$:clarification, $Elab$:explanation…) introduce a subordinate topic which, once resolved, is merged into the dominant topic,
- An A closes the topic,
- An I stays within the same topic (with the restriction on incidence types indicated above).

13.6 Analysis of a Doctor-Patient Dialogue

The analysis proceeds in two steps:

- The annotation,
- The statistics.

13.6.1 Annotation of the Dialogue

For each dialogue act, we annotate:

1. The illocutionary force of the dialogue act Fp,
2. The goal of the dialogue act (the dialogue goal, subject to the goal of the task)—some acts don't have a goal other than maintaining the progression of the dialogue (here especially for the psychoanalyst): these are phatics,
3. The doctor's goal G_D and the patient's goal G_P,
4. The strategy: S = directive, reactive, negotiated, constructive, cooperative,
5. The rhetorical relation RR,
6. The topic T.

To simplify the presentation, we will analyze the dialogue strategies (S) of the doctor only, and the rhetorical relations (RR) for only the patient's utterances. A final

SDRS schema is given for a fragment of the dialogue. In the presentation below, the doctor's interventions are justified to the left and those of the patient justified to the right.

13.6.1.1 Analysis Tableau

Analysis Tableau

Doctor (D) Patient (P)

....

$G_P = 0$

Good morning, please sit down. Were you told that you would see me this morning?
G_D = "*to get the patient to talk about himself*" $= F_P^{FK} P$
S = Directive

Yes.

Alright, so I'm listening.
S = Directive

But they didn't tell me why, sir. They told me, they told this morning that I was supposed to have a consultation downstairs and that's all.
$RR = R - Elab$
Topic = Consultation

And that's all.
Phatic

And that's all.

Alright then, just talk to me about whatever comes to mind.
S = Cooperative

Uh, what do you want me to talk (to you) about? About my illness? About... about... I really don't see... on what subject? I mean now, you just leave me... Talking to you puts me in an awkward position. If you give me a topic, then I'm perfectly capable... but just like that, on the spot, well I don't really know what to say, no. Ask me some questions and..., and we'll see. I can't really say anything more.
$RR = Q - Elab$
Topic = $\exists \neg G_D$

Completely stopped?
S = Constructive

Completely, no, but after all, that wouldn't do any harm, you know! It would just be pointless, futile things that I could tell you about.
R = *Q* − *Sub*

Pointless, futile?

Yeah. I could just tell you anything. So if there's not a topic to discuss, or even a question to ask, what do I tell you? You ask me right away if... what do I... "talk to me!" but about what? It's exactly the same; I don't get it, or I just pick a subject and then just talk to you. No. You're putting me in an awkward position, honestly!
RR = *Elab*: clarification

What happens when you feel awkward?
S = Directive

Well, I'm a little ashamed, precisely.
RR = *QAP*

Ashamed?
Phatic

Ashamed... When one is taken by surprise like that, in front of an audience, a very friendly one, but still...
RR = *Elab*: explanation

Friendly?
Phatic

Yes. But still, you know, I feel taken by surprise. I wasn't expecting this when I came, you understand. I hadn't prepared myself for it.
RR = *Elab*: correction

You hadn't prepared yourself?
S = Reactive

That's it!
RR = *QAP*

And, not being prepared, what does that feel like?
S = Cooperative

Not being prepared, that makes me look like a fool! It leaves me kind of looking stupid in front of you, in front of...
RR = *Elab*: explanation

You have this impression?
S = Directive

I have the very clear impression because... well... of being sort of an imbecile, of not knowing what to say.
RR = *Elab*: explanation

But you tell me that it's up to me to ask you questions?
S = Constructive/Detour

Yes. Yes because you told me "talk to me!". That's all you told me. You asked me the question "talk to me!". Yes, but about what? That's fine with me to talk just like that, about one subject or an... but just about this and that, it's...

$RR = QAP$

So you'd like it to me who chooses? why shouldn't it be you?
S = Constructive

Ah! If I may! You tell me "talk to me!", but about what? Anything?

Retort

Why shouldn't it be you who chooses?
S = Cooperative

Oh sure, but about some random topic.

$RR = R - Elab$

Hm!
Phatic
An a priori mark of satisfaction The goal has been reached, and the patient begins to talk about himself End of the opening phase of the dialogue (long in this example), which is to establish the goal and topic of conversation. To reach this point, a set of strategies have been implemented by D(doctor)

$G_P = F_D^K P$

Topic1 = context (health, socio-familial)

For example, why I checked into the hospital... I checked into the hospital for observation for a prepyloric ulcer I've had for ten years, which hasn't been going very well, at least recently, and I went under observation for tests to see if they have to operate on me or not. I've been seeing Dr. Mignon for ten years. Not for ten years but for a few years, at least, always in the same department, since before it was Professor Vilain, before... now Professor Bonfils, and what can I say, I'm waiting for the results to know if they'll operate on me or not. On top of that, I have a bad gall bladder and I'm diabetic. Not much, one twenty, but still, I'm a little diabetic. It's hereditary, my father had it, my mother had it, my father died of it... there you go!

$RR = Elab$

Topic = Stay(me, hospital) $\wedge$ Illness(me, ulcer+gallbladder+diabetes) $\wedge$ Heridity(me, father)

(M1) Your father died of it?
S = Constructive

He died diabetic; he was 82 years old after all. **(P1)**

$RR = QAP$

Topic+ = Death(father, age 82) $\wedge$ Illness(father, diabetes)

After all?
S = Reactive

It's a pretty good age. My mother is 86, she's still alive, and me, I'll be 55 at the end of the year and I'm retiring. **(P2)**

$RR = Elab$

Topic+ = Alive(mother, age 86) $\wedge$ Alive(me, 55ans) $\wedge$ Plan(me, retirement)

You're retiring?
Phatic

On the trains, we retire at 55. **(P3)**
RR = *Elab*: clarification
Topic++ = Profession(me, SNCF)

On the trains?
Phatic

So I'm going to leave Paris, to go get some fresh air in the countryside. I have a house in the countryside, in Saumur, and I can't wait to get out of Paris, because gets suffocating and I hope it will do me good because every time I go there, I feel much better than staying here. I feel alive, in the countryside, and I never have stomach pains like when I come back to Paris after my weekends, or well, whenever I come back to Paris. There it is, it's starting again, twisting me up... Well it's... Well it doesn't hurt much, but well, let's say it's heavy, it's... I feel heavy, while in the countryside, it doesn't bother me... what do you want me to say? And that's all. **(P4)**
RR = *C*
Closing of first Topic T1. New Topic T2 = (me, health, countryside, Paris, suffocation)

Yes.
Phatic

Refining of Topic "health"
Well, now, what do you want me to talk about? There would be plenty for hours to just say anything... What would you like me to tell you, sir! I think they won't operate on me, because it's never pleasant. If I have a treatment... I followed it before, you know, more or less. It's sort of my fault, treatment for the stomach, there were some times, two or three months, where I did not take bismuth because I did not feel bad, then you understand that...
So, if it's really necessary, as Professor Vilain said, that it was for life with bismuth, I'll take it for life, but now, if he talks about operations, well then I have no idea. In any case, if they don't operate on me, I decided to retire, not to take on any more. My wife will leave too since I live at the hospital, my wife is at the hospital; she's an administrator by the way and she will try to retire at the same time as me. That's why, with both of us civil servants, we'll manage very well, we'll have a good retirement. I don't know, it's been 8 years that I've lived at Bichat, you know, I'm starting to... **(P5)**
RR = *Elab*
Topic+ = Health(me, treatment+operation)
Appearance of another Topic. Context(Spouse)
Topic3 = Profession(spouse, administrator) ∧ Residence(me+spouse, hospital) ∧ Plan(spouse, retirement)

(M6) That you've been living at Bichat?
S = Cooperative

Digressions on places/pollution

Yes, I'm starting to... I feel that it's still not the air I need, to know about all that happens here, we know quite a bit about it. **(P6)**
RR = I
New Topic T4= Bichat

(M7) It's not the air you need?
S = Reactive

Well, you know, it's still the air in Paris anyway, you know! **(P7)**
RR = IQAP

All that happens there, you were saying?
S = Directive

Well, it's a real city here, it's just as... After all, you see, there were at least four or five hundred cars; there are at least three thousand, the fifteen hundred people who pass through the hospital every day. It's a real city, if you count the patients, the..., the..., the nurses, everyone, it's a real town, this hospital! So you know, it's like if we were in Paris, it's sort of fouled. **(P8)**
RR = Elab: clarification

Fouled?
Phatic

With all these cars around, I can't even... Sometimes I can't even find a parking space, so, I'm telling you! I just put the car anywhere, it's unbearable...
What else to tell you? I have a sedentary job, in the offices, so, you know, the air in Paris, like I told you, it's... then on top of that in the overheated offices... that's why I'm hoping to retire, then leave for the countryside. **(P9)**
RR = Elab: explanation

(M9) You talk a lot about the air, the fouled air, the air in the offices!
S = Directive
Sub-goal "get the patient to talk about himself using his pet subjects"

Yes, because we're in the polluted air and it's true, it's true! I had an experience once coming back from Paris by car, with a blue sky but then when we looked toward Paris, the sky was grey. It's an experience I had. Maybe I'm not alone in having had it, but when you look at Paris, you see a completely grey sky while above you, the sky is blue. So obviously the air is polluted or fouled and we're all affected by it. **(P10)**
RR = QAP
Topic 4 Context(Pollution)
Topic4 = Pollution(Paris, air)

There's some bad stuff out there!
Phatic

Pardon?

There's some bad stuff out there.

Well, all of it together, gasoline, factories, we already have quite a lot around Bichat, in Saint-Ouen, the smoke, all of it, you know!
RR = *Elab*: explanation
Topic+ = Pollution(Bichat, air)

What's still difficult or painful..., for you? What was there that's still difficult or painful for you?
"Pet subjects" goal satisfied ⇒ Return to main goal,
S = Directive

For me, personally?
$RR = Elab_q$

Mm-hm!
S = Reactive

That requires some reflection. I don't know what to say just like that. I can't answer you because... difficult, everything is difficult, life is difficult, uh... I can't, I won't be able to explain to you how I feel, what I feel.
RR = *IQAP*

How you feel?
S = Cooperative

Yes... it's difficult. I can't really say anything, I can't find the word.
Change of context Topic = Context(Memory)
RR = *Elab*: explanation

Yes, what do you mean?
S = Directive

Yes, a lot. It's a fault of mine, it has been for several years already.
RR = *Elab*: explanation

How so?
S = Directive

Well, I could express myself very clearly before, but for a while now, there's... words elude me. Just like that, yep! Even simple words sometimes!
RR = *C*

For a while now, words elude you?
S = Reactive

Oh, for a while now, yes, for several years already.
RR = *C*

How does that happen?
S = Directive

Well... you notice, the... the... these are actually pretty complicated words, but sometimes, I find I just don't know how to say... a table, an ashtray. I... I'm looking for the word. But there are times! It happens to me once in a while.
RR = *C*

And so now, to describe a little bit what's happening within you, you lack the words, when I talk about difficult or painful things?
S = Cooperative

There's so much! There's so much! What do..., I'm not an orator!
RR = R

You've lived through a lot.
S = Directive

Yes, since the age of sixteen, yes.
RR = IQAP

Do the words to talk to me still escape you? How is it going with me since the beginning?
S = Directive
Sub-goal, get the patient to talk about himself using the situation

Well, you're embarrassing me, because...
RR = R

Explain that a little!
S = Directive

Well you're embarrassing me because... you're embarrassing me because, I'll tell you, because we haven't had a precise topic, a topic to discuss. You told me to talk to you, I repeat myself again... so now! Caught off guard.
RR = Elab: clarification

You don't like being caught off guard?
S = Reactive

No, no! I like to know what's happening... This morning, I didn't count on coming here, oh no!
RR = QAP

Does this remind you of something, this idea of being caught off guard, or the way it happens here?
S = Constructive

No.
RR = QAP

It's never happened to you?
S = Negotiated
The doctor, not satisfied with this complete answer, reformulates the question to work around the *QAP*.

Nothing comes to me at the moment. Maybe, but it's not coming to me. Maybe there are some cases, but...
RR = PQAP
This time the patient's partial answer leaves an opening for exploring the theme.

So, at the beginning, you found yourself caught off guard, embarrassed, not knowing what topic to discuss, and you have the impression that it's still the same thing? That you're still embarrassed?
S = Cooperative

Yes. Yes, because we always end up at the same place. What do you want me to talk about. Since... Let's say you want me to tell you about everything starting from the age of three... well, up until the age of fifty-five years, ok then, I can talk to you for two hours, if you want... About things that.... it wouldn't make any sense.
RR = QAP

It wouldn't make any sense?
Phatic

Well yeah, why would that interest you, from the age of three, what I've done until now? How would that interest you?
$RR = Elab_q$

But it would.
S = Reactive

For your profession surely, but for me, what would that get me?
RR = I

[.... continuation of the dialogue] (**M20**) I'm going to ask you one more thing, to tell me about a dream, the kinds of dreams that we have at night while we sleep.
Main goal
S = Directive
Introduction of a new topic by the psychoanalyst.

Yes. I don't dream very much, but when I dream, then, it's exactly like my father, I'm always flying!
RR = QAP
(**P20**)
Topic = Dream(me, flying) ∧ Dream(father, flying)

Yes.
Phatic

I feel myself leave.
RR = C
(**P21**)

(**M21**) Yes. But do you remember an anecdote from one of these dreams?
S = Directive

No. It's always the same. I feel myself flying and saying... having the impression of always being above the trees, you know, soaring like that, and it's always the same. Otherwise, I don't dream much. I don't have nightmares.
(**P22**)
RR = QAP

Fine. Well, I'm going to let you go back upstairs.
S = Directive

Goodbye, ladies and gentlemen, I'm sorry if...
RR = R
Closing of the Topic

....

13.6.2 Analysis

We begin by showing some statistics of the doctor's acts, over a total of 47 interventions:

	Directive	Reactive	Coop.	Const.	Negotiated	Phatic
Number	16	7	6	5	1	12
%	35	15	13	5	0.02	26

The doctor uses a lot of phatics to support his strategies, with a mainly directive approach. The further the dialogue advances the more directive it becomes (i.e., with a greater proportion of directives toward the end of the dialogue).

Regarding his goals:

The first goal—to get the patient to talk about himself—is only reached after 16 interventions, which is relatively long. To achieve this first goal, the doctor starts by being directive but does not succeed, and must vary his strategies by being more cooperative or constructive, as shown in the following table.

	Directive	Reactive	Coop.	Const.	Negotiated	Phatic
Number	4	1	3	3	0	5
%	25	1	21	21	0	32

The doctor then lets the patient talk about himself for nine dialogue turns (taking a mainly reactive strategy with phatics), and orients him toward a first sub-goal "get to know his pet subjects" which he achieves in two interventions (directive and phatic). After this, he aims for a second sub-goal "get to know his difficulties" which he achieves in nine interventions (essentially still in a directive style), then finally he approaches a third sub-goal "get to know the feeling of the situation" of the patient with the same strategy, which has by now been well established. Towards the end of the dialogue, the doctor sets up and achieves a final goal "hear about a dream" with a completely directive approach, and quickly concludes the dialogue by a single and somewhat abrupt directive.

All the goals of the dialogue are satisfied for the doctor, who has put into place a progressively dominant directive strategy. As is often the case in psychoanalysis, he uses phatics to encourage the patient when he is on a path that satisfies the doctor. In this analysis, we recognize a lot of "classic" behavior for this type of doctor during a consultation.

The patient, meanwhile, has no particular goal in the beginning, and takes time to understand and accept the physician's goal before definitively adopting it. In this first part, his rhetoric is based on elaborations ($Q - Elab$, $R - Elab$, $Elab$, $Q - Sub$), a few partial responses (QAP), and a Retort that seems to challenge the questioning of the doctor. In the second part, the patient essentially constructs his discourse by elaboration of a series of topics, mainly QAP and $Elab$:explanation (see Fig. 13.3). We will note that there are not many digressions (I), which may be a

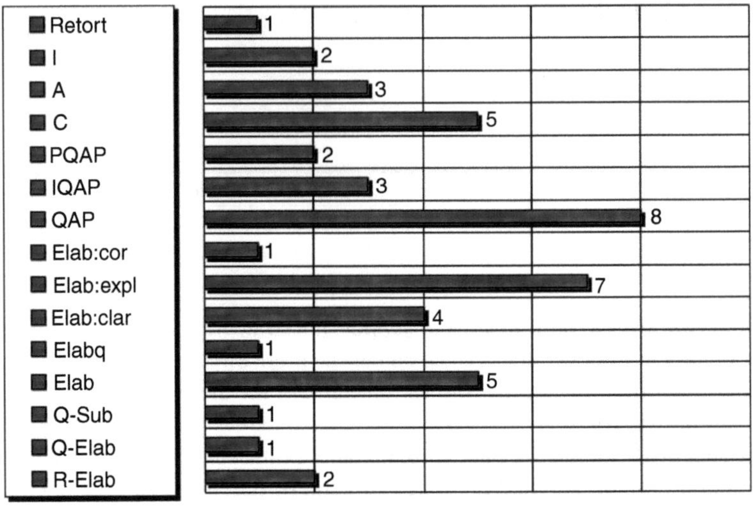

Fig. 13.3 The distribution of rhetorical relations is a sign of a certain behavior in the dialogue

sign that the patient is not psychotic, but it would be imprudent to assert this without being a specialist. The patient does not make many corrections either.

The Structure of the Dialogue Is the Following

Opening: Topic0 = Consultation
Negotiation of goals $G_p = 0, G_D = F^{FK} pP$
Body of the dialogue
    Topic1 = Context (Health, socio-familial)
    Topic1 = Stay(me, hospital) ∧ Illness(me, ulcer+gallbladder+diabetes) ∧ Heridity(me, father)
        Topic+ = Death(father, age 82) ∧ Illness(father, diabetes)
        Topic+ = Alive(mother, age 86) ∧ Alive(me, 55ans) ∧ Plan(me, retirement)
            Topic++ = Profession(me, SNCF)
    Topic2 = Health(me, suffocation)
        Topic2 += Health(me, treatment+operation)
    Topic3 = Context(Spouse)
    Topic3 = Profession(spouse, administrator) ∧ Residence(me+spouse, hospital) ∧ Plan(spouse, retirement)
    Topic4 = Context(Pollution)
    Topic4 = Pollution(Paris, air)
        Topic4 += Pollution(Bichat, air)
    Topic5 = Context(Memory)
    ....
    Topic6 = Context(Dream)
    Topic6 = Dream(me, flying) ∧ Dream(father, flying)
Closure: Closing of the Topic

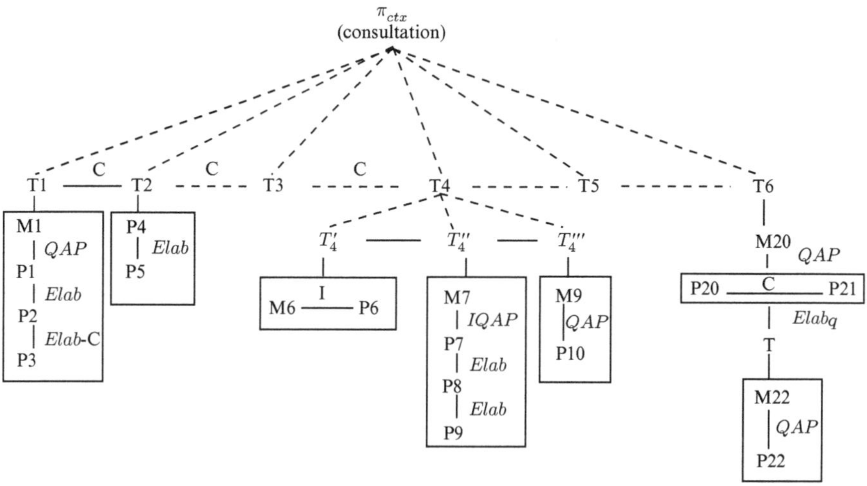

Fig. 13.4 SDRS of the dialog

It is made up of an opening, a negotiation phase, the body of the dialogue proper as a series of exchanges related to different topics, and finished with a relatively brief closing. There is no re-activation of topics during the dialogue, so the sequence is linear.

13.6.2.1 The Global SDRS

For better readability, we present only four topics in detail: T1, T2, T4, T6.

The SDRS (see Fig. 13.4) is composed of six topics T1 to T6, coordinated by relations of Continuation. Topics T1 and T2 are formed mainly by sequences of subordinate elaborations by the patient on his own statements. The topic is developed "in depth". Topic T4 is itself composed of three coordinated sub-topics. At the end of dialogue, topic T6 contains more resolving answers (QAP relations). It consists of two question-answer pairs connected by an elaboration.

13.7 Discussion and Conclusion

The analysis in terms of dialogue goals and strategies clearly allows the process underlying the entanglement of dialogue and action to emerge. It highlights the process underlying the dialogue, the source of which is in the action (praxeology), but which is implemented in dialogue with a specific 'dialogue game'. Avoiding recourse to fixed rules of a dialogue schema, or any model of beliefs and intentions, this analysis of dialogue as a strategic game shows that dialogue is in itself an action-oriented practice. Thus, we show two interlocking games:

- The dialogue game (or conversational game)
- The action game (the world)

The strategies implemented in the dialogue game are subordinated to the pursuit of the action game, the psychological consultation; we cannot model the dialogue game without completely immersing it in the context of this action game in which it originates, and where its effects are produced. The dynamic of interaction, highlighted by the analysis of the participants' goals and strategies, reveals their tactics, along with their role. The structure of the topics shows the progressive co-construction of shared knowledge (what is said, negotiated, accepted or denied), while the arrangement of rhetorical relations reveals the details of this construction (the "how").

The structure of the dialogue shows the evolution of the action and its phases; the dialogue acts are the building blocks whose distribution can also be illuminating. Thus, by recalling Wittgenstein (1953) (on the purpose of language-games), "the speaking of language is part of an activity, or a form of life.", we can see that it is possible starting from a pragmatic analysis of a dialogue, to trace this activity back to a form of life (here, the consultation), which articulates the dialogue game as the "form of life" in which it is always immersed.

It is also interesting to note that a "classical" method of linguistic analysis (syntax, lexicon) of the same dialogue led to the following conclusions Pouder (1977, 1997): "The discursive polarities in relation are clearly differentiated at all levels, lexical, syntactic, inter-sentential—the therapist's speech exhibits specific features that distinguish it very clearly from the speech of patients. In certain aspects (e.g., syntactic), it resembles the speech of other interviews. In fact, it additionally turns out to be very specialized on the lexical level as soon as it goes beyond repetitions of patients' words. With respect to the spoken registers of modern French, the patient's discourse is similar to unplanned dialogues between middle class French speakers (common lexical and syntactic aspects): the patient speaks "like everyone" or at least like most people. The common claims of psychosomaticians concerning the language deficiencies of their patients are not substantiated at the linguistic level. We can not even relate the linguistic code of these patients to the restricted code of B. Bernstein. These discourses are all centered on the first person, exhibiting various levels of hierarchical structure. On the other hand, reality seems to pose a real problem for these patients, judging from the general arrangement of their stories. It is here that we run up against the inadequacy of a purely linguistic analysis; indeed, the deficiency of the language of psychosomatic patients is not properly characterized as a linguistic deficiency, but as a "functional" deficiency, but as such, it does not favor the integration of libidinal energies. In addition, it is usually analyzed in comparison to the 'richness' of other forms of discourse."

This concludes in favor of a pragmatic analysis of dialogue.

References

J.C. Anscombre, O. Ducrot, *L'Argumentation dans la langue* (Mandarga, Bruxelles, 1983)
N. Asher, A. Lascarides, *Logics of Conversation* (Cambridge University Press, Cambridge, 2003)
J. Caelen, Stratégies de dialogue, in *Conférence MFI'03 (Modèles Formels de l'Interaction)*, Lille, 2003. Cépaduès éd
J. Caelen, A. Xuereb, *Interaction et pragmatique: jeux de dialogue et de langage*. Collection science informatique et SHS (sous la direction de C. Garbay). Hermès éd., Paris, 2007, p. 332
O. Ducrot, *Le Dire et le Dit* (Éditions de Minuit, Paris, 1984)
H.P. Grice, Logic and conversation, in *Syntax and Semantics, Volume 3: Speech Acts*, ed. by P. Cole, J.L. Morgan (Academic, New York, 1975), pp. 41–58
B.J. Grosz, C.L. Sidner, Attention, intentions, and the structure of discourse. Comput. Linguist. **12**(3), 175–204 (1986)
D. Luzzati, *Recherches sur le dialogue Homme-Machine : modèles linguistiques et traitement automatique*. PhD thesis, Paris III, 1989. Thèse d'État
W.C. Mann, S. Thompson, Rhetorical structure theory: toward a functional theory of text organization. Text Interdiscip. J. Study Discourse **8**(3), 243–281 (1988)
H. Nguyen, J. Caelen, Generic manager for spoken dialogue systems, in *Proceedings of 7th Workshop on the Semantics and Pragmatics of Dialogue, DiaBruck*, Saarbrucken, 2003, ed. by I. Kruijff-Korbayova, C. Kosny
M.-Ch. Pouder, Étude linguistique du dialogue psychosomatique. *Langage et situations de communication* **26**(mai-juin), 104–123 (1977). Études de Linguistique Appliquée
M.-Ch. Pouder, Aspects pragmatiques de la modification des rôles discursifs dans une psychothérapie d'enfant (retard de parole et langage). *Rééducation orthophonique* **35**(191), 239–264 (1997)
L. Prévot, *Structures sémantiques et pragmatiques pour la modélisation de la cohérence dans des dialogues finalisés*. PhD thesis, Université Paul Sabatier, Toulouse, 2004
J.R. Searle, D. Vanderveken, *Foundations of Illocutionary Logic* (Cambridge University Press, Cambridge, 1985)
D. Vanderveken, *Meaning and Speech Acts* (Cambridge University Press, Cambridge, 1990)
D. Vanderveken, La logique illocutoire et l'analyse de discours, in *Le Dialogique*, ed. by D. Luzzati et al. (Peter Lang, Bern, 1997)
D. Vernant, *Du discours à l'action* (Presses Universitaires de France, Paris, 1997)
L. Wittgenstein, *Philosophical Investigations* (Blackwell, Oxford, 1953) (Transl. by G.E.M Anscombe)
A. Xuereb, J. Caelen, Topics dialogiques, in *Actes de TALN 2005, XIIème Conférence sur le Traitement Automatique des Langues Naturelles*, Dourdan, 2005, pp. 273–282

Chapter 14
Investigating Discourse Specificities in Schizophrenic Disorders

Michel Musiol and Frédéric Verhaegen

14.1 Introduction

Our aim is to help determine what the features of schizophrenic speech are, how they deviate from those of normal speech, and what accounts for the feeling that such speech constitutes 'crazy talk'. Confronted with a pathological conversation, any ordinary speaker intuitively feels that there are some incoherencies and discontinuities. Based on our view that verbal interaction is the "natural locus of symptom expression", our approach to schizophrenia is drawn from linguistics, pragmatics, cognitive psychology and discourse analysis. This approach allows us to uncover—in the most objective way possible—the discontinuities found in verbal interactions between a schizophrenic patient and a normal interlocutor. Our aim is, first, to detect discourse and dialogue discontinuities as objectively and "decisively" as possible (by "decisively", we mean that there is a high probability of finding pathological dysfunction behind the pathological behavior). We will then look at the potential relationship between these discontinuities and the syndrome's specificities, and at a more general level, we will discuss how they relate to the question of incoherence and thought disorders.

The model that we propose at this point in our investigation describes four clearly distinguishable types of discontinuity. The discontinuities we have detected can be ascribed to the patients' discursive and dialoguing behavior. They are

M. Musiol (✉)
MSH Lorraine (USR 3261) CNRS, ATILF (UMR 7118), Université de Lorraine,
44, avenue de la Libération, 54063 Nancy, France
e-mail: Michel.Musiol@univ-lorraine.fr

F. Verhaegen
MSH Lorraine (USR 3261) CNRS, Laboratoire APEMAC, EPSaM (EA 4360),
Université de Lorraine, Campus Lettres et Sciences Humaines, 3, Place Godefroy
de Bouillon, 54015 Nancy, France
e-mail: frederic.verhaegen@univ-lorraine.fr

M. Rebuschi et al. (eds.), *Interdisciplinary Works in Logic, Epistemology, Psychology and Linguistics*, Logic, Argumentation & Reasoning 3,
DOI 10.1007/978-3-319-03044-9_14, © Springer International Publishing Switzerland 2014

the formal pragmatic reflection, in the patients' discourse and dialogue, of the incongruous or even incoherent behavior likely to be exhibited by schizophrenics. The different types of discontinuity observed are compared empirically to some of the diagnostic and psychopharmacological specificities of the disorganized and paranoid syndromes. Our approach thus has some diagnostic power, as it is grounded in a well-informed clinical foundation and a methodology that consists of building models aligned with the modes of expression specific to these patients' language behaviors and language use during verbal interaction. Our approach provides an accurate picture of the impact of these specificities, and allows us to contemplate the possibility of interpreting these behaviors as a sign of an underlying perturbation of the processes through which schizophrenics understand and compute the communicative intentions of their interlocutor. Moreover, this chapter focuses on language production in schizophrenia as opposed to receptive language ability, occurring in discourse insofar as language production in schizophrenia is impaired mainly at the macrolinguistic level of processing. Schizophrenic speech is disordered and filled with irrelevant pieces of information and derailments. Such erratic discourse may be linked to an inability to use pragmatic rules as well as to cognitive deficits involving factors such as attention, action planning, ordering and sequencing (Marini 2008). Such deficits may also be tied into thought processes that address either the rationality of representational, meta-representational and intentional capacities or the thought-content itself (Amblard et al. 2014).

14.2 Symptomatological Characteristics of Schizophrenia

Schizophrenia is no doubt one of the most controversial psychotic disorders when it comes to describing the symptomatological characteristics (or syndrome groups) that define it. It has no syndrome-specific pathognomonic sign, and its etiology remains poorly understood. A century of inquiries supported by considerable progress, especially recent advancements in electrophysiology, imaging, molecular biology, eye-tracking and even cognitive psychology (including evolutionary psychology), have not yet supplied the needed answers. As a result, it is still impossible to come up with a single definition of schizophrenia. Even today, this disease remains an ill-defined reality. Many studies have suggested that one problem with schizophrenia is its heterogeneity (Heinrich 1993, to name but one), an idea supported not only by the discovery of the disease's multiple clinical manifestations but also and especially because it is difficult to find characteristics or features that are shared by all individuals diagnosed with this disease.

In this chapter, we will not address the issue of the potential cognitive or neuropsychological processes underlying the symptoms of schizophrenia. Whatever they may be, we believe that the illness will necessarily manifest itself in interactive and discursive settings, whether experimental or clinical; we hypothesize accordingly that under certain conditions—at least in the natural conditions of language use—the verbal behavior of schizophrenics is likely to reflect some important specificities of their disease (Musiol and Trognon 2000). Locating and analyzing any such specificities should improve diagnostic strategies in the medium term. Clinical research on schizophrenia has been making significant progress for nearly 40 years now. In the 1970s and 1980s, inquiries into the well-foundedness of its classification into clinical psychiatric subtypes (paranoid, disorganized, catatonic, etc.) paved the way for new descriptive models of the disease (Andreasen 1979, 1984; Andreasen and Olsen 1982; Crow 1980; Liddle 1987). The results of these increasingly numerous studies, were contradictory, however, so their heuristic relevance was to some extent discredited. The heterogeneity of such findings led investigators to steer their research towards the establishment of more accurate criteria so as to obtain greater homogeneity in the populations under study. The development of a number of clinical information-gathering methods aimed at producing more comprehensive symptom-assessment scales exemplifies this latter approach. New tools like Kay et al. (1987) PANSS (Positive and Negative Syndrome Scale) and Andreasen's (1983, 1984) SANS (Scale for the Assessment of Negative Symptoms) and SAPS (Scale for the Assessment of Positive Symptoms) became the first methods designed and used for the specific purpose of evaluating the negative and positive symptoms of schizophrenia. All of these early scales are still widely used today.

The work that produced these tools was based on psychometric analysis (mostly factor analysis). Schizophrenia was described first in two dimensions (Andreasen 1983, 1984; Andreasen and Olsen 1982; Crow 1980), then in three Liddle (1987): positive (or productive), negative (or deficient), and disorganized, i.e., characterized by formal thought disorders (impoverished and incoherent discourse). Schizophrenics also frequently suffer from cognitive deficits affecting their attention, memory, and executive functions. Such impairment can be massive and is relatively well correlated not only with negative-symptom severity, but also, though to a lesser extent, with positive-symptom severity (Berman et al. 1997; Harvey et al. 1996). These new directions proved promising and sparked considerable interest, thanks in part to their good diagnostic and statistical validity due to high rates of inter-judge reliability. These psychometric instruments have also been deemed very useful in evaluating the effectiveness of neuroleptic medication with or without pragmatic tools (Verhaegen and Musiol 2011). The idea that language abnormalities pervade the discourse of schizophrenic patients is now widely acknowledged by the scientific community. However, although language and communication disorders are among the most widely studied, they are hardly ever examined in an interactive context. Taking a classical clinical approach, Andreasen (1979) drew up an extensive inventory of these disorders based on the symptom-assessment scales she developed for describing the language-related anomalies specific to schizophrenic discourse. She picked such specificities from the verbal output of patients in clinical interviews, not with any formal tool but rather using psychiatric and DSM criteria. Her work is still valid today Bazin et al. (2002), Bazin et al. (2005), Liddle et al. (2002), and Olivier et al. (1997).

Clinical observation has also helped a great deal in describing these impairments. From the very first descriptions of schizophrenic symptoms, a preponderant concern was language, or even thought disorders (Bleuler 1993; Chaslin 1912; Kraepelin 1919). It was, in fact, within a language- and communication-centered Bleulerian perspective that Andreasen designed her scale for assessing dissociation (Scale for Assessment of Thought, Language and Communication or TLC) in an attempt to make the concept of "formal thought disorders" fully operational. Such disorders are indeed key symptoms for researchers and clinicians interested in the cognitive side of this complex mental illness. There have been more and more studies attempting to gain finer insight into the symptomatology of schizophrenia via a clinical approach. It has become clear, however, that although these concepts—"formal thought disorder", "incoherence", "disorganized thought"—have been addressed in terms of their relationship to language problems, little research has been conducted to look into how they really relate to language or verbal interaction.

14.3 Specificities of Schizophrenic Language

Instruments based on quantification, including psychometric scales, do not paint an accurate picture of the cognitive specificities of schizophrenic language and communication disorders. Such instruments are developed using a static methodology that is hardly compatible with the naturally dynamic aspects of communication. Furthermore, concepts such as "incoherence" and "formal thought disorders" are only defined in terms of the items included in the scales (Bazin et al. 2002; Andreasen and Grove 1986), i.e., solely in terms of the overt behaviors assumed to be associated with the concepts, with reference neither to the utterances and discourse contexts from which said behaviors arise, nor to the psycholinguistic and/or inferential types of cognitive processes that provide a basis for those behaviors. In parallel with this clinical and psychometric approach, a pragmatic and linguistic methodology also began to develop in the 1970s. It focused on the language and communication disorder in situ, with as much emphasis on the speech act itself as on the syntactic-semantic structure of the utterance or the contextual and co-textual dimensions of the uttering process, grasped in context (Chaïka 1974; Fromkin 1975; Labov and Fanshel 1977; Rochester and Martin 1979). By then the goal was to understand more than just the schizophrenic language disorder itself; researchers wanted to comprehend the impaired way in which schizophrenic individuals use language in a communicative setting (be it a clinical interview or therapy session). Over the past four decades, few have challenged the idea that one of the greatest difficulties (if not the greatest of all) presented by schizophrenic patients is pragmatic in nature: how they use signs in communicative contexts.

According to the linguist Elaine O. Chaïka (1974), schizophrenic language is caused by a disruption in the ability to order linguistic elements into meaningful structures. This disruption affects different levels of language at different times, even in the same patient, giving us six definable characteristics of schizophrenic speech:

- Sporadic disruption in the ability to match semantic features with sound strings comprising actual lexical items in the language;
- Preoccupation with too many of the semantic features of a word in discourse;
- Inappropriate noting of phonological features of words in discourse;
- Production of sentences according to phonological and semantic features of previously uttered words, rather than according to a topic;
- Disruption in the ability to apply rules of syntax and discourse;
- Failure to self-monitor, e.g., not noting errors when they occur.

The author assumes that "all of these characteristics suggest a disruption in the ability to apply those rules which organize linguistic elements, such as phonemes, words, and sentences, into corresponding meaningful structures, namely words, sentences, and discourse." There is also the possibility of a disruption in the hierarchy of linguistic rules (Chaïka 1974, p. 275). She explains, however, that the deviance of schizophrenic discourse cannot always be accounted for simply by intrusive word associations, intonation breaks, or pronominilization. These disruptions in the ability to apply linguistic rules do not affect all levels of speech at once, nor is any one level affected all the time. It becomes apparent that when a given level is affected, all the rules of that level are not equally affected.

According to further investigations, and as Fromkin argued in 1975, most of the linguistic deviations that Chaïka (1974) singles out as characteristic of schizophrenic speech also occur in normal production. It may be shown, says Fromkin, that except for the disruption of the sequencing of ideas in discourse, which can be attributed to non-linguistic factors (Fromkin 1975, p. 498), all these features are prevalent in normal speech, as exemplified by slips of the tongue and other commonplace speaking errors. Such questions are still under investigation in both linguistics (pragmatics) and cognitive psychopathology.

Chaïka explains that, viewed in comparison with normal language, the features of schizophrenic speech are (Chaïka 1990, p. 7): gibberish, neologisms, opposite speech and other erroneous retrievals of words, glossomania, rhyme and alliteration inappropriate to the context, intrusive errors, word salad and other syntactic disruptions, perseveration and other repetitions.

14.4 Features of Discontinuity in Schizophrenic Discourse

14.4.1 Grasping the Oddity of Schizophrenic Speech

The model of schizophrenic speech and incoherency that we propose in this chapter relies above all on discourse impairment and thematic disruption. We will assume at this point in our investigation that, as Chaïka pointed out in the early 1970s, the first rule violated in schizophrenic speech is that the speaker is supposed to pay attention only to those semantic features of an item that are pertinent to the context (i.e., the conversational context in our model); the second rule is that discourse is about something external to the elements of the discourse itself, usually termed "the topic". But like many other authors, Chaïka provides no specific tools for distinguishing between incoherent conversational contexts and coherent ones. Both aforementioned rules might be violated in different ways by schizophrenic speakers in discourse. The author provides no precise or specific axioms; instead she reasons in the following terms. As far back as her research on schizophrenic speech goes, Chaïka claims that the oddity of the patient's utterances seems mostly to be caused by aberrations in the discourse structure. She argues that there is no rigid boundary between the syntax of the sentence and the structure of the discourse. Certain rules, notably those of pronominalization, deletion, and selection of tense and aspect, obviously overlap, with the choice of alternatives governed both by the general context and by the requirements of individual sentences. Other rules, notably those governing the selection of markers used for temporal or logical sequencing, ("then", "finally", "thus", "this proves"), announcing a coming contradiction ("but", "however"), announcing a coming similarity ("and", "similarly"), or changing subjects ("not to change the subject", "Oh, that reminds me"), clearly belong to the discourse level. These rules enable a hearer to perceive sentences as belonging together, as being part of a whole. Normal discourse is centered on topics, what Ervin-Tripp calls (Ervin-Tripp 1964, p. 88) "the manifest content or referent of speech. This includes both gross categories such as subject matter (economics, household affairs, gossip) and the propositional content of utterances".

As Chaïka explains, we may observe that in schizophrenic conversational speech the propositional content of individual sentences is usually understandable, but not subordinated to any particular subject matter. Or, if it is, what is absent is the discourse markers necessary to show connections and orient listeners in relation to the topic. But it cannot truly be said that the schizophrenic's sentences are produced at random, for there is often an obvious connection between them. The problem is that the type of connection is not usual in normal discourse. Just as erratic discourse may be described according to constraints on logical sequencing as the test of social relevance (Fromkin 1975) or pragmatic relevance (Marini 2008; Musiol and Rebuschi 2011), what is being discussed in our method is not only linguistic competence but also social competence (or psychological competence), and the connection between the two.

14.4.2 Discontinuity, Dynamic Organization of Discourse and Hierarchical Structure

Few investigators have attempted to develop tools suited to the ways in which these disorders are expressed during verbal interaction, i.e., tools that take the process-based, dynamic nature of interaction into account. We thus propose to approach discourse disorders using a discontinuity-analysis model designed to account for schizophrenic language use and its interrelatedness both with patients' discourse and with their conversational behavior as manifested especially in the turn-taking process. The many properties of verbal interaction—turn-taking, reciprocity, the hierarchical and dynamic organization of constituents, and the interlocutory roles the communicating subjects occupy in the turn-taking process (initiator/speaker versus reacting-partner/listener)—should all be seen as factors likely to have an impact on our understanding of the significance of a symptom (Musiol 2009), such that verbal interaction can be regarded as the natural locus of expression for psychopathological phenomena. Because of its specific properties and the constraints it imposes on the interlocutors' behavior, the conversational transaction is the perfect place, methodologically speaking, to observe certain interpretive and inferential processes as well as their potential dysfunction. Our task here is to build a model describing the properties of the inferential processes underlying certain forms of incoherence in dialogue, which in our case should be revealed in the behaviors that schizophrenic and ordinary interlocutors are led to adopt. The idea is to build a dialogical and pragmatic model capable of accounting for the dynamic properties of verbal interaction sequences in which a discontinuity appears.[1] The skills examined are related not exclusively to the cognitive processes used to manage the properties extracted from the various components of the primary communication units that generate the verbal interaction. These units are elementary illocutionary acts, also called speech acts or discourse acts (Searle and Vanderveken 1985).

Empirically speaking, our research in this area over the past 15 or so years has enabled us to hypothesize that conversations involving a schizophrenic patient will exhibit many incongruities and discontinuities. Our studies have also led to the hypothesis that the discontinuities formally detected and delineated within a verbal interaction with a schizophrenic fall into two main categories (Musiol 2009), defined by the so-called hierarchical and functional properties of discourse structure. In terms of this "hierarchical and functional" structure of discourse (Roulet et al. 1985), let us call the first category "non-decisive" and the second "decisive". Only decisive discontinuities come with a high probability of finding pathological dysfunction behind the schizophrenic's behavior in the collective course of verbal action (Sect. 14.4.4).

The idea that discourse should be approached as a verbal interaction, at least in linguistics, dates back to the 1930s and Bakhtine and Volochinov (1930/1981), but the concept of hierarchical structure itself was introduced by Pike in the late 1960s (Pike 1967). Pike incorporates the study of language (both languages and discourse) into a unified theory of the structure of human behavior. In this theory, any event involving human behavior (a religious service, for example) can first be broken down into a certain number of constituents linked by specific functions; each constituent can in turn be broken down into lower-level constituents, and so on down to units of behavior such as the utterance or individual word. In this view—as sometimes in the linguistics of argumentation (Roulet et al. 1985) or the psychology of communication (Trognon 2002)—the discourse can be seen as

[1] Here, we interpret the notion of incoherence in terms of discontinuity.

a negotiation process, which makes its structure and function easier to grasp; the conversational transaction can then be considered the relevant unit of analysis. Let us define conversational transactions as follows: the most elementary component is the simple or complex speech act (the illocution); illocutions are defined as acts that apply forces to propositional content (Searle and Vanderveken 1985); the force defines the type of action (assertive, commissive, directive, declarative, expressive) that the speech act accomplishes, and can be described in terms of a number of properties, of which the illocutionary goal and its direction of fit are among the most important. At a higher level, conversational transactions are regular groups of structures, and structures are regular groups of exchanges and interventions. Accordingly, the exchange is the basic unit of the interlocution, where "basic" means that it is the smallest dialogical unit of the interaction (Goffman 1974; Roulet et al. 1985). From a microscopic point of view, the exchange is made up of interventions, and the minimal intervention is made up of speech acts (or illocutions). Macroscopically, on the other hand, exchanges and interventions are organized into structures. Some of these structures exhibit a typical organization and can be interpreted functionally as if realizing a collective intentionality. Examples include communicating information, debating, discussing, negotiating, leading a group, making a group decision, and conducting or participating in a clinical interview or a psychotherapy session.

14.4.3 Properties of Non-decisive Discontinuity

Earlier studies (see below) have shown that schizophrenic interlocutions (i.e., those involving a person diagnosed as schizophrenic) exhibit many discontinuities between adjacent segments of discourse at both the exchange and intervention levels. These discontinuities occur either when the schizophrenic patient is the second speaker and is attempting to adjust her reply to the interlocutor's previous intervention, or when the patient is expressing her train of thought while accomplishing multiple speech acts within the same discursive intervention. We will use the term "between-intervention breaks" to refer to coherence problems or discontinuities resulting from a violation of the chaining constraints that guarantee continuity between the speaking turns of two separate interlocutors in an exchange, and "within-intervention breaks" to refer to coherence problems or discontinuities resulting from violation of between-act chaining constraints within a single intervention.

Note that in discourse there exist complex interventions that contain subparts made up of one or more embedded interaction exchanges (Roulet et al. 1985). Failure to satisfy any of these constraints whatsoever is enough to produce a discontinuity. Also note that chaining constraints apply locally first, between adjacent speaking turns, but the possibility of embedded exchange sequences authorizes deferred constraint satisfaction (until after such a sequence is over), which then takes place farther along in the discourse. It is also possible to recursively double up embedded sequences (one can always make a parenthetical remark within another parenthetical remark), which means that the interlocutors must be capable of managing a recursive exchange structure, and that the formal analyst of the exchange must be able to take its hierarchical structure into account. To be exact, one must make the distinction between proximal breaks, which result from the violation of a chaining constraint between adjacent interventions, and distal breaks, which occur between non-adjacent interventions. Both occur insofar as the intervention called the speaker's initiative contains the directing utterance that conveys the hypothetical speaker's intended meaning; the listener's reactive intervention contains the directing utterance that carries the linguistic trace of the addressee's interpretation of the initial directing utterance.

The non-decisive nature of incoherence thus appears at the transaction level in two types of structures, called "between-intervention breaks" and "within-intervention breaks".

Below we present a non-decisive discontinuity exemplifying a between-intervention break. We hypothesize that we can account for chaining phenomena in speech using linguistic rules. There exist, in discourse, chaining rules associated with the correct formation of exchanges (Roulet et al. 1985); these rules are found in the form of constraints. For Roulet and colleagues, constraints associated with the correct formation of exchanges are expressed through four conditions: the "thematic condition", the "propositional-content condition", the "illocutionary condition" and the "argumentative-orientation condition". We will draw on these constraints to establish the notion of discontinuity proposed below.

14.4.3.1 Discontinuity of the Sequence

These are, by definition, discontinuities in exchanges consisting, discursively, of a pair of adjacent interventions (Ii, Ij) the second of which, Ij, is not in a relation of continuity with the intervention that precedes it (Ii) in the conversation. The first element, Ii, is seen as a source variable that imposes constraints on the second element, Ij. Following Roulet et al. (1985), the source variable(Ii) thus defines the set of all between-intervention constraints linked to a question with a closed set of possible responses. These constraints are as follows:

- *Thematic condition*: obligation to reply on the theme addressed in the question.
- *Propositional-content condition*: obligation to give a reply whose content is related to the question's content in an implicative, antonymic, or paraphrastic way.
- *Illocutionary condition*: obligation to express the content of one's reply in the corresponding illocutionary mode.
- *Argumentative-orientation condition*: obligation to reply in the expected way, i.e., to confirm the content of the question or its argumentative orientation.

We posit that discontinuity exists as soon as the second element in the pair does not totally or partially satisfy the constraints imposed by the first element (Fig. 14.1).

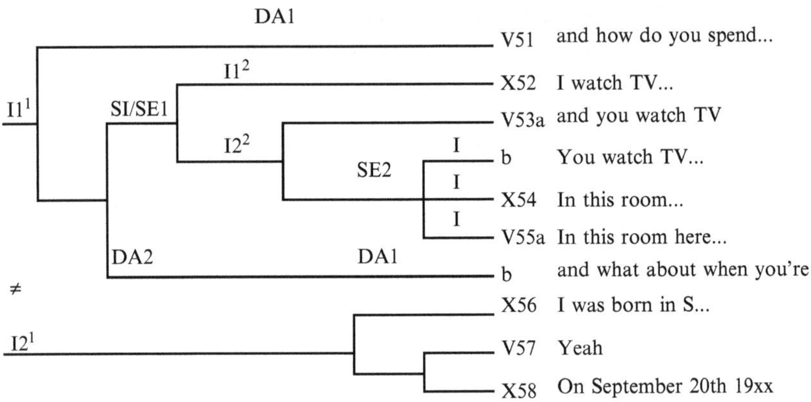

Legend:
SI1: Subordinate Intervention 1.
SI/SE1: subordinate exchange.
I1[1]: complex intervention 1 (principal structure on the left and subordinate structure on the right).
I2[1]: complex intervention 2 (principal structure on the left and subordinate structure on the right).
DA1: directing actin each principal complex intervention, i.e., V51 and X56.
SI/SE1: subordinate intervention / subordinate exchange 1.
SE2: subordinate exchange 2.
V: interlocutor V.X: interlocutor X. #: discontinuity.

Fig. 14.1 Hierarchical diagram of Example 1 with commentary

14.4.3.2 Example 1 (X is the Schizophrenic Interlocutor)[2]

V51 : (. . .) et qu'est-ce que vous faites de vos journées sinon (↑) +5+
X52 : Je regarde la télé
V53 : Vous regardez la télé et vous regardez la télé où (↑)
X54 : Dans la salle là
V55 : Dans la salle là ici et sinon quand vous n'êtes pas ici (↑) lorsque vous êtes ailleurs
X56 : Je suis né S. (ville)
V57 : Ouais
X58 : Le 20 septembre 19xx (. . .)

[2]Transcription conventions: (. . .) stands for the beginning or end of a conversational sequence; (→) stands for prolonged pronunciation of a linguistic sound; (↑) stands for rising intonation; (↓) stands for falling intonation; (inaudible) means that the passage was inaudible (sometimes with duration indicated); capital letters mean that the speaker stressed the word; +5+ stands for a silence of 5 s. Information likely to be important for understanding and analyzing the transcription is given in parentheses. Ambiguous passages are shown in brackets. For ethical reasons, names, places, and dates have been changed to guarantee the anonymity of all participants.

This exchange consists of two principal interventions ($I1^1$ and $I2^1$), corresponding to two conversational contributions from two different speakers, starting with the normal interlocutor (hetero-initiated from the patient's point of view). This first intervention, $I1^1$, is considered complex. It contains five speaking turns (V51 to V55), and is made up of a directing intervention (represented by intervention V51/DA1, a first-level directing act) and a subordinate structure, SI1, which takes place between X52 and V55. This subordinate intervention will be called complex too (following Roulet et al. 1985); it consists of a directing act, V55b/DA2 (second-level directing act in the whole structure $I1^1$), and a subordinate exchange, SI/SE1 (X52-V55a), which constitutes its subordinate part insofar as V55b retroactively subordinates this substructure (namely SI/SE1) and inhibits the schizophrenic's explicative development. Because the normal interlocutor's intervention, $I2^1$, unfolds between X56 and X58 (with a directing constituent conveyed by X56),[3] one can assume that $I1^1$'s directing component is carried by the utterance acts performed in DA1 (V51) and DA2 (V55b) as a directive type of complex speech act as [DA1-DA2] would do: "*How do you spend your time when you're not here?*".

A hierarchical and functional analysis of this sequence thus assigns X56 the role of initiative-interpretive reaction to the initiating directing component. A discontinuity nevertheless appears; the break is the result of the lack of continuity between $I1^1$/DA1-DA2 (V51/V55b) and $I2^1$/DA1 (X56).

According to our definition of the discontinuity of the sequence (above), V51/V55b (I1/DA1-DA2) is the first element in the pair, Ii, and X56 (I2/DA1) is the second element in the pair, Ij. The discontinuity is generated by the violation of three out of four conditions: thematic (the patient introduced a new topic), propositional content, and argumentative orientation (the new topic actually introduced a new discourse universe). The second element in the pair, Ij, was an unexpected response to the first element, Ii, in the framework of the general theme of the conversational transaction introduced by the normal interlocutor.

14.4.3.3 The Specificity of Non-decisive Discontinuous Sequences

This discontinuity, however, as in any 'between-intervention break' might be called non-decisive. Unfortunately, such a pragmatic and linguistic analysis provides no certification that the schizophrenic interlocutor was cognitively incoherent insofar as the he or she was simply insufficiently cooperative (or not cooperative at all). Under this hypothesis, discontinuities of the non-decisive type may be linked to cognitive dysfunction affecting, for example, the a person's conversational capacities or

[3]The utterance act performed in X56, "*I was born in S*" is the constituent which, given the argumentative structure of I2, should in theory satisfy the discursive constraints imposed by $I1^1$'s directing component.

cognitive-linguistic processes (intentional, inferential, and so on). But according to available formalizations of such discursive and dialogical phenomena, we are not justified in assuming the existence of an impairment.

This evaluation is equally relevant for within-intervention break discourse sequences, which may be described as involving non-decisive within-intervention chaining constraints that pertain to the subject's coordination of her own discourse. These are discourse planning constraints, and planning operates at various levels depending on the complexity of the discourse (Musiol 2009).

14.4.4 Properties of Decisive Discontinuity

In our model's current state of development, there are two types[4] of decisive discontinuity. We call the first type "conversational gear-shifting" (Trognon 1987; Trognon and Musiol 1996) and the second "defective conversational initiative" (Musiol 2009; Verhaegen and Musiol 2011). By analyzing numerous sequences from pathological verbal interactions, we were able to discern several characteristics of the type of discontinuity called manifest or decisive (Musiol 2009). Although a patient's utterance discontinuity or discourse incongruity may be counteracted in conversation by his interlocutor's verbal behavior, it is clear that conversational discontinuities of the within- or between-intervention type retain some degree of non-decisiveness. Only conversational gear-shifting and sequences containing conversational initiative defectiveness can currently be seen as transactions wherein the patient's behavior might be considered "incoherent". Furthermore, the mere fact of detecting incoherence does not imply that there is a thought disorder, and therefore does not itself authorize an interpretation of this deficient interlocutionary behavior in terms of dysfunctional thought. What we do hypothesize, however, is that the detection of *decisive* incoherence reflects an intermediate stage, i.e., *a sufficient but non-necessary condition* for any attempted interpretation in terms of psychopathology. Under this hypothesis, discontinuities of the decisive type are a sign of cognitive dysfunction affecting, for example, cognitive-linguistic processes, cognitive-inferential processes, or the interface between the two. The absence of such discontinuities in a corpus is not equivalent to the absence of any given pathology (the model may simply be insensitive to it).

Thus, the decisive nature of incoherence becomes manifest at the transaction level in two types of structures:

- In an exchange, understood a priori as a balanced dialogic unit involving a speaker (e.g., a patient) opposite his/her interlocutor (e.g., a therapist); the conversational transaction is structured on the basis of at least three symmetrical directing moves (conversational gear-shifting);

[4] A third type of decisive discontinuity will be published in 2013.

- In a complex intervention, understood as an asymmetrical dialogic unit wherein the argumentation of one interlocutor (e.g., the patient) overrides that of his/her addressee; the conversational transaction is analyzed on the basis of hierarchical and functional relations between at least three discursive segments detected in the main discourse; the hierarchical and functional relations between these three or more constituents subsume and support the unfolding of the interlocutor's argumentation (defective conversational initiative).

14.4.4.1 Conversational Gear-Shifting as a Type of Decisive Discontinuity

Discontinuities of the conversational gear-shifting type disrupt the turn-taking process while sequentially satisfying the chaining constraints of two directing interventions. They are characterized by a surreptitious change in the course of action, instigated by the speaker (the schizophrenic patient) despite the fact that she was the original initiator. As a result of this, the referential context changes without any indication of that change expressed by the speaker. Conversational gear-shifting can in fact be formally described in the following manner. Let I1, I2, and I3 be three interventions (directing interventions) that follow each other in a conversation, although not necessarily consecutively. Of the three component pairs in this sequence, (I1, I2), (I1, I3), (I2, I3), two exhibit continuity and one exhibits discontinuity. The continuous pairs are (I1, I2) and (I2, I3). Intuitively, these pairs exhibit continuity because their components—for example, I1 and I2 for the pair (I1, I2)—belong to the same discourse universe. However, the thematic universes of (I1, I2) and (I2, I3) are disjoint, albeit non-contradictory. Furthermore, abstractly speaking, the meaning of I2 is the union of the meanings at play in (I1, I2) and (I2, I3). It thus seems that this three-intervention sequence has formed two parallel thematic series, with I2 serving as a switch from one series to the other. This is precisely what makes the (I1, I3) pair discontinuous. In switching from the first series to the second, I2 loses some of its properties.

Two sets of properties typically characterize a conversational component. The first includes the semantic-pragmatic properties attached to the component's literal meaning; illocutionary force belongs to this set. The second set includes those properties that describe how the component fits into the organization of the conversation, such as whether the component is directing or subordinate. So, the meaning of I2 in the second series now retains only the semantic-pragmatic properties of this element, as though I2 could somehow be withdrawn from the conversational structure to which it belongs in order to be treated abstractly and literally (Trognon and Musiol 1996). Analyses of specific cases of conversational gear-shifting can be found in Musiol and Rebuschi (2011) and Verhaegen and Musiol (2011).

14.4.4.2 Defective Conversational Initiatives as a Type of Decisive Discontinuity

Our model involves a second type of decisive discontinuity called a "defective conversational initiative". Granted, this type of within-intervention discontinuity consists of chainings that sequentially satisfy the interactional constraints governing the organization of the exchange-level subcomponents of the complex transaction unit. Yet it specifically involves discontinuities that are inherent in the hierarchical and functional relations governing the sequentialization of speech acts at different levels (in that an act can impose interactive constraints on the constituent following or even preceding it, while still being dependent upon it hierarchically and functionally), which subsume or support the argumentation of the interlocutor who initiated the conversational transaction, e.g., the schizophrenic patient.

The definition of the defective conversational initiative discontinuity type that we propose (Musiol 2009) assumes that it is possible to account for chaining phenomena in speech using linguistic rules (Roulet et al. 1985). Here, we rely on chaining constraints illustrated by Roulet and colleagues using three conditions: the thematic condition, the argumentative-relation condition, and the argumentative-orientation condition.

14.4.4.3 Discontinuity of the Sequence

Hierarchically and functionally speaking, within-intervention constraints pertain to the proper formulation of interventions. Roulet's book defines them as follows (Roulet et al. 1985).

- *Thematic condition*: obligation in the intervention to pursue the object of discourse presented in the intervention's first constituent, whether implicitly or explicitly.
- *Argumentative-relation condition*: obligation to pursue the intervention using a constituent capable of entering into an argumentative relation with (being an argument or conclusion of) the intervention's first constituent.
- *Argumentative-orientation condition*: obligation, within the intervention, to continue with a constituent that does not contradict the argumentative orientation of the intervention's first constituent.

A complex intervention exhibiting discontinuity is theoretically composed of various act-level components, exchange-level components, and intervention-level components. These various components may be nested (e.g., an intervention can contain an exchange as a subpart of itself) and combined into more complex units (hierarchically and functionally interrelated). We will call these units the subcomponents of the complex intervention. These units are deemed relevant to analyzing this type of conversational transaction, and are related to each other via domination relations at the rhetorical level: a given subcomponent of the complex intervention always either directs or is subordinate to one or more associated units. In addition, each potential subcomponent has its own internal coherence (if it consists of more than one speech act) and is functionally dependent on the subcomponents that surround it both upstream and downstream, but here again, in a more or less distant way. The functions operating inside a subcomponent are necessarily of the interactional and interactive type (they must satisfy both between- and within-intervention constraints), but the functions that associate the subcomponents amongst each other are solely of the interactive type.

Sequences exhibiting conversational initiative defectiveness contain at least three directing acts, e1, e2, e3, in a hierarchical and functional relation of domination derived from simple or complex intervention-level constituents. The domination relation defines three pairs [e1, e2], [e2, e3], and [e1, e3] whose dialogical rationality is such that the first element in each pair, e (the source element) puts the second element, e′ (the target element) in a strategic interactive relationship with itself that is based on three conditions: the thematic condition, whereby e′ must implicitly or explicitly continue with the object of discourse presented in e; the argumentative-relation condition, whereby e′ must be an argument or a conclusion of e; and the argumentative-orientation condition, whereby e′ must not contradict e in any way. Conversational initiative defectiveness is considered to exist if e3 does not satisfy one or more of the three interactive conditions imposed on it by e2 in the pair [e2, e3] or by e1 in the pair [e1, e3], or if e3 does not satisfy one of more of the three interactive conditions imposed on it by e2 in the pair [e2, e3] and e2 does not satisfy one or more of the three interactive conditions imposed on it by e1 in the pair [e1, e2] (Fig. 14.2).

14.4.4.4 Example 2 (J Is the Schizophrenic Interlocutor)

This hierarchical and functional diagram reveals a complex structure. The intervention will be called self-initiated—in this case, initiated by the schizophrenic patient. It can be subdivided into two parts. The first has a single constituent, J142, which is the transaction's directing constituent at the intervention level. The second is a complex exchange-level constituent that progresses through eight other speaking turns in the transaction; it is the subordinate component of the exchange-level transaction that extends from V143 to J150.

The two directing constituents of this exchange are V143, a simple intervention (I1) performed by the normal interlocutor; and a complex intervention (I2), which runs from J144 to J150 and is itself made up of two complex parts: DI2, conveyed by speech act J144a—an act of confirmation and the directing element of this intervention; and SI2, a subordinate intervention that progresses across J144b and J150d. The second part of this intervention will also be called complex. Its dynamic progression from J144b to J150d unfolds upon first analysis via two subcomponents, themselves endowed with a complex structure: SI2-D (J144b to J144f) and SI2-S (J144g to J150d). The first-level directing act of this constituent is accomplished in J144b, i.e., "*well somebody practically knocked me over*". Only as the discursive segments of this complex intervention (SI2) progress and are each linked together in turn do we gradually uncover the salient features of the defectiveness of the patient's conversational initiative. Statement 144b will be called the directing act (DA1) of the first-level directing constituent of this complex intervention-level component. Likewise, 144b is the directing constituent of directing intervention SI2-D, which itself forms the directing part of the complex component (SI2). The SI2-D substructure thus dominates SI2-S, itself highly complex, and as such dominates the key act of this substructure, here again called "directing". We are referring to the act

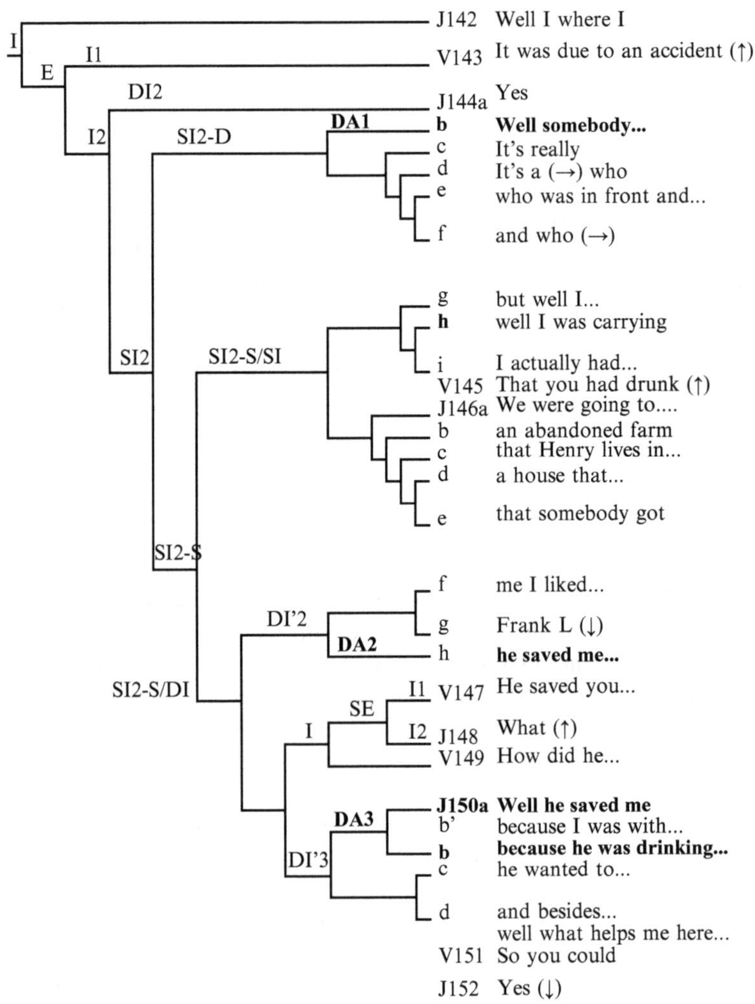

Legend:
E: exchange. SE: subordinate exchange. I: intervention. DI: directing intervention. SI: subordinate intervention. DA: directing act. V: interlocutor V. J: interlocutor J.

Fig. 14.2 Hierarchical diagram of Example 2 with commentary

J 142 :	enfin moi où j'ai quand même souffert c'est quand j'ai eu mon traumatisme crânien
V143 :	C'est dû à un accident (↑)
J 144 :	Oui enfin on m'avait pratiquement culbuté (↓) c'est quand même bien un (→) ç'en est un (→) qui m'a balancé (→) qu'était devant et puis moi derriére et qui m'a (→) mais enfin je m'en fous parce que (→) enfin j'étais chargé j'avais quand même 5 litres de vin de (→) de pineau, 5 litres de biére, plus 1 ou 2 (inaud.)
V145 :	Que vous aviez bu (↑)
J 146 :	On allait dans la ferme à S. (lieu) (↓) une ferme abandonnée (↓) qu'habite qu'est (→) qu'appartient à Henry (inaud.) euh (→) une maison qu'est qu'on a fait qu'on a fait (→) qu'on a touchée (↓) + moi j'aimais j'aime bien Franck (↓) Franck L (nom) (↓ il m'a sauvé (→) avec son frère (inaud)
V147 :	Il vous a sauvé comment ça (↑)
J 148 :	Comment (↑)
V149 :	Comment ça il vous a sauvé (↑)
J 150 :	Ah mais euh (→) qui euh (→) ben il m'a sauvé euh parce que j'étais avec lui parce qu'il (→) buVAIT quoi (↓) il voulait me (→) taper dessus + et en plus son frangin il m'a enlevé (↓) +2+ ben ce qui m'aide là c'est quelqu'un de bien c'est Damien (↓) ben heureusement qu'il m'a fait ça parce que (→) il il faisait comme ça il se faisait disparaître +1+ et je peux le faire moi disparaître +1+
V151 :	Donc vous pouviez disparaître et réapparaître (↑)
J 152 :	Oui (↓)

Fig. 14.2 (continued)

accomplished in J146h, i.e., "*he and his brother saved me.*" This subordinate part, SI2-S, runs across J144g and J150d. SI2-S in turn includes a subordinate part extending from J144g to J146e (SI2-S/SI) and a directing part extending from J146f to J150d (SI2-S/DI). Hierarchically and functionally speaking, SI2-S/DI is comprised of two complex intervention-level constituents in a subordination relation: DI′2, which extends from J146f to J146h with J146h as its directing act (DA2); and DI′3, which spans J150a to J150d. The directing act of this intervention is complex; it is composed of two segments, 150a and 150b, linked around the connective "*because*", which fulfills a causal function. Moreover, directing act DA3 is interactively associated with subordinate act J150b′ (preparatory function), which is incorporated into the directing act's structure and into subordinate acts J150c and J150d, both of which perform a function of justification. Insofar as we are describing the structure of a complex intervention-level component, namely SI2-S-DI, we will acknowledge—drawing on Roulet's model (Roulet et al. 1985)—that DA2 imposes constraints of the interactive type on DA3. Likewise, insofar as the SI2-S-DI component is itself an integral part of complex intervention SI2, of which SI2-D is the directing element, we will acknowledge that DA1 imposes interactive constraints on both DA2 and DA3. Indeed, DA1 is the directing constituent of complex intervention SI2-D, which subordinates SI2-S globally, i.e., dominates both DA2 and DA3.

We can see here that, at the dialogical level, the discontinuity is generated by a multi-layered process in that DA3 (namely utterance J150a-b "*he saved me because he was DRINKing I mean*") satisfies neither the argumentative-relation constraint imposed by DA2 (namely utterance J146h, "*he and his brother saved me*") nor the argumentative-relation constraint imposed more distally by DA1 (namely utterance J144b, "*well somebody practically knocked me over*"). Clearly, the utterance act performed in DA3, "*he saved me because he was DRINKing I mean*" (just like the acts that contribute more globally to the coherence of the subcomponent dominated by DA2, such as "*he and his brother saved me*") can in no way be seen as a discursive constituent of the rhetorical argument-conclusion relations imposed by discursive constituent DA2, which plays the role of argument here. We can also see that this same constituent, DA2, does not satisfy the constraints imposed on it by the constituent DA1, which dominates it hierarchically. Hence, "*he and his brother saved me*" (DA2) does not satisfy the interactive constraints—which once again are argumentative-relation constraints—theoretically imposed on it by DA1, "*well somebody practically knocked me over*". We will agree in addition, based on a hierarchical analysis of this sequence, that DA3 is no better at satisfying the interactive constraints imposed on it by DA1. The rest of the sequence conveys other artefacts and incongruities, but we will stop our commentary there because the points of analysis presented so far suffice for our demonstration.

More generally, J150 is made up of another series of speech acts that introduce a new topic to which the interlocutor will contribute. We are thus in the presence of two distinct conversational transactions: the first (analyzed above) stops precisely at the end of J150d; the second begins with the dialogue-resumption segment "*well what helps me here*".

14.4.4.5 Heuristic Aspect of Decisive Discontinuity

Through the pragmatic-dialogical formalization of the sequences analyzed above (conversational gear-shifting and conversational initiative defectiveness), we were able to paint a more precise picture of the form and basic properties of decisive discontinuity. This kind of discontinuity is not sustained by the simple proposition, the speech act, or even the exchange, but by conversational transactions whose structure is based on rhetorical and semantic relations between at least three discursive segments. The relevant unit is the conversational transaction, not the act, the utterance, or the two- or three-turn exchange. Thus we may grasp not only the neurocognitive processes underlying discourse (taking the process-based, dynamic nature of interaction into account: action plan, reciprocity, and so on) but also the intentional and inferential processes involved. More precisely, this kind of formalization of disorganized discursive sequences may help to account for the accomplishment of inter-comprehension and its interrelationships both with the patient's language acts and with the interlocutor's communicational behavior as manifested particularly in discourse. Because of their specific properties and the constraints they impose on each interlocutor's behavior, these verbal transactions are the perfect place, methodologically speaking, to observe certain interpretive and inferential processes as well as any assessment or dysfunction thereof.

Our investigative strategy sheds light on the extent to which clinicians can make valid intuitive judgments about a patient's linguistic and/or communicative deficiencies based on the patient's behavior. We claim that an apparent communication deficiency in a schizophrenic patient may not imply a thought disorder, even if a thought disorder most likely means impaired communication (i.e., non-decisive discontinuity). From a diagnostic standpoint, this pragmatic approach to cognitive psychopathology allows us to contemplate the possibility of clarifying or even operationalizing the notion of formal thought disorders. Generally speaking, this investigation contributes to advancing our understanding of language and communication in relation to schizophrenia (Crow 2010; Titone 2010).

14.5 Study

14.5.1 Method

The purpose of this study was to use a pragmatic-dialogic model to link any verbal-behavior discontinuities detected in a patient to that patient's clinical manifestations (or syndromes) as diagnosed on the basis of DSM-IV criteria. The merits of this model are clear: it provides a more accurate description of the symptomatic manifestations of schizophrenia—as expressed in verbal interaction in the form of syndrome-specific discontinuities—and thereby allows us to show how these discontinuities co-occur with the clinical manifestations generally described in disease classification systems. From this, we should be able to set forth some specific hypotheses about the potentially distinct properties of the underlying cognitive processes. The models that account for non-decisive discontinuity in verbal interaction are congruent with a potential dysfunction in psychophysiological or neurocognitive processes such as those involved in planning, for example. The models that account for decisive discontinuity in verbal interaction are congruent with potential impairment of representational or meta-representational cognitive processes (complex thought processes such as intentional or inferential processes).

The features of our empirical corpus (Table 14.1) also make it possible to control for the potential impact of antipsychotic medication on the expression of symptoms in verbal interaction. As stated at the beginning of this article, psychometric scales have traditionally been used to measure the efficacy of neuroleptic treatments, and research in this area has mainly focused on the ability of these scales to assess the comparative effects of conventional (first-generation) and atypical (second-generation) neuroleptics on schizophrenia symptoms. While few studies contest the efficacy of neuroleptics on schizophrenia symptoms (especially positive ones), their mechanisms of action and their repercussions on cognition are still widely debated. Although some studies have shown that the cognitive performance of schizophrenic patients improves more with atypical than with conventional neuroleptic medication (Goldberg and Weinberger 1995; Harvey et al. 2003; Meltzer and McGurk 1999), the efficacy of such drugs is still being questioned.

Table 14.1 Characteristics of the investigation corpus

	SCH (n = 22)		CTR (n = 8)	
	SCH-P (n = 14) (SCH-P-A/SCH-P-N) M+SD	SCH-D (n = 8) (SCH-D-A/SCH-D-N) M+SD	M+SD	Total
Sex (M-F)	(10–4)	(4–4)	(4–4)	
Age in years	45.6 ± 17.0	43.9 ± 13.4	32.1 ± 14.3	
Education (in no. of years of schooling from first grade on)	9.4 ± 1.7	7.3 ± 3.5	9.1 ± 1.4	
Chlorpromazine equivalent in mg per day	182 ± 161 (283 ± 100/0)	208 ± 170 (277 ± 133/0)		
Time since onset	10.1 ± 12.2	5.6 ± 4.7		
Number of interviews	14 (9/5)	8 (6/2)	8	30
Number of conversational transactions	208 (146/62)	150 (108/42)	45	403

Legend. *SCH-P* Paranoid schizophrenics, *SCH-D* Disorganized schizophrenics, *SCH-N* Schizophrenics with no treatment, *SCH-A* Schizophrenics under antipsychotic treatment, *CTR* Participants with no diagnosed psychiatric disorders, *n* Number of patients, *M* Mean, *SD* Standard deviation

14.5.2 Participants

Table 14.1 provides information about the group from which the corpus originated (Verhaegen and Musiol 2009). Thirty native French-speaking adults (18 men and 12 women, age 41.5 ± 16) participated in the study. Twenty-two participants (14 men and 8 women, age 45.0 ± 15.4) were assigned to the schizophrenic group (SCH), and eight (4 men and 4 women, age 32.1 ± 14.3) were assigned to the control group (CTR).

Of the 22 schizophrenic participants included satisfying the DSM-IV criteria, 15 were being treated with antipsychotic drugs (SCH-A: mean dose equivalent to 281 ± 118 mg/day of chlorpromazine) and 7 were taking no medication (SCH-N). Clinical types of schizophrenia were as follows: there were 14 paranoid schizophrenics (SCH-P) (5 of whom were taking antipsychotic drugs) and 8 disorganized schizophrenics (SCH-D) (2 of whom were not taking any antipsychotic medication). The antipsychotic medication taken by the 15 schizophrenic patients was atypical (second generation), conventional (first generation), or a combination of the two. The patients had no neurological disorders and had neither suffered from alcohol intoxication nor used any toxic substances for at least 3 months before the study. The schizophrenia diagnosis was made by experienced psychiatrists who did not take part in the study.

The schizophrenic patients came from two different clinical institutions. Seven were in a psychiatric emergency ward (Temporary Psychiatric Hospitalization Unit in Troyes, France). They were apparently having their first encounter with psychiatry and were not taking antipsychotic drugs. For these participants, no data indicating prior hospitalization in a psychiatric ward could be found. Given that a diagnosis of schizophrenia cannot be pronounced unless the signs of the disorder persist for at least 6 months (APA, 1994), we were to verify required diagnoses half a year later. Diagnoses were indeed confirmed in all cases, although once again, data were collected at time of hospitalization. The other 15 patients had been under treatment in a psychiatric ward for at least 3 years (Specialized Hospital of La Rochelle, France). They received daily antipsychotic treatment. Of these 15 patients, 5 were encountered in the specialized hospital where they were inpatients. The other ten were hospitalized only intermittently.

The control participants had no neurological disorders and, like the schizophrenic patients, had not suffered from alcohol intoxication or used toxic substances for at least 3 months. They had no diagnosed psychiatric disorders and were not taking any psychotropic medication. Control subjects were recruited in public places.

For the sociodemographic variables, pairwise comparison (Student's t-test for independent samples) of our groups (SCH-P vs. SCH-D, SCH-P vs. CTR, SCH-D vs. CTR) yielded no significant differences in education level ($t[1,20] = 1.580$, $p = 0.138$; $t[1,20] = 0.430$, $p = 0.673$; $t[1,14] = -1.334$, $p = 0.207$), age ($t[1,20] = 0.242$, $p = 0.811$; $t[1,20] = 1.887$, $p = 0.074$, marginally significant; $t[1,14] = 1.697$, $p = 0.112$), or sex (corrected chi-squarred: $p = 0.45$). Regarding the neuroleptic treatment of these two groups (mean chlorpromazine-equivalent dose in mg/day), no significant difference was found ($t[1,20] = -0.348$, $p = 0.732$). Given that both patient groups contained neuroleptic-treated and untreated individuals, we also compared the treated paranoid schizophrenics (SCH-P-A) to the treated disorganized schizophrenics (SCH-D-A): no significant difference was found here either ($t[1,13] = 0.111$, $p = 0.913$). The medication factor should therefore not interfere with results.

14.5.3 Procedure

The study was based on a pragmatic and dialogic analysis of verbal transactions taken from a corpus of 30 interviews. In all cases, the interviewer was a research psychologist and the interviewee was either a schizophrenic patient or an individual with no psychiatric disorders. All interviewees agreed to have the conversation recorded so that we could compile our corpus. They were told why they were being recorded, and we did not conceal the fact that they were participating in a study. The instructions were simply to talk to the interviewer (approximately during 30 min).

If the interviewee initially said he/she was having trouble expressing him/herself, the interviewer started with a relatively general topic of conversation (everyday activities and/or concerns). The corpus was transcribed by two researchers, one of whom was not involved in this study. Transcriptions were compared, differences discussed (with other colleagues when necessary), and a final transcription chosen. The (↑) and (↓) arrows respectively indicate a rising or falling intonation. The (→) arrow indicates a pause in the flow of speech for 2–5 s.

The breakdown of the entire interview corpus yielded 403 conversational sequences (or transactions).

14.6 Results

14.6.1 Classification of Conversational Sequences by Type of Interlocutor

Our first step was to label the sequences according to whether they contained or did not contain a discontinuity, for each group of interlocutors. Again, the interlocutors were schizophrenics of the paranoid (SCH-P) or disorganized type (SCH-D), or individuals with no diagnosed psychiatric disorders (CTR).

Comparisons of the sequences with and without a discontinuity (whether decisive or non-decisive) across participant groups showed that the schizophrenics' conversational sequences (SCH) contained more discontinuities than the normal participants' sequences. These two groups were significantly different ($Chi^2 = 21.175, p < 0.001$). There were also more discontinuous sequences in the disorganized-schizophrenic subcorpus than in the control-participant subcorpus ($Chi^2 = 17.347, p < 0.001$) and more discontinuous sequences in the paranoid-schizophrenic subcorpus than in the control subcorpus ($Chi^2 = 22.323, p < 0.001$). These results suggest that the models we devised to account for discourse discontinuity are good at differentiating between pathological conversations and normal conversations in terms of coherence. This does not seem to hold true, however, in comparing the two groups of schizophrenics defined on the basis of clinical type. The sequences in the paranoid-schizophrenic subcorpus did not have more discontinuities than those in the disorganized-schizophrenic subcorpus. These two subgroups did not differ significantly ($\mathrm{Chi}^2 = 0.991$, $\mathrm{p} = 0.319$). Thus, irrespective of the medication variable and the type of discontinuity at play, the model failed to detect the specificities of each clinical type of schizophrenia. Our next step, then, will be to look at other variables in order to determine the specificities of each schizophrenic subtype (Table 14.2).

Table 14.2 Presence or absence of discontinuity, by participant group

	SCH-P	SCH-D	CTR	*p*-value SCH *vs* CTR	SCH-P *vs* CTR	SCH-D *vs* CTR	SCH-P *vs* SCH-D
Sequences with discontinuity	80 (38 %)	50 (33 %)	1 (2 %)	<0.001	<0.001	<0.001	p = 0.319
Sequences without discontinuity	128 (62 %)	100 (67 %)	44 (98 %)				
Total	208	150	45				

Legend. *SCH* Schizophrenics, *SCH-P* Paranoid schizophrenics, *SCH-D* Disorganized schizophrenics, *CTR* Participants with no diagnosed psychiatric disorders

Table 14.3 Presence or absence of non-decisive discontinuity, by participant group

	SCH-P	SCH-D	CTR	*p*-value SCH *vs* CTR	SCH-P *vs* CTR	SCH-D *vs* CTR	SCH-P *vs* SCH-D
Sequences with non-decisive discontinuity	71 (36 %)	50 (33 %)	1 (2 %)	<0.001	<0.001	<0.001	0.649
Sequences without discontinuity	128 (64 %)	100 (67 %)	44 (98 %)				
Total	199	150	45				

Legend. *SCH-P* Paranoid schizophrenics, *SCH-D* Disorganized schizophrenics, *SCH* Schizophrenics, *CTR* Individuals with no diagnosed psychiatric disorder

14.6.2 Conversational Sequences with or Without a Non-decisive Discontinuity, by Group of Interlocutors

Now let us look at the number of sequences with or without the type of discontinuity we call "non-decisive", for each group of interlocutors. The distribution of these sequences across groups is shown in Table 14.3, which also gives the significance level in each case. Sequences containing a decisive discontinuity (nine in all) were not included in the table, so the comparison shown here is between non-decisive discontinuous sequences and sequences with no discontinuities.

These results are very similar to those presented above in that non-decisive discontinuities were more frequent in the schizophrenic subcorpus. When we compare the sequences with a non-decisive discontinuity to those with no discontinuity across participant groups, we can see that the schizophrenics' conversational sequences contained more such discontinuities than those of the normal individuals. These two groups differed significantly ($Chi^2 = 19.633, p < 0.001$). We also found more

Table 14.4 Conversational sequences with or without a non-decisive discontinuity, by presence/absence of antipsychotic medication and clinical type of schizophrenia

		SCH-P	SCH-D
SCH-N	Sequences with non-decisive discontinuity	12 (20 %)	28 (67 %)
	Sequences with no discontinuity	47 (80 %)	(33 %)
	Total	59	42
SCH-A	Sequences with non-decisive discontinuity	59 (42 %)	22 (20 %)
	Sequences with no discontinuity	81 (58 %)	86 (80 %)
	Total	140	108

Legend. *SCH-P* Paranoid schizophrenics, *SCH-D* Disorganized schizophrenics, *SCH-N* Schizophrenics with no treatment, *SCH-A* Schizophrenics under treatment

non-decisive discontinuous sequences in the disorganized-schizophrenic subcorpus than in the control-participant subcorpus ($Chi^2 = 17.347, p < 0.001$), and more non-decisive discontinuous sequences in the paranoid-schizophrenic subcorpus than in the control-participant subcorpus ($Chi^2 = 19.749, p < 0.001$). Comparing the sequences with or without a non-decisive discontinuity across clinical types of schizophrenia, we can see that these two patient groups were not significantly different ($Chi^2 = 0.208, p = 0.649$): the paranoid-schizophrenic sequences did not contain more non-decisive discontinuities than the disorganized-schizophrenic ones.

However, as suggested above and called for by our experimental design (see Table 14.1), additional information is needed regarding the potential interaction between the "clinical type of schizophrenia" and "medication" variables (Verhaegen and Musiol 2011). We thus attempted to find out, firstly, whether SCH-P-N conversational sequences had fewer, as many, or more non-decisive discontinuities than other sequences as compared to SCH-D-N conversational sequences; and secondly, whether SCH-P-A conversational sequences had fewer, as many, or more non-decisive discontinuities than other sequences as compared to SCH-D-A conversational sequences (see Table 14.4). For the schizophrenics not under treatment (SCH-N), there were more non-decisive discontinuities in the SCH-D subgroup than in the SCH-P subgroup ($Chi^2 = 22.015, p < 0.001$). By contrast, for the patients taking antipsychotic medication (SCH-A), the non-decisive discontinuities were more frequent in the SCH-P subgroup than in the SCH-D subgroup ($Chi^2 = 13.141, p < 0.001$).

14.6.3 Conversational Sequences with a Decisive Discontinuity, by Clinical Type of Schizophrenia

Lastly, we looked at the sequences with and without decisive discontinuities for each patient group. All nine sequences that were compatible with our decisive-discontinuity model occurred in the paranoid-schizophrenic subcorpus. This subgroup differed significantly from both the disorganized-schizophrenic group (binomial test $p = 0.002$) and the normal group (binomial test $p = 0.002$). Among these nine paranoid schizophrenics, three were from the no-medication group (SCH-P-N) and six were from the antispsychotic-medication group (SCH-P-A).

14.7 Concluding Remarks

Our results indicate that the pragmatic and dialogic discontinuity models we developed (decisive and non-decisive models) turned out to be good at discriminating schizophrenic patients from individuals with no psychiatric disorders in terms of conversational coherence. In addition, they accounted for certain coherence-related specificities of the discursive and dialogical productions of patients with either of the subtypes of schizophrenia we studied (paranoid and disorganized). We were able to point out a strong correlation between the paranoid clinical type and a particular kind of discontinuous verbal behavior, namely decisive discontinuity, for paranoid schizophrenics both with and without antipsychotic treatment. Our decisive-discontinuity model thus allowed us to propose some possible explanations for the dysfunctional interpretive and inferential thought processes of schizophrenics of the paranoid type, with the help of an additional model based on formal semantics (Musiol and Rebuschi 2011; next chapter in this book). On the other hand, it did not permit us to draw any conclusions about possible similar dysfunctions among schizophrenics of the disorganized type. We are therefore forced to acknowledge that, at this point in our research, it is impossible to decide which of the following possibilities is correct: either the specific characteristics of verbal interactions between a disorganized schizophrenic patient and a normal interlocutor are not captured by the discontinuity model we have developed, or such disorganized patients do not exhibit significant incoherency in their dialogue.

Questions surrounding what kind of process might support this sort of incoherence arise as soon as we compare the specificities of these incongruous or even incoherent behaviors with theoretical and interpretive models of congruent discourse, such as models of dialogical and pragmatic analysis. We hypothesize that the processes at work are those underlying the comprehension and calculation of communicative intentions in Sperber's sense of the term: "Comprehension (or its pragmatic layer) is an inferential process, using as input the output of linguistic decoding and aiming at discovering the speaker's meaning. Comprehension consists, therefore, in inferring a mental state (an intention of a specific kind) from behavior (an utterance)" (Sperber 2000, p. 129). Furthermore, we know that decisive verbal-interaction discontinuities have some highly specific properties (Musiol 2009). They appeared here solely over the course of self-initiated conversational sequences (i.e., initiated by the patient). From this standpoint, our model is not only capable of accounting for defective processes that can be grasped in terms of action-planning deficits, as in experimental cognitive neuropsychology for example, but is also and especially very effective at capturing dysfunctions affecting certain cognitive-inferential processes related to spared rationality. This capability is not offered by experimentation, questionnaires, or structured and semi-structured interviews, where the subject (here, the patient) is always in the position of "reactor" and is therefore led to react and adapt to the presentation of a stimulus in the discourse of another person (e.g., in the task instructions given by an investigator).

While no link was found here between non-decisive discontinuous transaction sequences and the clinical form of a schizophrenic interlocutor's pathology when the medication variable was not controlled, such was no longer the case when we did control for this factor. For the schizophrenics who were not under any kind of antipsychotic treatment, we found more non-decisive discontinuities among patients of the disorganized type than among paranoid ones. For those taking antipsychotic drugs, we found more non-decisive discontinuities among the paranoid schizophrenics than among the disorganized ones. These results once again stress the merits of taking the medication variable into account when researching this disorder. Although we are not the first to make this recommendation, there are still few studies that look at the impact of medication on dialogue behavior (and not just verbal behavior) or on cognitive-inferential processes. Taking this type of variable into account has another advantage: it brings up the issue of the specificities of the cognitive processes underlying these disorders. Indeed, the statistical results presented here suggest that only the model of non-decisive discontinuity was able to bring out a significant effect of medication on incoherence type (Verhaegen and Musiol 2011), firstly in terms of a decrease in discontinuity, i.e., the reestablishment of certain forms of coherence solely for disorganized schizophrenics; secondly, in terms of an increase in discontinuity for the paranoid patients.

These findings enable us to define communication disorders in a more precise way than was possible prior to the late 1980s, when the term "pragmatic impairment" was used to mean the same thing as impaired language use. Today, the pragmatic approach in cognitive psychopathology addresses various theoretical and practical dimensions of cognitive psychology and neurocognition. From an empirical point of view, however, descriptions of certain features of severe illnesses (psychoses and neurological disorders) remain inadequate. Again, we still do not have a precise symptom-classification system for describing the interpretive and inferential thought disorders seen in patients. Pragmatics-oriented psychology studies have attempted to grasp and formalize this type of cognitive activity, putting this approach in a position to supply new knowledge not only for defining incoherence but also for describing it using data obtained through a pragmatic perspective on neurocognitive conceptions of schizophrenia (Musiol 2009). A formal semantic approach should then allow us to gain new and better insight into the psychocognitive processes implicated in thought disorders (Musiol and Rebuschi 2011). We are also working on interfacing our pragmatic-dialogical analysis of decisive sequences with a formal semantic model with a view to accessing the properties and rationality underlying the semantic representations (see Rebuschi, Amblard and Musiol, pp. 343–368) of subjects with a psychiatric disorder, i.e., their intentional, interpretive, or inferential thought processes.

References

M. Amblard, M. Musiol, M. Rebuschi, L'interaction conversationnelle à l'épreuve du handicap schizophrénique. *Recherches sur la Philosophie et le Langage*, forthcoming, 2014

N.C. Andreasen, Thought, language and communication disorders. I-Clinical assessments definition of terms, and evaluation of their reliability. Arch. Gen. Psychiatry **36**, 1315–1324 (1979)

N.C. Andreasen, *Scale for the Assessment of Negative Symptoms (SANS)* (University of Iowa, Iowa City, 1983)

N.C. Andreasen, *Scale for the Assessment of Positive Symptoms (SAPS)* (University of Iowa, Iowa City, 1984)

N.C. Andreasen, W.N. Grove, Thought, language and communication in schizophrenia: diagnosis and prognosis. Schizophren. Bull. **12**, 348–359 (1986)

N.C. Andreasen, S. Olsen, Negative versus positive schizophrenia. Arch. Gen. Psychiatry **39**, 789–794 (1982)

M. Bakhtine, V.N. Volochinov, La structure de l'énoncé. in *Mikhaïl Bakhtine, le principe dialogique*, ed. by T. Todorov (Éditions du Seuil, Paris, 1930/1981), pp. 287–316

N. Bazin, F. Lefrère, C. Passerieux, Y. Sarfati, M.-C. Hardy-Bayle, Troubles formels de la pensée: traduction franÃ§aise de l'échelle d'évaluation de la pensée, du langage et de la communication (Scale for the Assessment of Thought, Language and Communication: TLC). L'Encéphale **28**, 109–119 (2002)

N. Bazin, Y. Sarfati, F. Lefrère, C. Passerieux, M.-C. Hardy-Bayle, Scale for the evaluation of communication disorders in patients with schizophrenia: a validation study. Schizophren. Res. **77**(1), 75–84 (2005)

I. Berman, B. Viegner, A. Merson, E. Allan, D. Pappas, A.I. Green, Relationships between positive and negative symptoms and neuropsychological deficits in schizophrenia. Schizophren. Res. **25**(1), 1–10 (1997)

E. Bleuler, *Dementia praecox ou groupe des schizophrénies* (E.P.E.L., G.R.E.C, 1911), French translation of 1993

E.O. Chaïka, A linguist looks at 'schizophrenic' language. Brain Lang. **I**, 257–276 (1974)

E.O. Chaïka, *Understanding Psychotic Speech: Beyond Freud and Chomsky* (Charles C. Thomas Publisher, Springfield, 1990)

P. Chaslin, Groupe provisoire des folies discordantes, in *Eléments de sémiologie et clinique mentales* (Editions Asselin et Houzeau, Paris, 1912)

T.J. Crow, Molecular pathology of schizophrenia: more than one disease process? Br. Med. J. **280**, 66–68 (1980)

T.J. Crow, The nuclear symptoms of schizophrenia reveal the four quadrant structure of language and its deficit frame. J. Neurolinguistics **23**(1), 1–9 (2010)

S. Ervin-Tripp, Imitation and structural change in children's language in *New Directions in the Study of Language*, ed. by E.H. Lenneberg, (MIT, Cambridge, 1964), pp. 163–189

V.A. Fromkin, A linguist looks at "a linguist looks at schizophrenic language". Brain Lang. **2**, 498–503 (1975)

E. Goffman, *Les Rites d'interaction* (Éditions de Minuit, Paris, 1974)

T.E. Goldberg, D.R. Weinberger, Thought disorder, working memory and attention: interrelationships and the effects of neuroleptic medications. Int. Clin. Psychopharmacol. **10**(3), 99–104 (1995)

P.D. Harvey, J. Lombardi, M. Leibman, L. White, M. Parrella, P. Powchik, M. Davidson, Cognitive impairment and negative symptoms in geriatric chronic schizophrenic patients: a follow-up study. Schizophren. Res. **22**(3), 223–231 (1996)

P.D. Harvey, M.F. Green, S.R. McGurk, H.Y. Meltzer, Changes in cognitive functioning with risperidone and olanzapine treatment: a large-scale, double-blind, randomized study. Psychopharmacology **69**, 404–411 (2003)

R.W. Heinrichs, Schizophrenia and the brain: conditions for a neuropsychology of madness. Am. Psychol. **48**(3), 221–233 (1993)
S.R. Kay, A. Fiszbein, L.A. Opler, The Positive and Negative Syndrome Scale (PANSS) for schizophrenia. Schizophren. Bull. **13**, 261–276 (1987)
E. Kraepelin, *Dementia Praecox and Paraphrenia* (Krieger RE, New York, 1919). Trans. R.M. Barclay and G.M. Robertson (Eds.) (1971)
W. Labov, D. Fanshel, *Therapeutic Discourse: Psychotherapy a Conversation* (Academic, New York, 1977)
P.F. Liddle, The symptoms of chronic schizophrenia. a re-examination of the positive-negative dichotomy. Br. J. Psychiatry **151**, 145–151 (1987)
P.F. Liddle, E.T.C. Ngan, S.L. Caissie, C.M. Anderson, A.T. Bates, D.J. Quested, R. White, R. Weg, Thought and language index: an instrument for assessing thought and language in schizophrenia. Br. J. Psychiatry **181**, 326–330 (2002)
A. Marini et al., The language of schizophrenia: an analysis of micro and macrolinguistic abilities and their neuropsychological correlates. Schizophren. Res. **105**(1–3), 145–155 (2008)
H.Y. Meltzer, S. McGurk, The effects of clozapine, ripseridone and olanzapine on cognitive function in schizophrenia. Schizophren. Bull. **25**, 233–255 (1999)
M. Musiol, Incohérence et formes psychopathologiques dans l'interaction verbale schizophrénique in *Des neurosciences à la psychopathologie: Action, Langage, Imaginaire*, ed. by N. Franck, J. Rozenberg, C. Hervé (De Boeck, Bruxelles, 2009), pp. 219–238
M. Musiol, M. Rebuschi, Towards a two-step formalisation of verbal interaction in schizophrenia: a case study, in *Dialog's logical properties*, ed. by A. Trognon, M. Batt, J. Caelen, D. Vernant (Presses Universitaires de Nancy, Nancy, 2011), pp. 187–225
M. Musiol, A. Trognon, *Èléments de Psychopathologie Cognitive. Le discours schizophrène* (Armand Colin, Paris, 2000)
V. Olivier, M.C. Hardy-Bayle, S. Lancrenon, J. Fermanian, Y. Sarfati, C. Passerieux, J.F. Chevalier, Rating scale for the assessment of communication disorders in schizophrenics. Eur. Psychiatry **12**, 356–361 (1997)
K. Pike, *Language in Relation to Unified Theory of the Structure of Human Behavior* (Mouton, The Hague, 1967)
S. Rochester, J.R. Martin, *Crazy Talk. A Study of the Discourse of Schizophrenic Speakers* (Plenum, London, 1979)
E. Roulet, A. Auchlin, J. Moeschler, C. Rubattel, M. Schelling, *L'articulation du discours en français contemporain* (Peter Lang, Bern, 1985)
J.R. Searle, D. Vanderveken, *Foundations of Illocutionary Logic* (Cambridge University Press, Cambridge, 1985)
D. Sperber, Metarepresentations in an evolutionary perspective, in *Metarepresentations: An Multidisciplinarity Perspective*, ed. by D. Sperber (Oxford University Press, Oxford, 2000), pp. 117–137
D. Titone, Language, communication, & schizophrenia. J. Neurolinguistics **23**, 173–175 (2010)
A. Trognon, Débrayages conversationnels. DRLAV **36–37**, 105–122 (1987)
A. Trognon, Speech acts and the logic of mutual understanding in *Essays in Speech Act Theory*, ed. by D. Vanderveken, S. Kubo (John Benjamins Publishing Company, Amsterdam/Philadelphia, 2002), pp. 121–133
A. Trognon, M. Musiol, L'accomplissement interactionnel du trouble schizophrénique, in *Raisons Pratiques (La folie dans la place)*, ed. by I. Joseph, J. Proust (Éditions de l'École des Hautes Études en Sciences Sociales, Paris, 1996), pp. 179–209
F. Verhaegen, M. Musiol, Symptomatologie schizophrénique et processus psychopharmacologiques: contribution empirique. Annales Medico-Psychologiques **167**, 728–735 (2009)
F. Verhaegen, M. Musiol, Verbal behavior analysis as a diagnostic and psychopharmalogical strategy for differentiating paranoid and disorganized schizophrenics, in *Psychiatric Disorders. Trends and Developments*, ed. by T. Uehara (InTech, Rijeka, 2011)

Chapter 15
Using SDRT to Analyze Pathological Conversations: Logicality, Rationality, and Pragmatic Deviances

Manuel Rebuschi, Maxime Amblard, and Michel Musiol

15.1 Introduction

Schizophrenia is well-known among mental illnesses for the severity of the thought disorders it involves, and for their widespread and spectacular manifestations ranging from deviant social behavior to delusion, not to mention affective and sensory distortions. The goal of this paper is twofold: (i) to discuss how the concepts of rationality and logicality may apply to conversational contexts in which one of the speakers is schizophrenic, and (ii) to present the initial steps of a scientific research project on one specific manifestation, namely disorders in conversational speech.

This paper aims to present an overview of ongoing interdisciplinary research that started with the DiaRaFor project at the MSH Lorraine in Nancy. Certain materials have already been collected in Rebuschi et al. (2013). We are grateful to the audiences at JSM 2010 and CAuLD (Nancy, 2010), MSH-Alpes (Grenoble, 2011), and TALN 2011 (Montpellier, 2011), where versions of this paper were presented. We wish to thank Bruno Ambroise, Valérie Aucoututier, Denis Bonnay, and Eric Grillo for their critical comments and helpful suggestions.

M. Rebuschi (✉)
LHSP – Archives H. Poincaré (UMR 7117), MSH Lorraine (USR 3261) CNRS, Université de Lorraine, 91, avenue de la Libération, BP 454, 54001 Nancy, France
e-mail: manuel.rebuschi@univ-lorraine.fr

M. Amblard
LORIA, UMR 7503, Université de Lorraine, CNRS, Inria, Campus Scientifique, F-54506 Vandœuvre-lès-Nancy, France
e-mail: maxime.amblard@loria.fr

M. Musiol
MSH Lorraine (USR 3261) CNRS, ATILF (UMR 7118), Université de Lorraine, 44, avenue de la Libération, 54063 Nancy, France
e-mail: michel.musiol@univ-lorraine.fr

M. Rebuschi et al. (eds.), *Interdisciplinary Works in Logic, Epistemology, Psychology and Linguistics*, Logic, Argumentation & Reasoning 3,
DOI 10.1007/978-3-319-03044-9_15, © Springer International Publishing Switzerland 2014

Our data are taken from transcriptions of real conversations between a psychologist and a schizophrenic patient. Data collection and selection relied on theoretical hypotheses from psychiatry and psychopathology. Confronted with such a pathological conversation, any "ordinary" speaker intuitively feels that there are some incoherencies or discontinuities. The aim of this research is to account for these using both pragmatics and formal semantics. Linguistics, especially semantics and pragmatics, is thus central to this work. Moreover, since speech incongruities raise the issue of the nature of rationality and its connections with logicality, the interpretative part of our research is naturally related to fields such as philosophy, philosophy of mind, and philosophy of logic.

This paper is organized as follows. In Sect. 15.2, we discuss the relationships between logicality, rationality, and schizophrenia. This reflection then leads us to a specific strategy to account for pathological conversations, based on semantic and pragmatic theorizing. In Sect. 15.3, we briefly present the theoretical background both psycholinguistic and formal of our empirical analyses. Section 15.4 introduces the corpus: the choice of participants, i.e. schizophrenic patients, and the procedure followed from live conversation and transcription to the selection of relevant excerpts, as well as the formal framework used to construe conversations. In Sect. 15.5, we provide two example analyses. Lastly, in our conclusion, we discuss a few epistemological implications of our research.

15.2 Logic, Rationality, and Schizophrenics

The delirium of schizophrenia is marked in psychiatry as one of the most radically deviant forms of thinking. Schizophrenia is often approached based on analysis of verbal productions (scales, tests, experiments) and patient speech. Should we consider that insanity means a complete loss of logicality or rationality? Does assuming so help us understand schizophrenia? In this section, we shall explain why not.

15.2.1 Interpretation and Charity

Can we understand insanity? In the most radical of schizophrenic delusions, this seems impossible when referring to the classical canons of rationality. Denial of reality and seemingly contradictory thoughts, which are characteristic of the disease, would urge us to give up. Should we thus content ourselves with a purely external third-person approach to the mental life of insane persons?

We will argue against this impossibility. We do not deny the relevance of explanations from the third-person point of view, such as neurobiology, psychoanalysis, etc. What we reject is the hypothesis that reductionist explanations can completely account for insanity. We claim that insanity does not exclude rationality in the subject, even if it is deviant rationality. Consequently, a first-person perspective on such illnesses is defensible.

15.2.1.1 The Principle of Charity

In order to address the question of rationality (and logicality) in schizophrenics, we will start with a discussion of the principle of charity. Quine (1960), and later Davidson (1980), have defended the need for the principle of charity in mutual interpretation. The idea is to maximize the truth of others' beliefs, but above all to assume their consistency, i.e. their logical non-contradiction. The so-called principle of charity actually includes several variants, which we can cite from highest to lowest:

- A postulate of *strong logicality*: the person interpreted is consistent with classical logic[1];
- A postulate of *weak logicality*: the person interpreted is consistent with the principle of contradiction (i.e., she does not simultaneously allow A and non-A);
- A postulate of *rationality*: the person interpreted is rational.

One can obviously defend the principle of contradiction without adopting classical logic,[2] and this is why we have labelled the first two versions, respectively, "strong" and "weak". Following the assumption of logicality in its weak version, the subject complies with the principle of contradiction, but nothing is said about her general logic that can be non-standard. The postulate of rationality is itself relatively independent from the assumption of logicality, since one can consider a subject who does not comply with the latter even in its weak version, and hence who does not respect the principle of contradiction, but who would nevertheless be judged *rational*.[3]

Quine has defended the need for the principle of charity as strong assumption of logicality in a context of "radical translation", i.e. in some hypothetical and ideal situation where an anthropologist meets people who have had no previously contact with the outside world:

> To take an extreme case, let us suppose that certain natives are said to accept as true certain sentences translatable in the form '*p* and not *p*'. Now this claim is absurd under our semantic criteria … Wanton translation can make natives sound as queer as one pleases. Better translation imposes our logic upon them, and would beg the question of prelogicality if there were a question to beg (Quine 1960, Sect. 13).

But the principle should go back home. The translation (i.e. the interpretation in which we project our own assumptions) is not so much used with the Indians of

---

[1]Of course, it is not required that subjects reason as through deductions within some logical calculus, but that their reasoning tend to conform to the standards of classical logic.

[2]Most non-classical logics (relevance logic, intuitionistic logic, etc.) nonetheless retain the principle of contradiction.

[3]We provide no precise definition of rationality here, but merely rely on usual mutual attributions of rationality by subjects in interaction. Such attributions are generally based on the observation of behavioral coherence, the defeasible assumption of a minimal amount of shared background beliefs and ways of reasoning, or other implicit criteria.

a particular tribe as with people around us, who are apparently speaking the same language as us:

> That fair translation preserves logical laws is implicit in practice even where, to speak paradoxically, no foreign language is involved. Thus when to our querying of an English sentence an English speaker answers 'Yes and no', we assume that the queried sentence is meant differently in the affirmation and negation; this rather than that he would be so silly as to affirm and deny the same thing. ... [O]ne's interlocutor's silliness, beyond a certain point, is less likely than bad translation – or, in the domestic case, linguistic divergence (Quine 1960, Sect. 13).

Interpretation and the possibility of rival and incompatible interpretations also arise in this more familiar case because, to put it simply, there is no (empirical) *fact* to determine the meanings our interlocutors want to communicate to us. According to Davidson, assuming rationality and logicality is thus a precondition for understanding others:

> Crediting people with a large degree of consistency cannot be counted mere charity: it is unavoidable if we are to be in a position to accuse them meaningfully of error and some degree of irrationality. Global confusion, like universal mistake, is unthinkable, not because imagination boggles, but because too much confusion leaves nothing to be confused about and massive error erodes the background of true belief against which alone failure can be construed. ... To the extent that we fail to discover a coherent and plausible pattern in the attitudes and actions of others we simply forego the chance of treating them as persons. (Davidson 1980, 221–222)

The justification of the principle of charity is then not only methodological, i.e. the principle is not only made indispensable for interpretation. It is also a conceptual justification, in the sense that rationality is here conceived of as constitutive of (the concepts of) true beliefs as well as subjects' other attitudes (see Bonnay and Cozic 2011).

15.2.1.2 Understanding Insane People

The issue is, now, what happens when our interlocutors are insane? Very often, what insane persons are saying is not considered serious, and whay they say is not even considered to be taken seriously for a good analysis of insanity. The dominant views are indeed *reductionist*. According to such views, insanity should be *fully* explained either by brain dysfunction (neurobiological or genetic reductionism), or by the subconscious (psychoanalytic reductionism). The explanation is then constrained to an external *third-person* perspective on the subject. The intended analysis is that of a causal explanation. If there is a kind of rationalization of insanity via the analysis, the only rationality at work is that of the psychologist. A psychiatrist and a linguist assumed the same hypothesis in the early 1980s according to some experimental research (Rochester and Martin 1979).

The American philosopher and psychologist Louis A. Sass (1994, 2003) challenges these reductionist approaches and defends an analysis that takes into account the internal, *first-person* point of view. The issue is not only to explicate but also to *understand* what motivates the insane in terms of *reasons*. This means acknowledging *the subject's rationality*, in contrast to what appears in the standard diagnostic criteria in psychiatry (see the critique of DSM-IV by Henriksen (2011)).

This first-person approach was seen by Wilhelm Dilthey (1989) as the only appropriate one for the "sciences of the mind" (*Geisteswissenschaften*). Let us emphasize that it is perfectly *compatible* with the explanations offered in the third-person perspective by neurobiology and/or genetics, which are dominant in psychiatry. It is our intention neither to verify the value thereof, nor to discuss the classification of psychiatric disease summarized in the DSM. What we take issue with is *reductionism*. We dispute the idea that the perception of the illness can be fully supported by third-person explanations.

Understanding the insane involves adopting their rationality, but their rationality is deviant. Where should we locate such a deviance? We will focus on schizophrenia, a pathology giving rise to the most radically deviant delusions and inconsistencies. While speaking of the insane's *rationality*, especially about schizophrenics, we assume, in part, the principle of charity.

Schizophrenic persons are *apparently* contradictory. This is what emerges from the analysis of conversations with schizophrenics. There are frequent conversational *breaks* or discontinuities. In some cases, these breaks occur at times when, clearly, the schizophrenic *appears* to accept (and generate) contradictory judgments. How can we account for this?

15.2.2 Locating Failures

Locating conversational breaks depends on perspective. From the "ordinary" speaker's point of view, failures are spontaneously placed in semantics and seen as a mere contradictions. However, postulating logicality for schizophrenics leads us to take into account their own viewpoints on conversation, where failures must be grounded elsewhere.

15.2.2.1 The Semantic Content

If we follow Quine and his conception of the principle of charity, wherein rationality is synonymous with (first-order) classical logic, that is to say where charity is designed as a postulate of strong logicality, we have the choice between[4]: (1) considering that the principle of charity is not valid in the case of schizophrenics, but then denying them any rationality and returning to the reductionist approaches mentioned above, thus renouncing understanding, and (2) considering the principle of charity as fully applicable, i.e. that subjects are logical and even classical, but

[4]This is not the place to discuss the positions that Quine might have defended, but rather to see what positions are consistent with his strong conception of charity.

that schizophrenics do not understand the meaning of words as we do and that we do not have translation manual between their language and ours, which makes understanding them impossible for us.

One can challenge Quine's conception of charity and follow Graham Priest (2003), for whom the postulates of logicality (strong or weak) and rationality must be separated. The schizophrenic would be rational, but she would not be logical in the sense of conforming to classical logic. She would not even comply with the principle of contradiction. She would have a different logic, a *paraconsistent* one, tolerant to contradictions. This would account for the fact that delusion sometimes seems to have formal meaning for the subject (in a first-person perspective), even though we consider that this is insanity, and hence non-logical thought (in a third-person perspective). This duality of perspectives results in a logical duality. Priest would certainly be very unhappy to learn that paraconsistent logic is restricted to the thought patterns of schizophrenics, but this is incidental to our purpose. However, according to this position, one comes to take on different logics between insane and not insane at least when they converse together. This also leads us to consider that we, who are not insane, cannot understand the insane, simply because we do not have the same logic they have.

In his 1910 study of the principle of contradiction in Aristotle, Łukasiewicz (2000) advocates the idea that the psychological version of the principle of contradiction should be empirically tested, but not proven a priori. The psychological version of the principle of contradiction is the impossibility of having *contrary beliefs*, i.e. the impossibility of beliefs whose contents are contradictory judgments (A and not-A). Schizophrenics would thus show at little cost that the psychological principle of contradiction does not hold (in respect to themselves at least).

But this is moving a little fast. Łukasiewicz draws on a naive epistemology. If we are to determine empirically vs. A priori the validity of the principle, we must assume some kind of *raw psychological facts*. But in psychology as elsewhere there are no such raw facts: psychological facts are theory-laden, that is to say that the data are always interpreted in terms of our theoretical assumptions. Regarding the phenomenon of apparent contradiction, the question of the location of the inconsistency remains open.

15.2.2.2 The Presentation of Content

In line with other theorists, Louis Sass (1994) denies that the *reality-testing deficit*, usually included among the symptoms of schizophrenia, adequately characterizes the thinking of schizophrenic subjects. The reality-testing deficit is an impermeability to reality that would result in the production of false and contradictory beliefs. Sass disputes this notion since it brings the deficit to the *content* of mental states, whereas we should consider that the defect involves the *states* themselves. To put it in other words, what is at stake is the mode of presentation of the content rather than the content itself. According to Sass, where we see *beliefs*, the schizophrenic entertains *states* of a type far less committed vis-à-vis reality. For Campbell (2001), these are *framework propositions*, a concept which can be approached through Searle's *background capacities* (Searle 1992; Henriksen 2011).

According to Sass, the mental attitude of schizophrenics is closed to that underlying philosophical solipsism as per Wittgenstein. Let us call *schizo-beliefs* such belief-like attitudes of schizophrenics. The idea is that, far from objectifying the contents of her schizo-beliefs, the subject would tend to subjectivize them, that is to say, to deny them any genuine status. This is consistent with a widespread questioning of perceptions implied by the radical skepticism of solipsism. The delusional thoughts and states resulting from perceptions are treated in the same fashion, as schizo-beliefs rather than beliefs.[5]

How does playing on the container (the type of mental state) empty the content of contradictions? This is difficult to describe here since schizo-beliefs are characteristic of schizophrenic thinking. They belong to a type of mental states that non-schizophrenics do not have, which explains the difficulty of understanding (e.g. by empathy) schizophrenic subjects.[6] Our proposal is to account for the first-person perspective using third-person methods, in a way similar to Dennett's *heterophenomenology* (Dennett 1991).

However, we can try to illustrate the issue using a type of custom-built deviant mental state that cannot be found anywhere. Such states would generate contradictions in content in cases where normal mental states would not. Let us call this imaginary kind of mental state *imadaynation*. This state lasts 1 day and corresponds to imagination continuous over time, say until the next phase of sleep. If I *imadayne* now that it's raining, that means I imagine that it is raining until tonight. So if I *imadayne* it is raining, and a minute later I *imadayne* it is *not* raining, I will thus entertain *imadaynation* states whose contents are contradictory. Whereas if I never *imadayne* anything, but just imagine, then I can imagine it is raining, a minute later imagine it is not raining, and not have (imagination) states whose contents are contradictory. In short: *the type of state in question is crucial in determining whether the contents of two states are contradictory or not*. Just as the same contents imagined produce no contradiction, whereas they produce one when *imadayned*, we must conceive that the same content, even though contradictory as contents of beliefs, would cease to be contradictory if they were the contents of schizo-beliefs.

---

[5]It is noteworthy that this point converges with formal approaches to contradiction by paraconsistent logicians. E.g. Villadsen proposes an analysis of paraconsistent assertions whose principle is to suspend judgment on a claim (by assigning them an indeterminate truth value). This strategy makes it possible for contradictory assertions to coexist (see Villadsen 2004, 106).

[6]The idea that understanding requires empathy underlies the alternative to the principle of charity proposed by Bonnay and Cozik (2011). They argue that cognitive science suggests that our understanding of others is mainly based on simulation mechanisms. However, in the case of schizophrenia, the subject's strangeness is such that simulation can not work. So here we defend a conception of the first-person perspective which does not require empathy or simulation.

15.2.2.3 Pragmatic Inconsistencies

The strategy we will develop for the analysis of conversations is not based on a new classification of mental states. However, we agree with Sass that the problem of schizophrenic thinking, as expressed in conversation, is not a problem of inconsistency of content. We postulate that schizophrenic speakers perfectly conform to classical logic; hence we assume that the principle of charity à la Quine obtains in their case too.[7] But we place the deviance of rationality in the *rules of language use*, i.e. in language conventions of rhetorical and pragmatic types.

What emerges from our approach differs from Brunet's (2010) idea that the separation between reasoning (dynamic processes involving states) and argument (logically binding contents) must be modeled on the distinction between, respectively, third-person point of view and first-person perspective. In our conception, the first-person view, which aims to account for a subject's rational thinking, is irreducible to a mere evaluation of contents. The way contents are structured (for a particular type of mental state in Sass's approach to delusion, by such and such pragmatic relations in the analysis of pathological conversations we develop) is an essential component of rationality. In short, rationality is not reducible to logicality.

Our empirical analyses focus on transcripts of conversations between a schizophrenic subject and a psychologist (ordinary subject). Conversations lead to breaks which are perceived by ordinary subjects, but not necessarily by the schizophrenic interlocutor causing them. The analysis involves constructing representations of conversations based on the formalism of SDRT, briefly presented in the next section. These representations include two levels: semantic representation (i.e. the content of the conversation), and pragmatic representation (i.e. the hierarchical structure of the speech acts that constitute the conversation).

To analyze pathological conversations, we propose the systematic construction of two simultaneous conversational representations, one for each interlocutor. On the schizophrenic's side, according to the principle of charity, there are no semantic contradictions. If there are failures, they occur at the pragmatic level, via violation of SDRT tree construction rules. The situation is not the same on the other side. In the conversations studied, the ordinary speaker is a psychologist asked to continue the interview. She does so in such a way as to repair the conversational structure after a break that would normally cause the interruption of a conversation. We then assume a corresponding postulate according to which the construction of a representation must respect pragmatic constraints. This option causes the appearance of inconsistencies at the semantic level.

The duality of conversational representations reflects the duality of views on the conversation: the schizophrenic subject seems to contradict ordinary subjects, so the conversation works, but the representation of the co-constructed world is inconsistent (in third-person terms). Conversely, because the schizophrenic's

---

[7]That is to say neither more nor less than for non-schizophrenics. A general discussion on the status of logic is obviously not our purpose in this paper.

Table 15.1 The duality of views on a single conversation

Ordinary interlocutor (Third-person point of view)	Schizophrenic interlocutor (First-person point of view)
Pragmatic correctness	Pragmatic deviance
⇓	⇑
Semantic deviance	Semantic correctness
Contradictory content: *apparent* contradiction!	Consistent content: *everything is OK!*

conversational dysfunction is pragmatic in nature, her own representation of the world built through the conversation does not suffer from this defect (first-person point of view). The resulting situation is summarized in Table 15.1.

15.3 Theoretical Background

Before turning to empirical data and checking whether the interpretational strategy just presented can produce relevant analyses, we will present the theoretical background of our work, which relies both on psycholinguistics and on formal semantics.

15.3.1 Psycholinguistics

The goal of this research is to address the problem of thought disorders by drawing on the study of the mental illnesses that cause them. In psychology, the issue of abnormal thinking in a broad sense is usually discussed on the basis of three main approaches:

(i) A psychometric approach that emphasizes investigation by self- or interviewer-administrated questionnaires;
(ii) An experimental approach;
(iii) A pragmatic and psycholinguistic approach.

The first two methodologies provide, above all, pieces of information concerning the emotional sphere or the basic cognitive operations of the patient's mind, subject to dysfunction. The pragmatic approach enables psychologists to address the rationality of representational, meta-representational, and intentional capacities of the mind. Our research program falls into this third perspective and focuses, methodologically, on the analysis of verbal interaction. Among the various mental illnesses that are usually preferred in research on pathological cognitive processes, schizophrenia appears particularly suitable. Indeed, according to the diagnostic criteria commonly used internationally (DSM-IV, Coll 1994), schizophrenic patients are known first and foremost to suffer from thought disorders. This assumption is mainly based on the psychometric approach, which until now has been offering the most interpretative models of the term "thought disorder".[8] In addressing schizophrenics' speech in clinical interviews, pragmatic and linguistic-minded researchers are providing more and more precise descriptions of the specific features of disorders affecting language and language-use. But there is little objective – let alone pathognomonic – evidence of psychiatric disorders available from the scientific literature. Moreover, the pragmatic and dialogic indications uncovered in empirical data almost never lead to research on the semantic side. As a result, schizophrenics' thought processes, specific or defective, and potentially involving language, are still largely unknown.

Nevertheless, either in clinical practice or in research, all attempts to approach this illness, from the most academic to the most empirical, must in one way or another be subjected to an interactional, discursive framework, if only an experimental one. For 40-some years now, research into psychiatric or cognitive disorders – just like the study of thought patterns – has inspired a large body of experimental and theoretical work in almost every branch of psychology, linguistics, and neuroscience, and in the cognitive sciences in general. It is clear, however, that only a small minority of these scientific publications have dared to approach thought processes in depth while simultaneously attempting to grasp any potential disorders likely to be expressed in context. Very few studies have approached the interface between these two domains by looking into how a given disorder and its associated thought patterns might be interrelated to the properties of the language, discourse, and conversation exhibited by the patient. This is despite the fact that increasingly accurate analytical tools, themselves derived from improvements in theoretical and methodological knowledge in several fields, are now available. Our pragmatic and conversational approach to abnormal cognitive psychology relies on the hypothesis that interlocution is a "natural" place for the expression of psychological and thought disorders. The interlocutory framework is equally applicable to clinical interviews, casual conversations, and even interactions set up experimentally. Consequently, the pragmatic approach to analyzing psychopathological conversations necessarily also describes the interpretive activity of each interlocutor, be that person "ordinary" or a patient. For example, this approach identifies the strategies an interlocutor implements in order to maintain a conversation based on certain processes or regularities that ensure turn-taking or make it possible to grasp the meaning of utterances and mental processes activated by communicating subjects.

In this epistemological and methodological context, this chapter will examine the conditions under which a basic technique for analyzing thought disorders can be developed, i.e. one that combines advances in the pragmatic conversational

[8]It may be questionable to use the categories from DSM while claiming to account for a first-person perspective on pathological reasoning through conversations. However, our purpose is not to define schizophrenia, but rather to offer a fine-grained conception of what is going on in conversations with schizophrenic people. Reference to the DSM classification provides us with the starting point for our research, not the final destination.

analysis of pathological interactions with progress in the formal analysis of verbal interaction. But for such an undertaking to be possible, even if only in the medium term, we need a pragmatic model of conversation capable of accounting for the dynamic properties of sequences containing a discontinuity (Musiol 2009). In order to develop such an analytical method, it must be possible (through a semantic approach) to devise a formal method capable of incorporating the properties of conversational discontinuity in such a way as to optimally describe and interpret it, and thus uncover and analyze the rationality of the underlying psychological (or cognitive) processes.

15.3.2 Formal Framework

The formal framework used in this paper is that of Segmented Discourse Representation Theory (SDRT), presented by Asher and Lascarides in their *Logics of conversation* (2003). SDRT combines two levels of analysis in order to account for the interpretive process at work in conversations: semantic content and conversational pragmatics. The first is analyzed via Segmented Discourse Representation Structures (SDRS) inspired by the DRS of Discourse Representation Theory (DRT), which is a syntactic construction updated by conversational flow (Kamp and Reyle 1993). Conversation also implies pragmatic relations between speech acts, the complexity of which gives rise to a hierarchical structure first described in linguistics in the 1980s (Roulet et al. 1985). We propose formalizing this relationship with the rhetorical relations in SDRT. A conversation is then interpreted via a double construction: that of a hierarchical tree linking actions, and that of the DRS representing the semantic content of segments. The assumption we make is that schizophrenic persons do not always conform to the rules that prevail in this double construction, which explains the phenomenon of conversational failure perceived by "ordinary" speakers.

The rhetorical structures of SDRT link the actions of speakers and are represented as hierarchical trees with vertical, horizontal and diagonal relations depending on the type under consideration. The tree structure (hierarchical ordering) encodes properties of the discourse and can be used to resolve semantic effects (e.g. prediction of attachment sites or resolution of anaphora). A discourse relation is viewed as a binary relation between propositions. A narration is thus typically a horizontal relationship (same hierarchical level), as well as the answer to a question, while an elaboration is a vertical relationship (subordinated to what it elaborates on) and a question an oblique relationship (vertical, and thus subordinated, but also horizontal because requiring an answer).

An example of SDRT structure, taken from Lascarides and Asher (1993) and slightly modified, is shown in Fig. 15.1. The tree is updated throughout the discourse. Each subsequent intervention by one of the interlocutors is supposed to be related to the conversational representation already built. The structure then allows us to identify general constraints affecting the attachment sites. The main constraint

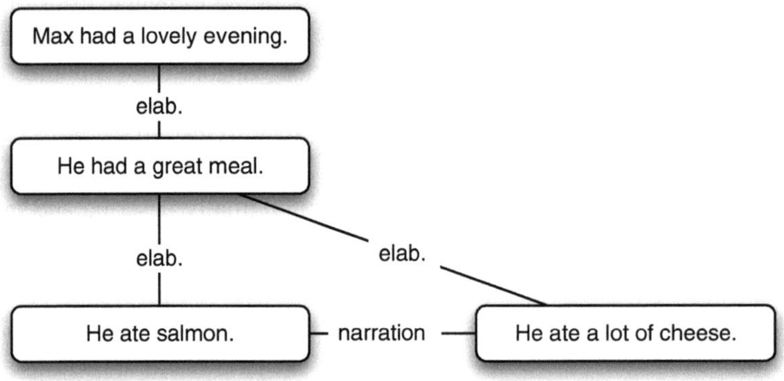

Fig. 15.1 A simple representation of the structure of a discourse

is the so-called right-frontier constraint, forcing the connection to the nodes located on the right side of the tree. Based on this example, the assertion "He found it really wonderful" is ambiguous, since the pronoun ("it") can take multiple values. As indicated by the right-frontier constraint, this sentence cannot be linked to "He ate salmon", and therefore "it" cannot refer to the salmon, but it can be related to any other node of the tree, and thus "it" may refer to the cheese, the meal, or the evening.[9]

Here, we will focus only on the SDRT tree, but we assume that propositions are DRSs. However, we also introduce themes, which should be supported by the DRSs. Themes are coherent sets of DRSs, and we mark them with boxes. We assume that a DRS cannot simultaneously belong to two different themes, unless one is included in the other, in which case these boxes represent a hierarchy: inclusion between boxes is allowed, but overlapping is not.

15.4 Analyzing Empirical Data

As Perkins claims (Perkins 1998, 295), we can all think of people who are "poor communicators" in spite of good linguistic ability. But in cases where a communication deficit is directly linked to an illness diagnosable according to independent clinical criteria, we have a clearer starting point. Detailed indications about the participants in the corpus are available from Musiol and Verhaegen's chapter (Musiol and Verhaegen 2014, Sects. 14.5.2 and 14.5.3). Here we present the way relevant excerpts are selected, in Sect. 14.5.3. The last step is devoted to formalization, which is briefly presented in Sect. 15.4.2.

[9]SDRT also introduces variables representing the conjunction of elaborations. The right-frontier constraint thus provides access to the statement containing salmon, though not to the salmon itself.

15.4.1 Selection of Relevant Excerpts

The study was based on a pragmatic and dialogic analysis of verbal transactions taken from a corpus of 30 interviews. In all cases, the interviewer was a research psychologist and the interviewee was either a schizophrenic patient or an individual with no psychiatric disorders. All interviewees agreed to have the conversation recorded so that we could compile our corpus. They were told why they were being recorded, and we did not conceal the fact that they were participating in a study. The instructions were simply to talk to the interviewer. If the interviewee initially said he/she was having trouble expressing him/herself, the interviewer started with a relatively general topic of conversation (everyday activities and/or concerns). The corpus was transcribed by two researchers, one of whom was not involved in this study. Transcriptions were compared, differences discussed (with other colleagues when necessary), and a final transcription chosen. The (↑) and (↓) arrows respectively indicate a rising or falling intonation. The (→) arrow indicates a pause in the flow of speech for 2–5 s.

The breakdown of the entire interview corpus yielded 403 conversational sequences (or transactions). These transactions are built on the basis of sequences of elementary acts, also called speech acts or discourse acts. Empirically speaking, our research in this area over the past 15 or so years (Musiol and Verhaegen 2009) has enabled us to hypothesize that conversations involving a schizophrenic patient exhibit many incongruities and discontinuities. Our studies have also led us to the hypothesis that the discontinuities formally detected and delineated within a verbal interaction with a schizophrenic fall into two main categories, defined by the so-called hierarchical and functional properties of the discourse structure. In this "hierarchical and functional" structure of discourse (Roulet et al. 1985), we will call the first category "non-decisive" and the second "decisive". In our model's current state of development, there are two types of decisive discontinuity.

We call the first type "conversational gear shifting" (Trognon 1992; Musiol and Trognon 2000). Discontinuities of this type disrupt the turn-taking process while sequentially satisfying the chaining constraints of two leading interventions. They are characterized by a surreptitious change in the speaker's course of action (here, the schizophrenic patient), despite the fact that he/she was the initiator. The referential context thus changes without any indication of that change from the speaker.

Our model involves a second type of decisive discontinuity, qualified as a "defective conversational initiative" (Musiol 2009). Granted, this type of within-intervention discontinuity consists in chainings that sequentially satisfy the interactional constraints governing the organization of the exchange-level subcomponents of the complex transaction unit; yet it consists specifically of discontinuities that are inherent to the hierarchical and functional relations governing the sequencing of speech acts at different levels (in the sense that an act can impose interactive constraints on the constituent that follows or even precedes it, while still being dependent upon it hierarchically and functionally). In this case, the schizophrenic patient has initiated the conversational transaction and supports the argumentation of the "ordinary" interlocutor. Nine sequences were compatible with our decisive discontinuity model. All nine sequences occurred in the paranoid schizophrenic subcorpus. This subgroup differed significantly from both the disorganized schizophrenic group (binomial test $p = 0.002$) and the "ordinary" group (binomial test $p = 0.002$). Among these nine paranoid schizophrenics, three were from the no-medication group (SCH-P-N) and six were from the antipsychotic medication group (SCH-P-A). Our decisive discontinuity model thus allows us to propose some possible explanations for the dysfunctional interpretive and inferential thought processes of schizophrenics of the paranoid type, with help from an additional analysis based on formal semantics.

15.4.2 Formalization

In order to formalize pathological conversations, we make a double conjecture:

1. Schizophrenics are logically consistent; therefore, conversational breaks occur in the construction process of the pragmatic structure of conversations (i.e., on the rhetorical relationships between SDRS); and
2. Under-specification (ambiguity) plays a central role in these failures, which could be summarized by the phrase: a choice is never definitive!

The first conjecture is nothing but the implementation of the principle of charity. The second conjecture, which is primarily based on empirical observation, is a heuristic for the location of remedial strategies in action by the "ordinary" speaker. When there is the appearance of discontinuity, the speaker uses the underspecified relations in order to maintain the pragmatic consistency of the dialogue. In other words, the flexibility of underspecified relations enables one to build a conversational representation under any circumstance.

We had to extend the basic set of rhetorical relations in SDRT to account for the complexity of the dialogic interaction, especially taking into account the meta-conversational adjustments absent from the original theory. Studying of the corpus led us to identify the types of relationships summarized in Table 15.2.

The formalization of conversations is reduced to the elements relevant to our analysis, which means that we abandon anything that does not seem to play a role in explaining the breaks. The representation of semantic content is thus stripped to a minimum, namely to the conversational topic. Each conversational sequence is indeed built around a theme, which is the main contextual element relevant to disambiguating the underspecified terms.[10]

---

[10] The fact that many ruptures take place around underspecified expressions reinforces our choice to represent the thematic element in the formalization.

Table 15.2 Pragmatic relation types

Horizontal relations	Vertical relations	Diagonal relations
Narration	Elaboration	Question
Answer	Elaboration: explanation	Question: driving
Phatic answer	Elaboration: instruction	Meta-question
Continuation and illustration	Evaluation	Elaboration requirement
	Phatic	Driving
	Counter-elaboration	
	Justification	

The conversational theme usually changes after a conventional signal (e.g., "Well, but..." or "Moreover..."), or another form of closure of the current conversational sequence. Maintaining the ongoing theme enables the continuation of a tree, while a theme shift implies a rise through the tree to relate to a dominant node which corresponds to a sequence preceding the exchange. Our formalization introduces *thematic sets* (represented by either boxes or colors), which are consistent sets of units of speech that can be mutually inclusive (without duplication),[11] and the rule of climbing in a SDRT tree, which is allowed only if the current thematic box is properly closed.

To analyze pathological conversations, we always offer the simultaneous construction of two representations, one for each speaker. For the schizophrenic, the postulate of logicality means that the representation is devoid of contradictions at the semantic level. If there are breakdowns, they operate at the pragmatic level, with a departure from the rules for constructing the SDRT tree. The situation is different on the other side. In the conversations that constitute the corpus studied, the "ordinary" interlocutor is a psychologist in charge of continuing the interview. He or she does so in such a way as to "fix" the conversational structure after a break, even if this break would have caused the interruption of a conversation in another situation.

We then admit a postulate corresponding to this requirement, namely the construction of a pragmatic representation within the constraints. This option causes the appearance of inconsistencies on the semantic side. As we argued above, dual conversational representations reflect a duality of views on the conversation. According to the "ordinary" subject, the schizophrenic apparently contradicts the dialogical behavior so that the conversation works, but the representation of the co-constructed world is inconsistent. Conversely, when we assume dysfunction in a schizophrenic's management of pragmatic relations, the representation of the world built by the conversation does not suffer from this defect.

[11] Since it pertains to semantics, the thematic criterion could in principle be represented by a marker inside the SDRS. As it is the only semantic element expected to appear in our simplified representations, we have chosen to waive SDRS, leaving only the pragmatic tree and a mere pictorial thematic marker.

We assume that exchanges are excerpts from larger exchanges, whose starting point is a particular semantically empty node. Thus, whatever the treatment, this root node can be used to link to a new proposition in the pragmatic representation. Analysis of excerpts leads us to highlight two transgressions of the standard SDRT rules: breaks of the right frontier and rises through the structure without any acceptable closing (inconsistency of representation). For the second phenomenon, it is indeed common in corpora to identify items that are used both to close a part of the exchange and to open a new one. But the schizophrenic sometimes does not respect this dual effect and creates an incomplete representation that is not interpretable in a usual way.

15.5 Two Examples

We will focus on two non-canonical uses of SDRT: break of the right frontier and rise through the structure without completeness. Throughout the corpus, we identified three ruptures of the right frontier and five rises without completeness. We will go back over two examples from the corpus, each of which highlights one of these phenomena.

15.5.1 Break of the Right Frontier

The first excerpt is shown in Table 15.3. In this exchange between a psychologist (K) and a schizophrenic patient (J), there is ambiguity about the meaning of "here". It can mean either (a) *in the hospital*, or (b) *in the room*. In principle, there could be many other meanings, but the conversational context restricts the set of possible interpretations to (a) and (b). Any residual ambiguity should be resolved by context updating through the conversational exchange. In this exchange, while it is acknowledged that the conversation has moved from the (a)-meaning to the (b)-meaning of "here", the schizophrenic shifts back to (a) with no warning (Trognon and Musiol 1996). As we will see, this shift is made irrespective of the right frontier constraint.

Figures 15.2 and 15.3 provide two SDRT-like representations of the excerpt, the former according to the ordinary speaker, the latter according to her shizophrenic interlocutor. The two representations are similar until K_{14}. They then diverge radically, as will be explained.

The starting point of the exchange is K_1, which is linked to the initial node (an abstract root node of the tree). It consists of a question (*quest*, oblique relation) from the psychologist, in which a first token of "here" occurs with obvious ambiguity. The schizophrenic answers (*ans*, horizontal relation) in J_1, interpreting "here" as *in the hospital* (a). The answer splits into two parts. The second part is an elaboration (*elab*, vertical relation) on the beginning.

Table 15.3 Extract from a pathological conversation "*Here*, where?"

(K_1) Pourquoi vous êtes ici (↑)	(K_1) Why are you here (↑)
(J_1) [D'accord (*ton concédant*)(→) parce que je sais pas (*accentué*) quoi faire tout seul (→)]^1 [et il faut tout le temps un qui m'aide (→)]^2	(J_1) [Okay (*conceding*)(→) because I dunno (*emphasis*) what to do on my own (→)]^1 [somebody always has to help me (→)]^2
(K_2) [Oui (→)]^1 [et ici alors (↑)]^2	(K_2) [Yes (→)]^1 [and so here (↑)]^2
(J_2) Mmm (*respire fort*) (→) je sais pas moi pour-quoi (*détaché*) (→) oh je sais pas (→) la la la Tania elle m'a dit (→) (*soupir*)	(J_2) Hmm (*breathing hard*) (→) I dunno why (*detached*) (→) oh I dunno (→) the the the Tania told me (→) (*sighing*)
(K_3) Tania (↑)	(K_3) Tania (↑)
(J_3) [Oui la la (→) l'infirmière Madame Tania (→)]^1 [elle m'a dit comme ça (→) allez voir ici (→) y'a pt'être quelque chose qui vous (→)]^2	(J_3) [Yes the the (→) nurse Mrs Tania (→)]^1 [she told me just (→) go see here (→) maybe there's something that might (→)]^2
(K_4) Y'a quelque chose (↑)	(K_4) There's something (↑)
(J_4) Qui vous intéresse	(J_4) That might be interesting for you
(K_5) Ah (→) elle vous a dit ça (↑)	(K_5) Ah (→) she told you that (↑)
(J_5) Mmm	(J_5) Mm-hmm
(K_6) Et alors (↑)	(K_6) And so (↑)
(J_6) [(→) Mm cinq minutes (*marmonne*) (→)]^1 [je sais pas à quoi ça sert]^2	(J_6) [(→) Hmm five minutes (*mumbling*) (→)]^1 [I dunno what the point is]^2
(K_7) Enfin je vous avais vu lundi dernier pour vous expliquer un peu (→) lundi dernier (→) j'étais venue au pavillon pour vous demander s'il était possible de vous voir aujourd'hui	(K_7) Well I saw you last Monday to explain a bit (→) last Monday (→) I came to the pavilion to ask you if we could meet today
(J_7) L'année dernière (↑)	(J_7) Last year (↑)
(K_8) Lundi dernier	(K_8) Last Monday
(J_8) Ah lundi (*accentué*) dernier OK	(J_8) Oh last Monday (*emphasis*) okay
(K_9) Donc heu aujourd'hui quand heu (→) Tania vous a dit de venir ici (→) vous ne vous souveniez plus de (→)	(K_9) So uh today when uh (→) Tania told you to come here (→) you couldn't remember (→)
(J_9) Mmmmm (*chantonne*) de quoi il s'agissait (↑)	(J_9) Hmm-mm (*humming*) what it was about (↑)
(K_{10}) Comment (↑)	(K_{10}) Sorry (↑)
(J_{10}) De quoi il s'agissait	(J_{10}) What it was about
(K_{11}) Oui	(K_{11}) Yes
(J_{11}) Ah je m'en rappelle plus bien	(J_{11}) Oh I can't really remember
(K_{12}) Ah bon	(K_{12}) Ah okay
(J_{12}) Vous fumez (↑)	(J_{12}) Do you smoke (↑)
(K_{13}) Je ne fume pas (→) non	(K_{13}) I don't smoke (→) no
(J_{13}) [Oh c'est dommage (→)]^1 [ça fait déjà quatre fois]^2	(J_{13}) [Oh that's too bad (→)]^1 [that makes four times now]^2
(K_{14}) Ça fait déjà quatre fois (↑)	(K_{14}) That makes four times (↑)

(continued)

Table 15.3 (continued)

(J_{14}) [Ah je sais je sais je sais (→) moi qu'est-ce qui m'intéresse (→)][1] [pourquoi je suis venu ici (→) ou bien pourquoi que (→) pourquoi que (→) pourquoi que (→) on m'a envoyé ici (→) parce que (*respire fort*) (→) bon][2]	(J_{14}) [Oh I know I know I know (→) what's interesting for me (→)][1] [why I came here (→) or why it is (→) why it is (→) why it is (→) they sent me here (→) because (*breathing hard*) (→) yeah][2]
(K_{15}) On vous a envoyé ici (↑)	(K_{15}) You were sent here (↑)
(J_{15}) Comment (↑)	(J_{15}) Sorry (↑)
(K_{16}) On vous a envoyé ici (↑)	(K_{16}) You were sent here (↑)
(J_{16}) [Oui (→)][1] [depuis le premier jour que je suis arrivé (→) de l'année dernière le deux février][2]	(J_{16}) [Yes (→)][1] [since the first day I got here (→) last year February second][2]

But, this was not the psychologist's intended meaning. In K_2^1, she closes the starting exchange, asserting "Yes", which is a phatic (*phat*, here horizontal), then asks her question (*quest*) again in K_2^2. Since this question does not relate to any previous box, it is linked to the root node. Now it is clear for both interlocutors that "here" means *in the room* (b). In the SDRSs, we represent the thematic variability with colors. The boxes corresponding to acts interpreted relative to (a) are grey, whereas those corresponding to (b) are white. The agreement between the interlocutors is corroborated by the patient's answer (*ans*) J_2, which clearly refers to the (b)-meaning.

In K_3, the psychologist asks a meta-question (*meta-quest*, oblique), i.e. not a question directly about the main topic, but a metaconversational question about what was stated by her interlocutor (here, about the name "Tania"). In J_3^1, the schizophrenic answers this question and closes the subdialogue. He then continues his narration (*narr*, horizontal) with J_3^2, which is attached to J_2. K_4 is a phatic (*phat*, here vertical), or maybe a driving. However, the schizophrenic does not take K_4 into account and goes on with his narration in J_4. K_5 is a confirmation question by the psychologist, and J_5 its immediate answer ("Mm-hmm" meaning here *Yes*).

In K_6, the psychologist requests elaboration (*elab-request*, oblique) on the narration (her act is not attached to the answer just given by the patient, but to J_4.) The schizophrenic starts answering in J_6^1, then (critically) evaluates (*eval*, vertical) the whole situation in J_6^2. The psychologist disputes this evaluation, starting a counter-elaboration (*counter-elab*, vertical) with K_7. Since the patient falsely understands "last year" instead of "last Monday", he opens a subdialogue with a meta-question in J_7, which he closes with a phatic in J_8. In K_9, the psychologist carries on with her (counter-)elaboration.

The segment between J_9 and K_{11} has a complex attachment to what precedes it. It starts like a question, but this is actually the question that the psychologist would have asked if her interlocutor had let her finish her sentence. The question is therefore mixed with a driving (*driving*, also oblique), i.e. with an utterance designed to help the interlocutor to continue. After a short metaconversational

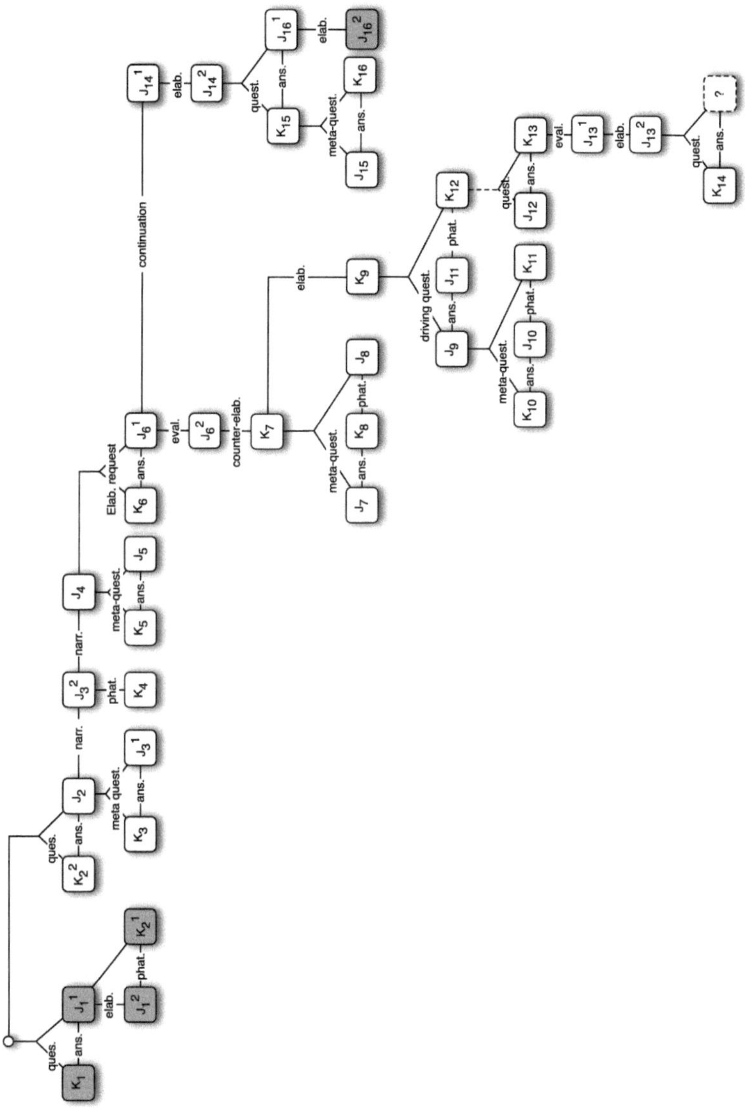

Fig. 15.2 Representation by the ordinary speaker (K)

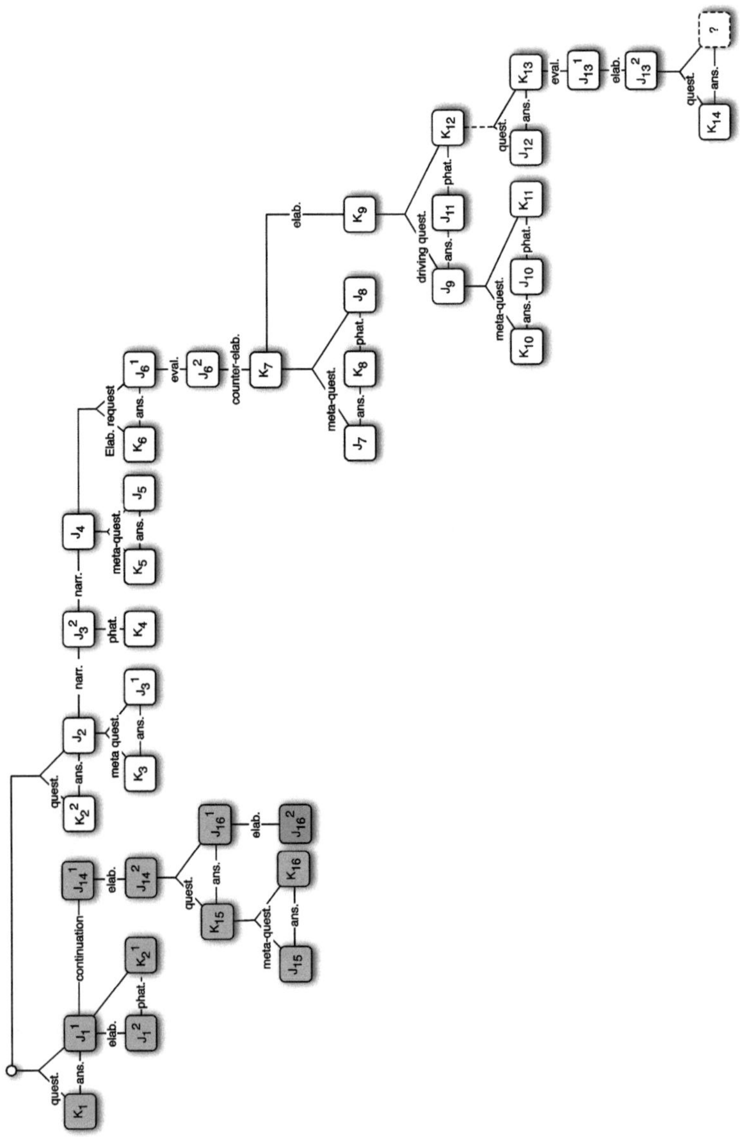

Fig. 15.3 Representation by the schizophrenic speaker (J)

exchange about J_9, between K_{10} and K_{11}, the schizophrenic finally answers the question with J_{11}. The psychologist then uses a phatic in K_{12}, which could close the subtree.

The schizophrenic opens a subdialogue about *smoking*, i.e. about features of the extra-conversational context. The subtree J_{12}–K_{14} corresponds to this subdialogue, and is conventionally attached to the closest preceding box, K_{12}, even though it is not related to the semantic content of K_{12}.[12] Just like its start, the subdialogue's ending is not correct because there is no answer to the question asked by the psychologist in K_{14}. Hence the subtree is not closed. This might be justified by the fact that the schizophrenic interlocutor then resumes the main conversation.

We have now reached the point where the interlocutors start diverging. Let us first look at the psychologist's point of view (Fig. 15.2). In J_{14}^1, when the schizophrenic asserts he knows what is interesting for him, this appears to be a delayed answer to the elaboration request K_6. The utterance is thus attached to J_6^1, the beginning of the answer, as a continuation (*continuation*, horizontal). Let us keep in mind that this elaboration request happened after an answer to the initial question asked by the psychologist, "why are you here?". This is therefore what the interlocutor is expected to carry on answering. In J_{14}^2, the patient elaborates on his answer and says for the first time that he was sent here. The psychologist asks him for an explanation, or at least a confirmation, with K_{15}. After a two-round metaconversational adjustment (J_{15}–K_{16}), the schizophrenic answers the question in J_{16}^1, then elaborates on his answer in J_{16}^2. But the semantic content of J_{16}^2 is clearly inappropriate in the current conversational context. The schizophrenic has shifted back to the first interpretation of "here", indicating a blatant inconsistency.

Let us now look at the schizophrenic's perspective (Fig. 15.3). We will assume semantic consistency, i.e., in our representation, thematic coherence. As evidenced by the psychologist's point of view, with J_{14}^1, the schizophrenic starts answering a question that was asked earlier. It seems as though the speaker is lost and does not know where to attach his utterance. What is most plausible in order to preserve the speaker's consistency is that J_{14}^1 is attached to J_1^1 as a continuation. From a semantic/thematic viewpoint, J_{14}^1 fits perfectly with the (a)-interpretation of "here" as *in the hospital*, which is relevant to J_1^1. However, while making this attachment, the speaker breaks the right frontier constraint.

Both views are questionable for any ordinary speaker, who would accept neither semantic inconsistencies, nor pragmatic fallacies. Nevertheless, we can conjecture that the conversational situation is acceptable for the schizophrenic since he is the speaker whose utterances generate the apparent breaks. This entails that pragmatic rules like the right frontier constraint are relaxed for him, whereas logical norms still apply.

---

[12]This conventional attachment grants that the closest preceding node will remain available for further attachment. Another possibility would be to leave the subtree with no attachment, since it corresponds to a subdialogue with no connection to the current conversation.

15.5.2 Rise Through the Structure with Inconsistency

The second pathological use of exchange conventions is more complex to express in a non-logical framework. When an interlocutor shifts topics, she is conventionally expected to make this obvious via by some linguistic marker. This is generally required for the dialogue to go on. Schizophrenic interlocutors, however, sometimes change the subject and continue their narration without respecting this convention. In our context, the prototypical case corresponds to the psychologist's expectation of an answer on a specific theme (or a question), which the schizophrenic never gives. The lack of a target for such switches produces an inconsistency in the structure. Breaks of the right frontier, though they constitute violations of a hard constraint, do not stop the building of a tree structure for the rhetorical representation. The issue raised here is the lack of information for a complete representation. For instance, bindings are introduced in an ad hoc way that relates the current segment to some abstract point that does not make sense. Assuming such bindings ensures that an acceptable structure is available for the exchange to continue.

An illustration of this case is presented in the second excerpt, in Fig. 15.4. In this short dialogue, the psychologist performs a rise through the structure (but with consistency). Next, the schizophrenic rises with inconsistency. The schizophrenic plays on the ambiguity of the loss (feel lost vs. lose someone or something). The main part of the exchange goes normally. But now, the schizophrenic is driving the dialogue. The psychologist loses control and at some point his understanding of the conversation. The first sign of this is the question from the schizophrenic, G^2_{86}, which seems too abstract for this dialogue. Then, the psychologist closes the subpart of the tree and starts a new theme attached to G^3_{82}. The psychologist's challenge is to deal with how the schizophrenic feels. By doing this, he closes the question and waits for the rest. In the formal representation, the V_{87} node (the darkest one in Fig. 15.4) is duplicated, and a dotted line links the two V_{87} nodes.

After this admissible rise, the schizophrenic accepts the climb, but instead of responding in G_{88} with an answer (or an elaboration), he or she rises again through the structure to a higher node. This could be either a previous node, possibly not defined in this excerpt, where they discussed the loss of someone, or at least the root node. In any case, he or she can rise if and only if the subparts are correctly closed (just by answering the question). He or she does not do so here, and that is why it is not possible to duplicate G_{88} in Fig. 15.4 so as to properly answer V_{87}. The psychologist continues the dialogue without knowing from where in the tree.

Even if it is difficult to define the target of the duplication in sentences (a word, a relation, etc.), it is perfectly admissible for the psychologist to follow the standard rhetorical rules and for the schizophrenic not to. From here, we could argue that the problem comes from the psychologist who started the rise. But the key point in this example shows that the issue is not the rise, but the consistency.

This phenomenon is the most frequent discontinuity in the corpus. An important remark on this structural (and not strictly logical) inconsistency is that in all exchanges, schizophrenics always use ambiguity as support. It may be lexical (as in

G_{82}: (...) [l'an dernier euh (→) j'savais pas comment faire j'étais perdue]^{1} [et pourtant j'avais pris mes médicaments]^{2} [j'suis dans un état]^{3} [vous voyez même ma bouche elle est sèche j'suis dans un triste état]^{4}

V_{83}: Vous êtes quand même bien (↑)

G_{84}: [J'pense que ma tête est bien mais on croirait à moitié]^{1} (↓) [la moitié qui va et la moitié qui va pas j'ai l'impression de ça vous voyez]^{2} (↑)

V_{85}: D'accord

G_{86}: [Ou alors c'est la conscience peut être la conscience]^{1} [est-ce que c'est ça]^{2} (↑)

V_{87}: Vous savez ça arrive à tout le monde d'avoir des moments biens et des moments où on est perdu

G_{88}: Oui j'ai peur de perdre tout le monde

V_{89}: Mais ils vont plutôt bien vos enfants (↑)

G_{90}: [Ils ont l'air ils ont l'air mais ils ont des allergies ils ont]^{1} (→) [mon petit fils il s'est cassé le bras à l'école tout ça]^{2}

(G_{82}) (...) [last year uh (→) I didn't know how to do, I was lost]^{1} [but I had taken my medication.]^{2} [I'm in a state!]^{3} [you see even my mouth is dry. I'm in bad shape]^{4}

(V_{83}) You are still fine (↑)

(G_{84}) [I think my head is fine but one would believe half]^{1} (↓) [half right and half wrong. I fell like that you see]^{2} (↑)

(V_{85}) Right

(G_{86}) [Or it is consciousness, consciousness maybe]^{1}, [is it that]^{2} (↑)

(V_{87}) You know, everyone sometimes well and sometimes lost.

(G_{88}) Yes, I'm afraid to lose everybody

(V_{89}) But, they are rather OK (↑)

(G_{90}) [They look like, they look like, but they have allergies, they have]^{1} (→) [my grandson he broke his arm at school you see]^{2}

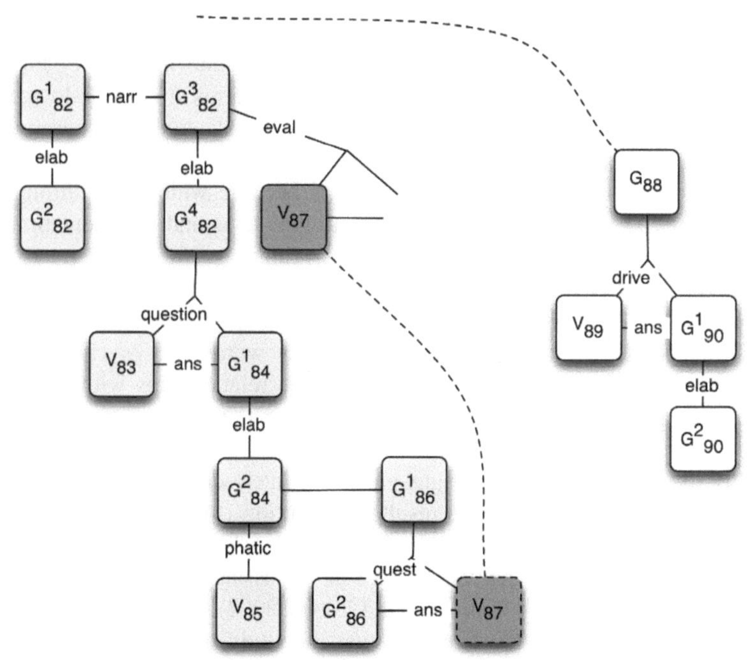

Fig. 15.4 Rise over the sub-structure

the present example about loss), semantic (the switch of an entity of the universe of discourse based on the name of the entity), or caused by any underspecified relation. Formalization requires resolving this ambiguity before continuing, and when a choice is made, it is assumed in what follows. But the schizophrenic still considers this relation unbounded, such that he or she may go back on the chosen interpretation.

15.6 Concluding Remarks

We argue that rationality, while not reducible to logicality, contributes to the dynamics of clinical interviews. Moreoever, since schizophrenia appears to be more pragmatic than semantic in nature, our investigations focused not only on the relations between two interlocutors' speech acts, but also on the relationships that link each communicating subject to the dialogical context, and especially to his or her interlocutor. In cognitive terms, our analyses have to take into account the two speakers' thought management strategies, as well as the thought contents themselves.

Pragmatic relations that contribute to the balance of trade in schizophrenic pathological exchanges are indeed also an expression of cognitive processes, namely intentional ones, since the protagonists of the exchange are in a position to "interpret" one another. The principle of rationality, e.g. as defined in Popper (1969), states that human beings act according to reason, i.e., based on considerations that have some normative force and are binding, and that justify their actions. This principle can be translated into intentional terms from a dialogical perspective. Each of the two interactive subjects sets up adaptive procedures in order to handle the needs and peculiarities of his or her interlocutor. In cognitive psychology and philosophy of mind, this view has become widespread through the assumption that agents act by virtue of intentional states and representations with contents that are the causes of their actions (Engel 1996). For these two disciplines, and especially for evolutionary psychology, the principle of rationality is at the heart of the "interpreter's strategy", a.k.a. "intentional stance" (Dennett 1987). Common sense or folk psychology, in other words the psychological background on which one spontaneously settles one's relationships with others, involves rational calculation that can be expressed in terms of desires, expectations and beliefs.

This ability to manage both the dialogue and one's interlocutor in a situation of interaction is assumed to be partly the result of evolution (Musiol and Rebuschi 2007). Since some schizophrenic disorders are likely to be accounted for by explanations of an evolutionary nature, at least as far as language (Crow 2010), reasoning (Corcoran et al. 1995; Cosmides and Tooby 2002), and social behavior (Burns 2004) are concerned, we can expect that the study of such pathological interactions will tell us something about the rationality of the cognitive processes listed above. Indeed, the manifestation of the disorder during interactions and the need to maintain the link cause the schizophrenic interlocutor to adopt a compensatory management strategy. This strategy is presumably based on archaic cognitive processes, which are actually harder to detect in ordinary conversations than in this type of clinical interview.

Thought disorders are one of the best areas for investigating for the pragmatic and semantic perspectives on the incoherence of speech. Thanks to our methodology and focus on the intentionality of the mind and of thought, our approach complements many papers in neuroscience and cognitive science on the same subjects. This approach is also probably relevant to the investigation of psychiatric disorders and the diagnostic criteria associated with them, as well as to the question of the existence of pathognomonic signs in mental illness, and to the more general question of the relationships between discourse and cognition.

We hope to have shown that mental illness in general and schizophrenia in particular raise issues of great interest not only to psychopathology and psychiatry, but also to linguistics and epistemology. This research needs to be expanded to bigger corpuses. By looking at natural language in its interactive dimension, our work opens new perspectives on the study of schizophrenic behavioral deviancies in psychology. Linguistically speaking, empirical data from pathological conversations offer a new challenge. Theoretical models must account for such data in a non-standard way because they are deviant. The main epistemological difficulty lies in the complex picture that emerges from such studies, for there are no longer two, but three terms to include in a notion of reflexive equilibrium: linguistic norms (accounted for by linguistic theory), normal performance, and deviant performance. The evaluation of the impact of this new kind of data is left to future work.

References

N. Asher, A. Lascarides, *Logics of Conversation* (Cambridge University Press, Cambridge/New York, 2003)

D. Bonnay, M. Cozic, Principe de charité et sciences de l'homme, in *Les sciences humaines sont-elles des sciences?* ed. by T. Martin (Vuibert, Paris, 2011)

J. Brunet, Théorie du raisonnement et perspective de la première personne. Philosophiques **37**(2), 411–437 (2010)

J. Burns, An evolution theory of schizophrenia: cortical connectivity, metarepresentation and the social brain. Behav. Brain Sci. **27**(6), 831–855 (2004)

J. Campbell, Rationality, meaning, and the analysis of delusion. Philos. Psychiatry Psychol. **8**(2/3), 89–100 (2001)

Coll, *Diagnostic and Statistical Manual of Mental Disorders DSM-IV-TR. Fourth Edition (Text Revision)* (American Psychiatric Association, Washington DC, 1994)

R. Corcoran, G. Mercer, C.D. Frith, Schizophrenia, symptomatology and social inference: investigating "theory of mind" in people with schizophrenia. Schizophr. Res. **17**, 5–13 (1995)

L. Cosmides, J. Tooby, Cognitive adaptations for social exchange, in *The Adapted Mind*, ed. by J.H. Barkow, L. Cosmides, J. Tooby (Oxford University Press, New York/Oxford, 2002), pp. 163–228

T.J. Crow, The nuclear symptoms of schizophrenia reveal the four quadrant structure of language and its deficit frame. J. Neurolinguistics **23**(1), 1–9 (2010)

D. Davidson, Mental events. in *Essays on Actions and Events*, Chap. 20 (Oxford University Press, Oxford, 1980), pp. 137–149

D. Dennett, *The Intentional Stance* (MIT, Cambridge, 1987)

D. Dennett, *Consciousness Explained* (Little, Brown and Company, Boston/New York, 1991)

W. Dilthey, *Introduction to the Human Sciences. Selected Works*, Number 1 (Princeton University Press, Princeton, 1989)

P. Engel, *Philosophie et psychologie* (Gallimard/Folio, Paris, 1996)

M.G. Henriksen, On incomprehensibility in schizophrenia. Phenomenol. Cogn. Sci. **12**(1), 105–129 (2013)

H. Kamp, U. Reyle, *From Discourse to Logic: Introduction to Model Theoretic Semantics of Natural Language, Formal Logic and Discourse Representation Theory*. Studies in Linguistics and Philosophy (Kluwer Academic, Dordrecht, 1993)

A. Lascarides, N. Asher, Temporal interpretation, discourse relations and commonsense entailment. Linguist. Philos. **16**, 437–493 (1993)

J. Łukasiewicz, *Du principe de contradiction chez Aristote (O zasadzie sprzeczności u Arystotelesa)*, (1910) edn. (L'Éclat, Paris, 2000)

M. Musiol, Incohérence et formes psychopathologiques dans l'interaction verbale schizophrénique. in *Des neurosciences à la psychopathologie: Action, Langage, Imaginaire*, ed. by J. Rozenberg, N. Franck, C.Hervé (De Boeck, Bruxelles, 2009) pp. 219–238

M. Musiol, M. Rebuschi, La rationalité de l'incohérence en conversation schizophrène (analyse pragmatique conversationnelle et sémantique formelle). Psychologie française **52**(2), 137–169 (2007)

M. Musiol, A. Trognon, *Eléments de psychopathologie cognitive. Le discours schizophrène* (Coll. U. Armand Colin, Paris, 2000)

M. Musiol, F. Verhaegen, Appréhension et catégorisation de l'expression de la symptomatologie schizophrénique dans l'interaction verbale. Annales Médico-Psychologiques **167**, 717–727 (2009)

M. Musiol F. Verhaegen, Investigating discourse specificities in schizophrenic disorders, in *Interdisciplinary Works in Logic, Epistemology, Psychology and Linguistics: Dialogue, Rationality, Formalism* (Springer, Cham, 2014)

M. R. Perkins, Is pragmatics epiphenomenal? evidence from communication disorders. J. Pragmat. **29**, 291–311, (1998)

K. Popper, *Conjectures and Refutations*, 3rd edn. (Routledge & K. Paul, London, 1969)

G. Priest, On alternative geometries, arithmetics, and logics: a tribute to łukasiewicz. Studia Logica **74**, 441–468, (2003)

M. Rebuschi, M. Amblard, M. Musiol, Schizophrénie, logicité et compréhension en première personne. *L'Evolution psychiatrique* **78**(1), 127–141 (2013)

S. Rochester, J.R. Martin, *Crazy Talk. A Study of the Discourse of Schizophrenic Speakers* (Plenum, London, 1979)

E. Roulet, A. Auchlin, M. Schelling, J. Moeschler, C. Rubattel, *L'articulation du discours en français contemporain*. (Peter Lang, Berne, 1985)

L.A. Sass, *The Paradoxes of Delusion: Wittgenstein, Schreber, and the Schizophrenic Mind* (Cornell, New York, 1994)

L.A. Sass, Incomprehensibility and understanding: on the interpretation of severe mental illness. Philos. Psychiatry Psychol. **10**(2), 125–132, (2003)

J.R. Searle, *The Rediscovery of the Mind* (MIT, Cambridge, 1992)

A. Trognon, L'approche pragmatique en psychopathologie cognitive. Psychologie française **44**(4), 189–202, (1992)

A. Trognon, M. Musiol, L'accomplissement interactionnel du trouble schizophrénique. Raisons Prat. **7**, 179–209, (1996)

J. Villadsen, Paraconsistent assertions, in Multiagent System Technologies (MATES), Erfurt. Lecture Notes in Computer Science, vol. **3187** (Springer, 2004), pp. 99–113

Willard Van Orman Quine, *Word and Object* (MIT, Cambridge, 1960)

Index

M. Rebuschi et al. (eds.), *Interdisciplinary Works in Logic, Epistemology, Psychology and Linguistics*, Logic, Argumentation & Reasoning 3,
DOI 10.1007/978-3-319-03044-9, © Springer International Publishing Switzerland 2014

T

U

V

MIX
Papier aus verantwortungsvollen Quellen
Paper from responsible sources
FSC® C105338

If you have any concerns about our products, you can contact us on
ProductSafety@springernature.com

In case Publisher is established outside the EU, the EU authorized representative is:
Springer Nature Customer Service Center GmbH
Europaplatz 3, 69115 Heidelberg, Germany

Printed by Libri Plureos GmbH
in Hamburg, Germany